Continuous Stochastic Calculus with Applications to Finance

APPLIED MATHEMATICS
Editor: R.J. Knops

This series presents texts and monographs at graduate and research level covering a wide variety of topics of current research interest in modern and traditional applied mathematics, in numerical analysis and computation.

(Full details concerning this series, and more information on titles in preparation are available from the publisher.)

Continuous Stochastic Calculus with Applications to Finance

MICHAEL MEYER, Ph.D.

CRC Press
Taylor & Francis Group
Boca Raton London New York

CRC Press is an imprint of the
Taylor & Francis Group, an **informa** business
A CHAPMAN & HALL BOOK

First published 2001 by Chapman and Hall

Published 2019 by CRC Press
Taylor & Francis Group
6000 Broken Sound Parkway NW, Suite 300
Boca Raton, FL 33487-2742

First issued in paperback 2019

No claim to original U.S. Government works

ISBN-13: 978-0-367-45543-9 (pbk)
ISBN-13: 978-1-58488-234-3 (hbk)

Visit the Taylor & Francis Web site at
http://www.taylorandfrancis.com

and the CRC Press Web site at
http://www.crcpress.com

Library of Congress Card Number 00-064361

Library of Congress Cataloging-in-Publication Data

Meyer, Michael (Michael J.)
    Continuous stochastic calculus with applications to finance / Michael Meyer.
        p.   cm.--(Applied mathematics ; 17)
    Includes bibliographical references and index.
    ISBN 1-58488-234-4 (alk. paper)
    1. Finance--Mathematical models. 2. Stochastic analysis. I. Title. II. Series.

HG173 .M49 2000
332'.01'5118—dc21   00-064361

PREFACE

The current, prolonged boom in the US and European stock markets has increased interest in the mathematics of security markets most notably the theory of stochastic integration. Existing books on the subject seem to belong to one of two classes. On the one hand there are rigorous accounts which develop the theory to great depth without particular interest in finance and which make great demands on the prerequisite knowledge and mathematical maturity of the reader. On the other hand treatments which are aimed at application to finance are often of a nontechnical nature providing the reader with little more than an ability to manipulate symbols to which no meaning can be attached. The present book gives a rigorous development of the theory of stochastic integration as it applies to the valuation of derivative securities. It is hoped that a satisfactory balance between aesthetic appeal, degree of generality, depth and ease of reading is achieved

Prerequisites are minimal. For the most part a basic knowledge of measure theoretic probability and Hilbert space theory is sufficient. Slightly more advanced functional analysis (Banach Alaoglu theorem) is used only once. The development begins with the theory of discrete time martingales, in itself a charming subject. From these humble origins we develop all the necessary tools to construct the stochastic integral with respect to a general continuous semimartingale. The limitation to continuous integrators greatly simplifies the exposition while still providing a reasonable degree of generality. A leisurely pace is assumed throughout, proofs are presented in complete detail and a certain amount of redundancy is maintained in the writing, all with a view to make the reading as effortless and enjoyable as possible.

The book is split into four chapters numbered I, II, III, IV. Each chapter has sections 1,2,3 etc. and each section subsections a,b,c etc. Items within subsections are numbered 1,2,3 etc. again. Thus III.4.a.2 refers to item 2 in subsection a of section 4 of Chapter III. However from within Chapter III this item would be referred to as 4.a.2. Displayed equations are numbered (0), (1), (2) etc. Thus II.3.b.eq.(5) refers to equation (5) of subsection b of section 3 of Chapter II. This same equation would be referred to as 3.b.eq.(5) from within Chapter II and as (5) from within the subsection wherein it occurs.

Very little is new or original and much of the material is standard and can be found in many books. The following sources have been used:
[Ca,Cb] I.5.b.1, I.5.b.2, I.7.b.0, I.7.b.1;
[CRS] I.2.b, I.4.a.2, I.4.b.0;
[CW] III.2.e.0, III.3.e.1, III.2.e.3;

[DD] II.1.a.6, II.2.a.1, II.2.a.2;
[DF] IV.3.e;
[DT] I.8.a.6, II.2.e.7, II.2.e.9, III.4.b.3, III.5.b.2;
[J] III.3.c.4, IV.3.c.3, IV.3.c.4, IV.3.d, IV.5.e, IV.5.h;
[K] II.1.a, II.1.b;
[KS] I.9.d, III.4.c.5, III.4.d.0, III.5.a.3, III.5.c.4, III.5.f.1, IV.1.c.3;
[MR] IV.4.d.0, IV.5.g, IV.5.j;
[RY] I.9.b, I.9.c, III.2.a.2, III.2.d.5.

To
my mother

TABLE OF CONTENTS

Chapter I Martingale Theory

Chapter IV   Application to Finance

SUMMARY OF NOTATION

Sets and numbers. $\mathbb{N}$ denotes the set of natural numbers ($\mathbb{N} = \{1, 2, 3, \ldots\}$), R the set of real numbers, $R_+ = [0, +\infty)$, $\overline{R} = [-\infty, +\infty]$ the extended real line and R^n Euclidean n-space. $\mathcal{B}(R)$, $\mathcal{B}(\overline{R})$ and $\mathcal{B}(R^n)$ denote the Borel σ-field on R, $\overline{R}$ and R^n respectively. $\mathcal{B}$ denotes the Borel σ-field on R_+. For $a, b \in \overline{R}$ set $a \vee b = max\{a, b\}$, $a \wedge b = min\{a, b\}$, $a^+ = a \vee 0$ and $a^- = -a \wedge 0$.

$\Pi = [0, +\infty) \times \Omega$ . . . . domain of a stochastic process

$\mathcal{P}_g$ . . . . the progressive σ-field on Π (III.1.a).

$\mathcal{P}$ . . . . the predictable σ-field on Π (III.1.a).

$[\![S, T]\!] = \{(t, \omega) \mid S(\omega) \le t \le T(\omega)\}$ . . . stochastic interval.

Random variables. $(\Omega, \mathcal{F}, P)$ the underlying probability space, $\mathcal{G} \subseteq \mathcal{F}$ a sub-σ-field. For a random variable X set $X^+ = X \vee 0 = 1_{[X>0]}X$ and $X^- = -X \wedge 0 = -1_{[X<0]}X = (-X)^+$. Let $\mathcal{E}(P)$ denote the set of all random variables X such that the expected value $E_P(X) = E(X) = E(X^+) - E(X^-)$ is defined ($E(X^+) < \infty$ or $E(X^-) < \infty$). For $X \in \mathcal{E}(P)$, $E_\mathcal{G}(X) = E(X|\mathcal{G})$ is the unique $\mathcal{G}$-measurable random variable Z in $\mathcal{E}(P)$ satisfying $E(1_G X) = E(1_G Z)$ for all sets $G \in \mathcal{G}$ (the conditional expectation of X with respect to $\mathcal{G}$).

Processes. Let $X = (X_t)_{t \ge 0}$ be a stochastic process and $T : \Omega \to [0, \infty]$ an optional time. Then X_T denotes the random variable $(X_T)(\omega) = X_{T(\omega)}(\omega)$ (sample of X along T, I.3.b, I.7.a). X^T denotes the process $X_t^T = X_{t \wedge T}$ (process X stopped at time T). $\mathcal{S}$, $\mathcal{S}_+$ and $\mathcal{S}^n$ denote the space of continuous semimartingales, continuous positive semimartingales and continuous R^n-valued semimartingales respectively. Let $X, Y \in \mathcal{S}$, $t \ge 0$, $\Delta = \{0 = t_0 < t_1 < \ldots, t_n = t\}$ a partition of the interval $[0, t]$ and set $\Delta_j X = X_{t_j} - X_{t_{j-1}}$, $\Delta_j Y = Y_{t_j} - Y_{t_{j-1}}$ and $\|\Delta\| = max_j(t_j - t_{j-1})$.

$Q_\Delta(X) = \sum(\Delta_j X)^2$ . . . . . I.9.b, I.10.a, I.11.b.

$Q_\Delta(X, Y) = \sum \Delta_j X \Delta_j Y$ . . I.10.a.

$\langle X, Y \rangle$ . . . . covariation process of X, Y (I.10.a, I.11.b).

$\qquad \qquad \qquad \langle X, Y \rangle_t = \lim_{\|\Delta\| \to 0} Q_\Delta(X, Y)$ (limit in probability).

$\langle X \rangle = \langle X, X \rangle$ . . . . . . quadratic variation process of X (I.9.b).

u_X . . . . (additive) compensator of X (I.11.a).

U_X . . . . multiplicative compensator of $X \in \mathcal{S}_+$ (III.3.f).

$\mathbf{H}^2$ . . . . space of continuous, L^2-bounded martingales M with norm $\|M\|_{\mathbf{H}^2} = \sup_{t \ge 0} \|M_t\|_{L^2(P)}$ (I.9.a).

$\mathbf{H}_0^2 = \{M \in \mathbf{H}^2 \mid M_0 = 0\}$.

Multinormal distribution and Brownian motion.

W . . . . Brownian motion starting at zero.

$\mathcal{F}_t^W$ . . . . Augmented filtration generated by W (II.2.f).

$N(m, C)$ . . . . Normal distribution with mean $m \in R^k$ and covariance matrix C (II.1.a).

$N(d) = P(X \le d)$ . . . . X a standard normal variable in R^1.

$n_k(x) = (2\pi)^{-k/2} exp(-\|x\|^2/2)$ . . Standard normal density in R^k (II.1.a).

Stochastic integrals, spaces of integrands. $H \bullet X$ denotes the integral process $(H \bullet X)_t = \int_0^t H_s \cdot dX_s$ and is defined for $X \in \mathcal{S}^n$ and $H \in L(X)$. $L(X)$ is the space of X-integrable processes H. If X is a continuous local martingale, $L(X) = L^2_{loc}(X)$ and in this case we have the subspaces $L^2(X) \subseteq \Lambda^2(X) \subseteq L^2_{loc}(X) = L(X)$. The integral processes $H \bullet X$ and associated spaces of integrands H are introduced step by step for increasingly more general integrators X:

Scalar valued integrators. Let M be a continuous local martingale. Then

μ_M . . . . . Doleans measure on $(\Pi, \mathcal{B} \times \mathcal{F})$ associated with M (III.2.a)
$$\mu_M(\Delta) = E_P\left[\int_0^\infty 1_\Delta(s,\omega) d\langle M\rangle_s(\omega)\right], \ \Delta \in \mathcal{B} \times \mathcal{F}.$$

$L^2(M)$ . . . . space $L^2(\Pi, \mathcal{P}_g, \mu_M)$ of all progressively measurable processes H satisfying $\|H\|^2_{L^2(M)} = E_P\left[\int_0^\infty H_s^2 d\langle M\rangle_s\right] < \infty.$

For $H \in L^2(M)$, $H \bullet M$ is the unique martingale in $\mathbf{H}_0^2$ satisfying $\langle H \bullet M, N\rangle = H \bullet \langle M, N\rangle$, for all continuous local martingales N (III.2.a.2). The spaces $\Lambda^2(M)$ and $L(M) = L^2_{loc}(M)$ of M-integrable processes H are then defined as follows:

$\Lambda^2(M)$ . . . . space of all progressively measurable processes H satisfying $1_{[0,t]} H \in L^2(M)$, for all $0 < t < \infty$.

$L(M) = L^2_{loc}(M)$ . . space of all progressively measurable processes H satisfying $1_{[0,T_n]} H \in L^2(M)$, for some sequence (T_n) of optional times increasing to infinity, equivalently $\int_0^t H_s^2 d\langle M\rangle_s < \infty$, P-as., for all $0 < t < \infty$ (III.2.b).

If $H \in L^2(M)$, then $H \bullet M$ is a martingale in $\mathbf{H}^2$. If $H \in \Lambda^2(M)$, then $H \bullet M$ is a square integrable martingale (III.2.c.3).

Let now A be a continuous process with paths which are almost surely of bounded variation on finite intervals. For $\omega \in \Omega$, $dA_s(\omega)$ denotes the (signed) Lebesgue-Stieltjes measure on finite subintervals of $[0, +\infty)$ corresponding to the bounded variation function $s \mapsto A_s(\omega)$ and $|dA_s|(\omega)$ the associated total variation measure.

$L^1(A)$ . . . . . the space of all progressively measurable processes H such that $\int_0^\infty |H_s(\omega)| |dA_s|(\omega) < \infty$, for P-ae. $\omega \in \Omega$.

$L^1_{loc}(A)$ . . . . the space of all progressively measurable processes H such that $1_{[0,t]} H \in L^1(A)$, for all $0 < t < \infty$.

For $H \in L^1_{loc}(A)$ the integral process $I_t = (H \bullet A)_t = \int_0^t H_s dA_s$ is defined pathwise as $I_t(\omega) = \int_0^t H_s(\omega) dA_s(\omega)$, for P-ae. $\omega \in \Omega$.

Assume now that X is a continuous semimartingale with semimartingale decomposition $X = A + M$ ($A = u_X$, M a continuous local martingale, I.11.a). Then $L(X) = L^1_{loc}(A) \cap L^2_{loc}(M)$. Thus $L(X) = L^2_{loc}(X)$, if X is a local martingale. For $H \in L(X)$ set $H \bullet X = H \bullet A + H \bullet M$. Then $H \bullet X$ is the unique continuous semimartingale satisfying $(H \bullet X)_0 = 0$, $u_{H \bullet X} = H \bullet u_X$ and $\langle H \bullet X, Y\rangle = H \bullet \langle X, Y\rangle$, for all $Y \in \mathcal{S}$ (III.4.a.2). In particular $\langle H \bullet X\rangle = \langle H \bullet X, H \bullet X\rangle = H^2 \bullet \langle X\rangle$. In other words $\langle H \bullet X \rangle_t = \int_0^t H_s^2 d\langle X \rangle_s$. If the integrand H is continuous we have the representation

$$\int_0^t H_s dX_s = \lim_{\|\Delta\| \to 0} S_\Delta(H, X)$$

(limit in probability), where $S_\Delta(H, X) = \sum H_{t_{j-1}}(X_{t_j} - X_{t_{j-1}})$ for Δ as above (III.2.e.0). The (deterministic) process $\mathbf{t}$ defined by $\mathbf{t}(t) = t$, $t \geq 0$, is a continuous semimartingale, in fact a bounded variation process. Thus the spaces $L(\mathbf{t})$ and $L^1_{loc}(\mathbf{t})$ are defined and in fact $L(\mathbf{t}) = L^1_{loc}(\mathbf{t})$.

Vector valued integrators. Let $X \in \mathcal{S}^d$ and write $X = (X^1, X^2, \ldots, X^d)'$ (column vector), with $X^j \in \mathcal{S}$. Then $L(X)$ is the space of all R^d-valued processes $H = (H^1, H^2, \ldots, H^d)'$ such that $H^j \in L(X^j)$, for all $j = 1, 2, \ldots, d$. For $H \in L(X)$,

$$H \bullet X = \sum_j H^j \bullet X^j, \quad (H \bullet X)_t = \int_0^t H_s \cdot dX_s = \sum_j \int_0^t H_s^j dX_s^j,$$

$$dX = (dX^1, dX^2, \ldots, dX^d)', \quad H_s \cdot dX_s = \sum_j H_s^j dX_s^j.$$

If X is a continuous local martingale (all the X^j continuous local martingales), the spaces $L^2(X)$, $\Lambda^2(X)$ are defined analogously. If $H \in \Lambda^2(X)$, then $H \bullet X$ is a square integrable martingale; if $H \in L^2(X)$, then $H \bullet X \in \mathbf{H}^2$ (III.2.c.3, III.2.f.3).

In particular, if W is an R^d-valued Brownian motion, then

$L^2(W)$ . . . . space of all progressively measurable processes H such that $\|H\|^2_{L^2(W)} = E_P \int_0^\infty \|H_s\|^2 ds < \infty$.

$\Lambda^2(W)$ . . . . . space of all progressively measurable processes H such that $1_{[0,t]}H \in L^2(W)$, for all $0 < t < \infty$.

$L(W) = L^2_{loc}(W)$ . . space of all progressively measurable processes H such that $\int_0^t \|H_s\|^2 ds < \infty$, P-as., for all $0 < t < \infty$.

If $H \in L^2(W)$, then $H \bullet W$ is a martingale in $\mathbf{H}^2$ with $\|H \bullet W\|_{\mathbf{H}^2} = \|H\|_{L^2(W)}$. If $H \in \Lambda^2(W)$, then $H \bullet W$ is a square integrable martingale (III.2.f.3, III.2.f.5).

Stochastic differentials. If $X \in \mathcal{S}^n$, $Z \in \mathcal{S}$ write $dZ = H \cdot dX$ if $H \in L(X)$ and $Z = Z_0 + H \bullet X$, that is, $Z_t = Z_0 + \int_0^t H_s \cdot dX_s$, for all $t \geq 0$. Thus $d(H \bullet X) = H \cdot dX$. We have $dZ = dX$ if and only if $Z - X$ is constant (in time). Likewise $KdZ = HdX$ if and only if $K \in L(Z)$, $H \in L(X)$ and $K \bullet Z = H \bullet X$ (III.3.b). With the process $\mathbf{t}$ as above we have $d\mathbf{t}(t) = dt$.

Local martingale exponential. Let M be a continuous, real valued local martingale. Then the local martingale exponential $\mathcal{E}(M)$ is the process

$$X_t = \mathcal{E}_t(M) = exp\left(M_t - \tfrac{1}{2}\langle M \rangle_t\right).$$

$X = \mathcal{E}(M)$ is the unique solution to the exponential equation $dX_t = X_t dM_t$, $X_0 = 1$. If $\gamma \in L(M)$, then all solutions X to the equation $dX_t = \gamma_t X_t dM_t$ are given by $X_t = X_0 \mathcal{E}_t(\gamma \bullet M)$. If W is an R^d-valued Brownian motion and $\gamma \in L(W)$, then all solutions to the equation $dX_t = \gamma_t X_t \cdot dW_t$ are given by

$$X_t = X_0 \mathcal{E}_t(\gamma \bullet W) = X_0 exp\left(-\tfrac{1}{2} \int_0^t \|\gamma_s\|^2 ds + \int_0^t \gamma_s \cdot dW_s\right) \quad \text{(III.4.b)}.$$

Finance. Let B be a market (IV.3.b), $Z \in \mathcal{S}$ and $A \in \mathcal{S}_+$.

$Z_t^A = Z_t/A_t$ . . . Z expressed in A-numeraire units.

$B(t,T)$ . . . . . Price at time t of the zero coupon bond maturing at time T.

$B_0(t)$ . . . . . . Riskless bond.

P_A . . . . A-numeraire measure (IV.3.d).

P_T . . . . Forward martingale measure at date T (IV.3.f).

W_t^T . . . . . . Process which is a Brownian motion with respect to P_T.

$L(t,T_j)$ . . . . . Forward Libor set at time T_j for the accrual interval $[T_j, T_{j+1}]$

$L(t)$ . . . . Process $\big(L(t,T_0), \ldots, L(t,T_{n-1})\big)$ of forward Libor rates.

CHAPTER I

Martingale Theory

Preliminaries. Let $(\Omega, \mathcal{F}, P)$ be a probability space, $\overline{R} = [-\infty, +\infty]$ denote the extended real line and $\mathcal{B}(\overline{R})$ and $\mathcal{B}(R^n)$ the Borel σ-fields on $\overline{R}$ and R^n respectively.

A *random object* on $(\Omega, \mathcal{F}, P)$ is a measurable map $X : (\Omega, \mathcal{F}, P) \to (\Omega_1, \mathcal{F}_1)$ with values in some measurable space $(\Omega_1, \mathcal{F}_1)$. P_X denotes the distribution of X (appendix B.5). If Q is any probability on $(\Omega_1, \mathcal{F}_1)$ we write $X \sim Q$ to indicate that $P_X = Q$. If $(\Omega_1, \mathcal{F}_1) = (R^n, \mathcal{B}(R^n))$ respectively $(\Omega_1, \mathcal{F}_1) = (\overline{R}, \mathcal{B}(\overline{R}))$, X is called a *random vector* respectively *random variable*. In particular random variables are extended real valued.

For extended real numbers a, b we write $a \wedge b = min\{a, b\}$ and $a \vee b = max\{a, b\}$. If X is a random variable, the set $\{\, \omega \in \Omega \mid X \geq 0 \,\}$ will be written as $[X \geq 0]$ and its probability denoted $P([X \geq 0])$ or, more simply, $P(X \geq 0)$. We set $X^+ = X \vee 0 = 1_{[X>0]}X$ and $X^- = (-X)^+$. Thus $X^+, X^- \geq 0$, $X^+ X^- = 0$ and $X = X^+ - X^-$.

For nonnegative X let $E(X) = \int_\Omega X dP$ and let $\mathcal{E}(P)$ denote the family of all random variables X such that at least one of $E(X^+)$, $E(X^-)$ is finite. For $X \in \mathcal{E}(P)$ set $E(X) = E(X^+) - E(X^-)$ *(expected value* of X). This quantity will also be denoted $E_P(X)$ if dependence on the probability measure P is to be made explicit.

If $X \in \mathcal{E}(P)$ and $A \in \mathcal{F}$ then $1_A X \in \mathcal{E}(P)$ and we write $E(X; A) = E(1_A X)$. The expression "P-almost surely" will be abbreviated "P-as.". Since random variables X, Y are extended real valued, the sum $X + Y$ is not defined in general. However it is defined (P-as.) if both $E(X^+)$ and $E(Y^+)$ are finite, since then $X, Y < +\infty$, P-as., or both $E(X^-)$ and $E(Y^-)$ are finite, since then $X, Y > -\infty$, P-as.

An *event* is a set $A \in \mathcal{F}$, that is, a measurable subset of Ω. If (A_n) is a sequence of events let $[A_n \, i.o.] = \bigcap_m \bigcup_{n \geq m} A_n = \{\, \omega \in \Omega \mid \omega \in A_n$ for infinitely many $n \,\}$.

Borel Cantelli Lemma. *(a) If $\sum_n P(A_n) < \infty$ then $P(A_n \, i.o.) = 0$.*

(b) If the events A_n are independent and $\sum_n P(A_n) = \infty$ then $P(A_n \, i.o.) = 1$.

(c) If $P(A_n) \geq \delta$, for all $n \geq 1$, then $P(A_n i.o.) \geq \delta$.

Proof. (a) Let $m \geq 1$. Then $0 \leq P(A_n \, i.o.) \leq \sum_{n \geq m} P(A_n) \to 0$, as $m \uparrow \infty$.

(b) Set $A = [A_n \, i.o.]$. Then $P(A^c) = \lim_m P\left(\bigcap_{n \geq m} A_n^c\right) = \lim_m \prod_{n \geq m} P(A_n^c) = \lim_m \prod_{n \geq m}(1 - P(A_n)) = 0$. (c) Since $P(A_n i.o.) = \lim_m P\left(\bigcup_{n \geq m} A_n\right)$. ∎

1. CONVERGENCE OF RANDOM VARIABLES

1.a Forms of convergence. Let X_n, X, $n \geq 1$, be random variables on the probability space $(\Omega, \mathcal{F}, P)$ and $1 \leq p < \infty$. We need several notions of convergence $X_n \to X$:

(i) $X_n \to X$ *in* L^p, if $\|X_n - X\|_p^p = E(|X_n - X|^p) \to 0$, as $n \uparrow \infty$.

(ii) $X_n \to X$, *P-almost surely* (*P*-as.), if $X_n(\omega) \to X(\omega)$ in $\overline{R}$, for all points ω in the complement of some P-null set.

(iii) $X_n \to X$ *in probability on the set* $A \in \mathcal{F}$, if $P([|X_n - X| > \epsilon] \cap A) \to 0$, $n \uparrow \infty$, for all $\epsilon > 0$. Convergence $X_n \to X$ *in probability* is defined as convergence in probability on all of Ω, equivalently $P(|X_n - X| > \epsilon) \to 0$, $n \uparrow \infty$, for all $\epsilon > 0$.

Here the differences $X_n - X$ are evaluated according to the rule $(+\infty) - (+\infty) = (-\infty) - (-\infty) = 0$ and $\|Z\|_p$ is allowed to assume the value $+\infty$. Recall that the finiteness of the probability measure P implies that $\|Z\|_p$ increases with $p \geq 1$. Thus $X_n \to X$ in L^p implies that $X_n \to X$ in L^r, for all $1 \leq r \leq p$.

Convergence in L^1 will simply be called *convergence in norm*. Thus $X_n \to X$ in norm if and only if $\|X_n - X\|_1 = E(|X_n - X|) \to 0$, as $n \uparrow \infty$. Many of the results below make essential use of the finiteness of the measure P.

1.a.0. *(a) Convergence P-as. implies convergence in probability.*
(b) Convergence in norm implies convergence in probability.

Proof. (a) Assume that $X_n \not\to X$ in probability. We will show that that $X_n \not\to X$ on a set of positive measure. Choose $\epsilon > 0$ such that $P([|X_n - X| \geq \epsilon]) \not\to 0$, as $n \uparrow \infty$. Then there exists a strictly increasing sequence (k_n) of natural numbers and a number $\delta > 0$ such that $P(|X_{k_n} - X| \geq \epsilon) \geq \delta$, for all $n \geq 1$.

Set $A_n = [|X_{k_n} - X| \geq \epsilon]$ and $A = [A_n \text{ i.o.}]$. As $P(A_n) \geq \delta$, for all $n \geq 1$ it follows that $P(A) \geq \delta > 0$. However if $\omega \in A$, then $X_{k_n}(\omega) \not\to X(\omega)$ and so $X_n(\omega) \not\to X(\omega)$. (b) Note that $P(|X_n - X| \geq \epsilon) \leq \epsilon^{-1}\|X_n - X\|_1$. ∎

1.a.1. *Convergence in probability implies almost sure convergence of a subsequence*

Proof. Assume that $X_n \to X$ in probability and choose inductively a sequence of integers $0 < n_1 < n_2 < \ldots$ such that $P(|X_{n_k} - X| \geq 1/k) \leq 2^{-k}$. Then $\sum_k P(|X_{n_k} - X| \geq 1/k) < \infty$ and so the event $A = [|X_{n_k} - X| \geq \frac{1}{k} \text{ i.o.}]$ is a nullset. However, if $\omega \in A^c$, then $X_{k_n}(\omega) \to X(\omega)$. Thus $X_{k_n} \to X$, *P*-as. ∎

Remark. Thus convergence in norm implies almost sure convergence of a subsequence. It follows that convergence in L^p implies almost sure convergence of a subsequence. Let $L^0(P)$ denote the space of all (real valued) random variables on $(\Omega, \mathcal{F}, P)$. As usual we identify random variables which are equal P-as. Consequently $L^0(P)$ is a space of equivalence classes of random variables.

It is interesting to note that convergence in probability is metrizable, that is, there is a metric d on $L^0(P)$ such that $X_n \to X$ in probability if and only i

$d(X_n, X) \to 0$, as $n \uparrow \infty$, for all $X_n, X \in L^0(P)$. To see this let $\rho(t) = 1 \wedge t$, $t \geq 0$, and note that ρ is nondecreasing and satisfies $\rho(a+b) \leq \rho(a) + \rho(b)$, $a, b \geq 0$. From this it follows that $d(X, Y) = E(\rho(|X - Y|)) = E(1 \wedge |X - Y|)$ defines a metric on $L^0(P)$. It is not hard to show that $P(|X - Y| \geq \epsilon) \leq \epsilon^{-1} d(X, Y)$ and $d(X, Y) \leq P(|X - Y| \geq \epsilon) + \epsilon$, for all $0 < \epsilon < 1$. This implies that $X_n \to X$ in probability if and only if $d(X_n, X) \to 0$. The metric d is translation invariant $(d(X + Z, Y + Z) = d(X, Y))$ and thus makes $L^0(P)$ into a metric linear space. In contrast it can be shown that convergence P-as. cannot be induced by any topology.

1.a.2. *Let $A_k \in \mathcal{F}$, $k \geq 1$, and $A = \bigcup_k A_k$. If $X_n \to X$ in probability on each set A_k, then $X_n \to X$ in probability on A.*

Proof. Replacing the A_k with suitable subsets if necessary, we may assume that the A_k are disjoint. Let $\epsilon, \delta > 0$ be arbitrary, set $E_m = \bigcup_{k > m} A_k$ and choose m such that $P(E_m) < \delta$. Then

$$P\left([|X_n - X| > \epsilon] \cap A\right) \leq \sum_{k \leq m} P\left([|X_n - X| > \epsilon] \cap A_k\right) + P(E_m),$$

for all $n \geq 1$. Consequently $\limsup_n P\left([|X_n - X| > \epsilon] \cap A\right) \leq P(E_m) < \delta$. Since here $\delta > 0$ was arbitrary, this lim sup is zero, that is, $P\left([|X_n - X| > \epsilon] \cap A\right) \to 0$, as $n \uparrow \infty$. ∎

1.b Norm convergence and uniform integrability. Let X be a random variable and recall the notation $E(X; A) = E(1_A X) = \int_A X dP$. The notion of uniform integrability is motivated by the following observation:

1.b.0. *X is integrable if and only if $\lim_{c \uparrow \infty} E(|X|; [|X| \geq c]) = 0$. In this case X satisfies $\lim_{P(A) \to 0} E(|X| 1_A) = 0$.*

Proof. Assume that X is integrable. Then $|X| 1_{[|X| < c]} \uparrow |X|$, as $c \uparrow \infty$, on the set $[|X| < +\infty]$ and hence P-as. The Monotone Convergence Theorem now implies that $E(|X|; [|X| < c]) \uparrow E(|X|) < \infty$ and hence

$$E(|X|; [|X| \geq c]) = E(|X|) - E(|X|; [|X| < c]) \to 0, \quad \text{as } c \uparrow \infty.$$

Now let $\epsilon > 0$ be arbitrary and choose c such that $E(|X|; [|X| \geq c]) < \epsilon$. If $A \in \mathcal{F}$ with $P(A) < \epsilon/c$ is any set, we have

$$E(|X| 1_A) = E(|X|; A \cap [|X| < c]) + E(|X|; A \cap [|X| \geq c])$$
$$\leq cP(A) + E(|X|; [|X| \geq c]) < \epsilon + \epsilon = 2\epsilon.$$

Thus $\lim_{P(A) \to 0} E(|X| 1_A) = 0$. Conversely, if $\lim_{c \uparrow \infty} E(|X|; [|X| \geq c]) = 0$ we can choose c such that $E(|X|; [|X| \geq c]) \leq 1$. Then $E(|X|) \leq c + 1 < \infty$. Thus X is integrable. ∎

This leads to the following definition: a family $F = \{ X_i \mid i \in I \}$ of random variables is called *uniformly integrable* if it satisfies

$$\lim_{c \uparrow \infty} \sup_{i \in I} E(|X_i|; [|X_i| \geq c]) = 0,$$

that is, $\lim_{c\uparrow\infty} E(|X_i|; [|X_i| \geq c]) = 0$, uniformly in $i \in I$. The family F is called *uniformly P-continuous* if it satisfies

$$\lim_{P(A)\to 0} \sup_{i\in I} E(1_A |X_i|) = 0,$$

that is, $\lim_{P(A)\to 0} E(1_A |X_i|) = 0$, uniformly in $i \in I$. The family F is called L^1-*bounded*, iff $\sup_{i\in I} \|X_i\|_1 < +\infty$, that is, $F \subseteq L^1(P)$ is a bounded subset.

1.b.1 Remarks. (a) The function $\phi(c) = \sup_{i\in I} E(|X_i|; [|X_i| \geq c])$ is a nonincreasing function of $c \geq 0$. Consequently, to show that the family $F = \{ X_i \mid i \in I \}$ is uniformly integrable it suffices to show that for each $\epsilon > 0$ there exists a $c \geq 0$ such that $\sup_{i\in I} E(|X_i|; [|X_i| \geq c]) \leq \epsilon$.

(b) To show that the family $F = \{ X_i \mid i \in I \}$ is uniformly P-continuous we must show that for each $\epsilon > 0$ there exists a $\delta > 0$ such that $\sup_{i\in I} E(1_A |X_i|) < \epsilon$, for all sets $A \in \mathcal{F}$ with $P(A) < \delta$. This means that the family $\{ \mu_i \mid i \in I \}$ of measures μ_i defined by $\mu_i(A) = E(1_A |X_i|)$, $A \in \mathcal{F}$, $i \in I$, is uniformly absolutely continuous with respect to the measure P.

(c) From 1.b.0 it follows that each finite family $F = \{ f_1, f_2, \ldots, f_n \} \subseteq L^1(P)$ of integrable functions is both uniformly integrable (increase c) and uniformly P-continuous (decrease δ).

1.b.2. *A family $F = \{ X_i \mid i \in I \}$ of random variables is uniformly integrable if and only if F is uniformly P-continuous and L^1-bounded.*

Proof. Let F be uniformly integrable and choose ρ such that $E(|X_i|; [|X_i| \geq \rho]) < 1$, for all $i \in I$. Then $\|X_i\|_1 = E((|X_i|; [|X_i| \geq \rho]) + E((|X_i|; [|X_i| < \rho]) \leq 1 + \rho$, for each $i \in I$. Thus the family F is L^1-bounded.

To see that F is uniformly P-continuous, let $\epsilon > 0$. Choose c such that $E((|X_i|; [|X_i| \geq c]) < \epsilon$, for all $i \in I$. If $A \in \mathcal{F}$ and $P(A) < \epsilon/c$, then

$$\begin{aligned} E(1_A |X_i|) &= E(|X_i|; A \cap [|X_i| < c]) + E(|X_i|; A \cap [|X_i| \geq c]) \\ &\leq cP(A) + E((|X_i|; [|X_i| \geq c]) < \epsilon + \epsilon = 2\epsilon, \quad \text{for every } i \in I. \end{aligned}$$

Thus the family F is uniformly P-continuous. Conversely, let F be uniformly P-continuous and L^1-bounded. We must show that $\lim_{c\uparrow\infty} E((|X_i|; [|X_i| \geq c]) = 0$, uniformly in $i \in I$. Set $r = \sup_{i\in I} \|X_i\|_1$. Then, by Chebycheff's inequality,

$$P([|X_i| \geq c]) \leq c^{-1} \|X_i\|_1 \leq r/c,$$

for all $i \in I$ and all $c > 0$. Let now $\epsilon > 0$ be arbitrary. Find $\delta > 0$ such that $P(A) < \delta \Rightarrow E(1_A |X_i|) < \epsilon$, for all sets $A \in \mathcal{F}$ and all $i \in I$. Choose c such that $r/c < \delta$. Then we have $P([|X_i| \geq c]) \leq r/c < \delta$ and so $E((|X_i|; [|X_i| \geq c]) < \epsilon$, for all $i \in I$. ∎

1.b.3 Norm convergence. *Let $X_n, X \in L^1(P)$. Then the following are equivalent:*
(i) $X_n \to X$ in norm, that is, $\|X_n - X\|_1 \to 0$, as $n \uparrow \infty$.
(ii) $X_n \to X$ in probability and the sequence (X_n) is uniformly integrable.
(iii) $X_n \to X$ in probability and the sequence (X_n) is uniformly P-continuous.

Remark. Thus, given convergence in probability to an integrable limit, uniform integrability and uniform P-continuity are equivalent. In general this is not the case.

Proof. $(i) \Rightarrow (ii)$: Assume that $\|X_n - X\|_1 \to 0$, as $n \uparrow \infty$. Then $X_n \to X$ in probability, by 1.a.0. To show that the sequence (X_n) is uniformly integrable let $\epsilon > 0$ be arbitrary. We must find $c < +\infty$ such that $\sup_{n \geq 1} E(|X_n|; [|X_n| \geq c]) \leq \epsilon$. Choose $\delta > 0$ such that $\delta < \epsilon/3$ and $P(A) < \delta$ implies $E(1_A|X|) < \epsilon/3$, for all sets $A \in \mathcal{F}$. Now choose $c \geq 1$ such that

$$E(|X|; [|X| \geq c - 1]) < \epsilon/3 \tag{0}$$

and finally N such that $n \geq N$ implies $\|X_n - X\|_1 < \delta < \epsilon/3$ and let $n \geq N$. Then $|X_n| \leq |X_n - X| + |X|$ and so

$$E(|X_n|; [|X_n| \geq c]) \leq E(|X_n - X|; [|X_n| \geq c]) + E(|X|; [|X_n| \geq c])$$
$$\leq \|X_n - X\|_1 + E(|X|; [|X_n| \geq c]) < \tfrac{\epsilon}{3} + E(|X|; [|X_n| \geq c]).$$

Let $A = [|X_n| \geq c] \cap [|X| < c - 1]$ and $B = [|X_n| \geq c] \cap [|X| \geq c - 1]$. Then $|X_n - X| \geq 1$ on the set A and so $P(A) \leq E(1_A|X_n - X|) \leq \|X_n - X\|_1 < \delta$ which implies $E(1_A|X|) < \epsilon/3$. Using (0) it follows that

$$E(|X|; [|X_n| \geq c]) = E(1_A|X|) + E(1_B|X|) < \epsilon/3 + \epsilon/3.$$

Consequently $E(|X_n|; [|X_n| \geq c]) < \epsilon$, for all $n \geq N$. Since the X_n are integrable, we can increase c suitably so as to obtain this inequality for $n = 1, 2, \ldots, N-1$ and consequently for all $n \geq 1$. Then $\sup_{n \geq 1} E(|X_n|; [|X_n| \geq c]) \leq \epsilon$ as desired.

$(b) \Rightarrow (c)$: Uniform integrability implies uniform P-continuity.

$(c) \Rightarrow (a)$: Assume now that the sequence (X_n) is uniformly P-continuous and converges to $X \in L^1(P)$ in probability. Let $\epsilon > 0$ and set $A_n = [|X_n - X| \geq \epsilon]$. Then $P(A_n) \to 0$, as $n \uparrow \infty$. Since the sequence (X_n) is uniformly P-continuous and $X \in L^1(P)$ is integrable, we can choose $\delta > 0$ such that $A \in \mathcal{F}$ and $P(A) < \delta$ imply $\sup_{n \geq 1} E(1_A|X_n|) < \epsilon$ and $E(1_A|X|) < \epsilon$. Finally we can choose N such that $n \geq N$ implies $P(A_n) < \delta$. Since $|X_n - X| \leq \epsilon$ on A_n^c, it follows that

$$n \geq N \Rightarrow \|X_n - X\|_1 = E(|X_n - X|; A_n) + E(|X_n - X|; A_n^c)$$
$$\leq E(|X_n|; A_n) + E(|X|; A_n) + \epsilon P(A_n^c) \leq \epsilon + \epsilon + \epsilon = 3\epsilon.$$

Thus $\|X_n - X\|_1 \to 0$, as $n \uparrow \infty$. ∎

1.b.4 Corollary. *Let $X_n \in L^1(P)$, $n \geq 1$, and assume that $X_n \to X$ almost surely. Then the following are equivalent:*

(i) $X \in L^1(P)$ and $X_n \to X$ in norm.

(ii) The sequence (X_n) is uniformly integrable.

Proof. $(i) \Rightarrow (ii)$ follows readily from 1.b.3. Conversely, if the sequence (X_n) is uniformly integrable, especially L^1-bounded, then the almost sure convergence $X_n \to X$ and Fatou's lemma imply that $\|X\|_1 = E(|X|) = E(\liminf_n |X_n|) \leq \liminf_n E(|X_n|) < \infty.$ ∎

Next we show that the uniform integrability of a family $\{\, X_i \mid i \in I \,\}$ of random variables is equivalent to the L^1-boundedness of a family $\{\, \phi \circ |X_i| : i \in I \,\}$ of suitably enlarged random variables $\phi(|X_i|)$.

1.b.5 Theorem. *The family $F = \{\, X_i \mid i \in I \,\} \subseteq L^0(P)$ is uniformly integrable if and only if there exists a function $\phi : [0, +\infty[\to [0, +\infty[$ such that*

$$\lim_{x \uparrow \infty} \phi(x)/x = +\infty \quad and \quad \sup_{i \in I} E(\phi(|X_i|)) < \infty. \tag{1}$$

The function ϕ can be chosen to be convex and nondecreasing.

Proof. ($\Leftarrow$): Let ϕ be such a function and $C = \sup_{i \in I} E(\phi(|X_i|)) < +\infty$. Set $\rho(a) = \mathrm{Inf}_{x \geq a} \phi(x)/x$. Then $\rho(a) \to \infty$, as $a \uparrow \infty$, and $\phi(x) \geq \rho(a)x$, for all $x \geq a$. Thus

$$E(|X_i|; [|X_i| \geq a]) = \rho(a)^{-1} E(\rho(a)|X_i|; [|X_i| \geq a])$$
$$\leq \rho(a)^{-1} E(\phi(|X_i|); [|X_i| \geq a])) \leq C/\rho(a) \to 0,$$

as $a \uparrow \infty$, where the convergence is uniform in $i \in I$.

($\Rightarrow$): Assume now that the family F is uniformly integrable, that is

$$\delta(a) = \sup_{i \in I} E(|X_i|; [|X_i| \geq a]) \to 0, \quad as \ a \to \infty.$$

According to 1.b.2 the family F is L^1-bounded and so $\delta(0) = \sup_{i \in I} \|X_i\|_1 < \infty$. We seek a piecewise linear convex function ϕ as in (1) with $\phi(0) = 0$. Such a function has the form $\phi(x) = \phi(a_k) + \alpha_k(x - a_k)$, $x \in [a_k, a_{k+1}]$, with $0 = a_0 < a_1 < \ldots < a_k < a_{k+1} \to \infty$ and increasing slopes $\alpha_k \uparrow \infty$.

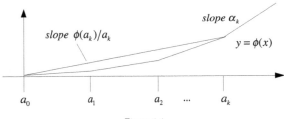

Figure 1.1

The increasing property of the slopes α_k implies that ϕ is convex. Observe that $\phi(x) \geq \alpha_k(x - a_k)$, for all $x \geq a_k$. Thus $\alpha_k \uparrow \infty$ implies $\phi(x)/x \to \infty$, as $x \uparrow \infty$. We must choose a_k and α_k such that $\sup_{i \in I} E(\phi(|X_i|)) < \infty$. If $i \in I$, then

$$E(\phi(|X_i|)) = \sum_{k=0}^{\infty} E\big(\phi(|X_i|); [a_k \leq |X_i| < a_{k+1}]\big)$$

$$= \sum_{k=0}^{\infty} E\big(\phi(a_k) + \alpha_k(|X_i| - a_k); [a_k \leq |X_i| < a_{k+1}]\big)$$

$$\leq \sum_{k=0}^{\infty} \big\{\phi(a_k)P(|X_i| \geq a_k) + \alpha_k E\big(|X_i|; [|X_i| \geq a_k]\big)\big\}.$$

Using the estimate $P([|X_i| \geq a_k]) \leq a_k^{-1} E(|X_i|; [|X_i| \geq a_k])$ and observing that $\phi(a_k)/a_k \leq \alpha_k$ by the increasing nature of the slopes (Figure 1.1), we obtain

$$E(\phi(|X_i|)) \leq \sum_{k=0}^{\infty} 2\alpha_k E\big(|X_i|; [|X_i| \geq a_k]\big) \leq \sum_{k=0}^{\infty} 2\alpha_k \delta(a_k).$$

Since $\delta(a) \to 0$, as $a \to \infty$, we can choose the sequence $a_k \uparrow \infty$ such that $\delta(a_k) < 3^{-k}$, for all $k \geq 1$. Note that a_0 cannot be chosen $(a_0 = 0)$ and hence has to be treated separately. Recall that $\delta(a_0) = \delta(0) < \infty$ and choose $0 < \alpha_0 < 2$ so that $\alpha_0 \delta(a_0) < 1 = (2/3)^0$. For $k \geq 1$ set $\alpha_k = 2^k$. It follows that

$$E(\phi(|X_i|)) \leq \sum_{k=0}^{\infty} 2 (2/3)^k = 6, \quad \text{for all } i \in I. \blacksquare$$

1.b.6 Example. If $p > 1$ then the function $\phi(x) = x^p$ satisfies the assumptions of Theorem 1.b.5 and $E(\phi(|X_i|)) = E(|X_i|^p) = \|X_i\|_p^p$. It follows that a bounded family $F = \{X_i \mid i \in I\} \subseteq L^p(P)$ is automatically uniformly integrable, that is, L^p-boundedness (where $p > 1$) implies uniform integrability. A direct proof of this fact is also easy:

1.b.7. *Let $p > 1$. If $K = \sup_{i \in I} \|X_i\|_p < \infty$, then the family $\{X_i \mid i \in I\} \subseteq L^p$ is uniformly integrable.*

Proof. Let $i \in I$, $c > 0$ and q be the exponent conjugate to p $(1/p + 1/q = 1)$. Using the inequalities of Hoelder and Chebycheff we can write

$$E\big(|X_i|1_{[|X_i| \geq c]}\big) \leq \|1_{[|X_i| \geq c]}\|_q \|X_i\|_p = P\big(|X_i| \geq c\big)^{\frac{1}{q}} \|X_i\|_p$$

$$\leq \big(c^{-p}\|X_i\|_p^p\big)^{\frac{1}{q}} \|X_i\|_p = c^{-\frac{p}{q}} K^{1+\frac{p}{q}} \to 0,$$

as $c \uparrow \infty$, uniformly in $i \in I$. $\blacksquare$

2. CONDITIONING

2.a Sigma fields, information and conditional expectation. Let $\mathcal{E}(P)$ denote the family of all extended real valued random variables X on $(\Omega, \mathcal{F}, P)$ such that $E(X^+) < \infty$ or $E(X^-) < \infty$ (i.e., $E(X)$ exists). Note that $\mathcal{E}(P)$ is not a vector space since sums of elements in $\mathcal{E}(X)$ are not defined in general.

2.a.0. *(a) If $X \in \mathcal{E}(P)$, then $1_A X \in \mathcal{E}(P)$, for all sets $A \in \mathcal{F}$.*
(b) If $X \in \mathcal{E}(P)$ and $\alpha \in R$, then $\alpha X \in \mathcal{E}(P)$.
(c) If $X_1, X_2 \in \mathcal{E}(P)$ and $E(X_1) + E(X_2)$ is defined, then $X_1 + X_2 \in \mathcal{E}(P)$.

Proof. We show only (c). We may assume that $E(X_1) \le E(X_2)$. If $E(X_1) + E(X_2)$ is defined, then $E(X_1) > -\infty$ or $E(X_2) < \infty$. Let us assume that $E(X_1) > -\infty$ and so $E(X_2) > -\infty$, the other case being similar. Then $X_1, X_2 > -\infty$, P-as and hence $X_1 + X_2$ is defined P-as. Moreover $E(X_1^-), E(X_2^-) < \infty$ and, since $(X_1 + X_2)^- \le X_1^- + X_2^-$, also $E\big((X_1 + X_2)^-\big) < \infty$. Thus $X_1 + X_2 \in \mathcal{E}(P)$. ∎

2.a.1. *Let $\mathcal{G} \subseteq \mathcal{F}$ be a sub-σ-field, $D \in \mathcal{G}$ and $X_1, X_2 \in \mathcal{E}(P)$ $\mathcal{G}$-measurable.*
(a) If $E(X_1 1_A) \le E(X_2 1_A)$, $\forall A \subseteq D, A \in \mathcal{G}$, then $X_1 \le X_2$ as. on D.
(b) If $E(X_1 1_A) = E(X_2 1_A)$, $\forall A \subseteq D, A \in \mathcal{G}$, then $X_1 = X_2$ as. on D.

Proof. (a) Assume that $E(X_1 1_A) \le E(X_2 1_A)$, for all $\mathcal{G}$-measurable subsets $A \subseteq D$. If $P\big([X_1 > X_2] \cap D\big) > 0$ then there exist real numbers $\alpha < \beta$ such that the event $A = [X_1 > \beta > \alpha > X_2] \cap D \in \mathcal{G}$ has positive probability. But then $E(X_1 1_A) \ge \beta P(A) > \alpha P(A) \ge E(X_2 1_A)$, contrary to assumption. Thus we must have $P\big([X_1 > X_2] \cap D\big) = 0$. (b) follows from (a). ∎

We should now develop some intuition before we take up the rigorous development in the next section. The elements $\omega \in \Omega$ are the possible states of nature and one among them, say δ, is the true state of nature. The true state of nature is unknown and controls the outcome of all random experiments. An event $A \in \mathcal{F}$ occurs or does not occur according as $\delta \in A$ or $\delta \notin A$, that is, according as the random variable 1_A assumes the value one or zero at δ.

To gain information about the true state of nature we determine by means of experiments whether or not certain events occur. Assume that the event A of probability $P(A) > 0$ has been observed to occur. Recalling from elementary probability that $P(B \cap A)/P(A)$ is the conditional probability of an event $B \in \mathcal{F}$ given that A has occurred, we replace the probability measure P on $\mathcal{F}$ with the probability $Q_A(B) = P(B \cap A)/P(A)$, $B \in \mathcal{F}$, that is we pass to the probability space $(\Omega, \mathcal{F}, Q_A)$. The usual extension procedure starting from indicator functions shows that the probability Q_A satisfies

$$E_{Q_A}(X) = P(A)^{-1} E(X 1_A), \quad \text{for all random variables } X \in \mathcal{E}(P).$$

At any given time the family of all events A, for which it is known whether they occur or not, is a sub-σ-field of $\mathcal{F}$. For example it is known that $\emptyset$ does not occur

Ω does occur and if it is known whether or not A occurs, then it is known whether or not A^c occurs etc. This leads us to define the information in any sub-σ-field $\mathcal{G}$ of $\mathcal{F}$ as the information about the occurrence or nonoccurrence of each event $A \in \mathcal{G}$, equivalently, the value $1_A(\delta)$, for all $A \in \mathcal{G}$. Define an equivalence relation $\sim_{\mathcal{G}}$ on Ω as $\omega_1 \sim_{\mathcal{G}} \omega_2$ iff $1_A(\omega_1) = 1_A(\omega_2)$, for all events $A \in \mathcal{G}$. The information in $\mathcal{G}$ is then the information which equivalence class contains the true state δ.

Each experiment adds to the information about the true state of nature, that is, enlarges the σ-field of events of which it is known whether or not they occur. Let, for each $t \geq 0$, $\mathcal{F}_t$ denote the σ-field of all events A for which it is known by time t whether or not they occur. The $\mathcal{F}_t$ then form a *filtration* on Ω, that is, an increasing chain of sub-σ-fields of $\mathcal{F}$ representing the increasing information about the true state of nature available at time t.

Events are special cases of random variables and a particular experiment is the observation of the value $X(\delta)$ of a random variable X. Indeed this is the entire information contained in X. Let $\sigma(X)$ denote the σ-field generated by X. If A is an event in $\sigma(X)$, then $1_A = g \circ X$, for some deterministic function g (appendix B.6.0). Thus the value $X(\delta)$ determines the value $1_A(\delta)$, for each event $A \in \sigma(X)$ and the converse is also true, since X is a limit of $\sigma(X)$-measurable simple functions. Consequently the information contained in X (the true value of X) can be identified with the information contained in the σ-field generated by X.

Thus we will say that X contains no more information than the sub-σ-field $\mathcal{G} \subseteq \mathcal{F}$, if and only if $\sigma(X) \subseteq \mathcal{G}$, that is, iff X is $\mathcal{G}$-measurable. In this case X is constant on the equivalence classes of $\sim_{\mathcal{G}}$ since this is true of all $\mathcal{G}$-measurable simple functions and X is a pointwise limit of these. This is as expected as the observation of the value $X(\delta)$ must not add to further distinguish the true state of nature δ.

Let $X = X_1 + X_2$, where X_1, X_2 are independent random variables and assume that we have to make a bet on the true value of X. In the absence of any information our bet will be the mean $E(X) = E(X_1) + E(X_2)$. Assume now that it is observed that $X_1 = 1$ (implying nothing about X_2 by independence). Obviously then we will refine our bet on the value of X to be $1 + E(X_2)$. More generally, if the value of X_1 is observed, our bet on X becomes $X_1 + E(X_2)$.

Let now $X \in \mathcal{E}(P)$ and $\mathcal{G} \subseteq \mathcal{F}$ any sub-σ-field. We wish to define the conditional expectation $Z = E(X|\mathcal{G})$ to give a rigorous meaning to the notion of a best bet on the value of X in light of the information in the σ-field $\mathcal{G}$. From the above it is clear that Z is itself a random variable. The following two properties are clearly desirable:

(i) Z is $\mathcal{G}$-measurable (Z contains no more information than $\mathcal{G}$).
(ii) $Z \in \mathcal{E}(P)$ and $E(Z) = E(X)$.

These two properties do not determine the random variable Z but we can refine (ii). Rewrite (ii) as $E(Z1_\Omega) = E(X1_\Omega)$ and let $A \in \mathcal{G}$ be any event. Given the information in $\mathcal{G}$ it is known whether A occurs or not. Assume first that A occurs and $P(A) > 0$. We then pass to the probability space $(\Omega, \mathcal{F}, Q_A)$ and (ii) for this new space becomes $E_{Q_A}(Z) = E_{Q_A}(X)$, that is, after multiplication with $P(A)$,

$$E(Z1_A) = E(X1_A). \tag{0}$$

This same equation also holds true if $P(A) = 0$ (regardless of whether A occurs or not). Likewise, if $B \in \mathcal{G}$ does not occur, then $A = B^c$ occurs and (0) and (ii) then imply that $E(Z1_B) = E(X1_B)$. In short, equation (0) holds for all events $A \in \mathcal{G}$. This, in conjunction with the $\mathcal{G}$-measurability of Z uniquely determines Z up to a P-null set (2.a.1.(b)). The existence of Z will be shown in the next section. Z is itself a random variable and the values $Z(\omega)$ should be interpreted as follows: By $\mathcal{G}$-measurability Z is constant on all equivalence classes of $\sim_{\mathcal{G}}$. If it turns out that $\delta \sim_{\mathcal{G}} \omega$, then $Z(\omega)$ is our bet on the true value of X.

If we wish to avoid the notion of true state of nature and true value of a random variable, we may view the random variable Z as a best bet on the random variable X as a whole using only the information contained in $\mathcal{G}$. This interpretation is supported by the following fact (2.b.1):
If $X \in L^2(P)$, then $Z \in L^2(P)$ and $Y = Z$ minimizes the distance $\|X - Y\|_{L^2}$ over all $\mathcal{G}$-measurable random variables $Y \in L^2(P)$.

Example. Assume that $\mathcal{G} = \sigma(X_1, \ldots, X_n)$ is the σ-field generated by the random variables $X_1, \ldots, X_n$. The information contained in $\mathcal{G}$ is then equivalent to an observation of the values $X_1(\delta) = x_1, \ldots, X_n(\delta) = x_n$. Moreover, since $Z = E(X|\mathcal{G})$ is $\mathcal{G}$-measurable, we have $Z = g(X_1, X_2, \ldots, X_n)$, for some Borel measurable function $g : R^n \to \overline{R}$, that is, Z is a deterministic function of the values $X_1, \ldots, X_n$ (appendix B.6.0). If the values $X_1(\delta) = x_1, \ldots, X_n(\delta) = x_n$ are observed, our bet on the value of X becomes $Z(\delta) = g(x_1, x_2, \ldots, x_n)$.

2.b Conditional expectation. Let $\mathcal{G}$ be a sub-σ-field of $\mathcal{F}$ and $X \in \mathcal{E}(P)$. A *conditional expectation of* X given the sub-σ-field $\mathcal{G}$ is a $\mathcal{G}$-measurable random variable $Z \in \mathcal{E}(P)$ such that

$$E(Z1_A) = E(X1_A), \quad \forall A \in \mathcal{G}. \tag{0}$$

2.b.0. *A conditional expectation of* X *given* $\mathcal{G}$ *exists and is P-as. uniquely determined. Henceforth it will be denoted* $E(X|\mathcal{G})$ *or* $E_{\mathcal{G}}(X)$.

Proof. Uniqueness. Let Z_1, Z_2 be conditional expectations of X given $\mathcal{G}$. Then $E(Z_1 1_A) = E(X1_A) = E(Z_2 1_A)$, for all sets $A \in \mathcal{G}$. It will suffice to show that $P(Z_1 < Z_2) = 0$. Otherwise there exists numbers $\alpha < \beta$ such that the event $A = [Z_1 \leq \alpha < \beta \leq Z_2] \in \mathcal{G}$ has probability $P(A) > 0$. Then $E(Z_1 1_A) \leq \alpha P(A) < \beta P(A) \leq E(Z_2 1_A)$, a contradiction.

Existence. (i) Assume first that $X \in L^2(P)$ and let $L^2(\mathcal{G}, P)$ be the space of all equivalence classes in $L^2(P)$ containing a $\mathcal{G}$-measurable representative. We claim that the subspace $L^2(\mathcal{G}, P) \subseteq L^2(P)$ is closed. Indeed, let $Y_n \in L^2(\mathcal{G}, P)$, $Y \in L^2(P)$ and assume that $Y_n \to Y$ in $L^2(P)$. Passing to a suitable subsequence of Y_n if necessary, we may assume that $Y_n \to Y$, P-as. Set $\tilde{Y} = \limsup_n Y_n$. Then $\tilde{Y}$ is $\mathcal{G}$-measurable and $\tilde{Y} = Y$, P-as. This shows that $Y \in L^2(\mathcal{G}, P)$.

Let Z be the orthogonal projection of X onto $L^2(\mathcal{G}, P)$. Then $X = Z + U$, where $U \in L^2(\mathcal{G}, P)^{\perp}$, that is $E(UV) = 0$, for all $V \in L^2(\mathcal{G}, P)$, especially $E(U1_A) = 0$, for all $A \in \mathcal{G}$. This implies that $E(X1_A) = E(Z1_A)$, for all $A \in \mathcal{G}$, and consequently Z is a conditional expectation for X given $\mathcal{G}$.

(ii) Assume now that $X \geq 0$ and let, for each $n \geq 1$, Z_n be a conditional expectation of $X \wedge n \in L^2(P)$ given $\mathcal{G}$. Let $n \geq 1$. Then $E(Z_n 1_A) = E((X \wedge n)1_A) \leq E((X \wedge (n+1))1_A) = E(Z_{n+1}1_A)$, for all sets $A \in \mathcal{G}$, and this combined with the $\mathcal{G}$-measurability of Z_n, Z_{n+1} shows that $Z_n \leq Z_{n+1}$, P-as. (2.a.1.(a)). Set $Z = \limsup_n Z_n$. Then $Z \geq 0$ is $\mathcal{G}$-measurable and $Z_n \uparrow Z$, P-as. Let $A \in \mathcal{G}$. For each $n \geq 1$ we have $E(Z_n 1_A) = E((X \wedge n)1_A)$ and letting $n \uparrow \infty$ it follows that $E(Z1_A) = E(X1_A)$, by monotone convergence. Thus Z is a conditional expectation of X given $\mathcal{G}$.

(iii) Finally, if $E(X)$ exists, let Z_1, Z_2 be conditional expectations of X^+, X^- given $\mathcal{G}$ respectively. Then $Z_1, Z_2 \geq 0$, $E(Z_1 1_A) = E(X^+ 1_A)$ and $E(Z_2 1_A) = E(X^- 1_A)$, for all sets $A \in \mathcal{G}$. Letting $A = \Omega$ we see that $E(Z_1) < \infty$ or $E(Z_2) < \infty$ and consequently the event $D = [Z_1 < \infty] \cup [Z_2 < \infty]$ has probability one. Clearly $D \in \mathcal{G}$. Thus the random variable $Z = 1_D(Z_1 - Z_2)$ is defined everywhere and $\mathcal{G}$-measurable. We have $Z^+ \leq Z_1$ and $Z^- \leq Z_2$ and consequently $E(Z^+) < \infty$ or $E(Z^-) < \infty$, that is, $E(Z)$ exists. For each set $A \in \mathcal{G}$ we have $E(Z1_A) = E(Z_1 1_{A \cap D}) - E(Z_2 1_{A \cap D}) = E(X^+ 1_{A \cap D}) - E(X^- 1_{A \cap D}) = E(X1_{A \cap D}) = E(X1_A)$. Thus Z is a conditional expectation of X given $\mathcal{G}$. ∎

Remark. By the very definition of the conditional expectation $E_{\mathcal{G}}(X)$ we have $E(X) = E\big(E_{\mathcal{G}}(X)\big)$, a fact often referred to as the *double expectation theorem*. Conditioning on the sub-σ-field $\mathcal{G}$ before evaluating the expectation $E(X)$ is a technique frequently applied in probability theory. Let us now consider some examples of conditional expectations. Throughout it is assumed that $X \in \mathcal{E}(P)$.

2.b.1. *If $X \in L^2(P)$, then $E_{\mathcal{G}}(X)$ is the orthogonal projection of X onto the subspace $L^2(\mathcal{G}, P)$.*

Proof. We have seen this in (i) above. ∎

2.b.2. *If X is independent of $\mathcal{G}$, then $E_{\mathcal{G}}(X) = E(X)$, P-as.*

Proof. The constant $Z = E(X)$ is a $\mathcal{G}$-measurable random variable. If $A \in \mathcal{G}$, then X is independent of the random variable 1_A and consequently $E(X1_A) = E(X)E(1_A) = ZE(1_A) = E(Z1_A)$. Thus $Z = E_{\mathcal{G}}(X)$. ∎

Remark. This is as expected since the σ-field $\mathcal{G}$ contains no information about X and thus should not allow us to refine our bet on X beyond the trivial bet $E(X)$.

The *trivial* σ-field is the σ-field generated by the P-null sets and consists exactly of these null sets and their complements. Every random variable X is independent of the trivial σ-field and consequently of any σ-field $\mathcal{G}$ contained in the trivial σ-field. It follows that $E_{\mathcal{G}}(X) = E(X)$ for any such σ-field $\mathcal{G}$. Thus the ordinary expectation $E(X)$ is a particular conditional expectation.

2.b.3. *(a) If A is an atom of the σ-field $\mathcal{G}$, then $E_{\mathcal{G}}(X) = P(A)^{-1}E(X1_A)$ on A.*
(b) If $\mathcal{G}$ is the σ-field generated by a countable partition $\mathcal{P} = \{A_1, A_2, \ldots\}$ of Ω satisfying $P(A_n) > 0$, for all $n \geq 1$, then $E_{\mathcal{G}}(X) = \sum_n P(A_n)^{-1}E(X1_{A_n})1_{A_n}$.

Remark. The σ-field $\mathcal{G}$ in (b) consists of all unions of sets A_n and the A_n are the atoms of $\mathcal{G}$. The σ-field $\mathcal{G}$ is countable and it is easy to see that every countable σ-field is of this form.

Proof. (a) The $\mathcal{G}$-measurable random variable $Z = E_{\mathcal{G}}(X)$ is constant on the atom A of $\mathcal{G}$. Thus we can write $E(X1_A) = E(Z1_A) = ZE(1_A) = ZP(A)$. Now divide by $P(A)$. (b) Since each A_n is an atom of $\mathcal{G}$, we have $E_{\mathcal{G}}(X) = P(A_n)^{-1}E(X1_{A_n})$ on the set A_n. Since the A_n form a partition of Ω it follows that $E_{\mathcal{G}}(X) = \sum_n P(A_n)^{-1}E(X1_{A_n})1_{A_n}$. ∎

Remark. (b) should be interpreted as follows: exactly one of the events A_n occurs and the information contained in $\mathcal{G}$ is the information which one it is. Assume it is the event A_m, that is, assume that $\delta \in A_m$. Our bet on the value of X then becomes $E_{\mathcal{G}}(X)(\delta) = P(A_m)^{-1}E(X1_{A_m})$.

2.b.4. *Let $\mathcal{G} \subseteq \mathcal{F}$ be a sub-σ-field, $\mathcal{P}$ a π-system which generates the σ-field $\mathcal{G}$ ($\mathcal{G} = \sigma(\mathcal{P})$) and which contains the set Ω, $X, Y \in \mathcal{E}(P)$ and assume that Y is $\mathcal{G}$-measurable. Then*
  (i) $Y \leq E_{\mathcal{G}}(X)$ if and only if $E(Y1_A) \leq E(X1_A)$, for all sets $A \in \mathcal{G}$.
  (ii) $Y = E_{\mathcal{G}}(X)$ if and only if $E(Y1_A) = E(X1_A)$, for all sets $A \in \mathcal{G}$.
  (iii) If $X, Y \in L^1(P)$, then $Y = E_{\mathcal{G}}(X)$ if and only if $E(Y1_A) = E(X1_A)$, for all sets $A \in \mathcal{P}$.

Remark. Note that we can restrict ourselves to sets A in some π-system generating the σ-field $\mathcal{G}$ in (iii).

Proof. (i) Let $A \in \mathcal{G}$ and integrate the inequality $Y \leq E_{\mathcal{G}}(X)$ over the set A, observing that $E\big(E_{\mathcal{G}}(X)1_A\big) = E(X1_A)$. This yields $E(Y1_A) \leq E(X1_A)$. The converse follows from 2.a.1.(a). (ii) follows easily from (i).

(iii) If $Y = E_{\mathcal{G}}(X)$, then $E(Y1_A) = E(X1_A)$, for all sets $A \in \mathcal{G}$, by definition of the conditional expectation $E_{\mathcal{G}}(X)$. Conversely, assume that $E(Y1_A) = E(X1_A)$, for all sets $A \in \mathcal{P}$. We have to show that $E(Y1_A) = E(X1_A)$, for all sets $A \in \mathcal{G}$. Set $\mathcal{L} = \{ A \in \mathcal{F} \mid E(Y1_A) = E(X1_A) \}$. We must show that $\mathcal{G} \subseteq \mathcal{L}$. The integrability of X and Y and the countable additivity of the integral imply that $\mathcal{L}$ is a λ-system. By assumption, $\mathcal{P} \subseteq \mathcal{L}$. The π-λ-Theorem (appendix B.3) now shows that $\mathcal{G} = \sigma(\mathcal{P}) = \lambda(\mathcal{P}) \subseteq \mathcal{L}$. ∎

2.b.5. *Let $X, X_1, X_2 \in \mathcal{E}(P)$, α a real number and $D \in \mathcal{G}$ a $\mathcal{G}$-measurable set.*
(a) If X is $\mathcal{G}$-measurable, then $E_\mathcal{G}(X) = X$.
(b) If $\mathcal{H} \subseteq \mathcal{G}$ is a sub-σ-field, then $E_\mathcal{H}(E_\mathcal{G}(X)) = E_\mathcal{H}(X)$.
(c) $E_\mathcal{G}(\alpha X) = \alpha E_\mathcal{G}(X)$.
(d) $X_1 \leq X_2$, P-as. on D, implies $E_\mathcal{G}(X_1) \leq E_\mathcal{G}(X_2)$, P-as. on D.
(e) $X_1 = X_2$, P-as. on D, implies $E_\mathcal{G}(X_1) = E_\mathcal{G}(X_2)$, P-as. on D.
(f) $|E_\mathcal{G}(X)| \leq E_\mathcal{G}(|X|)$.
(g) If $E(X_1) + E(X_2)$ is defined, then $X_1 + X_2$, $E_\mathcal{G}(X_1 + X_2)$ and $E_\mathcal{G}(X_1) + E_\mathcal{G}(X_2)$
are defined and $E_\mathcal{G}(X_1 + X_2) = E_\mathcal{G}(X_1) + E_\mathcal{G}(X_2)$, P-as.

Proof. (a) and (c) are easy and left to the reader. (b) Set $Z = E_\mathcal{H}(E_\mathcal{G}(X))$. Then $Z \in \mathcal{E}(P)$ is $\mathcal{H}$-measurable and $E(Z 1_A) = E(E_\mathcal{G}(X) 1_A) = E(X 1_A)$, for all sets $A \in \mathcal{H}$. It follows that $Z = E_\mathcal{H}(X)$.

(d) Assume that $X_1 \leq X_2$, P-as. on D and set $Z_j = E_\mathcal{G}(X_j)$. If A is any $\mathcal{G}$-measurable subset of D, then $E(Z_1 1_A) = E(X_1 1_A) \leq E(X_2 1_A) = E(Z_2 1_A)$. This implies that $Z_1 \leq Z_2$, P-as. on the set D (2.a.1).

(e) If $X_1 = X_2$, P-as. on D, then $X_1 \leq X_2$, P-as. on D and $X_2 \leq X_1$, P-as. on D. Now use (e).

(f) $-|X| \leq X \leq |X|$ and so, using (c) and (d), $-E_\mathcal{G}(|X|) \leq E_\mathcal{G}(X) \leq E_\mathcal{G}(|X|)$, that is, $|E_\mathcal{G}(X)| \leq E_\mathcal{G}(|X|)$, P-as. on Ω.

(g) Let Z_1, Z_2 be conditional expectations of X_1, X_2 given $\mathcal{G}$ respectively and assume that $E(X_1) + E(X_2)$ is defined. Then $X_1 + X_2$ is defined P-as. and is in $\mathcal{E}(P)$ (2.a.0). Consequently the conditional expectation $E_\mathcal{G}(X_1 + X_2)$ is defined. Moreover $E(X_1) > -\infty$ or $E(X_2) < +\infty$.

Consider the case $E(X_1) > -\infty$. Then Z_1, Z_2 are defined everywhere and $\mathcal{G}$-measurable and $E(Z_1) = E(X_1) > -\infty$ and so $Z_1 > -\infty$, P-as. The event $D = [Z_1 > -\infty]$ is in $\mathcal{G}$ and hence $Z = 1_D(Z_1 + Z_2)$ defined everywhere and $\mathcal{G}$-measurable. Since $Z = Z_1 + Z_2$, P-as., it will now suffice to show that Z is a conditional expectation of $X_1 + X_2$ given $\mathcal{G}$.

Note first that $E(1_D Z_1) + E(1_D Z_2) = E(X_1) + E(X_2)$ is defined and so $Z = 1_D Z_1 + 1_D Z_2 \in \mathcal{E}(P)$ (2.a.0.(c)). Moreover, for each set $A \in \mathcal{G}$, we have $E(Z 1_A) = E(Z_1 1_{A \cap D}) + E(Z_2 1_{A \cap D}) = E(X_1 1_{A \cap D}) + E(X_2 1_{A \cap D}) = E(X_1 1_A) + E(X_2 1_A) = E((X_1 + X_2) 1_A)$, as desired. The case $E(X_2) < +\infty$ is dealt with similarly. ∎

Remark. The introduction of the set D in the proof of (g) is necessary since the σ-field $\mathcal{G}$ is not assumed to contain the null sets.

Since $\mathcal{E}(P)$ is not a vector space, $E_\mathcal{G} : X \in \mathcal{E}(P) \mapsto E_\mathcal{G}(X)$ is not a linear operator. However when its domain is restricted to $L^1(P)$, then $E_\mathcal{G}$ becomes a nonnegative linear operator.

2.b.6 Monotone Convergence. *Let $X_n, X, h \in \mathcal{E}(P)$ and assume that $X_n \geq h$ $n \geq 1$, and $X_n \uparrow X$, P-as. Then $E_{\mathcal{G}}(X_n) \uparrow E_{\mathcal{G}}(X)$, P-as. on the set $\left[E_{\mathcal{G}}(h) > -\infty\right]$*

Remark. If h is integrable, then $E(E_{\mathcal{G}}(h)) = E(h) > -\infty$ and so $E_{\mathcal{G}}(h) > -\infty$ P-as. In this case $E_{\mathcal{G}}(X_n) \uparrow E_{\mathcal{G}}(X)$, P-as.

Proof. For each $n \geq 1$ let Z_n be a conditional expectation of X_n given $\mathcal{G}$. Especially Z_n is defined everywhere and $\mathcal{G}$-measurable. Thus $Z = \limsup_n Z_n$ is $\mathcal{G}$-measurable From 2.b.5.(d) it follows that $Z_n \uparrow$ and consequently $Z_n \uparrow Z$, P-as. Now le $D = \left[Z_0 > -\infty\right]$ and $D_m = \left[Z_0 \geq -m\right]$, for all $m \geq 1$. We have $X_0 \geq h$ and s $Z_0 \geq E_{\mathcal{G}}(h)$, P-as., according to 2.b.5.(d). Thus $\left[E_{\mathcal{G}}(h) > -\infty\right] \subseteq D$, P-as. (tha is, on the complement of a P-null set). It will thus suffice to show that $Z = E_{\mathcal{G}}(X)$ P-as. on D.

Fix $m \geq 1$ and let A be an arbitrary $\mathcal{G}$-measurable subset of D_m. Note tha $-m \leq 1_A Z_0 \leq 1_A Z$ and so $1_A Z \in \mathcal{E}(P)$. Moreover $-m \leq E(1_A Z_0) = E(1_A X_0)$ Since $1_A Z_n \uparrow 1_A Z$ and $1_A X_n \uparrow 1_A X$, the ordinary Monotone Convergence Theorem shows that $E(1_A Z_n) \uparrow E(1_A Z)$ and $E(1_A X_n) \uparrow E(1_A X)$. But by definition of Z_n we have $E(1_A Z_n) = E(1_A X_n)$, for all $n \geq 1$. It follows that $E(1_A 1_{D_m} Z) = E(1_A Z) =$ $E(1_A X)$, where the random variable $1_{D_m} Z$ is in $\mathcal{E}(P)$. Using 2.b.4.(ii) it follows that $Z = 1_{D_m} Z = E_{\mathcal{G}}(X)$, P-as. on D_m. Taking the union over all $m \geq 1$ we se that $Z = E_{\mathcal{G}}(X)$, P-as. on D. $\blacksquare$

2.b.7 Corollary. *Let α_n be real numbers and $X_n \in \mathcal{E}(P)$ with $\alpha_n, X_n \geq 0$, $n \geq 1$ Then $E_{\mathcal{G}}\left(\sum_n \alpha_n X_n\right) = \sum_n \alpha_n E_{\mathcal{G}}(X_n)$, P-as.* $\blacksquare$

Recall the notation $\underline{\lim} = \liminf$ and $\overline{\lim} = \limsup$.

2.b.8 Fatou's Lemma. *Let $X_n, g, h \in \mathcal{E}(P)$ and assume that $h \leq X_n \leq g$, $n \geq 1$ Then, among the inequalities,*

$$E_{\mathcal{G}}\left(\underline{\lim}_n X_n\right) \leq \underline{\lim}_n E_{\mathcal{G}}(X_n) \leq \overline{\lim}_n E_{\mathcal{G}}(X_n) \leq E_{\mathcal{G}}\left(\overline{\lim}_n X_n\right)$$

the middle inequality trivially holds P-as.
(a) If $\underline{\lim}_n X_n \in \mathcal{E}(P)$, the first inequality holds P-as. on the set $\left[E_{\mathcal{G}}(h) > -\infty\right]$.
(b) If $\overline{\lim}_n X_n \in \mathcal{E}(P)$, the last inequality holds P-as. on the set $\left[E_{\mathcal{G}}(g) < \infty\right]$.

Proof. (a) Assume that $\underline{X} = \liminf_n X_n \in \mathcal{E}(P)$. Set $Y_n = \inf_{k \geq n} X_k$. The $Y_n \uparrow \underline{X}$. Note that Y_n may not be in $\mathcal{E}(P)$. Fix $m \geq 1$, set $D_m = \left[E_{\mathcal{G}}(h) > -m\right]$ an note that $E(h 1_{D_m}) = E\left(E_{\mathcal{G}}(h) 1_{D_m}\right) \geq -m$. Thus $E\left((h 1_{D_m})^-\right) < \infty$. Moreove $Y_n \geq h$ thus $1_{D_m} Y_n \geq 1_{D_m} h$ and consequently $(1_{D_m} Y_n)^- \leq (1_{D_m} h)^-$. It follows that $E\left((1_{D_m} Y_n)^-\right) < \infty$ especially $1_{D_m} Y_n \in \mathcal{E}(P)$, for all $n \geq 1$.

From $1_{D_m} Y_0 \geq 1_{D_m} h = h$, P-as. on $D_m \in \mathcal{G}$, it follows that $E_{\mathcal{G}}\left(1_{D_m} Y_0\right) \geq$ $E_{\mathcal{G}}(h) > -m$, P-as. on D_m. Thus $\left[E_{\mathcal{G}}\left(1_{D_m} Y_0\right) > -\infty\right] \supseteq D_m$. Let $n \uparrow \infty$. The $1_{D_m} Y_n \uparrow 1_{D_m} \underline{X}$ and so 2.b.6 and 2.b.5.(e) yield

$$E_{\mathcal{G}}\left(1_{D_m} Y_n\right) \uparrow E_{\mathcal{G}}\left(1_{D_m} \underline{X}\right) = E(\underline{X}|\mathcal{G}), \quad \text{P-as. on the set } D_m.$$

Moreover $X_n \geq Y_n = 1_{D_m} Y_n$, P-as. on D_m, and so $E_{\mathcal{G}}(X_n) \geq E_{\mathcal{G}}\left(1_{D_m} Y_n\right)$, P-as on D_m, according to 2.b.5.(d). It follows that

$$\liminf_n E_{\mathcal{G}}(X_n) \geq \liminf_n E_{\mathcal{G}}\left(1_{D_m} Y_n\right) = \lim_n E_{\mathcal{G}}\left(1_{D_m} Y_n\right) = E_{\mathcal{G}}(\underline{X}),$$

P-as. on D_m. Taking the union over all sets D_m gives the desired inequality on th set $D = \bigcup_m D_m = \left[E_{\mathcal{G}}(h) > -\infty\right]$. (b) follows from (a). $\blacksquare$

2.b.9 Dominated Convergence Theorem. *Assume that $X_n, X, h \in \mathcal{E}(P)$, $|X_n| \le h$ and $X_n \to X$, P-as. Then $E_\mathcal{G}(|X_n - X|) \to 0$, P-as. on the set $[E_\mathcal{G}(h) < \infty]$.*

Remark. If $E(X_n) - E(X)$ is defined, then $\left|E_\mathcal{G}(X_n) - E_\mathcal{G}(X)\right| \le E_\mathcal{G}(|X_n - X|)$, for all $n \ge 1$, and it follows that $\left|E_\mathcal{G}(X_n) - E_\mathcal{G}(X)\right| \to 0$, that is $E_\mathcal{G}(X_n) \to E_\mathcal{G}(X)$, P-as.

Proof. We do have $|X_n - X| \le 2h$ and so, according to 2.b.8.(b),

$$0 \le \overline{\lim}_n E_\mathcal{G}(|X_n - X|) \le E_\mathcal{G}(\overline{\lim}_n |X_n - X|) = 0, \ P\text{-as. on } [E_\mathcal{G}(2h) < \infty].\ \blacksquare$$

2.b.10. *If Y is $\mathcal{G}$-measurable and $X, XY \in \mathcal{E}(P)$, then $E_\mathcal{G}(XY) = Y E_\mathcal{G}(X)$.*

Proof. (i) Assume first that $X, Y \ge 0$. Since Y is the increasing limit of $\mathcal{G}$-measurable simple functions, 2.b.6 shows that we may assume that Y is such a simple function. Using 2.b.5.(c),(g) we can restrict ourselves to $Y = 1_A$, $A \in \mathcal{G}$. Set $Z = Y E_\mathcal{G}(X) = 1_A E_\mathcal{G}(X) \in \mathcal{E}(P)$ and note that Z is $\mathcal{G}$-measurable. Moreover, for each set $B \in \mathcal{G}$ we have $E(Z1_B) = E(1_{A \cap B} E_\mathcal{G}(X)) = E(1_{A \cap B} X) = E(XY1_B)$. It follows that $Z = E_\mathcal{G}(XY)$.

(ii) Let now $X \ge 0$ and Y be arbitrary. Write $Y = Y^+ - Y^-$. Then $E(XY) = E(XY^+) - E(XY^-)$ is defined and so, using 2.b.5.(c),(g) we have $E_\mathcal{G}(XY) = E_\mathcal{G}(XY^+) - E_\mathcal{G}(XY^-) = Y^+ E_\mathcal{G}(X) - Y^- E_\mathcal{G}(X) = Y E_\mathcal{G}(X)$.

(iii) Finally, let both X and Y be arbitrary, write $X = X^+ - X^-$ and set $A = [X \ge 0]$ and $B = [X \le 0]$. Since $XY \in \mathcal{E}(P)$ we have $X^+ Y = 1_A XY \in \mathcal{E}(P)$, $X^- Y = -1_B XY \in \mathcal{E}(P)$ and $E(X^+ Y) - E(X^- Y) = E(XY)$ is defined. The proof now proceeds as in step (ii). $\blacksquare$

2.b.11. *Let $Z = f(X, Y)$, where $f : R^n \times R^m \to [0, \infty)$ is Borel measurable and X, Y are R^n respectively R^m-valued random vectors. If X is $\mathcal{G}$-measurable and Y independent of $\mathcal{G}$, then*

$$E_\mathcal{G}(Z) = E_\mathcal{G}(f(X, Y)) = \int_{R^m} f(X, y) P_Y(dy), \quad P\text{-as.} \tag{1}$$

Remark. The $\mathcal{G}$-measurable variable X is left unaffected while the variable Y, independent of $\mathcal{G}$, is integrated out according to its distribution. The integrals all exist by nonnegativity of f.

Proof. Introducing the function $G_f(x) = \int_{R^m} f(x, y) P_Y(dy) = E(f(x, Y))$, $x \in R^n$, equation (1) can be rewritten as $E_\mathcal{G}(Z) = E_\mathcal{G}(f(X, Y)) = G_f(X)$, P-as. Let $\mathcal{C}$ be the family of all nonnegative Borel measurable functions $f : R^n \times R^m \to R$ for which this equality is true.

We use the extension theorem B.4 in the appendix to show that $\mathcal{C}$ contains every nonnegative Borel measurable function $f : R^n \times R^m \to R$. Using 2.b.7, $\mathcal{C}$ is easily seen to be a λ-cone on $R^n \times R^m$.

Assume that $f(x, y) = g(x)h(y)$, for some nonnegative, Borel measurable functions $f : R^n \to [0, \infty)$ and $g : R^m \to [0, \infty)$. We claim that $f \in \mathcal{C}$.

Note that $Z = f(X,Y) = g(X)h(Y)$ and $G_f(x) = g(x)E(h(Y))$, $x \in R^n$, and so $W := G_f(X) = g(X)E(h(Y))$. We have to show that $W = E_{\mathcal{G}}(Z)$.

Since X is $\mathcal{G}$-measurable so is W and, if $A \in \mathcal{G}$, then $h(Y)$ is independent of $g(X)1_A$ and consequently $E(Z1_A) = E\big(g(X)h(Y)1_A\big) = E\big(g(X)1_A\big)E(h(Y)) = E\big(g(X)E(h(Y))1_A\big) = E(W1_A)$, as desired.

In particular the indicator function $f = 1_{A \times B}$ of each measurable rectangle $A \times B \subseteq R^n \times R^m$ ($A \subseteq R^n$, $B \subseteq R^m$ Borel sets) satisfies $f(x,y) = 1_A(x)1_B(y)$ and thus $f \in \mathcal{C}$. These measurable rectangles form a π-system generating the Borel-σ-field on $R^n \times R^m$. The extension theorem B.4 in the appendix now implies that $\mathcal{C}$ contains every nonnegative Borel measurable function $f : R^n \times R^m \to R$. ∎

Jensen's Inequality. Let $\phi : R \to R$ be a convex function. Then ϕ is known to be continuous. For real numbers a, b set $\phi_{a,b}(t) = at + b$ and let Φ be the set of all $(a,b) \in R^2$ such that $\phi_{a,b} \le \phi$ on all of R. The convexity of ϕ implies that the subset $C(\phi) = \{ (x,y) \in R^2 \mid y \ge \phi(x) \} \subseteq R^2$ is convex. From the Separating Hyperplane Theorem we conclude that

$$\phi(t) = \sup\{ \phi_{a,b}(t) \mid (a,b) \in \Phi \}, \quad \forall t \in R. \tag{2}$$

We will now see that we can replace Φ with a countable subset Ψ while still preserving (2). Note that the simplistic choice $\Psi = \mathbb{Q}^2$ does not work for example if $\phi(t) = at + b$, with a irrational. Let $D \subseteq R$ be a dense countable subset. Clearly, for each point $s \in D$, we can find a countable subset $\Phi(s) \subseteq \Phi$ such that

$$\phi(s) = \sup\{ \phi_{a,b}(s) \mid (a,b) \in \Phi(s) \}.$$

Now let $\Psi = \bigcup_{s \in D} \Phi(s)$. Then Ψ is a countable subset of Φ and we claim that

$$\phi(t) = \sup\{ \phi_{a,b}(t) \mid (a,b) \in \Psi \}, \quad \forall t \in R. \tag{3}$$

Consider a fixed $s \in D$ and $a, b \in \Psi$ and assume that $\phi_{a,b}(s) > \phi(s) - 1$. Combining this with the inequalities $\phi_{a,b}(s+1) \le \phi(s+1)$ and $\phi_{a,b}(s-1) \le \phi(s-1)$ easily yields $|a| \le |\phi(s-1)| + |\phi(s)| + |\phi(s+1)| + 1$. The continuity of ϕ now shows:

(i) For each compact interval $I \subseteq R$ there exists a constant K such that $s \in D$ and $\phi_{a,b}(s) > \phi(s) - 1$ implies $|a| \le K$, for all points $s \in I$.

Now let $t \in R$. We wish to show that $\phi(t) = \sup\{ \phi_{a,b}(t) \mid (a,b) \in \Psi \}$. Set $I = [t-1, t+1]$ and choose the constant K for the interval I as in (i) above. Let $\epsilon > 0$. It will suffice to show that $\phi_{a,b}(t) > \phi(t) - \epsilon$, for some $(a,b) \in \Psi$. Let $\rho > 0$ be so small that $(K+2)\rho < \epsilon$.

By continuity of ϕ and density of D we can choose $s \in I \cap D$ such that $|s-t| < \rho$ and $|\phi(s) - \phi(t)| < \rho$. Let $(a,b) \in \Psi(s) \subseteq \Psi$ such that $\phi_{a,b}(s) > \phi(s) - \rho > \phi(t) - 2\rho$. Since $|\phi_{a,b}(s) - \phi_{a,b}(t)| = |a(s-t)| < K\rho$, we have $\phi_{a,b}(t) > \phi_{a,b}(s) - K\rho > \phi(t) - \epsilon$, as desired. Defining $\phi(\pm\infty) = \sup\{ \phi_{a,b}(\pm\infty) \mid (a,b) \in \Psi \}$ we extend ϕ to the extended real line such that (2) holds for all $t \in [-\infty, \infty]$.

2.b.12 Jensen's Inequality. *Let* $\phi : R \to R$ *be convex and* $X, \phi(X) \in \mathcal{E}(P)$. *Then* $\phi(E_{\mathcal{G}}(X)) \leq E_{\mathcal{G}}(\phi(X))$, *P-as.*

Proof. Let $\phi_{a,b}$ and Ψ be as above. For $(a, b) \in \Psi$, we have $\phi_{a,b} \leq \phi$ on $[-\infty, \infty]$ and consequently $aX + b = \phi_{a,b}(X) \leq \phi(X)$ on Ω. Using 2.b.4.(c),(g) it follows that

$$aE_{\mathcal{G}}(X) + b \leq E_{\mathcal{G}}(\phi(X)), \quad P\text{-as.}, \tag{4}$$

where the exceptional set depends on $(a, b) \in \Psi$. Since Ψ is countable, we can find a P-null set N such that (4) holds on the complement of N, for all $(a, b) \in \Psi$. Taking the sup over all such (a, b) now yields $\phi(E_{\mathcal{G}}(X)) \leq E_{\mathcal{G}}(\phi(X))$ on the complement of N and hence P-as. ∎

2.b.13. *Let* $\{ \mathcal{F}_i \mid i \in I \}$ *be any family of sub-σ-fields* $\mathcal{F}_i \subseteq \mathcal{F}$, $X \in L^1(P)$ *an integrable random variable and* $X_i = E_{\mathcal{F}_i}(X)$, *for all* $i \in I$. *Then the family* $\{ X_i \mid i \in I \}$ *is uniformly integrable.*

Proof. Let $i \in I$ and $c \geq 0$. Since X_i is $\mathcal{F}_i$-measurable $[|X_i| \geq c] \in \mathcal{F}_i$. Integrating the inequality $|X_i| = |E_{\mathcal{F}_i}(X)| \leq E_{\mathcal{F}_i}(|X|)$ over Ω we obtain $\|X_i\|_1 \leq \|X\|_1$. Integration over the set $[|X_i| \geq c] \in \mathcal{F}_i$ yields $E(|X_i|; [|X_i| \geq c]) \leq E(|X|; [|X_i| \geq c])$, where, using Chebycheff's inequality,

$$P([|X_i| \geq c]) \leq c^{-1}\|X_i\|_1 \leq c^{-1}\|X\|_1 \to 0, \quad \text{uniformly in } i \in I \text{ as } c \uparrow \infty.$$

Let $\epsilon > 0$. Since X is integrable, we can choose $\delta > 0$ such that $E(|X|1_A) < \epsilon$, for all sets $A \in \mathcal{F}$ with $P(A) < \delta$. Now choose $c > 0$ such that $c^{-1}\|X\|_1 < \delta$. Then $P([|X_i| \geq c]) \leq c^{-1}\|X\|_1 < \delta$ and consequently

$$E(|X_i|; [|X_i| \geq c]) \leq E(|X|; [|X_i| \geq c]) < \epsilon, \quad \text{for each } i \in I.$$

Thus the family $\{ X_i \mid i \in I \}$ is uniformly integrable. ∎

Conditioning and independence. Recall that independent random variables X, Y satisfy $E(XY) = E(X)E(Y)$ whenever all expectations exist. For families $\mathcal{A}$, $\mathcal{B}$ of subsets of Ω we shall write $\sigma(\mathcal{A}, \mathcal{B})$ for the σ-field $\sigma(\mathcal{A} \cup \mathcal{B})$ generated by all the sets $A \in \mathcal{A}$ and $B \in \mathcal{B}$. With this notation we have

2.b.14. *Let* $\mathcal{A}, \mathcal{B} \subseteq \mathcal{F}$ *be sub-σ-fields and* $X \in \mathcal{E}(P)$. *If the σ-fields* $\sigma(\sigma(X), \mathcal{A})$ *and* $\mathcal{B}$ *are independent, then* $E_{\sigma(\mathcal{A}, \mathcal{B})}(X) = E_{\mathcal{A}}(X)$, *P-as.*

Remark. The independence assumption is automatically satisfied if $\mathcal{B}$ is the σ-field generated by the P-null sets ($\mathcal{B} = \{ B \in \mathcal{F} \mid P(B) \in \{0, 1\} \}$). This σ-field is independent of every other sub-σ-field of $\mathcal{F}$. In other words: augmenting the sub-σ-field $\mathcal{A} \subseteq \mathcal{F}$ by the P-null sets does not change any conditional expectation $E_{\mathcal{A}}(X)$, where $X \in \mathcal{E}(P)$.

Proof. (i) Assume first that $X \in L^1(P)$ and set $Y = E_{\mathcal{A}}(X) \in L^1(P)$. Then Y is $\sigma(\mathcal{A}, \mathcal{B})$-measurable. To see that $Y = E_{\sigma(\mathcal{A}, \mathcal{B})}(X)$, P-as., it will suffice to show that $E(1_D Y) = E(1_D X)$, for all sets D in some π-system $\mathcal{P}$ generating the σ-field $\sigma(\mathcal{A} \cup \mathcal{B})$ (2.b.4).

A suitable π-system is the family $\mathcal{P} = \{ A \cap B \mid A \in \mathcal{A}, B \in \mathcal{B} \}$. We now have to show that $E(1_{A \cap B} Y) = E(1_{A \cap B} X)$, for all sets $A \in \mathcal{A}$, $B \in \mathcal{B}$.

Indeed, for such A and B, 1_B is $\mathcal{B}$-measurable, $1_A Y$ is $\mathcal{A}$-measurable and the σ-fields $\mathcal{A}$, $\mathcal{B}$ are independent. It follows that 1_B and $1_A Y$ are independent. Thus $E(1_{A \cap B} Y) = E(1_B 1_A Y) = E(1_B) E(1_A Y)$.

But $E(1_A Y) = E(1_A X)$, as $Y = E_{\mathcal{A}}(X)$ and $A \in \mathcal{A}$. Thus $E(1_{A \cap B} Y) = E(1_B) E(1_A X)$. Now we reverse the previous step. Since 1_B is $\mathcal{B}$-measurable, $1_A X$ is $\sigma(\sigma(X), \mathcal{A})$-measurable and the σ-fields $\sigma(\sigma(X), \mathcal{A})$, $\mathcal{B}$ are independent, it follows that 1_B and $1_A X$ are independent. Hence $E(1_B) E(1_A X) = E(1_B 1_A X) = E(1_{A \cap B} X)$ and it follows that $E(1_{A \cap B} Y) = E(1_{A \cap B} X)$, as desired.

(ii) The case $X \geq 0$ now follows from (i) by writing $X = \lim_n (X \wedge n)$ and using 2.b.6, and the general case $X \in \mathcal{E}(P)$ follows from this by writing $X = X^+ - X^-$. ∎

The conditional expectation operator $E_{\mathcal{G}}$ on $L^p(P)$. Let $X \in L^1(P)$. Integrating the inequality $\big| E_{\mathcal{G}}(X) \big| \leq E_{\mathcal{G}}(|X|)$ over Ω yields $E_{\mathcal{G}}(X) \in L^1(P)$ and $\| E_{\mathcal{G}}(X) \|_1 \leq \| X \|_1$. Thus the conditional expectation operator

$$E_{\mathcal{G}} : X \in L^1(P) \to E_{\mathcal{G}}(X) \in L^1(P)$$

maps $L^1(P)$ into $L^1(P)$ and is in fact a contraction on $L^1(P)$. The same is true for $E_{\mathcal{G}}$ on the space $L^2(P)$, according to 2.b.1. We shall see below that it is true for each space $L^p(P)$, $1 \leq p < \infty$.

If $\mathcal{G}$ is the σ-field generated by the trivial partition $\mathcal{P} = \{\emptyset, \Omega\}$, then $E_{\mathcal{G}}(X) = E(X)$, for P-as. In this case the conditional expectation operator $E_{\mathcal{A}}$ is the ordinary integral. Thus we should view the general conditional expectation operator $E_{\mathcal{G}} : L^1(P) \to L^1(P)$ as a generalized (function valued) integral. We will see below that this operator has all the basic properties of the integral:

2.b.15. *Let $\mathcal{H}, \mathcal{G} \subseteq \mathcal{F}$ be sub-σ-fields and $X \in L^1(P)$. Then*
(a) $\mathcal{H} \subseteq \mathcal{G}$ implies $E_{\mathcal{H}} E_{\mathcal{G}} = E_{\mathcal{H}}$.
(b) $E_{\mathcal{G}}$ is a projection onto the subspace of all $\mathcal{G}$-measurable functions $X \in L^1(P)$.
(c) $E_{\mathcal{G}}$ is a positive linear operator: $X \geq 0$, P-as. implies $E_{\mathcal{G}}(X) \geq 0$, P-as.
(d) $E_{\mathcal{G}}$ is a contraction on each space $L^p(P)$, $1 \leq p < \infty$.

Proof. (a),(c) have already been shown in 2.b.5 and (b) follows from (a) and 2.b.5.(a). (d) Let $X \in L^p(P)$. The convexity of the function $\phi(t) = |t|^p$ and Jensen's inequality imply that $|E_{\mathcal{G}}(X)|^p \leq E_{\mathcal{G}}(|X|^p)$. Integrating this inequality over the set Ω, we obtain $\| E_{\mathcal{G}}(X) \|_p^p \leq \| X \|_p^p$. ∎

3. SUBMARTINGALES

3.a Adapted stochastic processes. Let $\mathcal{T}$ be a partially ordered index set. It is useful to think of the index $t \in \mathcal{T}$ as time. A *stochastic process* X on $(\Omega, \mathcal{F}, P)$ *indexed by* $\mathcal{T}$ is a family $X = (X_t)_{t \in \mathcal{T}}$ of random variables X_t on Ω. Alternatively, defining $X(t, \omega) = X_t(\omega)$, $t \in \mathcal{T}$, $\omega \in \Omega$, we can view X as a function $X : \mathcal{T} \times \Omega \to \overline{R}$ with $\mathcal{F}$-measurable sections X_t, $t \in \mathcal{T}$.

A $\mathcal{T}$-*filtration* of the probability space $(\Omega, \mathcal{F}, P)$ is a family $(\mathcal{F}_t)_{t \in \mathcal{T}}$ of sub-σ-fields $\mathcal{F}_t \subseteq \mathcal{F}$, indexed by $\mathcal{T}$ and satisfying $s \leq t \Rightarrow \mathcal{F}_s \subseteq \mathcal{F}_t$, for all $s, t \in \mathcal{T}$. Think of the σ-field $\mathcal{F}_t$ as representing the information about the true state of nature available at time t. A stochastic process X indexed by $\mathcal{T}$ is called $(\mathcal{F}_t)$-*adapted*, if X_t is $\mathcal{F}_t$-measurable, for all $t \in \mathcal{T}$. A $\mathcal{T}$-*filtration* $(\mathcal{F}_t)$ will be called *augmented*, if each σ-field $\mathcal{F}_t$ contains all the P-null sets. In this case, if X_t is $\mathcal{F}_t$-measurable and $Y_t = X_t$, P-as., then Y_t is $\mathcal{F}_t$-measurable.

If the partially ordered index set $\mathcal{T}$ is fixed and clear from the context, stochastic processes indexed by $\mathcal{T}$ and $\mathcal{T}$-filtrations are denoted (X_t) and $(\mathcal{F}_t)$ respectively. If the filtration $(\mathcal{F}_t)$ is also fixed and clear from the context, an $(\mathcal{F}_t)$-adapted process X will simply be called *adapted*. On occasion we will write $(X_t, \mathcal{F}_t)$ to denote an $(\mathcal{F}_t)$-adapted process (X_t).

An $(\mathcal{F}_t)$-adapted stochastic process X is called an $(\mathcal{F}_t)$-*submartingale*, if it satisfies $E(X_t^+) < \infty$ and $X_s \leq E(X_t | \mathcal{F}_s)$, P-as., for all $s \leq t$. Equivalently, X is a submartingale if $X_t \in \mathcal{E}(P)$ is $\mathcal{F}_t$-measurable, $E(X_t) < \infty$ and

$$E(X_s 1_A) \leq E(X_t 1_A), \quad \text{for all } s \leq t \text{ and } A \in \mathcal{F}_s \tag{0}$$

(2.b.4.(ii)). Thus a submartingale is a process which is expected to increase at all times in light of the information available at that time.

Assume that the $\mathcal{T}$-filtration $(\mathcal{G}_t)$ satisfies $\mathcal{G}_t \subseteq \mathcal{F}_t$, for all $t \in \mathcal{T}$. If the $(\mathcal{F}_t)$-submartingale X is in fact $(\mathcal{G}_t)$-adapted, then X is a $(\mathcal{G}_t)$-submartingale also. This is true in particular for the $\mathcal{T}$-filtration $\mathcal{G}_t = \sigma(X_s; s \leq t)$. Thus, if no filtration $(\mathcal{F}_t)$ is specified, it is understood that $\mathcal{F}_t = \sigma(X_s; s \leq t)$.

If X is a submartingale, then $X_t < \infty$, P-as., but $X_t = -\infty$ is possible on a set of positive measure. If X, Y are submartingales and α is a nonnegative number, then the sum $X + Y$ and scalar product αX are defined as $(X + Y)_t = X_t + Y_t$ and $(\alpha X)_t = \alpha X_t$ and are again submartingales. Consequently the family of $(\mathcal{F}_t)$-submartingales is a convex cone.

A process X is called an $(\mathcal{F}_t)$-*supermartingale* if $-X$ is an $(\mathcal{F}_t)$-*submartingale*, that is, if it is $(\mathcal{F}_t)$-adapted and satisfies $E(X_t^-) < \infty$ and $X_s \geq E(X_t | \mathcal{F}_s)$, P-as., for all $s \leq t$. Equivalently, X is an $(\mathcal{F}_t)$-supermartingale if $X_t \in \mathcal{E}(P)$ is $\mathcal{F}_t$-measurable, $E(X_t) > -\infty$ and $E(X_s 1_A) \geq E(X_t 1_A)$, for all $s \leq t$ and $A \in \mathcal{F}_s$ (2.b.4.(ii)). Thus a supermartingale is a process which is expected to decrease at all times in light of the information available at that time.

Finally X is called an $(\mathcal{F}_t)$-*martingale* if it is an $(\mathcal{F}_t)$-*submartingale* and an $(\mathcal{F}_t)$-*supermartingale*, that is, if $X_t \in L^1(P)$ is $\mathcal{F}_t$-measurable and $X_s = E(X_t | \mathcal{F}_s)$,

P-as., equivalently

$$E(X_t 1_A) = E(X_s 1_A), \quad \text{for all } s \leq t \text{ and } A \in \mathcal{F}_s. \qquad (1$$

Especially X_t is finite almost surely, for all $t \in \mathcal{T}$, and the family of $\mathcal{T}$-martingales forms a vector space. Let us note that $E(X_t) < \infty$ increases with $t \in \mathcal{T}$, if X is a submartingale, $E(X_t) > -\infty$ decreases with t, if X is a supermartingale, and $E(X_t$ is finite and remains constant, if X is a martingale. We will state most results for submartingales. Conclusions for martingales can then be drawn if we observe that X is a martingale if and only if both X and $-X$ are submartingales. Let now $\mathcal{T}$ be any partially ordered index set and $(\mathcal{F}_t)$ a $\mathcal{T}$-filtration on $(\Omega, \mathcal{F}, P)$.

3.a.0. *(a) If X_t, Y_t are both submartingales, then so is the process $Z_t = X_t \vee Y_t$.*
(a) If X_t is a submartingale, then so is the process X_t^+.

Proof. (a) Let X_t and Y_t be submartingales and set $Z_t = \max\{X_t, Y_t\}$. Then Z is $\mathcal{F}_t$-measurable and $Z_t^+ \leq X_t^+ + Y_t^+$, whence $E(Z_t^+) \leq E(X_t^+) + E(Y_t^+) < \infty$ If $s, t \in \mathcal{T}$ with $s \leq t$ then $Z_t \geq X_t$ and so $E_{\mathcal{F}_s}(Z_t) \geq E_{\mathcal{F}_s}(X_t) \geq X_s$. Similarly $E_{\mathcal{F}_s}(Z_t) \geq E_{\mathcal{F}_s}(Y_t) \geq Y_s$ and so $E_{\mathcal{F}_s}(Z_t) \geq X_t \vee Y_t = Z_t$, P-as. (b) follows from (a), since $X_t^+ = X_t \vee 0$. ∎

3.a.1. *Let $\phi : R \to R$ be convex and assume that $E(\phi(X_t)^+) < \infty$, for all $t \in \mathcal{T}$.*
(a) If (X_t) is a martingale, then the process $\phi(X_t)$ is a submartingale.
(b) If X_t is a submartingale and ϕ nondecreasing, then the process $\phi(X_t)$ is a submartingale.

Remark. Extend ϕ to the extended real line as in the discussion preceding Jensen's inequality (2.b.12).

Proof. The convex function ϕ is continuous and hence Borel measurable. Thus, if the process X_t is $(\mathcal{F}_t)$-adapted, the same will be true of the process $\phi(X_t)$.
(a) Let X_t be a martingale and $s \leq t$. Then $\phi(X_s) = \phi(E_{\mathcal{F}_s}(X_t)) \leq E_{\mathcal{F}_s}(\phi(X_t))$ by Jensen's inequality for conditional expectations. Consequently $(\phi(X_t))$ is a submartingale.
(b) If X_t is a submartingale and ϕ nondecreasing and convex, then $\phi(X_s) \leq \phi(E_{\mathcal{F}_s}(X_t)) \leq E_{\mathcal{F}_s}(\phi(X_t))$, where the first inequality follows from the submartingale condition $X_s \leq E_{\mathcal{F}_s}(X_t)$ and the nondecreasing nature of ϕ. Thus $\phi(X_t)$ is a submartingale. ∎

In practice only the following partially ordered index sets $\mathcal{T}$ are of significance:
(i) $\mathcal{T} = \{1, 2, \ldots, N\}$ with the usual partial order (finite stochastic sequences).
(ii) $\mathcal{T} = \mathbb{N} = \{1, 2, \ldots\}$ with the usual partial order. A $\mathcal{T}$-stochastic process X will be called a *stochastic sequence* and denoted (X_n). A $\mathcal{T}$-filtration $(\mathcal{F}_n)$ is an increasing chain of sub-σ-fields of $\mathcal{F}$. In this case the submartingale condition reduces to $E(X_n 1_A) \leq E(X_{n+1} 1_A)$, equivalently,

$$E(1_A(X_{n+1} - X_n)) \geq 0, \quad \forall n \geq 1, A \in \mathcal{F}_n,$$

with equality in the case of a martingale.

(iii) $T = \mathbb{N} = \{1, 2, \ldots\}$ with the usual partial order reversed. A T-filtration $(\mathcal{F}_n)$ is a decreasing chain of sub-σ-fields of $\mathcal{F}$. An $(\mathcal{F}_n)$-submartingale will be called a *reversed submartingale sequence* and a similar terminology applies to $(\mathcal{F}_n)$-supermartingale and $(\mathcal{F}_n)$-martingales. In this case the submartingale condition becomes $E(X_n|\mathcal{F}_{n+1}) \geq X_{n+1}$, $n \geq 1$, with equality in the case of a martingale.

(iv) $T = [0, +\infty) = R_+$ with the usual partial order. This is the most important case for us. A T-stochastic process X will simply be called a *stochastic process* and denoted (X_t).

(v) T the family of all finite measurable partitions of Ω and, for each $t \in T$, $\mathcal{F}_t$ the σ-field generated by the partition t (consisting of all unions of sets in t). We will use this only as a source of examples.

(vi) The analogue of (v) using countable partitions in place of finite partitions.

Here are some examples of martingales:

3.a.2 Example. Let $Z \in L^1(P)$, T any partially ordered index set and $(\mathcal{F}_t)$ any T-filtration. Set $X_t = E_{\mathcal{F}_t}(Z)$. Then (X_t) is an $(\mathcal{F}_t)$-martingale. This follows easily from 2.b.5.(b). The martingale (X_t) is uniformly integrable, according to 2.b.13.

3.a.3 Example. Let (X_n) be a sequence of independent integrable random variables with mean zero and set

$$S_n = X_1 + X_2 + \ldots + X_n, \quad \text{and} \quad \mathcal{F}_n = \sigma(X_1, X_2, \ldots, X_n), \quad n \geq 1.$$

Then (S_n) is an $(\mathcal{F}_n)$-martingale. Indeed $E(S_{n+1}|\mathcal{F}_n) = E(S_n + X_{n+1}|\mathcal{F}_n) = E(S_n|\mathcal{F}_n) + E(X_{n+1}|\mathcal{F}_n) = S_n + E(X_{n+1}) = S_n$, by $\mathcal{F}_n$-measurability of S_n and independence of X_{n+1} from $\mathcal{F}_n$.

3.a.4 Example. Let T be any partially ordered index set, $(\mathcal{F}_t)$ any T-filtration on $(\Omega, \mathcal{F}, P)$ and Q a probability measure on $\mathcal{F}$ which is absolutely continuous with respect to P. For $t \in T$, let $P_t = P|\mathcal{F}_t$, $Q_t = Q|\mathcal{F}_t$ denote the restrictions of P respectively Q to $\mathcal{F}_t$, note that $Q_t << P_t$ and let X_t be the Radon-Nikodym derivative $dQ_t/dP_t \in L^1(\Omega, \mathcal{F}_t, P)$. Then the density process (X_t) is $(\mathcal{F}_t)$-adapted and we claim that X is an $(\mathcal{F}_t)$-martingale. Indeed, for $s \leq t$ and $A \in \mathcal{F}_s \subseteq \mathcal{F}_t$, we have

$$E(X_s 1_A) = Q_s(A) = Q_t(A) = E(X_t 1_A).$$

Numerous other examples of martingales will be encountered below.

3.b Sampling at optional times. We now turn to the study of submartingale sequences. Let $\mathcal{T} = \mathbb{N}$ with the usual partial order and $(\mathcal{F}_n)$ be a fixed $\mathcal{T}$-filtration on $(\Omega, \mathcal{F}, P)$, $\mathcal{F}_\infty = \bigvee_n \mathcal{F}_n = \sigma \left(\bigcup_n \mathcal{F}_n \right)$ be the σ-field generated by $\bigcup_n \mathcal{F}_n$ and assume that $X = (X_n)$ is an $(\mathcal{F}_n)$-adapted stochastic sequence.

A *random time* T is a measurable function $T : \Omega \to \mathbb{N} \cup \{\infty\}$ (the value ∞ is allowed). Such a random time T is called $(\mathcal{F}_n)$-*optional*, if it satisfies $[T \leq n] \in \mathcal{F}_n$, for each $1 \leq n < \infty$. Since the σ-fields $\mathcal{F}_n$ are increasing this is equivalent with $[T = n] \in \mathcal{F}_n$, for all $1 \leq n < \infty$ and implies that $[T = \infty] \in \mathcal{F}_\infty$.

T can be viewed as a gambler's strategy when to stop a game. If the true state of nature turns out to be the state ω, then the gambler intends to quit at time $n = T(\omega)$. Of course it is never completely clear which state ω the true state of nature is. At time n the information at hand about the true state of nature ω is the information contained in the σ-field $\mathcal{F}_n$. The condition $[T = n] \in \mathcal{F}_n$ ensures that we know at time n (without knowledge of the future) if $\omega \in [T = n]$, that is, if $T(\omega) = n$, in short, if it is time to quit now.

Suppose now that T is an optional time. We call an event $A \in \mathcal{F}$ *prior to* T, if $A \cap [T \leq n] \in \mathcal{F}_n$, for all $1 \leq n \leq \infty$ and denote with $\mathcal{F}_T$ the family of all events $A \in \mathcal{F}$ which are prior to T. Equivalently, $A \in \mathcal{F}_T$ if and only if $A \cap [T = n] \in \mathcal{F}_n$, for all $1 \leq n \leq \infty$. Interpret $\mathcal{F}_n$ as the σ-field of all events for which it is known at time n whether they occur or not. Then $A \in \mathcal{F}_T$ means that, for each state $\omega \in \Omega$, it is known by time $n = T(\omega)$, whether $\omega \in A$ or not. Alternatively, if δ is the true state of nature, it is known by time $n = T(\delta)$ whether A occurs or not.

Sampling X at time T. Assume that X_∞ is some $\mathcal{F}_\infty$-measurable random variable (exactly which will depend on the context). The random variable $X_T : \Omega \to \overline{R}$ is defined as follows:

$$X_T(\omega) = X_{T(\omega)}(\omega), \quad \omega \in \Omega.$$

Note that $X_T = X_n$ on the set $[T = n]$ and $X_T = X_\infty$ on the set $[T = +\infty]$. In case $\lim_n X_n$ exists almost surely, the random variable X_∞ is often taken to be $X_\infty = \limsup_n X_n$ (defined everywhere, $\mathcal{F}_\infty$-measurable and equal to the limit $\lim_n X_n$ almost surely). Note that we have to be careful with random variables defined P-as. only, as the σ-fields $\mathcal{F}_n$ are not assumed to contain the P-null sets and so the issue of $\mathcal{F}_n$-measurability arises. For much that follows the precise nature of X_∞ is not important. The random variable X_∞ becomes completely irrelevant if the optional time T is *finite* in the sense that $T < \infty$ almost surely.

The random variable X_T represents a *sampling* of the stochastic sequence X_n at the random time T. Indeed X_T is assembled from disjoint pieces of all the random variables X_n, $0 \leq n \leq \infty$, as $X_T = X_n$ on the set $[T = n]$. The optional condition ensures that no knowledge of the future is employed. Optional times are the basic tools in the study of stochastic processes.

If $\mathcal{G}_n$, $\mathcal{G}$, $1 \leq n < \infty$, are σ-fields, we write $\mathcal{G}_n \uparrow \mathcal{G}$, if $\mathcal{G}_1 \subseteq \mathcal{G}_2 \subseteq \ldots$ and $\mathcal{G} = \bigvee_n \mathcal{G}_n = \sigma \left(\bigcup_n \mathcal{G}_n \right)$.

3.b.0. *Let S, T, T_n, $1 \leq n < \infty$, be optional times, Y a random variable and $X = (X_n)$ an $(\mathcal{F}_n)$-adapted stochastic sequence. Then*
(a) $\mathcal{F}_T$ is a sub-σ-field of $\mathcal{F}$.
(b) Y is $\mathcal{F}_T$-measurable $\Leftrightarrow Y1_{[T=n]}$ is $\mathcal{F}_n$-measurable, $\forall 1 \leq n \leq \infty$.
(c) T and X_T are $\mathcal{F}_T$-measurable.
(d) $S \leq T$ implies $\mathcal{F}_S \subseteq \mathcal{F}_T$.
(e) $S \wedge T$, $S \vee T$ are optional times.
(f) $[S \leq T], [S = T] \in \mathcal{F}_{S \wedge T}$.
(g) $A \in \mathcal{F}_T$ implies $A \cap [T \leq S], A \cap [T = S] \in \mathcal{F}_{S \wedge T}$.
(h) If $T_n \uparrow T < \infty$, then $\mathcal{F}_{T_n} \uparrow \mathcal{F}_T$.
(i) If the filtration $(\mathcal{F}_n)$ is augmented, then $\mathcal{F}_T$ contains the P-null sets.

Proof. (a) $\Omega \in \mathcal{F}_T$ since T is optional. Let $A \in \mathcal{F}_T$. Then $A \cap [T \leq k] \in \mathcal{F}_k$ and consequently $A^c \cap [T \leq k] = (\Omega \cap [T \leq k]) \setminus (A \cap [T \leq k]) \in \mathcal{F}_k$, for each $k \geq 1$. This shows that $A^c \in \mathcal{F}_T$. Closure under countable unions is straightforward.

(b) Set $Y_n = Y1_{[T=n]}$, for all $1 \leq n \leq \infty$. If B is a Borel set not containing zero we have $[Y_n \in B] = [Y \in B] \cap [T = n]$ and so $[Y \in B] \in \mathcal{F}_T$ if and only if $[Y_n \in B] \in \mathcal{F}_n$, for all $n \geq 1$.

(c) Let $1 \leq m \leq \infty$. The set $A = [T = m]$ satisfies $A \cap [T = n] = \emptyset$, if $n \neq m$, and $A \cap [T = n] = [T = n]$, if $n = m$. In any event $A \cap [T = n] \in \mathcal{F}_n$, for all $n \geq 1$. This shows that $A = [T = m] \in \mathcal{F}_T$ and implies that T is $\mathcal{F}_T$-measurable.

To see that X_T is $\mathcal{F}_T$-measurable, note that $1_{[T=n]}X_T = 1_{[T=n]}X_n$ is $\mathcal{F}_n$-measurable, for all $1 \leq n \leq \infty$ (X_∞ is $\mathcal{F}_\infty$-measurable), and use (b).

(d) Assume $S \leq T$ and hence $[T \leq k] \subseteq [S \leq k]$, for all $k \geq 1$. Let $A \in \mathcal{F}_S$. Then, for each $k \geq 1$, we have $A \cap [S \leq k] \in \mathcal{F}_k$ and consequently $A \cap [T \leq k] = (A \cap [S \leq k]) \cap [T \leq k] \in \mathcal{F}_k$. Thus $A \in \mathcal{F}_T$.

(e),(f) Set $R = S \wedge T$ and let $n \geq 1$. Then $[R \leq n] = [S \leq n] \cup [T \leq n] \in \mathcal{F}_n$. Thus R is optional. Likewise $[S \leq T] \cap [R = n] = [S \leq T] \cap [S = n] = [n \leq T] \cap [S = n] \in \mathcal{F}_n$, for all $n \geq 1$. Thus $[S \leq T] \in \mathcal{F}_R$. By symmetry $[T \leq S] \in \mathcal{F}_R$ and so $[S = T] \in \mathcal{F}_R$.

(g) Set $R = S \wedge T$ and let $A \in \mathcal{F}_T$ and $n \geq 1$. Then $A \cap [T \leq S] \cap [R = n] = A \cap [T \leq S] \cap [T = n] = (A \cap [T = n]) \cap [n \leq S] \in \mathcal{F}_n$. Thus $A \cap [T \leq S] \in \mathcal{F}_R$. Intersecting this with the set $[S \leq T] \in \mathcal{F}_R$ we obtain $A \cap [T = S] \in \mathcal{F}_R$.

(h) Set $\mathcal{G} = \bigvee_n \mathcal{F}_{T_n}$. We have to show that $\mathcal{F}_T = \mathcal{G}$. According to (d), $\mathcal{F}_{T_n} \subseteq \mathcal{F}_T$, for all $n \geq 1$, and consequently $\mathcal{G} \subseteq \mathcal{F}_T$. To see the reverse inclusion, let $A \in \mathcal{F}_T$. We wish to show that $A \in \mathcal{G}$. According to (c) all the T_k are $\mathcal{G}$-measurable and hence so is the limit $T = \lim_k T_k$. Thus $[T = n] \in \mathcal{G}$, for all $n \geq 1$. Moreover $A \cap [T_k = T] \in \mathcal{F}_{T_k} \subseteq \mathcal{G}$, for all $k \geq 1$, according to (g). Since T is finite and the T_n are integer valued, the convergence $T_n \uparrow T$ implies that $T_k = T$ for some $k \geq 1$ (which may depend on $\omega \in \Omega$). Thus $A = A \cap \bigcup_k [T_k = T] = \bigcup_k A \cap [T_k = T] \in \mathcal{G}$.
(i) is left to the reader. ∎

Remark. The assumption in (h) is that $T < \infty$ everywhere on Ω. If the filtration $(\mathcal{F}_n)$ is augmented, this can be relaxed to $P(T < \infty) = 1$.

Let T be a *bounded* optional time, say $T \leq N$, P-as. If $E(X_n^+) < \infty$, for all $n \geq 1$, then $E(X_T^+) < \infty$ also, since $X_T^+ = \sum_{k=1}^{N} 1_{[T=k]} X_k^+$, P-as. Likewise, if $E(X_n^-) < \infty$, for all $n \geq 1$, then $E(X_T^-) < \infty$ and, under either of these two assumptions, $X_T \in \mathcal{E}(P)$. The boundedness of T also eliminates the necessity to specify X_T on $[T = +\infty]$. Thus we do not need any random variable X_∞.

3.b.1 Baby Optional Sampling Theorem. *Let X_n be a submartingale and S, T bounded optional times with $S \leq T$. Then $X_S, X_T \in \mathcal{E}(P)$ and $E(X_T 1_A) \leq E(X_T 1_A)$, for all sets $A \in \mathcal{F}_S$, that is, $X_S \leq E(X_T | \mathcal{F}_S)$. In particular $E(X_S) \leq E(X_T)$.*

Proof. We have $E(X_n^+) < \infty$, for all $n \geq 1$, and so $E(X_S^+), E(X_T^+) < \infty$, especially $X_S, X_T \in \mathcal{E}(P)$. The submartingale condition for the stochastic sequence X can be written as

$$E\big(1_A (X_{k+1} - X_k)\big) \geq 0, \quad \forall k \geq 1, A \in \mathcal{F}_k.$$

Assume now that $S \leq T \leq N$, P-as., where N is some natural number. For each $\omega \in \Omega$ such that $T(\omega) < +\infty$ (and thus for P-ae. $\omega \in \Omega$) we have:

$$X_{T(\omega)}(\omega) - X_{S(\omega)}(\omega) = \sum_{k=S(\omega)}^{T(\omega)-1} \big(X_{k+1}(\omega) - X_k(\omega)\big).$$

The bounds in this sum depend on ω. The boundedness $P([T \leq N]) = 1$ can be used to rewrite this with bounds independent of ω:

$$X_T - X_S = \sum_{k=1}^{N} 1_{[S \leq k < T]} (X_{k+1} - X_k).$$

Consequently, if $A \in \mathcal{F}_S$ is any set, then

$$1_A (X_T - X_S) = \sum_{k=1}^{N} 1_{A \cap [S \leq k < T]} (X_{k+1} - X_k), \quad P\text{-as.} \tag{0}$$

As $A \in \mathcal{F}_S$, $A \cap [S \leq k] \in \mathcal{F}_k$ and so the set $A \cap [S \leq k < T] = A \cap [S \leq k] \cap [T \leq k]^c$ is in $\mathcal{F}_k$. By the submartingale condition, $E\big(1_{A \cap [S \leq k < T]} (X_{k+1} - X_k)\big) \geq 0$, for all $k = 1, 2, \ldots, N$. Taking expectations in (0) now yields $E\big(1_A (X_T - X_S)\big) \geq 0$, as desired. ∎

3.b.2 Corollary. *Let $(X_n, \mathcal{F}_n)$ be a submartingale (martingale) and (T_n) a nondecreasing sequence of bounded optional times. Then $(X_{T_n}, \mathcal{F}_{T_n})$ is a submartingale (martingale).*

Proof. The boundedness of T_n implies that $E\big(X_{T_n}^+\big) < \infty$. According to 3.b.0.(c) X_{T_n} is $\mathcal{F}_{T_n}$-measurable. Thus the sequence (X_{T_n}) is $(\mathcal{F}_{T_n})$-adapted. Moreover 3.b.1 applied to the bounded optional times $T_n \leq T_{n+1}$ yields $X_{T_n} \leq E(X_{T_{n+1}} | \mathcal{F}_{T_n})$. Thus $(X_{T_n}, \mathcal{F}_{T_n})$ is a submartingale. The proof for the martingale case is similar. ∎

Remark. It is the assumption of boundedness of the optional times S, T which makes 3.b.1 so elementary although even this version of the Optional Sampling Theorem is extremely useful.

The following example shows that 3.b.1 does not hold for all finite optional times and all submartingales: Let X_n denote the gambler's fortune after n tosses of a fair coin starting with initial capital 0 and betting 1 dollar on each toss (a negative fortune is allowed). More precisely, let $X_n = Y_1 + Y_2 + \ldots + Y_n$, where the Y_j are independent and identically distributed with $P(Y_j = 1) = P(Y_j = -1) = 1/2$. Then (X_n) is a martingale and $E(X_1) = 0$.

Now let S be the constant optional time $S = 1$ and define $T(\omega) = \inf\{n \geq 1 \mid X_n(\omega) = 1\}$ ($= +\infty$, if no such n exists). The gambler intends to stop when he is ahead by one. It is easy to see that $T < +\infty$ with probability one and that T is an optional time. However, by the very definition of T we have $X_T = 1$, P-as., and hence $E(X_T) = 1 \neq 0 = E(X_1) = E(X_S)$.

Stronger versions of the Optional Sampling Theorem explore conditions on the submartingale (X_n) which imply that 3.b.1 holds for all optional times. It will be seen later that the existence of a last element X_∞ for the submartingale (X_n) (which in turn follows from uniform integrability) is a suitable assumption. Finally, let us record a simple consequence of 3.b.1:

3.b.3. *Assume that T is an optional time bounded by the integer $N \geq 1$. Then*
(a) $E(|X_T|) \leq 2E(X_N^+) - E(X_1)$, if (X_n) is a submartingale.
(b) $E(|X_T|) \leq 2E(X_N^-) + E(X_1)$, if (X_n) is a supermartingale.

Proof. (a) Assume that (X_n) is a submartingale. Then so is the sequence (X_n^+). Thus $T \leq N$ implies that $E(X_T^+) \leq E(X_N^+)$ while $1 \leq T$ implies that $E(X_1) \leq E(X_T)$. Note now that $|X_T| = X_T^+ + X_T^-$ and $X_T = X_T^+ - X_T^-$ and so $X_T^- = X_T^+ - X_T$. It follows that $|X_T| = 2X_T^+ - X_T$ and consequently

$$E(|X_T|) = 2E(X_T^+) - E(X_T) \leq 2E(X_N^+) - E(X_1).$$

(b) If the sequence (X_n) is a supermartingale then $(-X_n)$ is a submartingale satisfying $(-X_n)^+ = X_n^-$. Replacing X with $-X$ in (a) now yields $E(|X_T|) \leq 2E(X_N^-) + E(X_1)$. ∎

3.c Application to the gambler's ruin problem. Let $(X_n)_{n \geq 1}$ be an iid sequence of random variable on $(\Omega, \mathcal{F}, P)$ which assume only the values $+1$ and -1 with respective probabilities $P(X_n = 1) = p$ and $P(X_n = -1) = q$. Set

$$S_n = X_1 + X_2 + \ldots + X_n, \ n \geq 1.$$

S_n will be interpreted as the sum total of wins and losses of a gambler, betting 1 dollar on the outcome $X_n = 1$, at the nth game. The random walk (S_n) is called *symmetric* (unbiased) if $p = q$ and *biased* otherwise. Since the bets are limited to exactly one dollar at each game, the random walk (S_n) is integer valued and proceeds in jumps of unity, that is, it cannot jump over any integer.

A question of great interest to us, the gamblers, is the following: starting with $d \geq 1$ dollars what is the probability that we win $b > 0$ dollars before we are bankrupt (lose all our d dollars)? This can be modeled as follows: We set $a := -d < 0$ and examine how long S_n (which starts at zero) remains in the interval $[a, b]$. Note that $a < 0 < b$ and let $\mathcal{F}_n = \sigma(X_1, X_2, \ldots, X_n)$, for all $n \geq 1$. Clearly the sequence (S_n) is $(\mathcal{F}_n)$-adapted. We set

$$T = min\{\, n \geq 1 \mid S_n \notin (a, b)\,\}.$$

It is easy to see that T is an optional time relative to the filtration $(\mathcal{F}_n)$. At time T the random walk leaves the interval (a, b) for the first time and since it cannot jump over the boundary points a, b we have

$$S_T \in \{a, b\}, \text{ on the set } [T < \infty].$$

We will soon see that $T < \infty$ almost surely, and thus we do not need a random variable S_∞ for the definition of S_T. If $S_T = a = -d$ we are bankrupt, while in case $S_T = b$, we have won b dollars before going bankrupt.

The unbiased case. Assume that $p = q = 1/2$. Then $E(X_n) = 0$. Note that $E(S_n | \mathcal{F}_n) = S_n$, by $\mathcal{F}_n$-measurability of S_n, and $E(X_{n+1} | \mathcal{F}_n) = E(X_{n+1}) = 0$, by independence of X_{n+1} from $\mathcal{F}_n$. It follows that

$$E(S_{n+1} | \mathcal{F}_n) = E(S_n | \mathcal{F}_n) + E(X_{n+1} | \mathcal{F}_n) = S_n,$$

that is, (S_n) is a martingale. Apply the conditional expectation operator $E_{\mathcal{F}_n}$ to both sides of the equation

$$\begin{aligned} S_{n+1}^2 &= S_n^2 + 2S_n X_{n+1} + X_{n+1}^2 \\ &= S_n^2 + 2S_n X_{n+1} + 1 \end{aligned}$$

and recall that $E(X_{n+1} | \mathcal{F}_n) = E(X_{n+1}) = 0$ and S_n is bounded ($|S_n| \leq n$) and $\mathcal{F}_n$-measurable. It follows that $E(2S_n X_{n+1} | \mathcal{F}_n) = 2S_n E(X_{n+1} | \mathcal{F}_n) = 0$ and so

$$E(S_{n+1}^2 | \mathcal{F}_n) = S_n^2 + 1.$$

Consequently the sequence $(S_n^2 - n)$ is a martingale. Set $Y_n = S_n^2 - n$ and $T_n = n \wedge T$ where T is as above. Then (Y_{T_n}) is a martingale (3.b.2) and since a martingale has a constant mean, we conclude that

$$E(S_{n \wedge T}^2 - n \wedge T) = E(Y_{T_n}) = E(Y_{T_1}) = E(Y_1) = 0;$$

in other words, $E(n \wedge T) = E(S_{n \wedge T}^2)$, for all $n \geq 0$. However $n \wedge T \leq T$ and T is the first time S_n leaves the interval (a, b). It follows that $S_{n \wedge T} \in [a, b]$ and consequently $|S_{n \wedge T}| \leq max\{|a|, |b|\} := K$. Thus $E(n \wedge T) \leq K^2$. Also $0 \leq n \wedge T \uparrow T$ and so, by monotone convergence, it follows that $E(n \wedge T) \uparrow E(T)$, as $n \uparrow \infty$. Consequently $E(T) \leq K^2 < \infty$ and this implies that $T < \infty$ almost surely.

It follows that S_T is defined and, as we have seen above, $S_T \in \{a, b\}$ almost surely. This implies that $E(S_T) = a\alpha + b\beta$, where

$$\alpha = P(S_T = a) \quad \text{and} \quad \beta = P(S_T = b).$$

On the other hand, using 3.b.2 again, $(S_{n \wedge T})$ is a martingale and as such has a constant mean. It follows that $E(S_{n \wedge T}) = E(S_{1 \wedge T}) = E(S_1) = 0$, for all $n \geq 0$. Also $S_{n \wedge T} \to S_T$ on the set $[T < \infty]$, and hence almost surely, as $n \uparrow \infty$. Because of $|S_{n \wedge T}| \leq K$ the Dominated Convergence Theorem yields $E(S_{n \wedge T}) \to E(S_T)$. It follows that $a\alpha + b\beta = E(S_T) = 0$. Also $\alpha + \beta = 1$, since $S_T \in \{a, b\}$ almost surely. We can solve the equations $a\alpha + b\beta = 0$ and $\alpha + \beta = 1$ to obtain

$$\alpha = \frac{b}{b-a} = \frac{b}{b+d} \qquad \text{(probability of ruin), and}$$

$$\beta = \frac{-a}{b-a} = \frac{d}{b+d} \qquad \text{(probability of success).}$$

We can also compute the expected time $E(T)$ to decision. We have seen above that $E(n \wedge T) = E\big(S_{n \wedge T}^2\big)$. Letting $n \uparrow \infty$ we conclude that

$$E(T) = E(S_T^2) = \alpha a^2 + \beta b^2 = -ab = bd.$$

The biased case. Assume now that $p \neq q$. Then $E(X_n) = p - q \neq 0$ and so $E(S_n) = n(p-q)$. Note first that

$$E(S_{n+1}|\mathcal{F}_n) = E(S_n|\mathcal{F}_n) + E(X_{n+1}|\mathcal{F}_n) = S_n + E(X_{n+1}) = S_n + (p-q).$$

Consequently $Y_n = S_n - n(p-q)$, $n \geq 1$, is a martingale and hence so is the sequence $(Y_{n \wedge T})$ (3.b.2). In particular this sequence has a constant mean, that is,

$$E(S_{n \wedge T} - (p-q)n \wedge T) = E(Y_{n \wedge T}) = E(Y_1) = E(S_1) - (p-q) = 0. \qquad (0)$$

Note that $S_{n \wedge T} \in [a, b]$. Thus $|S_{n \wedge T}| \leq \max\{|a|, |b|\} = K$ and so $|p-q|E(n \wedge T) = |E(S_{n \wedge T})| \leq K$,that is, $E(n \wedge T) \leq K/|p-q| < \infty$. Since $0 \leq n \wedge T \uparrow T$ we have $E(n \wedge T) \uparrow E(T)$ and hence $E(T) \leq K/|p-q| < \infty$, from which it follows that $T < \infty$ almost surely. Also $|S_{n \wedge T}| \leq K$ and $S_{n \wedge T} \to S_T$ on the set $[T < \infty]$ and hence almost surely. By bounded convergence it follows that $E(S_{n \wedge T}) \to E(S_T)$. Thus passing to the limit in the equation $(p-q)E(n \wedge T) = E(S_{n \wedge T})$, derived from (0), we obtain

$$(p-q)E(T) = E(S_T) = a\alpha + b\beta, \qquad (1)$$

where $\alpha = P(S_T = a)$ and $\beta = P(S_T = b)$, as above (note that $S_T \in \{a, b\}$ when $T < \infty$, and hence almost surely). In order to compute the unknown quantities

$E(T)$, α, β we must derive further equations. To do so let $A > 0$ and set $Z_n = A^{S_n}$. Then

$$E(Z_{n+1}|\mathcal{F}_n) = E(A^{S_n} A^{X_{n+1}}|\mathcal{F}_n) = A^{S_n} E(A^{X_{n+1}}|\mathcal{F}_n)$$
$$= Z_n E(A^{X_{n+1}}) = Z_n (pA + qA^{-1}) = Z_n B,$$

where $B = pA + qA^{-1}$. From this it follows that $(B^{-n}Z_n)$ is a martingale. This is particularly simple, if $B = 1$, that is $pA + qA^{-1} = 1$, which one solves easily for $A = 1, q/p$. Thus we set $r = q/p$ and use the fact that $Z_n = r^{S_n}$ defines a martingale. Using 3.b.2 the sequence $(Z_{n \wedge T})$ is also a martingale with $Z_{1 \wedge T} = Z_1$ and thus has a constant mean. It follows that

$$E(Z_{n \wedge T}) = E(Z_1) = pr + qr^{-1} = 1, \quad \text{for all } n \geq 1. \tag{2}$$

Now $Z_{n \wedge T} \to Z_T$ on the set $[T < \infty]$, and so almost surely. Since $S_{n \wedge T} \in [a, b]$ this convergence is bounded ($|Z_{n \wedge T}| \leq C$, where $C = \sup_{t \in [a,b]} r^t$) and passing to the limit in equation (2) yields $E(Z_T) = 1$. But $S_T \in \{a, b\}$ and hence $Z_T \in \{r^a, r^b\}$ almost surely and in fact $[Z_T = r^a] = [S_T = a]$ and $[Z_T = r^b] = [S_T = b]$. Consequently $1 = E(Z_T) = r^a P(S_T = a) + r^b P(S_T = b) = \alpha r^a + \beta r^b$. Combined with the equation $\alpha + \beta = 1$ this yields the system of equations

$$\alpha + \beta = 1, \quad \alpha a + \beta b = (p - q)E(T) \quad \text{and} \quad \alpha r^a + \beta r^b = 1,$$

which one solves for

$$\alpha = \frac{1 - r^b}{r^a - r^b}, \quad \beta = \frac{r^a - 1}{r^a - r^b}, \quad E(T) = \frac{1}{p - q} \left[\frac{br^a - ar^b + a - b}{r^a - r^b} \right].$$

In terms of our original data $d = -a$ and b we obtain

$$P(S_T = a) = \alpha = \frac{r^d - r^{b+d}}{1 - r^{b+d}} \qquad \text{(probability of defeat)},$$

$$P(S_T = b) = \beta = \frac{1 - r^d}{1 - r^{b+d}} \qquad \text{(probability of success)},$$

$$E(T) = \frac{1}{p - q} \left[\frac{b + dr^{b+d} - (b + d)r^d}{1 - r^{b+d}} \right] \qquad \text{(expected time to decision)}.$$

Here d is our initial capital, b the amount we want to win (in addition to our initial capital), $p = P(X_1 = 1)$ the probability in our favour and $q = P(X_1 = -1)$ the odds against us on each individual bet and finally $r = q/p \neq 1$.

4. CONVERGENCE THEOREMS

4.a Upcrossings. Let $(\Omega, \mathcal{F}, P)$ be a probability space, $(\mathcal{F}_n)_{n \geq 1}$ a filtration on $(\Omega, \mathcal{F}, P)$ and (X_n) an $(\mathcal{F}_n)$-submartingale. For $\omega \in \Omega$ the sequence $n \in \mathbb{N} \mapsto X_n(\omega)$ is called the *sample path* associated with the point ω. We are now interested in the oscillatory behaviour of sample paths, especially in the number of times such a path crosses up from a value $X_j(\omega) \leq \alpha$ to a later value $X_k(\omega) \geq \beta$.

4.a.0. *Let $N \geq 1$, B a Borel set and S an optional time. Set*

$$T(\omega) = N \wedge \inf\{\, 1 \leq k < N \mid k > S(\omega) \text{ and } X_k(\omega) \in B \,\}.$$

Then T is an optional time.

Remark. Recall the convention $\inf(\emptyset) = +\infty$. It follows that $T(\omega) = N$, if there does not exist k such that $S(\omega) < k < N$ and $X_k(\omega) \in B$, and $T(\omega)$ is the smallest such k, especially $T(\omega) < N$, if such k exists.

Proof. Since the sequence X is $(\mathcal{F}_n)$-adapted, we have $[X_k \in B] \in \mathcal{F}_k$, for all $k \geq 1$. If $n \geq N$, we have $[T \leq n] = \Omega \in \mathcal{F}_n$. Let now $n < N$. Then $T(\omega) \leq n$ if and only if there exists k such that $S(\omega) < k \leq n$ and $X_k(\omega) \in B$. Necessarily then $S(\omega) \in \{1, 2, \ldots, n-1\}$. Thus

$$[T \leq n] = \bigcup_{j=1}^{n-1} \bigcup_{k=j+1}^{n} [S = j] \cap [X_k \in B] \in \mathcal{F}_n. \ \blacksquare$$

Fix $N \geq 1$ and $-\infty < \alpha < \beta < +\infty$. A segment $(X_j(\omega), X_{j+1}(\omega), \ldots, X_k(\omega))$ of the sample path $(X_n(\omega))$ will be called an *upcrossing* of the interval (α, β) if we have $X_j(\omega) \leq \alpha$, k is the smallest index $n > j$ such that $X_n(\omega) \geq \beta$ and the difference $k - j$ is maximal subject to these constraints. In other words $j < k$ is the smallest index for which $X_j(\omega) \leq \alpha$ and k has the preceding property. This fixes the starting point j of an upcrossing as the time of the first dip below α since the last upcrossing and in consequence any two distinct upcrossings are disjoint. The upcrossing $(X_j(\omega), X_{j+1}(\omega), \ldots, X_k(\omega))$ is said to *occur before time N*, if $k < N$. The times j, k at which upcrossings start and end can be defined recursively and will then be seen to be $(\mathcal{F}_n)$-optional. For $\omega \in \Omega$ set

$$S_1(\omega) = N \wedge \inf\{\, 1 \leq k < N \mid X_k(\omega) \leq \alpha \,\} \quad \text{and}$$
$$T_1(\omega) = N \wedge \inf\{\, 1 \leq k < N \mid k > S_1(\omega) \text{ and } X_k(\omega) \geq \beta \,\}.$$

Assuming that $S_n(\omega)$, $T_n(\omega)$ have already been defined, we set

$$S_{n+1}(\omega) = N \wedge \inf\{\, 1 \leq k < N \mid k > T_n(\omega) \text{ and } X_k(\omega) \leq \alpha \,\} \quad \text{and}$$
$$T_{n+1}(\omega) = N \wedge \inf\{\, 1 \leq k < N \mid k > S_{n+1}(\omega) \text{ and } X_k(\omega) \geq \beta \,\}.$$

Note that

$$S_1(\omega) < T_1(\omega) < S_2(\omega) < T_2(\omega) < \ldots < \begin{cases} S_j(\omega) = N = T_j(\omega) = S_{j+1}(\omega) = \ldots \\ T_j(\omega) = N = S_{j+1}(\omega) = T_{j+1}(\omega) = \ldots, \end{cases}$$

that is, the sequence $(S_1, T_1, S_2, T_2, \ldots)$ is strictly increasing until one of its terms hits the value N, when all the following terms stabilize at N. Moreover $S_j(\omega)$, $T_j(\omega)$ equal N if and only if the condition for k in the defining infimum can no longer be satisfied. Clearly $S_N(\omega) = T_N(\omega) = N$.

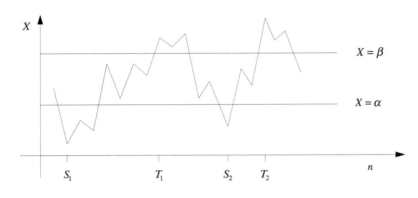

Figure 1.2

The upcrossings of the interval (α, β) which occur before time N are exactly the segments $(X_{S_1(\omega)}(\omega), \ldots, X_{T_1(\omega)}(\omega)), \ldots, (X_{S_n(\omega)}(\omega), \ldots, X_{T_n(\omega)}(\omega))$ with $n \geq 1$ the largest integer such that $T_n(\omega) < N$ (see Figure 1.2). In particular

$$U_N(\alpha, \beta)(\omega) = \sup\{\, n \geq 1 \mid T_n(\omega) < N \,\} \vee 0 \quad (= 0, \text{ if no such } n \geq 1 \text{ exists})$$

is the precise number of upcrossings of (α, β) by the sample path $(X_n(\omega))$ which occur before time N.

4.a.1. *(a) The T_n, S_n, $n \geq 1$, are bounded optional times.*
(b) $U_N(\alpha, \beta) : \Omega \to \{0, 1, 2, \ldots\}$ is measurable.
(c) We have $X_{T_j(\omega)}(\omega) - X_{S_j(\omega)}(\omega) \geq \beta - \alpha$, for all $j = 1, 2, \ldots, U_N(\alpha, \beta)(\omega)$.

Proof. (a) This follows from 4.a.0 by straightforward induction.
(b) The increasing nature of the T_n implies that $[U_N(\alpha, \beta) \leq m] = [T_{m+1} = N] \in \mathcal{F}$, for all $m \geq 0$. Since $U_N(\alpha, \beta)$ takes values in $\{0, 1, 2, \ldots\}$, it follows that $U_N(\alpha, \beta)$ is measurable.
(c) For $k = 1, 2, \ldots, U_N(\alpha, \beta)(\omega)$, the segment $(X_{S_k(\omega)}(\omega), \ldots, X_{T_k(\omega)}(\omega))$ is an upcrossing of (α, β) and thus in particular $X_{S_k(\omega)}(\omega) \leq \alpha$ and $X_{T_k(\omega)}(\omega) \geq \beta$. ∎

The crucial step in the proof of our convergence theorems is the following estimate of the expected number $E\big(U_N(\alpha, \beta)\big)$ of upcrossings of (α, β) by X before time N:

4.a.2 Upcrossing Lemma.

$$E\big(U_N(\alpha,\beta)\big) \leq \frac{E(X_N^+) + |\alpha|}{\beta - \alpha}.$$

Proof. For each $n \geq 1$ set $Y_n = (X_n - \alpha)^+$. Then $Y_n \geq 0$ is a submartingale and we have

$$X_k \leq \alpha \iff Y_k \leq 0 \quad \text{and} \quad X_k \geq \beta \iff Y_k \geq \beta - \alpha.$$

Thus the upcrossings of (α,β) by $(X_n(\omega))$ happen at exactly the same times as the upcrossings of $(0, \beta - \alpha)$ by $(Y_n(\omega))$. Setting $T_0 = 1$ and recalling that $T_N = N$ we can write

$$Y_N \geq Y_N - Y_1 = \sum_{k=1}^{N} \left(Y_{T_k} - Y_{T_{k-1}}\right) = \sum_{k=1}^{N} \left(Y_{T_k} - Y_{S_k}\right) + \sum_{k=1}^{N} \left(Y_{S_k} - Y_{T_{k-1}}\right).$$

If $S_k(\omega) < N$, then $Y_{S_k(\omega)}(\omega) = 0$, and if $S_k(\omega) = N$, then $T_k(\omega) = N$ also. In any case we have $(Y_{T_k} - Y_{S_k})(\omega) \geq 0$, for all $k = 1, 2, \ldots, N$. Moreover $U_N(\alpha,\beta)(\omega) \leq N$ and $(Y_{T_k} - Y_{S_k})(\omega) \geq \beta - \alpha$, for all $k = 1, 2, \ldots, U_N(\alpha,\beta)(\omega)$, according to 4.a.1.(c). Thus $\sum_{k=1}^{N} \left(Y_{T_k} - Y_{S_k}\right) \geq (\beta - \alpha)U_N(\alpha,\beta)$ at each point of Ω and consequently

$$Y_N \geq (\beta - \alpha)U_N(\alpha,\beta) + \sum_{k=1}^{N} \left(Y_{S_k} - Y_{T_{k-1}}\right).$$

Taking expectations we find that

$$E(Y_N) \geq (\beta - \alpha)E(U_N(\alpha,\beta)) + \sum_{k=1}^{N} \left(E(Y_{S_k}) - E(Y_{T_{k-1}})\right).$$

Applying the Optional Sampling Theorem 3.b.1 to the submartingale (Y_n) and bounded optional times $T_{k-1} \leq S_k$ yields $E(Y_{S_k}) \geq E(Y_{T_{k-1}})$, for all $k = 1, \ldots, N$. We conclude that

$$E(Y_N) \geq (\beta - \alpha)E(U_N(\alpha,\beta)),$$

equivalently, that $E(U_N(\alpha,\beta)) \leq E(Y_N)/(\beta - \alpha)$. It remains to be shown merely that $E(Y_N) \leq E(X_N^+) + |\alpha|$. This follows immediately from $Y_N = (X_N - \alpha)^+ \leq X_N^+ + |\alpha|$ upon taking expectations. ∎

4.a.3 Submartingale Convergence Theorem. *Assume that the submartingale (X_n) satisfies $K = \sup_n E(X_n^+) < \infty$. Then*
 (i) $X_\infty = \lim_n X_n \in \overline{R}$ exists P-as. and satisfies $E(X_\infty^+) < \infty$.
 (ii) If $E(X_n) > -\infty$, for some n, then $X_\infty \in L^1(P)$.
 (iii) We have $X_n \leq E(X_\infty|\mathcal{F}_n)$, for all $n \geq 1$, if and only if the family $\{X_n^+ | n \geq 1\}$ is uniformly integrable.
 (iv) Assume that $(X_n) \subseteq L^1(P)$. Then $X_\infty \in L^1(P)$ and $X_n \to X_\infty$ in $L^1(P)$, if and only if the submartingale (X_n) is uniformly integrable.

Proof. (i) Set $X_* = \liminf_{n\uparrow\infty} X_n$ and $X^* = \limsup_{n\uparrow\infty} X_n$. Then X_*, X^* are extended real valued random variables. We have to show that $P(X_* < X^*) = 0$.

As $[X_* < X^*]$ is the countable union of the sets $A(\alpha, \beta) = [X_* < \alpha < \beta < X^*]$ over all rational numbers α, β with $\alpha < \beta$, it will suffice to show that $P(A(\alpha, \beta)) = 0$ for all such α and β.

Now if $\omega \in A(\alpha, \beta)$ then $\liminf_{n \uparrow \infty} X_n(\omega) < \alpha < \beta < \limsup_{n \uparrow \infty} X_n(\omega)$ and consequently the sample path $(X_n(\omega))$ must drop below α infinitely often and must also exceed the value β infinitely often. In consequence it must cross up from below α to above β infinitely often, and so

$$U(\alpha, \beta)(\omega) := \lim_{N \uparrow \infty} U_N(\alpha, \beta)(\omega) = +\infty.$$

It will now suffice to show that this can happen only on a P-null set, equivalently that $U(\alpha, \beta) < \infty$, P-as. As $U(\alpha, \beta) = \lim_{N \uparrow \infty} U_N(\alpha, \beta)$ is measurable and nonnegative, it will suffice to show that $E(U(\alpha, \beta)) < \infty$. Indeed $0 \le U_N(\alpha, \beta) \uparrow U(\alpha, \beta)$ and so $E(U_N(\alpha, \beta)) \uparrow E(U(\alpha, \beta))$, as $N \uparrow \infty$. However, according to the Upcrossing Lemma, we have $E(U_N(\alpha, \beta)) \le (\beta - \alpha)^{-1}(K + |\alpha|)$, for each $N \ge 1$, and it follows that $E(U(\alpha, \beta)) \le (\beta - \alpha)^{-1}(K + |\alpha|) < \infty$.

Thus $X_\infty(\omega) = \lim_{n \uparrow \infty} X_n(\omega) \in \overline{R}$ exists almost surely. Extending X_∞ to all of Ω by setting $X_\infty = \limsup_n X_n$, X_∞ becomes a random variable (defined and measurable on all of Ω). Using Fatou's Lemma, we see that

$$E(X_\infty^+) = E(\lim_n X_n^+) = E(\liminf_n X_n^+) \le \liminf_n E(X_n^+) \le K < \infty.$$

(ii) Assume now that $m \ge 1$ and $E(X_m) > -\infty$. Recall that the expectations $E(X_n)$ are nondecreasing. If $n \ge m$, then $|X_n| = X_n^+ + X_n^- = 2X_n^+ - X_n$ and so $E(|X_n|) = 2E(X_n^+) - E(X_n) \le 2K - E(X_m)$. Another application of Fatou's Lemma now yields

$$E(|X_\infty|) = E(\liminf_n |X_n|) \le \liminf_n E(|X_n|) \le 2K - E(X_m) < \infty.$$

(iii) Assume first that $X_n \le E(X_\infty | \mathcal{F}_n)$, for all $n \ge 1$. Then the extended sequence $(X_n)_{1 \le n \le \infty}$ is still a submartingale and hence so is the extended sequence $(X_n^+)_{1 \le n \le \infty}$ (3.a.0). Consequently

$$0 \le X_n^+ \le E(X_\infty^+ | \mathcal{F}_n), \quad n \ge 1.$$

The uniform integrability of the family $\{ X_n^+ \mid n \ge 1 \}$ now follows from the uniform integrability of the family $\{ E_{\mathcal{F}_n}(X_\infty^+) \mid n \ge 1 \}$ (2.b.13).

Conversely, assume that the family $\{ X_n^+ \mid n \ge 1 \}$ is uniformly integrable (and hence L^1-bounded). Then $E(X_\infty^+) < \infty$, according to (i). We must show that $X_n \le E(X_\infty | \mathcal{F}_n)$, equivalently

$$E(X_n 1_A) \le E(X_\infty 1_A), \quad \forall n \ge 1, A \in \mathcal{F}_n. \tag{0.}$$

Fix $r \in R$ and set $X_n(r) = X_n \vee r$, $n \geq 1$. Then $(X_n(r))_n$ is a submartingale (3.a.0). Fix $n \geq 1$ and let $A \in \mathcal{F}_n$ and $m \geq n$. Then $E(X_n(r)1_A) \leq E(X_m(r)1_A)$. Letting $m \uparrow \infty$ and observing that the uniform integrability of $\{X_m^+ \mid m \geq 1\}$ implies the uniform integrability of $\{X_m(r) \mid m \geq 1\}$, we obtain

$$E(X_n(r)1_A) \leq E(X_\infty(r)1_A).$$

Letting $r \downarrow -\infty$ now yields (0), by decreasing convergence. Note that the families $\{X_n(r) \mid r \in R\}$ and $\{X_\infty(r) \mid r \in R\}$ are bounded above by the integrable functions X_n^+ respectively X_∞^+.

(iv) If $(X_n) \subseteq L^1(P)$, then norm convergence $X_n \to X_\infty \in L^1(P)$ implies the uniform integrability of the sequence (X_n). Conversely, the uniform integrability of the sequence (X_n) and almost sure convergence $X_n \to X_\infty$ imply that $X_\infty \in L^1(P)$ and $X_n \to X_\infty$ in norm (1.b.4). ∎

Remark. In general the limit X_∞ will not be integrable. For a trivial example set $\mathcal{F}_n = \{\emptyset, \Omega\}$ and $X_n = -\infty$, for all $n \geq 1$. The sequence $(X_n, \mathcal{F}_n)$ is a submartingale and $X_\infty = -\infty$ on all of Ω.

4.a.4 Corollary. *A submartingale sequence $(X_n) \subseteq L^1(P)$ is norm convergent to an integrable random variable X_∞ if and only if it is uniformly integrable.* ∎

Let now (X_n) be an L^1-bounded martingale and $K = \sup_n \|X_n\|_1 < \infty$. Then (X_n) and $(-X_n)$ are submartingale sequences with $\sup_n E(X_n^+), \sup_n E((-X_n)^+) = \sup_n E(X_n^-) < \infty$. An application of 4.a.3, 4.a.4 to both submartingales (X_n) and $(-X_n)$ now yields:

4.a.5 Martingale Convergence Theorem. *Let (X_n) be an L^1-bounded martingale. Then $X_\infty = \lim_n X_n$ exists P-as. and is an integrable random variable. Moreover the following conditions are equivalent:*

(i) $X_n = E(X_\infty | \mathcal{F}_n)$, for all $n \geq 1$.

(ii) $X_n \to X_\infty$ in L^1-norm.

(iii) (X_n) is uniformly integrable. ∎

Remark. The reader will have noticed that the filtration $(\mathcal{F}_n)$ does not enter the argument. If (X_n) is a submartingale with respect to any filtration $(\mathcal{F}_n)$, then (X_n) is a submartingale with respect to the filtration $\mathcal{G}_n = \sigma(X_1, X_2, \ldots, X_n)$ and this, conversely, is sufficient for all the results above.

4.b Reversed submartingales. Recall that a *reversed submartingale* is a sequence $(X_n, \mathcal{F}_n)_{n \geq 1}$ which is a martingale when the natural order on the index set $\mathbb{N}$ is reversed. In short $\mathcal{F}_1 \supseteq \mathcal{F}_2 \supseteq \mathcal{F}_3 \supseteq \ldots$, (X_n) is $(\mathcal{F}_n)$-adapted, $E(X_n^+) < \infty$ and

$$E_{\mathcal{F}_{n+1}}(X_n) \geq X_{n+1}, \quad \text{for all } n \geq 1. \tag{0}$$

If $X_n \in L^1(P)$ and equality holds here for each $n \geq 1$, then the sequence $(X_n, \mathcal{F}_n)$ is called a *reversed martingale*. The reversed order on $\mathbb{N}$ has a last element, namely 1, and so $X_n \leq E(X_1|\mathcal{F}_n)$, $n \geq 1$, with equality in the martingale case. This has far reaching consequences, as we shall see below. For example, if the sequence $(X_n, \mathcal{F}_n)$ is a reversed martingale, then $X_n = E(X_1|\mathcal{F}_n)$, for all $n \geq 1$, and it follows that (X_n) is uniformly integrable, especially L^1-bounded (2.b.13).

Let $(X_n, \mathcal{F}_n)$ be a *reversed submartingale* and set $\mathcal{F}_\infty = \bigcap_n \mathcal{F}_n$. The increasing property of the mean in the reversed order on $\mathbb{N}$ means that $E(X_n) \downarrow$, as $n \uparrow \infty$, and consequently $M = \lim_{n \uparrow \infty} E(X_n) \in \overline{R}$ exists. Moreover, for each finite N, the reversed sequence $((X_N, \mathcal{F}_N), (X_{N-1}, \mathcal{F}_{N-1}), \ldots, (X_1, \mathcal{F}_1))$ is a finite submartingale sequence with the usual order to which the Upcrossing Lemma can be applied. Thus, for $\alpha < \beta$,

$$E(U_N(\alpha, \beta)) \leq \frac{\|X_1\|_1 + |\alpha|}{\beta - \alpha}, \tag{1}$$

where $U_N(\alpha, \beta)(\omega)$ is the number of upcrossings of the interval (α, β) by the finite reversed sample path $(X_N(\omega), X_{N-1}(\omega), \ldots, X_1(\omega))$, which occur before time N. Since the right hand side of (1) does not depend on N, almost everywhere convergence follows without additional assumptions.

4.b.0 Theorem. *Let $(X_n, \mathcal{F}_n)_{n \geq 1}$ be a reversed submartingale and $M = \lim_n E(X_n)$. Then*

(i) The family $\{X_n^+ | n \geq 1\}$ is uniformly integrable.
(ii) $X_\infty = \lim_{n \uparrow \infty} X_n \in \overline{R}$ exists for P-as. and satisfies $E(X_\infty^+) < \infty$.
(iii) $X_\infty \leq E(X_n | \mathcal{F}_\infty)$, $n \geq 1$.
(iv) If $M > -\infty$, then the sequence (X_n) is L^1-bounded, and so $X_\infty \in L^1(P)$.
(v) If $M > -\infty$, then the sequence (X_n) is uniformly integrable.

Remark. Clearly (v) is stronger than (iv) but the proof is harder.

Proof. (i) According to 3.a.0, $(X_n^+, \mathcal{F}_n)$ is a reversed submartingale. Consequently $0 \leq X_n^+ \leq E(X_1^+ | \mathcal{F}_n)$, for all $n \geq 1$. By definition of a submartingale $X_1^+ \in L^1(P)$. The uniform integrability of the family $\{X_n^+ | n \geq 1\}$ now follows from the uniform integrability of $\{E(X_1^+ | \mathcal{F}_n) \mid n \geq 1\}$ (2.b.13).

(ii) The existence of the limit $X = \lim_{n \uparrow \infty} X_n \in \overline{R}$, P-as., is shown exactly as in the proof of 4.a.3 using estimate (1). By (i) the family $\{X_n^+ | n \geq 1\}$ is L^1-bounded. The finiteness of $E(X_\infty^+)$ now follows by the usual application of Fatou's lemma.

(iii) Extend X_∞ to all of Ω by setting $X_\infty = \limsup_{n\uparrow\infty} X_n$. It is easy to see that then X_∞ is $\mathcal{F}_n$-measurable, for all $n \geq 1$, and consequently X_∞ is $\mathcal{F}_\infty$-measurable. Thus it will suffice to show that

$$E(X_\infty 1_A) \leq E(X_n 1_A), \quad \forall n \geq 1, A \in \mathcal{F}_n. \tag{2}$$

Fix $r \in R$ and set $X_n(r) = X_n \vee r$, $n \geq 1$. Then $(X_n(r))_n$ is a reversed submartingale (3.a.0). Fix $n \geq 1$ and let $A \in \mathcal{F}_n$ and $m \geq n$. By the reversed submartingale property $E(X_m(r)1_A) \leq E(X_n(r)1_A)$. Letting $m \uparrow \infty$ and observing that the uniform integrability of $\{ X_m^+ \mid m \geq 1 \}$ implies the uniform integrability of $\{ X_m(r) \mid m \geq 1 \}$, we obtain

$$E(X_\infty(r)1_A) \leq E(X_n(r)1_A).$$

Letting $r \downarrow -\infty$ now yields (2), by decreasing convergence. Note that the families $\{ X_n(r) \mid r \in R \}$ and $\{ X_\infty(r) \mid r \in R \}$ are bounded above by the integrable functions X_n^+ respectively X_∞^+.

(iv) Assume that $M > -\infty$. From (i) it follows that $K = \sup_n E(X_n^+) < \infty$. Let $n \geq 1$. Then $E(X_n) \geq M$ (since $E(X_n) \downarrow M$) and $|X_n| = 2X_n^+ - X_n$. It follows that $E(|X_n|) \leq 2K - M < \infty$. The usual application of Fatou's lemma now shows that $E(|X_\infty|) \leq 2K - M < \infty$ also.

(v) Assume that $M > -\infty$. Because of (i) it will suffice to show that the family $\{ X_n^- \mid n \geq 1 \}$ is uniformly integrable, that is,

$$E\big(X_n^-; [X_n^- > a]\big) \to 0, \text{ uniformly in } n \geq 1, \text{ as } a \uparrow \infty. \tag{3}$$

Let $a > 0$. Recall that $E(X_n) \downarrow M$, especially $E(X_n) \geq M > -\infty$, $n \geq 1$. Combined with $\sup_n E(X_n^+) < \infty$ (from (i)) this shows that $C = \sup_n E(X_n^-) < \infty$. According to Chebycheff's inequality

$$P\big(X_n^- > a\big) \leq \frac{1}{a}E(X_n^-) \leq \frac{C}{a}$$

and consequently $P\big(X_n^- > a\big) \to 0$, uniformly in $n \geq 1$, as $a \uparrow \infty$. Now let $1 \leq m < n$. By the reversed submartingale property we have

$$E(X_n 1_A) \leq E(X_m 1_A), \quad \forall A \in \mathcal{F}_n. \tag{4}$$

Note that the event $A = [X_n^- \leq a]$ is in $\mathcal{F}_n$ and $X_n^- = -X_n$ on the set $[X_n^- > a]$. Thus

$$X_n^- 1_{[X_n^- > a]} = -X_n 1_{[X_n^- > a]} = X_n 1_{[X_n^- \leq a]} - X_n.$$

Using (4), it follows that

$$\begin{aligned}
0 \leq E\big(X_n^- 1_{[X_n^- > a]}\big) &= E\big(X_n 1_{[X_n^- \leq a]}\big) - E(X_n) \leq E\big(X_m 1_{[X_n^- \leq a]}\big) - E(X_n) \\
&= E(X_m) - E(X_n) - E\big(X_m 1_{[X_n^- > a]}\big) \\
&\leq E(X_m) - E(X_n) + E\big(|X_m| 1_{[X_n^- > a]}\big).
\end{aligned}$$

Now let $\epsilon > 0$ be arbitrary. Since $M = \lim_n E(X_n)$ is finite, we can choose m such that $n > m \Rightarrow E(X_m) - E(X_n) < \epsilon$. Moreover the integrability of X_m combined with the convergence $P(X_n^- > a) \to 0$, uniformly in $n \geq 1$, as $a \uparrow \infty$, shows that $\sup_n E(|X_m|1_{[X_n^- > a]}) \to 0$, as $a \uparrow \infty$. We can thus choose a_0 such that

$$\sup_n E(|X_m|1_{[X_n^- > a]}) < \epsilon, \quad \forall a \geq a_0.$$

Then
$$0 \leq \sup_{n \geq m} E(X_n^- 1_{[X_n^- > a]}) \leq \epsilon + \epsilon = 2\epsilon, \quad \forall a \geq a_0.$$

Increasing a_0 we can obtain $\sup_{n \geq 1} E(X_n^-; [X_n^- > a]) \leq 2\epsilon$, for all $a \geq a_0$. Thus the family $\{ X_n^- \mid n \geq 1 \}$ is uniformly integrable. ∎

4.c Levi's Theorem. Let $\mathcal{F}_n$, $\mathcal{G}$ be sub-σ-fields of $\mathcal{F}$, $n \geq 1$, and write $\mathcal{F}_n \uparrow \mathcal{G}$, if $\mathcal{F}_1 \subseteq \mathcal{F}_2 \subseteq \mathcal{F}_3 \subseteq \ldots$ and $\mathcal{F}_\infty = \sigma\left(\bigcup_{n \geq 1} \mathcal{F}_n\right)$. Similarly, write $\mathcal{F}_n \downarrow \mathcal{G}$, if $\mathcal{F}_1 \supseteq \mathcal{F}_2 \supseteq \mathcal{F}_3 \supseteq \ldots$ and $\mathcal{F}_\infty = \bigcap_{n \geq 1} \mathcal{F}_n$.

4.c.0 Theorem. *Let $(\mathcal{F}_n)_{n \geq 1}$ be a sequence of sub-σ-fields of $\mathcal{F}$, $X \in L^1(P)$ an integrable random variable and $X_n = E_{\mathcal{F}_n}(X)$, for all $n \geq 1$.*
(i) If $\mathcal{F}_n \uparrow \mathcal{G}$, then the sequence $(X_n, \mathcal{F}_n)$ is a uniformly integrable martingale and $X_n \to E_{\mathcal{G}}(X)$, P-as. and in norm.
(ii) If $\mathcal{F}_n \downarrow \mathcal{G}$, then the sequence $(X_n, \mathcal{F}_n)$ is a uniformly integrable reversed martingale and $X_n \to E_{\mathcal{G}}(X)$, P-as. and in norm.

Remark. The pointwise limit $Y = \lim_{n \uparrow \infty} X_n$, if it exists, must be $\mathcal{G}$-measurable and thus cannot be expected to be X itself.

Proof. (i) The martingale property follows from 2.b.5.(b). According to 2.b.13 the martingale (X_n) is uniformly integrable and hence L^1-bounded. Set $Y = \limsup_n X_n$. Then Y is defined everywhere and $\mathcal{F}_\infty$-measurable. By the Martingale Convergence Theorem 4.a.5 we have $X_n \to Y$, P-as. and in norm.

It remains to be shown only that $Y = E_{\mathcal{G}}(X)$ P-as. According to 2.b.4.(iii) it will now suffice to show that $E(Y1_A) = E(X1_A)$, for all sets A in the π-system $\mathcal{P} = \bigcup_{n \geq 1} \mathcal{F}_n$ which generates the σ-field $\mathcal{G}$. Indeed, let $A \in \mathcal{P}$ and choose $m \geq 1$ such that $A \in \mathcal{F}_m$. If $n \geq m$ then $A \in \mathcal{F}_n$ and the definition of X_n shows that

$$E(X_n 1_A) = E(X 1_A). \tag{5}$$

On the other hand the norm convergence $X_n \to Y$ implies that $E(X_n 1_A) \to E(Y1_A)$. Letting $n \uparrow \infty$ in (5) now shows that $E(Y1_A) = E(X1_A)$.

(ii) The reversed martingale property follows from 2.b.5.(b) and the uniform integrability of the sequence (X_n) follows from 2.b.13. Set $Y = \limsup_n X_n$. Then Y is defined everywhere and $\mathcal{F}_\infty$-measurable. According to 4.b.0 we have $X_n \to Y$, P-as. and so, because of the uniform integrability, also in norm.

It remains to be shown only that $Y = E_{\mathcal{G}}(X)$, that is, $E(Y1_A) = E(X1_A)$, for all sets $A \in \mathcal{G}$. If $A \in \mathcal{G}$, then $A \in \mathcal{F}_n$ and consequently

$$E(X_n 1_A) = E(X 1_A), \tag{6}$$

for each $n \geq 1$. On the other hand the norm convergence $X_n \to Y$ implies that $E(X_n 1_A) \to E(Y 1_A)$. Letting $n \uparrow \infty$ in (6) now shows that $E(Y 1_A) = E(X 1_A)$. ∎

Convergence for conditional expectations revisited. Levi's Theorem allows us to strengthen our dominated convergence theorem for conditional expectations: it will now be possible to cope with varying σ-fields also. Relatively weak assumptions establish norm convergence:

4.c.1. (a) *If $\mathcal{F}_n \uparrow \mathcal{G}$ and $X_n \to X$ in L^1, then $E_{\mathcal{F}_n}(X_n) \to E_{\mathcal{G}}(X)$ in L^1.*
(b) *If $\mathcal{F}_n \downarrow \mathcal{G}$ and $X_n \to X$ in L^1, then $E_{\mathcal{F}_n}(X_n) \to E_{\mathcal{G}}(X)$ in L^1.*

Proof. (a) Note first that $\|E_{\mathcal{F}_n}(X_n) - E_{\mathcal{F}_n}(X)\|_1 \leq \|X_n - X\|_1 \to 0$. Moreover $\|E_{\mathcal{F}_n}(X) - E_{\mathcal{G}}(X)\|_1 \to 0$, by 4.c.0. Thus $\|E_{\mathcal{F}_n}(X_n) - E_{\mathcal{G}}(X)\|_1 \to 0$, by the triangle inequality. The proof of (b) is similar. ∎

If we want to conclude P-as. convergence of the conditional expectations, we need stronger hypotheses:

4.c.2 Ultimate Dominated Convergence Theorem. *Let $\mathcal{F}_n, \mathcal{G} \subseteq \mathcal{F}$ be σ-fields, $X_n, X, Z \in L^1(P)$ and assume that $|X_n| \leq Z$ and $X_n \to X$, P-as. Then*
(i) *If $\mathcal{F}_n \uparrow \mathcal{G}$, then $E_{\mathcal{F}_n}(X_n) \to E_{\mathcal{G}}(X)$, P-as., as $n \uparrow \infty$.*
(ii) *If $\mathcal{F}_n \downarrow \mathcal{G}$, then $E_{\mathcal{F}_n}(X_n) \to E_{\mathcal{G}}(X)$, P-as., as $n \uparrow \infty$.*

Proof. For each $n \geq 1$ set $W_n = \sup_{k \geq n} |X_k - X|$. Then $0 \leq W_n \leq 2Z$ and hence $W_n \in L^1(P)$. Moreover $W_n \downarrow 0$, P-as. on Ω.
(i) Fix $N \geq 1$. For $n \geq N$ we have $|X_n - X| \leq W_n \leq W_N$ and so $E_{\mathcal{F}_n}(|X_n - X|) \leq E_{\mathcal{F}_n}(W_N)$. By Levi's theorem we have $E_{\mathcal{F}_n}(W_N) \to E_{\mathcal{G}}(W_N)$, as $n \uparrow \infty$, and so

$$\limsup_n E_{\mathcal{F}_n}(|X_n - X|) \leq \lim_n E_{\mathcal{F}_n}(W_N) = E_{\mathcal{G}}(W_N), \quad \text{for each } N \geq 1.$$

Let $N \uparrow \infty$. Since $2Z \geq W_N \downarrow 0$ we have $E_{\mathcal{G}}(W_N) \downarrow 0$, P-as., by monotone convergence (2.b.6). It follows that $\limsup_n E_{\mathcal{F}_n}(|X_n - X|) = 0$, P-as. Thus

$$|E_{\mathcal{F}_n}(X_n) - E_{\mathcal{F}_n}(X)| \leq E_{\mathcal{F}_n}(|X_n - X|) \to 0, \quad P\text{-as., as } n \uparrow \infty.$$

Again, by Levi's theorem we have $E_{\mathcal{F}_n}(X) \to E_{\mathcal{G}}(X)$, P-as., and it follows that

$$E_{\mathcal{F}_n}(X_n) = (E_{\mathcal{F}_n}(X_n) - E_{\mathcal{F}_n}(X)) + E_{\mathcal{F}_n}(X) \to E_{\mathcal{G}}(X), \quad P\text{-as., as } n \uparrow \infty.$$

The proof of (ii) is quite similar. ∎

Remark. Note that our hypotheses imply that $X_n \to X$ in L^1-norm (dominated convergence theorem for functions), that is, the assumptions of 4.c.2. But the conclusion is now *almost sure convergence* of the conditional expectations, a strong result with striking applications (even in its most elementary form; see the martingale proof of Kolmogoroff's Zero-One Law below) and does not follow from weaker assumptions, not even if the σ-fields $\mathcal{F}_n = \mathcal{G}$ are constant:

Example. [DT] If our assumption of dominated convergence $2Z \geq |X_n - X| \to 0$ P-as., is replaced with the following weaker assumption: (X_n) uniformly integrable and $X_n \to X$, P-as. (this implies $X_n \to X$ in norm), the almost sure convergence $E_{\mathcal{G}}(X_n) \to E_{\mathcal{G}}(X)$ no longer follows as the following example establishes Let (Y_n) and (Z_n) be sequences of independent random variables (the Y_n assumed independent of the Z_n also) such that

$$Y_n = \begin{cases} 1 & \text{with probability } 1/n \\ 0 & \text{otherwise,} \end{cases} \qquad Z_n = \begin{cases} n & \text{with probability } 1/n \\ 0 & \text{otherwise,} \end{cases}$$

and set $X_n = Y_n Z_n$ and $\mathcal{G} = \sigma(Y_1, Y_2, \ldots)$. Note first that the events $[Y_n > 1/2]$ are independent and satisfy $\sum_n P(Y_n > 1/2) = \infty$. This implies $P(Y_n > 1/2 \, i.o.) = 1$ especially $Y_n \not\to 0$, P-as. By independence of Y_n and Z_n we have

$$X_n = \begin{cases} n & \text{with probability } 1/n^2 \\ 0 & \text{otherwise.} \end{cases}$$

Thus $P(X_n > 0) = 1/n^2$. By the Borel Cantelli Lemma $P(X_n > 0 \, i.o.) = 0$ and so $X_n \to 0$, P-as. Moreover

$$E\big(|X_n|; [|X_n| \geq a]\big) \leq n\frac{1}{n^2} = \frac{1}{n},$$

for all $a > 0$. This implies that $E\big(|X_n|; [|X_n| \geq a]\big) \to 0$, $a \uparrow \infty$, uniformly in $n \geq 1$ (finitely many integrals for $n \leq N$ can be handled by making $a > 0$ large enough). In short the sequence (X_n) is uniformly integrable and $X_n \to 0$, P-as. Nonetheless $E_{\mathcal{G}}(X_n) \not\to 0$, P-as., since the $\mathcal{G}$-measurability of Y_n and independence of $\mathcal{G}$ of Z_n imply that $\quad E_{\mathcal{G}}(X_n) = E_{\mathcal{G}}(Y_n Z_n) = Y_n E_{\mathcal{G}}(Z_n) = Y_n E(Z_n) = Y_n \not\to 0$, P-as. ∎

4.d Strong Law of Large Numbers. As striking applications of Levi's theorem we prove the Kolmogoroff Zero One Law and the Strong Law of Large Numbers. Let $X = (X_n)$ be a sequence of random variables. The σ-field

$$\mathcal{T} = \bigcap_{n \geq 1} \sigma(X_n, X_{n+1}, X_{n+2}, \ldots)$$

is called the *tail-σ-field* with respect to the sequence X. A function $f : \Omega \to \overline{R}$ is called a *tail-function* of X if it is measurable with respect to the tail-σ-field $\mathcal{T}$ of X.

The events $A \in \mathcal{T}$ are called the *tail events* with respect to the sequence X Clearly A is a tail event with respect to X if and only if the indicator function 1_A is a tail function of X.

Let f be a tail function of X and $n \geq 1$. Then f is $\sigma(X_n, X_{n+1}, \ldots)$-measurable and hence $f = g_n(X_n, X_{n+1}, \ldots)$ for some measurable function $g_n : R^\infty \to R$ (R^∞ equipped with the product σ-field). Thus a tail function of X should be thought of as a measurable function of X which does not depend on any finite collection of the X_n. Obvious examples are $f = \limsup_n X_n$ and $f = \liminf_n X_n$.

Likewise $A \in \sigma(X)$ is a tail event if, for each $\omega \in \Omega$, it does not depend on any finite collection of values $X_1(\omega), X_2(\omega), \ldots, X_N(\omega)$ whether $\omega \in A$ or not, but merely on the values $X_n(\omega)$, $n \geq m$, where $m \uparrow \infty$. We will frequently use the following fact:

4.d.0. *Assume that $\mathcal{A}$ and $\mathcal{B}$ are independent σ-fields and X, Y random variables. If X is $\mathcal{A}$-measurable and Y is $\mathcal{B}$-measurable, then X and Y are independent.*

Proof. Then we have $\sigma(X) \subseteq \mathcal{A}$ and $\sigma(Y) \subseteq \mathcal{B}$ and the independence of $\sigma(X)$ and $\sigma(Y)$ follows. ∎

4.d.1 Kolmogoroff Zero One Law. *Assume that $X = (X_n)$ is a sequence of independent, integrable random variables. Then*
(i) Every integrable tail function f of X is constant, P-as.
(ii) Every tail event A with respect to X satisfies $P(A) = 0$ or $P(A) = 1$.

Proof. (i) Let f be an integrable tail function of X. Set $\mathcal{F}_n = \sigma(X_1, X_2, \ldots, X_n)$, for each $n \geq 1$, and $\mathcal{F}_\infty = \sigma\left(\bigcup_{n\geq 1} \mathcal{F}_n\right) = \sigma(X)$, as usual. We note that f is $\mathcal{F}_\infty$-measurable and hence $E_{\mathcal{F}_\infty}(f) = f$, P-as.

By independence of the sequence (X_n) the σ-fields $\mathcal{F}_n = \sigma(X_1, X_2, \ldots, X_n)$ and $\sigma(X_{n+1}, X_{n+2}, \ldots)$ are independent. Since f is $\sigma(X_{n+1}, X_{n+2}, \ldots)$-measurable, it follows that f is independent of the σ-field $\mathcal{F}_n$. Consequently $Z_n := E_{\mathcal{F}_n}(f) = E(f)$, P-as., for each $n \geq 1$ (2.b.2). On the other hand Levi's Theorem implies that $Z_n \to E_{\mathcal{F}_\infty}(f) = f$, P-as. Thus $f = \lim_{n\uparrow\infty} Z_n = E(f)$, P-as.

(ii) Let A be a tail event with respect to X. Then the indicator function 1_A is a tail function with respect to the sequence X and is thus constant P-as. This implies that $1_A = 0$, P-as., or $1_A = 1$, P-as., that is, $P(A) = 0$ or $P(A) = 1$. ∎

For the proof of the Strong Law of Large Numbers we need some preparation. Let $X = (X_n)$ be a sequence of *independent* and *identically distributed* (iid) integrable random variables. For $n \geq 1$ set $S_n = X_1 + X_2 + \ldots + X_n$ and let Y_n be the R^n-valued random vector $Y_n = (X_1, X_2, \ldots, X_n)$. By the iid property of X the distribution of Y_n is the product measure

$$P_{Y_n} = Y_n(P) = \nu \otimes \nu \otimes \ldots \otimes \nu, \tag{0}$$

where ν is the common distribution of the X_j on R. For $1 \leq j \leq n$ let $T : R^n \to R^n$ be the (linear) map which interchanges the first and jth coordinate and $\pi_j : R^n \to R$ the jth coordinate projection ($\pi_j(t) = t_j$, $t = (t_1, t_2, \ldots, t_n) \in R^n$). An application of T to the measure P_{Y_n} merely interchanges the first and jth factor in (0) and consequently the image measure $T(P_{Y_n})$ satisfies

$$T(P_{Y_n}) = P_{Y_n}. \tag{1}$$

Note also that we have $\pi_j = \pi_1 \circ T$. We claim that

$$E(X_j; [S_n \leq a]) = E(X_1; [S_n \leq a]), \quad \forall a \in R. \tag{2}$$

Let $a \in R$ and set $A = [S_n \leq a]$ and $B = \{t \in R^n \mid t_1 + t_2 + \ldots + t_n \leq a\}$. Then $A = [Y_n \in B] = Y_n^{-1}(B)$. Using the image measure theorem (appendix B.5), it now follows that

$$\int_A X_j dP = \int_{[Y_n \in B]} \pi_j(Y_n) dP = \int_B \pi_j dP_{Y_n}$$

$$= \int_B (\pi_1 \circ T) dP_{Y_n} = \int_B \pi_1 dT\left(P_{Y_n}\right) = \int_B \pi_1 dP_{Y_n} = \int_A X_1 dP,$$

as desired. For random variables $Z \in \mathcal{E}(P), W_1, W_2, \ldots$ write $E(Z|W_1, W_2, \ldots) = E\left(Z|\sigma(W_1, W_2, \ldots)\right)$. With this notation we claim that

$$E(X_j|S_n) = E(X_1|S_n). \tag{3}$$

Set $Y = E(X_j|S_n)$. We want to show that $Y = E(X_1|S_n)$. According to 2.b.4.(iii) it will suffice to show that $E(Y1_A) = E(X_11_A)$, equivalently $E(X_j1_A) = E(X_11_A)$, for all sets A in some π-system generating the σ-field $\sigma(S_n)$. In fact, according to (2) the sets $[S_n \leq a]$, $a \in R$, form such a π-system.

4.d.2 Strong Law of Large Numbers. *Let $(X_n)_{n \geq 1}$ be a sequence of independent, identically distributed, integrable random variables and $S_n = X_1 + X_2 + \ldots + X_n$. If μ denotes the common mean of the X_n, we have*

$$\frac{S_n}{n} \to \mu, \quad P\text{-as. and in norm.}$$

Proof. Let $n \geq 1$. As $E(X_j|S_n) = E(X_1|S_n)$, for all $j = 1, 2, \ldots, n$, we have

$$nE(X_1|S_n) = \sum_{j=1}^{n} E(X_j|S_n) = E\left(\sum_{j=1}^{n} X_j|S_n\right) = E(S_n|S_n) = S_n,$$

and so $S_n/n = E(X_1|S_n) = E(X_1|\mathcal{A})$ with $\mathcal{A} = \sigma(S_n)$. Let $\mathcal{B} = \sigma(X_{n+1}, X_{n+2}, \ldots)$. By independence of the sequence (X_n) the σ-fields $\sigma(X_1, X_2, \ldots, X_n)$ and $\mathcal{B}$ are independent. Since $\sigma(\sigma(X_1), \mathcal{A}) \subseteq \sigma(X_1, X_2, \ldots, X_n)$, the σ-fields $\sigma(\sigma(X_1), \mathcal{A})$ and $\mathcal{B}$ are independent also. According to 2.b.14 this implies that

$$\frac{S_n}{n} = E(X_1|S_n) = E(X_1|\mathcal{A}) = E(X_1|\sigma(\mathcal{A}, \mathcal{B})) = E(X_1|S_n, X_{n+1}, X_{n+2}, \ldots).$$

Since $\sigma(S_n, X_{n+1}, X_{n+2}, \ldots) = \sigma(S_n, S_{n+1}, S_{n+2}, \ldots)$, it follows that

$$\frac{S_n}{n} = E(X_1|S_n, S_{n+1}, S_{n+2}, \ldots) = E_{\mathcal{F}_n}(X_1),$$

where $\mathcal{F}_n = \sigma(S_n, S_{n+1}, S_{n+2}, \ldots)$. But these $\mathcal{F}_n$ form a decreasing chain of sub-σ-fields of $\mathcal{F}$. By Levi's theorem $(S_n/n, \mathcal{F}_n)$ is a reversed martingale which converges P-as. and in norm to some integrable limit $Y \in L^1(P)$. Moreover we can take $Y = \limsup_{n \uparrow \infty} S_n/n$ (which is defined everywhere).

We claim that Y is a tail function with respect to the iid sequence (X_n), that is, Y is $\sigma(X_k, X_{k+1}, \ldots)$-measurable, for each $k \geq 1$. Let $k \geq 1$ be arbitrary. Then we have

$$Y = \limsup_{n \uparrow \infty} \frac{S_n}{n} = \limsup_{n \uparrow \infty} \left[\frac{X_1 + \ldots + X_{k-1}}{n} + \frac{X_k + \ldots + X_n}{n} \right]$$

$$= \limsup_{n \uparrow \infty} \frac{(X_k + \ldots + X_n)}{n},$$

at each point of Ω. It follows that Y is $\sigma(X_k, X_{k+1}, \ldots)$-measurable. Thus Y is a tail function with respect to the sequence (X_n). By the Kolmogoroff 0-1 Law, Y is constant P-as. and hence $Y = E(Y)$, P-as. As $S_n/n \to Y$ in norm, it follows that $E(S_n/n) \to E(Y)$. But $E(S_n/n) = \mu$, for all $n \geq 1$, and so $E(Y) = \mu$, hence $Y = \mu$, P-as. It follows that $S_n/n \to \mu$, P-as. and in norm. ∎

5. OPTIONAL SAMPLING OF CLOSED SUBMARTINGALE SEQUENCES

5.a Uniform integrability, last elements, closure. A *last element* for the partially ordered index set $\mathcal{T}$ is an element $\infty \in \mathcal{T}$ satisfying $t \leq \infty$, for all $t \in \mathcal{T}$. Such an element is uniquely determined, if it exists. A submartingale $X = (X_t, \mathcal{F}_t)_{t \in \mathcal{T}}$ is called *closed*, if the index set $\mathcal{T}$ has a last element. In this case the random variable X_∞ is called the *last element of* X and satisfies

$$ X_t \leq E(X_\infty | \mathcal{F}_t), \quad \forall t \in \mathcal{T}. $$

Closed supermartingales and closed martingales are defined similarly. The last element X_∞ of a closed martingale X satisfies $X_t = E(X_\infty | \mathcal{F}_t)$, for all $t \in \mathcal{T}$. The existence of last elements has strong consequences:

5.a.0. *(i) If the submartingale $X = (X_t)$ is closed, then the family $\{ X_t^+ \mid t \in \mathcal{T} \}$ is uniformly integrable.*
(ii) If the martingale $X = (X_t)$ is closed, then X itself is uniformly integrable.

Proof. (i) Let $X = (X_t)$ be a submartingale with a last element. Then so is the process (X_t^+), according to 3.a.0. Thus $0 \leq X_t^+ \leq E(X_\infty^+ | \mathcal{F}_t)$, $t \in \mathcal{T}$, and the uniform integrability of the family $\{ X_t^+ \mid t \in \mathcal{T} \}$ now follows from the uniform integrability of the family $\{ E_{\mathcal{F}_t}(X_\infty^+) \mid t \in \mathcal{T} \}$ (2.b.13). (ii) follows directly from 2.b.13. ∎

Consider now a submartingale $X = (X_t, \mathcal{F}_t)_{t \in \mathcal{T}}$, where the index set $\mathcal{T}$ does not have a last element. Choosing $\infty \notin \mathcal{T}$ and decreeing that $t \leq \infty$, for all $t \in \mathcal{T}$, $\mathcal{T}$ can be enlarged to a partially ordered index set $\mathcal{T} \cup \{\infty\}$ with last element ∞. The filtration $(\mathcal{F}_t)$ can also be extended by setting

$$ \mathcal{F}_\infty = \sigma \left(\bigcup_{t \in \mathcal{T}} \mathcal{F}_t \right). $$

The question is now if the submartingale X can be extended also, that is, if there exists a random variable X_∞ such that the process $(X_t, \mathcal{F}_t)_{t \in \mathcal{T} \cup \{\infty\}}$ is still a submartingale, that is, such that X_∞ is $\mathcal{F}_\infty$-measurable, $E(X_\infty^+) < \infty$ and $X_t \leq E(X_\infty | \mathcal{F}_t)$, for all $t \in \mathcal{T}$. A random variable X_∞ having these properties will be called a *last element for the submartingale* X. The submartingale X will be called *closeable* if there exists a last element X_∞ for X. In this case $(X_t, \mathcal{F}_t)_{t \in \mathcal{T} \cup \{\infty\}}$ is a closed submartingale extending X.

A last element for the supermartingale X is not uniquely determined: If X_∞ is a last element for X and $Z \geq 0$ is $\mathcal{F}_\infty$-measurable with $E(Z)$ finite, then $X_\infty + Z$ is also a last element for X.

Closeable supermartingales and martingales and last elements for these are defined similarly. Note that X_∞ is a last element for the martingale X if and only if $X_\infty \in L^1(P)$ is $\mathcal{F}_\infty$-measurable and $X_t = E(X_\infty | \mathcal{F}_t)$, for all $t \in \mathcal{T}$. Equivalently X_∞ is a last element for the martingale X if and only if it is a last element for X both as a submartingale and as a supermartingale.

Note for example that each nonnegative supermartingale $X = (X_t)$ has a last element, namely $X_\infty = 0$. However, if X happens to be a martingale, then $X_\infty = 0$ will be a last element for the martingale X only if $X_t = 0$, for all $t \in T$.

In the case of martingale sequences, that is, $T = \mathbb{N}$ with the usual order, $\mathcal{F}_\infty = \sigma\left(\bigcup_{n \geq 1} \mathcal{F}_n\right)$ and the convergence theorems yield the following:

5.a.1. *(i) The submartingale sequence $X = (X_n, \mathcal{F}_n)$ is closeable, if and only if the sequence (X_n^+) is uniformly integrable. In this case $X_\infty = \lim_n X_n$ exists P-as. and is a last element for X.*

(ii) The martingale sequence $(X_n, \mathcal{F}_n)$ is closeable, if and only if it is uniformly integrable. In this case the last element X_∞ is uniquely determined as $X_\infty = \lim_n X_n$, P-as.

Proof. (i) From 5.a.0 it follows that the sequence (X_n^+) is uniformly integrable, if X is closeable. Conversely, if the sequence (X_n^+) is uniformly integrable (and hence L^1-bounded), then, according to the Submartingale Convergence Theorem 4.a.3.(i),(iii) $X_\infty = \limsup_n X_n$ (defined everywhere and $\mathcal{F}_\infty$-measurable) is a last element for the submartingale X.

(ii) This follows similarly from 5.a.0 and 4.a.5. Only the uniqueness of the last element X_∞ requires additional argument. Indeed, let Z be any last element for X, that is $Z \in L^1(P)$ $\mathcal{F}_\infty$-measurable and $X_n = E(Z|\mathcal{F}_n)$, for all $n \geq 1$. Then, from Levi's theorem, $X_n \to Z$, P-as., that is, $Z = \lim_n X_n$, P-as. ∎

Remark. The uniform integrability of the sequence (X_n^+) follows, for example, if $X_n \leq Z$, $n \geq 1$, for some integrable random variable Z.

5.a.2 Example. Here we construct a nonzero, nonnegative martingale $X = (X_n)$ which converges to zero almost surely. The nonnegativity implies that $\|X_n\|_1 = E(X_n) = E(X_1) > 0$, for all $n \geq 1$. Thus the martingale X is L^1-bounded and does not converge to zero in norm. It follows that X is not uniformly integrable. Consequently X does not admit a last element, although it converges almost surely.

To obtain such X let Ω be $[0, 1[$ equipped with the Borel sets and Lebesgue measure. Inductively define a sequence $(\mathcal{P}_n)$ of partitions of Ω into intervals as follows: $\mathcal{P}_0 := \{[0, 1]\}$ and the intervals in $\mathcal{P}_{n+1}$ arise from those in $\mathcal{P}_n$ by bisection. In short, $\mathcal{P}_n$ consists of the dyadic intervals $I_k^n := [k/2^n, (k+1)/2^n[$, $k = 0, 1, \ldots, 2^n - 1$.

Now let $\mathcal{F}_n := \sigma(\mathcal{P}_n)$ and set $X_n := 2^n 1_{I_0^n} = 2^n 1_{[0, 1/2^n[}$. Clearly $X_n \geq 0$ and $X_n \to 0$ at all points $\omega \neq 0$. We have to show that $(X_n, \mathcal{F}_n)$ is a martingale. Since $I_0^n \in \mathcal{F}_n$, X_n is $\mathcal{F}_n$-measurable. It remains to be shown that $E(X_{n+1}1_A) = E(X_n 1_A)$, for all sets $A \in \mathcal{F}_n$. Since each set $A \in \mathcal{F}_n$ is a (finite) union of intervals I_k^n, $k = 0, 1, \ldots, 2^n - 1$, it will suffice to show that $E(X_{n+1}1_{I_k^n}) = E(X_n 1_{I_k^n})$, for all $k = 0, 1, \ldots, 2^n - 1$. Indeed, both integrals equal one, if $k = 0$, and both are equal to zero, for all other k.

5.b Sampling of closed submartingale sequences. Let $(\mathcal{F}_n)$ be a filtration on $(\Omega, \mathcal{F}, P)$, $\mathcal{F}_\infty = \bigvee \mathcal{F}_n = \sigma\left(\bigcup_n \mathcal{F}_n\right)$ and set $\mathbb{N}_\infty := \mathbb{N} \cup \{\infty\}$. Assume that $X = (X_n, \mathcal{F}_n)_{1 \leq n < \infty}$ is a submartingale sequence. Recall that a *last element* Z for the submartingale X is an $\mathcal{F}_\infty$-measurable random variable Z such that $E(Z^+) < \infty$ and

$$X_n \leq E(Z|\mathcal{F}_n), \quad 1 \leq n < \infty. \tag{1}$$

Thus, if we set $X_\infty = Z$, then $(X_n)_{1 \leq n \leq \infty}$ is again a submartingale. Inequality (1) is reversed in the case of a last element of a supermartingale and replaced with an equality in the case of a martingale.

We have seen in 5.a.1 that a submartingale sequence has a last element if and only if the sequence (X_n^+) is uniformly integrable. In this case $X_\infty = \lim_n X_n$ exists P-as. and is a last element for X. More precisely, since $\mathcal{F}_\infty$ is not assumed to contain the P-null sets, $Z = \limsup_n X_n$, which is defined everywhere, $\mathcal{F}_\infty$-measurable and equals the limit $\lim_n X_n$ almost surely, is a last element for X.

A last element Z provides a random variable $X_\infty := Z$ which closes the submartingale $(X_n)_{1 \leq n < \infty}$, that is, the extended sequence $(X_n)_{1 \leq n \leq \infty}$ is still a submartingale (and hence a closed submartingale). Moreover the random variable X_T is now defined for each optional time $T : \Omega \to \mathbb{N}_\infty$. Here we set $X_T = X_\infty = Z$ on the set $[T = \infty]$.

We will now show that a closed submartingale $X = (X_n)_{1 \leq n \leq \infty}$ satisfies the Optional Sampling Theorem 3.b.1 for *all* optional times $S, T : \Omega \to \mathbb{N}_\infty$. The general case will be put together from the following two special cases:

(i) X has the form $X_n = E(Z|\mathcal{F}_n)$ (5.b.0).
(ii) X is a *nonnegative* supermartingale and thus a supermartingale with last element $X_\infty = 0$ (5.b.1).

5.b.0. *Let $Z \in \mathcal{E}(P)$ with $E(Z^+) < \infty$ and set $X_n = E(Z|\mathcal{F}_n)$ for $1 \leq n \leq \infty$. Then for any two optional times $S, T : \Omega \to \mathbb{N}_\infty$ we have*
(a) $E(X_S^+) < \infty$ and $X_S = E(Z|\mathcal{F}_S)$.
(b) $S \leq T$ implies $X_S = E(X_T|\mathcal{F}_S)$.

Remark. If $Z \in L^1(P)$, then (X_n) is a martingale with last element Z.

Proof. (a) We have $X_n^+ \leq E_{\mathcal{F}_n}(Z^+)$ (2.b.12) and so $E\left(1_A X_n^+\right) \leq E\left(1_A Z^+\right)$, for all sets $A \in \mathcal{F}_n$. It follows that

$$E(X_S^+) = \sum_{1 \leq n \leq \infty} E(X_n^+; [S = n]) \leq \sum_{1 \leq n \leq \infty} E(Z^+; [S = n]) = E(Z^+) < \infty.$$

Thus $X_S \in \mathcal{E}(P)$. As X_S is $\mathcal{F}_S$-measurable (3.b.0.(c)), it will now suffice to show that $E\left(1_A X_S\right) = E\left(1_A Z\right)$, for all sets $A \in \mathcal{F}_S$. If $A \in \mathcal{F}_S$, then $A \cap [S = n] \in \mathcal{F}_n$ for all $n \in \mathbb{N}_\infty$, and it follows that

$$E\left(1_A X_S\right) = \sum_{1 \leq n \leq \infty} E(X_S; A \cap [S = n]) = \sum_{1 \leq n \leq \infty} E(X_n; A \cap [S = n])$$
$$= \sum_{1 \leq n \leq \infty} E(Z; A \cap [S = n]) = E\left(1_A Z\right).$$

(b)   If $S \leq T$, then $\mathcal{F}_S \subseteq \mathcal{F}_T$ and so, using (a), $E(X_T|\mathcal{F}_S) = E\left(E(Z|\mathcal{F}_T) \mid \mathcal{F}_S\right) = E(Z|\mathcal{F}_S) = X_S$. ∎

5.b.1. *Assume that $(X_n)_{1 \leq n < \infty}$ is a nonnegative supermartingale. Then $X_\infty = 0$ is a last element for X. If $S, T : \Omega \to \mathbb{N}_\infty$ are any optional times with $S \leq T$, then $X_S, X_T \in L^1(P)$ and we have $X_S \geq E(X_T | \mathcal{F}_S)$.*

Remark. Here we set $X_S = X_\infty = 0$ on the set $[S = \infty]$ and the same for X_T.

Proof. Let us first show that X_S is integrable. For $n \geq 1$ apply the Optional Sampling Theorem 3.b.1 to the bounded optional times $1, S \wedge n \geq 1$ to conclude that $E(X_{S \wedge n}) \leq E(X_1)$. Since $X_n \geq 0 = X_\infty$, we have $X_S \leq \liminf_n X_{S \wedge n}$ and Fatou's Lemma now shows that $E(X_S) \leq \liminf_n E(X_{S \wedge n}) \leq E(X_1) < \infty$. Combined with the nonnegativity of X_S this shows that $X_S \in L^1(P)$.

Assume now that $S \leq T$. To see that $X_S \geq E(X_T | \mathcal{F}_S)$ we must show that $E(1_A X_S) \geq E(1_A X_T)$, for all sets $A \in \mathcal{F}_S$. Let $A \in \mathcal{F}_S$ and $n \geq 1$. Then $A \cap [S \leq n] \in \mathcal{F}_{S \wedge n}$ (3.b.0.(g)). Thus the Optional Sampling Theorem 3.b.1 applied to the bounded optional times $S \wedge n \leq T \wedge n$ yields

$$E(X_{S \wedge n}; A \cap [S \leq n]) \geq E(X_{T \wedge n}; A \cap [S \leq n]) \geq E(X_{T \wedge n}; A \cap [T \leq n]),$$

the second inequality following from $A \cap [S \leq n] \supseteq A \cap [T \leq n]$ and $X_{T \wedge n} \geq 0$. Since $X_{S \wedge n} = X_S$ on the set $[S \leq n]$ (and a similar fact for $X_{T \wedge n}$), this can be rewritten as $E(X_S; A \cap [S \leq n]) \geq E(X_T; A \cap [T \leq n])$. Letting $n \uparrow \infty$ and using increasing convergence it follows that

$$E(X_S; A \cap [S < \infty]) \geq E(X_T; A \cap [T < \infty]).$$

As $X_S = X_\infty = 0$ on the set $[S = \infty]$ and $X_T = 0$ on the set $[T = \infty]$, this can be rewritten as $E(1_A X_S) \geq E(1_A X_T)$, as desired. ∎

5.b.2 Discrete Optional Sampling Theorem. *Let $X = (X_n)_{1 \leq n \leq \infty}$ be a closed submartingale sequence. Then we have $E(X_T^+) < \infty$ and $X_S \leq E(X_T | \mathcal{F}_S)$, for all optional times $S, T : \Omega \to \mathbb{N}_\infty$ with $S \leq T$.*

Proof. Let $Z = X_\infty$. Then $E(Z^+) < \infty$ and $X_n \leq E(Z | \mathcal{F}_n)$. Set $A_n = E(Z | \mathcal{F}_n)$. Then A_n and $-X_n$ are supermartingales and so $B_n = A_n - X_n$ is a nonnegative supermartingale satisfying $X_n = A_n - B_n$. Defining $A_\infty = E(Z | \mathcal{F}_\infty) = Z = X_\infty$ and $B_\infty = 0$ we have $X_\infty = A_\infty - B_\infty$. Here 5.b.0 and 5.b.1 apply to A and B respectively: If $S, T : \Omega \to \mathbb{N}_\infty$ are optional times with $S \leq T$, then $B_T \in L^1(P)$ and $X_S = A_S - B_S$, $X_T = A_T - B_T$. Moreover $B_S \geq E(B_T | \mathcal{F}_S)$ and $A_S = E(A_T | \mathcal{F}_S)$ and thus

$$X_S = A_S - B_S \leq E(A_T | \mathcal{F}_S) - E(B_T | \mathcal{F}_S) = E(X_T | \mathcal{F}_S).$$

It remains to be shown only that $E(X_T^+) < \infty$. Since $B_T \geq 0$ we have $X_T^+ \leq A_T^+ = 1_{[A_T \geq 0]} A_T$. Moreover, according to 5.b.0, $A_T = E(Z | \mathcal{F}_T)$ and integrating this equality over the set $[A_T \geq 0] \in \mathcal{F}_T$ yields

$$E(X_T^+) \leq E(A_T^+) = E(1_{[A_T \geq 0]} A_T) = E(1_{[A_T \geq 0]} Z) \leq E(Z^+) < \infty. \quad \blacksquare$$

Remark. X_S is $\mathcal{F}_S$-measurable (3.b.0.(c)). According to 2.b.4.(i) the inequality $X_S \le E(X_T | \mathcal{F}_S)$ is thus equivalent with $E(1_A X_S) \le E(1_A X_T)$, for all sets $A \in \mathcal{F}_S$, and implies in particular that $E(X_S) \le E(X_T)$. The corresponding fact for closed supermartingales (all inequalities reversed) follows easily from this. If X is a closed martingale, then it is both a closed supermartingale and a closed submartingale with the same last element. The conclusion of 5.b.2 then becomes $X_T \in L^1(P)$ and $X_S = E(X_T | \mathcal{F}_S)$, for all optional times $S, T : \Omega \to \mathbb{N}_\infty$ with $S \le T$.

6. MAXIMAL INEQUALITIES FOR SUBMARTINGALE SEQUENCES

6.a Expectations as Lebesgue integrals. Let X be a random variable.

6.a.0. *Assume that $X \geq 0$ and that $h : [0, +\infty) \to [0, +\infty)$ is continuously differentiable, nondecreasing and satisfies $h(0) = 0$. Then*

$$E(h \circ X) = \int_\Omega h(X(\omega))P(d\omega) = \int_0^{+\infty} h'(t)P(X > t)\,dt = \int_0^{+\infty} h'(t)P(X \geq t)\,dt.$$

Proof. For each $\omega \in \Omega$

$$h(X(\omega)) = h(X(\omega)) - h(0) = \int_0^{X(\omega)} h'(t)dt$$

$$= \int_0^{+\infty} h'(t)1_{[0,X(\omega)]}(t)dt = \int_0^{+\infty} h'(t)1_{[0,X(\omega)[}(t)dt.$$

The last two integrals are equal, since they are integrals with respect to Lebesgue measure on the line and their integrands differ only at the point $t = X(\omega)$. As $1_{[0,X(\omega)]}(t) = 1_{[X \geq t]}(\omega)$ and $1_{[0,X(\omega)[}(t) = 1_{[X > t]}(\omega)$ we can write this as

$$h(X(\omega)) = \int_0^{+\infty} h'(t)1_{[X \geq t]}(\omega)dt \quad \text{and} \quad h(X(\omega)) = \int_0^{+\infty} h'(t)1_{[X > t]}(\omega)dt. \quad (0)$$

Using the first equality in (0) we can show $E(h \circ X) = \int_0^{+\infty} h'(t)P([X \geq t])\,dt$ by an application of Fubini's theorem (justified by the σ-finiteness of Lebesgue measure and the positivity of the integrand $h'(t)1_{[X \geq t]}(\omega)$ below):

$$E(h \circ X) = \int_\Omega h(X(\omega))P(d\omega) = \int_\Omega \left(\int_0^{+\infty} h'(t)1_{[X \geq t]}(\omega)dt \right) P(d\omega)$$

$$= \int_0^{+\infty} h'(t) \left(\int_\Omega 1_{[X \geq t]}(\omega)P(d\omega) \right) dt = \int_0^{+\infty} h'(t)P([X \geq t])\,dt.$$

The proof of the equality $E(h \circ X) = \int_0^{+\infty} h'(t)P([X > t])\,dt$ is exactly the same starting from the second equality in (0). ∎

Remark. 6.a.0 applies for example also to the function $h(t) = \sqrt{t}$, which is not differentiable at the point 0, since this function h also satisfies $h(x) = \int_0^x h'(t)dt$, for all $x \geq 0$. We will need this in 9.d below.

6.a.1. (a) *If $X \geq 0$ then $E(X) = \int_\Omega X(\omega)P(d\omega) = \int_0^{+\infty} P(X > t)dt$.*
(b) *If $p \geq 1$ then $\|X\|_p^p = E(|X|^p) = \int_0^{+\infty} pt^{p-1}P(|X| > t)dt$.*

Proof. (a) Apply 6.a.0 with $h(t) = t$. (b) Apply 6.a.0 to the nonnegative random variable $|X|$ and the function $h(t) = t^p$. ∎

6.b Maximal inequalities for submartingale sequences. Let $(X_k)_{k=1}^N$ be a (finite) submartingale and set $\mathcal{F}_k = \sigma(X_j; j \leq k)$ and $X_N^* = \max_{1 \leq k \leq N} X_k$.

For $\lambda > 0$ we have the trivial inequality $\lambda P(X_N^* \geq \lambda) \leq E(X_N^*; [X_N^* \geq \lambda])$. Since the submartingale $(X_k)_{k=1}^N$ has a tendency to increase we would expect the random variable X_N to play a large role in the computation of the maximum X_N^*. Indeed, in the previous integral, X_N^* can be replaced with the smaller X_N:

6.b.0. $\lambda P\left(\left[X_N^* \geq \lambda\right]\right) \leq E\left(X_N; \left[X_N^* \geq \lambda\right]\right) \leq E(X_N^+)$, *for all $\lambda > 0$.*

Proof. The second inequality above being clear, we concern ourselves only with the first. Set $X_k = X_N$ and $\mathcal{F}_k = \mathcal{F}_N$, for $k \geq N$. Then $(X_k)_{k \geq 1}$ is a submartingale sequence. Let $\lambda > 0$ and define

$$T(\omega) = \min\{\, k \in \{1, \ldots, N\} \mid X_k(\omega) \geq \lambda \,\} \wedge (N+1)$$

$(= N+1$, if no such k exists). We claim that $T : \Omega \to \{1, 2, \ldots, N+1\}$ is an optional time for the filtration $(\mathcal{F}_k)$. Indeed, for $k \leq N$,

$$[T \leq k] = [X_1 \geq \lambda] \cup [X_2 \geq \lambda] \cup \ldots \cup [X_k \geq \lambda] \in \mathcal{F}_k, \tag{0}$$

while for $k > N$ we have $[T \leq k] = \Omega \in \mathcal{F}_k$. Let now A be the event

$$A = [X_N^* \geq \lambda] = [X_1 \geq \lambda] \cup [X_2 \geq \lambda] \cup \ldots \cup [X_N \geq \lambda] = [T \leq N].$$

Since T is $\mathcal{F}_T$-measurable (3.b.0.(c)), we have $A \in \mathcal{F}_T$. By definition of T we have $X_T \geq \lambda$ on A. Recalling that $X_{N+1} = X_N$ and applying the Optional Sampling Theorem 3.b.1 to the bounded optional times $T \leq N+1$ it follows that

$$\lambda P\left([X_N^* \geq \lambda]\right) = \lambda P(A) \leq E\left(1_A X_T\right)$$
$$\leq E(1_A X_{N+1}) = E(1_A X_N) = E\left(X_N; [X_N^* \geq \lambda]\right). \quad \blacksquare$$

6.b.1. *Assume that $(X_k)_{k=1}^N$ is a martingale and $p \geq 1$. If $E(|X_N|^p) < \infty$, then $\left(|X_k|^p\right)_{k=1}^N$ is a submartingale.*

Proof. Assume that $E(|X_N|^p) < \infty$. Since the function $\phi(t) = |t|^p$ is convex, it will suffice to show that $E(|X_k|^p) < \infty$, for all $k = 1, \ldots, N$ (3.a.1). By the martingale property $|X_k| = \left|E_{\mathcal{F}_k}(X_N)\right| \leq E_{\mathcal{F}_k}(|X_N|)$ and so, by Jensen's inequality and the convexity of ϕ,

$$|X_k|^p \leq E_{\mathcal{F}_k}\left(|X_N|\right)^p \leq E_{\mathcal{F}_k}\left(|X_N|^p\right), \quad P\text{-as.}$$

Integrating this inequality over the set Ω, we obtain $E(|X_k|^p) \leq E(|X_N|^p) < \infty$, as desired. $\blacksquare$

6.b.2. *Assume that $(X_k)_{k=1}^N$ is a martingale and set $S^* = \max_{1 \leq k \leq N} |X_k|$. Then*

$$P(S^* \geq \lambda) \leq \lambda^{-p} E(|X_N|^p), \quad \text{for all } \lambda > 0 \text{ and } p \geq 1.$$

Proof. We may assume that $E(|X_N|^p) < \infty$ (otherwise the inequality is trivial). Set $Y_k = |X_k|^p$ and $Y_N^* = \max_{1 \leq k \leq N} Y_k$. Then $(Y_k)_{k=1}^N$ is a submartingale (6.b.1). Moreover $[S^* \geq \lambda] = [Y_N^* \geq \lambda^p]$. Applying 6.b.0 to (Y_k) and λ^p now yields

$$\lambda^p P(S^* \geq \lambda) = \lambda^p P\left(Y_N^* \geq \lambda^p\right) \leq E(Y_N^+) = E(Y_N) = E(|X_N|^p). \quad \blacksquare$$

6.b.3. *Let $(X_k)_{k=1}^N$ be a martingale and set $S^* = \max_{1 \le k \le N} |X_k|$. Then*

$$\|X_N\|_p \le \|S^*\|_p \le \frac{p}{p-1}\|X_N\|_p, \quad \forall p > 1.$$

Proof. If $\|X_N\|_p = \infty$, there is nothing to prove. Thus assume that $X_N \in L^p(P)$. Then $X_k \in L^p(P)$, $1 \le k \le N$ (6.b.1) and so $S^* \in L^p(P)$ also. Moreover $(|X_k|)_{k=1}^N$ is a submartingale sequence and thus, according to 6.b.0,

$$tP\left([S^* \ge t]\right) \le \int_\Omega |X_N| 1_{[S^* \ge t]}, \quad t \ge 0. \tag{1}$$

Using 6.a.0 with $h(t) = t^p$, we can now write

$$\frac{1}{p} E((S^*)^p) = \int_0^{+\infty} t^{p-1} P(S^* \ge t)dt = \int_0^{+\infty} t^{p-2} t P(S^* \ge t)dt \le \text{ (using (1))} \le$$

$$\le \int_0^{+\infty} \left[\int_\Omega t^{p-2} |X_N(\omega)| 1_{[S^* \ge t]}(\omega) P(d\omega)\right] dt = \text{ (Fubini) } =$$

$$= \int_\Omega \left[\int_0^{+\infty} |X_N| t^{p-2} 1_{[0, S^*(\omega)]}(t)dt\right] P(d\omega) = E\left[|X_N| \int_0^{S^*(\omega)} t^{p-2}dt\right]$$

$$= \frac{1}{p-1} E\left(|X_N|(S^*)^{(p-1)}\right).$$

Now let q denote the exponent conjugate to p, given by $\frac{1}{p} + \frac{1}{q} = 1$ and so $q = \frac{p}{p-1}$. Multiplying the above inequality with p and using Holder's inequality we obtain

$$E((S^*)^p) \le qE\left(|X_N|(S^*)^{(p-1)}\right) \le qE(|X_N|^p)^{\frac{1}{p}} E\left((S^*)^{(p-1)q}\right)^{\frac{1}{q}}$$

$$= q\|X_N\|_p E\left((S^*)^p\right)^{\frac{1}{q}}.$$

Divide by $E\left((S^*)^p\right)^{\frac{1}{q}}$ using $1 - \frac{1}{q} = \frac{1}{p}$ to obtain $E((S^*)^p)^{\frac{1}{p}} \le q\|X_N\|_p$. This is the second inequality in 6.b.3. The first inequality is trivial. ∎

7. CONTINUOUS TIME MARTINGALES

7.a Filtration, optional times, sampling. We now turn to the study of martingales indexed by the set $T = [0, \infty)$ with the usual order. A T-filtration $(\mathcal{F}_t)_{t \geq 0}$ on $(\Omega, \mathcal{F}, P)$ is called *right continuous* if it satisfies

$$\mathcal{F}_t = \bigcap_{s>t} \mathcal{F}_s, \quad \text{and all } t \geq 0;$$

equivalently, if $s_n \downarrow t$ implies that $\mathcal{F}_{s_n} \downarrow \mathcal{F}_t$, for all sequences $(s_n) \subseteq R$ and all $t \geq 0$. Recall also that the filtration $(\mathcal{F}_t)$ is called augmented if $\mathcal{F}_0$ (and hence each σ-field $\mathcal{F}_t$) contains the family of P-null sets. As in the discrete case we set $\mathcal{F}_\infty = \sigma\left(\bigcup_{t \geq 0} \mathcal{F}_t\right)$. The theory now proceeds under the following

7.a.0 Assumption. *The probability space $(\Omega, \mathcal{F}, P)$ is complete and the filtration $(\mathcal{F}_t)_{t \geq 0}$ on $(\Omega, \mathcal{F}, P)$ right continuous and augmented.*

Augmentation eliminates measurability problems on null sets. Let $X = (X_t)$, $Y = (Y_t)$, $X(n) = (X_t(n))$ be stochastic processes on $(\Omega, \mathcal{F}, P)$ indexed by $T = [0, \infty)$, and $t \geq 0$. If X_t is $\mathcal{F}_t$-measurable and $Y_t = X_t$, P-as., then Y_t is $\mathcal{F}_t$-measurable. Likewise, if $X_t(n)$ is $\mathcal{F}_t$-measurable, for all $n \geq 1$, and $X_t(n) \to X_t$, P-as., as $n \uparrow \infty$, then X_t is $\mathcal{F}_t$-measurable. If $\omega \in \Omega$, the function

$$t \in [0, \infty) \mapsto X_t(\omega) \in \overline{R}$$

is called the *path* of X in state ω. The process X is called $(right, left)$ *continuous* if X is $(\mathcal{F}_t)$-adapted and P-ae. path of X is finitely valued and (right, left) continuous. Let us call the processes X, Y *versions of each other* and write $X = Y$ if they satisfy

$$X_t = Y_t, \quad P\text{-as., for all } t \geq 0. \tag{0}$$

Since the filtration $(\mathcal{F}_t)$ is augmented, each version of an $(\mathcal{F}_t)$-adapted process is again $(\mathcal{F}_t)$-adapted.

The exceptional null set $[X_t \neq Y_t]$ in (0) is allowed to depend on t. If this null set can be made independent of $t \geq 0$, that is, if there is a P-null set $N \subseteq \Omega$ such that $X_t(\omega) = Y_t(\omega)$, for all $\omega \in \Omega \setminus N$ and all $t \geq 0$, then we call the processes X and Y *indistinguishable*. Clearly X and Y are indistinguishable if and only if the paths $t \in [0, \infty) \mapsto X_t(\omega)$ and $t \in [0, \infty) \mapsto Y_t(\omega)$ are identical, for P-ae. $\omega \in \Omega$. These notions of equality agree for right continuous processes, to which mostly we shall confine our attention:

7.a.1. *Assume that the right continuous processes X and Y are versions of each other. Then they are indistinguishable.*

Proof. For each rational number $r \geq 0$ choose a null set $E_r \subseteq \Omega$ such that $X_r = Y_r$ on the complement E_r^c and let $E \supseteq \bigcup_r E_r$ be a null set such that the paths $t \mapsto X_t(\omega)$ and $t \mapsto Y_t(\omega)$ are right continuous, for each $\omega \in E^c$. If $\omega \in E^c$ then the paths $t \mapsto X_t(\omega)$ and $t \mapsto Y_t(\omega)$ are right continuous and satisfy $X_r(\omega) = Y_r(\omega)$, for all $r \in [0, \infty) \cap Q$ and so $X_t(\omega) = Y_t(\omega)$, for all $t \geq 0$. ∎

Recall that an $(\mathcal{F}_t)$-optional time is a function $T : \Omega \to [0, +\infty]$ satisfying

$$[T < t] \in \mathcal{F}_t, \quad 0 \leq t < \infty. \tag{1}$$

The value $T = \infty$ is allowed. It follows easily that (1) also holds for $t = \infty$. The right continuity of the filtration $(\mathcal{F}_t)$ implies that condition (1) is equivalent with

$$[T \leq t] \in \mathcal{F}_t, \quad 0 \leq t < \infty. \tag{2}$$

Indeed, assuming (1), the set $[T \leq t] = \bigcap_{r > s > t} [T < s]$ is in $\mathcal{F}_r$, for each $r > t$, and thus $[T \leq t] \in \mathcal{F}_t$. Conversely, assuming (2), the set $[T < t] = \bigcup_{s < t} [T \leq s] \in \mathcal{F}_t$. The equivalence of (1) and (2) is very useful and greatly simplifies the statements and proofs of results below.

Let T be an optional time. Then all the sets $[T < t]$, $[T > t]$ and $[T = t]$ are in $\mathcal{F}_t$, for each $t \geq 0$. We set

$$\begin{aligned} \mathcal{F}_T := &\{ A \in \mathcal{F}_\infty \mid A \cap [T < t] \in \mathcal{F}_t, \ \forall 0 \leq t < \infty \} \\ = &\{ A \in \mathcal{F}_\infty \mid A \cap [T \leq t] \in \mathcal{F}_t, \ \forall 0 \leq t < \infty \} \\ = &\{ A \subseteq \Omega \mid A \cap [T \leq t] \in \mathcal{F}_t, \ \forall 0 \leq t \leq \infty \}, \end{aligned} \tag{3}$$

the second equality again due to the right continuity of the filtration $(\mathcal{F}_t)$ and the last being trivial. $\mathcal{F}_T$ is the family of events of which it is known prior to time T whether they have occurred or not. More precisely, for $\omega \in \Omega$ it is known by time $T(\omega)$, whether $\omega \in A$ or not, that is, the value $1_A(\omega)$ is known by time $T(\omega)$.

7.a.2. *Assume that T_n, $n = 1, 2, \ldots$ are optional times. Then each of the following are optional times also:*

(a) $\sup_n T_n$, $\inf_n T_n$, $T_1 \wedge T_2$, $T_1 \vee T_2$ *and* $T_1 + T_2$.

(b) $\limsup_n T_n$ *and* $\liminf_n T_n$.

Proof. (a) Set $T = \sup_n T_n$. For each $t \geq 0$ we have $[T \leq t] = \bigcap_n [T_n \leq t] \in \mathcal{F}_t$. Similarly, if $S = \inf_n T_n$, then $[S < t] = \bigcup_n [T_n < t] \in \mathcal{F}_t$. Using the equivalent conditions (1) and (2) for optionality, this shows that S and T are optional times. The optionality of $T_1 \wedge T_2$ and $T_1 \vee T_2$ follows as a special case. Finally set $T = T_1 + T_2$. Then, for each $t \geq 0$, $[T < t] = \bigcup_{r, s \in Q, r + s < t} [T_1 < r] \cap [T_2 < s] \in \mathcal{F}_t$. Thus T is optional. (b) $\liminf_n T_n = \sup_n \inf_{m \geq n} T_m$ and $\limsup_n T_n = \inf_n \sup_{m \geq n} T_m$ are optional, by (a). ∎

7.a.3. *Let S, T, T_n, $n \geq 1$, be optional times, $\tilde{T} : \Omega \to [0, \infty]$ and Z a random variable. Then*
(a) $S \leq T$ implies $\mathcal{F}_S \subseteq \mathcal{F}_T$.
(b) $\mathcal{F}_T$ is a σ-field and T is $\mathcal{F}_T$-measurable.
(c) Z is $\mathcal{F}_T$-measurable if and only if $Z1_{[T<t]}$ is $\mathcal{F}_t$-measurable, for each $t \geq 0$.
(d) $[S < T], [S = T] \in \mathcal{F}_{S \wedge T}$.
(e) If the filtration $(\mathcal{F}_t)$ is augmented, then $\mathcal{F}_T$ contains all the null sets.
(f) If $T_n \downarrow T$, then $\mathcal{F}_{T_n} \downarrow \mathcal{F}_T$.
(g) If $T_n \uparrow T$ and $\bigcup_n [T_n = T] = \Omega$, then $\mathcal{F}_{T_n} \uparrow \mathcal{F}_T$.
(h) $\mathcal{F}_T$ contains the P-null sets.
(i) If $\tilde{T} = T$, P-as., then $\tilde{T}$ is an optional time and $\mathcal{F}_{\tilde{T}} = \mathcal{F}_T$.
(j) If $A \in \mathcal{F}_S$ then $A \cap [S \leq T] \in \mathcal{F}_{S \wedge T}$.

Remark. The condition $\bigcup_n [T_n = T] = \Omega$ in (g) means that the limit $T = \lim_n T_n$ is hit in finite time at each point $\omega \in \Omega$. This condition is satisfied for example if the T_n are of the form $T_n = S \wedge S_n$, where $S < \infty$ and $S_n \uparrow \infty$ almost surely.

Proof. (e) is obvious. (a) Assume that $S \leq T$. Then $[T < t] \subseteq [S < t]$ and $[T < t] \in \mathcal{F}_t$, for each $t \geq 0$. Let $A \in \mathcal{F}_S$ and $t \geq 0$. Then $A \cap [S < t] \in \mathcal{F}_t$ and so $A \cap [T < t] = (A \cap [S < t]) \cap [T < t] \in \mathcal{F}_t$. Thus $A \in \mathcal{F}_T$.

(b) It is easy to see that $\emptyset \in \mathcal{F}_T$ and that $\mathcal{F}_T$ is closed under countable unions. Let $A \in \mathcal{F}_T$ and $t \geq 0$. Then $A^c \cap [T < t] = [T < t] \setminus (A \cap [T < t]) \in \mathcal{F}_t$. Thus $A^c \in \mathcal{F}_T$ and $\mathcal{F}_T$ is closed under complements. One easily verifies that $[T < r] \in \mathcal{F}_T$, for each $r \in R$, and this shows that T is $\mathcal{F}_T$-measurable.

(c) ($\Rightarrow$) Assume that Z is $\mathcal{F}_T$-measurable. We wish to show that $Z1_{[T<t]}$ is $\mathcal{F}_t$-measurable, for each $t \geq 0$. We follow the usual extension procedure from indicator functions. Assume first that $Z = 1_F$, where $F \in \mathcal{F}_T$ and let $t \geq 0$ be arbitrary. Then $F \cap [T < t] \in \mathcal{F}_t$; equivalently, $Z1_{[T<t]} = 1_{F \cap [T<t]}$ is $\mathcal{F}_t$-measurable. By linearity it follows that $Z1_{[T<t]}$ is $\mathcal{F}_t$-measurable, for each $t \geq 0$, whenever Z is an $\mathcal{F}_T$-measurable simple function.

Next let Z be a nonnegative $\mathcal{F}_T$-measurable function and $t \geq 0$. Choose a sequence (Z_n) of nonnegative $\mathcal{F}_T$-measurable simple functions such that $Z_n \uparrow Z$. Then $Z_n 1_{[T<t]} \uparrow Z1_{[T<t]}$. By the previous step, $Z_n 1_{[T<t]}$ is $\mathcal{F}_t$-measurable, for each $n \geq 1$, and it follows that $Z1_{[T<t]}$ is $\mathcal{F}_t$-measurable. The extension to arbitrary $\mathcal{F}_T$-measurable Z is accomplished by decomposing such Z as $Z = Z^+ - Z^-$.

($\Leftarrow$) Assume now that $Z1_{[T<t]}$ is $\mathcal{F}_t$-measurable, for each $t \geq 0$. To see that Z is $\mathcal{F}_T$-measurable, it will suffice to show that $[Z \geq r] \in \mathcal{F}_T$, for all real numbers r; equivalently, $[Z \geq r] \cap [T < t] \in \mathcal{F}_t$, for all $t \geq 0$ and $r \in R$. Indeed, for such r and t we have $[Z \geq r] \cap [T < t] = [Z1_{[T<t]} \geq r] \cap [T < t] \in \mathcal{F}_t$, where we have used $[T < t] \in \mathcal{F}_t$, by optionality of the random time T.

(d) $[S < T] \cap [S \wedge T < t] = [S < T] \cap [S < t] = \bigcup \{ [S < q < T] : q \in Q \cap [0, t] \} \in \mathcal{F}_t$, for all $t \geq 0$. This shows that $[S < T] \in \mathcal{F}_{S \wedge T}$. By symmetry $[T < S] \in \mathcal{F}_{S \wedge T}$ and so $[S = T] = ([S < T] \cup [T < S])^c \in \mathcal{F}_{S \wedge T}$.

(f) Assume that $T_N \downarrow T$, as $N \uparrow \infty$. From (a) it follows that $\mathcal{F}_{T_1} \supseteq \mathcal{F}_{T_2} \supseteq \ldots$ and $\mathcal{F}_T \subseteq \bigcap_N \mathcal{F}_{T_N}$. Thus it remains to be shown only that $\bigcap_N \mathcal{F}_{T_N} \subseteq \mathcal{F}_T$.

Let $A \in \mathcal{F}_{T_N}$, for all $N \geq 1$. Then $A \cap [T_N < t] \in \mathcal{F}_t$, for all $t \geq 0$ and all $N \geq 1$. Let $t \geq 0$. As $T_N \downarrow T$, $N \uparrow \infty$, we have $[T < t] = \bigcup_N [T_N < t]$ and so $A \cap [T < t] = \bigcup_N (A \cap [T_N < t]) \in \mathcal{F}_t$. Thus $A \in \mathcal{F}_T$. This shows that $\mathcal{F}_T = \bigcap_N \mathcal{F}_{T_N}$.

(g) Set $\mathcal{G} = \sigma \left(\bigcup_N \mathcal{F}_{T_N} \right)$. From (a) it follows that $\mathcal{F}_{T_1} \subseteq \mathcal{F}_{T_2} \subseteq \ldots \subseteq \mathcal{F}_T$ and so $\mathcal{G} \subseteq \mathcal{F}_T$. Thus it remains to be shown only that $\mathcal{F}_T \subseteq \mathcal{G}$. Let $A \in \mathcal{F}_T$. We claim that $A_N := A \cap [T = T_N] \in \mathcal{F}_{T_N}$, for all $N \geq 1$.

Since $[T = T_N] \in \mathcal{F}_{T \wedge T_N} \subseteq \mathcal{F}_T$ we have $A_N \in \mathcal{F}_T$. Let $t \geq 0$. Since $T = T_N$ on the set A_N, we have $A_N \cap [T_N < t] = A_N \cap [T < t] \in \mathcal{F}_t$. This shows that $A_N \in \mathcal{F}_{T_N} \subseteq \mathcal{G}$. From $\bigcup_N [T = T_N] = \Omega$ it now follows that $A = \bigcup_N A_N \in \mathcal{G}$, as desired. (h), (i) follow easily from the fact that $\mathcal{F}_t$ contains the P-null sets, for each $t \geq 0$ (assumption 7.a.0).

(j) Let $A \in \mathcal{F}_S$ and $r \geq 0$. To verify $A \cap [S \leq T] \in \mathcal{F}_{S \wedge T}$ we must show that $A \cap [S \leq T] \cap [S \wedge T \leq r] \in \mathcal{F}_r$. Indeed $A \cap [S \leq r] \in \mathcal{F}_r$, the optional times $T \wedge r$, $S \wedge r$ are $\mathcal{F}_r$-measurable (7.a.3.(a),(b)) and so $[S \wedge r \leq T \wedge r] \in \mathcal{F}_r$. Consequently $A \cap [S \leq T] \cap [S \wedge T \leq r] = A \cap [S \leq T] \cap [S \leq r] = A \cap [S \leq r] \cap [S \wedge r \leq T \wedge r] \in \mathcal{F}_r$, as desired. ∎

Remark. Measurability with respect to $\mathcal{F}_T$ should be interpreted as follows: A random variable Z is $\mathcal{F}_T$-measurable, if the value $Z(\omega)$ is known by time $T(\omega)$, for each $\omega \in \Omega$.

Sampling a process X. Let now $X = X_t(\omega) = X(t, \omega)$ be any adapted process on the filtered probability space $(\Omega, \mathcal{F}, (\mathcal{F}_t), P)$ and $T : \Omega \to [0, \infty]$ a random time. The random variable X_T, to be interpreted as the process X sampled at time T, is defined as follows

$$(X_T)(\omega) = X_{T(\omega)}(\omega), \quad \omega \in \Omega.$$

Here provisions have to be made for the case $T(\omega) = \infty$. We set $X_T = X_\infty$ on the set $[T = \infty]$, where X_∞ is some previously specified, $\mathcal{F}_\infty$-measurable random variable (exactly which will depend on the context).

The most common choice for X_∞ is $X_\infty = \limsup_n X_n$ in case $\lim_{t \uparrow \infty} X_t \in \overline{R}$ exists almost surely. Then X_∞ is defined everywhere, $\mathcal{F}_\infty$-measurable and satisfies $X_\infty = \lim_{t \uparrow \infty} X_t \in \overline{R}$, P-as. On occasion the choice $X_\infty = 0$ is made. This is the case in particular if X_T is to be interpreted as the reward for quitting a game at time T (no reward if we have to wait infinitely long).

At present it is not even clear that X_T, so defined, is measurable. We will turn to this problem several times below. The following lemma is the basic tool which will allow us to reduce many questions from continuous time martingales to martingale *sequences*: It approximates arbitrary optional times by optional times with *countable range*. Recall that $[x]$ denotes the greatest integer not exceeding x.

7.a.4 Discretization Lemma. *Let T be an optional time. For each $N \geq 1$ set*

$$T_N(\omega) := \big([2^N T(\omega)] + 1\big)/2^N \quad (= \infty, \text{ if } T(\omega) = \infty), \quad \omega \in \Omega. \tag{4}$$

Then each T_N is an optional time and $T_N \downarrow T$, pointwise on Ω, as $N \uparrow \infty$.

Proof. For $N \geq 1$ set $D_N := \{\, k2^{-N} \mid k = 0, 1, 2, \ldots\}$. The points in D_N are the endpoints of *dyadic intervals* $[k/2^N, (k+1)/2^N)$ of degree N, which form a partition of the interval $[0, \infty)$. For $t \in [0, \infty]$ set

$$b_N(t) = \inf\{\, \beta \in D_N \mid \beta > t\} \quad \text{and} \quad a_N(t) = b_N(t) - 2^{-N}.$$

Thus, if $t < \infty$, $t \in [a_N(t), b_N(t))$ and so $[a_N(t), b_N(t))$ is the unique dyadic interval $[k/2^N, (k+1)/2^N)$ of degree N which contains the point t. If $t = \infty$, then $b_N(t) = \infty$ also. One verifies easily that $b_N(t) = \big([2^N t] + 1\big)/2^N$ and so

$$T_N(\omega) = b_N(T(\omega)), \quad \omega \in \Omega. \tag{5}$$

Note that $t \leq b_N(t) \leq t + 2^{-N}$ and $D_N \subseteq D_{N+1}$ which implies $b_{N+1}(t) \leq b_N(t)$. Consequently $b_N(t) \downarrow t$, as $N \uparrow \infty$, for each $t \in [0, \infty]$. From (5) it now follows that $T_N \downarrow T$ pointwise everywhere on Ω. It remains to be shown only that the T_N are optional. Let $N \geq 1$, $\omega \in \Omega$ and $t \geq 0$. Then $T_N(\omega) = b_N(T(\omega)) \leq t$ if and only if the degree N dyadic interval containing t is to the right of the degree N dyadic interval containing $T(\omega)$ and this is equivalent with $a_N(t) > T(\omega)$. Thus $[T_N \leq t] = [T < a_N(t)] \in \mathcal{F}_{a_N(t)} \subseteq \mathcal{F}_t$. ∎

7.a.5. *Assume that the process $X = (X_t)$ has right continuous paths almost surely, X_∞ is any $\mathcal{F}_\infty$-measurable random variable and that T is an optional time. Then X_T is $\mathcal{F}_T$-measurable.*

Proof. Let T_N be as in 7.a.4. If $\omega \in \Omega$ is such that the path $t \mapsto X_t(\omega)$ is right continuous, then the convergence $T_N(\omega) \downarrow T(\omega)$ implies that

$$(X_{T_N})(\omega) = X_{T_N(\omega)}(\omega) \to X_{T(\omega)}(\omega) = (X_T)(\omega), \quad \text{as } N \uparrow \infty.$$

Thus we have $X_{T_N} \to X_T$, as $N \uparrow \infty$, P-as. Moreover the random time T has countable range in the set $D_N = \{\, k2^{-N} \mid k = 0, 1, 2, \ldots\}$. Thus the random variable X_{T_N} can be viewed as a sample of the *sequential process* $(X_{k2^{-N}})_{k \geq 1}$ at time T_N. It follows from the sequential theory (3.b.0.(c)) that X_{T_N} is $\mathcal{F}_{T_N}$ measurable, for each $N \geq 1$. According to 7.a.3.(f) we have $\mathcal{F}_{T_N} \downarrow \mathcal{F}_T$. It is easily verified that the limit $Y = \limsup_n X_{T_n} = \limsup_{n \geq N} X_{T_n}$ is $\mathcal{F}_{T_N}$-measurable, for each $N \geq 1$.

   Since $\mathcal{F}_T = \bigcap_{N \geq 1} \mathcal{F}_{T_N}$ it follows that Y is $\mathcal{F}_T$-measurable. Finally, since $X_T = Y$, P-as. and the σ-field $\mathcal{F}_T$ contains the null sets, it follows that X_T is $\mathcal{F}_T$-measurable. ∎

7.a.6 Examples. (1) It is easy to see that the constant time $T = t$ is optional. To get a more interesting example, let $A \in \mathcal{F}$, $0 \le s < t$ and set $T = s1_{A^c} + t1_A$. Then, for each real number r we have

$$[T \le r] = \begin{cases} \emptyset & \text{if } r < s, \\ A^c & \text{if } s \le r < t, \\ \Omega & \text{if } r \ge t. \end{cases}$$

Thus the requirement for optionality of T, $[T \le r] \in \mathcal{F}_r$, $r \ge 0$, translates into the condition $A^c \in \mathcal{F}_s$. In other words, T is an optional time if and only if $A \in \mathcal{F}_s$. In particular the random time $T = t1_A$ is optional if and only if $A \in \mathcal{F}_0$.

(2) Let $\mathcal{P} = \{A_1, A_2, \ldots\}$ be a countable partition of Ω and $0 \le t_1 < t_2 < \ldots$ and set $T = \sum_n t_n 1_{A_n}$. If T is optional, then $A_1 = [T \le t_1] \in \mathcal{F}_{t_1}$, $A_1 \cup A_2 = [T \le t_2] \in \mathcal{F}_{t_2}$ and so $A_2 \in \mathcal{F}_{t_2}$. Continuing in this fashion we see that $A_n \in \mathcal{F}_{t_n}$, for all $n \ge 1$. Conversely this condition implies that T is optional. This characterizes all optional times T with countable range. If X is any process, then $X_T = \sum_n 1_{A_n} X_{t_n}$.

(3) *Hitting times.* Let E be a Polish space (complete separable metric space), $\mathcal{E}$ the Borel σ-field on E and assume that the process $X = (X_t)$ takes values in the $(E, \mathcal{E})$. More precisely we assume that $X_t : (\Omega, \mathcal{F}) \to (E, \mathcal{E})$ is measurable, for each $t \ge 0$. For a subset $A \subseteq E$ we define the *hitting time* T_A and *first exit time* τ_A as follows:

$$T_A := \inf\{t > 0 \mid X_t \in A\}$$
$$\tau_A := \inf\{t > 0 \mid X_t \notin A\}.$$

Then $\tau_A = T_{A^c}$. From the definition it is clear that $A \subseteq B \Rightarrow T_A \ge T_B$.

7.a.7. *Assume that the process X is adapted and has continuous paths, P-as. Then the hitting time T_A is optional, for each open and each closed subset $A \subseteq E$.*

Proof. We may assume that *all* paths $t \mapsto X_t(\omega)$ are continuous. Otherwise we can replace X with a process which has this property and is indistinguishable from X. This affects hitting times only on P-null sets and has no effect on optionality since the filtration $(\mathcal{F}_t)$ is augmented.

Assume first that the set A is open and $t > 0$. The path continuity of X implies that $[T_A < t] = \bigcup_{q \in Q, q < t}[X_q \in A] \in \mathcal{F}_t$, for all $t \ge 0$. Thus T_A is optional.

Assume now that the set A is closed and set $G_n = \{x \in E \mid dist(x, A) < 1/n\}$, $n > 0$. Then $G_n \downarrow A$, since A is closed. Since each set G_n is open, T_{G_n} is optional, for each $n > 0$. According to 7.a.2.(b) it will now suffice to show that $T_{G_n} \uparrow T_A$, as $n \uparrow \infty$.

Indeed, $G_n \downarrow$ implies $T_{G_n} \uparrow$ and consequently $T_{G_n} \uparrow T$, where $T = \sup_n T_{G_n}$. It will thus suffice to show that $T_A = T$. From $G_n \supseteq A$ it follows that $T_{G_n} \le T_A$, for each $n > 0$, and consequently $T \le T_A$. Thus it remains to be shown only that $T_A \le T$.

Indeed, let $\omega \in \Omega$ and $r > T(\omega)$ be arbitrary. Then, for each $n > 0$, we have $r > T_{G_n}(\omega)$ and consequently there exists $t_n < r$ such that $X_{t_n}(\omega) \in G_n$. Replacing the sequence (n) with a suitable subsequence (k_n) if necessary (this maintains the relationship $G_n \downarrow A$), we may assume that $t_n \to t \leq r$. The continuity of the path $s \to X_s(\omega)$ now implies that $X_{t_n}(\omega) \to X_t(\omega)$. From this and $dist(X_{t_n}(\omega), A) < 1/n$ it follows that $dist(X_t(\omega), A) = 0$, that is, $X_t(\omega) \in A$, by closedness of the set A. Thus $T_A(\omega) \leq t \leq r$. Since here $r > T(\omega)$ was arbitrary we conclude that $T_A(\omega) \leq T(\omega)$, as desired. ∎

7.b Pathwise continuity. The Upcrossing Lemma implies certain continuity proper-ties of submartingale paths. Indeed, we will see below (7.b.3) that every martingale has a right continuous version.

7.b.0. *Let $(X_t)_{t \geq 0}$ be a submartingale and $S \subseteq [0, +\infty)$ a countable dense subset. Then, for P-ae. $\omega \in \Omega$,*
(i) the limits $\lim_{S \ni s \downarrow t} X(s, \omega)$ and $\lim_{S \ni s \uparrow t} X(s, \omega)$ exist in $[-\infty, +\infty)$ for each $t \geq 0$ respectively $t > 0$.
(ii) The set $\{ X(s, \omega) \mid s \in I \cap S \} \subseteq [-\infty, +\infty)$ is bounded above, for each bounded interval $I \subseteq [0, +\infty)$.

Remark. (a) Here the *value* of the limits in (i) does not depend on the countable dense subset $S \subseteq [0, +\infty)$ (given any two such sets the union is another such set) but the exceptional null set on which the limits may fail to exist does depend on the set S. Thus it is in general not true that $\lim_{s \downarrow t} X(s, \omega)$ exists, for each $t \geq 0$, P-as. This question of right continuity of the paths will be dealt with later.

(b) We claim that the limits in (i) are less than $+\infty$. Note that this property follows from (ii).

(c) In the supermartingale case the limits exist and are bigger than $-\infty$ and the set in (ii) is bounded from below. In the martingale case the limits exist and are finite and the set in (ii) is bounded both above and below.

Proof. (i)   Let $m \geq 1$. For a finite subset $T = \{ t_1 < t_2 < \ldots < t_n \} \subseteq S \cap [0, m]$ and real numbers $\alpha < \beta$ let $U_T(\alpha, \beta)(\omega)$ denote the number of times the sample path $(X_{t_1}(\omega), X_{t_2}(\omega), \ldots, X_{t_n}(\omega))$ crosses from below α to above β. Applying the Upcrossing Lemma to the finite submartingale sequence $(X_{t_1}, X_{t_2}, \ldots, X_{t_n}, X_m)$ we obtain

$$E\left(U_T(\alpha, \beta)\right) \leq \frac{E(X_m^+) + |\alpha|}{\beta - \alpha}, \quad \text{for all finite subsets } T \subseteq S \cap [0, m]. \qquad (0)$$

Now write the countable set $S \cap [0, m]$ as the increasing union $S \cap [0, m] = \bigcup_n T_n$ for some increasing sequence of finite subsets $T_n \subseteq S \cap [0, m]$. Then the sequence of random variables $U_{T_n}(\alpha, \beta)$ increases at each point of Ω and we set

$$U_{S \cap [0, m]}(a, \beta)(\omega) = \lim_{n \uparrow \infty} U_{T_n}(\alpha, \beta)(\omega), \quad \omega \in \Omega,$$

to be interpreted (vaguely) as the number of upcrossings of the sample path $t \in S \cap [0, m] \to X_t(\omega)$ from below α to above β. If $T \subseteq S \cap [0, m]$ is any finite subset then $T \subseteq T_n$, for some $n \geq 1$, and consequently

$$U_T(\alpha, \beta) \leq U_{S \cap [0, m]}(a, \beta) \text{ on } \Omega, \text{ for each finite subset } T \subseteq S \cap [0, m]. \qquad (1)$$

By monotone convergence we have

$$E\left(U_{S\cap[0,m]}(a,\beta)\right) = \lim_n E\left(U_{T_n}(a,\beta)\right) \le \frac{E(X_m^+) + |\alpha|}{\beta - \alpha} < \infty, \qquad (2)$$

and in particular thus $U_{S\cap[0,m]}(a,\beta) < \infty$, P-as., where the exceptional set may still depend on $m \ge 1$. Since a countable union of null sets is again a null set, it follows that there exists a null set $N \subseteq \Omega$ such that

$$U_{S\cap[0,m]}(a,\beta)(\omega) < \infty, \quad \text{for all } \omega \in \Omega \setminus N,\ m \ge 1,$$
$$\text{and all pairs of rational numbers } (\alpha,\beta) \text{ with } \alpha < \beta. \qquad (3)$$

Let $\omega \in \Omega \setminus N$. We claim that the one sided limit $\lim_{S \ni s \downarrow t} X(s,\omega)$ exists for each $t \ge 0$ and the one sided limit $\lim_{S \ni s \uparrow t} X(s,\omega)$ exists for each $t > 0$. Indeed let $t > 0$ and assume that $\lim_{S \ni s \uparrow t} X(s,\omega)$ does not exist. Then there exist rational numbers $\alpha < \beta$ such that

$$\liminf_{S \ni s \uparrow t} X(s,\omega) < \alpha < \beta < \limsup_{S \ni s \uparrow t} X(s,\omega).$$

Fix $m \ge t$ and let $N \ge 1$. Then there exists a finite subset $T \subseteq S \cap [0,t) \subseteq S \cap [0,m]$ such that the sample path $t \in T \mapsto X_t(\omega)$ crosses from below α to above β more than N times. Thus, using (1), $U_{S\cap[0,m]}(a,\beta)(\omega) \ge U_T(a,\beta)(\omega) > N$. Since here N was arbitary, it follows that $U_{S\cap[0,m]}(a,\beta)(\omega) = \infty$ in contradiction to (3). The existence of the limit $\lim_{S \ni s \downarrow t} X(s,\omega)$, for $t \ge 0$, is shown similarly.

(ii)   We still have to show that the limits in (i) are less than $+\infty$ but this will follow from (ii), that is, the existence of a further null set $F \subseteq \Omega$ such that for every point $\omega \in \Omega \setminus F$ the subset $\{\, X(s,\omega) \mid s \in I \cap S \,\} \subseteq [-\infty, +\infty)$ is bounded above, for each bounded interval $I \subseteq [0, +\infty)$. Clearly it will suffice to have this boundedness for all intervals $I = [0,m]$, $m \ge 1$. Since a countable union of null sets is again a null set, it will suffice to show that for each $m \ge 1$ the set $\{\, X(s,\omega) \mid s \in S \cap [0,m] \,\}$ is bounded above, for P-ae. $\omega \in \Omega$; equivalently,

$$P(\sup_{t \in S\cap[0,m]} X_t^+ = +\infty) = 0, \quad m \ge 1. \qquad (4)$$

Let $m \ge 1$ and $T = \{\, t_1 < t_2 < \ldots < t_n \,\} \subseteq S \cap [0,m]$ a finite subset. The maximal inequality 6.b.0 applied to the finite submartingale sequence $(X_{t_1}^+, X_{t_2}^+, \ldots, X_{t_n}^+, X_m^+)$ yields

$$P\left(\sup_{t \in T} X_t^+ \ge \lambda\right) \le \lambda^{-1} E(X_m^+), \quad \forall \lambda > 0. \qquad (5)$$

Fix $\lambda > 0$ and write the set $S \cap [0,m]$ as the increasing union $S \cap [0,m] = \bigcup_n T_n$, for some increasing sequence of finite subsets $T_n \subseteq S \cap [0,m]$. Then

$$\left[\sup_{t \in T_n} X_t^+ > \lambda\right] \uparrow \left[\sup_{t \in S\cap[0,m]} X_t^+ > \lambda\right], \quad \text{as } n \uparrow \infty.$$

Note the strict inequalities. From (5) we now conclude that

$$P\left(\sup_{t \in S\cap[0,m]} X_t^+ > \lambda\right) \le \lambda^{-1} E(X_m^+).$$

Letting $\lambda \uparrow \infty$ now yields (4). ∎

7.b.1. *Let* $(X_t)_{t \geq 0}$ *be a submartingale. Assume that almost every sample path is right continuous at each point. Then almost every sample path has left limits at each point and is bounded above on each finite interval.*

Proof. Choose a countable dense subset $S \subseteq [0, +\infty)$. Continuing with the notation of the proof of 7.b.0 we have $U_{S \cap [0,m]}(\alpha, \beta) < \infty$, P-as., for all $\alpha < \beta$, and the sample path $f(t) = X_t(\omega)$ is right continuous at each point and has the property that the set $\{ X(s, \omega) \mid s \in S \cap I \} \subseteq [-\infty, +\infty)$ is bounded above, for each bounded interval $I \subseteq [0, +\infty)$, for P-ae. $\omega \in \Omega$. The right continuity of f and density of S now imply that f itself is bounded above on any bounded interval $I \subseteq [0, +\infty)$.

   If f does not have a left limit at the point t, then there exist rational numbers $\alpha < \beta$ such that $f(t)$ crosses infinitely often from strictly below α to strictly above β on the interval $[0, t)$ (in fact on each left neighborhood of the point t). The right continuity of f and density of S now imply that the restriction $f|_{S \cap [0,t)}$ crosses infinitely often from below α to above β. But then $U_{S \cap [0,m]}(\alpha, \beta) = \infty$, for any integer m with $t \leq m$, and this is impossible P-almost surely. ∎

7.b.2. *Let* $f : [0, +\infty) \to R$ *and* $S \subseteq [0, +\infty)$ *be a countable dense subset such that* $f(t+) = \lim_{S \ni s \downarrow t} f(s)$ *exists for each* $t \geq 0$ *and* $f(t-) = \lim_{S \ni s \uparrow t} f(s)$ *exists for each* $t > 0$ *and both are finite. Then the function* $g(t) = f(t+)$ *is right continuous and the function* $h(t) = f(t-)$ *is left continuous on* $[0, +\infty)$.

Remark. Here $h(0) = f(0-) := f(0)$.

Proof. We show merely the right continuity of $g(t)$. Let $t \geq 0$ and assume that $t_n \downarrow t$, as $n \uparrow \infty$. We have to show that $g(t_n) \to g(t) = \lim_{S \ni s \downarrow t} f(s)$, as $n \uparrow \infty$.

   Let $n \geq 1$. As $g(t_n) = \lim_{S \ni s \downarrow t_n} f(s)$ we can choose $s_n \in S$ such that $t_n < s_n < t_n + \frac{1}{n}$ and $|f(s_n) - g(t_n)| < \frac{1}{n}$. Then $S \ni s_n \downarrow t$ and so $f(s_n) \to g(t)$. This implies $g(t_n) \to g(t)$, as desired. ∎

7.b.3. *Every martingale* $(X_t, \mathcal{F}_t)_{t \geq 0}$ *has a right continuous version.*

Proof. Let $S \subseteq [0, +\infty)$ be a countable dense set and choose, according to 7.b.0, a null set $N \subseteq \Omega$ such that the right limit $X(t+, \omega) = \lim_{S \ni s \downarrow t} X_s(\omega) \in R$ exists for all $\omega \in \Omega \setminus N$. Define

$$Y_t(\omega) = \begin{cases} X(t+, \omega) & t \geq 0 \text{ and } \omega \in \Omega \setminus N \\ 0 & t \geq 0 \text{ and } \omega \in N. \end{cases}$$

We claim that Y_t is $\mathcal{F}_t$ measurable: Since the filtration $(\mathcal{F}_t)$ is augmented, 1_N is $\mathcal{F}_r$-measurable, for each $r \geq 0$. Now if $r > t$, then Y_t is the pointwise limit

$$Y_t = \lim_{s \in S, s < r, s \downarrow t} 1_N X_s$$

on all of Ω, and thus is $\mathcal{F}_r$-measurable. Since this is true for each $r > t$, it follows that Y_t is measurable with respect to the σ-field $\mathcal{F}_t = \bigcap_{r > t} \mathcal{F}_r$. This shows that the process Y is adapted to the filtration $(\mathcal{F}_t)$.

From 7.b.2 it follows that every sample path $f(t) = Y_t(\omega)$ of the process Y is right continuous on $[0, +\infty)$. It remains to be shown only that $Y_t = X_t$, P-as., for each $t \geq 0$. Let $t \geq 0$ and choose $s_n \in S$, $n \geq 1$, such that $s_n \downarrow t$. Then $X_{s_n} \to Y_t$, P-as.

Now choose any number r such that $s_n \leq r$, for all $n \geq 1$ and set $Z = X_r$. Then, by the martingale property, $X_{s_n} = E(Z \mid \mathcal{F}_{s_n})$, for all $n \geq 1$, and so the family $\{ X_{s_n} \mid n \geq 1 \}$ is uniformly integrable (2.b.13). It follows that $X_{s_n} \to Y_t$ in norm (1.b.4) and so, since the conditional expectation operators are contractions on $L^1(P)$,

$$E(X_{s_n}|\mathcal{F}_t) \to E(Y_t|\mathcal{F}_t) = Y_t, \text{ in norm, as } n \uparrow \infty.$$

On the other hand $E(X_{s_n}|\mathcal{F}_t) = X_t$, for all $n \geq 1$, by the martingale property. Since a limit in $L^1(P)$-norm is uniquely determined, it follows that $X_t = Y_t$, P-almost surely. ∎

7.c Convergence theorems.

7.c.0 Submartingale Convergence Theorem. *Assume that the right continuous submartingale (X_t) satisfies $K = \sup_t E(X_t^+) < \infty$. Then*
(i) *$X_\infty = \lim_{t \uparrow \infty} X_t \in \overline{R}$ exists P-as. and satisfies $E(X_\infty^+) < \infty$.*
(ii) *If $E(X_t) > -\infty$, for some t, then $X_\infty \in L^1(P)$.*
(iii) *We have $X_t \leq E(X_\infty|\mathcal{F}_t)$, for all $t \geq 0$, if and only if the family $\{ X_t^+ \mid t \geq 0 \}$ is uniformly integrable.*
(iv) *If (X_t) is uniformly integrable then $X_\infty \in L^1(P)$ and $X_t \to X_\infty$ in $L^1(P)$, as $t \uparrow \infty$.*

Proof. (i) Let $S \subseteq [0, +\infty)$ be a countable dense set. With the notation of the proof of 7.b.0 we set, for real numbers $\alpha < \beta$,

$$U_S(\alpha, \beta) = \sup\{ U_T(\alpha, \beta) \mid T \subseteq S \text{ finite} \}.$$

Since every finite subset $T \subseteq S$ is contained in $S \cap [0, m]$, for some $m \geq 1$, it follows that $U_{S \cap [0,m]}(\alpha, \beta) \uparrow U_S(\alpha, \beta)$, as $m \uparrow \infty$, at each point of Ω. By monotone convergence and 7.b.eq.(2) above, we have

$$E\left(U_S(\alpha, \beta)\right) = \lim_m E\left(U_{S \cap [0,m]}(\alpha, \beta)\right) \leq \frac{K + |\alpha|}{\beta - \alpha} < \infty.$$

In particular $U_S(\alpha, \beta) < \infty$, P-as. Assume now that $\omega \in \Omega$ is such that the sample path $f(t) = X_t(\omega)$ is right continuous but $\lim_{t \uparrow \infty} X_t(\omega)$ does not exist (in $\overline{R}$). Choose real numbers α, β such that $\liminf_{t \uparrow \infty} X_t(\omega) < \alpha < \beta < \limsup_{t \uparrow \infty} X_t(\omega)$. Then the sample path $f(t)$ crosses infinitely often from strictly below α to strictly above β. By right continuity the restriction $f|_S$ crosses infinitely often from below α to above β and this implies that $U_S(\alpha, \beta)(\omega) = \infty$. This is impossible for P-ae. $\omega \in \Omega$ and so the limit $X_\infty(\omega) = \lim_{t \uparrow \infty} X_t(\omega)$ exists in $\overline{R}$, for P-ae. $\omega \in \Omega$. Moreover, using Fatou's lemma, $E(X_\infty^+) = E\left(\liminf_n X_n^+\right) \leq \liminf_n E(X_n^+) \leq K < \infty$.

(ii) Note that $E(X_t) \uparrow$ and that $X_\infty = \lim_n X_n$. If $E(X_t) > -\infty$, for some $t \geq 0$, then $E(X_n) > -\infty$, for some $n \geq 1$, and (ii) now follows from the corresponding result 4.a.3.(ii) in the discrete case.

(iii) Assume first that $X_t \leq E(X_\infty | \mathcal{F}_t)$, for all $t \geq 1$. Then the extended process $(X_t)_{0 \leq t \leq \infty}$ is still a submartingale and hence so is the process $(X_t^+)_{0 \leq t \leq \infty}$ (3.a.0). Consequently
$$0 \leq X_t^+ \leq E(X_\infty^+ | \mathcal{F}_t), \quad t \geq 0.$$
The uniform integrability of the family $\{ X_t^+ \mid t \geq 0 \}$ now follows from the uniform integrability of the family $\{ E_{\mathcal{F}_t}(X_\infty^+) \mid t \geq 0 \}$ (2.b.13).

Conversely, assume that the family $\{ X_t^+ \mid t \geq 0 \}$ is uniformly integrable (and hence L^1-bounded). Then $E(X_\infty^+) < \infty$, according to (i). We must show that $X_t \leq E(X_\infty | \mathcal{F}_t)$; equivalently (since X_t is $\mathcal{F}_t$-measurable),
$$E(X_t 1_A) \leq E(X_\infty 1_A), \quad \forall t \geq 0, A \in \mathcal{F}_0. \tag{0}$$
Fix $r \leq 0$ and set $X_t(r) = X_t \vee r$. Then $(X_t(r))_t$ is a submartingale (3.a.0). Fix $t \geq 0$ and let $A \in \mathcal{F}_t$ and $m \geq t$. Then $E(X_t(r)1_A) \leq E(X_m(r)1_A)$. Letting $m \uparrow \infty$ and observing that the uniform integrability of $\{ X_m^+ \mid m \geq 1 \}$ implies the uniform integrability of $\{ X_m(r) \mid m \geq 1 \}$, we obtain
$$E(X_t(r)1_A) \leq E(X_\infty(r)1_A).$$
Letting $r \downarrow -\infty$ now yields (0), by decreasing convergence. Note that the families $\{ X_t(r) \mid r \leq 0 \}$ and $\{ X_\infty(r) \mid r \leq 0 \}$ are bounded above by the integrable functions X_t^+ respectively X_∞^+.

(iv) Note that $X_t \to X_\infty$ in $L^1(P)$, as $t \uparrow \infty$, if and only if $X_{t_n} \to X_\infty$ in $L^1(P)$, as $n \uparrow \infty$, for each sequence $t_n \uparrow \infty$, and apply 4.a.3.(iv). ∎

Remark. A converse of (iv) such as in 4.a.3 is no longer possible. Consider any martingale $(X_t)_{t \in [0,1)}$ which is not uniformly integrable and satisfies $X_t \leq 0$. Now set $X_t = 0$, for $t \geq 1$. Then $X = (X_t)_{t \geq 0}$ is a submartingale with $X_t \to 0$ in norm, but X is not uniformly integrable. The converse can be established in the martingale case. See 7.c.2.

7.c.1. *The right continuous submartingale $X = (X_t)$ is closeable if and only if the family $\{ X_t^+ \mid t \geq 0 \}$ is uniformly integrable.*

Proof. ($\Rightarrow$) Let Z be a last element for X. Then $E(Z^+) < \infty$ and the extended process $(X_t)_{0 \leq t \leq \infty}$, where $X_\infty = Z$, is still a submartingale. It follows that the process $(X_t^+)_{0 \leq t \leq \infty}$ is a submartingale (3.a.0) and consequently
$$0 \leq X_t^+ \leq E(Z^+ | \mathcal{F}_t), \quad t \geq 0.$$
The uniform integrability of the family $\{ X_t^+ \mid t \geq 0 \}$ now follows from the uniform integrability of the family $\{ E(Z^+ | \mathcal{F}_t) \mid t \geq 0 \}$ (2.b.13).

($\Leftarrow$) If the family $\{ X_t^+ \mid t \geq 0 \}$ is uniformly integrable, then $X_\infty = \lim_{t \uparrow \infty} X_t$ exists almost surely and is a last element for X, according to 7.c.0 (note that $\mathcal{F}_\infty$ contains the null sets by assumption 7.a.0). ∎

Let now (X_t) be a right continuous martingale with $K = \sup_t \|X_t\|_1 < \infty$. Then (X_t) and $(-X_t)$ are right continuous submartingales satisfying $\sup_t E(X_t^+)$, $\sup_t E((-X_t)^+) \leq K < \infty$. An application of 7.c.0 to both submartingales (X_t) and $(-X_t)$ now yields:

7.c.2 Martingale Convergence Theorem. *Let $X = (X_t)_{t \geq 0}$ be a right continuous, L^1-bounded martingale. Then $X_\infty = \lim_{t \uparrow \infty} X_t$ exists P-as. and is an integrable random variable. Moreover the following conditions are equivalent:*

(i) $X_t = E(X_\infty | \mathcal{F}_t)$, for all $t \geq 0$.

(ii) (X_t) is uniformly integrable.

(iii) $X_t \to X_\infty$ in L^1-norm, as $t \uparrow \infty$.

Proof. (i) $\Rightarrow$ (ii): follows from 2.b.13.

(ii) $\Rightarrow$ (iii): Note that $X_t \to X_\infty$ in L^1-norm, as $t \uparrow \infty$, if and only if $X_{t_n} \to X_\infty$ in L^1-norm, as $n \uparrow \infty$, for each sequence $t_n \uparrow \infty$, and use 1.b.4.

(iii) $\Rightarrow$ (i): Assume that $X_t \to X_\infty$ in L^1-norm, as $t \uparrow \infty$. Fix $t \geq 0$. We wish to show that $X_t = E(X_\infty | \mathcal{F}_t)$; equivalently (since X_t is $\mathcal{F}_t$-measurable), $E(X_t 1_A) = E(X_\infty 1_A)$, for all sets $A \in \mathcal{F}_t$.

Let A be such a set. Then $E(X_t 1_A) = E(X_n 1_A)$, for all $n \geq t$, by the martingale property. Let $n \uparrow \infty$. Then $E(X_n 1_A) \to E(X_\infty 1_A)$, by the norm convergence $X_n \to X_\infty$. It follows that $E(X_t 1_A) = E(X_\infty 1_A)$. ∎

7.c.3 Corollary. *Let $Z \in L^1(P)$ and let $X = (X_t)$ be a right continuous version of the martingale $E(Z|\mathcal{F}_t)$, $t \geq 0$. Then $X_t \to E(Z|\mathcal{F}_\infty)$, as $t \uparrow \infty$, almost surely and in L^1.*

Proof. The martingale X_t is right continuous and uniformly integrable. According to 7.c.2, $X_t \to X_\infty$, $t \uparrow \infty$, P-as. and in norm, for some integrable random variable X_∞ satisfying

$$E(Z|\mathcal{F}_t) = X_t = E(X_\infty | \mathcal{F}_t), \quad t \geq 0. \tag{1}$$

In fact we can take $X_\infty = \limsup_n X_n$, which is defined everywhere and $\mathcal{F}_\infty$-measurable. It remains to be shown that $X_\infty = E(Z|\mathcal{F}_\infty)$. According to 2.b.4 it will now suffice to show that $E(X_\infty 1_A) = E(Z 1_A)$, for all sets A in some π-system $\mathcal{P}$ which generates the σ-field $\mathcal{F}_\infty$. From (1) it follows easily that the π-system $\mathcal{P} = \bigcup_{t \geq 0} \mathcal{F}_t$ has this property. ∎

7.c.4 Corollary. *For a right continuous martingale $X = (X_t)_{t \geq 0}$ the following conditions are equivalent:*

(i) X is closeable.

(ii) X is uniformly integrable.

(iii) $X_t \to Z$ in L^1-norm, as $t \uparrow \infty$, for some integrable random variable Z.

Proof. (i) $\Rightarrow$ (ii): If $X_\infty \in L^1(P)$ is a last element for X, then $X_t = E(X_\infty | \mathcal{F}_t)$, for all $t \geq 0$, and the uniform integrability of X follows from 2.b.13.

(ii) $\Rightarrow$ (iii): follows from 7.c.2.

(iii) $\Rightarrow$ (i): Assume that $X_t \to Z \in L^1(P)$ in L^1-norm, as $t \uparrow \infty$. We claim that $X_\infty = E(Z|\mathcal{F}_\infty)$ is a last element for X. Since X_∞ is $\mathcal{F}_\infty$-measurable and satisfies $E(X_\infty | \mathcal{F}_t) = E(Z|\mathcal{F}_t)$, $t \geq 0$, it will suffice to show that $X_t = E(Z|\mathcal{F}_t)$, $t \geq 0$. The proof is identical to the proof of (iii) $\Rightarrow$ (i) in theorem 7.c.2. ∎

7.d Optional Sampling Theorem. Let us now extend the discrete parameter Optional Sampling Theorem 5.b.2 to the case of a continuous parameter.

7.d.0 Optional Sampling Theorem. *Let $(X_t)_{0 \le t \le \infty}$ be a right continuous, closed submartingale. Then we have $E(X_S^+), E(X_T^+) < \infty$ and*

$$X_S \le E(X_T | \mathcal{F}_S) \tag{0}$$

for all optional times $S \le T$ (not necessarily finitely valued).

Remark. A similar statement holds for closed supermartingales (the inequality in (0) is reversed) and closed martingales (with equality in (0)).

Proof. Let S, T be optional times satisfying $S \le T$.
(i) Assume first that $E(X_0) > -\infty$ (equivalently that $(X_t) \subseteq L^1(P)$). The discretization lemma yields optional times $S_n, T_n : \Omega \to \{ k2^{-n} \mid k \ge 0 \} \cup \{\infty\}$ which satisfy

$$S_n \le T_n, \quad S_n \downarrow S \quad \text{and} \quad T_n \downarrow T.$$

By the special nature of the range of S_n, T_n, the variables X_{S_n}, X_{T_n} can be viewed as samplings of the closed submartingale sequence $(X_{k2^{-n}})_{0 \le k \le \infty}$. Thus the discrete case 5.b.2 applies and shows that $E(X_{S_n}^+), E(X_{T_n}^+) < \infty$ and

$$X_{S_n} \le E(X_{T_n} | \mathcal{F}_{S_n}), \quad \forall n \ge 1. \tag{1}$$

Moreover we have $\mathcal{F}_{S_n} \downarrow \mathcal{F}_S$, by right continuity of the filtration $(\mathcal{F}_t)$ (7.a.3.(f)) as well as $X_{S_n} \to X_S$ and $X_{T_n} \to X_T$, almost surely, by right continuity of X. To pass to the limit as $n \uparrow \infty$ in (1) we need L^1-convergence (4.c.1) which follows from almost sure convergence if we can show that the sequences $(X_{S_n}), (X_{T_n})$ are uniformly integrable.

Note first that the discrete Optional Sampling Theorem 5.b.2 applied to the closed submartingale sequence $(X_{k2^{-n}})_{0 \le k \le \infty}$ and optional times $0 \le S_n$ implies that $E(X_{S_n}) \ge E(X_0) > -\infty$. Moreover the filtration $(\mathcal{F}_{S_n})$ is nonincreasing and the inequality $S_{n+1} \le S_n$ and a similar application of 5.b.2 implies that

$$X_{S_{n+1}} \le E(X_{S_n} | \mathcal{F}_{S_{n+1}}).$$

Thus the sequence (X_{S_n}) is a reversed submartingale with $E(X_{S_n}) \ge E(X_0) > -\infty$. According to 4.b.0 this implies that the sequence (X_{S_n}) is uniformly integrable and the same is true of the sequence (X_{T_n}). Consequently the pointwise convergence $X_{S_n} \to X_S$ and $X_{T_n} \to X_T$ implies that $X_S, X_T \in L^1(P)$ and $X_{S_n} \to X_S$ and $X_{T_n} \to X_T$ in $L^1(P)$. It follows that $E(X_{T_n} | \mathcal{F}_{S_n}) \to E(X_T | \mathcal{F}_S)$ in $L^1(P)$ also (4.c.1) and so, upon passing to a suitable subsequence, almost surely. Thus, letting $n \uparrow \infty$, (1) implies that $X_S \le E(X_T | \mathcal{F}_S)$, as desired.

(ii) In the general case let $m \leq 0$ be any integer and set $X_t(m) = X_t \vee m$, $t \geq 0$. Then $(X_t(m))_t$ is a right continuous submartingale with $E(X_0(m)) \geq m > -\infty$. Thus, according to (i), $X_T \vee m \in L^1(P)$ and

$$X_S \leq X_S \vee m \leq E(X_T \vee m \mid \mathcal{F}_S). \tag{2}$$

Since $X_T^+ \leq (X_T \vee m)^+$, it follows that $E(X_T^+) < \infty$. Likewise $E(X_S^+) < \infty$. Moreover the random variables $X_T \vee m$, $m \leq 0$, are bounded above by the integrable random variable X_T^+. Now let $m \downarrow -\infty$. The Monotone Convergence Theorem for conditional expectations (2.b.6) yields $E(X_T \vee m \mid \mathcal{F}_S) \downarrow E(X_T \mid \mathcal{F}_S)$, P-as., and so (0) follows from (2). ∎

Remarks. (a) If the right continuous submartingale $X = (X_t)_{0 \leq t < \infty}$ is not closed, then it is closeable if and only if the family $\{ X_t^+ \mid t \geq 0 \}$ is uniformly integrable. In this case the limit $X_\infty = \lim_{t \uparrow \infty} X_t$ exists P-as. and is a last element for the submartingale X (note that $\mathcal{F}_\infty$ contains the null sets by assumption 7.a.0).

(b) If the optional times S, T satisfy $S \leq T < \infty$, P-as., then we do not need X_∞ to define X_S, X_T. Nonetheless we need the closeability of the submartingale X for 7.d.0 to hold. See example 3.b.3 in the discrete case. However, if the optional times S, T are bounded, say $S \leq T \leq C < \infty$, the conclusion of 7.d.1 holds for all submartingales $X = (X_t)$. Indeed the closed submartingale $X^C = (X_{t \wedge C})_{0 \leq t \leq +\infty}$ satisfies $X_S = X_S^C$ and $X_T = X_T^C$.

7.d.1 Corollary. *Let $X = (X_t, \mathcal{F}_t)_{0 \leq t \leq \infty}$ be a closed, right continuous submartingale and $(T_t)_{0 \leq t < \infty}$ a nondecreasing family of optional times. Then the family $(X_{T_t}, \mathcal{F}_{T_t})_{0 \leq t < \infty}$ is a submartingale.*

Proof. According to 7.a.1 the process $(X_{T_t})_t$ is $(\mathcal{F}_{T_t})$-adapted. Let $0 \leq s \leq t$. Then, according to 7.d.0, $E(X_{T_s}^+), E(X_{T_t}^+) < +\infty$ and $X_{T_s} \leq E(X_{T_t} \mid \mathcal{F}_{T_s})$, as desired. ∎

Remark. It is assumed that the optional times T_t satisfy $s \leq t \Rightarrow T_s \leq T_t$. If the T_t are individually bounded, that is if $T_t \leq C_t$, P-as., for some constant C_t, then the assumption of closedness of X is not necessary. The proof remains the same. 7.d.1 will be applied primarily to bounded optional times T_t of the form $T_t = t \wedge T$, where T is a fixed optional time.

7.d.2 Corollary. *Let X be a closed, right continuous submartingale and S, T any optional times. Then $E(X_T \mid \mathcal{F}_S) \geq X_{S \wedge T}$, P-as.*

Remark. This generalizes the Optional Sampling Theorem in that it is no longer assumed that $S \leq T$. If the optional times S, T are bounded, then the submartingale X need not be closed. In the martingale case we have equality.

Proof. Since $X_{S \wedge T}$ is $\mathcal{F}_S$-measurable (7.a.5, 7.a.3.(a)) it is to be shown only that

$$E(X_T; D) \geq E(X_{S \wedge T}; D), \quad \text{for all sets } D \in \mathcal{F}_S, \tag{3}$$

(2.b.4). Let $D \in \mathcal{F}_S$. Then $D \cap [T \geq S] \in \mathcal{F}_{S \wedge T}$ (7.a.3.(j)). By the Optional Sampling Theorem, $E(X_T \mid \mathcal{F}_{S \wedge T}) \geq X_{S \wedge T}$ and so

$$E(X_T; D \cap [T \geq S]) \geq E(X_{S \wedge T}; D \cap [T \geq S]). \tag{4}$$

Also
$$E(X_T; D \cap [T < S]) = E(X_{S \wedge T}; D \cap [T < S]), \tag{5}$$

as $X_T = X_{S \wedge T}$ on the set $[T < S]$. Adding (4) and (5) now yields (3). ∎

7.e Continuous time L^p-inequalities. We now turn to the continuous time version of the maximal inequalities of 6.b.2, 6.b.3.

7.e.0. *If $(X_t)_{0 \leq t \leq T}$ is a right continuous process then $S^* := \sup_{0 \leq t \leq T} |X_t|$ is a random variable, that is, measurable.*

Remark. By completeness of $(\Omega, \mathcal{F}, P)$ it will show that $S^* = S_0^*$, P-as., for some random variable S_0^*.

Proof. Let $D \subseteq [0, T]$ be any countable dense subset with $T \in D$. Then $S_0^* := \sup_{t \in D} |X_t|$ is measurable. If the path $t \in [0, T] \to X_t(\omega) \in R$ is right continuous, it follows that $S^*(\omega) = S_0^*(\omega)$. Here we are using that $T \in D$, as right continuity on $[0, T]$ has no implications at the point T. Thus $S_0^* = S^*$, P-as. ∎

7.e.1 L^p-inequalities. *Let $(X_t)_{0 \leq t \leq T}$ be a right continuous martingale and $S^* = \sup_{0 \leq t \leq T} |X_t|$. Then*

(a) $P(S^* \geq \lambda) \leq \lambda^{-p} E(|X_T|^p)$ *for all $\lambda > 0$, $p \geq 1$.*

(b) $\|S^*\|_p \leq \frac{p}{p-1} \|X_T\|_p$, *for all $p > 1$.*

Proof. Let $D \subseteq [0, T]$ be a countable dense subset with $T \in D$. Then $S^* = \sup_{t \in D} |X_t|$, P-as. Enumerate the set D as $D = \{t_n\}_{n \geq 1}$. For $N \geq 1$, set $I_N = \{t_1, t_2, \ldots, t_N, T\}$, $S_N^* = \max_{t \in I_N} |X_t|$ and note that

$$S_N^* \uparrow S^*, \quad P\text{-as., as } N \uparrow \infty. \tag{0}$$

With the understanding that the index t ranges through the elements of I_N in increasing order, the finite sequence $(X_t)_{t \in I_N}$ is a martingale. From 6.b.2 we get

$$P(S_N^* \geq \lambda) \leq \lambda^{-p} E(|X_T|^p), \quad \lambda > 0, \ p \geq 1. \tag{1}$$

Let $N \uparrow \infty$. From (0) it follows that $[S_N^* > \lambda] \uparrow [S^* > \lambda]$ on the complement of a null set. Here the use of strict inequalities is essential. Thus (1) yields

$$P(S^* > \lambda) = \lim_{N \uparrow \infty} P(S_N^* > \lambda) \leq \lambda^{-p} E(|X_T|^p). \tag{2}$$

Choose $\lambda_n > 0$ such that $\lambda_n < \lambda$ and $\lambda_n \uparrow \lambda$, as $n \uparrow \infty$. (2) applied to λ_n instead of λ yields

$$P(S^* \geq \lambda) \leq P(S^* > \lambda_n) \leq (\lambda_n)^{-p} E(|X_T|^p).$$

Letting $n \uparrow \infty$ now yields (a). 6.b.3 applied to the finite martingale sequence $(X_t)_{t \in I_N}$ yields $\|S_N^*\|_p \leq (p/(p-1)) \|X_T\|_p$, for all $N \geq 1$. Let $N \uparrow \infty$. Then $0 \leq S_N^* \uparrow S^*$, P-as., and so $\|S_N^*\|_p \uparrow \|S^*\|_p$. This establishes (b). ∎

8. LOCAL MARTINGALES

Recall that the filtration $(\mathcal{F}_t)_{t\geq0}$ on $(\Omega, \mathcal{F}, P)$ is assumed to be right continuous and augmented and that $\mathcal{F}_\infty = \bigvee_t \mathcal{F}_t \subseteq \mathcal{F}$. The process of localization, described below, is another interesting application of sampling (here stopping) a process by optional times.

8.a Localization. Let $X = X_t(\omega)$ be an adapted process and $T : \Omega \to [0, \infty]$ an optional time (the value ∞ is allowed). The process X^T, defined by $X_t^T := X_{t\wedge T}$, $t \geq 0$, is called the process X *stopped at time T*. If $\omega \in \Omega$ then

$$X_t^T(\omega) = \begin{cases} X_t(\omega), & \text{if } t \leq T(\omega) \\ X_{T(\omega)}(\omega) & \text{if } t > T(\omega) \end{cases},$$

i.e., the path $t \mapsto X_t(\omega)$ is stopped at time $t = T(\omega)$, when it turns constant. This justifies the terminology and shows that the process X^T inherits all continuity properties of the process X: clearly, if the path $t \mapsto X_t(\omega)$ is (left, right) continuous, then the same is true of the path $t \mapsto X_t^T(\omega)$. Note that

$$\left(X^S\right)^T = X^{S\wedge T} \tag{0}$$

and in particular $(X^T)^T = X^T$. Stopping X at a constant time $T = a$ is equivalent to redefining $X_t := X_a$, for $t \geq a$; equivalently, $X_t^a = X_a$, for all $t \geq a$.

8.a.0. *The filtration $(\mathcal{F}_{t\wedge T})_t$ is also right continuous. If X is a right continuous submartingale then the same is true of the process X^T relative to the filtration $(\mathcal{F}_{t\wedge T})_t$.*

Proof. Let us first show that the filtration $(\mathcal{F}_{t\wedge T})_t$ is right continuous. It has to be shown that $\bigcap_{s>t} \mathcal{F}_{s\wedge T} \subseteq \mathcal{F}_{t\wedge T}$, for all $t \geq 0$. Let $t \geq 0$ and $A \in \bigcap_{s>t} \mathcal{F}_{s\wedge T}$. We wish to show that $A \in \mathcal{F}_{t\wedge T}$, that is, $A \cap [t \wedge T < r] \in \mathcal{F}_r$, for all $r \geq 0$.

Let $r \geq 0$. Since $A \in \mathcal{F}_{s\wedge T}$, we have $A \cap [s \wedge T < r] \in \mathcal{F}_r$, for all $s > t$. Choose a sequence (s_n) such that $s_n > t$ and $s_n \downarrow t$, as $n \uparrow \infty$. Then $s_n \wedge T \downarrow t \wedge T$ pointwise and consequently $[s_n \wedge T < r] \uparrow [t \wedge T < r]$, whence $A \cap [s_n \wedge T < r] \uparrow A \cap [t \wedge T < r]$, as $n \uparrow \infty$. Since $A \cap [s_n \wedge T < r] \in \mathcal{F}_r$, for all $n \geq 1$, it follows that $A \cap [t \wedge T < r] \in \mathcal{F}_r$, as desired. This shows the right continuity of the filtration $(\mathcal{F}_{t\wedge T})_t$.

According to 7.a.5 the process $X^T = (X_{t\wedge T})_t$ is adapted to the filtration $(\mathcal{F}_{t\wedge T})_t$. The right continuity is inherited from the process X. The rest now follows from 7.d.1 applied to the bounded optional times $T_t = t \wedge T$. ∎

Let $A \in \mathcal{F}$ be a measurable subset of Ω. If $X = (X_t)$ is a stochastic process we define the stochastic process $Y = 1_A X$ as $Y_t(\omega) = 1_A(\omega)X_t(\omega)$, $t \geq 0$, $\omega \in \Omega$. Thus, multiplication of X by 1_A affects the paths of X in a very simple way: the path $t \mapsto Y_t(\omega)$ agrees with the path $t \mapsto X_t(\omega)$, if $\omega \in A$, and is identically zero otherwise. If X is $(\mathcal{F}_t)$-adapted and $A \in \mathcal{F}_0$, then $Y = 1_A X$ is $(\mathcal{F}_t)$-adapted also. Now let T be an optional time. Then $A = [T > 0] \in \mathcal{F}_0$. Thus, if X is an adapted process, then so is the process $1_{[T>0]}X$.

8.a.1 Definition. *An optional time T is said to reduce the process X, if the process $1_{[T>0]}X_t^T$ is an $(\mathcal{F}_{t\wedge T})$-martingale. The process X is called a local martingale if there exists a sequence (T_n) of optional times such that*
(a) $T_n \uparrow \infty$, P-as., and
(b) T_n reduces X, for each $n \geq 1$.
In this case we will say that the sequence (T_n) reduces X.

Remark. The definition of a local martingale depends on the underlying filtration $(\mathcal{F}_t)$ and we should therefore speak more properly of (F_t)-local martingales. However, unless varying filtrations are involved, we shall stick with the simpler term "local martingale".

If the process X is adapted and right continuous, then the process $1_{[T>0]}X_t^T$ is adapted to the filtration $(\mathcal{F}_{t\wedge T})$ (7.a.5). We use this filtration rather than $(\mathcal{F}_t)$ to facilitate the application of the Optional Sampling Theorem 7.d.0 and streamline the development. However, this is not crucial. See the remark following 8.a.2 below.

The special provision on the set $[T = 0]$ (cutoff to zero) is designed to be able to handle nonintegrable X_0 but is also useful otherwise (see proof of 8.a.5 below). If X_0 is integrable, then T reduces X if and only if X_t^T is a martingale (see 8.a.2.(b) below), that is the factor $1_{[T>0]}$ can be dropped in definition 8.a.1.

Assume that X is right continuous and let (T_n) be a reducing sequence of optional times for X. Fix $t \geq 0$. Then $1_{[T_n>0]}X_t^{T_n}$ is $\mathcal{F}_t$-measurable, for all $n \geq 1$ (7.a.5), and $1_{[T_n>0]}X_t^{T_n} \to X_t$, P-as., as $n \uparrow \infty$. It follows that X_t is $\mathcal{F}_t$-measurable. Thus a right continuous local martingale is automatically $(\mathcal{F}_t)$-adapted.

If X is a martingale, then $E(|X_t|) < \infty$ and it follows that $|X_t| < \infty$, P-as., for each $t \geq 0$. It is now easy to see that local martingales have the same property. In consequence local martingales X, Y can be added by means of $(X + Y)_t = X_t + Y_t$ and are easily seen to form a vector space. We will see below that this vector space is not closed under multiplication. This will be the starting point of important developments.

8.a.2. *Let X_t, Y_t be right continuous, adapted processes and S, T optional times.*
(a) Let $Y_t = X_t^T$ or $Y_t = 1_{[T>0]}X_t^T$. Then Y_t is an $(\mathcal{F}_{t\wedge T})$-martingale if and only if it is an $(\mathcal{F}_t)$-martingale.
(b) If X is an $(\mathcal{F}_t)$-martingale, then so are X_t^T and $1_A X$, for each set $A \in \mathcal{F}_0$. In particular X is a local martingale.
(c) If X is a local martingale, then so are X^T, $1_A X$ and $Y_t = X_t - X_0$, for each set $A \in \mathcal{F}_0$.
(d) If X_t^T is a martingale, then T reduces X. Conversely, if X_0 is integrable and T reduces X, then X_t^T is a martingale.
(e) If T reduces X and $S \leq T$, then S reduces X.
(f) Let X be a local martingale. Then there exists a reducing sequence (T_n) for X such that $T_n \uparrow \infty$ at each point of Ω and $(1_{[T_n>0]}X_t^{T_n})_t$ is a uniformly integrable martingale, for each $n \geq 1$.

Remark. Assume that X is right continuous and adapted. From 7.a.1 it follows that the process X_t^T is $(\mathcal{F}_{t\wedge T})$-adapted and hence so is $Y_t = 1_{[T>0]}X_t^T$. Applying

(a) to this process, we see that it is irrelevant whether we use the filtration $(\mathcal{F}_{t \wedge T})$ or the filtration $(\mathcal{F}_t)$ in definition 8.a.1.

Proof. (a) ($\Leftarrow$) The filtration $(\mathcal{F}_{t \wedge T})_t$ satisfies $\mathcal{F}_{t \wedge T} \subseteq \mathcal{F}_t$, for all $t \geq 0$. However, if Y_t is a martingale with respect to the filtration $(\mathcal{F}_t)$, then it is also a martingale with respect to any filtration $(\mathcal{G}_t)$ which satisfies $\mathcal{G}_t \subseteq \mathcal{F}_t$, $t \geq 0$, and to which it is adapted. To see this, note that for $0 \leq s < t$ the conditional expectation $E(Y_t | \mathcal{F}_s) = Y_s$ is in fact $\mathcal{G}_s$-measurable and so $Y_s = E(Y_t | \mathcal{F}_s) = E(Y_t \mid \mathcal{G}_s)$, as desired.

($\Rightarrow$) Assume now that Y_t is a martingale relative to the filtration $(\mathcal{F}_{t \wedge T})_t$. To get to the larger filtration $(\mathcal{F}_t)$ we must show that

$$E(Y_t; A) = E(Y_s; A), \quad 0 \leq s \leq t, \tag{1}$$

for all sets $A \in \mathcal{F}_s$, and this is known to be true for all sets $A \in \mathcal{F}_{s \wedge T}$. Assume that $0 \leq s \leq t$ and let $A \in \mathcal{F}_s$. Split the set A as $A = (A \cap [T \leq s]) \cup (A \cap [T > s])$. The set $B = A \cap [T > s]$ is in $\mathcal{F}_{s \wedge T}$ (7.a.3.(j),(d)) and so

$$E(Y_t; A \cap [T > s]) = E(Y_s; A \cap [T > s]). \tag{2}$$

On the set $A \cap [T \leq s]$ we have $X_{t \wedge T} = X_T = X_{s \wedge T}$ and so $Y_t = Y_s$. Thus

$$E(Y_t; A \cap [T \leq s]) = E(Y_s; A \cap [T \leq s]). \tag{3}$$

Adding (2) and (3) now yields (1).

(b)   Let X be an $(\mathcal{F}_t)$-martingale. Then, by 7.d.1, X_t^T is an $(\mathcal{F}_{t \wedge T})$-martingale. From (a) it follows that it is an $(\mathcal{F}_t)$-martingale. Now let $A \in \mathcal{F}_0$. The process $Y = 1_A X$ is defined by $Y_t(\omega) = 1_A(\omega) X_t(\omega)$. Thus the integrability of Y_t follows from the integrability of X_t. Let $0 \leq s < t$. Since the function 1_A is bounded and $\mathcal{F}_s$-measurable, we have $E(Y_t | \mathcal{F}_s) = E(1_A X_t | \mathcal{F}_s) = 1_A E(X_t | \mathcal{F}_s) = 1_A X_s = Y_s$ (2.b.10). Thus Y_t is an $(\mathcal{F}_t)$-martingale.

(c)   Let (T_n) be a reducing sequence of optional times for X. Fix $n \geq 1$. Using (a), $1_{[T_n > 0]} X^{T_n}$ is an $(\mathcal{F}_t)$-martingale. In particular $1_{[T_n > 0]} X_0 = 1_{[T_n > 0]} X_0^{T_n} \in L^1(P)$. Thus $1_{[T_n > 0]} Y_t^{T_n} = 1_{[T_n > 0]} X_t^{T_n} - 1_{[T_n > 0]} X_0$ is a martingale (indexed by t) also. Consequently the sequence (T_n) reduces Y.

Likewise, using (c), $1_{[T_n > 0]} (X^T)^{T_n} = (1_{[T_n > 0]} X^{T_n})^T$ is an $(\mathcal{F}_t)$-martingale. Thus the sequence (T_n) reduces X^T.

Now let $A \in \mathcal{F}_0$. For each optional time T we have $(1_A X)^T = 1_A X^T$ and so $1_{[T_n > 0]} (1_A X)^{T_n} = 1_A \left(1_{[T_n > 0]} X^{T_n} \right)$ which is an $(\mathcal{F}_t)$-martingale, according to (c). Thus the sequence (T_n) reduces $1_A X$ as well.

(d)   If X_t^T is a martingale, then so is $1_{[T > 0]} X_t^T$, that is, T reduces X. Conversely assume that X_0 is integrable and T reduces X, that is, $1_{[T > 0]} X_t^T$ is a martingale. Then $X_t^T = 1_{[T > 0]} X_t^T + 1_{[T = 0]} X_t^T = 1_{[T > 0]} X_t^T + 1_{[T = 0]} X_0$ is a martingale also.

(e)   Assume that T reduces X and $S \leq T$. Then $M_t = 1_{[T>0]} X_{t \wedge T}$ is a martingale and $[S > 0] \subseteq [T > 0]$ and thus $1_{[S>0]} = 1_{[S>0]} 1_{[T>0]}$. By 7.d.1 applied to the optional times $T_t = t \wedge S$ and (c), $1_{[S>0]} X_{t \wedge S} = 1_{[S>0]} M_{t \wedge S}$ is a martingale, that is, S reduces X.

(f)   Let (R_n) be a reducing sequence for X and choose a null set $N \subseteq \Omega$ such that $T_n(\omega) \uparrow \infty$, for all $\omega \in N^c$. Set $S_n = n 1_N + R_n 1_{N^c}$. Then $S_n \uparrow \infty$ at each point of Ω and $S_n = R_n$, P-as. Since the filtration $(\mathcal{F}_t)$ is augmented, it follows that S_n is an optional time also. Let $n \geq 1$. Then $1_{[S_n>0]} X_t^{S_n} = 1_{[R_n>0]} X_t^{R_n}$, P-as., for each $t \geq 0$, and it follows that $1_{[S_n>0]} X_t^{S_n}$ is a martingale. Thus (S_n) reduces X.

   Now set $T_n = S_n \wedge n$. Then $T_n \uparrow \infty$ everywhere. According to (e), the sequence (T_n) reduces X. Fix $n \geq 1$. Then $Y_t = 1_{[S_n>0]} X_t^{S_n}$ is a martingale. We can write $1_{[T_n>0]} X_t^{T_n} = 1_{[T_n>0]} Y_{t \wedge n}$. Since $Y_{t \wedge n}$ is a martingale with last element Y_n and hence uniformly integrable, the same is true of $1_{[T_n>0]} X_t^{T_n}$. ∎

Remark. Local martingales are considerably more general than martingales. If integrability is understood in the extremely strong form of uniform integrability in 8.a.3 below, then a local martingale is a martingale if and only if it is integrable. However, weaker forms of integrability do not suffice. A local martingale can be contained in $L^p(P)$ for each $p > 1$ without being a martingale. It can be uniformly integrable without being a martingale. See example 8.a.6 below. The correct integrability condition which forces the martingale property on a local martingale is given as follows:

   For each $a > 0$ let $\mathcal{T}_a$ denote the class of all optional times $T : \Omega \to [0, a]$. The right continuous and adapted process X is said to be of *class DL*, if the family of random variables $(X_T)_{T \in \mathcal{T}_a}$ is uniformly integrable, for each $a > 0$. This is a strengthening of the uniform integrability of the families $(X_t)_{t \in [0,a]}$, $a > 0$.

8.a.3. *A right continuous local martingale is a martingale if and only if it is of class DL.*

Proof. Let $X = (X_t)$ be a right continuous martingale. If $T \in \mathcal{T}_a$ is any optional time, then the Optional Sampling Theorem 7.d.0 applied to the bounded optional times $T \leq a$ yields $X_T = E(X_a | \mathcal{F}_T)$. The uniform integrability of the family $\{ X_T \mid T \in \mathcal{T}_a \}$ now follows from 2.b.13. Thus X is of class DL.

   Conversely, let X_t be a right continuous local martingale which is of class DL and (T_n) a reducing sequence for X. For $n \geq 1$ set $Y_t^n = 1_{[T_n>0]} X_{t \wedge T_n}$. Using 8.a.2.(a), $(Y_t^n)_t$ is an $(\mathcal{F}_t)$-martingale, for each $n \geq 1$. Fix $n \geq 1$ and $0 \leq s < t$. Then

$$Y_s^n = E(Y_t^n | \mathcal{F}_s). \qquad (4)$$

Let $n \uparrow \infty$. Then $Y_s^n \to X_s$ and $Y_t^n \to X_t$ almost surely. Since X is of class DL, the sequences $\left(Y_s^n\right)_n$, $\left(Y_t^n\right)_n$ are uniformly integrable. Consequently $X_s, X_t \in L^1(P)$ and $Y_s^n \to X_s$ and $Y_t^n \to X_t$ in norm. Thus $E(Y_t^n | \mathcal{F}_s) \to E(X_t | \mathcal{F}_s)$ in norm and it follows from (4) that $X_s = E(X_t | \mathcal{F}_s)$. ∎

Remark. For $a > 0$ set $S_a^* = \sup_{t \leq a} |X_t|$. If $E(S_a^*) < \infty$, for each $a > 0$, then X is of class DL, as $0 \leq |X_T| \leq S_a^*$, for all optional times $T \in \mathcal{T}_a$. Especially if X is uniformly bounded, then X is of class DL.

8.a.4. *If the right continuous local martingale X is uniformly bounded or satisfies $E\left(\sup_{t\le a}|X_t|\right) < \infty$, for each $a > 0$, then it is a martingale.* ∎

The next fact shows that there is always a canonical reducing sequence for a *continuous* local martingale:

8.a.5. *Let X be a continuous local martingale. Then $T_n := \inf\{\, t \ge 0 \mid |X_t| > n \,\}$ defines a reducing sequence (T_n) of optional times for X. In fact, any sequence (S_n) of optional times which satisfies $S_n \uparrow \infty$ and $S_n \le T_n$ reduces X and satisfies*

$$\left|1_{[S_n>0]}X_t^{S_n}\right| \le n. \tag{5}$$

Thus the martingale $\left(1_{[S_n>0]}X_t^{S_n}\right)_t$ is uniformly bounded and hence uniformly integrable, for each $n \ge 1$.

Proof. Let us first show that T_n is an optional time, for each $n \ge 1$. Let $t \ge 0$. Then $T_n(\omega) < t$ if and only if $|X_q(\omega)| > n$, for some rational number $q < t$. Thus $[T_n < t] = \bigcup\{\, [|X_q| > n] \mid q \in Q \cap [0,t) \,\} \in \mathcal{F}_t$.

Let now (S_n) be any sequence of optional times such that $S_n \le T_n$, for all $n \ge 1$. Fix $n \ge 1$. The left continuity of the process X implies that $|X_t^{S_n}| \le n$, as., on the set $[T_n > 0]$ and hence on its subset $[S_n > 0]$, which implies (5). According to 8.a.2.(c) the process $(1_{[S_n>0]}X_t^{S_n})_t$ is a local martingale, which is uniformly bounded and hence is a martingale. Thus the sequence (S_n) reduces X. ∎

8.a.6 Example. Our example uses Brownian motions which are introduced in chapter II. Here we need only the following properties: if B is a Brownian motion in R^2 starting at x, then the distribution of B_t has density

$$h(t,y) = (2\pi t)^{-1}e^{-\|x-y\|^2/2t}, \quad y \in R^2, \tag{6}$$

and the process $X_t = \log\|B_t\|$ is a local martingale (III.3.g below). We will see that this process is highly integrable in the sense that $X_t \in L^p(P)$, for all $p \ge 1$, $t \ge 0$ and yet $E(X_t) \to \infty$, as $t \uparrow \infty$. Thus X_t does not have a constant mean and hence cannot be a martingale. Indeed, using the density (6),

$$E(X_t) = E\left(\log\|B_t\|\right) = (2\pi t)^{-1}\int_{R^2} h(t,y)\log\|y\|\,dy, \tag{7}$$

if this latter integral exists. Integration by parts shows that $\int_0^1 r\log(r)dr > -\infty$. Integration using polar coordinates now shows that the function $f(y) = \log\|y\|$ is integrable near zero:

$$\int_{B_1(0)} \log\|y\|dy = 2\pi \int_0^1 r\log(r)dr > -\infty.$$

As the exponential kills off everything near infinity, the integral on the right of (7) exists and is finite. Fix $n \geq 1$ and write $B_n(0) = \{ y \mid \|y\| \leq n \}$. Since $log\|y\| \geq log(n)$ on $R^2 \setminus B_n(0)$, we have

$$\int_{R^2} h(t,y)log\|y\| \, dy = \int_{R^2 \setminus B_n(0)} h(t,y)log\|y\| \, dy + \int_{B_n(0)} h(t,y)log\|y\| \, dy$$

$$\geq log(n) \int_{R^2 \setminus B_n(0)} h(t,y) dy + \int_{B_n(0)} h(t,y)log\|y\| \, dy.$$

Multiply with $(2\pi t)^{-1}$ and let $t \uparrow \infty$. The second integral converges to zero, by the integrability of $log\|y\|$ near zero and the boundedness $0 \leq h(t,y) = e^{-\|x-y\|^2/2t} \leq 1$. Thus

$$\liminf_{t \uparrow \infty} E(X_t) = \liminf_{t \uparrow \infty} \frac{1}{2\pi t} \int_{R^2} h(t,y)log\|y\| \, dy$$

$$\geq log(n) \liminf_{t \uparrow \infty} \frac{1}{2\pi t} \int_{R^2 \setminus B_n(0)} h(t,y) dy$$

$$= log(n) \liminf_{t \uparrow \infty} \frac{1}{2\pi t} \int_{R^2} h(t,y) dy$$

$$= log(n) \liminf_{t \uparrow \infty} \frac{1}{2\pi t} \int_{R^2} e^{-\|y\|^2/2t} \, dy.$$

Integration using polar coordinates yields

$$\int_{R^2} e^{-\|y\|^2/2t} \, dy = 2\pi \int_0^\infty r e^{-r^2/2t} dr = 2\pi t.$$

Thus $\liminf_{t \uparrow \infty} E(X_t) \geq log(n)$ and this is true for all $n \geq 1$. It follows that $\liminf_{t \uparrow \infty} E(X_t) = +\infty$, that is, $E(X_t) \to +\infty$, as $t \uparrow \infty$. Similarly, for each $p \geq 1$ and $0 < \epsilon \leq t \leq a$ we have

$$E\left(|X_t|^p\right) = E\left(\left|log\|B_t\|\right|^p\right) = (2\pi t)^{-1} \int_{R^2} e^{-\|x-y\|^2/2t} |log(\|y\|)|^p \, dy$$

$$\leq (2\pi \epsilon)^{-1} \int_{R^2} e^{-\|x-y\|^2/2a} |log(\|y\|)|^p \, dy.$$

The last integral is finite (integrability of $|log(\|y\|)|^p$ near zero) and independent of t. It follows that $(X_t)_{t \in [\epsilon,a]} \subseteq L^p(P)$ is bounded and hence uniformly integrable (1.b.7). If a is chosen large enough the mean $E(X_t)$ will not be constant on the interval $[0,a]$.

8.a.7. *Let X_t be a nonnegative local martingale. Then X is a supermartingale. Consequently X is a martingale if and only if it has a constant mean.*

Proof. Since $E(X_t^-) = 0$ we have to show only that $E(X_t|\mathcal{F}_s) \leq X_s$, for all $0 \leq s \leq t$. Consider such s and t and let (T_n) be a reducing sequence of optional times for X. Then $T_n \uparrow \infty$, P-as., as $n \uparrow \infty$, and $1_{[T_n>0]}X_{t \wedge T_n}$ is a martingale (indexed by t), for each $n \geq 1$. Fix such n. Then

$$E\big(1_{[T_n>0]}X_{t \wedge T_n}|\mathcal{F}_s\big) = 1_{[T_n>0]}X_{s \wedge T_n}. \tag{8}$$

Letting $n \uparrow \infty$ and using Fatou's Lemma I.2.b.8 for conditional expectations (with $h = 0$), we obtain

$$E(X_t|\mathcal{F}_s) = E\left(\liminf_n 1_{[T_n>0]}X_{t \wedge T_n} \mid \mathcal{F}_s\right) \leq \liminf_n E\left(1_{[T_n>0]}X_{t \wedge T_n} \mid \mathcal{F}_s\right)$$
$$= \liminf_n 1_{[T_n>0]}X_{s \wedge T_n} = X_s.$$

Thus X is a supermartingale. If X is a martingale, then it has a constant mean. Assume conversely that $t \geq 0 \mapsto E(X_t)$ is constant. By the supermartingale property we have $E(X_t|\mathcal{F}_s) \leq X_s$, P-as., for all $0 \leq s < t$. If X were not a martingale we would have $P\left(E(X_t|\mathcal{F}_s) < X_s\right) > 0$, for some $0 \leq s < t$. Integration over Ω then yields $E(X_t) = E\left(E(X_t|\mathcal{F}_s)\right) < E(X_s)$ in contradiction to the constancy of the mean. ∎

Remark. If $X_0 \in L^1(P)$ then the inequality $E(X_t|\mathcal{F}_0) \leq X_0$ integrated over Ω yields $E(X_t) \leq E(X_0) < \infty$. Combined with $X_t \geq 0$ this shows that $X_t \in L^1(P)$, for all $t \geq 0$.

8.b Bayes Theorem. The Bayes theorem handles the elementary aspects of changing from the probability measure P to another probability measure Q. Assume that $(\Omega, \mathcal{F}, (\mathcal{F}_t)_{t \geq 0}, P)$ is a filtered probability space, Q another probability measure on $\mathcal{F}$ and let $P_t = P|\mathcal{F}_t$ and $Q_t = Q|\mathcal{F}_t$ denote the restrictions of P and Q to the σ-field $\mathcal{F}_t$, for all $t \geq 0$.

The probability measures P and Q are called $(\mathcal{F}_t)$-*locally equivalent*, if the measures P_t and Q_t on $\mathcal{F}_t$ are equivalent, for each $t \geq 0$. This does not imply that P and Q are equivalent on $\mathcal{F}_\infty$. In fact P and Q can even be mutually singular on $\mathcal{F}_\infty$. Examples will be encountered in III.4.c below. Set

$$M_t = \frac{dQ_t}{dP_t} = \frac{d(Q|\mathcal{F}_t)}{d(P|\mathcal{F}_t)}, \quad t \geq 0.$$

Then, for each $t \geq 0$ and each set $A \in \mathcal{F}_t$, we have $Q(A) = Q_t(A) = E_{Q_t}(1_A) = E_{P_t}(M_t 1_A) = E_P(M_t 1_A)$. The usual extension procedure now implies that

$$E_Q(f) = E_{Q_t}(f) = E_{P_t}(M_t f) = E_P(M_t f), \tag{0}$$

for each nonnegative $\mathcal{F}_t$-measurable function f. Thus, if f is any $\mathcal{F}_t$-measurable function, then $f \in L^1(Q) \iff M_t f \in L^1(P)$ in which case $E_Q(f) = E_P(M_t f)$. The following theorem generalises this relation to conditional expectations:

8.b.0 Bayes Theorem. *Assume that P and Q are locally equivalent. Then*
(a) M_t is a strictly positive P-martingale.
(b) For $0 \le t < T$ and each function $f \in L^1(Q, \mathcal{F}_T)$ we have

$$E_Q\left(f|\mathcal{F}_t\right) = \frac{E_P\left(M_T f|\mathcal{F}_t\right)}{M_t} = \frac{E_P\left(M_T f|\mathcal{F}_t\right)}{E_P\left(M_T|\mathcal{F}_t\right)}.$$

Proof. (a) Fix $0 \le t < T$. The equivalence of P_t and Q_t on $\mathcal{F}_t$ implies that $M_t = dQ_t/dP_t > 0$, P-as. and $M_t \in L^1(P, \mathcal{F}_t)$, especially M_t is $\mathcal{F}_t$-measurable, by definition of the Radon-Nikodym derivative. Moreover for $A \in \mathcal{F}_t \subseteq \mathcal{F}_T$ we have $E_P(1_A M_t) = Q(A) = E_P(1_A M_T)$ (see (0)). This shows that $M_t = E_P\left(M_T|\mathcal{F}_t\right)$.

(b) Let $0 \le t < T$, $f \in L^1(Q, \mathcal{F}_T)$ and $h = E_Q(f|\mathcal{F}_t)$. We want to show that $M_t h = E_P\left(M_T f|\mathcal{F}_t\right)$. Let $A \in \mathcal{F}_t$ and note that h is $\mathcal{F}_t$-measurable and satisfies $E_Q(1_A h) = E_Q(1_A f)$. Using the $\mathcal{F}_t$-measurability of $1_A h$, the $\mathcal{F}_T$-measurability of $1_A f$ and (0), we can now write this as $E_P(1_A M_t h) = E_P(1_A M_T f)$. Since $M_t h$ is $\mathcal{F}_t$-measurable this implies that $M_t h = E_P\left(M_T f|\mathcal{F}_t\right)$, as desired. ∎

Remark. Recalling that $M_T = dP_T/dQ_T$, (b) can also be written as

$$E_Q\left(f|\mathcal{F}_t\right) = \frac{E_P\left((dQ_T/dP_T)f \mid \mathcal{F}_t\right)}{E_P\left(dQ_T/dP_T \mid \mathcal{F}_t\right)}, \quad \forall\, 0 \le t < T,\ f \in L^1(Q, \mathcal{F}_T).$$

We are mainly interested in the following

8.b.1 Corollary. *The adapted process (X_t) is a Q-martingale (Q-local martingale) if and only if the process $(M_t X_t)$ is a P-martingale (P-local martingale).*

Proof. Regarding the martingale case we have, using 8.b.0.(b),

$$
\begin{aligned}
(X_t) \text{ is a } Q\text{-martingale} \iff & \ X_t \in L^1(Q) \text{ and } X_t = E_Q\left(X_T|\mathcal{F}_t\right),\ \forall\, 0 \le t < T \\
\iff & \ M_t X_t \in L^1(P) \text{ and } M_t X_t = E_P\left(M_T X_T|\mathcal{F}_t\right), \\
& \ \forall\, 0 \le t < T \\
\iff & \ (M_t X_t) \text{ is a } P\text{-martingale.}
\end{aligned}
$$

Turning to the case of local martingales, assume that $X = (X_t)$ is a Q-local martingale and let (T_n) be a reducing sequence of optional times for X such that $T_n \uparrow \infty$ at each point of Ω (8.a.2.(f)). Then $1_{[T_n>0]} X_{t \wedge T_n}$ is a Q-martingale (indexed by t) and so $Y_t = M_t 1_{[T_n>0]} X_{t \wedge T_n}$ a P-martingale and hence so is $Y_t^{T_n} = 1_{[T_n>0]} M_{t \wedge T_n} X_{t \wedge T_n}$, for each $n \ge 1$. Thus (T_n) is a reducing sequence for the process $(M_t X_t)$ with respect to the probability measure P. Consequently $(M_t X_t)$ is a P-local martingale. The converse can be shown similarly or follows from this by interchanging P and Q and observing that $dP_t/dQ_t = M_t^{-1}$. ∎

9. QUADRATIC VARIATION

9.a Square integrable martingales. A martingale (M_t) is called *square integrable* if it satisfies $E(M_t^2) < \infty$, that is, $M_t \in L^2(P)$, for all $t \geq 0$. In this case M_t^2 is a submartingale (3.a.1) and hence the function $t \mapsto E(M_t^2)$ nondecreasing. The martingale M_t is called *L^2-bounded* if it is square integrable and satisfies $\sup_t E(M_t^2) < \infty$. In this case the martingale M_t is uniformly integrable (1.b.7) and consequently has a last element M_∞ which satisfies $M_\infty = \lim_{t \uparrow \infty} M_t$, P-as. (7.c.2). Fatou's lemma now implies that

$$E(M_\infty^2) = E\left(\liminf_n M_n^2\right) \leq \liminf_n E(M_n^2). \tag{0}$$

On the other hand, using Jensen's inequality (2.b.12) for conditional expectations, $M_t^2 = E(M_\infty | \mathcal{F}_t)^2 \leq E(M_\infty^2 | \mathcal{F}_t)$. Integration over Ω yields $E(M_t^2) \leq E(M_\infty^2)$. Combining this with (0), we see that

$$E(M_\infty^2) = \sup_t E(M_t^2) = \lim_{t \uparrow \infty} E(M_t^2), \tag{1}$$

especially $M_\infty \in L^2(\Omega, \mathcal{F}_\infty, P)$. Let $\mathcal{H}^2$ denote the space of all L^2-bounded, right continuous martingales and set

$$\|M\|_2 := \sup_t \|M_t\|_{L^2} = \|M_\infty\|_{L^2}, \quad M \in \mathcal{H}^2.$$

Identifying martingales which are versions of each other, we see that $\|\cdot\|_2$ is a norm on $\mathcal{H}^2$ and the map

$$M \in \mathcal{H}^2 \mapsto M_\infty \in L^2(\Omega, \mathcal{F}_\infty, P)$$

is an isometry. It is also surjective: if $f \in L^2(\Omega, \mathcal{F}_\infty, P)$, then the martingale $M_t = E(f | \mathcal{F}_t)$ has a right continuous version (7.b.3). From Jensen's inequality for conditional expectations, $M_t^2 \leq E(f^2 | \mathcal{F}_t)$. Integrating this over Ω, we obtain $E(M_t^2) \leq E(f^2)$. Taking the sup over all $t \geq 0$, it follows that $\|M\|_2 \leq \|f\|_{L^2} < \infty$. Thus $M \in \mathcal{H}^2$. Moreover $M_\infty = f$, according to 7.c.3. Consequently the space $\mathcal{H}^2$ is isometrically isomorphic to the Hilbert space $L^2(\Omega, \mathcal{F}_\infty, P)$ and so is a Hilbert space itself. It follows that the inner product on $\mathcal{H}^2$ is given by

$$(M, N)_{\mathcal{H}^2} = \left(M_\infty, N_\infty\right)_{L^2} = E[M_\infty N_\infty], \quad M, N \in \mathcal{H}^2.$$

For $M \in \mathcal{H}^2$ set $M_\infty^* = \sup_{t \geq 0} |M_t|$. The right continuity of M implies that M_∞^* is measurable and hence a nonnegative random variable. M_∞^* is called the *maximal function* of the process M. We claim that

$$\|M\|_2 \leq \|M_\infty^*\|_{L^2} \leq 2\|M\|_2. \tag{2}$$

Since $M_t^2 \leq (M_\infty^*)^2$ we have $E[M_t^2] \leq E[(M_\infty^*)^2]$. Taking the sup over all $t \geq 0$ shows the left inequality. Fix $n \geq 1$ and set $M_n^* = \sup_{t \leq n} |M_t|$. By Doob's L^2-inequality (7.e.1.(b)) we have $E[(M_n^*)^2] \leq 4E[M_n^2] \leq 4\|M\|_2^2$. Letting $n \uparrow \infty$ it follows that $E[(M_\infty^*)^2] \leq 4\|M\|_2^2$. The right inequality in (2) follows upon taking square roots.

Consequently, for $M \in \mathcal{H}^2$, the maximal function M_∞^* is square integrable and $\|M\| = \|M_\infty^*\|_{L^2}$ defines an equivalent norm on $\mathcal{H}^2$. However with respect to this norm $\mathcal{H}^2$ is no longer a Hilbert space. Let $\mathbf{H}^2$ be the space of *continuous* L^2-bounded martingales and $\mathbf{H}_0^2 = \{M \in \mathbf{H}^2 \mid M_0 = 0\}$. Clearly $\mathbf{H}_0^2 \subseteq \mathbf{H}^2 \subseteq \mathcal{H}^2$ are subspaces of $\mathcal{H}$.

9.a.0. *The subspaces* $\mathbf{H}^2$, $\mathbf{H}^2_0$ *are closed in* $\mathcal{H}^2$.

Proof. We show closedness in $\mathcal{H}^2$ in the equivalent norm $\|M\| = \|M^*_\infty\|_{L^2}$ on $\mathcal{H}^2$. Let $(M(n)) \subseteq \mathbf{H}^2$, $M \in \mathcal{H}^2$ and assume that $\|M(n)-M\| = \|(M(n)-M)^*_\infty\|_{L^2} \to 0$ as $n \uparrow \infty$. Replacing $M(n)$ with a suitable subsequence if necessary we may assume that $(M(n) - M)^*_\infty \to 0$, P-as., equivalently that $M(n)_t \to M_t$ uniformly in $t \geq 0$ P-as. on Ω (1.a.0,1.a.1). Thus, for P-ae. $\omega \in \Omega$, the path $t \mapsto M_t(\omega)$ is the uniform limit of the continuous paths $t \mapsto M(n)_t(\omega)$, and hence itself continuous. This shows that M is continuous and hence $M \in \mathbf{H}^2$. Thus $\mathbf{H}^2$ is closed in $\mathcal{H}^2$. If in fact $(M(n)) \subseteq \mathbf{H}^2_0$ and so $M(n)_0 = 0$, for all $n \geq 1$, then $M_0 = \lim_n M(n)_0 = 0$ and so $M \in \mathbf{H}^2_0$. It follows that $\mathbf{H}^2_0$ is closed in $\mathcal{H}^2$. ∎

A martingale M_t will be called *uniformly bounded*, if it satisfies $|M_t| \leq K < \infty$ P-as., for all $t \geq 0$ and some constant K. Clearly such a martingale is in $\mathcal{H}^2$ with $\|M\|_2 \leq K$.

9.b Quadratic variation. A process A will be called a *bounded variation process*, if the path $t \geq 0 \mapsto A_t(\omega)$ is of bounded variation on finite intervals, for P-ae. $\omega \in \Omega$. Clearly each increasing process A has this property.

Consider a continuous, square integrable martingale M. Then M_t^2 is a submartingale but it is not a martingale if it is not constant in time (seen below). It will now be seen that M_t^2 differs from a martingale by a uniquely determined continuous, increasing process A_t with $A_0 = 0$, called the *quadratic variation of* M. The root of much that is to follow is the following simple observation:

9.b.0. *Let M_t be a square integrable martingale. Then*

$$E\left[(M_t - M_s)^2 \middle| \mathcal{F}_a\right] = E[M_t^2 - M_s^2 | \mathcal{F}_a], \quad 0 \leq a \leq s \leq t. \tag{0}$$

Proof. Let $0 \leq a \leq s \leq t$. Then $E[M_s(M_t - M_s)|\mathcal{F}_s] = M_s E[M_t - M_s|\mathcal{F}_s] = 0$ (2.b.10). Conditioning on $\mathcal{F}_a$, we obtain $E[M_s(M_t - M_s)|\mathcal{F}_a] = 0$. Observing that $(M_t^2 - M_s^2) - (M_t - M_s)^2 = 2M_s(M_t - M_s)$, equation (0) follows by taking the conditional expectation. ∎

Remark. Let $0 \leq a \leq b \leq s \leq t$. As above one shows that $E[M_a(M_t - M_s)|\mathcal{F}_a] = 0$. Integrating this over the set Ω we obtain $E\left[M_a(M_t - M_s)\right] = 0$, i.e., $M_a \perp M_t - M_s$ in the Hilbert space $L^2(P)$. It follows that $M_b - M_a \perp M_t - M_s$. Unsurprisingly this relation is referred to as the *orthogonality of martingale increments*.

9.b.1. *Assume that the continuous local martingale M is also a bounded variation process. Then M is constant (in time), that is, $M_t = M_0$, P-as., for each $t > 0$.*

Proof. Replacing M_t with the continuous local martingale $M_t - M_0$ we may assume that $M_0 = 0$ and must prove that $M_t = 0$, P-as., for each $t \geq 0$. Let $V_t(\omega)$ denote the total variation of the path $s \mapsto M_s(\omega)$ on the interval $[0, t]$. It is known that the increasing function $t \mapsto V_t(\omega)$ is continuous, whenever the path $t \mapsto M_t(\omega)$ is continuous and of bounded variation on finite intervals, and so for P-ae. $\omega \in \Omega$.

(A)   Assume first that M is a martingale satisfying $|V_t| \leq K$, P-as., for all $t \geq 0$ and some constant K. Because of $M_0 = 0$ we have $|M_t| = |M_t - M_0| \leq V_t \leq K$, P-as., for all $t \geq 0$, as well.

Fix $t > 0$ and let $\Delta = \{0 = t_0 < \ldots < t_n = t\}$ be any partition of the interval $[0, t]$. Set $\|\Delta\| = max_{j<n}|t_{j+1} - t_j|$. Then, using 9.b.0 integrated over Ω,

$$E\big[M_t^2\big] = E\big[M_t^2 - M_0^2\big] = E\left[\sum_{j=1}^n (M_{t_j}^2 - M_{t_{j-1}}^2)\right] = E\left[\sum_{j=1}^n (M_{t_j} - M_{t_{j-1}})^2\right]$$
$$\leq E\left[V_t \cdot \sup_{1 \leq j \leq n}|M_{t_j} - M_{t_{j-1}}|\right].$$

Now let $\|\Delta\| \to 0$. Then the integrand $V_t \sup_j |M_{t_j} - M_{t_{j-1}}|$ converges to zero at all points $\omega \in \Omega$ for which $V_t(\omega) < \infty$ and the path $s \in [0, t] \mapsto M_t(\omega)$ is continuous (and hence uniformly continuous) on the interval $[0, t]$, and hence at P-ae. point $\omega \in \Omega$. Moreover this integrand is uniformly bounded by the constant $2K^2$. The Dominated Convergence Theorem now shows that

$$E\left[V_t \cdot \sup_j |M_{t_j} - M_{t_{j-1}}|\right] \to 0.$$

Thus $E\big[M_t^2\big] = 0$ and hence $M_t = 0$, P-as., as desired.

(B)   Let now M_t be a continuous local martingale as in 9.b.1 and set, for each $n \geq 1$,
$$T_n = \inf\{t \geq 0 \mid V_t > n\} \quad (= \infty \text{ on the set } [V_t \leq n, \forall t \geq 0]).$$

According to 7.a.7, T_n is an optional time. The finiteness of V_t implies that $T_n \uparrow \infty$, P-as., as $n \uparrow \infty$. Fix $n \geq 1$. Then the process $M_t^{T_n}$ is a local martingale with $M_0^{T_n} = 0$ and thus its variation process $V_t(M^{T_n})$ satisfies $|M_t^{T_n}| \leq |V_t(M^{T_n})| \leq n$. Thus $M_t^{T_n}$ is a uniformly bounded local martingale and hence a martingale as in step (A). It follows that $M_t^{T_n} = 0$, P-as., for each $t \geq 0$. Letting $n \uparrow \infty$ it follows that $M_t = 0$, P-as., for each $t \geq 0$. ∎

Corollary 9.b.2. *Let X_t be any process. Then there is at most one continuous bounded variation process A_t such that $A_0 = 0$ and the difference $X_t - A_t$ is a local martingale.*

Proof. If A_t, B_t are continuous bounded variation processes such that $A_0 = B_0 = 0$ and both $X_t - A_t$ and $X_t - B_t$ are local martingales, then by subtraction, $B_t - A_t$ is a continuous local martingale which is also a bounded variation process. By 9.b.1 it follows that $B_t - A_t = B_0 - A_0 = 0$, P-as., for each $t \geq 0$. ∎

The quadratic variation process. Let X be a process and $0 \leq a < b$. For a partition $\Delta = \{ a = t_0 < \ldots < t_n = b \}$ of the interval $[a, b]$ let $\|\Delta\| = max_{j<n} |t_{j+1} - t_j|$ and define the *random variable* $Q_\Delta(X)$ by

$$Q_\Delta(X) = \sum_{j=1}^{n} \left(X_{t_j} - X_{t_{j-1}} \right)^2. \tag{1}$$

More generally, if $\Delta = \{ 0 = t_0 < \ldots < t_n < \ldots \}$ is any partition of the interval $[0, \infty)$ which has only finitely many points in each finite interval, we define the *process* $Q_t^\Delta(X)$ by

$$Q_t^\Delta(X) = (X_t - X_{t_k})^2 + \sum_{j=1}^{k(t)} \left(X_{t_j} - X_{t_{j-1}} \right)^2, \quad t \geq 0, \tag{2}$$

where the index $k(t)$ is defined by $k(t) = max\{ k \geq 0 \mid t_k \leq t \}$. Thus

$$Q_t^\Delta(X) = Q_{\Delta(t)}(X),$$

where $\Delta(t)$ is the partition $\Delta(t) = \left(\Delta \cup \{t\} \right) \cap [0, t]$ of the interval $[0, t]$. If the partition Δ contains the point t, then (2) simplifies to

$$Q_t^\Delta(X) = \sum_{j=1}^{n} \left(X_{t_j} - X_{t_{j-1}} \right)^2, \tag{3}$$

where the index n is defined by $t = t_n$. This is the case in particular if Δ is a partition of the interval $[0, t]$ which can be regarded as a partition of $[0, \infty)$ containing the point t. In this case $Q_t^\Delta(X) = Q_\Delta(X)$.

9.b.3 Theorem. *Let M be a continuous, uniformly bounded martingale. Then there exists a unique continuous bounded variation process A such that $A_0 = 0$ and the difference $M_t^2 - A_t$ is a martingale. The process A is called the quadratic variation of M, denoted $\langle M \rangle$. The quadratic variation $\langle M \rangle$ is an adapted and increasing process and we have $\langle M \rangle_t \in L^2(P)$ and*

$$\langle M \rangle_t = \lim_{\|\Delta\| \to 0} Q_\Delta(M) \text{ in } L^2(P), \quad \text{for each } t \geq 0, \tag{4}$$

where the limit is taken over all partitions Δ of the interval $[0, t]$.

Proof. The uniqueness of the process A has already been dealt with in 9.b.2. If $M_t^2 - A_t$ is a martingale and hence adapted, the process $A_t = M_t^2 - (M_t^2 - A_t)$ is automatically adapted also. Let us now turn to the construction of the process A_t. Choose a constant $K < \infty$ such that

$$|M_t| \leq K, \quad P\text{-as.}, \, \forall t \geq 0. \tag{5}$$

(a) *Motivation.* Fix $t > 0$ and consider any partition $\Delta = \{ 0 = t_0 < \ldots < t_n = t \}$ of $[0, t]$. If the process $M_t^2 - A_t$ is to be a martingale, a rearrangement of terms in the martingale equation combined with 9.b.0 yields

$$E \left[A_r - A_s | \mathcal{F}_s \right] = E \left[M_r^2 - M_s^2 | \mathcal{F}_s \right] = E \left[(M_r - M_s)^2 | \mathcal{F}_s \right].$$

Assume now that the increment $r - s$ is small. The continuity of the processes A, M and the right continuity of the filtration $(\mathcal{F}_t)$ leads us to believe that the increments $A_r - A_s$ and $M_r - M_s$ are almost $\mathcal{F}_s$-measurable and so dropping the conditional expectations will result in an approximate equality $A_r - A_s \approx (M_r - M_s)^2$.

Thus, if $\|\Delta\|$ is small, then $A_{t_j} - A_{t_{j-1}} \approx (M_{t_j} - M_{t_{j-1}})^2$ and summing over $j = 1, \ldots, n$, telescoping the left hand side, observing that $A_0 = 0$ and a healthy dose of optimism lead to the approximate equality

$$A_t \approx \sum_{j=1}^{n} (M_{t_j} - M_{t_{j-1}})^2 = Q_\Delta(M)$$

with hopes that this will turn into an equality in the limit, as $\|\Delta\| \to 0$.

(b)   *Let* $\Delta = \{\, 0 = t_0 < \ldots < t_n < \ldots \}$ *be any partition of the interval* $[0, \infty)$ *which has only finitely many points in each finite interval. Then the process* $M_t^2 - Q_t^\Delta(M)$ *is a continuous martingale.*

Clearly the process $H_t = M_t^2 - Q_t^\Delta(M)$ is continuous and satisfies $H_t \in L^1(P)$, for all $t \geq 0$. After rearrangement of terms the martingale equation for H becomes

$$E\left[Q_t^\Delta(M) - Q_s^\Delta(M) | \mathcal{F}_s\right] = E\left[M_t^2 - M_s^2 | \mathcal{F}_s\right], \tag{6}$$

for all $0 \leq s < t$. Consider such s and t and set $m = k(s) = max\{\, k \mid t_k \leq s \,\}$ and $n = k(t)$. Then we have $m \leq n$,

$$Q_t^\Delta(M) = (M_t - M_{t_n})^2 + \sum_{j=1}^{n} \left(M_{t_j} - M_{t_{j-1}}\right)^2,$$

$$Q_s^\Delta(M) = (M_s - M_{t_m})^2 + \sum_{j=1}^{m} \left(M_{t_j} - M_{t_{j-1}}\right)^2, \quad \text{and so}$$

$$Q_t^\Delta(M) - Q_s^\Delta(M) = -(M_s - M_{t_m})^2 + \sum_{j=m+1}^{n} \left(M_{t_j} - M_{t_{j-1}}\right)^2 + (M_t - M_{t_n})^2.$$

Using 9.b.0 and telescoping the sum on the right yields $E\left[Q_t^\Delta(M) - Q_s^\Delta(M) | \mathcal{F}_s\right] = E_{\mathcal{F}_s}\left[(M_{t_m}^2 - M_s^2) + \sum_{j=m+1}^{n} \left(M_{t_j}^2 - M_{t_{j-1}}^2\right) + (M_t^2 - M_{t_n}^2)\right] = E\left[M_t^2 - M_s^2 | \mathcal{F}_s\right]$, as desired.

(c)   *For* $r > 0$ *the limit* $\tilde{A}_r = \lim_{\|\Delta\| \to 0} Q_r^\Delta(M)$ *exists in* $L^2(P)$.

Recall that a partition Δ of $[0, r]$ can be viewed as a partition of $[0, \infty)$ containing the point r. Consequently

$$Q_r^\Delta(X) = Q_\Delta(X) = \sum_{j=1}^{n} \left(X_{t_j} - X_{t_{j-1}}\right)^2, \quad \text{where } t_n = r. \tag{7}$$

Fix $r > 0$. By completeness of $L^2(P)$ it will suffice to show that

$$\|Q_r^{\Delta_1}(M) - Q_r^{\Delta_2}(M)\|_{L^2} \to 0, \quad \text{as } \|\Delta_1\| + \|\Delta_2\| \to 0. \tag{8}$$

Let now Δ_1, Δ_2 be any two partitions of $[0, r]$ and let $\Delta = \{\, 0 = s_0 < \ldots < s_m = r \,\}$ denote their common refinement. According to (b), the processes $M_t^2 - Q_t^{\Delta_1}(M)$

and $M_t^2 - Q_t^{\Delta_2}(M)$ are both martingales. Taking the difference we see that the process

$$X_t = Q_t^{\Delta_1}(M) - Q_t^{\Delta_2}(M)$$

is a martingale also, which is again continuous and uniformly bounded. Applying (b) to X instead of M we see that $X_t^2 - Q_t^{\Delta}(X)$ is a martingale and hence has a constant mean. Since $X_0 = 0$, this process vanishes at $t = 0$ and it follows that the constant mean is zero. Thus

$$\|Q_r^{\Delta_1}(M) - Q_r^{\Delta_2}(M)\|_{L^2}^2 = E(X_r^2) = E\left(Q_r^{\Delta}(X)\right). \tag{9}$$

Set $Y_t = Q_t^{\Delta_1}(M)$ and $Z_t = Q_t^{\Delta_2}(M)$. Then $X_t = Y_t - Z_t$ and thus $Q_r^{\Delta}(X)$ is a sum of squares of the form $\left[(Y_{s_j} - Y_{s_{j-1}}) + (Z_{s_j} - Z_{s_{j-1}})\right]^2$. Using the estimate $(a-b)^2 \leq 2(a^2+b^2)$ on each summand we see that $Q_r^{\Delta}(X) \leq 2\left[Q_r^{\Delta}(Y) + Q_r^{\Delta}(Z)\right]$. In view of (9) and by symmetry it will now suffice to show that

$$E\left(Q_r^{\Delta}(Y)\right) \to 0, \quad \text{as } \|\Delta_1\| + \|\Delta_2\| \to 0. \tag{10}$$

Note that
$$Q_r^{\Delta}(Y) = \sum_{k=1}^{m}(Y_{s_k} - Y_{s_{k-1}})^2$$

and denote the points of the partition Δ_1 by t_j with $t_n = r$. To get an estimate for $Q_r^{\Delta}(Y)$, let $k \leq m$ and choose the index j such that $t_j \leq s_{k-1} < s_k \leq t_{j+1}$. This is possible since Δ refines Δ_1. From definition (2) it follows that

$$Y_{s_k} - Y_{s_{k-1}} = Q_{s_k}^{\Delta_1}(M) - Q_{s_{k-1}}^{\Delta_1}(M) = \left(M_{s_k} - M_{t_j}\right)^2 - \left(M_{s_{k-1}} - M_{t_j}\right)^2$$
$$= \left(M_{s_k} - M_{s_{k-1}}\right)\left(M_{s_k} + M_{s_{k-1}} - 2M_{t_j}\right),$$

and so
$$\left(Y_{s_k} - Y_{s_{k-1}}\right)^2 \leq C(\|\Delta_1\|)\left(M_{s_k} - M_{s_{k-1}}\right)^2, \tag{11}$$

where, for $\delta > 0$,
$$C(\delta) = \sup |M_s + M_q - 2M_t|^2$$

and the *sup* is taken over all numbers $s, q, t \in [0, r]$ such that $t \leq q < s$ and $s - t < \delta$. Because of the continuity of M we can restrict ourselves to rational numbers t, q, s and it follows that $C(\delta)$ is measurable and hence a nonnegative random variable. Recall that $|M| \leq K$. Thus $|C(\delta)| \leq 16K^2$. If $\omega \in \Omega$ is such that the path $t \in [0, r] \mapsto M_t(\omega)$ is continuous and hence uniformly continuous, we have $C(\delta)(\omega) \to 0$, as $\delta \downarrow 0$. In particular

$$C(\delta) \to 0, \quad P\text{-as., as } \delta \downarrow 0. \tag{12}$$

Summing the inequalities in (11) over all subintervals of Δ we obtain

$$Q_r^{\Delta}(Y) \leq C(\|\Delta_1\|)Q_r^{\Delta}(M).$$

The Cauchy-Schwartz inequality now implies that

$$E\left(Q_r^\Delta(Y)\right) \le E\left[C^2\left(\|\Delta_1\|\right)\right]^{\frac{1}{2}} E\left[Q_r^\Delta(M)^2\right]^{\frac{1}{2}}. \tag{13}$$

As $\|\Delta_1\| \to 0$ we have $E\left[C^2\left(\|\Delta_1\|\right)\right] \to 0$, by bounded, almost sure convergence of the integrand. To verify (10) it will thus suffice to show that the second factor on the right of (13) remains bounded by a constant independent of Δ_1 and Δ. Write $Q_t^\Delta = Q_t^\Delta(M)$. Recalling that $r = s_m$ we have

$$Q_r^\Delta = \sum\nolimits_{k=1}^{m}\left(M_{s_k} - M_{s_{k-1}}\right)^2.$$

Square this and note that the sum of the mixed products can be written as

$$\sum\nolimits_{1 \le k < j \le m}\left(M_{s_k} - M_{s_{k-1}}\right)^2\left(M_{s_j} - M_{s_{j-1}}\right)^2$$
$$= \sum\nolimits_{k=1}^{m}\left(M_{s_k} - M_{s_{k-1}}\right)^2 \sum\nolimits_{j=k+1}^{m}\left(M_{s_j} - M_{s_{j-1}}\right)^2$$
$$= \sum\nolimits_{k=1}^{m}\left(M_{s_k} - M_{s_{k-1}}\right)^2\left(Q_r^\Delta - Q_{s_k}^\Delta\right) = \sum\nolimits_{k=1}^{m}\left(Q_{s_k}^\Delta - Q_{s_{k-1}}^\Delta\right)\left(Q_r^\Delta - Q_{s_k}^\Delta\right).$$

It follows that

$$Q_r^\Delta(M)^2 = 2\sum\nolimits_{k=1}^{m}\left(Q_{s_k}^\Delta - Q_{s_{k-1}}^\Delta\right)\left(Q_r^\Delta - Q_{s_k}^\Delta\right) + \sum\nolimits_{k=1}^{m}\left(M_{s_k} - M_{s_{k-1}}\right)^4. \tag{14}$$

Now take expectations. From the martingale property of $M_t^2 - Q_t^\Delta(M)$ and 9.b.0

$$E\left[Q_r^\Delta - Q_{s_k}^\Delta \middle| \mathcal{F}_{s_k}\right] = E\left[M_r^2 - M_{s_k}^2 \middle| \mathcal{F}_{s_k}\right] = E\left[(M_r - M_{s_k})^2 \middle| \mathcal{F}_{s_k}\right].$$

Since the factor $Q_{s_k}^\Delta - Q_{s_{k-1}}^\Delta$ is bounded and $\mathcal{F}_{s_k}$-measurable 2.b.10 yields

$$E\left[\left(Q_{s_k}^\Delta - Q_{s_{k-1}}^\Delta\right)\left(Q_r^\Delta - Q_{s_k}^\Delta\right)\middle| \mathcal{F}_{s_k}\right] = E\left[\left(Q_{s_k}^\Delta - Q_{s_{k-1}}^\Delta\right)(M_r - M_{s_k})^2\middle| \mathcal{F}_{s_k}\right].$$

Integrating over Ω and observing that $(M_t - M_s)^2 \le 4K^2$ yields

$$E\left[\left(Q_{s_k}^\Delta - Q_{s_{k-1}}^\Delta\right)\left(Q_r^\Delta - Q_{s_k}^\Delta\right)\right] = E\left[\left(Q_{s_k}^\Delta - Q_{s_{k-1}}^\Delta\right)(M_r - M_{s_k})^2\right]$$
$$\le E\left[4K^2\left(Q_{s_k}^\Delta - Q_{s_{k-1}}^\Delta\right)\right],$$

where we have used that $Q_{s_k}^\Delta - Q_{s_{k-1}}^\Delta \ge 0$. Thus, taking expectations in (14) and telescoping the sum of differences $Q_{s_k}^\Delta - Q_{s_{k-1}}^\Delta$ to the value $Q_r^\Delta - Q_0^\Delta = Q_r^\Delta$ yields

$$E\left[Q_r^\Delta(M)^2\right] \le E\left[8K^2 Q_r^\Delta + \sum\nolimits_{k=1}^{m}\left(M_{s_k} - M_{s_{k-1}}\right)^4\right].$$

Using the estimate $\left(M_{s_k} - M_{s_{k-1}}\right)^4 \le 4K^2\left(M_{s_k} - M_{s_{k-1}}\right)^2$ this becomes

$$E\left[Q_r^\Delta(M)^2\right] \le E\left[8K^2 Q_r^\Delta + 4K^2 Q_r^\Delta\right] = 12K^2 E\left[Q_r^\Delta(M)\right].$$

Since the process $M_t^2 - Q_t^{\Delta}(M)$ is a martingale and thus has a constant mean, we have $E\left[Q_r^{\Delta}(M)\right] = E(M_r^2 - M_0^2) \leq E(M_r^2) \leq K^2$. It follows that $E\left[Q_r^{\Delta}(M)^2\right] \leq 12K^4$, as desired. This proves (c).

We now have the existence of the limit $\tilde{A}_t = \lim_{\|\Delta\| \to 0} Q_t^{\Delta}(M) \in L^2(P)$, for each $t \geq 0$, but this does not yet provide us with the desired process $t \mapsto A_t$. We must show that the random variables A_t can be chosen consistently within the equivalence class $\tilde{A}_t$ in L^2 so that the resulting process $t \mapsto A_t$ has the desired properties. The process A will be constructed path by path rather than random variable by random variable.

Fix $r > 0$ and let Δ_n be a sequence of partitions of $[0, r]$ such that $\Delta_n \subseteq \Delta_{n+1}$ and $\bigcup_n \Delta_n$ is dense in $[0, r]$. Necessarily then $\|\Delta_n\| \to 0$, as $n \uparrow \infty$. Write $Q_t^{\Delta_n} = Q_t^{\Delta_n}(M)$. Then the sequence $Q_r^{\Delta_n}$ converges in $L^2(P)$ and, replacing (Δ_n) with a suitable subsequence if necessary, we may assume that

$$\sum_n \|Q_r^{\Delta_{n+1}} - Q_r^{\Delta_n}\|_{L^2} < \infty.$$

Fix $n \geq 1$, observe $\|f\|_{L^1} \leq \|f\|_{L^2}$ and apply Doob's L^2-inequality (7.e.1.(b) with $p = 2$) to the martingale $Q_t^{\Delta_{n+1}} - Q_t^{\Delta_n}$ to obtain

$$E\left[\sum_n \sup_{t \leq r} |Q_t^{\Delta_{n+1}} - Q_t^{\Delta_n}|\right] \leq \sum_n \| \sup_{t \leq r} |Q_t^{\Delta_{n+1}} - Q_t^{\Delta_n}|\|_{L^2}$$

$$\leq 2\sum_n \|Q_r^{\Delta_{n+1}} - Q_r^{\Delta_n}\|_{L^2} < \infty$$

and so $\sum_n \sup_{t \leq r} |Q_t^{\Delta_{n+1}} - Q_t^{\Delta_n}| < \infty$, P-as.

Let $\omega \in \Omega$ be in the set where the above sum is finite. As $n \uparrow \infty$ the continuous paths $t \in [0, r] \mapsto Q_t^{\Delta_n}(\omega)$ converge uniformly to some path $t \in [0, r] \mapsto A_t(\omega)$ which is therefore itself continuous.

It follows in particular that $Q_t^{\Delta_n} \to A_t$, P-as., for each $t \in [0, r]$. For such t

$$E\left(M_r^2 - Q_r^{\Delta_n}|\mathcal{F}_t\right) = M_t^2 - Q_t^{\Delta_n}, \quad \forall n \geq 1. \tag{15}$$

Let now $n \uparrow \infty$. On the left $Q_r^{\Delta_n} \to A_r$, P-as. Since the sequence $Q_r^{\Delta_n}$ also converges in $L^2(P)$ it follows that $A_r \in L^2(P)$ and $Q_r^{\Delta_n} \to A_r$ in $L^2(P)$ and hence in $L^1(P)$. Thus

$$E\left(M_r^2 - Q_r^{\Delta_n}|\mathcal{F}_t\right) \to E\left(M_r^2 - A_r|\mathcal{F}_t\right)$$

in $L^1(P)$ and so P-as., if Δ_n is replaced with a suitable subsequence (1.a.0,1.a.1). Likewise, on the right $Q_t^{\Delta_n} \to A_t$, P-as. Thus (15) implies that

$$E\left(M_r^2 - A_r|\mathcal{F}_t\right) = M_t^2 - A_t, \quad P\text{-as.}$$

Hence the process $M_t^2 - A_t$ is a martingale on the interval $[0, r]$. Finally, let us establish the increasing nature of the paths $t \in [0, r] \mapsto A_t(\omega)$. The processes Q_t^{Δ}

are not increasing because of the last term in the summation in (2). However, if $s, t \in \Delta$ and $s < t$, then $Q_s^\Delta \leq Q_t^\Delta$ (everywhere).

If now $s, t \in D := \bigcup_n \Delta_n \subseteq [0, r]$ with $s < t$, then there exists an index n_0 such that $s, t \in \Delta_n$, for all $n \geq n_0$. For such n we have $Q_s^{\Delta_n} \leq Q_t^{\Delta_n}$ and, letting $n \uparrow \infty$, $A_s \leq A_t$, P-as. Here the exceptional set can depend on s and t but, since the set D is countable, it follows that

$$A_s \leq A_t, \quad \text{for all } s, t \in D \text{ with } s < t, \quad P\text{-as.,}$$

that is, P-ae every path $t \in [0, r] \mapsto A_t(\omega)$ increases on the subset $D \subseteq [0, r]$. By continuity and density of D it must increase on all of $[0, r]$.

Let us now verify the representation (4). Fix $t \in [0, r]$. According to (c), $B = L^2\text{-}\lim_{\|\Delta\| \to 0} Q_\Delta(M)$ exists, if this limit is taken over all partitions Δ of $[0, t]$. From our construction, $Q_t^{\Delta_n} \to A_t$, P-as. Note that $Q_t^{\Delta_n} = Q_{\Delta_n(t)}(M)$, where $\Delta_n(t) = (\Delta_n \cup \{t\}) \cap [0, t]$ is a sequence of partitions of $[0, t]$ with $\|\Delta_n(t)\| \to 0$. It follows that $Q_t^{\Delta_n} \to B$ in L^2. Consequently

$$A_t = B = L^2\text{-}\lim_{\|\Delta\| \to 0} Q_\Delta(M), \quad P\text{-as.}$$

This gives us the desired process A_t on each finite interval $[0, r]$. Because of the uniqueness on each of these intervals, we can extend A_t uniquely to a process defined on $[0, \infty)$ with the desired properties. ∎

The definition of the quadratic variation will now be extended to continuous local martingales using the localization procedure. For this we need

9.b.4. *Let (M_t) be a continuous, uniformly bounded martingale and T any optional time. Then*

(a) $E[\langle M \rangle_t] = E\big[(M_t - M_0)^2\big]$, for all $t \geq 0$.

(b) M^T is a continuous, uniformly bounded martingale and $\langle M^T \rangle = \langle M \rangle^T$.

Proof. (a) The martingale $M_t^2 - \langle M \rangle_t$ has a constant mean. Thus $E[M_t^2 - \langle M \rangle_t] = E[M_0^2 - \langle M \rangle_0] = E[M_0^2]$. Using 9.b.0 it follows that $E[\langle M \rangle_t] = E[M_t^2 - M_0^2] = E[(M_t - M_0)^2]$.

(b) According to 8.a.2.(b), M^T is an $(\mathcal{F}_t)$-martingale. It is clearly again uniformly bounded. Thus the quadratic variation $\langle M^T \rangle$ is defined and is the unique continuous bounded variation process A such that $(M^T)^2 - A$ is a martingale.

Stopping the martingale $M^2 - \langle M \rangle$ at time T yields the martingale $(M^T)^2 - \langle M \rangle^T$. Since $\langle M \rangle^T$ is again a continuous, bounded variation process, it follows that $\langle M \rangle^T = A = \langle M^T \rangle$. ∎

9.b.5 Theorem. *Let X be a continuous local martingale. Then there exists a unique continuous, bounded variation process A such that $A_0 = 0$ and $X^2 - A$ is a local martingale. The process A is called the quadratic variation of X, denoted $\langle X \rangle$. The quadratic variation $\langle X \rangle$ is an adapted and increasing process and we have*

$$\langle X \rangle_t = \lim_{\|\Delta\| \to 0} Q_\Delta(X) \text{ in probability, for each } t \geq 0, \tag{16}$$

where the limit is taken over all partitions Δ of the interval $[0, t]$.

Proof. The uniqueness of A follows from 9.b.2. The adaptedness of A is automatic, if $X^2 - A$ is a local martingale and hence adapted. Let us now show the existence of A.

As X is indistinguishable from a process every path of which is continuous, we may assume that X itself has this property. Then the reducing sequence (T_n) given in 8.a.5 satisfies $T_n \uparrow \infty$, as $n \uparrow \infty$, at all points of Ω, and the process $X(n) = 1_{[T_n > 0]} X^{T_n}$ is a continuous, uniformly bounded martingale, for each $n \geq 1$.

Thus, for each $n \geq 1$, there exists a unique continuous increasing process $A(n)$ such that the difference $X(n)^2 - A(n)$ is a martingale. Since $T_n \leq T_{n+1}$ we have $[T_n > 0] \subseteq [T_{n+1} > 0]$ and so $1_{[T_n > 0]} 1_{[T_{n+1} > 0]} = 1_{[T_n > 0]}$. It follows that

$$X(n) = 1_{[T_n > 0]} X(n+1)^{T_n}. \tag{17}$$

Fix $n \geq 1$ and stop the martingale $X(n+1)^2 - A(n+1)$ at T_n to conclude that $\left(X(n+1)^{T_n} \right)^2 - A(n+1)^{T_n}$ is a martingale. Multiplying this with $1_{[T_n > 0]}$ and observing (17) shows that $X(n)^2 - 1_{[T_n > 0]} A(n+1)^{T_n}$ is a martingale also (8.b.1.(b)). From the characteristic property of $A(n)$ we now conclude that

$$A(n) = 1_{[T_n > 0]} A(n+1)^{T_n}, \tag{18}$$

along P-ae. path. A routine modification along paths indexed by points ω in a suitable null set yields this equality along every path, that is, as an equality of functions on $\Pi = R_+ \times \Omega$. Then (18) shows that $A(n) = A(n+1)$ on the set $\Pi_n = \{ (t, \omega) \in R_+ \times \Omega \mid T_n(\omega) > 0 \text{ and } t \leq T_n(\omega) \} \subseteq R_+ \times \Omega$. The sets Π_n are increasing and so
$$A(n) = A(n+1) = A(n+2) = \ldots, \quad \text{on } \Pi_n.$$

Since $\Pi_n \uparrow \Pi$ we can define a process A on Π by setting

$$A = A(n) \text{ on } \Pi_n, \quad n \geq 1. \tag{19}$$

Fix $t \geq 0$. If $\omega \in \Omega$, then we have $A_t(\omega) = A_t(n)(\omega)$, for all $n \geq 1$ such that $T_n(\omega) > 0$ and $t \leq T_n(\omega)$, that is, for all but finitely many $n \geq 1$. Thus $A_t(\omega) = \lim_n A_t(n)(\omega)$ and so A_t is an $\mathcal{F}_t$-measurable random variable. From (19) it follows that

$$1_{[T_n > 0]} A^{T_n} = 1_{[T_n > 0]} A(n)^{T_n} = A(n), \tag{20}$$

the second equality because of (18). It follows that

$$X(n)^2 - A(n) = \left(1_{[T_n>0]}X^{T_n}\right)^2 - 1_{[T_n>0]}A^{T_n} = 1_{[T_n>0]}\left(X^2 - A\right)^{T_n}$$

and in particular that this last expression is a martingale. Thus the sequence (T_n) reduces the process $X^2 - A$. It follows that $X^2 - A$ is a local martingale. Because of (20) the process $1_{[T_n>0]}A^{T_n}$ is continuous and of bounded variation, for each $n \geq 1$. It follows that the process A has the same property. Finally $A_0 = \lim_n A_0(n) = 0$. This establishes the existence of A.

Fix $t \geq 0$. With Δ ranging through partitions of $[0, t]$ we have $Q_t^\Delta(X(n)) \to A_t(n)$, as $\|\Delta\| \to 0$, in $L^2(P)$ and hence in probability. Since $X(n) = X$ and $A(n) = A$ on the set $\Pi_n \subseteq R_+ \times \Omega$, the process $Q_\cdot^\Delta(X(n))$ satisfies $Q_\cdot^\Delta(X(n)) = Q_\cdot^\Delta(X)$ on Π_n as well. Thus $Q_t^\Delta(X(n)) = Q_t^\Delta(X)$ and $A_t(n) = A_t$ on the t-section $\Omega_n := [T_n > 0] \cap [t \leq T_n] \subseteq \Omega$ of Π_n. It follows that

$$Q_t^\Delta(X) \to A_t, \quad \text{as } \|\Delta\| \to 0, \tag{21}$$

in probability on the set Ω_n. Since $\Omega_n \uparrow \Omega$, the convergence (21) holds in probability on all of Ω (1.a.2). $\blacksquare$

9.b.6. *Let X be a continuous local martingale and T an optional time. Then*
(a) $\langle X \rangle$ is a continuous increasing process with $\langle X \rangle_0 = 0$. Especially $\langle X \rangle \geq 0$.
(b) $\langle X^T \rangle = \langle X \rangle^T$.
(c) $\langle X \rangle = 0$ if and only if X is constant (in time).
(d) If $A \in \mathcal{F}_0$ then $\langle 1_A X \rangle = 1_A \langle X \rangle$.

Proof. (a) Clear. (b) Stopping the local martingale $X^2 - \langle X \rangle$ at time T produces the local martingale $\left(X^T\right)^2 - \langle X \rangle^T$ (8.a.2.(d)). It follows that $\langle X^T \rangle = \langle X \rangle^T$, since $\langle X \rangle^T$ is a continuous bounded variation process.

(c) If $X_t = X_0$, for all $t \geq 0$, then X^2 is a local martingale and hence $\langle X \rangle = 0$. Conversely assume now that $\langle X \rangle = 0$. Then $\langle X^T \rangle = \langle X \rangle^T = 0$, for each optional time T. Since X can be reduced to a sequence of uniformly bounded martingales, we may assume that X is itself such a martingale. Then 9.b.4.(a) implies that $E\left[(X_t - X_0)^2\right] = E\left[\langle X \rangle_t\right] = 0$ and thus $X_t = X_0$, P-as., for each $t \geq 0$.

(d) This follows at once from the limit representation of $\langle 1_A X \rangle$ in 9.b.5 and the effect multiplication with A has on the paths of X. $\blacksquare$

Remark. From the very definition of the process $\langle X \rangle$ it follows that X^2 is again a local martingale if and only if $\langle X \rangle = 0$. Thus (a) shows that X^2 is again a local martingale if and only if X is constant (in time).

Let us now show a path by path version of property (c). To this end we introduce the notation $\langle X \rangle_a^b = \langle X \rangle_b - \langle X \rangle_a$, whenever $a < b$. From 9.b.5 it follows that

$$\langle X \rangle_a^b = \lim_{\|\Delta\| \to 0} Q_\Delta(X) \quad \text{in probability}, \tag{22}$$

where this limit is taken over all partitions Δ of $[a, b]$.

9.b.7. *Let X be a continuous local martingale. Then, for P-ae. $\omega \in \Omega$ we have, for all $0 \le a < b$, $\langle X \rangle_a^b(\omega) = 0 \iff X_t(\omega) = X_a(\omega), \ \forall\, t \in [a, b]$.*

Remark. Recalling that $\langle X \rangle$ is an increasing process, this means that the paths $t \mapsto X_t(\omega)$ and $t \mapsto \langle X \rangle_t(\omega)$ have exactly the same intervals of constancy, for P-ae. $\omega \in \Omega$.

Proof. Fix $0 \le a < b$. For a suitable sequence Δ_n of partitions of $[a, b]$ we have almost sure convergence in (22). If ω is in this set of convergence and the path $t \mapsto X_t(\omega)$ is constant on $[a, b]$, then it follows trivially that $\langle X \rangle_a^b(\omega) = 0$. This shows ($\Leftarrow$) with an exceptional null set depending on the interval $[a, b]$.

To see the other direction, set $N_t = X_{t+a} - X_a$. Then N is a continuous $(\mathcal{F}_{t+a})$-local martingale with $N_t - N_s = X_{t+a} - X_{s+a}$. Thus, for each partition Δ of $[0, t]$, we have $Q_\Delta(N) = Q_{a+\Delta}(X)$, where $a + \Delta$ (translate of Δ) is a partition of $[a, a + t]$ which satisfies $\|a + \Delta\| = \|\Delta\|$. Letting $\|\Delta\| \to 0$ we obtain

$$\langle N \rangle_t = \langle X \rangle_a^{a+t}, \quad P\text{-as., for each } t \ge 0. \tag{23}$$

Now consider the $(\mathcal{F}_{t+a})$-optional time $T = \inf\{\, s > 0 \mid \langle N \rangle_s > 0 \,\}$ (7.a.7). We have $\langle N^T \rangle = \langle N \rangle^T = 0$. Thus N^T is constant in time. Since $N_0^T = N_0 = 0$, we have $N^T = 0$. That means that the path $t \mapsto X_t(\omega)$ is constant on the interval $[a, a + T(\omega)]$, for P-ae. $\omega \in \Omega$. Consider such ω which also satisfies (23) with $t = b - a$. If $\langle X \rangle_a^b(\omega) = \langle N \rangle_{b-a}(\omega) = 0$, then $T(\omega) \ge b - a$ and consequently the path $t \mapsto X_t(\omega)$ is constant on the interval $[a, b]$. This establishes the direction ($\Rightarrow$) again with an exceptional null set depending on the interval $[a, b]$.

The dependence of the exceptional set on $[a, b]$ is now removed as usual. By countability we obtain an exceptional null set for simultaneously all intervals $[a, b]$ with rational endpoints. The rest follows from the almost sure continuity of the paths $t \mapsto X_t(\omega)$ and $t \mapsto \langle X \rangle_t(\omega)$. ∎

Remarks. (1) If M is a uniformly bounded, continuous martingale (and hence also a local martingale), then the quadratic variation of M viewed as a martingale agrees with the quadratic variation of M viewed as a local martingale. This follows from the limit representations

$$\langle M \rangle_t = \lim\nolimits_{\|\Delta\| \to 0} Q_t^\Delta(M)$$

in 9.b.3, 9.b.5. Note that convergence in L^2 implies convergence in probability and that limits in probability are unique. In other words: if A is a continuous, bounded variation process such that $M^2 - A$ is a local martingale, then $A = \langle M \rangle$ and consequently $M^2 - A$ is a martingale.

(2) The limit representation (17) shows that the quadratic variation process $\langle M \rangle$ is unaffected if the filtration $(\mathcal{F}_t)$ is replaced with some other (right continuous and augmented) filtration $(\mathcal{G}_t)$ with respect to which X is still a local martingale. The quadratic variation process $\langle M \rangle$ is also unaffected if the probability measure

P is replaced with some absolutely continuous probability measure $Q << P$, with respect to which X is still a local martingale. This follows from the fact that convergence in P-probability implies convergence in Q-probability.

Example. Let us compute the quadratic variation process of a one dimensional Brownian motion $B = (B_t)$ with associated filtration $(\mathcal{F}_t)$. Brownian motions are introduced in chapter II. Here we need only the following properties:
(a) B is a continuous square integrable martingale.
(b) The increment $B_t - B_s$ is independent of $\mathcal{F}_s$, for all $0 \le s < t$.
(c) $B_t - B_s$ is a normal variable with mean zero and variance $t - s$, for all $0 \le s < t$.
We claim that the process $B_t^2 - t$ is also a martingale. To see this, we have to show that $E\left[B_t^2 - t \mid \mathcal{F}_s\right] = B_s^2 - s$; equivalently $E\left[B_t^2 - B_s^2 \mid \mathcal{F}_s\right] = t - s$, for all $0 \le s < t$. Indeed, for such s and t we have

$$E\left[B_t^2 - B_s^2 \mid \mathcal{F}_s\right] = E\left[(B_t - B_s)^2 \mid \mathcal{F}_s\right] = E\left[(B_t - B_s)^2\right] = Var(B_t - B_s) = t - s.$$

Here the first equality follows from (a) and 9.b.0, the second equality from (b) and the third from (c). The uniqueness part of 9.b.5 now shows that $\langle B \rangle_t = t$ for all $t \ge 0$, that is, the quadratic variation of a Brownian motion is indistinguishable from the nonrandom process $V_t = t$. This can also be shown using the representation (16), as follows: fix $t \ge 0$ and consider, for each $n \ge 1$, the following partition Δ_n of the interval $[0, t]$:

$$\Delta_n = \{0 < \tfrac{t}{n} < \ldots < \tfrac{(j-1)t}{n} < \tfrac{jt}{n} < \ldots < \tfrac{(n-1)t}{n} < t\}.$$

We will show that $Q_{\Delta_n}(B) \to t$ in $L^2(P)$, as $n \uparrow \infty$. Set $H_j = B_{jt/n} - B_{(j-1)t/n}$ and note that $Q_{\Delta_n}(B) - t = \sum_{j=1}^n (H_j^2 - \tfrac{t}{n})$. Thus

$$E\left[(Q_{\Delta_n}(B) - t)^2\right] = E\left[\left(\sum_{j=1}^n [H_j^2 - \tfrac{t}{n}]\right)^2\right] = E\left[\left(\sum_{j=1}^n Z_j\right)^2\right],$$

where $Z_j = H_j^2 - \tfrac{t}{n}$, for all $j = 1, \ldots, n$. The Z_j are independent, mean zero variables and consequently orthogonal in $L^2(P)$. Thus

$$E\left[(Q_{\Delta_n}(B) - t)^2\right] = E\left[\left(\sum_{j=1}^n Z_j\right)^2\right] = \sum_{j=1}^n E(Z_j^2), \quad \text{where}$$

$$E(Z_j^2) = E\left[(H_j^2 - \tfrac{t}{n})^2\right] = E\left[H_j^4 - \tfrac{2t}{n}H_j^2 + \tfrac{t^2}{n^2}\right]$$

and the increment $H_j = B_{jt/n} - B_{(j-1)t/n}$ is a mean zero normal variable with variance $\sigma^2 = t/n$. Such a variable has moment generating function $M_{H_j}(s) = exp(\sigma^2 s^2/2)$. Clearly $E(H_j^2) = \sigma^2 = t/n$ and the moment $E(H_j^4)$ can be found as the derivative $M_{H_j}^{(4)}(0) = 3\sigma^4 = 3t^2/n^2$. Consequently

$$E(Z_j^2) = \tfrac{3t^2}{n^2} - \tfrac{2t}{n} \cdot \tfrac{t}{n} + \tfrac{t^2}{n^2} = \tfrac{2t^2}{n^2},$$

and so $\qquad E\left[(Q_{\Delta_n}(B) - t)^2\right] = \sum_{j=1}^n E(Z_j^2) = \tfrac{2t^2}{n} \to 0$, as $n \uparrow \infty$.

Thus $\langle B \rangle_t = \lim_{n \uparrow \infty} Q_{\Delta_n}(B) = t$, P-a.s., for each $t \ge 0$. ∎

9.c Quadratic variation and L^2-bounded martingales. Recall that $\mathbf{H}^2$ is the space of all continuous, L^2-bounded martingales M with norm

$$\|M\|_2 = \sup_{t \geq 0}\|M_t\|_{L^2} = \|M_\infty\|_{L^2},$$

where $M_\infty = \lim_{t \uparrow \infty} M_t$ is the last element of M. For $M \in \mathbf{H}^2$ the maximal function $M_\infty^* = \sup_{t \geq 0}|M_t|$ is square integrable and satisfies $\|M\|_2 \leq \|M_\infty^*\|_{L^2} \leq 2\|M\|_2$ The quadratic variation $\langle M \rangle$ is an increasing process and hence

$$\langle M \rangle_\infty = \lim_{t \uparrow \infty}\langle M \rangle_t = \lim_{n \uparrow \infty}\langle M \rangle_n$$

exists and defines an extended real valued, nonnegative random variable on Ω. Let us call the process $\langle M \rangle$ *integrable*, if $E\big[\langle M \rangle_\infty\big] < \infty$. We will see below (9.c.1) that for $M \in \mathbf{H}_0^2 = \{\, M \in \mathbf{H}^2 \mid M_0 = 0 \,\}$,

$$\|M\|_2 = \|M_\infty\|_{L^2} = E\big[\langle M \rangle_\infty\big]^{\frac{1}{2}} = \big\|\langle M \rangle_\infty^{1/2}\big\|_{L^2}.$$

Note that a martingale $M \in \mathbf{H}^2$ need not be uniformly bounded and hence the quadratic variation $\langle M \rangle$ has to be computed as the quadratic variation of a local martingale.

9.c.0. *Let M be a continuous local martingale. Then the following are equivalent:*
(a) M is in $\mathbf{H}^2$.
(b) $M_0 \in L^2$ and the process $\langle M \rangle$ is integrable, that is, $E\big[\langle M \rangle_\infty\big] < \infty$.
In this case $M_t^2 - \langle M \rangle_t$ is a uniformly integrable martingale.

Proof. Choose a sequence T_n of optional times such that $M(n) = 1_{[T_n > 0]}M^{T_n}$ is a uniformly bounded martingale, for each $n \geq 1$, and $T_n \uparrow \infty$, P-as., as $n \uparrow \infty$. Then $Z_t = M(n)_t^2 - \langle M(n) \rangle_t$ is a martingale and thus has a constant mean. Noting that $\langle M(n) \rangle = 1_{[T_n > 0]}\langle M \rangle^{T_n}$ (9.b.6.(b),(d)), the equality $E(Z_t) = E(Z_0)$ can be written as

$$E\big[1_{[T_n > 0]}M_{t \wedge T_n}^2\big] - E\big[1_{[T_n > 0]}\langle M \rangle_{t \wedge T_n}\big] = E\big[1_{[T_n > 0]}M_0^2\big]. \tag{0}$$

(a)$\Rightarrow$(b) Let $M \in \mathbf{H}^2$. Then $M_0 \in L^2$. In fact $M_\infty^* \in L^2$. Since $(M_\infty^*)^2$ dominates $1_{[T_n > 0]}M_{t \wedge T_n}^2$, we can go first with $n \uparrow \infty$, to obtain $E\big[M_t^2\big] - E\big[\langle M \rangle_t\big] = E\big[M_0^2\big]$ and then with $t \uparrow \infty$, to obtain $E\big[M_\infty^2\big] - E\big[\langle M \rangle_\infty\big] = E\big[M_0^2\big]$ and thus

$$E\big[\langle M \rangle_\infty\big] = E\big[M_\infty^2\big] - E\big[M_0^2\big] = \|M\|_2^2 - \|M_0\|_2^2 < \infty.$$

(b)$\Rightarrow$(a) Assume that (b) is satisfied and set $K = E\big[\langle M \rangle_\infty\big] + E\big[M_0^2\big] < \infty$. Then (0) implies

$$E\big[1_{[T_n > 0]}M_{t \wedge T_n}^2\big] \leq K. \tag{1}$$

We have $E(M_t^2) = E\big[\liminf_n 1_{[T_n > 0]}M_{t \wedge T_n}^2\big] \leq \liminf_n E\big[1_{[T_n > 0]}M_{t \wedge T_n}^2\big] \leq K$, for all $t \geq 0$, by Fatou's Lemma, and it follows that the local martingale M is L^2 bounded. It remains to be shown that M is a martingale. Fix $0 \leq s < t$. Since $M(n)$ is a martingale, we have

$$E\big[1_{[T_n > 0]}M_{t \wedge T_n}|\mathcal{F}_s\big] = 1_{[T_n > 0]}M_{s \wedge T_n}. \tag{2}$$

Because of (1), the sequence $1_{[T_n>0]}M^2_{t\wedge T_n}$ is L^2-bounded, hence uniformly integrable. Moreover $1_{[T_n>0]}M_{t\wedge T_n} \to M_t$ almost surely and hence also in L^1-norm (by uniform integrability). We can thus pass to the limit in the conditional expectation in (2) to obtain $E[M_t|\mathcal{F}_s] = M_s$, P-as. (4.c.1). Finally to show that the process $M^2 - \langle M\rangle$ is uniformly integrable it suffices to note that

$$\sup_{t\geq 0}\left|M_t^2 - \langle M\rangle_t\right| \leq (M_\infty^*)^2 + \langle M\rangle_\infty,$$

where the right hand side is an integrable random variable. ∎

In general the norm and inner product on $\mathbf{H}^2$ are given by

$$\|M\|_2 = \|M_\infty\|_{L^2} \quad \text{and} \quad (M,N)_{\mathbf{H}^2} = \left(M_\infty, N_\infty\right)_{L^2} = E[M_\infty N_\infty].$$

However, on the subspace $\mathbf{H}_0^2 \subseteq \mathbf{H}^2$, the norm can also be written as follows:

9.c.1. *For $M \in \mathbf{H}_0^2$ we have $\|M\|_2 = E[\langle M\rangle_\infty]^{\frac{1}{2}} = \|\langle M\rangle_\infty^{1/2}\|_{L^2}$.*

Proof. In the proof of 9.c.0 we have seen that $E[M_\infty^2] - E[\langle M\rangle_\infty] = E[M_0^2]$. If $M_0 = 0$ it follows that
$$\|M\|_2^2 = \|M_\infty\|_{L^2}^2 = E[\langle M\rangle_\infty] = \|\langle M\rangle_\infty^{1/2}\|_{L^2}^2. \quad ∎$$

Remark. All our results extend easily to local martingales $(M_t)_{t\in[0,a]}$ defined on a finite time interval. By simply setting $M_t = M_a$, for $t > a$, we extend M to a local martingale M defined on $[0,\infty)$ satisfying $M_\infty = M_a$ and $\langle M\rangle_\infty = \langle M\rangle_a$. For example 9.c.0 becomes

9.c.2. *For a continuous local martingale $(M_t)_{t\in[0,a]}$ the following are equivalent:*
(a) M is an L^2-bounded martingale.
(b) $M_0 \in L^2$ and $E[\langle M\rangle_a] < \infty$. ∎

The following gives a glimpse of the significance of the quadratic variation process:

9.c.3. *Let M be a continuous local martingale. Then $\lim_{t\uparrow\infty} M_t$ exists P-as. on the set $[\langle M\rangle_\infty < \infty]$.*

Proof. We may assume $M_0 = 0$. Fix $n \geq 1$ and set $T_n = \inf\{t \geq 0 \mid \langle M\rangle_t > n\}$ with the usual provision that $inf(\emptyset) = \infty$. Because of the continuity of the process $\langle M\rangle$, T_n is an optional time (7.a.7). Moreover $\langle M^{T_n}\rangle = \langle M\rangle^{T_n} \leq n$. Thus the process $\langle M^{T_n}\rangle$ is integrable and hence M^{T_n} an L^2-bounded martingale. Consequently the limit $\lim_{t\uparrow\infty} M_t^{T_n}$ exists almost surely. The exceptional set can be made independent of n and so, for P-ae. $\omega \in [\langle M\rangle_\infty < \infty]$, the limit $\lim_{t\uparrow\infty} M_t^{T_n}(\omega)$ exists for all $n \geq 1$. If $n > \langle M\rangle_\infty(\omega)$, then $T_n(\omega) = \infty$ and consequently $M_t^{T_n}(\omega) = M_t(\omega)$, for all $t \geq 0$, and it follows that the limit $\lim_{t\uparrow\infty} M_t(\omega)$ exists. ∎

For the construction of the stochastic integral we need the following result:

9.c.4. *For a right continuous, adapted process X the following are equivalent:*
(a) X is a martingale.
(b) $X_T \in L^1$ and $E(X_T) = E(X_0)$, for each bounded optional time T.

Proof. (a)$\Rightarrow$(b) This follows from the Optional Sampling Theorem 7.d.0.
(b)$\Rightarrow$(a) By assumption $X_t \in L^1$, for all $t \geq 0$. Fix $0 \leq s < t$. We must show that $E(X_t | \mathcal{F}_s) = X_s$. Since X_s is $\mathcal{F}_s$-measurable, it will suffice to show that $E(X_t 1_A) = E(X_s 1_A)$, for all sets $A \in \mathcal{F}_s$.

Let $A \in \mathcal{F}_s$. Then $T = t1_{A^c} + s1_A$ is a bounded optional time (7.a.6). Note that $X_T = 1_{A^c} X_t + 1_A X_s$. Likwise t itself is a bounded optional time and so, by assumption (b), we have

$$E(X_0) = E(X_T) = E(X_t 1_{A^c}) + E(X_s 1_A) \quad \text{and}$$
$$E(X_0) = E(X_t) = E(X_t 1_{A^c}) + E(X_t 1_A).$$

By subtraction it follows that $E(X_t 1_A) = E(X_s 1_A)$, as desired. ∎

9.d Quadratic variation and L^1-bounded martingales. Let M be a continuous local martingale with $M_0 = 0$ and $\langle M \rangle_\infty = \lim_{t \uparrow \infty} \langle M \rangle_t$. In section 9.b we have seen that M is an L^2-bounded martingale if and only if $E(\langle M \rangle_\infty) < \infty$. Now we will see that the condition $E\left(\langle M \rangle_\infty^{1/2}\right) < \infty$ implies that M is a uniformly integrable martingale.

9.d.0 Lemma. *Let X, A be (adapted) continuous, nonnegative processes with A nondecreasing. Set $X_t^* = \sup_{s \in [0,t]} X_s$ and assume that $E(X_\tau) \leq E(A_\tau)$, for each bounded optional time τ. Then*

$$E\left(\sqrt{X_t^*}\right) \leq 3E\left(\sqrt{A_t}\right), \quad t \geq 0. \tag{0}$$

Proof. Define $A_\infty = \sup_{s \geq 0} A_s$, let $u, t \geq 0$ and set $\sigma = \inf\{ s \mid X_s \geq u \}$. If τ is any bounded optional time then $X_\tau^* \geq u \Rightarrow \sigma \leq \tau$ and hence $X_{\tau \wedge \sigma} = X_\sigma \geq u$ on the set $B = [X_\tau^* \geq u]$. Thus

$$P(X_\tau^* \geq u) = P(B) \leq u^{-1} E(X_{\tau \wedge \sigma} 1_B) \leq u^{-1} E(X_{\tau \wedge \sigma})$$
$$\leq u^{-1} E(A_{\tau \wedge \sigma}) \leq u^{-1} E(A_\tau). \tag{1}$$

Now set $\rho = \inf\{ s \mid A_s \geq u \}$. If $A_t < u$, then $\rho \geq t$, by the nondecreasing nature of the process A, and so $X_t^* = X_{t \wedge \rho}^*$ on the set $[A_t < u]$. Applying (1) to the bounded optional time $\tau = t \wedge \rho$, it follows that

$$P(X_t^* \geq u, A_t < u) \leq P(X_{t \wedge \rho}^* \geq u) \leq u^{-1} E(A_{t \wedge \rho}) \leq u^{-1} E(u \wedge A_t), \quad \text{thus}$$
$$P(X_t^* \geq u) \leq P(X_t^* \geq u, A_t < u) + P(A_t \geq u) \leq u^{-1} E(u \wedge A_t) + P(A_t \geq u).$$

Consequently, using 6.a.0 (and subsequent remark),

$$E\left(\sqrt{X_t^*}\right) = \int_0^\infty \frac{1}{2\sqrt{u}} P(X_t^* \geq u)\, du$$
$$\leq \int_0^\infty \frac{1}{2u^{3/2}} E(u \wedge A_t)\, du + \int_0^\infty \frac{1}{2\sqrt{u}} P(A_t \geq u)\, du. \tag{2}$$

The second integral on the right is simply $E(\sqrt{A_t})$. Using Fubini's Theorem to interchange the integral and expectation, the first integral becomes

$$E\left(\int_0^\infty \frac{u \wedge A_t}{2u^{3/2}}\, du\right) = E\left(\int_0^{A_t} \frac{1}{2\sqrt{u}}\, du + A_t \int_{A_t}^\infty \frac{1}{2u^{3/2}}\, du\right)$$

$$= E\left(\sqrt{A_t} + A_t A_t^{-1/2}\right) = 2E(\sqrt{A_t}).$$

Thus (0) follows from (2). ∎

9.d.1. *Let M be a continuous local martingale, $M_0 = 0$ and $M_t^* = \sup_{0 \le s \le t} |M_s|$. Then*

$$E(M_t^*) \le 3E\left(\langle M \rangle_t^{1/2}\right), \quad t \ge 0. \tag{3}$$

Proof. (a) Assume first that M is a uniformly bounded martingale. Then $M_t^2 - \langle M \rangle_t$ is a martingale vanishing at zero and so $E(M_\tau^2 - \langle M \rangle_\tau) = 0$, that is, $E(M_\tau^2) = E(\langle M \rangle_\tau)$, for all bounded optional times τ. Using 9.d.0 with $X_t = M_t^2$ and $A_t = \langle M \rangle_t$ and observing that $\sqrt{X_t^*} = M_t^*$ now yields (3).

(b) Assume now that M is a local martingale and choose a sequence (T_n) of optional times such that $T_n \uparrow \infty$ and M^{T_n} is a uniformly bounded martingale, for each $n \ge 1$ (8.a.5). Observing that $\left(M^{T_n}\right)_t^* = M_{t \wedge T_n}^*$, (a) implies that $E(M_{t \wedge T_n}^*) \le 3E(\langle M^{T_n} \rangle_t^{1/2}) = 3E(\langle M \rangle_{t \wedge T_n}^{1/2})$. Letting $n \uparrow \infty$ and using the Monotone Convergence Theorem now establishes (3). ∎

9.d.2 Corollary. *Let M be a continuous local martingale with $M_0 = 0$.*
(a) If $T > 0$ and $E(\langle M \rangle_T^{1/2}) < \infty$, then M is a martingale on the interval $[0, T]$.
(b) If $E(\langle M \rangle_\infty^{1/2}) < \infty$, then M is a uniformly integrable martingale.

Proof. (a) follows from (b) applied to the local martingale M^T.
(b) Assume $E(\langle M \rangle_\infty^{1/2}) < \infty$. Then, for all $t \ge 0$, $E(M_t^*) \le 3\,E(\langle M \rangle_\infty^{1/2})$, where $M_t^* = \sup_{0 \le s \le t} |M_s|$. Letting $t \uparrow \infty$ we see that $E(M_\infty^*) < \infty$. This implies that M is a uniformly integrable martingale (8.a.4). ∎

10. THE COVARIATION PROCESS

10.a Definition and elementary properties. Let X, Y be continuous local martingales. Then the product XY is not in general a local martingale. However, using the polarization identity

$$XY = \frac{1}{4}\left[(X+Y)^2 - (X-Y)^2\right] \tag{0}$$

we see that the process

$$\langle X, Y\rangle := \frac{1}{4}\left[\langle X+Y\rangle - \langle X-Y\rangle\right]$$

is a continuous bounded variation process such that $\langle X, Y\rangle_0 = 0$ and the process $XY - \langle X, Y\rangle$ is a local martingale. From 9.b.2 it follows that $\langle X, Y\rangle$ is the unique continuous bounded variation process with this property. Moreover, the product XY is a local martingale if and only if $\langle X, Y\rangle = 0$. Note that $\langle X, X\rangle = \langle X\rangle$ is the quadratic variation process of X. Set

$$Q_\Delta(X, Y) = \sum_{j=1}^{n}(X_{t_j} - X_{t_{j-1}})(Y_{t_j} - Y_{t_{j-1}}),$$

for each $t > 0$ and each partition $\Delta = \{0 = t_0 < \ldots < t_n = t\}$ of the interval $[0, t]$. The polarization identity (0) yields

$$Q_\Delta(X, Y) = \frac{1}{4}\left[Q_\Delta(X+Y) - Q_\Delta(X-Y)\right].$$

From 9.b.3 and 9.b.5 it now follows that

$$Q_\Delta(X, Y) \to \langle X, Y\rangle_t, \text{ in probability, as } \|\Delta\| \to 0. \tag{1}$$

Here the limit is taken over all partitions Δ of the interval $[0, t]$. If X and Y are uniformly bounded martingales, then the convergence is also in $L^2(P)$.

This limit representation shows that the covariation process $\langle X, Y\rangle$ is not affected if the filtration $(\mathcal{F}_t)$ is replaced with some other (right continuous and augmented) filtration $(\mathcal{G}_t)$ with respect to which X, Y are still local martingales. The covariation process $\langle X, Y\rangle$ is also unaffected if the probability measure P is replaced with some absolutely continuous probability measure $Q << P$, with respect to which X, Y are still local martingales. This follows from the fact that convergence in P-probability implies convergence in Q-probability.

The bracket $\langle X, Y\rangle$ has many properties of an inner product: it is *symmetric*, *bilinear* and *nonnegative* and even satisifies $\langle X\rangle = 0 \Rightarrow X = 0$, if we restrict ourselves to processes X with $X_0 = 0$. The bilinearity of $\langle X, Y\rangle$ is easily established from the universal property. For example $(\alpha X)Y - \alpha\langle X, Y\rangle = \alpha(XY - \langle X, Y\rangle)$ is a local martingale. Since the process $\alpha\langle X, Y\rangle$ is a continuous bounded variation process vanishing at time zero and $\langle \alpha X, Y\rangle$ is the unique continuous bounded variation process A vanishing at time zero such that $(\alpha X)Y - A$ is a local martingale, it follows that $\alpha\langle X, Y\rangle = \langle \alpha X, Y\rangle$.

10.a.0. *Let X, Y be continuous local martingales and T an optional time. Then*

$$\langle X^T, Y^T \rangle = \langle X^T, Y \rangle = \langle X, Y \rangle^T.$$

Proof. (a) Stopping the local martingale $XY - \langle X, Y \rangle$ at time T we see that $X^T Y^T - \langle X, Y \rangle^T$ is a local martingale and thus that $\langle X^T, Y^T \rangle = \langle X, Y \rangle^T$.

(b) To see that $\langle X^T, Y \rangle = \langle X^T, Y^T \rangle$, it suffices to show that $\langle X^T, Y - Y^T \rangle = 0$; equivalently, $X^T(Y - Y^T)$ is a local martingale. Intuitively, the factor X^T is constant after time T so that the product $X^T(Y - Y^T)$ is a constant multiple of the local martingale $Y - Y^T$ after time T, while before time T the factor $Y - Y^T$ is zero.

More precisely set $Z = X^T$ and $W = Y - Y^T$. We must show that $\langle Z, W \rangle = 0$. Fix $\omega \in \Omega$. Then the path $s \mapsto Z_s(\omega)$ is constant for $s \geq T(\omega)$ while the path $s \mapsto W_s(\omega)$ is identically zero for $s \leq T(\omega)$.

Fix $t \geq 0$ and let $\Delta = \{0 = t_0 < \ldots < t_n = t\}$ be a partition of $[0, t]$. The preceding shows that the product $\left(Z_{t_j}(\omega) - Z_{t_{j-1}}(\omega)\right)\left(W_{t_j}(\omega) - W_{t_{j-1}}(\omega)\right)$ is nonzero only if $t_{j-1} < T(\omega) < t_j$. Thus, for $\omega \in \Omega$, we have

$$Q_\Delta(Z, W)(\omega) = \begin{cases} 0 & \text{if } T(\omega) > t \\ \left(Z_{t_j}(\omega) - Z_{t_{j-1}}(\omega)\right)\left(W_{t_j}(\omega) - W_{t_{j-1}}(\omega)\right) & \text{if } T(\omega) \leq t \end{cases}, \quad (2)$$

where $t_j = t_j(\omega)$ satisfies $t_{j-1} < T(\omega) \leq t_j$. It follows that $Q_\Delta(Z, W)(\omega) \to 0$, as $\|\Delta\| \to 0$, for each $\omega \in \Omega$ such that the paths $s \mapsto Z_s(\omega)$ and $s \mapsto W_s(\omega)$ are continuous, and so for P-ae. $\omega \in \Omega$. Replacing Δ with a sequence Δ_n such that $\|\Delta_n\| \to 0$ and recalling that almost sure convergence implies convergence in probability (1.a.0), it follows that $\langle Z, W \rangle_t = P\text{-lim}_n Q_{\Delta_n}(Z, W) = 0$, as desired. ∎

10.b Integration with respect to continuous bounded variation processes. Recall that $(\Omega, \mathcal{F}, P, (\mathcal{F}_t))$ is a complete filtered probability space. Let A be a continuous bounded variation process, which is adapted to the filtration $(\mathcal{F}_t)$. For each $t \geq 0$ let $|A|_t$ denote the total variation of A on the interval $[0, t]$ defined pathwise, that is, $|A|_t(\omega)$ is the total variation of the path $s \in [0, t] \mapsto A_s(\omega)$, for each $\omega \in \Omega$. Then $|A|_t$ is a continuous increasing $(\mathcal{F}_t)$-adapted process and the same is true of the process $|A|_t - A_t$. Thus $A_t = |A|_t - (|A|_t - A_t)$ provides a canonical decomposition of A as a difference of continuous increasing $(\mathcal{F}_t)$-adapted processes.

Let $\omega \in \Omega$. If the path $A_\omega : s \in [0, +\infty) \mapsto A_s(\omega)$ is continuous and of bounded variation on finite intervals, then it induces a unique signed Borel measure μ_ω^t on each finite interval $I = [0, t]$ such that $\mu_\omega^t([a, b]) = A_\omega(b) - A_\omega(a)$, for all subintervals $[a, b] \subseteq I$. A_ω does not in general induce a measure on all of $[0, +\infty)$ but the measures μ_ω^t satisfy $\mu_\omega^r = \mu_\omega^t|_{[0,r]}$, for all $0 < r \leq t$. We shall thus drop the dependence on t and use the simpler notation μ_ω. It is customary to write $\mu_\omega(ds) = dA_s(\omega)$, that is,

$$\int_0^t f(s) dA_s(\omega) = \int_0^t f(s)\mu_\omega(ds),$$

whenever this integral exists. If the path A_ω is nondecreasing, then it does induce a unique positive Borel measure μ_ω on $[0, +\infty)$ satisfying $\mu_\omega([a, b]) = A_\omega(b) - A_\omega(a)$, for all finite intervals $[a, b] \subseteq [0, +\infty)$. This is the case in particular for P-ae. path $s \in [0, +\infty) \mapsto |A|_s(\omega)$ of the variation process $|A|$. The corresponding measure is the total variation $|\mu_\omega|$ of the measure μ_ω. We use the notation $|\mu_\omega|(ds) = |dA_s|(\omega)$ that is, we write

$$\int_0^t f(s)|dA_s|(\omega) = \int_0^t f(s)|\mu_\omega|(ds),$$

whenever this integral exists. Assume now that H_s is a process with measurable paths $s \mapsto H_s(\omega)$ satisfying

$$\int_0^t |H_s(\omega)|\,|dA_s|(\omega) < \infty, \quad P\text{-as., for each } t \geq 0. \tag{0}$$

Then, for each $t \geq 0$, the stochastic integral $I_t = \int_0^t H_s dA_s$ is defined pathwise as $I_t(\omega) = \int_0^t H_s(\omega)dA_s(\omega)$, for P-ae. $\omega \in \Omega$.

Let $\mathcal{B}$, $\mathcal{B}_t$ denote the Borel σ-fields on $[0, \infty)$, $[0, t]$ respectively. Call the process $H = H(s, \omega) : R_+ \times \Omega \to \overline{R}$ (jointly) measurable, if it is measurable for the product σ-field $\mathcal{B} \times \mathcal{F}$ on $R_+ \times \Omega$. Call H *progressively measurable*, if the restriction of H to $[0, t] \times \Omega$ is $\mathcal{B}_t \times \mathcal{F}_t$-measurable, for all $t \geq 0$.

Since the measurability with respect to a product σ-field implies the measurability of all sections, it follows that a measurable process H has Borel measurable paths $s \mapsto H_s(\omega)$ and that a progressively measurable process H_t is adapted to the filtration $(\mathcal{F}_t)$. Clearly a progressively measurable process H is measurable.

Let $L_{loc}^1(A)$ denote the family of all real valued, jointly measurable processes H satisfying (0). The subscript signifies local integrability, that is, the finiteness of the integral over compacts, equivalently, over sufficiently small neighborhoods of points. For $H \in L_{loc}^1(A)$ and $t \geq 0$ the integral $I_t = \int_0^t H_s dA_s$ is a function defined P-as. on Ω.

10.b.0. *Let $H \in L_{loc}^1(A)$. Then $I_t = \int_0^t H_s dA_s$ is a random variable, that is, measurable on Ω, for each $t \geq 0$. If H is progressively measurable, then I_t is $\mathcal{F}_t$-measurable for each $t \geq 0$, that is, the process I_t is $(\mathcal{F}_t)$-adapted.*

Proof. Let us first show that I_t is measurable. Recalling that the process A can be written as a difference of continuous increasing $(\mathcal{F}_t)$-adapted processes we may assume that A is itself increasing and hence the associated measures μ_ω positive. It will then suffice to conduct the proof for nonnegative H. Linearity and the usual approximation of H as an increasing limit of $\mathcal{B} \times \mathcal{F}$-measurable simple functions on $R_+ \times \Omega$ shows that we can restrict ourselves to the case $H = 1_\Gamma$, where $\Gamma \subseteq R_+ \times \Omega$ is a $\mathcal{B} \times \mathcal{F}$-measurable set. Application of the π-λ-Theorem (appendix B.3) now shows that we can limit ourselves to measurable rectangles Γ of the form $\Gamma = [a, b] \times F$ where $0 \leq a < b < \infty$ and $F \in \mathcal{F}$. However, if $H = 1_{[a,b] \times F}$, an easy computation shows that $I_t = 1_F(A_{t \wedge b} - A_{t \wedge a})$, P-as., for all $t \geq 0$, which is measurable on Ω.

Assume now that the process H is progressively measurable and fix $t \geq 0$. In the computation of the integral $I_t = \int_0^t H_s dA_s$ we make use only of the restriction

$H|_{[0,t]\times\Omega}$ which is $\mathcal{B}_t \times \mathcal{F}_t$-measurable. Thus, in the preceding argument we can stop the filtration $\mathcal{F}_s$ and the process A_s at time t and replace the σ-field $\mathcal{F}$ with $\mathcal{F}_t$. Then the preceding argument shows that I_t is $\mathcal{F}_t$-measurable. ∎

Assume that $H \in L^1_{loc}(A)$. Then the process $I_t = \int_0^t H_s dA_s$ is also denoted $H \bullet A$, that is, we set

$$(H \bullet A)_t = \int_0^t H_s dA_s, \quad t \geq 0.$$

The integral process $H \bullet A$ is a continuous bounded variation process. If H is progressively measurable, then this process is also adapted. The family of all jointly measurable processes H satisfying the stronger condition

$$\int_0^\infty |H_s(\omega)| \, |dA_s|(\omega) < \infty, \quad P\text{-as.}, \tag{1}$$

is denoted $L^1(A)$. Note $L^1(A) \subseteq L^1_{loc}(A)$. For $H \in L^1(A)$ the stochastic integral $\int_0^\infty H_s dA_s$ is defined pathwise as the limit $\int_0^\infty H_s dA_s = \lim_{t\uparrow\infty} \int_0^t H_s(\omega) dA_s(\omega)$, for P-ae. $\omega \in \Omega$. The existence of the limit is ensured by (1). The random variable $\int_0^\infty H_s dA_s$ is also denoted $(H \bullet A)_\infty$.

For an optional time T define the *stochastic interval* $[\![0, T]\!]$ as the set

$$[\![0, T]\!] = \{ (t, \omega) \in R_+ \times \Omega \mid 0 \leq t \leq T(\omega) \} \subseteq R_+ \times \Omega.$$

Thus $X = 1_{[\![0,T]\!]}$ is a stochastic process satisfying $X_t(\omega) = 1_{[0,T(\omega)]}(t)$. It follows that the process $Z = 1_{[\![0,T]\!]}H$ is given by $Z_t(\omega) = 1_{[0,T(\omega)]}(t)H_t(\omega)$. In short, multiplication by $1_{[\![0,T]\!]}$ cuts the process H off to zero after time T. Let us now gather the properties of the integral process $H \bullet A$ which are relevant for the definition of more general stochastic integrals below:

10.b.1. *Let A be a continuous, bounded variation process, $H \in L^1_{loc}(A)$ and T be any optional time. Then*

(a) *$H \bullet A = \int_0^{\cdot} H_s dA_s$ is a continuous bounded variation process. If H is progressively measurable, then the process $H \bullet A$ is adapted.*

(b) *$H \bullet A$ is bilinear in H and A.*

(c) *$H \bullet (A^T) = (1_{[\![0,T]\!]}H) \bullet A = (H \bullet A)^T$.*

(d) *$L^1_{loc}(A) = L^1_{loc}(A - A_0)$ and $H \bullet A = H \bullet (A - A_0)$, for all $H \in L^1_{loc}(A)$.*

(e) *$A^T = A_0 + 1_{[\![0,T]\!]} \bullet A$, especially $A = A_0 + 1 \bullet A$.*

Proof. This follows from standard results in Real Analysis in a path by path manner. (c) Note that the pathwise Lebesgue-Stieltjes measures corresponding to the paths $s \to A_s^T(\omega)$ do not charge the interval $(T(\omega), \infty) \subseteq R$. Consequently the process $H \bullet A^T$ remains constant on this interval. The same is obviously true of the processes $(1_{[\![0,T]\!]}H) \bullet A$ and $(H \bullet A)^T$. Moreover all three processes agree on the interval $[\![0, T]\!]$.

(d) Note that the pathwise Lebesgue-Stieltjes measures corresponding to A and $A - A_0$ coincide. (e) Note that for $t \geq 0$,

$$\left(A_0 + 1_{[\![0,T]\!]} \bullet A\right)_t(\omega) = A_0(\omega) + \int_0^t 1_{[0,T(\omega)]}(s) dA_s(\omega)$$

$$= A_0(\omega) + \int_0^{t \wedge T(\omega)} 1 dA_s(\omega) = A_{t \wedge T(\omega)}(\omega). \ \blacksquare$$

The following associative property is particularly important in the theory of stochastic integration. It is this property which supports the formalism of stochastic differentials developed in chapter III.

10.b.2. *If $K \in L^1_{loc}(A)$ and $H \in L^1_{loc}(K \bullet A)$, then $HK \in L^1_{loc}(A)$ and we have $H \bullet (K \bullet A) = (HK) \bullet A$.*

Proof. The equality $(K \bullet A)_t(\omega) = \int_0^t K_s(\omega) dA_s(\omega)$ implies that

$$d(K \bullet A)_t(\omega) = K_t(\omega) dA_t(\omega) \tag{2}$$

for P-ae. $\omega \in \Omega$. This equality is to be interpreted as follows: For P-ae. $\omega \in \Omega$, the function $t \mapsto K_t(\omega)$ is the Radon Nikodym derivative of the Lebesgue-Stieltjes measure corresponding to the path $t \mapsto (K \bullet A)_t(\omega)$ with respect to the Lebesgue-Stieltjes measure corresponding to the path $t \mapsto A_t(\omega)$. Recall that this implies the same relation $|d(K \bullet A)_t|(\omega) = |K_t(\omega)| \, |dA_t|(\omega)$ for the associated total variation measures. Thus, for $t \geq 0$, we have $\int_0^t |H_s K_s| \, |dA_s| = \int_0^t |H_s| \, |d(K \bullet A)_s| < \infty$, P-as., since $H \in L^1_{loc}(K \bullet A)$. It follows that $HK \in L^1_{loc}(A)$. Moreover, using (2),

$$\left((HK) \bullet A\right)_t = \int_0^t H_s K_s dA_s = \int_0^t H_s d(K \bullet A)_s = \left(H \bullet (K \bullet A)\right)_t, \quad P\text{-as. on } \Omega. \ \blacksquare$$

10.b.3 Remark. If the integrator A is a continuous increasing process, and hence the associated Lebesgue-Stieltjes measures nonnegative, then the stochastic integral $\int_0^\infty H_s dA_s$ is defined also for each jointly measurable process $H \geq 0$ and is a random variable, that is, measurable. Likewise the integral process $H \bullet A$ is defined and satisfies 10.b.2, 10.b.3 with proofs similar to the above.

10.c Kunita-Watanabe inequality. Let M, N be continuous local martingales and $t > 0$. The considerations of 10.b will now be applied to the continuous bounded variation processes $A = \langle M, N \rangle, \langle M \rangle, \langle N \rangle$. For $\omega \in \Omega$ let μ_ω, ν_ω, σ_ω denote the following Lebesgue-Stieltjes measures

$$\mu_\omega(ds) = d\langle M, N \rangle_s(\omega), \quad \nu_\omega(ds) = d\langle M \rangle_s(\omega) \quad \text{and} \quad \sigma_\omega(ds) = d\langle N \rangle_s(\omega)$$

on the Borel subsets of finite intervals $[0, t]$. Let us now study the relation of the measures μ_ω, ν_ω and σ_ω. Note that all these measures vanish on singletons as the path $s \mapsto A_s(\omega)$ is continuous, for all A as above. Recall that $|\mu_\omega|$ denotes the absolute variation of the signed measure μ_ω.

10.c.0. *For P-ae.* $\omega \in \Omega$ *we have* $|\mu_\omega|([a,b]) \leq \nu_\omega([a,b])^{1/2}\,\sigma_\omega([a,b])^{1/2}$, *for all subintervals* $[a,b] \subseteq [0,t]$.

Proof. *Step 1.* Fix a subinterval $[a,b] \subseteq [0,t]$. We show that $|\mu_\omega([a,b])| \leq \nu_\omega([a,b])^{1/2}\,\sigma_\omega([a,b])^{1/2}$, equivalently, by definition of the measures μ_ω, ν_ω, σ_ω, that

$$\left|\langle M,N\rangle_a^b(\omega)\right| \leq \langle M\rangle_a^b(\omega)^{1/2}\langle N\rangle_a^b(\omega)^{1/2}, \quad \text{for } P\text{-ae. } \omega \in \Omega. \tag{0}$$

Choose a sequence (Δ_n) of partitions of $[a,b]$ such that $\|\Delta_n\| \to 0$, as $n \uparrow \infty$. Then

$$Q_{\Delta_n}(M,N) \to \langle M,N\rangle_a^b \quad Q_{\Delta_n}(M) \to \langle M\rangle_a^b \quad \text{and} \quad Q_{\Delta_n}(N) \to \langle N\rangle_a^b, \tag{1}$$

in probability. Replacing (Δ_n) with a suitable subsequence the convergence will be almost sure. Consider any $\omega \in \Omega$ such that the convergence (1) holds at the point ω. If $\Delta = \{a = t_0 < t_1 < \ldots < t_n = b\}$ is any partition of the interval $[a,b]$, then, using the Cauchy-Schwartz inequality,

$$\left|Q_\Delta(M,N)\right|^2 = \left|\sum (M_{t_j} - M_{t_{j-1}})(N_{t_j} - N_{t_{j-1}})\right|^2$$
$$\leq \sum (M_{t_j} - M_{t_{j-1}})^2 \sum (N_{t_j} - N_{t_{j-1}})^2 = Q_\Delta(M)Q_\Delta(N).$$

Taking square roots, replacing Δ with Δ_n, evaluating the inequality at the point ω and letting $n \uparrow \infty$, we obtain (0).

Step 2. We observe that the exceptional P-null set in step 1 can be made independent of the interval $[a,b] \subseteq [0,t]$. This follows by taking the countable union of the exceptional sets for all intervals $[a,b] \subseteq [0,t]$ with rational endpoints a, b and approximating the general subinterval $[a,b] \subseteq [0,t]$ with these.

Step 3. Let $[a,b]$ be a subinterval of $[0,t]$ and $\Delta = \{a = t_0 < t_1 < \ldots < t_n = b\}$ a partition of $[a,b]$. According to step 1 we have

$$\left|\mu_\omega([t_{j-1},t_j])\right| \leq \nu_\omega([t_{j-1},t_j])^{1/2}\,\sigma_\omega([t_{j-1},t_j])^{1/2},$$

for P-ae. $\omega \in \Omega$ and all $j = 1,2,\ldots,n$. Summing and using the Cauchy-Schwartz inequality, we obtain

$$\sum \left|\mu_\omega([t_{j-1},t_j])\right| \leq \left\{\sum \nu_\omega([t_{j-1},t_j])\right\}^{1/2}\left\{\sum \sigma_\omega([t_{j-1},t_j])\right\}^{1/2}$$
$$= \nu_\omega([a,b])^{1/2}\sigma_\omega([a,b])^{1/2}.$$

Here the exceptional set does not depend on the partition Δ (step 2). Taking the sup over all such partitions Δ of $[a,b]$ we obtain $|\mu_\omega|([a,b]) \leq \nu_\omega([a,b])^{1/2}\,\sigma_\omega([a,b])^{1/2}$, as desired. Recall that in the computation of the total variation $|\mu_\omega|([a,b])$ of the (continuous) Lebesgue-Stieltjes measure μ_ω on $[a,b]$ it suffices to consider partitions of $[a,b]$ into subintervals (rather than general measurable sets). Note that the exceptional set is independent of the interval $[a,b]$ (see step 2). ∎

10.c.1. *For P-ae.* $\omega \in \Omega$ *we have* $|\mu_\omega|(A) \leq \nu_\omega(A)^{1/2}\,\sigma_\omega(A)^{1/2}$, *for all Borel sets* $A \subseteq [0,t]$.

Proof. Since the measures $|\mu_\omega|$, ν_ω, σ_ω all vanish on singletons, it will suffice to establish the claim for all Borel sets $A \subseteq [0,t)$. Let $\omega \in \Omega$ be such that 10.c.1 holds for all intervals $[a,b] \subseteq [0,t]$.

The family $\mathcal{G}$ of all finite disjoint unions of intervals of the form $[a,b) \subseteq [0,t)$ is a field of sets which generates the Borel-σ-field on $[0,t)$. If $A \subseteq [0,t)$ a Borel set then, according to appendix B.9.0, there exists a sequence of sets $A_n \in \mathcal{G}$ such that $(|\mu_\omega| + \nu_\omega + \sigma_\omega)(A \Delta A_n) \to 0$ and consequently

$$|\mu_\omega|(A_n) \to |\mu_\omega|(A),\quad \nu_\omega(A_n) \to \nu_\omega(A) \text{ and } \sigma_\omega(A_n) \to \sigma_\omega(A), \quad \text{as } n \uparrow \infty.$$

It will thus suffice to establish the claim for all sets $A \in \mathcal{G}$. Indeed, if $A = [a_1, b_1) \cup [a_2, b_2) \cup \ldots \cup [a_n, b_n)$, where $0 \leq a_1 < b_1 \leq a_2 < b_2 \leq \ldots \leq a_n < b_n$, then, using 10.c.1 and the Cauchy-Schwartz inequality,

$$|\mu_\omega|(A) = \sum |\mu_\omega|([a_j, b_j)) \leq \sum \nu_\omega([a_j, b_j))^{1/2}\sigma_\omega([a_j, b_j))^{1/2}$$

$$\leq \left\{\sum \nu_\omega([a_j, b_j))\right\}^{1/2} \left\{\sum \sigma_\omega([a_j, b_j))\right\}^{1/2} = \nu_\omega(A)^{1/2}\,\sigma_\omega(A)^{1/2}.\ \blacksquare$$

10.c.2. *For P-ae.* $\omega \in \Omega$ *we have*

$$\int_0^t fg\,d|\mu_\omega| \leq \left\{\int_0^t f^2 d\nu_\omega\right\}^{1/2} \left\{\int_0^t g^2 d\sigma_\omega\right\}^{1/2},$$

for all nonnegative Borel measurable functions $f, g : [0,t] \to \overline{R}$.

Proof. Let $\omega \in \Omega$ be such that 10.c.2 holds for all Borel sets $A \subseteq [0,t]$. It will suffice to establish the claim for Borel measurable simple functions f, g. Such f, g can be written as

$$f = \sum \alpha_j 1_{A_j} \quad \text{and} \quad g = \sum \beta_j 1_{A_j},$$

where $\mathcal{P} = \{A_1, A_2, \ldots, A_n\}$ is a Borel measurable partition of $[0,t]$. Then

$$f^2 = \sum \alpha_j^2 1_{A_j}, \quad g^2 = \sum \beta_j^2 1_{A_j} \quad \text{and} \quad fg = \sum \alpha_j \beta_j 1_{A_j}.$$

Thus, using 10.c.2 and the Cauchy-Schwartz inequality,

$$\int_0^t fg\,d|\mu_\omega| = \sum \alpha_j \beta_j |\mu_\omega|(A_j) \leq \sum \alpha_j \beta_j \nu_\omega(A_j)^{1/2}\,\sigma_\omega(A_j)^{1/2}$$

$$\leq \left\{\sum_{j=1}^n \alpha_j^2 \nu_\omega(A_j)\right\}^{1/2} \left\{\sum_{j=1}^n \beta_j^2 \sigma_\omega(A_j)\right\}^{1/2}$$

$$= \left\{\int_0^t f^2 d\nu_\omega\right\}^{1/2} \left\{\int_0^t g^2 d\sigma_\omega\right\}^{1/2}.\ \blacksquare$$

10.c.3 Kunita-Watanabe Inequality. *Let M, N be continuous local martingales, U, V be $\mathcal{B} \times \mathcal{F}$-measurable processes and $t \geq 0$. Then*

$$\int_0^t |U_s V_s| \, |d\langle M, N\rangle_s| \leq \left\{ \int_0^t U_s^2 d\langle M\rangle_s \right\}^{1/2} \left\{ \int_0^t V_s^2 d\langle N\rangle_s \right\}^{1/2}, \quad P\text{-as.} \quad (2)$$

Proof. Let $\omega \in \Omega$ be such that 10.c.3 holds for all nonnegative Borel measurable functions $f, g : [0, t] \to \overline{R}$ and let $f(s) = U_s(\omega)$ and $g(s) = V_s(\omega)$. Recalling that $|\mu_\omega|(ds) = |d\langle M, N\rangle_s|(\omega)$, $\nu_\omega(ds) = d\langle M\rangle_s(\omega)$ and $\sigma_\omega(ds) = d\langle N\rangle_s(\omega)$, 10.c.3 shows that (2) holds at the point ω. ∎

10.c.4 Remark. The special case $U = V = 1$ (already contained in 10.c.1) is useful and yields

$$\left|\langle M, N\rangle_t\right| \leq \langle M\rangle_t^{1/2} \langle N\rangle_t^{1/2}, \quad P\text{-as.} \ \forall \, t \geq 0.$$

11. SEMIMARTINGALES

11.a Definition and basic properties. Recall that $(\Omega, \mathcal{F}, P, (\mathcal{F}_t))$ is a filtered probability space with $(\mathcal{F}_t)$ a right continuous and augmented filtration. The family of continuous local martingales with respect to this probability space is a real vector space but is not closed under multiplication. Indeed, if X, Y are continuous local martingales, then even the square X^2 is a local martingale only if X itself is constant ($X_t = X_0$). However the processes X^2 and XY differ from a local martingale only by a continuous bounded variation process. In fact

$$X^2 = M + A \quad \text{and} \quad XY = N + B,$$

where $M = X^2 - \langle X \rangle$ and $N = XY - \langle X, Y \rangle$ are continuous local martingales and $A = \langle X \rangle$, $B = \langle X, Y \rangle$ are continuous bounded variation processes. This suggests that we enlarge the class of continuous local martingales and define

11.a.0 Definition. *The process X is called a continuous semimartingale if it can be represented as a sum $X_t = M_t + A_t$, $t \geq 0$, where M is a continuous local martingale and A a continuous (adapted) bounded variation process satisfying $A_0 = 0$.*

Equivalently, X is a continuous semimartingale if and only if there exists a continuous bounded variation process A such that $X - A$ is a local martingale. The condition $A_0 = 0$ can always be satisfied by replacing A with $A_t - A_0$.

   The requirement $A_0 = 0$ ensures that the decomposition $X = M + A$ is unique. Indeed, using 9.b.2, A is the unique continuous bounded variation process such that $A_0 = 0$ and $X - A$ is a local martingale, and $M = X - A$. The decomposition $X = M + A$ is referred to as the *semimartingale decomposition* of X, the process M is called the *local martingale part* of X and the process A the *compensator of* X, denoted

$$A = u_X.$$

Note that each continuous bounded variation process A is a semimartingale with local martingale part $M_t = A_0$ and compensator $u_A(t) = A_t - A_0$. More precisely a continuous semimartingale X is a bounded variation process if and only if its compensator satisfies $u_X(t) = X_t - X_0$. If $X_0 = 0$, then X is a bounded variation process if and only if $u_X = X$ and X is a local martingale if and only if $u_X = 0$.

Example. If X, Y are continuous local martingales, then X^2 and XY are semimartingales with compensator $u_{X^2} = \langle X \rangle$ and $u_{XY} = \langle X, Y \rangle$ respectively.

   Let $\mathcal{S}$ denote the family of all continuous semimartingales with respect to $(\Omega, \mathcal{F}, P, (\mathcal{F}_t))$. It is easily seen that $\mathcal{S}$ is a real vector space. However, at present it is not even clear that $\mathcal{S}$ is closed under multiplication. Miraculously the Ito formula of the Stochastic Calculus will show that $\mathcal{S}$ is in fact closed under the application of all twice continuously differentiable multivariable functions. That is, if $f \in C^2(R^n)$ and if $X_1, \ldots, X_n$ are continuous semimartingales, then $Y = f(X_1, \ldots, X_n)$ is also a continuous semimartingale. The Ito formula will also provide a formula for the local martingale part and compensator u_Y of Y. It thus turns out that the choice of the space $\mathcal{S}$ of continuous semimartingales is extremely fortunate.

11.b Quadratic variation and covariation. If X, Y are continuous semimartingales, we define the covariation process $\langle X, Y \rangle$ as
$$\langle X, Y \rangle = \langle M, N \rangle,$$

where M and N are the local martingale parts of X, Y respectively. In particular, if A is a continuous bounded variation process, then A is a continuous semimartingale with constant martingale part. It follows easily that $\langle X, A \rangle = 0$, for each continuous semimartingale X. The following justifies our definition of $\langle X, Y \rangle$:

11.b.0. *Let X, Y be continuous semimartingales, A a continuous bounded variation process and $t \geq 0$. Then*
(a) $Q_\Delta(X, A) \to 0$, P-as., as $\|\Delta\| \to 0$, and
(b) $Q_\Delta(X, Y) \to \langle X, Y \rangle_t$ in probability, as $\|\Delta\| \to 0$.
Here the limits are taken over all partitions Δ of the interval $[0, t]$.

Proof. (a) Let $\omega \in \Omega$ be such that the path $s \to A_s(\omega)$ is of bounded variation and the path $s \to X_s(\omega)$ is continuous and hence uniformly continuous on the interval $[0, t]$. This is the case for P-ae. $\omega \in \Omega$. Let $|A|_t(\omega) < \infty$ denote the total variation of the path $s \to A_s(\omega)$ on the interval $[0, t]$ and set, for any partition $\Delta = \{ 0 = t_0 < t_1 < \ldots < t_n = t \}$ of the interval $[0, t]$,

$$C_\Delta(\omega) = \sup_{1 \leq j \leq n} |X_{t_j}(\omega) - X_{t_{j-1}}(\omega)|.$$

The uniform continuity of the path $s \to X_s(\omega)$ on the interval $[0, t]$ implies that $\lim_{\|\Delta\| \to 0} C(\Delta)(\omega) = 0$. Thus

$$\left| Q_\Delta(X, A)(\omega) \right| \leq \sum |X_{t_j}(\omega) - X_{t_{j-1}}(\omega)| \, |A_{t_j}(\omega) - A_{t_{j-1}}(\omega)|$$
$$\leq C_\Delta(\omega) \sum |A_{t_j}(\omega) - A_{t_{j-1}}(\omega)| \leq C_\Delta(\omega) |A|_t(\omega) \to 0,$$

as $\|\Delta\| \to 0$. This shows (a).

(b) Let $X = M + \tilde{A}$ and $Y = N + B$ be the semimartingale decompositions of X, Y. Fix $t \geq 0$ and let $\Delta = \{ 0 = t_0 < t_1 < \ldots < t_n = t \}$ be a partition of the interval $[0, t]$. By elementary algebra

$$Q_\Delta(X, Y) = \sum \left[(M_{t_j} - M_{t_{j-1}}) + (\tilde{A}_{t_j} - \tilde{A}_{t_{j-1}}) \right] \left[(N_{t_j} - N_{t_{j-1}}) + (B_{t_j} - B_{t_{j-1}}) \right]$$
$$= Q_\Delta(\tilde{A}, Y) + Q_\Delta(M, N) + Q_\Delta(M, B).$$

Now let $\|\Delta\| \to 0$. Then we have $Q_\Delta(\tilde{A}, Y), Q_\Delta(M, B) \to 0$ according to (a) and, $Q_\Delta(M, N) \to \langle M, N \rangle_t$, according to 10.a.eq.(1), in probability, as $n \uparrow \infty$. It follows that $Q_\Delta(X, Y) \to \langle M, N \rangle_t = \langle X, Y \rangle_t$, in probability. ∎

Let X be a continuous semimartingale and $X = M + A$ the semimartingale decomposition of X. If T is any optional time X^T is again a continuous semimartingale with semimartingale decomposition $X^T = M^T + A^T$. Most properties of the co-variation process $\langle M, N \rangle$ of continuous local martingales M, N extend easily to the case of continuous semimartingales X, Y.

It is of course no longer true that $X^2 - \langle X \rangle$ is a local martingale (it *is* a continuous semimartingale, but this is no longer interesting, since much stronger statements are true for the space $\mathcal{S}$). Thus, it is also no longer true that $u_{X^2} = \langle X \rangle$. Likewise $\langle X \rangle = 0$ no longer implies that X is constant in time, merely that X is a bounded variation process. We collect these results below:

11.b.1. *Let* X, Y *be continuous semimartingales,* T *an optional time and* C *an* $\mathcal{F}_0$-*measurable random variable satisfying* $P(|C| < \infty) = 1$. *Then*
(a) If X *is a local martingale, then so is the process* CX.
(b) $\langle X, Y \rangle$ *is a continuous bounded variation process and* $\langle X \rangle$ *a continuous increasing process both vanishing at time zero.*
(c) $\langle X \rangle = 0$ *if and only if* X *is a bounded variation process.*
(d) $\langle X^T, Y^T \rangle = \langle X^T, Y \rangle = \langle X, Y \rangle^T$.
(e) The bracket $\langle \cdot, \cdot \rangle$ *is symmetric, bilinear and nonnegative.*
(f) $\langle X + A, Y + B \rangle = \langle X, Y \rangle$, *for all continuous bounded variation processes* A, B.
(g) $\langle CX, Y \rangle = C \langle X, Y \rangle$.

Proof. (a) Set $T_n = \inf\{\, t \geq 0 \mid |CX_t| \vee |X_t| > n.\,\}$. From the continuity of X and the fact that C is almost surely finitely valued, it follows that $T_n \uparrow \infty$, P-as. If X is a continuous local martingale then the sequence (T_n) reduces X (8.a.5), that is, $X(n) = 1_{[T_n > 0]} X^{T_n}$ is a martingale, for each $n \geq 1$. It will now suffice to show that (T_n) reduces the process CX also, that is, the process $1_{[T_n > 0]}(CX)^{T_n} = CX(n)$ is a martingale, for each $n \geq 1$.

Fix $n \geq 1$ and note that $|CX(n)| \leq n$, by definition of the optional time T_n. Now let $0 \leq s < t$. Then $X(n)_t, CX(n)_t \in \mathcal{E}(P)$ and so, using the $\mathcal{F}_0$-measurability of C, 2.b.10 and the martingale property of $X(n)$, it follows that $E(CX(n)_t | \mathcal{F}_s) = C E(X(n)_t | \mathcal{F}_s) = CX(n)_s$. Thus $CX(n)$ is a martingale.

(b)-(f) now follow immediately from the definitions and 10.a.1.

(g) Since C is $\mathcal{F}_0$-measurable, CX is adapted. Let $X = M + A$ be the semimartingale decomposition of X. According to (a), CM is a local martingale and CA a bounded variation process. Thus $CX = CM + CA$ is a semimartingale. Let $t \geq 0$ and Δ be any partition of $[0, t]$. Then $Q_\Delta(CX, Y) = C Q_\Delta(X, Y)$. Letting $\|\Delta\| \to 0$ it follows that $\langle CX, Y \rangle_t = C \langle X, Y \rangle_t$. ∎

Remark. The useful property (e) shows that bounded variation summands can be dropped from a covariation process. This is the case in particular if A, B are random variables (viewed as processes constant in time).

If X, Y are continuous local martingales, then the process $XY - \langle X, Y \rangle$ is a local martingale but it is known to be a martingale only if X, Y are uniformly bounded martingales. In fact the following is true:

11.b.2. *(a) If $M, N \in \mathbf{H}^2$, then $MN - \langle M, N \rangle$ is a uniformly integrable martingale.*
(b) If M, N are square integrable martingales, then $MN - \langle M, N \rangle$ is a martingale.

Proof. (a) We may assume that $M, N \in \mathbf{H}_0^2$. Then the functions $M_\infty^* = \sup_{t \geq 0} |M_t|$, N_∞^*, $\langle M \rangle_\infty^{1/2}$, $\langle N \rangle_\infty^{1/2}$ are all square integrable (9.c.1). Let $t \geq 0$. From 10.c.4 we have $|\langle M, N \rangle_t| \leq \langle M \rangle_t^{1/2} \langle N \rangle_t^{1/2}$ and so

$$f = \sup_{t \geq 0} |M_t N_t - \langle M, N \rangle_t| \leq M_\infty^* N_\infty^* + \langle M \rangle_\infty^{1/2} \langle N \rangle_\infty^{1/2} \quad \text{is integrable.}$$

Thus $M_t N_t - \langle M, N \rangle_t$ is a uniformly integrable local martingale of class DL and hence a martingale.

(b) Let $X = MN - \langle M, N \rangle$ and $a > 0$. Then $X^a = M^a N^a - \langle M^a, N^a \rangle$, where $M^a, N^a \in \mathbf{H}^2$. Thus X^a is a martingale by (a). It follows that X is a martingale. $\blacksquare$

11.b.3. *The Kunita-Watanabe inequality 10.c.4 still holds if the local martingales M, N are replaced with semimartingales $X, Y \in \mathcal{S}$.*

Proof. If $X = L + A$, $Y = M + B$ are the semimartingale decompositions of X and Y then $\langle X, Y \rangle = \langle M, N \rangle$, $\langle X \rangle = \langle M \rangle$ and $\langle Y \rangle = \langle N \rangle$. $\blacksquare$

11.b.4 Remark. Let $X, Y \in \mathcal{S}$. The limit representation

$$\langle X, Y \rangle_t = \lim_{\|\Delta\| \to 0} Q_\Delta(X, Y) = \lim_{\|\Delta\| \to 0} \sum (X_{t_j} - X_{t_{j-1}})(Y_{t_j} - Y_{t_{j-1}}), \qquad (0)$$

where the limit is taken over partitions $\Delta = \{ t_j \}$ of the interval $[0, t]$, shows that the covariation process $\langle X, Y \rangle$ is unaffected if the filtration $(\mathcal{F}_t)$ is replaced with some other (right continuous and augmented) filtration $(\mathcal{G}_t)$ with respect to which X, Y are still semimartingales. We will see below that the family $\mathcal{S}$ of continuous P-semimartingales is invariant under change to a locally equivalent probability measure Q. Since convergence in P-probability implies convergence in Q-probability it follows from (0) that the covariation $\langle X, Y \rangle$ is unaffected if P is replaced with Q.

Let $0 \leq t < T$. From (0) it follows that $\langle X, Y \rangle_t^T = \langle X, Y \rangle_T - \langle X, Y \rangle_t$ has a similar limit representation where the limit is taken along partitions of the interval $[t, T]$. Thus this quantity is a measure of the aggregate comovement of the processes X and Y over the interval $[t, T]$. Normalization (10.c.4) yields the quantity

$$\frac{\langle X, Y \rangle_t^T}{\sqrt{\langle X \rangle_t^T} \sqrt{\langle Y \rangle_t^T}} \in [-1, 1]$$

which is a measure of the aggregate correlation of X and Y on the interval $[t, T]$.

CHAPTER II

Brownian Motion

1. GAUSSIAN PROCESSES

Recall that $(\Omega, \mathcal{F}, P)$ is a complete probability space. The elements of Euclidean space R^k will be viewed as column vectors and we denote the dot product on R^k by (t, x) or $t \cdot x$, that is,

$$(t, x) = t \cdot x = \sum_{j=1}^{k} t_j x_j,$$

for all vectors $t = (t_1, t_2, \ldots, t_k)'$, $x = (x_1, x_2, \ldots, x_k)' \in R^k$. Here the prime denotes transposition as usual. Let $\{ e_1, e_2, \ldots, e_k \}$ denote the standard basis of R^k.

1.a Gaussian random variables in R^k. The normal distribution $N = N(\mu, \sigma^2)$ on R with mean μ and variance σ^2 is defined by

$$N(dx) = \frac{1}{\sigma\sqrt{2\pi}} \, exp\left(-\frac{(x-\mu)^2}{2\sigma^2}\right) dx$$

The characteristic function (Fourier transform) of this distribution is given by

$$\hat{N}(t) = \int_R e^{itx} N(dx) = exp\left(i\mu t - \frac{1}{2}\sigma^2 t^2\right), \quad t \in R.$$

In the case of a mean zero normal distribution $N = N(0, \sigma^2)$ this becomes

$$N(dx) = \frac{1}{\sigma\sqrt{2\pi}} e^{-x^2/2\sigma^2} \, dx, \quad \text{and} \quad \hat{N}(t) = e^{-\sigma^2 t^2/2}, \quad t \in R$$

and the *standard normal distribution* $N(0, 1)$ satisfies

$$N(0,1)(dx) = \frac{1}{\sqrt{2\pi}} e^{-x^2/2} \, dx, \quad \text{and} \quad \widehat{N(0,1)}(t) = e^{-t^2/2}, \quad t \in R.$$

For $\sigma^2 = 0$ the distribution $N(0, \sigma^2) = N(0, 0)$ is not defined by the above density but is interpreted to be the point measure $N(0, 0) = \epsilon_0$ concentrated at 0. With this interpretation the formula for the characteristic function $\widehat{N(0,0)}(t) = \hat{\epsilon}_0(t) = 1 = e^{-\sigma^2 t^2/2}$ holds in this case also.

The characteristic function of a random vector $X : \Omega \to R^k$ is defined to be the characteristic function of the distribution P_X of X, that is, the function

$$F_X(t) = \hat{P}_X(t) = \int_{R^k} e^{i(t,x)} P_X(dx) = E\big(e^{i(t,X)}\big), \quad t \in R^k.$$

Recall that the components $X_1, \ldots, X_k$ of the random vector $X = (X_1, \ldots, X_k)'$ are independent if and only if the joint distribution P_X is the product measure $P_{X_1} \otimes P_{X_2} \otimes \ldots \otimes P_{X_k}$. This is easily seen to be equivalent with the factorization

$$F_X(t) = F_{X_1}(t_1) F_{X_2}(t_2) \ldots F_{X_k}(t_k), \quad \forall t = (t_1, t_2, \ldots, t_k)' \in R^k.$$

Covariance matrix. The $k \times k$-matrix C defined by $C_{ij} = E\big[(X_i - m_i)(X_j - m_j)\big]$, where $m_i = EX_i$, is called the *covariance matrix* C of X. Here it is assumed that all relevant expectations exist. Set $m = (m_1, m_2, \ldots, m_k)'$ and note that the matrix $\big((X_i - m_i)(X_j - m_j)\big)_{ij}$ can be written as the product $(X - m)(X - m)'$ of the column vector $(X - m)$ with the row vector $(X - m)'$. Taking expectations entry by entry, we see that the covariance matrix C of X can also be written as $C = E\big[(X - m)(X - m)'\big]$ in complete formal analogy to the covariance in the one dimensional case. Clearly C is symmetric. Moreover, for each vector $t = (t_1, \ldots, t_k)' \in R^k$ we have

$$0 \le Var(t_1 X_1 + \ldots + t_k X_k) = \sum_{ij} t_i t_j Cov(X_i X_j) = \sum_{ij} C_{ij} t_i t_j = (Ct, t)$$

and it follows that the covariance matrix C is positive semidefinite. Let us note the effect of affine transformations on characteristic functions:

1.a.0. *Let $X : \Omega \to R^k$ be a random vector, $A : R^k \to R^n$ a linear map and $y_0 \in R^n$. Then the random vector $Y = y_0 + AX : \Omega \to R^n$ has characteristic function $F_Y(t) = e^{i(t,y_0)} F_X(A't)$, for all $t \in R^n$.*

Proof. For $t \in R^n$ we have $F_Y(t) = E\left[exp(i(t,Y))\right] = E\left[exp(i(t, y_0 + AX))\right] = E\left[e^{(t,y_0)} exp(i(t, AX))\right] = e^{(t,y_0)} E\left[exp(i(A't, X))\right] = e^{(t,y_0)} F_X(A't).$ ∎

1.a.1. *Let $X = (X_1, X_2, \ldots, X_k)' : \Omega \to R^k$ be a random vector.*

(a) *If $F_X(t) = exp\big(-\frac{1}{2} \sum_{j=1}^n \lambda_j t_j^2\big)$, $t \in R^k$, then the components X_j are independent normal variables with $X_j \sim N(0, \lambda_j)$. In particular $E(X_j) = 0$, $E(X_j^2) = \lambda_j$ and $E(X_i X_j) = 0$, for $i \neq j$.*

(b) *If $F_X(t) = exp\big(i(t, m) - \frac{1}{2}(Ct, t)\big)$, for some vector $m \in R^k$ and some symmetric real $k \times k$ matrix C, then $m = EX$ and C is the covariance matrix of X. Consequently C is positive semidefinite.*

Proof. (a) Assume that $F_X(t) = E\left[e^{i(t,X)}\right] = exp\left(-\frac{1}{2} \sum_{j=1}^n \lambda_j t_j^2\right)$ for all $t \in R^n$. Let $j \in \{1, 2, \ldots, n\}$ and $s \in R$. Setting $t = se_j = (0, \ldots, 0, s, 0, \ldots 0) \in R^k$ in the characteristic function of X yields

$$F_{X_j}(s) = E\left[e^{isX_j}\right] = E\left[e^{i(se_j, X)}\right] = F_X(se_j) = e^{-\frac{1}{2}\lambda_j s^2},$$

and this is the characteristic function of a real valued normal $N(0, \lambda_j)$-variable. Thus in particular $E(X_j) = 0$ and $E(X_j^2) = Var(X_j) = \lambda_j$. Moreover, for each $t = (t_1, t_2, \ldots, t_k)' \in R^k$, we have

$$F_X(t) = exp\left(-\tfrac{1}{2}\sum_{j=1}^{n} \lambda_j t_j^2\right) = \prod_{j=1}^{n} e^{-\frac{1}{2}\lambda_j t_j^2} = \prod_{j=1}^{n} F_{X_j}(t_j),$$

and this shows the independence of the random variables $X_1, X_2, \ldots, X_k$. In particular it follows that $E(X_i X_j) = E(X_i)E(X_j) = 0$, for $i \neq j$.

(b)   Set $Y = X - m$. We have to show that $EY = 0$ and $E(Y_i Y_j) = C_{ij}$. Indeed, using 1.a.0,
$$F_Y(t) = e^{-i(t,m)} F_X(t) = exp\left(-\tfrac{1}{2}(Ct, t)\right), \quad \forall t \in R^k.$$

The expectations $E(Y_i)$, $E(Y_i Y_j)$ can be computed from the characteristic function of Y as $E(Y_i) = -i(\partial F_Y/\partial t_i)(0)$ and $E(Y_i Y_j) = -(\partial^2 F_Y/\partial t_i \partial t_j)(0)$. Using the product rule and symmetry of C we have $(\partial/\partial t_i)(Ct, t) = (Ce_i, t) + (Ct, e_i) = 2(Ce_i, t)$. Consequently repeated differentiation yields

$$\partial F_Y/\partial t_i = -(Ce_i, t) exp\left(-\tfrac{1}{2}(Ct, t)\right) \quad \text{and}$$

$$\partial^2 F_Y/\partial t_i \partial t_j = -\left\{(Ce_i, e_j) - (Ce_i, t)(Ce_j, t) exp\left(-\tfrac{1}{2}(Ct, t)\right)\right\}.$$

Setting $t = 0$ now yields $E(Y_i) = 0$ and $E(Y_i Y_j) = (Ce_i, e_j) = C_{ij}$. ∎

1.a.2. *If $m \in R^k$ and C is a positive semidefinite, symmetric real $k \times k$ matrix, then there exists an R^k-valued random vector X with $F_X(t) = exp\left(i(t, m) - \tfrac{1}{2}(Ct, t)\right)$, for all $t \in R^k$. For such X the distribution P_X satisfies $P_X(m + range(C)) = 1$, that is, $X \in m + range(C)$ almost surely.*

Proof. Step 1. We show that there exists a random vector $Y : \Omega \to R^k$ with characteristic function $F_Y(t) = exp(-\|t\|^2/2)$, $t \in R^k$. Indeed, let $(\Omega, \mathcal{F}, P)$ be any probability space which supports *independent* standard normal real valued random variables $Y_1, Y_2, \ldots, Y_k$. Then $F_{Y_j}(s) = exp(-s^2/2)$, $s \in R$. Let $Y = (Y_1, \ldots, Y_k)'$. By independence of the coordinates we have

$$F_Y(t) = F_{Y_1}(t_1) \ldots F_{Y_k}(t_k) = e^{-t_1^2/2} \ldots e^{-t_k^2/2} = e^{-\|t\|^2/2}, \quad \text{for all } t \in R^k.$$

Step 2. Let now $m \in R^k$ be a vector, C a real, symmetric, positive semidefinite $k \times k$ matrix, write $C = QQ'$ as in appendix C and note that $(Ct, t) = \|Q't\|^2$, for all $t \in R^k$. According to step 1 there exists a random vector $Y : \Omega \to R^k$ such that $F_Y(t) = exp(-\|t\|^2/2)$. Set $X = m + QY$. Using 1.a.0 we have

$$F_X(t) = e^{i(t,m)} F_Y(Q't) = e^{i(t,m)} e^{-\|Q't\|^2/2} = exp\left(i(t, m) - \tfrac{1}{2}(Ct, t)\right),$$

for each $t \in R^k$, as desired. Recall now from appendix C that $range(C) = range(Q)$. Thus $X = m + QY \in m + range(Q) = m + range(C)$ always. It follows that $P_X(m + range(C)) = 1$, at least for our special random vector X as above. If now Z is any random vector in R^k such that $F_Z(t) = exp\left(i(t, m) - \tfrac{1}{2}(Ct, t)\right)$, then $\hat{P}_Z(t) = F_Z(t) = F_X(t) = \hat{P}_X(t)$, for all $t \in R^k$, and since the Fourier transform determines a measure uniquely, $P_Z = P_X$. It follows that $P_Z(m + range(C)) = 1$. ∎

Definition. *For any vector $m \in R^k$ and real, symmetric, positive semidefinite $k \times k$ matrix C the Gaussian measure $N(m, C)$ is the unique probability measure P on R^k which has Fourier transform*

$$\hat{P}(t) = exp\left(i(t, m) - \tfrac{1}{2}(Ct, t)\right), \quad \forall t \in R^k.$$

Remark. This measure is concentrated on the affine space $m + range(C)$. The parameters m and C are called the *mean* and *covariance matrix* of P respectively. This terminology is justified by 1.a.1.(b). If X is any R^k-valued random vector such that $P_X = N(m, C)$, then $m = EX = (EX_1, EX_2, \ldots, EX_k)' \in R^k$ is the mean of X and $C_{ij} = Cov(X_i, X_j)$. In this case the random vector X will be called *Gaussian* and we write $X \sim N(m, C)$. Each random vector X as in 1.a.2 has this property and this shows the existence of the Gaussian measure $N(m, C)$. Let us now record some of the properties of Gaussian distributions:

1.a.3. *Let $X : \Omega \to R^n$ be a random vector.*
(a) If X is Gaussian, so is $Y = y + AX$, for every linear map $A : R^n \to R^k$ and every vector $y \in R^k$.
(b) X is Gaussian if and only if $\Lambda X : \Omega \to R$ is a normal variable, for each linear functional $\Lambda : R^n \to R$.

Proof. (a) Assume that $X \sim N(m, C)$, that is, $F_X(t) = exp\left(i(t, m) - \tfrac{1}{2}(Ct, t)\right)$, $t \in R^n$, for some vector $m \in R^n$ and some symmetric, positive semidefinite $n \times n$ matrix C. Let $y \in R^k$, $A : R^n \to R^k$ be a linear map and $Y = y + AX$. Using 1.a.0,

$$F_Y(t) = F_{y+AX}(t) = e^{i(t,y)}F_X(A't) = e^{i(t,y)}exp\left(i(A't, m) - \tfrac{1}{2}(CA't, A't)\right)$$
$$= e^{i(t,y)}exp\left(i(t, Am) - \tfrac{1}{2}(ACA't, t)\right) = exp\left(i(t, y + Am) - \tfrac{1}{2}(ACA't, t)\right),$$

for all $t \in R^k$. Here $y + Am \in R^k$ and ACA' is a positive semidefinite $k \times k$ matrix. It follows that $Y \sim N(y + Am, ACA')$ is Gaussian.

(b) ($\Rightarrow$). This follows from (a). ($\Leftarrow$). Assume now that ΛX is a normal variable, for each linear functional $\Lambda : R^k \to R$. We wish to show that X is itself Gaussian, that is, $F_X(t) = exp\left(i(t, m) - \tfrac{1}{2}(Ct, t)\right)$, for all $t \in R^k$, where $m = EX \in R^k$ and $C_{ij} = Cov(X_i, X_j)$ (this matrix C is automatically symmetric and positive semidefinite). Fix $t = (t_1, t_2, \ldots, t_k)' \in R^k$, consider the linear functional $\Lambda(x) = (t, x)$, $x \in R^k$ and let $s \in R$. Since $\Lambda X = (t, X) = t_1 X_1 + t_2 X_2 + \ldots + t_k X_k$ is a normal variable,

$$E\left[exp(is(t, X)\right] = E\left[exp(is\Lambda X)\right] = F_{\Lambda X}(s) = e^{is\mu - s^2\sigma^2/2}, \quad \text{where}$$

$$\mu = \hat{E}\Lambda X = \Lambda EX = (t, EX) = (t, m) \quad \text{and}$$
$$\sigma^2 = Var(\Lambda X) = Var(t_1 X_1 + \ldots + t_k X_k) = (Ct, t).$$

Setting $s = 1$, $F_X(t) = E\left[exp(i(t, X))\right] = exp(i\mu - \sigma^2/2) = exp\left(i(t, m) - \tfrac{1}{2}(Ct, t)\right)$, that is, $X \sim N(m, C)$. $\blacksquare$

Remark. Our results about Gaussian random vectors can be reinterpreted as results about Gaussian measures: Recall that for any random vector X and measurable map ϕ on the range space of X we have $\phi(P_X) = P_{\phi(X)}$, where here $\phi(P_X)$ denotes the image of the measure P_X under ϕ. Since every probability measure Q on R^k is the distribution $Q = P_X$ of some random vector in R^k, 1.a.3 can be reinterpreted as follows: every affine image of a Gaussian measure is itself a Gaussian measure. A probability measure Q on R^n is Gaussian if and only if the image $\Lambda(Q)$ is a normal distribution on R, for every linear functional Λ on R^k.

1.a.4. *If $X_j : \Omega \to R$, $j = 1, \dots, k$ are independent normal variables, then the random vector $X = (X_1, X_2, \dots, X_k)'$ is Gaussian.*

Proof. Assume that $X_j \sim N(m_i, \sigma_j^2)$ and hence $F_{X_j}(s) = exp\left(ism_j - \sigma_j^2 s^2/2\right)$. Let $t \in R^k$. From the independence of the X_j it follows that,

$$
\begin{aligned}
F_X(t) &= \textstyle\prod_{j=1}^{k} F_{X_j}(t_j) \\
&= \textstyle\prod_{j=1}^{k} e^{-it_j m_j - \sigma_j^2 t_j^2/2} \\
&= exp\left(i(t,m) - \tfrac{1}{2}\textstyle\sum_{j=1}^{n} \sigma_j^2 t_j^2\right) \\
&= exp\left(i(t,m) - \tfrac{1}{2}(Ct,t)\right),
\end{aligned}
$$

where $m = (m_1, \dots, m_k)' \in R^k$ and $C = diag(\sigma_j^2)$. Thus $X \sim N(m, C)$. ∎

1.a.5 Normal Correlation Theorem. *Let $X_1, \dots, X_k : \Omega \to R$ be random variables. If the joint distribution of the X_j is Gaussian (i.e., if $X = (X_1, \dots, X_k)'$ is a Gaussian random variable), then the X_j are independent if and only if they are pairwise uncorrelated.*

Proof. Since independence implies pairwise independence which implies pairwise uncorrelatedness, we need to concern ourselves only with the converse. Thus assume that $X = (X_1, X_2, \dots, X_k)' \sim N(m, C)$ is a Gaussian random variable and that the X_j are pairwise uncorrelated: Then $C_{ij} = Cov(X_i, X_j) = 0$, for all $i \neq j$ and hence $C = diag(\lambda_j)$ is a diagonal matrix. Let $Z = X - m$. Then $Z \sim N(0, C)$, that is,

$$
F_Z(t) = exp\left(-\tfrac{1}{2}(Ct,t)\right) = exp\left(-\tfrac{1}{2}\textstyle\sum_{j=1}^{n} \lambda_j t_j^2\right),
$$

for all $t \in R^k$. According to 1.a.1.(a) this implies that the components Z_j are independent and hence so are the $X_j = m_j + Z_j$. ∎

Standard Normal Distribution $N(0, I)$ **in** R^k. The Gaussian distribution $N(0, I)$ with mean zero and covariance matrix I (the $k \times k$ identity matrix) is called the *standard normal distribution* on R^k. If X is a standard normal random vector in R^k, then

$$F_X(t) = e^{-\|t\|^2/2}, \quad t \in R^k. \tag{0}$$

According to 1.a.1.(a) it follows that the components $X_j \sim N(0, 1)$ are *independent* standard normal variables in R and consequently their joint distribution $P_X = N(0, I)$ is the product measure

$$N(0, I) = N(0, 1) \otimes N(0, 1) \otimes \ldots \otimes N(0, 1).$$

Since $N(0, 1)(ds) = (2\pi)^{-\frac{1}{2}} e^{-s^2/2} ds$, it follows that $N(0, I)$ has density

$$n_k(x) = (2\pi)^{-k/2} e^{-x_1^2/2} e^{-x_2^2/2} \ldots e^{-x_k^2/2} = (2\pi)^{-k/2} e^{-\|x\|^2/2}, \tag{1}$$

with respect to Lebesgue measure λ_k on R^k. The characteristic function (0) is spherically symmetric, that is, invariant under orthogonal transformations of R^k. Indeed

$$F_{UX}(t) = F_X(U't) = e^{-\|U't\|^2/2} = e^{-\|t\|^2/2} = F_X(t).$$

It follows that UX is again a standard normal random vector in R^k. Thus the standard normal distribution $N(0, I)$ on R^k satisfies

$$U(N(0, I)) = U(P_X) = P_{U(X)} = N(0, I),$$

for every orthogonal transformation U of R^k. This can be used to give an easy proof of the invariance under orthogonal transformations of Lebesgue measure λ_k on R^k:

1.a.6. *Lebesgue measure λ_k on R^k satisfies $U(\lambda_k) = \lambda_k$, for each orthogonal transformation U of R^k.*

Proof. From (1) we have $N(0, I)(dx) = (2\pi)^{-k/2} exp(-\|x\|^2/2) \lambda_k(dx)$ and so $\lambda_k(dx) = f(x) N(0, I)(dx)$, where the function $f(x) = (2\pi)^{k/2} exp(\|x\|^2/2)$ satisfies $f(Ux) = f(x)$, $x \in R^k$, for each orthogonal transformation U of R^k. It follows that for each nonnegative measurable function g on R^k we have

$$\int g(x) \, U(\lambda_k)(dx) = \int g(Ux) \, \lambda_k(dx) = \int g(Ux) f(x) \, N(0, I)(dx)$$
$$= \int g(Ux) f(Ux) \, N(0, I)(dx) = \int g(x) f(x) \, [U(N(0, I))](dx)$$
$$= \int g(x) f(x) N(0, I)(dx) = \int g(x) \lambda_k(dx). \blacksquare$$

Remarks. (a) Note that $(U(\lambda_k))(A) = \lambda_k(U^{-1}(A)) = \lambda_k(U'(A))$. Thus the equality $U(\lambda_k) = \lambda_k$ means that $\lambda_k(U'(A)) = \lambda_k(A)$; equivalently, $\lambda_k(U(A)) = \lambda_k(A)$, for each orthogonal transformation U of R^k and each Borel set $A \subseteq R^k$.
(b)   For later use we note the following property of Gaussian random variables: Let π be any permutation of $\{1, 2, \ldots, k\}$. If $X = (X_1, X_2, \ldots, X_k)'$ is a random vector in R^k, then X is Gaussian if and only if the permuted vector $X_\pi = (X_{\pi 1}, X_{\pi 2}, \ldots, X_{\pi k})'$ is Gaussian. This follows immediately from 1.a.3.(a) and the fact that permutation of coordinates is an invertible linear map on R^k.

1.a.7 Integration with respect to Gaussian measures. It will suffice to consider integration with respect to the distribution $N(0,C)$ on R^k. We might now be tempted to derive the density of this distribution. It is however easier and more elegant to reduce integration with respect to $N(0,C)$ to integration with respect to the standard normal distribution $N(0,I)$ on R^k with known density

$$n_k(x) = (2\pi)^{-k/2} e^{-\frac{1}{2}\|x\|^2}, \quad x \in R^k.$$

To this end we represent the symmetric, positive semidefinite matrix C as $C = A'A$ for some $k \times k$ matrix A, i.e., $C_{ij} = \theta_i \cdot \theta_j$, where $\theta_j = c_j(A)$ denotes the jth column of A. Then $(Ct, t) = \|At\|^2$, for all $t \in R^k$. Now let X be any $N(0,I)$-random vector on R^k ($P_X = N(0,I)$). Then, using 1.a.0,

$$F_{A'X}(t) = F_X(At) = e^{-\frac{1}{2}\|At\|^2} = e^{-\frac{1}{2}(Ct,t)},$$

and so $A'X$ is an $N(0,C)$-variable. Thus $N(0,C) = P_{A'X} = A'(P_X) = A'(N(0,I))$ (image measure). The image measure theorem [appendix B.5] now shows that for all nonnegative measurable functions f on R^k and all $f \in L^1(N(0,C))$ we have

$$\int_{R^k} f(x) N(0,C)(dx) = \int_{R^k} f(A'x) N(0,I)(dx)$$
$$= \int_{R^k} f(\theta_1 \cdot x, \theta_2 \cdot x, \ldots, \theta_k \cdot x) N(0,I)(dx)$$
$$= \int_{R^k} f(\theta_1 \cdot x, \theta_2 \cdot x, \ldots, \theta_k \cdot x) n_k(x) dx.$$

The representation $C = A'A$ can be effected as follows: Let $\lambda_1, \lambda_2, \ldots, \lambda_k$ be the eigenvalues of C (these are nonnegative) and $u_1, u_2 \ldots, u_k$ be an orthonormal basis of eigenvectors of C satisfying $Cu_j = \lambda_j u_j$. Now let A be the $k \times k$ matrix with rows $r_j(A) = \sqrt{\lambda_j} u_j$. We claim that $C = A'A$. It will suffice to show that $A'Au_j = Cu_j$, for all $j = 1, \ldots, k$. Indeed, the orthonormality of the u_j implies that $Au_j = \sqrt{\lambda_j} e_j$ and so $A'Au_j = \sqrt{\lambda_j} A'e_j = \sqrt{\lambda_j} c_j(A') = \sqrt{\lambda_j} r_j(A) = \lambda_j u_j = Cu_j$, as desired.

1.b Gaussian Processes. In order to be able to introduce isonormal processes, it will be necessary to consider certain real valued stochastic processes indexed by a set T without order. A real valued stochastic process $X = (X_t)_{t \in T}$ indexed by T will now be viewed as a function $X : \omega \in \Omega \mapsto X(\omega) = (X_t(\omega))_{t \in T} \in R^T$.

Thus $X(\omega)$ is the path $t \in T \mapsto X_t(\omega)$, for each $\omega \in \Omega$. For each $t \in T$ let $\pi_t : R^T \to R$ denote the tth coordinate projection, and let $\mathcal{B}^T = \sigma(\pi_t; t \in T)$ denote the product σ-field on R^T. Then the measurability of the individual random variables $X_t = \pi_t \circ X$, $t \in T$, implies that $X : (\Omega, \mathcal{F}) \to (R^T, \mathcal{B}^T)$ is a measurable map. The process $X = (X_t)_{t \in T} : (\Omega, \mathcal{F}, P) \to (R^T, \mathcal{B}^T)$ is called *Gaussian* if the variable $X_F := (X_t)_{t\in F} : \Omega \to R^F$ is Gaussian, for each finite subset $F \subseteq T$, that is if all the finite dimensional marginal distributions of X are Gaussian. The absence o order on the index set T is irrelevant, since the Gaussian property is invariant unde permutations of coordinates. If X is Gaussian the distribution of the random vecto X_F on R^F is completely determined by its mean $m_F = E(X_F) = (E(X_t))_{t\in F}$ an covariance matrix $C_F = (C(s,t))_{s,t\in F} = (Cov(X_s, X_t))_{s,t\in F}$ which is selfadjoin and positive semidefinite. Thus the functions

$$m : t \in T \mapsto E(X_t) \in R \quad \text{and} \quad C : (s,t) \in T \times T \mapsto Cov(X_s, X_t) \in R$$

completely determine the finite dimensional marginal distributions and hence th distribution of X on $(R^T, \mathcal{B}^T)$. Conversely

1.b.0 Theorem. *Let T be an index set, $m : T \to R$, $C : T \times T \to R$ functions an assume that the matrix $C_F := (C(s,t))_{s,t\in F}$ is selfadjoint and positive semidefinite for each finite set $F \subseteq T$.*

Then there exists a probability P on the product space $(\Omega, \mathcal{F}) = (R^T, \mathcal{B}^T)$ suc that the coordinate maps $X_t : \omega \in \Omega \mapsto X_t(\omega) = \omega(t)$, $t \in T$, form a Gaussia process $X = (X_t)_{t\in T} : (\Omega, \mathcal{F}, P) \to (R^T, \mathcal{B}^T)$ with mean function $E(X_t) = m(t$ and covariance function $Cov(X_s, X_t) = C(s,t)$, $s,t \in T$.

Remark. Our choice of Ω and X_t implies that the process $X : (\Omega, \mathcal{F}) \to (R^T, \mathcal{B}^T$ is the identity map, that is, the path $t \in T \mapsto X_t(\omega)$ is the element $\omega \in R^T = \Omega$ itself, for each $\omega \in \Omega$.

Proof. Fix any linear order on T and use it to order vector components and matri entries consistently. For finite subsets $F \subseteq G \subseteq T$ let

$$\pi_F : x = (x_t)_{t\in T} \in \Omega = R^T \to (x_t)_{t\in F} \in R^F \quad \text{and}$$
$$\pi_{GF} : x = (x_t)_{t\in G} \in R^G \to (x_t)_{t\in F} \in R^F$$

denote the natural projections and set

$$m_F = (m(t))_{t\in F} \in R^F, \quad C_F = (C(s,t))_{s,t\in F} \quad \text{and} \quad X_F = (X_t)_{t\in F}.$$

Let P be any probability on $(\Omega, \mathcal{F}) = (R^T, \mathcal{B}^T)$. Since $X : (\Omega, \mathcal{F}, P) \to (R^T, \mathcal{B}^T$ is the identity map, the distribution of X on $(R^T, \mathcal{B}^T)$ is the measure P itself an $\pi_F(P)$ is the joint distribution of $X_F = (X_t)_{t\in F}$ on R^F. Thus X is a Gaussia process with mean function m and covariance function C on the probability spac $(\Omega, \mathcal{F}, P)$ if and only if the finite dimensional distribution $\pi_F(P)$ is the Gaussia Law $N(m_F, C_F)$, for each finite subset $F \subseteq T$. By Kolmogoroff's existence theorem (appendix D.5) such a probability measure on $(\Omega, \mathcal{F}) = (R^T, \mathcal{B}^T)$ exists if and only i the system of Gaussian Laws $\{ N(m_F, C_F) : F \subseteq T \text{ finite} \}$ satisfies the consistency condition

$$\pi_{GF}(N(m_G, C_G)) = N(m_F, C_F),$$

for all finite subsets $F \subseteq G \subseteq T$. To see that this is true, consider such sets F, G and let W be any random vector in R^G such that $P_W = N(m_G, C_G)$. Then $\pi_{GF}(N(m_G, C_G)) = \pi_{GF}(P_W) = P_{\pi_{GF}(W)}$ and it will thus suffice to show that $Y = \pi_{GF}(W)$ is a Gaussian random vector with law $N(m_F, C_F)$ in R^F, that is, with characteristic function

$$F_Y(y) = exp\left(i(y, m_F) - \tfrac{1}{2}(C_F y, y)\right), \quad y = (y_t)_{t \in F} \in R^F.$$

Since W is a Gaussian random vector with law $N(m_G, C_G)$ on R^G, we have

$$F_W(y) = exp\left(i(x, m_G) - \tfrac{1}{2}(C_G x, x)\right), \quad x = (x_t)_{t \in G} \in R^G,$$

and consequently (1.a.0), for $y \in R^F$,

$$F_Y(y) = F_{\pi_{GF}(W)}(y) = F_W(\pi'_{GF}y) = exp\left(i(\pi'_{GF}y, m_G) - \tfrac{1}{2}(C_G \pi'_{GF}y, \pi'_{GF}y)\right).$$

Here $\pi'_{GF} : R^F \to R^G$ is the adjoint map and so $(\pi'_{GF}y, m_G) = (y, \pi_{GF}m_G) = (y, m_F)$. Thus it remains to be shown only that $(C_G \pi'_{GF}y, \pi'_{GF}y) = (C_F y, y)$. Let $y = (y_t)_{t \in F} \in R^F$. First we claim that $\pi'_{GF}y = z$, where the vector $z = (z_t)_{t \in G} \in R^G$ is defined by

$$z_t = \begin{cases} y_t & \text{if } t \in F \\ 0 & \text{if } t \in G \setminus F \end{cases}, \quad \forall y = (y_t)_{t \in F} \in R^F.$$

Indeed, if $x = (x_t)_{t \in G} \in R^G$ we have $(y, \pi_{GF}x) = \sum_{t \in F} y_t x_t = \sum_{t \in G} z_t x_t = (z, x)$ and so $z = \pi'_{GF}y$. Thus $(C_G \pi'_{GF}y, \pi'_{GF}y) = (C_G z, z) = \sum_{s,t \in G} C(s,t) z_s z_t = \sum_{s,t \in F} C(s,t) y_s y_t = (C_F y, y)$. ∎

1.c Isonormal processes. Let H be a real Hilbert space and $(\Omega, \mathcal{F}, P)$ a probability space. An *isonormal process* on $(\Omega, \mathcal{F}, P)$ *indexed by* H is a real valued Gaussian process $X = (X_f)_{f \in H} : (\Omega, \mathcal{F}, P) \to (R^H, \mathcal{B}^H)$ which satisfies

$$EX_f = 0 \quad \text{and} \quad Cov(X_f, X_g) = E(X_f X_g) = (f, g)_H,$$

for all vectors $f, g \in H$.

1.c.0 Theorem. *If H is a real Hilbert space then there exists an isonormal process $X = (X_f)_{f \in H}$ indexed by H (on some suitable probability space $(\Omega, \mathcal{F}, P)$).*

Proof. According to 1.b.0 it will suffice to show that the covariance function $C(f, g) = (f, g)_H$ has the property that the matrix

$$\left(C(f_i, f_j)\right)_{ij=1}^n = \left((f_i, f_j)_H\right)_{ij=1}^n$$

is symmetric and positive semidefinite, for each finite subset $\{f_1, f_2, \ldots, f_n\} \subseteq H$. The symmetry of this matrix is an immediate consequence of the symmetry of the inner product in a real Hilbert space. Moreover

$$\sum_{i,j=1}^n C(f_i, f_j) t_i t_j = \sum_{i,j=1}^n t_i t_j (f_i, f_j)_H = \left(\sum_{i=1}^n t_i f_i, \sum_{j=1}^n t_j f_j\right)_H$$
$$= \left\|\sum_{i=1}^n t_i f_i\right\|^2 \geq 0,$$

for all $t_1, \ldots, t_n \in R$. Thus the matrix $\left(C(f_i, f_j)\right)_{ij=1}^n$ is positive semidefinite. ∎

2. ONE DIMENSIONAL BROWNIAN MOTION

2.a One dimensional Brownian motion starting at zero. Recall that $(\Omega, \mathcal{F}, P)$ is a complete probability space and let $B = (B_t)_{t \in I} : (\Omega, \mathcal{F}, P) \to (R^I, \mathcal{B}^I)$ be a real valued stochastic process with index set $I = [0, \infty)$. Then B is called a *Brownian motion* (starting at zero) if

(α) B is a Gaussian process.
(β) $B_0 = 0$ almost surely.
(γ) $E(B_t) = 0$ and $Cov(B_s, B_t) = E(B_s B_t) = s \wedge t$, for all $s, t \geq 0$, and
(δ) For every $\omega \in \Omega$ the path $t \in [0, \infty) \mapsto B_t(\omega) \in R$ is continuous.

Condition (β) is redundant (it follows from (γ): $E(B_0^2) = Cov(B_0, B_0) = 0$) and is included for ease of reference only. Brownian motion can be characterized by an equivalent set of conditions:

2.a.0. *The process $B = (B_t)_{t \geq 0}$ is a Brownian motion if and only if*

(a) *$B_0 = 0$ almost surely.*
(b) *For $0 \leq s < t$ the increment $B_t - B_s$ is normal with mean zero and variance $t - s$: $B_t - B_s \sim N(0, t - s)$.*
(c) *For all $0 \leq t_1 < t_2 < \ldots < t_n$ the variables $B_{t_1}, B_{t_2} - B_{t_1}, \ldots, B_{t_n} - B_{t_{n-1}}$ are independent.*
(d) *For every $\omega \in \Omega$ the path $t \in [0, \infty) \mapsto B_t(\omega) \in R$ is continuous.*

Proof. ($\Rightarrow$). Assume first that B is a Brownian motion starting at zero. Because of (β) and (δ) we have to show only that (b) and (c) hold.

Let $0 \leq s < t$. According to (γ) we have $E(B_s) = E(B_t) = 0$, $E(B_s^2) = E(B_s B_s) = s \wedge s = s$, similarly $E(B_t^2) = t$ and finally $E(B_s B_t) = s$. Moreover, according to (1), (B_s, B_t) is a two dimensional Gaussian variable and hence its linear image $B_t - B_s$ is a one dimensional normal variable with mean $E(B_t) - E(B_s) = 0$ and variance $Var(B_t - B_s) = E\left[(B_t - B_s)^2\right] = E\left[B_t^2 - 2B_t B_s + B_s^2\right] = t - s$. Thus $B_t - B_s \sim N(0, t - s)$. This shows (b).

(c) Let $0 \leq t_1 < \ldots < t_n$. By ($\alpha$) the random vector $(B_{t_1}, B_{t_2}, \ldots, B_{t_n})$ is Gaussian and hence so is its linear image $(B_{t_1}, B_{t_2} - B_{t_1}, \ldots, B_{t_n} - B_{t_{n-1}})$. According to 1.a.5 the independence of the variables $B_{t_1}, B_{t_2} - B_{t_1}, \ldots, B_{t_n} - B_{t_{n-1}}$ follows if we can show that they are pairwise uncorrelated, that is, $E\left[B_{t_1}(B_{t_j} - B_{t_{j-1}})\right] = 0$ and $E\left[(B_{t_j} - B_{t_{j-1}})(B_{t_k} - B_{t_{k-1}})\right] = 0$, for all $j \neq k$ (recall that all these variables have mean zero). Indeed, we may assume $k < j$ and thus $t_{k-1} < t_k \leq t_{j-1} < t_j$. It follows that $E\left[B_{t_1}(B_{t_j} - B_{t_{j-1}})\right] = E(B_{t_1} B_{t_j}) - E(B_{t_1} B_{t_{j-1}}) = t_1 \wedge t_j - t_1 \wedge t_{j-1} = t_1 - t_1 = 0$ and similarly

$$E\left[(B_{t_j} - B_{t_{j-1}})(B_{t_k} - B_{t_{k-1}})\right] = t_k - t_k - t_{k-1} + t_{k-1} = 0.$$

($\Leftarrow$). Assume now that (a)-(d) are satisfied. We must verify (α)-(δ). In view of (a) and (d) we need to show only (α) and (γ). Note first that $B_t = B_t - B_0$ is a normal variable, according to (a) and (b). Let now $0 \leq t_1 < \ldots < t_n$. According to (b), (c) and the preceding remark, $B_{t_1}, B_{t_2} - B_{t_1}, \ldots, B_{t_n} - B_{t_{n-1}}$ are independent normal variables. It follows that $(B_{t_1}, B_{t_2} - B_{t_1}, \ldots, B_{t_n} - B_{t_{n-1}})$ is a Gaussian vector (1.a.4) and hence so is its linear image $(B_{t_1}, B_{t_2}, \ldots, B_{t_n})$. Thus B is a Gaussian process. This shows (α).

To show (γ), note now that (a) and (b) with $s = 0$ imply that $B_t \sim N(0, t)$ and thus $E(B_t) = 0$ and $E(B_t^2) = t$. Let $0 \le s \le t$. Then $E(B_s B_t) = E[B_s(B_t - B_s)] + E(B_s^2) = E(B_s)E(B_t - B_s) + s = s$, where we have used the independence of B_s and $B_t - B_s$, according to (c). This shows (γ). ∎

Remark. Condition (b) implies that the increments $B_t - B_s$ are stationary, that is, the distribution of this increment depends on s, t only through $t - s$. From (a) and (b) it follows that $B_t \sim N(0, t)$, for all $t > 0$. Regarding the distribution $N(0, 0)$ as the point measure ϵ_0 concentrated at zero, this relation holds for $t = 0$ also.

Brownian motion on $(\Omega, \mathcal{F}, (\mathcal{F}_t), P)$. The reader will note that no filtration is involved in the definition of a Brownian motion. However condition (c), the "independence of increments", can be shown to be equivalent with the independence of $B_t - B_s$ from the σ-field $\mathcal{F}_s^0 = \sigma(B_r; r \le s)$, for all $0 \le s < t$ (2.e.1 below). This motivates the following terminology: the process B will be called a *Brownian motion on the filtered probability space* $(\Omega, \mathcal{F}, (\mathcal{F}_t), P)$ if it is adapted, satisfies conditions (a),(b),(d) of 2.a.0 and the increment $B_t - B_s$ is independent of the σ-field $\mathcal{F}_s$, for all $0 \le s < t$. Thus each Brownian motion B is a Brownian motion on $(\Omega, \mathcal{F}, (\mathcal{F}_t^0), P)$, where $\mathcal{F}_t^0 = \sigma(B_r; r \le t)$. Let us now show that a Brownian motion starting at zero exists. We need the following

2.a.1 Lemma. *Let* $a, \delta > 0$. *If the real valued random variable* X *has distribution* $N(0, \delta)$, *then*

$$P(|X| \ge a) \le \tfrac{\sqrt{\delta}}{a} e^{-a^2/2\delta}.$$

Proof. Recall that $N(0, \delta)(dx) = (2\pi\delta)^{-1/2} e^{-x^2/2\delta} dx$. Thus

$$N(0, \delta)([a, +\infty)) = \int_a^{+\infty} (2\pi\delta)^{-1/2} e^{-x^2/2\delta} dx \le \int_a^{+\infty} \tfrac{x}{a} \cdot (2\pi\delta)^{-1/2} e^{-x^2/2\delta} dx$$

$$\le \tfrac{\sqrt{\delta}}{2a} \int_a^{+\infty} \tfrac{x}{\delta} e^{-x^2/2\delta} dx = \tfrac{\sqrt{\delta}}{2a} \left[-e^{-x^2/2\delta} \right]_a^{+\infty} = \tfrac{\sqrt{\delta}}{2a} e^{-a^2/2\delta}.$$

Assume now that $X \sim N(0, \delta)$. From the symmetry of the normal distribution it follows that

$$P(|X| \ge a) = 2N(0, \delta)([a, +\infty)) \le \tfrac{\sqrt{\delta}}{a} e^{-a^2/2\delta}. \quad ∎$$

2.a.2 Theorem. *A Brownian motion* $B = (B_t)_{t \ge 0}$ *exists.*

Proof. Let H be the Hilbert space $L^2([0, +\infty))$ (with respect to Lebesgue measure on $[0, +\infty)$) and $L = (L(f))_{f \in H}$ an isonormal process with index set H. Set $X_t = L(1_{[0,t]})$, $t \ge 0$. Then $X = (X_t)_{t \ge 0}$ is a Gaussian process, since so is L. Also $E(X_t) = 0$ and $Cov(X_s, X_t) = E[X_s X_t] = (1_{[0,s]}, 1_{[0,t]})_H = s \wedge t$, by definition of an isonormal process. This implies that $E(X_0^2) = 0$ and hence $X_0 = 0$ almost surely. Thus X has all the properties of a Brownian motion except the continuity of the paths. We note in particular that this implies that the increment $X_t - X_s$ satisfies

$$X_t - X_s \sim N(0, t - s), \tag{0}$$

for all $0 \leq s < t$ (see proof of 2.a.0). We now show that a suitable version B of the process X has continuous paths. The process B then satisfies $B_t = X_t$ almost surely, for each $t \geq 0$, and this implies that B also has properties (α), (β), (γ) above. Combined with the continuity of paths this will show that B is in fact a Brownian motion starting at zero.

(a) Let us first observe that the map $t \in [0, +\infty) \to X_t$ is continuous in probability, that is, $t_n \to t$ implies $X_{t_n} \to X_t$ in probability. Set $\delta_n = |t_n - t|$, $n \geq 1$. According to (0), $X_{t_n} - X_t \sim N(0, \delta_n)$ and consequently, using 2.a.1, $P\left(|X_{t_n} - X_t| \geq \epsilon\right) \leq (\sqrt{\delta_n}/\epsilon) exp\left(-\epsilon^2/2\delta_n\right) \to 0$, as $\delta_n = |t_n - t| \to 0$, for each $\epsilon > 0$.

(b) Fix $n \geq 1$, let $D_n = \{ k/2^n \mid k \geq 0 \}$ and set $a_n(t) = \max\{ r \in D_n \mid r \leq t \} = [2^n t]/2^n$, for each $t \geq 0$. Thus $a_n(t) \in D_n$ and $|a_n(t) - t| \leq 2^{-n}$. Since $D_n \subseteq D_{n+1}$, it follows that $a_n(t) \uparrow t$, as $n \uparrow \infty$. Now let

$$\Delta_n = \{ X_{r+2^{-n}} - X_r \mid r \in D_n \cap [0, n] \}.$$

The set Δ_n consists of $n2^n + 1$ random variables Y all of which have distribution $N(0, 2^{-n})$. Set $M_n = \max_{Y \in \Delta_n} |Y|$. Using lemma 2.a.1 every random variable $Y \in \Delta_n$ satisfies $P\left(|Y| \geq 1/n^2\right) \leq n^2 2^{-n/2} exp\left(-2^{n-1}/n^4\right) \leq n^2 exp\left(-2^{n-1}/n^4\right)$ and so

$$P\left(M_n \geq 1/n^2\right) \leq \sum_{Y \in \Delta_n} P\left(|Y| \geq 1/n^2\right)$$
$$\leq (1 + n2^n)n^2 exp\left(-2^{n-1}/n^4\right) := p_n.$$

We have $2^{n-1} > n^5$ and so $p_n \leq (1 + n2^n)n^2 e^{-n}$, for all sufficiently large n. It follows that

$$\sum_n P(M_n \geq 1/n^2) \leq \sum_{n \geq 1} p_n < \infty.$$

The Borel Cantelli Lemma now shows that $P\left(M_n \geq 1/n^2 \, i.o.\right) = 0$. In particular the series $\sum M_n$ converges almost surely.

Now let $n \geq t \geq 0$. Then $a_n(t), a_{n+1}(t) \in D_{n+1} \cap [0, n+1]$ and $a_{n+1}(t) - a_n(t) = 0, 2^{-(n+1)}$ and so $\left|X_{a_{n+1}(t)} - X_{a_n(t)}\right| \leq M_{n+1}$. Thus

$$\sum_{n \geq t} \left|X_{a_{n+1}(t)} - X_{a_n(t)}\right| \leq \sum_{n \geq 1} M_n < \infty, \quad P\text{-as.,} \tag{1}$$

and it follows that $Z_t := \lim_{n \uparrow \infty} X_{a_n(t)} \in R$ exists on the set $\left[\sum M_n < \infty\right]$ and hence almost surely with exceptional set independent of $t \geq 0$.

We have $X_{a_n(t)} \to Z_t$ almost surely and hence in probability. Also $a_n(t) \to t$ and hence $X_{a_n(t)} \to X_t$ in probability, according to (a). As limits in probability are almost surely uniquely determined, we have $Z_t = X_t$ almost surely. Next we wish to show that almost every path $t \mapsto Z_t(\omega)$ is continuous. Let $D := \bigcup_n D_n$ be the family of all dyadic rationals and observe that

(c) If $r \in D$ is dyadic rational with $r \le m$, then $|X_r - X_{a_m(r)}| \le \sum_{j>m} M_j$.

If $r = a_m(r)$ (equivalently if $r \in D_m$), there is nothing to prove. If $a_m(r) < r$ we can write

$$r = a_m(r) + \sum_{j=m+1}^{m+p} \epsilon_j/2^j,$$

with $\epsilon_j \in \{0,1\}$, for all $j = m+1, m+2,\ldots, m+p$. Set $r_k = a_m(r) + \sum_{j=m+1}^{m+k} \epsilon_j/2^j$, $k = 0, 1,\ldots, p$. Then $r_0 = a_m(r)$, $r_p = r$, and $r_{k+1}, r_k \in D_{m+k+1} \cap [0, m+k+1]$ and $r_{k+1}-r_k = 0, 1/2^{k+1}$ and hence $|X_{r_{k+1}} - X_{r_k}| \le M_{m+k+1}$, for all $k = 0, 1,\ldots, p-1$. Thus

$$|X_r - X_{a_m(r)}| = |X_{r_p} - X_{r_0}| \le \sum_{k=0}^{p-1} |X_{r_{k+1}} - X_{r_k}|$$
$$\le \sum_{k=0}^{p-1} M_{m+k+1} \le \sum_{j>m} M_j.$$

(d) If $r, s \in D \cap [0, m]$ with $|r - s| \le 2^{-m}$, then $|X_r - X_s| \le 2\sum_{j\ge m} M_j$.

If $|r - s| \le 2^{-m}$, then $a_m(r), a_m(s) \in D_m \cap [0, m]$ and $|a_m(r) - a_m(s)| = 0, 2^{-m}$ and it follows that $|X_{a_m(r)} - X_{a_m(s)}| \le M_m$. Thus, using (c),

$$|X_r - X_s| \le |X_r - X_{a_m(r)}| + |X_{a_m(r)} - X_{a_m(s)}| + |X_{a_m(s)} - X_s|$$
$$\le M_m + 2\sum_{j>m} M_j \le 2\sum_{j\ge m} M_j.$$

(e) The path $t \in [0, +\infty) \mapsto Z_t(\omega)$ is continuous, for almost every $\omega \in \Omega$, indeed for each ω such that $\sum_{j\ge 1} M_j(\omega) < \infty$.

Consider such $\omega \in \Omega$ and recall from (1) that then $X_{a_n(s)}(\omega) \to Z_s(\omega)$, for each $s \ge 0$. Fix $t \ge 0$ and consider any sequence of nonnegative numbers t_k such that $t_k \to t$. We want to show that $Z_{t_k}(\omega) \to Z_t(\omega)$, as $k \uparrow \infty$.

Let $\epsilon > 0$ be arbitrary, choose $m \ge t, \sup_k t_k$ such that $\sum_{j\ge m} M_j(\omega) < \epsilon$ and consider any k such that $|t_k - t| < 2^{-m}$. Since $X_{a_n(t_k)}(\omega) \to Z_{t_k}(\omega)$ and $X_{a_n(t)}(\omega) \to Z_t(\omega)$, we can choose $n \ge m$ such that $|X_{a_n(t_k)}(\omega) - Z_{t_k}(\omega)| < \epsilon$ and $|X_{a_n(t)}(\omega) - Z_t(\omega)| < \epsilon$. Then $a_n(t_k), a_n(t) \in D \cap [0, m]$ and $|t_k - t| < 2^{-m}$ implies $|a_n(t_k) - a_n(t)| \le 2^{-m}$ and so $|X_{a_n(t_k)}(\omega) - X_{a_n(t)}(\omega)| \le 2\sum_{j\ge m} M_j(\omega) < 2\epsilon$, according to (d). It follows that

$$|Z_{t_k}(\omega) - Z_t(\omega)| \le |Z_{t_k}(\omega) - X_{a_n(t_k)}(\omega)| + |X_{a_n(t_k)}(\omega) - X_{a_n(t)}(\omega)| +$$
$$|X_{a_n(t)}(\omega) - Z_t(\omega)| \le \epsilon + 2\epsilon + \epsilon = 4\epsilon.$$

Thus the path $s \mapsto Z_s(\omega)$ is continuous at the point $s = t$.

Finally we make a trivial modification which forces all paths to be continuous. Choose a null set $N \subseteq \Omega$ such that the path $t \in [0, +\infty) \mapsto Z_t(\omega)$ is continuous, for each $\omega \in \Omega \setminus N$ and set $B = (1 - 1_N)Z$. Then the path $t \mapsto B_t(\omega)$ is continuous, for each $\omega \in \Omega$ and $B_t = Z_t = X_t$ almost surely, for each $t \ge 0$. It follows that the process $B = (B_t)_{t\ge 0}$ inherits properties (α)-(γ) of a Brownian motion from the process X. Thus B is a Brownian motion starting at zero. ∎

2.b Pathspace and Wiener measure. Let $B = (B_t)_{t \geq 0}$ be a Brownian motion starting at zero on the complete probability space $(\Omega, \mathcal{F}, P)$ and let $\mathcal{B}$ denote the Borel σ-field on R. We can view B as a measurable map $B : (\Omega, \mathcal{F}, P) \to (R^I, \mathcal{B}^I)$, where $I = [0, +\infty)$ and $\mathcal{B}^I$ is the product σ-field, that is, $\mathcal{B}^I = \sigma(X_t : t \geq 0)$ is the σ-field generated by the coordinate maps

$$X_t : x = (x_t)_{t \geq 0} \in R^I \mapsto x_t \in R. \tag{0}$$

The measurability of B follows from the measurability of the compositions $B_t = X_t \circ B : (\Omega, \mathcal{F}) \to (R, \mathcal{B})$. The product space $(R^I, \mathcal{B}^I)$ exhibits many pathological properties. For example it is not metrizable and the product σ-field $\mathcal{B}^I$ is weaker than the Borel σ-field generated by the product topology on R^I. The pathwise continuity of B however allows us to restrict the range of B to a far smaller and more managable space. Let

$$C := C(I, R) = \{ f \mid f : I = [0, +\infty) \to R \text{ is continuous} \}.$$

Then C is a real vector space (and obviously a miniscule subspace of the product space R^I). Equipped with the seminorms $\|f\|_n := \sup_{t \in [0,n]} |f(t)|$, $f \in C$, $n \geq 1$, C becomes a Fréchet space. The metric topology on C is the topology of uniform convergence on compact subsets of I and is far stronger than the trace of the product topology (the topology of pointwise convergence) on R^I. It is not difficult to see that the metric space C is in fact separable: Piecewise linear functions with graphs whose vertices have rational coordinates and which are eventually constant form a countable dense subset of C. Thus C is a complete, separable metric space. For $t \geq 0$ the evaluation functional

$$X_t : f \in C \to f(t) \in R \tag{1}$$

is simply the restriction to C of the coordinate functional X_t in (0) and we let $\mathcal{C} := \sigma(X_t; t \geq 0)$ be the σ-field generated by these functionals. Then $\mathcal{C} = \{ C \cap A \mid A \in \mathcal{B}^I \}$ is the trace of the product σ-field $\mathcal{B}^I$ on the subset $C \subseteq R^I$.

The subsets $A \subseteq R^I$ such that the indicator function 1_A depends on only countably many coordinates X_t are easily seen to form a σ-field $\mathcal{G}$ containing the generators $X_t^{-1}(A)$, $t \geq 0$, $A \in \mathcal{B}(R)$, of the product σ-field $\mathcal{B}^I$ and hence all of $\mathcal{B}^I$. Since continuity is not a property depending on the value at only countably many points, the subset $C \subseteq R^I$ is not in $\mathcal{G}$ and hence not in $\mathcal{B}^I$.

On the product space R^I the product σ-field $\mathcal{B}^I$ is weaker than the Borel σ-field generated by the product topology. However, on the smaller space C the two σ-fields agree:

2.b.0. $\mathcal{C}$ *is the Borel σ-field generated by the metric topology of the space C.*

Proof. Let $\mathcal{B}(C)$ denote the Borel σ-field generated by the metric topology on C. Since each map $X_t : C \to R$ is continuous (and hence Borel measurable), it follows that $\mathcal{C} = \sigma(X_t; t \geq 0) \subseteq \mathcal{B}(C)$. On the other hand the Borel σ-field is generated by the closed balls

$$B_{n,r}(f) := \{\, g \in C \mid \|f - g\|_n \leq r \,\}, \quad n \geq 1, \; r > 0, \; f \in C.$$

Thus the reverse inclusion $\mathcal{B}(C) \subseteq \mathcal{C}$ will be established, if we can show that $B_{n,r}(f) \in \mathcal{C}$, for all such n, r and f. Indeed

$$
\begin{aligned}
B_{n,r}(f) &= \{\, g \in C \mid \sup_{t \in [0,n]} |g(t) - f(t)| \leq r \,\} \\
&= \{\, g \in C \mid |g(t) - f(t)| \leq r, \; \forall t \in Q \cap [0,n] \,\} \\
&= \{\, g \in C \mid X_t(g) \in [f(t) - r, f(t) + r], \; \forall t \in Q \cap [0,n] \,\} \\
&= \bigcap_{t \in Q \cap [0,n]} X_t^{-1}\left([f(t) - r, f(t) + r]\right) \in \sigma(X_t; t \geq 0) = \mathcal{C}. \; \blacksquare
\end{aligned}
$$

Terminology. The measurable space $(C, \mathcal{C})$ is called *path space*. It is a complete, separable metric space together with its Borel σ-field $\mathcal{C}$. We keep in mind however that $\mathcal{C}$ is also the σ-field generated by the evaluation functionals X_t in (2). Due to the continuity of all paths, our Brownian motion $B : (\Omega, \mathcal{F}, P) \to (R^I, \mathcal{B}^I)$ actually takes values in path space, that is, $B : (\Omega, \mathcal{F}, P) \to (C, \mathcal{C})$ is a measurable map.

Let P_B denote the distribution of B on path space $(C, \mathcal{C})$, and set $X = (X_t)_{t \geq 0}$. Then $X : (C, \mathcal{C}, P_B) \to (C, \mathcal{C})$ is a stochastic process on $(C, \mathcal{C}, P_B)$ and in fact

$$X : f \in C \to (X_t(f))_{t \geq 0} = f \in C$$

is the identity map. It follows that the distribution of X is identical to the distribution of B ($P_X = X(P_B) = P_B$) and in particular X is another Brownian motion starting at zero. By the special nature of X, the entire information about the stochastic process X is concentrated in the underlying probability measure $Q = P_X = P_B$ on path space $(C, \mathcal{C})$. This measure is called the *Wiener measure*. The measure Q is easily seen to be independent of the probability space $(\Omega, \mathcal{F}, P)$ and Brownian motion $B : (\Omega, \mathcal{F}, P) \to (C, \mathcal{C})$. It is completely determined by its finite dimensional marginal distributions. If $F \subseteq I = [0, +\infty)$ is a finite subset and $\pi_F : C \to R^F$ the corresponding coordinate projection, then $\pi_F(Q) = \pi_F(P_B) = P_{\pi_F \circ B} = P_{(B_t)_{t \in F}} = N(0, D)$, where the Gaussian measure $N(0, D)$ is completely determined by its covariance function $D(s, t) = s \wedge t$ and is thus independent of the special choices of $(\Omega, \mathcal{F}, P)$ and B. In short we may assume that our Brownian motion B is defined on the probability space $(\Omega, \mathcal{F}, P)$, where

$$
\begin{aligned}
&\Omega = C = \{\, \omega \mid \omega : I = [0, +\infty) \to R \text{ is continuous}\,\}, \\
&B_t = X_t : \omega \in \Omega = C \mapsto \omega(t) \in R, \quad t \geq 0, \\
&\mathcal{F} = \mathcal{C} = \sigma(X_t; t \geq 0) \quad \text{and} \\
&P = Q \text{ is the Wiener measure.}
\end{aligned}
\tag{2}
$$

In this case we might be tempted to use the natural filtration $\mathcal{F}_t^0 := \sigma(B_s; s \leq t)$, $t \geq 0$, to which the process B is adapted. This filtration however is not right continuous, a very serious flaw: indeed the set $\{\omega \in \Omega = C \mid \lim_{t \downarrow 0+} t^{-1}\omega(t) = 0\}$ is in $\bigcap_{t>0} \mathcal{F}_t^0$ but not in $\mathcal{F}_0^0$. This problem will be overcome below, where it is shown that augmentation of the σ-field $\mathcal{F}$ and of filtration $(\mathcal{F}_t^0)$ by the null sets makes this filtration right continuous.

2.c The measures P_x. Consider the Brownian motion B on the probability space $(C, \mathcal{C}, Q)$, where Q is the Wiener measure and $B_t(\omega) = \omega(t)$, for all $\omega \in \Omega$. Then $B : (C, \mathcal{C}) \to (C, \mathcal{C})$ is the identity map and $B_0 = 0$ almost surely.

Often it is more desirable to start the Brownian motion at some other point $x \in R$, while maintaining properties 2.a.0.(b)-(d) above.

Set $B^x = x + B$, that is, $B_t^x = x + B_t$, $t \geq 0$. Then obviously $B_0^x = x$, P-as., while the process B^x has the same increments as the process B and hence the properties 2.a.0.(b)-(d) remain in force for B^x with respect to the underlying probability measure Q. However it is better to leave the process B unchanged and force the desired property by a change of the underlying probability measure Q.

Since $B : (C, \mathcal{C}) \to (C, \mathcal{C})$ is the identity map, $Q = B(Q) = Q_B$ is also the distribution of the process B. The above suggests that we let $P_x = B^x(Q) = Q_{B^x}$ be the distribution of the process B^x:

2.c.0 Definition. *For $x \in R$ set $P_x = B^x(Q) = Q_{B^x}$, where $B^x = x + B$.*

Recalling that B is the identity map, we have $B(P_x) = P_x = B^x(Q)$, that is, the distribution of the process B under the measure P_x is identical to the distribution of the process B^x under the measure Q. Thus, with respect to the probability measure P_x, the process B satisfies:
(a) $B_0 = x$ almost surely,
(b) For all $0 \leq s < t$ the increment $B_t - B_s$ has distribution $N(0, t-s)$,
(c) For all $0 \leq t_1 < t_2 < \ldots < t_n$ the variables $B_{t_1}, B_{t_2} - B_{t_1}, \ldots, B_{t_n} - B_{t_{n-1}}$ are independent,
(d) For every $\omega \in \Omega$ the path $t \in [0, \infty) \mapsto B_t(\omega) \in R$ is continuous,

since this is true of the process B^x relative to the probability measure Q. In particular, relative to the underlying measure P_x we have $B_t \sim N(x, t)$, that is, B_t is normal with mean x and variance t. Note that, relative to P_x, B remains a path continuous process with stationary and independent increments.

2.d Brownian motion in higher dimensions. Let $d \geq 1$. A d-dimensional Brownian motion B starting at $0 \in R^d$ on the probability space $(\Omega, \mathcal{F}, P)$ is an R^d-valued stochastic process, $B_t = (B_t^1, B_t^2, \ldots, B_t^d)'$, such that the the coordinate processes

$$B^j : (\Omega, \mathcal{F}, P) \to (C, \mathcal{C}), \quad j = 1, 2, \ldots, d$$

are *independent* one dimensional Brownian motions on $(\Omega, \mathcal{F}, P)$ starting at $0 \in R$. The independence here is the usual independence of random objects and implies in particular the independence of the random variables $f_1(B^1), f_2(B^2), \ldots, f_d(B^d)$, for all measurable functions $f_j : (C, \mathcal{C}) \to R$. One verifies easily:

(a) $B_0 = 0$ almost surely.

(b) The increment $B_t - B_s$ is a Gaussian variable with distribution $N(0, (t-s)I)$, for all $0 \le s < t$.

(c) For all $0 \le t_1 < t_2 < \ldots < t_n$ the variables $B_{t_1}, B_{t_2} - B_{t_1}, \ldots, B_{t_n} - B_{t_{n-1}}$ are independent.

(d) For every $\omega \in \Omega$ the path $t \in [0, \infty) \mapsto B_t(\omega) \in R^d$ is continuous,

in close analogy to the one dimensional case. In particular B is a path continuous process with stationary and independent increments. Note that the process B can be viewed as a measurable map

$$B : (\Omega, \mathcal{F}, P) \to (C^d, \mathcal{C}^d) := (C, \mathcal{C})^d.$$

Let $I = [0, +\infty)$. The product $C^d = C(I, R)^d$ can be identified with the space $C(I, R^d)$ of all continuous functions $f : I \to R^d$. With seminorms analogous to the one dimensional case, $C(I, R^d)$ is a Fréchet space, its topology the product topology on C^d and hence the product σ-field $\mathcal{C}^d$ the Borel σ-field on $C(I, R^d)$.

Obviously properties (a)-(c) specify all the finite dimensional distributions of the process B and consequently uniquely determine the distribution of B on the space $(C^d, \mathcal{C}^d)$. Indeed, if $0 = t_0 < t_1 < \ldots < t_n$, then (a),(b),(c) specify the joint distribution of the random vector $(B_{t_0}, B_{t_1} - B_{t_0}, \ldots, B_{t_n} - B_{t_{n-1}})$ and hence the distribution of its (linear) image $(B_{t_0}, B_{t_1}, \ldots, B_{t_n})$. Thus a Brownian motion in R^d starting at zero is characterized by properties (a)-(d) above, that is, (a)-(d) imply that B is an R^d-valued Brownian motion starting at zero in R^d.

The existence of such Brownian motions follows easily from the existence in the one dimensional case: if $(\Omega, \mathcal{F}, P)$ is the d-fold product space $(C, \mathcal{C}, Q)^d$, where Q is the (one dimensional) Wiener measure, then the identity map

$$B : (\Omega, \mathcal{F}, P) \to (C, \mathcal{C})^d = (C^d, \mathcal{C}^d)$$

is such a process (the *standard Brownian motion* in R^d). The coordinates with respect to the product measure are independent and identically distributed and hence one dimensional Brownian motions as required above.

Consider this process B and let $x \in R^d$. Then the process $B^x = x + B$ and the probability measure $P_x := B^x(P)$ satisfy $B^x(P) = P_x = B(P_x)$, that is, the distribution of B under P_x is identical to the distribution of B^x under P. As in 2.c this implies that, relative to the probability measure P_x, the process B satisfies $B_0 = x$ almost surely and (b)-(d) as above.

The shift operators. The special nature of the space $(\Omega, \mathcal{F}, P) = (C, \mathcal{C}, Q)^d$ provides an additional useful structural element. On the set $\Omega = C^d = C(I, R^d)$ we can introduce the *shift operators* $\theta_s : \Omega \to \Omega$, $s \in I$, as follows

$$(\theta_s \omega)(t) = \omega(t + s), \quad \omega \in \Omega, \ s, t \in I = [0, +\infty).$$

The operator θ_s shifts us s seconds into the future. If B is the standard Brownian motion $B_t(\omega) = \omega(t)$, $\omega \in \Omega = C(I, R^d)$, then $B_t \circ \theta_s = B_{t+s}$. If $Y : \Omega \to R$ is any function, then $Y \circ \theta_s$ is the same function restricted to the future after time s. Let for example $Y = f(B_{t_1}, B_{t_2}, \ldots, B_{t_n})$, where $0 \le t_1 < t_2 < \ldots < t_n$ and $f : (R^d)^n \to R$. Then $Y \circ \theta_s = f(B_{t_1+s}, B_{t_2+s}, \ldots, B_{t_n+s})$. These relations will be useful in the formulation of the Markov property.

For the remainder of chapter II we assume that our probability space $(\Omega, \mathcal{F}, P)$ and Brownian motion B are of the above special form: $(\Omega, \mathcal{F}, P) = (C, \mathcal{C}, Q)^d$ and $B : (\Omega, \mathcal{F}, P) \to (C^d, \mathcal{C}^d)$ the identity map. In consequence we have the shift operators θ_s, $s \in [0, +\infty)$, and measures P_x, $x \in R^d$. Let $E_x = E_{P_x}$ denote expectation with respect to the measure P_x.

2.e Markov property. Let B be a Brownian motion in R^d and $\mathcal{F}_t^0 := \sigma(B_s; s \le t)$, $t \ge 0$, the associated filtration. We have noted above that this filtration is not satisfactory as it is not right continuous. It will be replaced with a more satisfactory filtration below.

At time s the development of the path $t \in [0, s] \mapsto B_t(\omega)$ has already been observed, that is, all the information in the σ-field $\mathcal{F}_s^0$ is at hand. A natural question is now what this implies about the future development of the path $t \mapsto B_t(\omega)$.

To investigate this, we study the conditional probabilities $P(B_t \in A \mid \mathcal{F}_s^0)$, for Borel subsets $A \subseteq R^d$, or, more generally and more elegantly, the conditional expectations $E\left(f(B_t) \mid \mathcal{F}_s^0\right)$, for $0 \le s < t$.

We will see that these depend only on the σ-field $\sigma(B_s)$ and not on all of $\mathcal{F}_s^0$, that is, the development of the path $t \mapsto B_t(\omega)$ from time $t = s$ onward depends only on the present state (value of $B_s(\omega)$), but not on its past $t \in [0, s) \mapsto B_t(\omega)$. For $t > 0$ and $x, y \in R^d$, set
$$q_t(x, y) := (2\pi t)^{-d/2} e^{-\|x-y\|^2/2t}.$$

From 1.a.7 it follows that the Gaussian measure $N(0, tI)$ with mean $0 \in R^d$ and covariance matrix tI has density $N(0, tI)(dy) = (2\pi t)^{-d/2} e^{-\|y\|^2/2t} dy$. It follows that the Gaussian measure $N(x, tI)$ has density
$$N(x, tI)(dy) = (2\pi t)^{-d/2} e^{-\|x-y\|^2/2t} dy = q_t(x, y) dy.$$

2.e.0. *We have* $q_t(x, y) = q_t(x + h, y + h)$, $q_t(x, y) = q_t(y, x) = q_t(x - y, 0)$ *and* $N(x, tI)(dy) = q_t(x, y) dy$ *especially* $\int_{R^d} q_t(x, y) dy = 1$, *for all* $x, y, h \in R^d$. ∎

Poisson kernels. Let $b(R^d)$ denote the Banach space of all bounded, measurable functions on $f : R^d \to R$. For $t \ge 0$ define the linear operator $P_t : b(R^d) \to b(R^d)$ as the convolution
$$P_t f = f * N(0, tI), \quad f \in b(R^d).$$

Consequently, for $x \in R^d$,
$$(P_t f)(x) = \int_{R^d} f(y) q_t(x, y) dy = E(f(W)), \tag{0}$$

where W is any random variable with distribution $N(x, tI)$. We will use the notation $P_t f = f * N(0, tI) = \int_{R^d} f(y) q_t(\cdot, y) dy$ for all measurable functions f, for which the corresponding integral exists, especially for nonnegative f.

From the Fourier transform $N\widehat{(0,tI)}(y) = exp\left(-(tIy, y)\right) = exp(-t\|y\|^2)$ we infer the semigroup property $N(0, sI) * N(0, tI) = N(0, (s+t)I)$, $s, t \geq 0$. The associativity of convolution now yields $P_s \circ P_t = P_{s+t}$; in other words the family $\{P_t\}_{t \geq 0}$ is a semigroup of operators on $b(R^d)$.

2.e.1. *Let $0 \leq s < t$. Then $B_t - B_s$ is independent of the σ-field $\mathcal{F}_s^0$ under all measures P_x, $x \in R^d$.*

Proof. Let $x \in R^d$, $0 \leq s_1 < s_2 < \ldots < s_n \leq s$ and set $\Delta = B_t - B_s$. Then the variables B_0, $B_{s_1} - B_0$, $B_{s_2} - B_{s_1}, \ldots$, $B_{s_n} - B_{s_{n-1}}$, Δ are independent under P_x (2.d.(c)) and so Δ is independent of the σ-field $\sigma(B_0, B_{s_1} - B_0, \ldots, B_{s_n} - B_{s_{n-1}}) = \sigma(B_0, B_{s_1}, \ldots, B_{s_n})$.

Consequently $\Pi = \bigcup\{\sigma(B_{s_1}, \ldots, B_{s_n}) \mid 0 \leq s_1 < \ldots < s_n \leq s\} \subseteq \mathcal{F}_s^0$ is a π-system which generates the σ-field $\mathcal{F}_s^0$ and satisfies $P_x(A \cap B) = P_x(A)P_x(B)$, for all sets $A \in \Pi$ and $B \in \sigma(\Delta)$. 2.e.1 now follows by applying appendix B.10.0 to each event $B \in \sigma(\Delta)$. ∎

2.e.2. *Let $0 \leq s < t$, $x \in R^d$ and $f : R^d \to R$ a bounded or nonnegative measurable function. Then*

(a) $E_x\left(f(B_t) \mid \mathcal{F}_s^0\right) = (P_{t-s}f)(B_s) = \int_{R^d} f(y)q_{t-s}(B_s, y)dy$.
(b) $E_x\left(f(B_t)\right) = (P_t f)(x) = \int_{R^d} f(y)q_t(x, y)dy$.
(c) $E_x\left(f(B_t) \mid \mathcal{F}_s^0\right) = E\left(f(B_t) \mid B_s\right)$.
(d) $E_x\left(f(B_t) \mid \mathcal{F}_s^0\right)(\omega) = E_{B_s(\omega)}\left(f(B_{t-s})\right)$, *for P-ae. $\omega \in \Omega$.*

Remark. Here $E\left(f(B_t) \mid B_s\right) = E\left(f(B_t) \mid \sigma(B_s)\right)$ as usual. The reader will note that the right hand sides of (a),(c) and (d) do not depend on x explicitly. It does not matter where B starts. It matters only where it is at time s.

Proof. (a)   Note that the random variable B_s is $\mathcal{F}_s^0$-measurable while the random variable $B_t - B_s$ is independent of the σ-field $\mathcal{F}_s^0$ under the measure P_x (2.e.1). Using I.2.b.11, we obtain

$$E_x\left(f(B_t) \mid \mathcal{F}_s^0\right) = E_x\left(f(B_s + (B_t - B_s)) \mid \mathcal{F}_s^0\right) = \int_{R^d} f(B_s + y)P_{B_t - B_s}(dy).$$

Since $B_t - B_s \sim N(0, (t-s)I)$ under P_x, we have $P_{B_t - B_s}(dy) = q_{t-s}(0, y)dy$. Thus

$$E_x\left(f(B_t) \mid \mathcal{F}_s^0\right) = \int_{R^d} f(B_s + y)q_{t-s}(0, y)dy = \int_{R^d} f(y)q_{t-s}(0, y - B_s)dy$$

$$= \int_{R^d} f(y)q_{t-s}(B_s, y)dy = (P_{t-s}f)(B_s).$$

(b)   Use (a) for $s = 0$ and note that the σ-field $\mathcal{F}_0^0$ consists only of events of P_x-probability zero or one. Thus $E_x\left(f(B_t) \mid \mathcal{F}_0^0\right) = E_x\left(f(B_t)\right)$. Moreover $B_0 = x$, P_x-as.

(c)   The right side of (a) is $\sigma(B_s)$-measurable. It follows that $E\left(f(B_t)\mid\mathcal{F}_s^0\right) = E\left(f(B_t)\mid\sigma(B_s)\right)$.

(d)   Let $w \in \Omega$. According to (b) with $x = B_s(w)$ and t replaced with $t - s$, the right hand side of (a) can be written as $(P_{t-s}f)\,(B_s(w)) = E_{B_s(w)}\,(f(B_{t-s}))$ and thus (d) follows from (a). ∎

Remark. 2.e.2 deals with random variables $Z : \Omega = C(I, R^d) \to R$ which are of the particularly simple form $Z = f(B_t)$. Note that (c) says that $E(Z\mid\mathcal{F}_s^0) = E(Z\mid B_s)$ that is, the future, given the entire past up to time s, is the same as the future given the state exactly at time s: the past influences the future only through the present.

Part (d) expresses this same fact in a more explicit way: At time s our path has arrived at the point $B_s(w)$. However, the process $Y_t = B_{t+s}$ has all the properties of a Brownian motion except $Y_0 = 0$. Thus we can view the path $t \geq s \mapsto B_t(w)$ as the path of a Brownian motion starting at the point $B_s(w)$ and consequently the future after time s should be evaluated through the measure P_x, where $x = B_s(w)$ The transition from time s to time t is then accomplished through the increment $B_t - B_s \sim N(0, (t-s)I) \sim B_{t-s}$.

The Markov property is the generalization of (d) to arbitrary bounded or nonnegative measurable random variables $Y : \Omega = C(I, R^d) \to R$. Let us see what would be an appropriate formulation: if in (d) we set $Y = f(B_{t-s})$, then $f(B_t) = Y \circ \theta_s$ and (d) becomes

$$E\left(Y \circ \theta_s \mid \mathcal{F}_s^0\right)(w) = E_{B_s(w)}\,(Y), \quad \text{for } P\text{-ae. } w \in \Omega.$$

Notice that $Y \circ \theta_s$ represents the random variable Y evaluated s seconds in the future and that, after s seconds, the state $B_s(w)$ is reached, so that evaluation should now proceed using the measure $E_{B_s(w)}$. Indeed we will be able to replace the σ-field $\mathcal{F}_s^0$ with the stronger σ-field $\mathcal{F}_s^+ = \bigcap_{r>s} \mathcal{F}_r^0$. This will have useful consequences.

2.e.3. *Let X, Y be R^m-valued random vectors and $T : R^m \to R^m$ an invertible linear map. If $X = T(Y)$ and $P_X(dx) = g(x)dx$ then $P_Y(dy) = g(T(y))|\det(T)|dy$.*

Proof. For each Borel subset $A \subseteq R^m$ we have

$$P(Y \in A) = P(X \in T(A)) = \int_{T(A)} g(x)dx = \int_A g(T(y))|\det(T)|dy,$$

where we have used the substitution formula for Lebesgue integrals and the fact that the Jacobian J_T of a linear map T satisfies $J_T(y) = T$, for all $y \in R^m$. ∎

2.e.4. *Let $x_0 \in R^d$, $0 = t_0 < t_1 < \ldots < t_n$, write $y = (y_1, y_2, \ldots, y_n) \in (R^d)^n$ and set $y_0 = x_0$. Then with respect to the probability measure P_{x_0} the random vector $Y = (B_{t_1}, B_{t_2}, \ldots, B_{t_n})$ in $(R^d)^n$ has density*

$$f(y) = \prod_{j=1}^{n} q_{t_j - t_{j-1}}(y_{j-1}, y_j) dy$$
$$= q_{t_1}(x_0, y_1) q_{t_2 - t_1}(y_1, y_2) \cdots q_{t_n - t_{n-1}}(y_{n-1}, y_n) dy_1 dy_2 \ldots dy_n.$$

Proof. Set $X_1 = Y_1 = B_{t_1}$, $X_2 = Y_2 - Y_1, \ldots, X_n = Y_n - Y_{n-1}$, in short $X = T(Y)$, where $T(y_1, y_2, \ldots, y_n) = (y_1, y_2 - y_1, \ldots, y_n - y_{n-1})$. Note that $T : (R^d)^n \to (R^d)^n$ is an invertible linear map with determinant one.

By stationarity of the increments of our Brownian motion B we have $X_j = B_{t_j} - B_{t_{j-1}} \sim N(0, (t_j - t_{j-1})I)$ and hence $P_{X_j}(dx_j) = q_{t_j - t_{j-1}}(0, x_j) dx_j$, for all $j = 2, 3, \ldots, n$, and $X_1 = B_0 + (B_{t_1} - B_0)$ with $B_{t_1} - B_0 \sim N(0, t_1 I)$ and $B_0 = x_0$. Thus $P_{X_1} = N(x_0, t_1 I)$ and so $P_{X_1}(dx_1) = q_{t_1}(x_0, x_1) dx_1$. Combining this with the independence of $X_1, X_2, \ldots, X_n$ it follows that the random vector $X = (X_1, X_2, \ldots, X_n)$ on $(R^d)^n$ has density

$$g(x) = q_{t_1}(x_0, x_1) q_{t_2 - t_1}(0, x_2) \cdots q_{t_n - t_{n-1}}(0, x_n) dx,$$
$$x = (x_1, x_2, \ldots, x_n) \in (R^d)^n.$$

Since $X = T(Y)$ and T is a linear map with determinant one, 2.e.3 yields that the random vector $Y = (B_{t_1}, B_{t_2} \ldots, B_{t_n})$ has density

$$f(y) = g(Ty) dy = q_{t_1}(x_0, y_1) q_{t_2 - t_1}(0, y_2 - y_1) \cdots q_{t_n - t_{n-1}}(0, y_n - y_{n-1})$$
$$= q_{t_1}(x_0, y_1) q_{t_2 - t_1}(y_1, y_2) \cdots q_{t_n - t_{n-1}}(y_{n-1}, y_n),$$

as desired. ∎

Finite dimensional cylinders. The sets $A = [B_{s_1} \in A_1, \ldots, B_{s_n} \in A_n,] \in \mathcal{F}$, where $0 < s_1 < \ldots < s_n$ and $A_j \subseteq R^d$ is a Borel set, for all $j = 1, 2, \ldots, n$, are called the finite dimensional cylinders. Note that $1_A = 1_{A_1}(B_{s_1}) 1_{A_2}(B_{s_2}) \ldots 1_{A_n}(B_{s_n})$.

Such a cylinder A is in the σ-field $\mathcal{F}_s^0$ if and only if $0 < s_1 < s_2 < \ldots < s_n \leq s$. Note the stipulation $s_1 > 0$. It is crucial for the following arguments. Thus a finite dimensional cylinder cannot put restrictions on the first coordinate $B_0(\omega) = \omega(0)$. Nonetheless the finite dimensional cylinders generate the σ-field $\mathcal{F}$. This is due to the continuity of Brownian motion paths at $t = 0$.

2.e.5. *The finite dimensional cylinders form a π-system which generates the σ-field $\mathcal{F} = \sigma(B_s; s \geq 0)$. For each $t > 0$ the finite dimensional cylinders in $\mathcal{F}_t^0$ form a π-system which generates the σ-field $\mathcal{F}_t^0$.*

Proof. It is easy to see that the intersection of two finite dimensional cylinders is another such cylinder, that is, the finite dimensional cylinders form a π-system.

Recall that $\mathcal{F}_t^0 = \sigma(B_s; 0 \leq s \leq t)$ and let $\mathcal{G}$ be the σ-field generated by all finite dimensional cylinders $A \in \mathcal{F}$. Then $\mathcal{G} \subseteq \mathcal{F}$ and to show that $\mathcal{G} = \mathcal{F}$ it suffices to show that each projection $B_s : \Omega \to R$ is $\mathcal{G}$-measurable. For $s > 0$ this follows from the fact that the set $A = [B_s \in D]$ is itself a finite dimensional cylinder, hence in $\mathcal{G}$, for each Borel set $D \subseteq R^d$. If $s = 0$, then $B_s = B_0 = \lim_{n \uparrow \infty} B_{1/n}$, at each point of Ω, because of the path continuity of our Brownian motion B. Since $B_{1/n}$ is $\mathcal{G}$-measurable, for each $n \geq 1$, so is B_0. The proof for the σ-field $\mathcal{F}_t^0$ is identical. ∎

Remark. The indicator function $Y = 1_A$ of a finite dimensional cylinder A is an example of a random variable $Y : (\Omega, \mathcal{F}) \to R$ of the form $Y(\omega) = \prod_{j=1}^n f_j(B_{t_j}(\omega))$, where the f_j are bounded measurable functions on R and $0 < t_1 < \ldots < t_n$. We now turn our attention to such random variables.

2.e.6 Corollary. *Let $Y = \prod_{j=1}^n f_j(B_{t_j}) : (\Omega, \mathcal{F}) \to R$, where the f_j are bounded measurable functions on R^d, $0 < t_1 < \ldots < t_n$ and $x \in R^d$. Then*

$$E_x(Y) = \int_{R^d} dy_1 \Big[q_{t_1}(x, y_1) f_1(y_1) \int_{R^d} dy_2 \Big[q_{t_2 - t_1}(y_1, y_2) f_2(y_2) \cdots$$
$$\cdots \int_{R^d} dy_n \big[q_{t_n - t_{n-1}}(y_{n-1}, y_n) f_n(y_n) \big] \cdots \Big].$$

Remark. The right hand side of 2.e.6 is an iterated integral with integration from the right to the left.

Proof. From the form 2.e.4 of the joint density for the distribution $P_{(B_{t_1}, B_{t_2}, \ldots, B_{t_n})}$ under the measure P_x it follows that

$$E_x(Y) = \int_{(R^d)^n} f_1(y_1) f_2(y_2) \cdots f_n(y_n) \\ q_{t_1}(x, y_1) q_{t_2 - t_1}(y_1, y_2) \cdots q_{t_n - t_{n-1}}(y_{n-1}, y_n) dy_1 dy_2 \ldots dy_n.$$

Integrating in the order $dy_n dy_{n-1} \ldots dy_1$, the right hand side can be written as the iterated integral 2.e.6. ∎

2.e.7 Lemma. *Let $Y = \prod_{k=1}^m f_k(B_{t_k}) : (\Omega, \mathcal{F}) \to R$, where the f_k are bounded measurable functions on R^d and $0 < t_1 < \ldots < t_m$. Then*

$$E_x[(Y \circ \theta_s)1_A] = E_x[\phi(B_{s+h}, h)1_A], \tag{1}$$

for all $x \in R^d$ and all sets $A \in \mathcal{F}_{s+h}^0$ with $s \geq 0$ and $0 < h < t_1$, where

$$\phi(y, h) = \int_{R^d} dy_1 \, q_{t_1 - h}(y, y_1) f_1(y_1) \int_{R^d} dy_2 \, q_{t_2 - t_1}(y_1, y_2) f_2(y_2) \cdots$$
$$\cdots \int_{R^d} dy_m \, q_{t_m - t_{m-1}}(y_m, y_{m-1}) f_m(y_m).$$

Proof. Assume first that $A \in \mathcal{F}_{s+h}$ is a finite dimensional cylinder, that is, $A = [B_{s_1} \in A_1, \ldots, B_{s_n} \in A_n,] \subseteq \Omega$, where $0 < s_1 < \ldots < s_n \leq s + h$ and $A_j \subseteq R^d$

a Borel set, for all $j = 1, 2, \ldots, n$. Then $1_A = \prod_{j=1}^{n} 1_{A_j}(B_{s_j})$. Let $s \geq 0$. Then $Y \circ \theta_s = \prod_{k=1}^{m} f_k(B_{t_k+s})$ and consequently

$$1_A(Y \circ \theta_s) = \prod_{j=1}^{n} 1_{A_j}(B_{s_j}) \cdot 1_{R^d}(B_{s+h}) \cdot \prod_{k=1}^{m} f_k(B_{t_k+s}),$$

where $0 < s_1 < s_2 < \ldots < s_n < h + s < t_1 + s < \ldots < t_m + s$. Likewise

$$1_A \phi(B_{s+h}, h) = 1_{A_1}(B_{s_1}) \ldots 1_{A_n}(B_{s_n}) \phi(B_{s+h}, h).$$

According to 2.e.6 both expectations $E_x[1_A(Y \circ \theta_s)]$ and $E_x(1_A \phi(B_{s+h}, h))$ can be written as

$$\int_{A_1} dx_1 \, q_{s_1}(x, x_1) \ldots \int_{A_n} dx_n \, q_{s_n - s_{n-1}}(x_{n-1}, x_n) \cdot \int_{R^d} dy \, q_{h+s-s_n}(x_n, y) \, \phi(y, h),$$

with $\phi(y, h)$ as above. In particular $E_x(Y \circ \theta_s; A) = E_x(\phi(B_{s+h}, h); A)$. Thus (1) is verified for all finite dimensional cylinders $A \in \mathcal{F}^0_{s+h}$. These cylinders form a π-system which generates the σ-field $\mathcal{F}^0_{s+h}$. Moreover the family of all sets $A \in \mathcal{F}^0_{s+h}$ for which (1) is true is a λ-system. An application of the π-λ-theorem (appendix B.3) now shows that (1) is true for all sets $A \in \mathcal{F}^0_{s+h}$. ∎

Definition. *For $s \geq 0$ set $\mathcal{F}^+_s = \bigcap_{r>s} \mathcal{F}^0_r$.*

Remark. Then $(\mathcal{F}^+_s)_s$ is a right continuous filtration which satisfies $\mathcal{F}^0_s \subseteq \mathcal{F}^+_s$, for all $s \geq 0$.

2.e.8. *Let $Y : (\Omega, \mathcal{F}) \to R$ be measurable and bounded or nonnegative. Then the function $g_Y(y) := E_y(Y)$, $y \in R^d$, is measurable on R^d.*

Proof. It will suffice to treat the nonnegative case. The family $\mathcal{L}$ of all functions $Y : (\Omega, \mathcal{F}) \to [0, +\infty)$ such that g_Y is measurable on R^d is easily seen to be a λ-cone on $(\Omega, \mathcal{F})$. By the extension theorem (appendix B.4) and 2.e.5 it will now suffice to show that $1_A \in \mathcal{L}$, for all finite dimensional cylinders A. The indicator function 1_A of such a cylinder has the form $1_A = \prod_{j=1}^{n} 1_{A_j}(B_{t_j})$ and an application of 2.e.6 now yields the measurability of $g(y) = E_y(1_A)$. ∎

2.e.9 Markov Property. *Let $Y : (\Omega, \mathcal{F}) \to R$ be any bounded or nonnegative random variable and $x \in R^d$. Then we have $E_x(Y \circ \theta_s \mid \mathcal{F}^+_s)(\omega) = E_{B_s(\omega)}(Y)$, for P-ae. $\omega \in \Omega$.*

Remark. It is interesting that we can use the stronger σ-field $\mathcal{F}^+_s$ instead of $\mathcal{F}^0_s$. This is possible because of the path continuity of Brownian motion (used in the proof of 2.e.5).

Proof. The right hand side is $g(w) = E_w(Y)$ evaluated at $w = B_s(\omega) \in R^d$. According to 2.e.8 the function $g = g(w)$, $w \in R^d$, is measurable on R^d. It follows that the function $H(\omega) = E_{B_s(\omega)}(Y) = g(B_s(\omega))$ is $\sigma(B_s)$-measurable and hence $\mathcal{F}_s^+$-measurable on Ω. Thus we have to show only that

$$E_x\left[(Y \circ \theta_s)1_A\right] = E_x\left[H1_A\right] = E_x\left[E_{B_s(\omega)}(Y)1_A(\omega)\right], \quad \text{for all sets } A \in \mathcal{F}_s^+. \quad (2)$$

Step 1. Assume first that Y has the form $Y = \prod_{k=1}^m f_k(B_{t_k})$, where the f_k are bounded measurable functions on R^d and $0 < t_1 < t_2 < \ldots < t_m$. If $A \in \mathcal{F}_s^+$, then $A \in \mathcal{F}_{s+h}^0$, for all $h > 0$. If in addition $0 < h < t_1$, then, using 2.e.7,

$$E_x\left(Y \circ \theta_s; A\right) = E_x\left(\phi(B_{s+h}, h); A\right), \quad \text{where}$$

$$\phi(y, h) = \int_{R^d} q_{t_1 - h}(y, y_1)\psi(y_1)dy_1 \quad \text{and}$$

$$\psi(y_1) = f_1(y_1)\int_{R^d} dy_2\, q_{t_2 - t_1}(y_1, y_2)f_2(y_2)\cdots$$

$$\cdots\int_{R^d} dy_m\, q_{t_m - t_{m-1}}(y_m, y_{m-1})f_m(y_m)$$

is bounded, since the functions $f_k(y_k)$ are bounded and the kernels $q_t(x, y)$ integrate to one (2.e.0). Thus the function $\phi(y, h)$ is seen to be continuous and bounded for $(y, h) \in R^d \times [0, \epsilon]$, where $0 < \epsilon < t_1$.

Let $h \downarrow 0$ and note that the continuity of ϕ and path continuity of B imply that $\phi(B_{s+h}, h) \to \phi(B_s, 0)$ everywhere and so $E_x\left[\phi(B_{s+h}, h)1_A\right] \to E_x\left[\phi(B_s, 0)1_A\right]$, by bounded convergence. It follows that

$$E_x\left[(Y \circ \theta_s)1_A\right] = E_x\left[\phi(B_s, 0)1_A\right], \quad \text{where} \quad (3)$$

$$\phi(y, 0) = \int_{R^d} dy_1\, q_{t_1}(y, y_1)f_1(y_1)\int_{R^d} dy_2\, q_{t_2 - t_1}(y_1, y_2)f_2(y_2)\cdots$$

$$\cdots\int_{R^d} dy_m\, q_{t_m - t_{m-1}}(y_m, y_{m-1})f_m(y_m) = E_y(Y),$$

for all $y \in R^d$. Consequently $\phi(B_s(\omega), 0) = E_{B_s(\omega)}(Y)$, for all $\omega \in \Omega$, and thus (3) implies (2). This concludes step 1.

Step 2. Step 1 verifies (3) in particular for $Y = 1_A = 1_{A_1}(B_{t_1})1_{A_2}(B_{t_2})\ldots 1_{A_n}(B_{t_n})$, the indicator function of a finite dimensional cylinder $A \in \mathcal{F}$. These sets form a π-system which generates the σ-field $\mathcal{F}$.

It is easy to see that the family $\mathcal{L}$ of all random variables $Y : (\Omega, \mathcal{F}) \to [0, +\infty)$ satisfying (3) is a λ-cone on $(\Omega, \mathcal{F})$. The extension theorem appendix B.4 now implies that Λ contains every nonnegative measurable function $Y : (\Omega, \mathcal{F}) \to R$. The extension to bounded Y now follows by writing $Y = Y^+ - Y^-$. ∎

Remark. Let $Y : (\Omega, \mathcal{F}) \to R$ be bounded and measurable. From 2.e.9

$$E_x\left(Y \circ \theta_s \mid \mathcal{F}_s^+\right)(\omega) = E_{B_s(\omega)}(Y), \quad \text{a.e. } \omega \in \Omega. \quad (4)$$

The function $g(y) = E_y(Y)$, $y \in R^d$, is measurable on R^d (2.e.8) and so the function $E_{B_s(\omega)}(Y) = g(B_s)$ is $\sigma(B_s)$-measurable and hence $\mathcal{F}_s^0$-measurable. Thus (4) implies that

$$E_x\left(Y \circ \theta_s \mid \mathcal{F}_s^+\right) = E_x\left(Y \circ \theta_s \mid \mathcal{F}_s^0\right) = E_x\left(Y \circ \theta_s \mid B_s\right). \quad (5)$$

Consequently the development $Y \circ \theta_s$ of Y after time s depends only on the present state B_s and not on any other information in the σ-field $\mathcal{F}_s^+$ including the infinitesimal future. The fact that we can even disregard the infinitesimal future is due to the path continuity of Brownian motion and has interesting consequences:

2.e.10. *If* $Z \in \mathcal{E}(P_x)$ *then* $E_x\left(Z \mid \mathcal{F}_s^+\right) = E_x\left(Z \mid \mathcal{F}_s^0\right)$, P_x*-as., for all* $x \in R^d$ *and all* $s \geq 0$.

Remark. Here Z is a random variable on d-dimensional pathspace $\Omega = C(I, R^d)$.
Proof. Clearly it will suffice to conduct the proof for nonnegative Z. Let $x \in R^d$ and $s \geq 0$. The family of all nonnegative measurable $Z : (\Omega, \mathcal{F}) \to R$ satisfying $E_x\left(Z \mid \mathcal{F}_s^+\right) = E_x\left(Z \mid \mathcal{F}_s^0\right)$, P_x-as., is easily seen to be a λ-cone on $(\Omega, \mathcal{F}, P_x)$. By the extension theorem B.4 (appendix) it will suffice to verify 2.e.10 for all $Z = 1_A$, where A ranges through a π-system generating the σ-field $\mathcal{F}$.

The finite dimensional cylinders $A = [\, B_{s_1} \in A_1, \ldots, B_{s_n} \in A_n \,]$, where the $A_j \subseteq R^d$ are Borel sets and $0 < s_1 < \ldots < s_n$, form such a π-system (2.e.5). For such A, $Z = 1_A = \prod_{j=1}^n 1_{A_j}(B_{s_j})$. We may assume that $s_n > s$. Now choose k such that $0 < s_1 < \ldots < s_k < s \leq s_{k+1} < \ldots < s_n$ and set $X = 1_{A_1}(B_{s_1}) \ldots 1_{A_k}(B_{s_k})$ and $Y = 1_{A_{k+1}}(B_{s_{k+1}-s}) \ldots 1_{A_n}(B_{s_n-s})$. Then X and Y are nonnegative and measurable and X is in fact $\mathcal{F}_s^0$-measurable. Moreover we have $Z = X(Y \circ \theta_s)$. Using (5) it follows that

$$E_x\left(Z \mid \mathcal{F}_s^+\right) = E_x\left(X\left(Y \circ \theta_s\right) \mid \mathcal{F}_s^+\right) = X\, E_x\left(Y \circ \theta_s \mid \mathcal{F}_s^+\right) = X\, E_x\left(Y \circ \theta_s \mid \mathcal{F}_s^0\right)$$
$$= E_x\left(X\left(Y \circ \theta_s\right) \mid \mathcal{F}_s^0\right) = E_x\left(Z \mid \mathcal{F}_s^0\right). \blacksquare$$

2.e.11 Corollary. *Let* $x \in R^d$ *and* $s \geq 0$. *For each set* $A \in \mathcal{F}_s^+$ *there exists a set* $B = B_x \in \mathcal{F}_s$ *such that* $P_x\left(A\Delta B\right) = 0$.

Proof. Let $A \in \mathcal{F}_s^+$. Then $g = E_x\left(1_A \mid \mathcal{F}_s\right) = E_x\left(1_A \mid \mathcal{F}_s^+\right) = 1_A$, P_x-as. (2.e.10), and so the function g is $\mathcal{F}_s$-measurable and $\{0,1\}$-valued P_x-as. Thus $g = 1_B$, P_x-as., where $B = [g = 1] \in \mathcal{F}_s$. It follows that $1_A = g = 1_B$, P_x-as., that is, $P_x\left(A\Delta B\right) = 0$. $\blacksquare$

Remark. The set $B = B_x$ depends on $x \in R^d$. Since $P_x\left([B_0 = x]\right) = 1$, the measures P_x are concentrated on the pairwise disjoint sets $[B_0 = x]$, $x \in R^d$, and hence are mutually singular. In consequence the P_x-null sets and P_y-null sets are completely unrelated, for $x \neq y$. Note that, for $x = 0 \in R^d$, $P_x = P = Q^d$ is the d-dimensional Wiener measure.

2.f The augmented filtration $(\mathcal{F}_t)$. We have seen above that the filtration $(\mathcal{F}_t^0)$ is not right continuous. The filtration $(\mathcal{F}_t^+)$ is right continuous by its very definition and satisfies $E\left(Z \mid \mathcal{F}_s^+\right) = E\left(Z \mid \mathcal{F}_s^0\right)$, P-as., for all $Z \in \mathcal{E}(P)$ and all $s \geq 0$ (2.e.10 for $x = 0 \in R^d$). In other words passage to the larger filtration $(\mathcal{F}_t^+)$ does not change any conditional expectations. However we have seen in chapter I that it is desirable to work with augmented filtrations, that is, we prefer the filtration $(\mathcal{F}_t)$ defined as

$$\mathcal{F}_t = \sigma(\mathcal{F}_t^0 \cup \mathcal{N}), \quad t \geq 0,$$

where $\mathcal{N}$ is the family of P-null sets. This filtration has all the desired properties:

2.f.0. *(a)* $\mathcal{F}_t = \{\, A \in \mathcal{F} \mid \exists B \in \mathcal{F}_t^0 : P(A\Delta B) = 0\,\}$, *for all* $t \geq 0$.
(b) $\mathcal{F}_t^0 \subseteq \mathcal{F}_t^+ \subseteq \mathcal{F}_t$, *for all* $t \geq 0$.
(c) The filtration $(\mathcal{F}_t)$ *is right continuous.*
(d) $E\left(Z|\mathcal{F}_t\right) = E\left(Z|\mathcal{F}_t^0\right)$, *P-as., for all* $Z \in \mathcal{E}(P)$ *and all* $t \geq 0$.

Proof. (a) Let $t \geq 0$. Then $\mathcal{G} = \{\, A \in \mathcal{F} \mid \exists B \in \mathcal{F}_t^0 : P(A\Delta B) = 0\,\}$ is easily seen to be a σ-field which contains $\mathcal{F}_t^0$ and $\mathcal{N}$ and hence also $\mathcal{F}_t$. Conversely, if $A \in \mathcal{G}$, then $P(A\Delta B) = 0$, for some set $B \in \mathcal{F}_t^0$ and it follows that $A = (B \cup (A \setminus B)) \setminus (B \setminus A) \in \sigma\left(\mathcal{F}_t^0 \cup \mathcal{N}\right) = \mathcal{F}_t$, since here $B \in \mathcal{F}_t^0$ and $A \setminus B, B \setminus A \in \mathcal{N}$.
(b) follows from (a) and 2.e.11 (with $x = 0 \in R^d$).
(c) We have to show that $\bigcap_{r>s} \mathcal{F}_r \subseteq \mathcal{F}_s$, for all $s \geq 0$. Consider such s, let $A \in \bigcap_{r>s} \mathcal{F}_r$ and choose a sequence $r_n \downarrow s$. For each $n \geq 1$ we have $A \in \mathcal{F}_{r_n}$ and so, using (a), we can choose $B_n \in \mathcal{F}_{r_n}^0$ such that $P(A\Delta B_n) = 0$. Set $C = [\, B_n \; io.\,] = \bigcap_n \bigcup_{m>n} B_m$. Then $C \in \mathcal{F}_s^+$ and $A\Delta C \subseteq \bigcup_n (A\Delta B_n)$ and consequently $P(A\Delta C) = 0$. Using 2.e.11 we can now choose $D \in \mathcal{F}_s^0$ such that $P(C\Delta D) = 0$. Then $D \in \mathcal{F}_s^0$ and $P(A\Delta D) = 0$ and so $A \in \mathcal{F}_s$, according to (a).
(d) Augmentation of a σ-field by null sets does not change conditional expectations with respect to that σ-field. See I.2.b.14 and subsequent remark. ∎

2.g Miscellaneous properties. Let B be a one dimensional Brownian motion.

2.g.0. *(a)* $B_t - B_s$ *is independent of the σ-field* $\mathcal{F}_s$, *for all* $0 \leq s < t$,
(b) B is a continuous square integrable martingale and
(c) $B_t^2 - t$ *is a martingale and so* $\langle B \rangle_t = t$, $t \geq 0$, *under all measures* P_x, $x \in R^d$.

Proof. Recall that $P = Q = P_0$ is the Wiener measure. Since the distribution of B under P_x is the distribution of $B^x = x + B$ under P (2.c.0) it will suffice to verify (a)-(c) for the process B^x relative to the probability measure P and it is now easy to see that we may assume $x = 0 \in R^d$.
(a) $B_t - B_s$ is independent of the σ-field $\mathcal{F}_s^0$ (2.e.1). According to B.10.2 this implies that $B_t - B_s$ is independent of $\mathcal{F}_s = \sigma(\mathcal{F}_s^0 \cup \mathcal{N})$.
(b) Let $0 \leq s < t$ and recall that $E(B_t) = E(B_s) = 0$. Writing $B_t = B_s + (B_t - B_s)$ and using (a) and I.2.b.2 it follows that $E(B_t|\mathcal{F}_s) = B_s + E(B_t - B_s) = B_s$, P-as. Thus B is a P-martingale.
(c) $A_t = \langle B \rangle_t$ is the unique continuous increasing process A such that $B^2 - A$ is a local martingale. It will thus suffice to show that the process $B_t^2 - t$ is also a martingale. To see this, we have to show that $E\left[B_t^2 - t \mid \mathcal{F}_s\right] = B_s^2 - s$, equivalently $E\left[B_t^2 - B_s^2 \mid \mathcal{F}_s\right] = t - s$, for all $0 \leq s < t$. Indeed, for such s and t we have $E\left[B_t^2 - B_s^2 \mid \mathcal{F}_s\right] = E\left[(B_t - B_s)^2 \mid \mathcal{F}_s\right] = E\left[(B_t - B_s)^2\right] = Var(B_t - B_s) = t - s$
Here the first equality follows from the martingale property of B (I.9.b.0), the second equality from the independence of the increment $B_t - B_s$ from the σ-field $\mathcal{F}_s$ and the third equality from the fact that $B_t - B_s$ is a normal variable with mean zero and variance $t - s$. ∎

Remark. Since $E(B_t^2) = t$, B is not L^2-bounded. However if B is stopped at any bounded optional time T, then it becomes L^2-bounded, that is, $B_t^T = B_{t \wedge T}$ is an L^2-bounded martingale. Likewise, one dimensional Brownian motion is not uniformly integrable; indeed the family $\{\, |B_t| \, : \, t \geq 0\,\}$ is not L^1-bounded.

2.g.1 Scaling. $B_t \sim \sqrt{t}B_1$ *(same distribution),* $t \geq 0$.

Proof. If the real valued random variable Z is $N(0,1)$, then $\sqrt{t}Z \sim N(0,t)$. Apply this to the coordinates of B_1 to obtain that the coordinates of $\sqrt{t}B_1$ are independent and distributed as $N(0,t)$. It follows that $\sqrt{t}B_1 \sim B_t$. ∎

2.g.2. *If* $\alpha > 1/2$ *then* $t^{-\alpha}B_t \to 0$, *as* $t \uparrow \infty$, *P-as.*

Proof. Fix $\alpha > 1/2$. Set $M_t := \sup_{0 \leq s \leq t} |B_s|$ and recall that B is a continuous martingale. It will suffice to show that $t^{-\alpha}M_t \to 0$. The increasing nature of M now implies that it suffices to show that $n^{-\alpha}M_n \to 0$, as $n \uparrow \infty$.

The L^p-estimate I.7.e.1 yields $E(M_n^p) \leq C_p E(B_n^p) = C_p E(n^{p/2}B_1^p) = n^{p/2}D_p$, where C_p is a constant depending only on p and $D_p = C_p E(B_1^p)$. Here we have used the scaling property 2.g.1. Multiplication with $n^{-\alpha p}$ yields

$$E\left[\left(n^{-\alpha}M_n\right)^p\right] \leq n^{p(1/2-\alpha)}D_p = n^{-k}D_p,$$

with $k = p(\alpha - 1/2)$. Choose $p > 1$ so large that $k = p(\alpha - 1/2) > 1$. Then

$$E\left[\sum_n \left(n^{-\alpha}M_n\right)^p\right] < \infty \quad \text{and so} \quad \sum_n \left(n^{-\alpha}M_n\right)^p < \infty, \text{ } P\text{-as.}$$

It follows that $n^{-\alpha}M_n \to 0$, P-a.s. ∎

Remarks. (a) The precise order of growth of $|B_t|$ is known to be $\sqrt{2t \log\log t}$ (Law of the Iterated Logarithm), see [KS, 9.23].

(b) Our treatment of Brownian motion has been rudimentary. We have merely assembled the necessary theory to support subsequent developments. For a fuller account see [KS, RY].

CHAPTER III

Stochastic Integration

1. MEASURABILITY PROPERTIES OF STOCHASTIC PROCESSES

Recall that $(\Omega, \mathcal{F}, (\mathcal{F}_t), P)$ is a complete filtered probability space with right continuous and augmented filtration $(\mathcal{F}_t)$, $\mathcal{F}_\infty = \sigma(\bigcup_t \mathcal{F}_t)$ and set $\Pi = [0, \infty) \times \Omega$. We can then view a stochastic process $X = (X_t)$ as a function $X : \Pi \to \overline{R}$ by setting $X(t, \omega) = X_t(\omega)$, for $t \in [0, \infty)$ and $\omega \in \Omega$. To simplify the exposition we introduce a further assumption on the filtration $(\mathcal{F}_t)$:

1.0 Assumption. *The σ-field $\mathcal{F}_0$ is trivial (consists of the null sets and their complements).*

In consequence the random variable X_0 is constant, P-almost surely, for every adapted process X_t. This allows us to rid ourselves of the cumbersome factor $1_{[T_n > 0]}$ in the reduction from local martingales to martingales (I.8.a.2.(b)). Assumption 1.0 is in accordance with our intuition that the value of each process at time zero (the present) is known. We will now introduce several σ-fields on the set $\Pi = [0, \infty) \times \Omega$ and corresponding measurability properties of X.

1.a The progressive and predictable σ-fields on Π. Let $\mathcal{B}_t$, $\mathcal{B}$ and $\overline{\mathcal{B}}$ denote the Borel σ-fields on $[0, t]$, $[0, \infty)$ and $\overline{R}$ respectively, for each $t \geq 0$. The product σ-field $\mathcal{B} \times \mathcal{F}$ is the strongest σ-field that will be considered on Π. The process X will be called *jointly measurable*, if it is measurable with respect to $\mathcal{B} \times \mathcal{F}$.

Recall from I.10.b that the process X is called *progressively measurable*, if the restriction of X to the set $[0, t] \times \Omega$ is $\mathcal{B}_t \times \mathcal{F}_t$-measurable, for each $t \geq 0$. A subset $\Delta \subseteq \Pi$ will be called *progressive* if 1_Δ is a progressively measurable process. This is equivalent with the requirement $\Delta \cap ([0, t] \times \Omega) \in \mathcal{B}_t \times \mathcal{F}_t$, for all $t \geq 0$. It is easily seen that the family $\mathcal{P}_g$ of all progressive subsets of Π forms a σ-field, the *progressive σ-field* on Π.

If $B \subseteq \overline{R}$ and $t \geq 0$, then $\left(X|_{[0,t] \times \Omega}\right)^{-1}(B) = X^{-1}(B) \cap ([0, t] \times \Omega)$. It follows that X is progressively measurable if and only if X is measurable with respect to the progressive σ-field.

Each progressively measurable process X is $(\mathcal{F}_t)$-adapted. This follows from the fact that measurability with respect to a product σ-field implies measurability of all sections. It is easily seen that a progressively measurable process X is jointly measurable. The notion of progressive measurability has already proven useful in I.10.b.0.

1.a.0. *Let X be a progressively measurable process and T an $(\mathcal{F}_t)$-optional time. Then the process X^T is progressively measurable and the random variable X_T is $\mathcal{F}_T$-measurable.*

Remark. Here $X_T = X_\infty$ on the set $[T = \infty]$, where X_∞ is any $\mathcal{F}_\infty$-measurable random variable.

Proof. Fix $t \geq 0$. The maps $(s, \omega) \in \big([0, t] \times \Omega, \ \mathcal{B}_t \times \mathcal{F}_t\big) \to u = T(\omega) \wedge s \in \big([0, t], \mathcal{B}_t\big)$ and $(s, \omega) \in \big([0, t] \times \Omega, \ \mathcal{B}_t \times \mathcal{F}_t\big) \to \omega \in \big(\Omega, \mathcal{F}_t\big)$ are measurable and hence so is

$$(s, \omega) \in \big([0, t] \times \Omega, \ \mathcal{B}_t \times \mathcal{F}_t\big) \to (u, \omega) = (T(\omega) \wedge s, \omega) \in \big([0, t] \times \Omega, \ \mathcal{B}_t \times \mathcal{F}_t\big).$$

Likewise the map $(u, \omega) \in \big([0, t] \times \Omega, \ \mathcal{B}_t \times \mathcal{F}_t\big) \to X(u, \omega) \in (\overline{R}, \overline{\mathcal{B}})$ is measurable by progressive measurability of X and hence so is the composition of the last two maps, that is the map

$$(s, \omega) \in \big([0, t] \times \Omega, \ \mathcal{B}_t \times \mathcal{F}_t\big) \to X(T(\omega) \wedge s, \omega) = X_s^T(\omega) \in (\overline{R}, \overline{\mathcal{B}}).$$

This shows that the process X^T is progressively measurable and hence in particular adapted. To see that the random variable X_T is $\mathcal{F}_T$-measurable let $B \subseteq \overline{R}$ be a Borel set. We must show that $[X_T \in B] \in \mathcal{F}_T$, equivalently $[X_T \in B] \cap [T \leq t] \in \mathcal{F}_t$, for all $0 \leq t \leq \infty$.

   If $t < \infty$ then $[X_T \in B] \cap [T \leq t] = [X_{t \wedge T} \in B] \cap [T \leq t] \in \mathcal{F}_t$, as $[T \leq t] \in \mathcal{F}_t$ and the process X^T is adapted. This implies that $[X_T \in B] \cap [T < \infty] \in \mathcal{F}_\infty$ and since $[X_T \in B] \cap [T = \infty] \in \mathcal{F}_\infty$, by $\mathcal{F}_\infty$-measurability of X_∞, it follows that $[X_T \in B] \cap [T \leq t] \in \mathcal{F}_t$ for $t = \infty$ also. ∎

   A set R of the form $R = \{0\} \times F$, where $F \in \mathcal{F}_0$, or $R = (s, t] \times F$, where $0 \leq s < t < \infty$ and $F \in \mathcal{F}_s$, is called a *predictable rectangle*. Note that the predictable rectangles form a π-system. The *predictable* σ-field is the σ-field $\mathcal{P}$ generated by the predictable rectangles on the set Π. The sets in $\mathcal{P}$ are called *predictable sets*. The process $X : \Pi \to \overline{R}$ is called *predictable*, if it is measurable relative to the predictable σ-field $\mathcal{P}$. The process X is called *simple predictable*, if it is a finite sum of processes of the form

$$Z_0(\omega) 1_{\{0\}}(t), \ Z(\omega) 1_{(a, b]}(t), \tag{0}$$

where $0 \leq a < b$, Z_0 is $\mathcal{F}_0$-measurable and Z is an $\mathcal{F}_a$-measurable random variable. If for example R is a predictable rectangle, then $X = 1_R$ is a simple predictable process.

1.a.1. *(a) A simple predictable process X is predictable.*
(b) A left continuous (adapted) process X is predictable.

Proof. (a) Since sums of measurable functions are measurable it will suffice to consider X as in (0). Let $X = Z(\omega)1_{(a,b]}(t)$ where Z is $\mathcal{F}_a$-measurable. If $B \subseteq \overline{R}$ is a Borel set with $0 \notin B$, then $[X \in B] = \{ (t,\omega) \mid t \in (a,b] \text{ and } Z(\omega) \in B \} = (a,b] \times Z^{-1}(B)$. Here $Z^{-1}(B) \in \mathcal{F}_a$, and so $[X \in B]$ is a predictable rectangle. Thus X is predictable. The case $X = Z_0(\omega)1_{\{0\}}(t)$ is handled similarly.

(b) Using (a) it will suffice to represent X as a pointwise limit of simple predictable processes X^N. For each $N \geq 1$ set $D_N = \{ k/2^N \mid k \geq 0 \}$ and write $r_N(t) = 0$, if $t = 0$, and

$$r_N(t) = \max\{ r \in D_N \mid r < t \}, \quad \text{if } t > 0.$$

Thus $r_N(t) = k/2^N$, for all $t \in \left(k/2^N, (k+1)/2^N\right]$. Since $D_N \subseteq D_{N+1}$, it follows that $r_N(t) \leq r_{N+1}(t)$ and it is now easy to see that $r_N(t) \uparrow t$, as $N \uparrow \infty$. Now set

$$X_t^N(\omega) = 1_{[0,N]}(t)X_{r_N(t)}(\omega), \quad \forall t \in [0,\infty), \ \omega \in \Omega.$$

As $r_N(t) \uparrow t$ the left continuity of X implies that $X^N \to X$ pointwise at each point $(t,\omega) \in \Pi$, as $N \uparrow \infty$. Moreover

$$X_t^N(\omega) = 1_{\{0\}}(t)X_0(\omega) + \sum_{k=0}^{N2^N-1} 1_{(k/2^N,(k+1)/2^N]}(t)X_{k2^{-N}}(\omega).$$

Since X is adapted it follows that X^N is simple predictable. ∎

Remark. The paths $t \mapsto X_t(\omega)$ of the elementary predictable processes in (0) are left continuous step functions. It follows that the same is true of the paths of all simple predictable processes. The left continuity is due to our choice of intervals $(s,t]$, left open and right closed, in our definition of simple predictable process. This choice is crucial also for the definition of the predictable σ-field $\mathcal{P}$. A left continuous process is very benign as the behaviour of each path at time t can be *predicted from its past* via $X_t(\omega) = \lim_{s \to t^-} X_s(\omega)$.

1.a.2. *Every predictable process X is progressively measurable.*

Proof. We use the Extension Theorem (appendix, B.4). The family $\mathcal{X}$ of nonnegative progressively measurable processes $X = X(t,\omega) : \Pi = [0,\infty) \times \Omega \to \overline{R}$ is a λ-cone on $(\Pi, \mathcal{P}_g)$. We wish to show that $\mathcal{X}$ contains every nonnegative predictable process. Since the predictable rectangles R form a π-system generating the predictable σ-field, it will now suffice to show that $\mathcal{X}$ contains the process $X = 1_R$, for each predictable rectangle R.

Let $X = 1_R$, where $R = (a,b] \times F$, with $F \in \mathcal{F}_a$. If $t \leq a$, then $X|_{[0,t] \times \Omega} = 0$ is $\mathcal{B}_t \times \mathcal{F}_t$-measurable. If $t > a$, then $X|_{[0,t] \times \Omega} = 1_{(a,b \wedge t] \times F}$, where $(a,b \wedge t] \times F \in \mathcal{B}_t \times \mathcal{F}_t$ and so $X|_{[0,t] \times \Omega}$ is again $\mathcal{B}_t \times \mathcal{F}_t$-measurable. Thus X is progressively measurable. The case $R = \{0\} \times F$, $F \in \mathcal{F}_0$, is handled similarly. ∎

1.b Stochastic intervals and the optional σ-field. For optional times $S, T : \Omega \rightarrow$ $[0, \infty]$ define the *stochastic interval* $[\![S, T]\!]$ to be the set

$$[\![S, T]\!] = \{\, (t, \omega) \in \Pi \mid S(\omega) \le t \le T(\omega) \,\}.$$

The stochastic intervals $]\!]S, T]\!]$, $[\![S, T[\![$ and $]\!]S, T[\![$ are defined similarly and are easily seen to be $\mathcal{B} \times \mathcal{F}$-measurable. A stochastic interval is a subset of Π and hence does not contain a point of the form (∞, ω), even if $T(\omega) = \infty$. It is not assumed that $S \le T$. If $S(\omega) > T(\omega)$ then the ω-section of any of the above stochastic intervals is empty. Note that

$$1_{[\![S,T]\!]}(t, \omega) = 1_{[S(\omega),T(\omega)]}(t),$$

and similar relations hold for all stochastic intervals. Real numbers $0 \le s < t$ can be interpreted as constant optional times. Then the stochastic interval $[\![s, t]\!]$ is the set $[s, t] \times \Omega \subseteq \Pi$.

Every predictable rectangle R is a stochastic interval. To see this, assume first that R is of the form $R = (s, t] \times F$, with $F \in \mathcal{F}_s$, $0 \le s < t$. Then we can write $R =]\!]S, T]\!]$, where $S = s$ and $T = s1_{F^c} + t1_F$. For the optionality of T see I.7.a.6 Note that the simpler representation $R =]\!]S, T]\!]$, where $S = s1_F$ and $T = t1_F$, does not work since in general neither of these is an optional time. In a similar way a predictable rectangle R of the form $R = \{0\} \times F$, with $F \in \mathcal{F}_0$, can be written as $R = [\![S, T]\!]$ with $T = 0$ and $S = 1_{F^c}$. S is optional since $F \in \mathcal{F}_0$.

The optional σ-field $\mathcal{O}$ on Π is the σ-field generated by the family of all stochastic intervals. The sets in $\mathcal{O}$ are called the *optional sets*. From the above it follows that $\mathcal{P} \subseteq \mathcal{O} \subseteq \mathcal{B} \times \mathcal{F}$.

A process $X : \Pi \rightarrow \overline{R}$ is called *optional* if it is measurable relative to the optional σ-field $\mathcal{O}$ on Π. Thus every predictable process is optional.

A more thorough investigation of the measurability properties of processes [CW] yields the following result (which we do not need):

1.b.0. *(a) Every optional process is progressively measurable.*
(b) Every right continuous process is optional. ∎

Certain stochastic intervals are predictable:

1.b.1. *Let S, T be optional times. Then the stochastic intervals $[\![0, T]\!]$ and $]\!]S, T]\!]$ are predictable sets.*

Proof. The processes $X = 1_{[\![0,T]\!]}$ and $Y = 1_{]\!]S,T]\!]}$ are left continuous and hence predictable. ∎

2. STOCHASTIC INTEGRATION WITH RESPECT TO CONTINUOUS SEMIMARTINGALES

2.a Integration with respect to continuous local martingales. Let M be a continuous *local* martingale. For suitable processes H and $t \geq 0$ we want to define the stochastic integral $I_t = \int_0^t H_s dM_s$. Here the process H will be called the *integrand* and M the *integrator*.

Since the paths $t \mapsto M_t(\omega)$ are no longer of bounded variation, a pathwise definition $I_t(\omega) = \int_0^t H_s(\omega) dM_s(\omega)$ is not possible and we have to use a global definition.

We could define the random variables I_t, $t \geq 0$, one by one but we will instead use a definition that introduces the *process* $(I_t)_{t \geq 0}$ through a universal property. First it is necessary to define the space of suitable integrands.

Doleans measure μ_M and space $L^2(M)$. Recall that $\Pi = [0, \infty) \times \Omega$ and $\mathcal{B}$ is the Borel σ-field on $[0, \infty)$. For each measurable set $\Delta \in \mathcal{B} \times \mathcal{F}$, the nonnegative function $\int_{s=0}^{s=\infty} 1_\Delta(s, \omega) d\langle M \rangle_s(\omega)$ on Ω is measurable (I.10.b.3) and hence we can set

$$\mu_M(\Delta) = E_P \left[\int_0^\infty 1_\Delta(s, \omega) d\langle M \rangle_s(\omega) \right]. \tag{0}$$

Clearly μ_M is a positive measure on $\mathcal{B} \times \mathcal{F}$. The usual extension procedure from indicator functions to simple functions to nonnegative measurable functions shows that, for each jointly measurable process $K \geq 0$, we have

$$\int_\Pi K d\mu_M = E_P \left[\int_0^\infty K(s, \omega) d\langle M \rangle_s(\omega) \right]. \tag{1}$$

Although μ_M is defined on the large σ-field $\mathcal{B} \times \mathcal{F}$, we will work only with its restriction to the progressive σ-field $\mathcal{P}_g$. The reason for this will become apparent during the proof of 2.a.1 below. Let now

$$L^2(M) = L^2(\Pi, \mathcal{P}_g, \mu_M).$$

In view of (1) and since progressive measurability is equivalent with measurability with respect to the progressive σ-field, $L^2(M)$ is the space of all progressively measurable processes H which satisfy

$$\|H\|^2_{L^2(M)} = E_P \left[\int_0^\infty H_s^2 d\langle M \rangle_s \right] < \infty. \tag{2}$$

Let T be an optional time, K a nonnegative progressively measurable process and $t \geq 0$. Letting $t \uparrow \infty$ in the equality $\left(K \bullet \langle M^T \rangle \right)_t = \left((1_{[0,T]} K) \bullet \langle M \rangle \right)_t$ (I.10.b.1.(c)) yields

$$\int_0^\infty K_s d\langle M^T \rangle_s = \int_0^\infty 1_{[0,T]}(s) K_s d\langle M \rangle_s = \int_0^T K_s d\langle M \rangle_s.$$

Thus, for any progressively measurable process H,

$$\|H\|_{L^2(M^T)}^2 = \left\|1_{[0,T]}H\right\|_{L^2(M)}^2 = E_P\left[\int_0^T H_s^2 d\langle M\rangle_s\right].$$

2.a.0. *Let T be an optional time. Then $\mu_{M^T}(\Delta) = \mu_M\big([0,T]\cap\Delta\big)$, for each set $\Delta \in \mathcal{B}\times\mathcal{F}$ and*

$$\|H\|_{L^2(M^T)}^2 = \left\|1_{[0,T]}H\right\|_{L^2(M)}^2 \tag{3}$$

and so $H\in L^2(M^T) \iff 1_{[0,T]}H \in L^2(M)$, for each measurable process H. In particular $L^2(M) \subseteq L^2(M^T)$. ∎

Note that $\mu_M(\Pi) = E_P\left[\int_0^\infty 1 d\langle M\rangle_s\right] = E_P\left[\langle M\rangle_\infty\right]$. It follows that the measure μ_M is finite if and only if $M\in\mathbf{H}^2$ (I.9.c.0). In general μ_M is σ-finite.

To see this note that M is indistinguishable from a process *every* path of which is continuous and we may thus assume that M itself has this property. Then the reducing sequence (T_n) of optional times given in I.8.a.5 satisfies $M^{T_n}\in\mathbf{H}^2$, $n\geq 1$, and $T_n\uparrow\infty$, at each point of Ω. Consequently $[0,T_n]\uparrow\Pi$, as $n\uparrow\infty$. Moreover

$$\mu_M\big([0,T_n]\big) = \mu_{M^{T_n}}(\Pi) < \infty,\quad \text{for each } n\geq 1.$$

Recall that $\mathbf{H}^2$ denotes the Hilbert space of continuous, L^2-bounded martingales N with norm $\|N\|_2 = \|N_\infty\|_{L^2(P)}$ and inner product $\left(I,N\right)_{\mathbf{H}^2} = E_P\left[I_\infty N_\infty\right]$, where $N_\infty = \lim_{t\uparrow\infty} N_t$ denotes the last element of the martingale $N\in\mathbf{H}^2$ and $\langle N\rangle_\infty = \lim_{t\uparrow\infty}\langle N\rangle_t$ is integrable (I.9.a, I.9.c.0).

Recall also from I.9.a.0 that $\mathbf{H}_0^2 = \{N\in\mathbf{H}^2 \mid N_0 = 0\} \subseteq \mathbf{H}^2$ is a closed subspace and hence a Hilbert space itself. On $\mathbf{H}_0^2$ the norm can also be written as (I.9.c.1)

$$\|N\|_2 = E_P\left[\langle N\rangle_\infty\right]^{1/2},\quad N\in\mathbf{H}_0^2.$$

2.a.1. *Let $H\in L^2(M)$. Then $H\in L^1\big(\langle M,N\rangle\big)$ and hence the process $H\bullet\langle M,N\rangle$ is defined and is a continuous, bounded variation process, for all $N\in\mathbf{H}^2$.*

Proof. Let $N\in\mathbf{H}^2$. Then $\langle M,N\rangle$ is a continuous bounded variation process and the increasing process $\langle N\rangle$ is integrable, that is $E_P\left[\langle N\rangle_\infty\right] < \infty$ (I.9.c.0). In particular we have $\langle N\rangle_\infty < \infty$, P-as. Similarly, from $H\in L^2(M)$ it follows that $\int_0^\infty H_s^2 d\langle M\rangle_s < \infty$, P-as. The Kunita-Watanabe inequality now shows that

$$\int_0^\infty |H_s|\,|d\langle M,N\rangle_s| \leq \left(\int_0^\infty H_s^2 d\langle M\rangle_s\right)^{1/2}\left(\int_0^\infty 1^2 d\langle N\rangle_s\right)^{1/2}$$

$$= \langle N\rangle_\infty^{1/2}\left(\int_0^\infty H_s^2 d\langle M\rangle_s\right)^{1/2} < \infty,\quad P\text{-as.} \tag{4}$$

Thus $H\in L^1\big(\langle M,N\rangle\big)$. The rest now follows from I.10.b.1.(a). ∎

The next theorem introduces the integral process $I = H\bullet M$ for $H\in L^2(M)$.

2.a.2 Theorem. *Let M be a continuous local martingale and $H \in L^2(M)$. Then there exists a unique continuous local martingale I vanishing at zero which satisfies*

$$\langle I, N \rangle = H \bullet \langle M, N \rangle, \tag{5}$$

for all continuous local martingales N. The process I is called the integral of H with respect to M and denoted $I = H \bullet M = \int_0^{\cdot} H_s dM_s$. In fact $I \in \mathbf{H}_0^2$ and the map $H \in L^2(M) \mapsto H \bullet M \in \mathbf{H}_0^2$ is a linear isometry.

Remark. Thus the defining property of the process $I = H \bullet M$ has the form

$(H \bullet M)_0 = 0$ and

$\langle H \bullet M, N \rangle = H \bullet \langle M, N \rangle$,   for all continuous local martingales N.

Proof. Uniqueness. Assume that I, L are continuous local martingales satisfying (5) and $I_0 = L_0 = 0$. Then $\langle I - L, N \rangle = \langle I, N \rangle - \langle L, N \rangle = 0$, for all continuous local martingales N. Letting $N = I - L$ we see that $\langle I - L \rangle = 0$. Thus $I - L$ is constant (I.9.b.6) and so $I - L = 0$.

Existence. Let $N \in \mathbf{H}_0^2$ and T be any optional time. Then $H \in L^1(\langle M, N \rangle)$, by 2.a.0, and so the process $H \bullet \langle M, N \rangle$ and the random variable $(H \bullet \langle M, N \rangle)_\infty = \int_0^\infty H_s d\langle M, N \rangle_s$ are defined. Using (4) we have

$$\left| (H \bullet \langle M, N \rangle)_T \right| \le \int_0^\infty |H_s| \, |d\langle M, N \rangle_s| \le \langle N \rangle_\infty^{1/2} \left(\int_0^\infty H_s^2 d\langle M \rangle_s \right)^{1/2}.$$

The Cauchy-Schwartz inequality now yields

$$\left\| (H \bullet \langle M, N \rangle)_T \right\|_{L^1(P)} \le \left(E_P[\langle N \rangle_\infty] \right)^{1/2} \left(E_P \left[\int_0^\infty H_s^2 d\langle M \rangle_s \right] \right)^{1/2}$$
$$= \|N\|_2 \|H\|_{L^2(M)}. \tag{6}$$

Here the equality $\|N\|_2 = \left(E_P[\langle N \rangle_\infty] \right)^{1/2}$ uses that $N \in \mathbf{H}_0^2$ (I.9.c.1). Combining the inequality $|E(f)| \le \|f\|_{L^1}$ with (6) for $T = \infty$ shows that

$$\Phi_H : N \in \mathbf{H}_0^2 \mapsto E_P \left[\int_0^\infty H_s d\langle M, N \rangle_s \right] = E_P \left[(H \bullet \langle M, N \rangle)_\infty \right]$$

defines a continuous linear functional on the Hilbert space $\mathbf{H}_0^2$. Consequently there exists a unique element $I \in \mathbf{H}_0^2$ satisfying

$$\Phi_H(N) = (I, N)_{\mathbf{H}^2} = E_P[I_\infty N_\infty], \quad \forall N \in \mathbf{H}_0^2.$$

It remains to be shown that the process I satisfies (5). Let us first verify (5) for $N \in \mathbf{H}_0^2$. Set $A = H \bullet \langle M, N \rangle$. Then A is known to be an *adapted* continuous bounded variation process vanishing at time zero. The progressive measurability of H ensures the adaptedness of the process A (I.10.b.0). This is why we have to restrict ourselves to progressively measurable processes H in our construction of the stochastic integral. We have to show that $\langle I, N \rangle = A$. By definition of the bracket $\langle I, N \rangle$, it will suffice to show that

$$X = IN - A = IN - H \bullet \langle M, N \rangle$$

is a local martingale. In fact we will show that X is a martingale. According to I.9.c.4 it will suffice to show that $X_T \in L^1(P)$ and $E_P(X_T) = E_P(X_0) = 0$; equivalently

$$E_P[I_T N_T] = E_P[(H \bullet \langle M, N \rangle)_T],$$

for each bounded optional time T. Indeed, according to (6), $(H \bullet \langle M, N \rangle)_T \in L^1(P)$ and the square integrability of the maximal functions I_∞^*, N_∞^* (I.9.a) now implies that $I_T N_T \in L^1(P)$. Thus $X_T \in L^1(P)$. Furthermore N^T is another martingale in $\mathbf{H}_0^2$ and consequently has a last element which clearly satisfies $N_\infty^T = N_T$. Thus

$$\begin{aligned}
E_P[I_T N_T] &= E_P\left[E_P[I_\infty | \mathcal{F}_T] N_T\right] = E_P[I_\infty N_T] = E_P[I_\infty N_\infty^T] \\
&= \Phi_H(N^T) = E_P\left[(H \bullet \langle M, N^T \rangle)_\infty\right] = E_P\left[(H \bullet \langle M, N \rangle^T)_\infty\right] \\
&= E_P\left[(H \bullet \langle M, N \rangle)_\infty^T\right] = E_P\left[(H \bullet \langle M, N \rangle)_T\right],
\end{aligned}$$

where we have used the $\mathcal{F}_T$-measurability of N_T, I.11.b.1.(c) and I.10.b.1.(c) to justify the 2nd, 5th and 6th equalities respectively.

Thus $I \in \mathbf{H}_0^2$ satisfies (5) for all $N \in \mathbf{H}_0^2$. Let now N be any continuous local martingale with $N_0 = 0$. According to I.8.a.5 there exist optional times $T_n \uparrow \infty$ such that $N^{T_n} \in \mathbf{H}_0^2$, for all $n \geq 1$. Then we have

$$\langle I, N \rangle^{T_n} = \langle I, N^{T_n} \rangle = H \bullet \langle M, N^{T_n} \rangle = (H \bullet \langle M, N \rangle)^{T_n},$$

for all $n \geq 1$. Letting $n \uparrow \infty$ we obtain $\langle I, N \rangle = H \bullet \langle M, N \rangle$. Finally, since replacing N with $N - N_0$ does not change the brackets (I.11.b.1.(e)), it follows that (5) holds for all continuous local martingales N and settles the existence of the process I.

To see the isometric property of the map $H \in L^2(M) \mapsto I = H \bullet M \in \mathbf{H}_0^2$, use (7) with $N = I = H \bullet M$ to obtain

$$\|I\|_2^2 = E_P[I_\infty^2] = \Phi_H(I) = E_P[(H \bullet \langle M, I \rangle)_\infty]. \tag{7}$$

The characteristic property (5) combined with the associative law I.10.b.2 shows that $H \bullet \langle M, I \rangle = H^2 \bullet \langle M \rangle$. Thus (7) can be rewritten as

$$\|I\|_2^2 = E_P[(H^2 \bullet \langle M \rangle)_\infty] = E_P\left[\int_0^\infty H_s^2 d\langle M \rangle_s\right] = \|H\|_{L^2(M)}^2,$$

as desired. The linearity of the map $H \mapsto I$ follows from the linearity of the covariation and uniqueness of I with regard to its defining property. ∎

Remark. We now set $\int_0^t H_s dM_s = (H \bullet M)_t$, $t \geq 0$.

This definition does not reveal why the random variable $I_t = (H \bullet M)_t$ should be called a stochastic integral (for this see 2.c.6, 2.c.7) but has the advantage of reducing all properties of the integral process $I = H \bullet M$ to the corresponding properties I.10.b of the integral process $H \bullet A$, where A is a continuous bounded variation process.

As $I = H \bullet M \in \mathbf{H}_0^2$ is an L^2-bounded martingale and so has a last element I_∞, we can set $\int_0^\infty H_s dM_s = \lim_{t \uparrow \infty} \int_0^t H_s dM_s = \lim_{t \uparrow \infty} I_t = I_\infty$.

2.a.3. *Let M, N be continuous local martingales, $H \in L^2(M)$, $K \in L^2(N)$ and T be any optional time. Then $H \bullet M, K \bullet N \in \mathbf{H}_0^2$ and*

(a) $\left\| \int_0^\infty H_s dM_s \right\|_{L^2(P)} = \|H \bullet M\|_2 = \|H\|_{L^2(M)}$.

(b) $H \bullet M$ *is bilinear in H and M.*

(c) $M^T = M_0 + 1_{[0,T]} \bullet M$, *especially* $M = M_0 + 1 \bullet M$.

(d) $H^T \bullet M^T = H \bullet (M^T) = (1_{[0,T]} H) \bullet M = (H \bullet M)^T$.

(e) $\langle H \bullet M, N \rangle_t = \int_0^t H_s d\langle M, N \rangle_s$, $t \geq 0$.

(f) $\langle H \bullet M, K \bullet N \rangle_t = \int_0^t H_s K_s d\langle M, N \rangle_s$, $t \geq 0$.

(g) $\langle H \bullet M \rangle_t = \int_0^t H_s^2 d\langle M \rangle_s$, $t \geq 0$.

(h) $\left\| \int_0^T H_s dM_s \right\|_{L^2(P)} = \left\| 1_{[0,T]} H \right\|_{L^2(M)}$.

Proof. (a) The last element $I_\infty = \int_0^\infty H_s dM_s$ of I satisfies $\|I_\infty\|_{L^2(P)} = \|I\|_2$. Now use the isometric nature of $H \in L^2(M) \mapsto I = H \bullet M \in \mathbf{H}^2$.

(b) Follows from the bilinearity of the covariation the uniqueness of $I = H \bullet M$ with regard to its defining property. (c) Clearly $1_{[0,T]} \in L^2(M)$. Since $M^T - M_0$ is a continuous local martingale which vanishes at zero, we need to show only that $\langle M^T - M_0, N \rangle = 1_{[0,T]} \bullet \langle M, N \rangle$, for all continuous local martingales N. Indeed, for such N,

$$\langle M^T - M_0, N \rangle = \langle M^T, N \rangle = \langle M, N \rangle^T = (\text{I.10.b.1.(e)}) = 1_{[0,T]} \bullet \langle M, N \rangle.$$

(d) To show that $H \bullet (M^T) = (H \bullet M)^T$ set $I = (H \bullet M)^T \in \mathbf{H}_0^2$ and let N be a continuous local martingale. Using I.11.b.1.(d) and the defining property of $H \bullet M$ we have $\langle I, N \rangle = \langle (H \bullet M)^T, N \rangle = \langle H \bullet M, N^T \rangle = H \bullet \langle M, N^T \rangle = H \bullet \langle M^T, N \rangle$. Thus $I = H \bullet M^T$. The proof of $H^T \bullet M^T = (H \bullet M)^T$ is similar and the equality $(1_{[0,T]} H) \bullet M = (H \bullet M)^T$ is reduced to the corresponding equality I.10.b.1.(c) when M is a bounded variation process in much the same way.

(e) This is the defining poperty $\langle H \bullet M, N \rangle = H \bullet \langle M, N \rangle$ of the process $H \bullet M$.

(f) The Kunita-Watanabe inequality implies that $HK \in L^1(\langle M, N \rangle)$. Moreover, according to (e) in differential form, $d\langle H \bullet M, N \rangle_t = H_t d\langle M, N \rangle_t$. Thus, using (e) again

$$\langle H \bullet M, K \bullet N \rangle_t = \int_0^t K_s d\langle H \bullet M, N \rangle_s = \int_0^t H_s K_s d\langle M, N \rangle_s.$$

(g) Let $K = H$ and $N = M$ in (e). (h) Replace H with $1_{[0,T]} H$ in (a). ∎

Remark. The following *associative law* is particularly important as it is the basis for the future stochastic differential formalism.

2.a.4. *Let M be a continuous local martingale, $K \in L^2(M)$ and $H \in L^2(K \bullet M)$. Then $HK \in L^2(M)$ and we have $H \bullet (K \bullet M) = (HK) \bullet M$.*

Proof. We have $\langle K \bullet M \rangle = K^2 \bullet \langle M \rangle$ and so $d\langle K \bullet M \rangle_s(\omega) = K_s^2(\omega)d\langle M \rangle_s(\omega)$, for P-ae. $\omega \in \Omega$ (2.a.2.(g)). Thus

$$\|HK\|_{L^2(M)}^2 = E_P\left[\int_0^\infty H_s^2 K_s^2 d\langle M \rangle_s\right] = E_P\left[\int_0^\infty H_s^2 d\langle K \bullet M \rangle_s\right]$$
$$= \|H\|_{L^2(K \bullet M)}^2 < \infty.$$

Consequently $HK \in L^2(M)$ and so $I = (HK) \bullet M \in \mathbf{H}^2$ is defined. For each continuous local martingale N, we have $\langle I, N \rangle = (HK) \bullet \langle M, N \rangle = $ (I.10.b.2) $= H \bullet (K \bullet \langle M, N \rangle) = H \bullet \langle K \bullet M, N \rangle$, and so $I = H \bullet (K \bullet M)$, as desired. ∎

2.b M-integrable processes. Let M be a continuous local martingale. We now define a larger space of integrands H as follows:

2.b.0. *A process H is called M-integrable if there exists a sequence (T_n) of optional times such that $T_n \uparrow \infty$, P-as., and $H \in L^2(M^{T_n})$, for all $n \geq 1$. Let $L_{loc}^2(M)$ denote the space of all M-integrable processes H.*

Remarks. (a) Obviously $L^2(M) \subseteq L_{loc}^2(M)$ (let $T_n = \infty$).

(b) The sequence of optional times (T_n) in 2.b.0 can always be chosen so as to satisfy $T_n(\omega) \uparrow \infty$, as $n \uparrow \infty$, at *each* point $\omega \in \Omega$.

Indeed, let (T_n) be as in 2.b.0 and $E \subseteq \Omega$ a null set such that $T_n(\omega) \uparrow \infty$ at each point $\omega \in E^c$. Set $\tau_n = T_n 1_{E^c} + n 1_E$, $n \geq 1$. Then $\tau_n \uparrow \infty$ everywhere. Let $n \geq 1$. Then $\tau_n = T_n$, P-as., and since the filtration $(\mathcal{F}_t)$ is augmented it follows that τ_n is again an optional time. Finally M^{τ_n} is indistinguishable from M^{T_n} and so $L^2(M^{\tau_n}) = L^2(M^{T_n})$ (see (0)).

(c) If $H \in L_{loc}^2(M)$ then H is progressively measurable and $H \in L^2(M^{T_n})$, that is $1_{[\![0,T_n]\!]}H \in L^2(M)$, $n \geq 1$, for a sequence (T_n) as in (a). Then $|H| < \infty$, μ_M-as on the set $[\![0,T_n]\!]$. Letting $n \uparrow \infty$ it follows that $|H| < \infty$, μ_M-as. on Π. This latter property ensures that $L_{loc}^2(M)$ is a vector space under the usual pointwise operations.

2.b.1. *For a progressively measurable process H the following are equivalent:*
(a) $H \in L_{loc}^2(M)$.
(b) There exist optional times $T_n \uparrow \infty$ such that $1_{[\![0,T_n]\!]}H \in L^2(M)$, for all $n \geq 1$.
(c) $\int_0^t H_s^2 d\langle M \rangle_s < \infty$, P-as., for each $t \geq 0$.

Proof. (a)$\Rightarrow$(b): Since $H \in L^2(M^T) \iff 1_{[\![0,T]\!]}H \in L^2(M)$ (2.a.0).

(b)$\Rightarrow$(c): Let T_n be a sequence of optional times as in (b). Then

$$E_P\left[\int_0^{T_n} H_s^2 d\langle M \rangle_s\right] < \infty \quad \text{and so} \quad \int_0^{T_n} H_s^2 d\langle M \rangle_s < \infty, \ P\text{-as.}, \quad \forall n \geq 1.$$

Let $t \geq 0$ and $\omega \in \Omega$ be such that this inequality holds simultaneously for all $n \geq 1$. Choose $n \geq 1$ such that $T_n(\omega) \geq t$. Then $\int_0^t H_s^2(\omega)d\langle M \rangle_s(\omega) < \infty$.

(c)⇒(a): As the process $H^2 \bullet \langle M \rangle$ is continuous and vanishes at zero, the optional times

$$T_n = \inf \{\, t \geq 0 \mid \int_0^t H_s^2 d\langle M \rangle_s > n \quad \text{or} \quad |M_t| > n \,\}$$

satisfy $T_n \uparrow \infty$ and

$$\int_0^{T_n} H_s^2 d\langle M \rangle_s \leq n, \quad P\text{-as.}$$

For $n > |M_0|$, M^{T_n} is a continuous local martingale with $|M^{T_n}| \leq n$. It follows that M^{T_n} is a martingale (I.8.a.3) and so $M^{T_n} \in \mathbf{H}^2$ and we have $\int_0^{T_n} H_s^2 d\langle M \rangle_s \leq n$; thus $\|H\|_{L^2(M^{T_n})}^2 = E_P \big[\int_0^{T_n} H_s^2 d\langle M \rangle_s \big] \leq n$ and consequently $H \in L^2(M^{T_n})$, for all $n \geq 1$. This shows $H \in L_{loc}^2(M)$. ∎

2.b.2. *Let $X(n)$ be a sequence of continuous martingales and T_n a sequence of optional times such that (a) $T_n \uparrow \infty$, P-as. and (b) $X(n+1)^{T_n} = X(n)$, $n \geq 1$. Then there exists a unique adapted process X such that $X^{T_n} = X(n)$, for all $n \geq 1$. X is a continuous local martingale.*

Proof. From (a) and (b) we can find a null set $E \subseteq \Omega$ such that $T_n(\omega) \uparrow \infty$ and $X(n+1)_t^{T_n}(\omega) = X(n)_t(\omega)$, for all $t \geq 0$, $n \geq 1$ and $\omega \in \Omega_0 := \Omega \setminus E$. Set $\Pi_0 = [0, \infty) \times \Omega_0$. Then the sets $[\![0, T_n]\!] \cap \Pi_0$ increase to Π_0 and $X(n+1) = X(n)$ at all points of $[\![0, T_n]\!] \cap \Pi_0$, for all $n \geq 1$. We can thus define $X : \Pi \to R$ by setting $X = X(n)$ on $[\![0, T_n]\!] \cap \Pi_0$ and $X = 0$ on $\Pi \setminus \Pi_0$.

Let $t \geq 0$. Then $X_t = X(n)_t$ on the set $[t \leq T_n] \cap \Omega_0 \subseteq \Omega$. Thus $X_t = \lim_{n \uparrow \infty} X(n)_t$ on Ω_0 and consequently P-as. Since each $X(n)_t$ is $\mathcal{F}_t$-measurable and $\mathcal{F}_t$ contains the null sets, it follows that X_t is $\mathcal{F}_t$-measurable. Thus the process X is adapted. The path $t \mapsto X_t(\omega)$ agrees with the path $t \mapsto X(n)_t(\omega)$ and so is continuous on the interval $[0, T_n(\omega)]$, for P-ae. $\omega \in \Omega$. It follows that X is a continuous process. From (b) it follows that $X(n)^{T_n} = X(n)$ and the definition of X now shows that $X_t^{T_n} = X(n)_t^{T_n} = X(n)_t$, on Ω_0 and hence P-as., for each $t \geq 0$. Thus $X^{T_n} = X(n)$ and so X^{T_n} is a martingale, for each $n \geq 1$. Consequently X a local martingale.

This shows the existence of the process X. To see uniqueness assume that X, Y are two processes satisfying $X^{T_n} = X(n) = Y^{T_n}$, for all $n \geq 1$, and let $t \geq 0$. Then $X_{t \wedge T_n} = X(n)_t = Y_{t \wedge T_n}$, P-as., for each $n \geq 1$. Letting $n \uparrow \infty$ we conclude that $X_t = Y_t$, P-as. Thus $X = Y$. ∎

We are now ready to introduce the stochastic integral of a process $H \in L_{loc}^2(M)$:

2.b.3 Theorem. *Let M be a continuous local martingale and $H \in L_{loc}^2(M)$. Then $H \in L_{loc}^1(\langle M, N \rangle)$, for each continuous local martingale N, and there exists a unique continuous local martingale $H \bullet M$ vanishing at zero such that $\langle H \bullet M, N \rangle = H \bullet \langle M, N \rangle$, for all continuous local martingales N.*

Proof. Let N be a continuous local martingale. If $t \geq 0$, then

$$\int_0^t |H_s|\, |d\langle M, N \rangle_s| \leq \langle N \rangle_t^{1/2} \left(\int_0^t H_s^2 d\langle M \rangle_s \right)^{1/2} < \infty, \quad P\text{-as.},$$

by the Kunita-Watanabe inequality and 2.b.1. Thus $H \in L^1_{loc}(\langle M, N \rangle)$. Uniqueness of the process $H \bullet M$ is shown as in the proof of 2.a.2. Let us now show the existence of $H \bullet M$.

Because of $H \in L^2_{loc}(M)$ we can choose a sequence $T_n \uparrow \infty$ of optional times such that $H \in L^2(M^{T_n})$, for all $n \geq 1$. Set $I(n) = H \bullet M^{T_n} \in \mathbf{H}^2_0$, $n \geq 1$. Then $I(n)$ is a continuous martingale with $I(n+1)^{T_n} = I(n)$, for all $n \geq 1$ (2.a.3.(d)).

According to 2.b.3 there exists a continuous local martingale I satisfying $I^{T_n} = I(n) = H \bullet M^{T_n}$, for all $n \geq 1$. Then, for each continuous local martingale N we have $\langle I, N \rangle^{T_n} = \langle I^{T_n}, N \rangle = \langle H \bullet M^{T_n}, N \rangle = H \bullet \langle M^{T_n}, N \rangle = (H \bullet \langle M, N \rangle)^{T_n}$, for all $n \geq 1$. Letting $n \uparrow \infty$, it follows that $\langle I, N \rangle = H \bullet \langle M, N \rangle$. ∎

Remark. We set $\int_0^t H_s dM_s = (H \bullet M)_t$, $H \in L^2_{loc}(M)$, $t \geq 0$, as in the case of integrands $H \in L^2(M)$. The integral process $H \bullet M$ will also be denoted $\int_0^\cdot H_s dM_s$. We should note that 2.b.3 produces an extension of the stochastic integral $H \bullet M$, where $H \in L^2(M)$:

2.b.4. *If $M \in \mathbf{H}^2$, then $L^2(M) \subseteq L^2_{loc}(M)$ and for each $H \in L^2(M)$ the integral process $H \bullet M$ of 2.b.3 coincides with the integral process $H \bullet M$ of 2.a.1.*

Proof. The process $H \bullet M$ of 2.b.3 satisfies the defining property 2.a.eq.(5) in 2.a.1. The inclusion $L^2(M) \subseteq L^2_{loc}(M)$ follows immediately from definition 2.b.0. ∎

2.c Properties of stochastic integrals with respect to continuous local martingales.

2.c.0. *Let M, N be continuous local martingales, $H \in L^2_{loc}(M)$, $K \in L^2_{loc}(N)$ and T any optional time.*
(a) $H \bullet M = \int_0^\cdot H_s dM_s$ is a continuous local martingale with $(H \bullet M)_0 = 0$.
(b) $H \bullet M$ is bilinear in H and M.
(c) $M^T = M_0 + 1_{[\![0,T]\!]} \bullet M$, especially $M = M_0 + 1 \bullet M$.
(d) $H^T \bullet M^T = H \bullet (M^T) = (1_{[\![0,T]\!]} H) \bullet M = (H \bullet M)^T$.
(e) $\langle H \bullet M, N \rangle_t = \int_0^t H_s d\langle M, N \rangle_s$, $t \geq 0$.
(f) $\langle H \bullet M, K \bullet N \rangle_t = \int_0^t H_s K_s d\langle M, N \rangle_s$, $t \geq 0$.
(g) $\langle H \bullet M \rangle_t = \int_0^t H_s^2 d\langle M \rangle_s$, $t \geq 0$.

Proof. Identical to the proof of 2.a.3 since the defining property of the process $H \bullet M$ is the same. ∎

Remark. Let $H \in L^2_{loc}(M)$ and let us rewrite the equality $(1_{[\![0,T]\!]} H \bullet M) = (H \bullet M)^T$ in a less abstract form. Set $Y = H \bullet M$, that is, $Y_t = \int_0^t H_s dM_s$, $t \geq 0$. In analogy to ordinary integration theory we define

$$\int_0^{t \wedge T} H_s dM_s = \int_0^t 1_{[\![0,T]\!]}(s) H_s dM_s, \quad t \geq 0. \tag{0}$$

Then $\int_0^{t \wedge T} H_s dM_s = (1_{[\![0,T]\!]} H \bullet M)_t = Y_t^T = Y_{t \wedge T}$. Thus (0) produces the desirable property

$$Y_t = \int_0^t H_s dM_s \quad \Rightarrow \quad Y_{t \wedge T} = \int_0^{t \wedge T} H_s dM_s.$$

2.c.1 Associativity. *Let M be a continuous local martingale. If $K \in L^2_{loc}(M)$ and $H \in L^2_{loc}(K \bullet M)$, then $HK \in L^2_{loc}(M)$ and we have $H \bullet (K \bullet M) = (HK) \bullet M$.*

Proof. From 2.c.0.(g) $\langle K \bullet M \rangle = K^2 \bullet \langle M \rangle$ and so $d\langle K \bullet M \rangle_s(\omega) = K_s^2(\omega)d\langle M \rangle_s(\omega)$, for P-ae. $\omega \in \Omega$. Using 2.b.1 and $H \in L^2_{loc}(K \bullet M)$ we have

$$\int_0^t H_s^2 K_s^2 d\langle M \rangle_s = \int_0^t H_s^2 d\langle K \bullet M \rangle_s < \infty, \quad P\text{-as.,} \quad \text{for each } t \geq 0.$$

Thus $HK \in L^2_{loc}(M)$ and consequently the process $I = (HK) \bullet M$ is defined and is a continuous local martingale. For each continuous local martingale N we have

$$\langle I, N \rangle = (HK) \bullet \langle M, N \rangle = (I.10.b.2) = H \bullet \big(K \bullet \langle M, N \rangle\big) = H \bullet \langle K \bullet M, N \rangle,$$

and so $I = H \bullet (K \bullet M)$, as desired. ∎

2.c.2 Review of spaces of integrands. Let M be a continuous local martingale. The largest space of processes H for which the integral process $I = H \bullet M$ is defined is the space $L^2_{loc}(M)$. Two processes $H, K \in L^2_{loc}(M)$ are identified if they satisfy $H = K$, μ_M-as. This is not equivalent with the usual identification of processes which are versions of each other or which are indistinguishable and implies that $H \bullet M = K \bullet M$ (note that $\langle (H-K) \bullet M \rangle_t = \int_0^t |H_s - K_s|^2 d\langle M \rangle_s$).

We follow the usual custom of neglecting a careful distinction between equivalence classes and their representatives. If $H \in L^2_{loc}(M)$, then the process I is a continuous local martingale with quadratic variation

$$\langle I \rangle_t = \langle H \bullet M \rangle_t = \int_0^t H_s^2 d\langle M \rangle_s, \ t \geq 0.$$

Thus $\langle I \rangle_\infty = \int_0^\infty H_s^2 d\langle M \rangle_s$. If now $H \in L^2(M)$ then

$$E_P\big(\langle I \rangle_\infty\big) = \|H\|^2_{L^2(M)} < \infty$$

and so $I = H \bullet M \in \mathbf{H}_0^2$ with $\|I\|_2 = E_P(\langle I \rangle_\infty) = \|H\|^2_{L^2(M)}$. Although this has already been established in 2.a.2, it points us to the following weaker condition $E(\langle I \rangle_t) < \infty$, $0 < t < \infty$, which implies that I is a square integrable martingale.

This suggests that we introduce the intermediate space $\Lambda^2(M)$ of all progressively measurable processes H satisfying

$$E_P\big[\int_0^t H_s^2 d\langle M \rangle_s\big] < \infty, \quad \forall t \geq 0, \quad \text{equivalently,}$$
$$\pi_n^2(H) = E_P\big[\int_0^n H_s^2 d\langle M \rangle_s\big] = \big\|1_{[0,n]}H\big\|^2_{L^2(M)} < \infty, \quad \text{for all } n \geq 1.$$

Thus $\Lambda^2(M)$ is the space of all progressively measurable processes H such that $1_{[0,n]}H \in L^2(M)$, for all $n \geq 1$. If $H \in \Lambda^2(M)$, then $1_{[0,n]}H \in L^2(M)$ and so, using I.10.b.1.(c), $(H \bullet M)^n = (1_{[0,n]}H) \bullet M \in \mathbf{H}_0^2$, for all $n \geq 1$. From this it follows that $H \bullet M$ is a square integrable martingale.

Two processes $H, K \in L^2(M)$ are identified if they satisfy $\left\| H - K \right\|_{L^2(M)} = 0$, equivalently $H = K$, μ_M-as. Likewise two processes $H, K \in \Lambda^2(M)$ will be identified if $\pi_n(H - K) = 0$, for all $n \geq 1$, which is again equivalent with $H = K$, μ_M-as.

With this identification $\Lambda^2(M)$ becomes a Fréchet space with increasing semi-norms π_n, $n \geq 1$, and $L^2(M)$ is continuously embedded in $\Lambda^2(M)$ as a subspace. From 2.b.1 it follows that

$$L^2(M) \subseteq \Lambda^2(M) \subseteq L^2_{loc}(M).$$

We collect these observations as follows:

2.c.3. *Let M be a continuous local martingale.*

(a) If $H \in L^2(M)$ then the increasing process $\langle H \bullet M \rangle$ is integrable, $H \bullet M$ is a martingale in $\mathbf{H}_0^2$ and the map $H \in L^2(M) \mapsto H \bullet M \in \mathbf{H}_0^2$ an isometry:

$$\left\| \int_0^\infty H_s dM_s \right\|_{L^2(P)}^2 = \left\| H \bullet M \right\|_2^2 = \left\| H \right\|_{L^2(M)}^2 = E_P \left[\int_0^\infty H_s^2 d\langle M \rangle_s \right].$$

(b) If $H \in \Lambda^2(M)$ then $H \bullet M$ is a square integrable martingale satisfying

$$\left\| \int_0^t H_s dM_s \right\|_{L^2(P)}^2 = \left\| 1_{[0,t]} H \right\|_{L^2(M)}^2 = E_P \left[\int_0^t H_s^2 d\langle M \rangle_s \right], \quad \forall t \geq 0.$$

Proof. (a) has already been verified above (2.a.2, 2.a.3). (b) Replace H with $1_{[0,T]} H$ in (a). $\blacksquare$

2.c.4 Example. If B is a one dimensional Brownian motion, then $\langle B \rangle_s = s$ and consequently the space $L^2(B)$ consists of all progressively measurable processes H satisfying $E_P \left[\int_0^\infty H_s^2 ds \right] < \infty$.

2.c.5. *Let M, N be continuous local martingales, $H \in \Lambda^2(M)$ and $K \in \Lambda^2(N)$. For $0 \leq r < t$ set $(H \bullet M)_r^t = (H \bullet M)_t - (H \bullet M)_r = \int_r^t H_s dM_s$ and define $(K \bullet N)_r^t$ accordingly. Then*

$$E_P \left[(H \bullet M)_r^t (K \bullet N)_r^t \mid \mathcal{F}_r \right] = E_P \left[\int_r^t H_s K_s d\langle M, N \rangle_s \mid \mathcal{F}_r \right], \quad and$$

$$E_P \left[(H \bullet M)_r^t (K \bullet N)_r^t \right] = E_P \left[\int_r^t H_s K_s d\langle M, N \rangle_s \right]. \tag{1}$$

Proof. Fixing $0 \leq r < t$ and replacing H and K with $1_{[0,t]} H$ and $1_{[0,t]} K$ (this does not change the above integrals), we may assume that $H \in L^2(M)$ and $K \in L^2(N)$. Then $X = H \bullet M$, $Y = K \bullet N$ are martingales in $\mathbf{H}^2$ and so $Z_t = X_t Y_t - \langle X, Y \rangle_t$ is a martingale (I.11.b.2.(a)). From 2.c.0.(f), $\langle X, Y \rangle_t = \int_0^t H_s K_s d\langle M, N \rangle_s$. Thus

$$Z_t = X_t Y_t - \langle X, Y \rangle_t = (H \bullet M)_t (K \bullet N)_t - \int_0^t H_s K_s d\langle M, N \rangle_s.$$

As X is a martingale, $E_P \left[(H \bullet M)_r^t \mid \mathcal{F}_r \right] = E_P \left[(H \bullet M)_t - (H \bullet M)_r \mid \mathcal{F}_r \right] = 0$. Since Z is a martingale, $E_P[Z_t - Z_r \mid \mathcal{F}_r] = 0$, that is,

$$E_P \left[(H \bullet M)_t (K \bullet N)_t - (H \bullet M)_r (K \bullet N)_r - \int_r^t H_s K_s d\langle M, N \rangle_s \mid \mathcal{F}_r \right] = 0.$$

Writing $(H \bullet M)_t (K \bullet N)_t = [(H \bullet M)_r + (H \bullet M)_r^t][(K \bullet N)_r + (K \bullet N)_r^t]$, multiplying out and cancelling the term $(H \bullet M)_r (K \bullet N)_r$ this becomes

$$E_P\left[(H \bullet M)_r (K \bullet N)_r^t + (K \bullet N)_r (H \bullet M)_r^t + (H \bullet M)_r^t (K \bullet N)_r^t \mid \mathcal{F}_r\right]$$
$$= E_P\left[\int_r^t H_s K_s d\langle M, N\rangle_s \mid \mathcal{F}_r\right].$$

Distribute the conditional expectation, pull out the $\mathcal{F}_r$-measurable factors $(H \bullet M)_r$, $(K \bullet N)_r$ and use that $E_P\left[(H \bullet M)_r^t \mid \mathcal{F}_r\right] = E_P\left[(K \bullet N)_r^t \mid \mathcal{F}_r\right] = 0$ to obtain

$$E_P\left[(H \bullet M)_r^t (K \bullet N)_r^t \mid \mathcal{F}_r\right] = E_P\left[\int_r^t H_s K_s d\langle M, N\rangle_s \mid \mathcal{F}_r\right].$$

The second equality in (1) follows by integration over Ω. ∎

Our next result shows that the stochastic integral $H \bullet M$ agrees with pathwise intuition, at least for suitably simple integrands H:

2.c.6. *Let M be a continuous local martingale, $S \leq T$ be optional times and Z a real valued $\mathcal{F}_S$-measurable random variable. Then $H = Z1_{]\!]S,T]\!]} \in L^2_{loc}(M)$ and $\int_0^t Z1_{]\!]S,T]\!]}(s)dM_s = Z(M_{t \wedge T} - M_{t \wedge S})$, $t \geq 0$.*

Proof. Let us first show that H is progressively measurable. Fix $t \geq 0$. The restriction of H to $[0, t] \times \Omega$ can be written as $Z1_{]\!]S \wedge t, T \wedge t]\!]} = Z1_{[S < t]}1_{]\!]S \wedge t, T \wedge t]\!]}$. Since the random variable Z is $\mathcal{F}_S$-measurable, the random variable $Z1_{[S<t]}$ is $\mathcal{F}_t$-measurable (I.7.a.3.(c)). Since the optional times $S \wedge t, T \wedge t : \Omega \to [0, t]$ are $\mathcal{F}_t$-measurable, the stochastic interval $]\!]S \wedge t, T \wedge t]\!]$ is $\mathcal{B}_t \times \mathcal{F}_t$-measurable. It follows that the restriction of H to $[0, t] \times \Omega$ is $\mathcal{B}_t \times \mathcal{F}_t$-measurable. Thus the process H is progressively measurable. From

$$\int_0^t H_s^2 d\langle M\rangle_s = Z^2 \int_0^t 1_{]\!]S,T]\!]} d\langle M\rangle_s = Z^2\left(\langle M\rangle_{t \wedge T} - \langle M\rangle_{t \wedge S}\right) < \infty, \quad P\text{-as.},$$

it follows that $H \in L^2_{loc}(M)$ (2.b.1). Our claim can now be written as $H \bullet M = Z(M^T - M^S)$. Set $Y = Z(M^T - M^S)$. Then $Y_0 = 0$. Let us show that Y is a continuous local martingale. Writing $Y_t = Z1_{[S<t]}\left(M_{t \wedge T} - M_{t \wedge S}\right)$ and recalling that $Z1_{[S<t]}$ is $\mathcal{F}_t$-measurable, it follows that Y is adapted. It is obviously continuous. Thus, by stopping we can reduce the claim to the case where both M and Y are uniformly bounded. In this case M is a martingale (I.8.a.4) and we show that Y is a martingale. Using I.9.c.4, it will suffice to show that $E(Y_A) = 0$, for each bounded optional time A. Indeed, for such A,

$$E(Y_A) = E\left[E(Y_A|\mathcal{F}_S)\right] = E\left[E(Z(M_{T \wedge A} - M_{S \wedge A}) \mid \mathcal{F}_S)\right]$$
$$= E\left[ZE(M_{T \wedge A} - M_{S \wedge A} \mid \mathcal{F}_S)\right] = 0,$$

where we use I.7.d.2 for the last equality.

Thus it remains to be shown only that $\langle Z(M^T - M^S), N \rangle = H \bullet \langle M, N \rangle$, for all continuous local martingales N. Indeed, using 2.c.0.(d), $\langle Z(M^T - M^S), N \rangle = Z\langle M^T - M^S, N \rangle = Z(\langle M, N \rangle^T - \langle M, N \rangle^S) = Z1_{]\!]S,T]\!]} \bullet \langle M, N \rangle = H \bullet \langle M, N \rangle$, for all such N. ∎

Remark. Let $L^2_{pred}(M) = L^2(\Pi, \mathcal{P}, \mu_M) \subseteq L^2(M)$ be the space of *predictable* processes $H \in L^2(M)$ and $\mathcal{R} \subseteq L^2_{pred}(M)$ denote the subspace generated by the indicator functions of predictable rectangles.

2.c.6 shows that the stochastic integral agrees with pathwise intuition for all integrands H as in 2.c.6 and so, by linearity, for all $H \in \mathcal{R}$. The following density result shows that the integral process $I = H \bullet M$ is uniquely determined from this and the continuity and linearity of the map $M \in L^2(M) \mapsto H \bullet M \in \mathbf{H}^2$, at least for predictable integrands $H \in L^2(M)$:

2.c.7. $\mathcal{R}$ *is dense in* $L^2_{pred}(M)$.

Proof. We must show that for each predictable process H,

$$H \in L^2(M) \quad \Rightarrow \quad \forall \epsilon > 0 \; \exists S \in \mathcal{R} : \|H - S\|_{L^2(M)} < \epsilon \tag{2}$$

and it will suffice to verify this for nonnegative H. Let $\mathcal{C}$ denote the family of all predictable processes $H \geq 0$ satisfying (2). Then $\mathcal{C}$ contains every nonnegative process $H \in \mathcal{R}$ and so in particular the indicator functions of predictable rectangles. Since the predictable rectangles are a π-system generating the predictable σ-field $\mathcal{P}$, the Extension Theorem (appendix B.4) shows that it will suffice to verify that $\mathcal{C}$ is a λ-cone on $(\Pi, \mathcal{P})$. Let us verify properties (a), (c) in the definition of a λ-cone. To simplify notation write $\| \cdot \|_{L^2(M)} = \| \cdot \|$.

(a) Assume $1 \in L^2(M)$. Then $\mu_M(\Pi) = \|1\|^2 < \infty$. Set $S_n = 1_{[0,n] \times \Omega} \in \mathcal{R}$. Then $\|1 - S_n\|^2 = \|1_{(n,\infty) \times \Omega}\|^2 = \mu_M((n,\infty) \times \Omega) \downarrow 0$, as $n \uparrow \infty$. Thus $1 \in \mathcal{C}$.

(c) Let $H_k \in \mathcal{C}$ and $\alpha_k > 0$, $k \geq 1$, and set $H = \sum_k \alpha_k H_k$ and $J_n = \sum_{k \leq n} \alpha_k H_k$, $n \geq 1$. We must show that $H \in \mathcal{C}$.

Assume that $H \in L^2(M)$ and let $\epsilon > 0$. Then $|H| < \infty$ and so $|H - J_n|^2 \to 0$ μ_M-as., as $n \uparrow \infty$. Moreover this convergence is dominated by the μ_M-integrable function H^2. Thus

$$\|H - J_n\|^2 = \int_\Pi |H - J_n|^2 d\mu_M \to 0$$

and so we can choose $n \geq 1$ such that $\|H - J_n\| < \epsilon/2$. From $H \in L^2(M)$ and $\alpha_k > 0$ it follows that $H_k \in L^2(M)$, $k \geq 1$, and we can thus choose $S_k \in \mathcal{R}$ such that $\|H_k - S_k\| < \epsilon/\alpha_k 2^{k+1}$, for all $k \leq n$. Set $S = \sum_{k \leq n} \alpha_k S_k \in \mathcal{R}$. Then $\|J_n - S\| \leq \sum_{k \leq n} \alpha_k \|H_k - S_k\| < \epsilon/2$ and it follows that $\|H - S\| < \epsilon$. ∎

2.d Integration with respect to continuous semimartingales. The extension of the stochastic integral to integrators which are continuous semimartingales is now a very small step. Let $\mathcal{S}$ denote the family of all (real valued) continuous semimartingales on $(\Omega, \mathcal{F}, (\mathcal{F}_t), P)$ and $X \in \mathcal{S}$ with semimartingale decomposition $X = M + A$, that is, M is a continuous local martingale and A a continuous bounded variation process vanishing at zero. Then we define the space $L(X)$ of X-integrable processes as $L(X) = L^2_{loc}(M) \cap L^1_{loc}(A)$. Thus $L(X)$ is the space of all progressively measurable processes H satisfying

$$\int_0^t H_s^2 d\langle M \rangle_s + \int_0^t |H_s|\, |dA_s| < \infty, \quad P\text{-as.}, \quad \forall\, t \geq 0.$$

For $H \in L(X)$ we set $H \bullet X = H \bullet M + H \bullet A$ and $\int_0^t H_s dX_s = (H \bullet X)_t$. In short

$$\int_0^t H_s dX_s = \int_0^t H_s dM_s + \int_0^t H_s dA_s, \quad t \geq 0.$$

Thus the case of a general integrator $X \in \mathcal{S}$ can often be reduced to the cases $X = M$ a local martingale and $X = A$ a bounded variation process by appeal to the semimartingale decomposition.

Since $H \bullet M$ is a local martingale and $H \bullet A$ a continuous bounded variation process vanishing at zero it follows that $H \bullet X$ is a continuous semimartingale with semimartingale decomposition $H \bullet X = H \bullet M + H \bullet A$. In particular $u_{H \bullet X} = H \bullet A = H \bullet u_X$ and $H \bullet X$ is a local martingale if and only if $H \bullet A = 0$.

2.d.0. *Let $X, Y \in \mathcal{S}$, $H, H' \in L(X)$, $K \in L(Y)$, $S \leq T$ optional times, W an $\mathcal{F}_S$-measurable random variable, $a \geq 0$ and Z an $\mathcal{F}_a$-measurable random variable. Then*

(a) $H \bullet X = \int_0^{\cdot} H_s dX_s$ is a continuous semimartingale with $(H \bullet X)_0 = 0$.

(b) $H \bullet X$ is bilinear in H and X.

(c) $X^T = X_0 + 1_{[\![0,T]\!]} \bullet X$, especially $X = X_0 + 1 \bullet X$.

(d) $H^T \bullet X^T = H \bullet (X^T) = \left(1_{[\![0,T]\!]} H\right) \bullet X = (H \bullet X)^T$.

(e) $\langle H \bullet X, Y \rangle_t = \int_0^t H_s d\langle X, Y \rangle_s$, $t \geq 0$.

(f) $\langle H \bullet X, K \bullet Y \rangle_t = \int_0^t H_s K_s d\langle X, Y \rangle_s$, $t \geq 0$.

(g) $\langle H \bullet X \rangle_t = \int_0^t H_s^2 d\langle X \rangle_s$, $t \geq 0$.

(h) $H(t, \omega) = 1_{\{a\}}(t) Z(\omega) \in L(X)$ and $H \bullet X = 0$.

(i) $H = W 1_{]\!]S,T]\!]} \in L(X)$ and $H \bullet X = W(X^T - X^S)$.

(j) If H and H' are indistinguishable then so are the processes $H \bullet X$ and $H' \bullet X$.

Proof. All except (h),(i),(j) follow by combining I.10.b.1, I.10.b.2 and 2.c.0. Let us show for example (e).

Here the claim is $\langle H \bullet X, Y \rangle = H \bullet \langle X, Y \rangle$. Let $X = M + A$ and $Y = N + B$ be the semimartingale decompositions of X and Y. Then $H \in L^2_{loc}(M) \cap L^1_{loc}(A)$. By 2.b.3 we have $\langle H \bullet M, N \rangle = H \bullet \langle M, N \rangle$. As $H \bullet A$ is a continuous bounded variation process and bounded variation summands can be dropped from covariations (I.11.b.1.(e)), we obtain $\langle H \bullet X, Y \rangle = \langle H \bullet M + H \bullet A, N + B \rangle = \langle H \bullet M, N \rangle = H \bullet \langle M, N \rangle = H \bullet \langle X, Y \rangle$, as desired.

(h) Since Z is $\mathcal{F}_a$-measurable, the process H is progressively measurable. If X is a local martingale the equations $(H \bullet X)_0 = 0$ and $\langle H \bullet X \rangle_t = \int_0^t H_s^2 d\langle X \rangle_s = 0$, P-as., for each $t \geq 0$, show $H \bullet X = 0$.

If X is a continuous, bounded variation process, standard Real Analysis arguments lead to the same conclusion. The general case follows using the semimartingale decomposition.

(i) The case where X is a local martingale has been treated in 2.c.6. If X is a continuous bounded variation process the result is obvious by pathwise integration.

(j) Assume that the path $t \mapsto H_t(\omega)$ is identically zero, for all ω in the complement of a null set $E \subseteq \Omega$. We must show that $H \bullet X$ is indistinguishable from zero. By continuity it will suffice to show that $\int_0^t H_s dX_s = 0$, P-as., for each $t \geq 0$.

If X is a bounded variation process, the result follows from the pathwise definition of the stochastic integral. If X is a local martingale, the result follows from 2.c.3.(b). The general case follows from the semimartingale decomposition of X. ∎

Likewise I.10.b.2 and 2.c.1 yield:

2.d.1 Associativity. *Let $X \in \mathcal{S}$. If $K \in L(X)$ and $H \in L(K \bullet X)$, then $HK \in L(X)$ and we have $H \bullet (K \bullet X) = (HK) \bullet X$.* ∎

Although the definition of the process $H \bullet X$ is global in nature, some pathwise properties can be established:

2.d.2. *Let $X \in \mathcal{S}$ and $H \in L(X)$. Then, for P-ae. $\omega \in \Omega$, the path $t \mapsto (H \bullet X)_t(\omega)$ is constant on any interval $[a, b]$ on which either*
(a) $H_t(\omega) = 0$, for all $t \in [a, b]$ or
(b) $X_t(\omega) = X_a(\omega)$, for all $t \in [a, b]$.

Proof. If X is a bounded variation process, then this follows in a path by path manner from the corresponding result from Real Analysis. If X is a local martingale the result follows from I.9.b.7, since (a) or (b) both imply that $\langle H \bullet X \rangle_a^b(\omega) = \left(H^2 \bullet \langle X \rangle \right)_a^b(\omega) = 0$. ∎

The space Λ_b of locally bounded integrands. The space $L(X)$ of X-integrable processes depends on the semimartingale X. We now introduce a space Λ_b of integrands which is independent of the integrator X.

Call a process H *locally bounded*, if there exists a sequence $T_n \uparrow \infty$ of optional times such that $|H^{T_n}| \leq C_n < \infty$ on all of $\Pi = R_+ \times \Omega$, for all $n \geq 1$, where the C_n are constants. Let Λ_b denote the space of all locally bounded, progressively measurable processes H.

If *every* path $t \mapsto H_t(\omega)$ of the adapted process H is continuous, then H is locally bounded. Indeed $T_n = \inf\{ t \geq 0 \mid |H_t| > n \}$ is a sequence of optional times $T_n \uparrow \infty$ such that $|H^{T_n}| \leq n$, for all $n > |H_0|$. Recall that by convention 1.0, H_0 is a constant.

If H is any continuous adapted process, then H is indistinguishable from a process K for which every path is continuous. Replacing H with K does not affect any stochastic integral $H \bullet X$ (2.d.0.(j)).

2.d.3. $\Lambda_b \subseteq L(X)$, *for each continuous semimartingale X.*

Proof. Let X be a continuous semimartingale with semimartingale decomposition $X = M + A$. Assume that $H \in \Lambda_b$ and let $T_n \uparrow \infty$ be a sequence of optional times such that $|H^{T_n}| \leq C_n < \infty$, for all $n \geq 1$, where the C_n are constants. Fix $t \geq 0$ and $\omega \in \Omega$ such that the path $s \mapsto A_s(\omega)$ is of bounded variation on finite intervals and let $V_t(\omega)$ denote the total variation of this path on the interval $[0,t]$. Then

$$\int_0^{t \wedge T_n(\omega)} |H_s(\omega)| \, |dA_s(\omega)| \leq C_n V_t(\omega) < \infty,$$

for all $n \geq 1$. Choosing n such that $T_n(\omega) > t$, we obtain $\int_0^t |H_s(\omega)| \, |dA_s(\omega)| < \infty$ and this inequality therefore holds for P-ae. $\omega \in \Omega$. Thus $H \in L^1_{loc}(A)$. Likewise

$$\int_0^{t \wedge T_n} H_s^2 d\langle M \rangle_s \leq C_n^2 \langle M \rangle_t < \infty,$$

for each $n \geq 1$. As above, this shows that $\int_0^t H_s^2 d\langle M \rangle_s < \infty$, P-as. on Ω. According to 2.b.0 this implies that $H \in L^2_{loc}(M)$. Thus $H \in L(X)$. ∎

2.d.4. *Let $X, Y \in \mathcal{S}$ and $H, K \in \Lambda_b$. Then, for P-ae. $\omega \in \Omega$, the difference $(H \bullet X)_t(\omega) - (K \bullet Y)_t(\omega)$ is constant on any interval $[a,b]$ satisfying*
(a) $H_t(\omega) = K_t(\omega)$, for all $t \in [a,b]$ and
(b) $X_t(\omega) = Y_t(\omega)$, for all $t \in [a,b]$.
In particular $(H \bullet X)_b(\omega) = (K \bullet Y)_b(\omega)$, for P-ae. $\omega \in \Omega$ such that $H_t(\omega) = K_t(\omega)$ and $X_t(\omega) = Y_t(\omega)$, for all $t \in [0,b]$.

Proof. Use 2.d.2, 2.d.3 and the equation $H \bullet X - K \bullet Y = H \bullet (X - Y) + (H - K) \bullet Y$. The last claim follows if we let $a = 0$ and note that $(H \bullet X)_a - (K \bullet X)_a = 0$. ∎

We also have the following analogue of the Dominated Convergence Theorem for stochastic integrals:

2.d.5 Dominated Convergence Theorem. *Let $X \in \mathcal{S}$ and $H(n)$ a sequence of locally bounded, progressively measurable processes satisfying $H(n) \to 0$ pointwise on $\Pi = R_+ \times \Omega$. If there exists a locally bounded progressively measurable process K such that $|H(n)| \leq K$, for all $n \geq 1$, then $\big(H(n) \bullet X\big)_t \to 0$ in probability, as $n \uparrow \infty$, for all $t \geq 0$.*

Remark. To simplify the wording of the proof it is assumed that $|H(n)| \leq K$ on all of $\Pi = R_+ \times \Omega$, for all $n \geq 1$. The result remains true if this inequality holds only along paths $t \mapsto H(n)_t(\omega)$, $t \mapsto K_t(\omega)$, where ω is in the complement of a null set E. Simply replace $H(n)$ with $H'(n) = 1_{[0,\infty) \times E} H(n)$ (then $H(n)$ is indistinguishable from $H'(n)$) and use 2.d.0.(j).

Proof. Assume first that X is a local martingale, let $H(n)$ and K be as above and choose a sequence $T_m \uparrow \infty$ of optional times such that simultaneously $X^{T_m} \in \mathbf{H}^2$ and $|K^{T_m}| \leq C_m < \infty$, for all $m \geq 1$, where the C_m are constants.

Fix $m \geq 1$. Then $\left|H(n)^{T_m}\right| \leq \left|K^{T_m}\right| \leq C_m < \infty$ and $H(n)^{T_m} \to 0$ pointwise on Π, as $n \uparrow \infty$. The ordinary Dominated Convergence Theorem implies that $H(n)^{T_m} \to 0$, in $L^2\left(\Pi, \mathcal{P}_g, \mu_{X^{T_m}}\right) = L^2\left(X^{T_m}\right)$ and consequently, by the isometric property 2.a.1, $\left(H(n) \bullet X\right)^{T_m} = H(n)^{T_m} \bullet X^{T_m} \to 0$, in $\mathbf{H}^2$, as $n \uparrow \infty$. Now let $t \geq 0$. Then $\left(H(n) \bullet X\right)_t^{T_m} \to 0$ in L^2 and consequently in probability. Thus we have $\left(H(n) \bullet X\right)_t \to 0$ in probability on the set $[T_m \geq t]$. Since here $m \geq 1$ was arbitrary and $\bigcup_m [T_m \geq t] = \Omega$, it follows that $\left(H(n) \bullet X\right)_t \to 0$ in probability on all of Ω (I.1.a.2).

The proof when X is a bounded variation process is quite similar. The convergence $\left(H(n) \bullet X\right)_t^{T_m} \to 0$ in L^2 is now obtained from the ordinary Dominated Convergence Theorem. ∎

2.e The stochastic integral as a limit of certain Riemann type sums. Let $X, Y \in \mathcal{S}$ and H be a continuous adapted process. Recall that $H \in \Lambda_b \subseteq L(X)$, by continuity. Fix $t > 0$, let $\Delta = \{0 = t_0 < t_1 < \ldots < t_n = t\}$ be a partition of the interval $[0, t]$ and set $\|\Delta\| = \max_{1 \leq j \leq n}(t_j - t_{j-1})$ and

$$S_\Delta(H, X) = \sum_{j=1}^{n} H_{t_{j-1}}(X_{t_j} - X_{t_{j-1}}). \tag{0}$$

Thus $S_\Delta(H, X)$ is the Δ-Riemann sum for the integral $\int_0^t H dX$, which evaluates the integrand H always at the left endpoint of each subinterval of the partition Δ. Using 2.d.0.(h),(i) we can write

$$S_\Delta(H, X) = \int_0^t R_\Delta(H)_s dX_s = \left(R_\Delta(H) \bullet X\right)_t,$$

where $R_\Delta(H)$ is the following simple predictable process:

$$R_\Delta(H, X) = 1_{\{0\}} H_0 + \sum_{j=1}^{n} H_{t_{j-1}} 1_{\rrbracket t_{j-1}, t_j \rrbracket}.$$

The first summand is superfluous but facilitates the proof of 2.e.0 below. The next fact shows that the stochastic integral $\int_0^t H_s dX_s$ is the limit in probability of these Riemann sums:

2.e.0. *Let $X \in \mathcal{S}$ and H be a continuous, adapted process. Then $\int_0^t H_s dX_s = \lim_{n \uparrow \infty} S_{\Delta_n}(H, X)$ in probability, for each sequence (Δ_n) of partitions of the interval $[0, t]$ such that $\|\Delta_n\| \to 0$, as $n \uparrow \infty$.*

Proof. Replacing H with a suitable version from which H is indistinguishable, we may assume that all paths of H are continuous.

(a) Assume first $|H| \leq C < \infty$, for some constant C and let Δ_n be as in 2.e.0. Then $R_{\Delta_n}(H) \to H$ pointwise on $\Pi = R_+ \times \Omega$ and $\left|R_{\Delta_n}(H)\right| \leq C$, for each $n \geq 1$. The Dominated Convergence Theorem 2.d.5 now implies that $S_{\Delta_n}(H, X) = \left(R_{\Delta_n}(H) \bullet X\right)_t \to (H \bullet X)_t$ in probability, as $n \uparrow \infty$.

(b) In general there exists a sequence $T_m \uparrow \infty$ of optional times with $\left| H^{T_m} \right| \leq m$, for all $m > |H_0|$ (recall that H_0 is a constant). For such m, according to (a),

$$S_{\Delta_n}\left(H^{T_m}, X\right) \to \left(H^{T_m} \bullet X\right)_t \quad \text{in probability,} \quad \text{as } n \uparrow \infty.$$

On the set $[T_m \geq t]$ we have $S_{\Delta_n}\left(H^{T_m}, X\right) = S_{\Delta_n}(H, X)$ and $\left(H^{T_m} \bullet X\right)_t = (H \bullet X)_t^{T_m} = (H \bullet X)_t$ (2.d.0.(d)). Thus $S_{\Delta_n}(H, X) \to (H \bullet X)_t$ in probability on the set $[T_m \geq t]$. Since $\bigcup_m [T_m \geq t] = \Omega$, it follows that $S_{\Delta_n}(H, X) \to (H \bullet X)_t$ in probability on all of Ω. (I.1.a.2) ∎

2.e.1. *Let $0 \leq a < b$, Z an $\mathcal{F}_a$-measurable, real valued random variable, H an adapted continuous process and $X \in \mathcal{S}$. Then $\int_a^b Z H_s dX_s = Z \int_a^b H_s dX_s$.*

Proof. By shifting time we may assume that $a = 0$. Then the process $t \mapsto Z H_t$ is continuous and adapted. For each partition Δ of $[a, b]$ we have $S_\Delta(ZH, X) = Z S_\Delta(H, X)$. 2.e.1 now follows from 2.e.0 by letting $\|\Delta\| \to 0$. ∎

Let us now derive a result similar to 2.e.0 for integrals with respect to the covariation $\langle X, Y \rangle$. For a partition $\Delta = \{0 = t_0 < \ldots < t_n = t\}$ of the interval $[0, t]$ set

$$SQ_\Delta(H, X, Y) = \sum_{j=1}^n H_{t_{j-1}}(X_{t_j} - X_{t_{j-1}})(Y_{t_j} - Y_{t_{j-1}}).$$

Similarly set $SQ_\Delta(H, X) = Q_\Delta(H, X, X)$, that is

$$SQ_\Delta(H, X) = \sum_{j=1}^n H_{t_{j-1}}(X_{t_j} - X_{t_{j-1}})^2.$$

Multiplying the equality

$$4\left(X_{t_j} - X_{t_{j-1}}\right)\left(Y_{t_j} - Y_{t_{j-1}}\right) = \left((X_{t_j} + Y_{t_j}) - (X_{t_{j-1}} + Y_{t_{j-1}})\right)^2$$
$$- \left((X_{t_j} - Y_{t_j}) - (X_{t_{j-1}} - Y_{t_{j-1}})\right)^2$$

with $H_{t_{j-1}}$ and summing for $j = 1, 2, \ldots, n$ yields

$$SQ_\Delta(H, X, Y) = \frac{1}{4}\left[SQ_\Delta(H, X + Y) - SQ_\Delta(H, X - Y)\right]. \tag{1}$$

2.e.2 Stochastic Product Rule. *Let $X, Y \in \mathcal{S}$. Then*

$$X_t Y_t = X_0 Y_0 + \int_0^t X_s dY_s + \int_0^t Y_s dX_s + \langle X, Y \rangle_t, \quad \text{for all } t \geq 0.$$

Proof. Let $\Delta = \{0 = t_0 < t_1 < \ldots < t_n = t\}$ be any partition of the interval $[0, t]$. Sum the equalities

$$X_{t_j} Y_{t_j} - X_{t_{j-1}} Y_{t_{j-1}} = \left(X_{t_j} - X_{t_{j-1}}\right)\left(Y_{t_j} - Y_{t_{j-1}}\right) + X_{t_{j-1}}\left(Y_{t_j} - Y_{t_{j-1}}\right)$$
$$+ Y_{t_{j-1}}\left(X_{t_j} - X_{t_{j-1}}\right)$$

over $j = 1, 2, \ldots, n$ to obtain $X_t Y_t - X_0 Y_0 = Q_\Delta(X, Y) + S_\Delta(X, Y) + S_\Delta(Y, X)$, with $Q_\Delta(X, Y)$ as in I.10.a. Now let $\|\Delta\| \to 0$ and use 2.e.0 and I.11.b.0. ∎

2.e.3. *Let X and H be as above and $0 < t$. Then $SQ_{\Delta_n}(H, X) \to \int_0^t H_s d\langle X \rangle_s$ in probability, for each sequence of partitions (Δ_n) of the interval $[0, t]$ such that $\|\Delta_n\| \to 0$.*

Proof. As in the proof of 2.e.0 we may assume that *all* paths of H and X are continuous and localization leads to the case where both processes H and X are bounded. The stochastic product rule with $X = Y$ yields

$$X_t^2 - X_0^2 = 2 \int_0^t X_s dX_s + \langle X \rangle_t.$$

Consequently, if $\Delta = \{0 = t_0 < \ldots < t_n = t\}$ is a partition of $[0, t]$ and $1 \leq j \leq n$,

$$X_{t_j}^2 - X_{t_{j-1}}^2 = 2 \int_{t_{j-1}}^{t_j} X_s dX_s + \left(\langle X \rangle_{t_j} - \langle X \rangle_{t_{j-1}} \right) \quad \text{and so}$$

$$\left(X_{t_j} - X_{t_{j-1}} \right)^2 = \left(X_{t_j}^2 - X_{t_{j-1}}^2 \right) - 2X_{t_{j-1}} \left(X_{t_j} - X_{t_{j-1}} \right)$$

$$= 2 \int_{t_{j-1}}^{t_j} X_s dX_s + \left(\langle X \rangle_{t_j} - \langle X \rangle_{t_{j-1}} \right) - 2X_{t_{j-1}} \left(X_{t_j} - X_{t_{j-1}} \right).$$

Multiply this with $H_{t_{j-1}}$, note that $H_{t_{j-1}} \int_{t_{j-1}}^{t_j} X_s dX_s = \int_{t_{j-1}}^{t_j} H_{t_{j-1}} X_s dX_s = \int_0^t 1_{]\!]t_{j-1}, t_j]\!]}(s) H_{t_{j-1}} X_s dX_s$ (2.e.1) and sum over $j = 1, \ldots, n$ to obtain

$$SQ_\Delta(H, X) = 2 \int_0^t R_\Delta(H)_s X_s dX_s + S_\Delta(H, \langle X \rangle) - 2S_\Delta(HX, X).$$

Now let $\|\Delta\| \to 0$. By continuity $R_\Delta(H)X \to HX$, pointwise on $\Pi = R_+ \times \Omega$. The stochastic Dominated Convergence Theorem now implies that $\int_0^t R_\Delta(H)_s X_s dX_s \to \int_0^t H_s X_s dX_s$ in probability. Likewise $S_\Delta(HX, X) \to \int_0^t H_s X_s dX_s$ in probability according to 2.e.0. Finally $S_\Delta(H, \langle X \rangle) \to \int_0^t H_s d\langle X \rangle_s$ in probability, according to 2.e.0 applied to the process $\langle X \rangle$ instead of X. It follows that $SQ_\Delta(H, X) \to \int_0^t H_s d\langle X \rangle_s$ in probability. ∎

2.e.4. *Let X, Y, H be as above and $0 < t$. Then $SQ_{\Delta_n}(H, X, Y) \to \int_0^t H_s d\langle X, Y \rangle_s$ in probability, for each sequence of partitions (Δ_n) of the interval $[0, t]$ such that $\|\Delta_n\| \to 0$.*

Proof. Using (1) and the equality $\langle X, Y \rangle = \frac{1}{4} \left(\langle X + Y \rangle - \langle X - Y \rangle \right)$ and multiplying with 4, our claim can be rewritten as

$$SQ_{\Delta_n}(H, X + Y) - SQ_{\Delta_n}(H, X - Y) \to \int_0^t H_s d\langle X + Y \rangle_s - \int_0^t H_s d\langle X - Y \rangle_s$$

and is thus an immediate consequence of 2.e.3. ∎

2.f Integration with respect to vector valued continuous semimartingales. It is now a very small step to generalize the above integration theory to integrands and integrators which are vector valued processes. Vectors in R^d will be viewed as column vectors and we write $x = (x^1, x^2, \ldots, x^d)'$, $x \in R^d$, where the prime denotes transposition. Let $x \cdot y = \sum_j x^j y^j$ denote the inner product on R^d as usual.

An R^d-valued process $X_t = (X_t^1, X_t^2, \ldots, X_t^d)'$ will be called *continuous*, a *(local) martingale*, a *semimartingale*, if each component process X_t^j, $j = 1, \ldots, d$, has the respective property. Let $\mathcal{S}^d$ denote the family of all R^d-valued, continuous semimartingales on $(\Omega, \mathcal{F}, (\mathcal{F}_t), P)$. For $X \in \mathcal{S}^d$ we define the quadratic variation $\langle X \rangle$ as $\langle X \rangle = \sum_{j=1}^d \langle X^j \rangle$. If X is a local martingale, then $\langle X \rangle$ is the unique continuous bounded variation process A vanishing at zero such that $\|X\|^2 - A$ is a local martingale. In fact $\langle X \rangle$ is an increasing process.

Call the process X *square integrable* if it satisfies $E(\|X_t\|^2) < \infty$, $t \geq 0$, that is, if all the component processes X_t^j are square integrable. If X is a continuous, square integrable martingale, then $\|X\|^2 - \langle X \rangle$ is a martingale, in analogy to the one dimensional case (I.11.b.2). For $X, Y \in \mathcal{S}^d$ define the covariation process $\langle X, Y \rangle$ as

$$\langle X, Y \rangle = \sum_{j=1}^d \langle X^j, Y^j \rangle. \tag{0}$$

If X, Y are local martingales, then $\langle X, Y \rangle$ is the unique continuous bounded variation process A vanishing at zero such that $X \cdot Y - A$ is a local martingale. If X and Y are square integrable martingales, then $X \cdot Y - A$ is a martingale (I.11.b.2).

Let $X^j = M^j + A^j$ be the semimartingale decomposition of X^j ($A^j = u_{X^j}$), for all $j = 1, \ldots, d$. Defining the compensator u_X of X to be the R^d-valued process $u_X = (A^1, A^2, \ldots, A^d)'$, u_X is the unique continuous, R^d-valued, bounded variation process A vanishing at zero such that $X - A$ is a local martingale.

If Z is a continuous scalar semimartingale, then the product ZX is the R^d-valued semimartingale $ZX = (ZX^1, ZX^2, \ldots, ZX^d)'$ and this suggests that we define the covariation $\langle Z, X \rangle$ as the R^d-valued process

$$\langle Z, X \rangle = (\langle Z, X^1 \rangle, \langle Z, X^2 \rangle, \ldots, \langle Z, X^d \rangle)'. \tag{1}$$

If Z, X are local martingales, then $\langle Z, X \rangle$ is again the unique continuous bounded variation process A vanishing at zero such that $ZX - A$ is an (R^d-valued) local martingale. In each of the above cases the uniqueness follows from I.9.b.2.

We now define the space $L(X)$ of X-integrable processes to be the space of all R^d-valued, progressively measurable processes $H = (H^1, H^2, \ldots, H^d)'$ such that $H^j \in L(X^j)$, for all $j = 1, \ldots, d$, that is, $L(X)$ is the direct product $L(X) = L(X^1) \times L(X^2) \times \ldots \times L(X^d)$. Setting $A_j = u_{X^j}$, $L(X)$ consists of all R^d-valued, progressively measurable processes $H = (H^1, H^2, \ldots, H^d)'$ such that

$$\sum_{j=1}^d \left\{ \int_0^t (H_s^j)^2 d\langle X^j \rangle_s + \int_0^t |H_s^j| \, |dA_s^j| \right\} < \infty, \quad P\text{-as.}, \quad \forall t \geq 0.$$

For $H \in L(X)$ we set $H \bullet X = \sum_{j=1}^{d} H^j \bullet X^j$ and write $(H \bullet X)_t = \int_0^t H_s \cdot dX_s$. Then

$$\int_0^t H_s \cdot dX_s = \sum_{j=1}^{d} \int_0^t H_s^j dX_s^j, \quad t \geq 0.$$

Thus we view the stochastic differential dX as a vector $dX = (dX^1, dX^2, \ldots, dX^d)'$ and consequently $H \cdot dX = \sum_{j=1}^{d} H^j dX^j$. Note that the quadratic variation $\langle X \rangle$, the covariation $\langle X, Y \rangle$ and the integral process $H \bullet X$ are *scalar* processes.

If X is a local martingale, then $L(X^j) = L_{loc}^2(X^j)$, $1 \leq j \leq d$, and so $L(X) = L_{loc}^2(X^1) \times \ldots \times L_{loc}^2(X^d)$. This space will then also be denoted $L_{loc}^2(X)$. We now have the perfect analogues of 2.d.0, 2.d.1:

2.f.0. *Let $Z \in \mathcal{S}$, $X, Y \in \mathcal{S}^d$ $H, H' \in L(X)$, $K \in L(Y)$ and T any optional time. Then*

(a) $H \bullet X = \int_0^{\cdot} H_s \cdot dX_s$ is a continuous scalar semimartingale with $(H \bullet X)_0 = 0$.

(b) $H \bullet X$ is bilinear in H and X.

(c) $X^T = X_0 + 1_{[0,T]} \bullet X$, especially $X = X_0 + 1 \bullet X$.

(d) $H \bullet (X^T) = (1_{[0,T]} H) \bullet X = (H \bullet X)^T$.

(e) $\langle Z, H \bullet X \rangle_t = \int_0^t H_s \cdot d\langle Z, X \rangle_s$, $t \geq 0$.

(f) $\langle H \bullet X, K \bullet Y \rangle_t = \sum_{i,j=1}^{d} \int_0^t H_s^i K_s^j d\langle X^i, Y^j \rangle_s$, $t \geq 0$.

(g) If H and H' are indistinguishable then so are the processes $H \bullet X$ and $H' \bullet X$.

Proof. (a)-(d),(g) follow immediately from 2.d.0.(a)-(d),(j).

(e) Here $d\langle Z, X \rangle = (d\langle Z, X^1 \rangle, d\langle Z, X^2 \rangle, \ldots, d\langle Z, X^d \rangle)'$ in accordance with definition (2). Using 2.d.0.(e) and the bilinearity of the covariation we get

$$\langle Z, H \bullet X \rangle_t = \sum_{j=1}^{d} \langle Z, H^j \bullet X^j \rangle_t = \sum_{j=1}^{d} (H^j \bullet \langle Z, X^j \rangle)_t$$
$$= \sum_{j=1}^{d} \int_0^t H_s^j d\langle Z, X^j \rangle_s = \int_0^t H_s \cdot d\langle Z, X \rangle_s.$$

(f) Follows from 2.d.0.(f) and the bilinearity of the covariation. $\blacksquare$

2.f.1 Associativity. *Let $X \in \mathcal{S}^d$. If $K \in L(X)$ and $H \in L(K \bullet X)$, then $HK \in L(X)$ and we have $H \bullet (K \bullet X) = (HK) \bullet X$.*

Proof. Note that here K is an R^d-valued process while H is a scalar process (since $K \bullet X$ is a scalar semimartingale). Thus $HK = (HK^1, HK^2, \ldots, HK^d)$ is an R^d-valued process. The result now follows easily from 2.d.1. $\blacksquare$

2.f.2 The spaces $L^2(M)$ and $\Lambda^2(M)$. The spaces $L^2(M)$ and $\Lambda^2(M)$ of 2.c.2 also have vector valued analogues. For an R^d-valued continuous local martingale $M = (M^1, M^2, \ldots, M^d)'$, we let $L^2(M)$ and $\Lambda^2(M)$ denote the spaces of all progressively measurable R^d-valued processes $H = (H^1, H^2, \ldots, H^d)'$ satisfying $H^j \in L^2(M^j)$ respectively $H^j \in \Lambda^2(M^j)$, for all $j = 1, \ldots, d$. Thus $L^2(M)$ is the direct product $L^2(M) = L^2(M^1) \times L^2(M^2) \times \ldots \times L^2(M^d)$ and so is a Hilbert space with norm

$$\left\| H \right\|_{L^2(M)}^2 = \sum\nolimits_{j=1}^d \left\| H^j \right\|_{L^2(M^j)}^2 = \sum\nolimits_{j=1}^d E_P \int_0^\infty \left(H_s^j \right)^2 d\langle M^j \rangle_s. \qquad (2)$$

Similarly $\Lambda^2(M)$ is the direct product $\Lambda^2(M) = \Lambda^2(M^1) \times \Lambda^2(M^2) \times \ldots \times \Lambda^2(M^d)$ and is thus a Fréchet space. As in the one dimensional case $\Lambda^2(M)$ consists of all R^d-valued processes H such that $1_{[0,t]} H \in L^2(M)$, for all $t \geq 0$, that is, all R^d-valued, progressively measurable processes H such that

$$\left\| 1_{[0,t]} H \right\|_{L^2(M)}^2 = \sum\nolimits_{j=1}^d \left\| 1_{[0,t]} H^j \right\|_{L^2(M^j)}^2, \quad \text{for all } t > 0. \qquad (3)$$

The subspaces of predictable processes H in $L^2(M)$ respectively $\Lambda^2(M)$ are closed. We have the inclusion

$$L^2(M) \subseteq \Lambda^2(M) \subseteq L_{loc}^2(M) = L(M).$$

Recall that $H \bullet M = \sum_{j=1}^d H^j \bullet M^j$, that is, $\int_0^t H_s \cdot dM_s = \sum_{j=1}^d \int_0^t H_s^j dM_s^j$, for all $H \in L_{loc}^2(M)$ and $t \geq 0$. If the components M^j of the local martingale M are orthogonal in the sense $\langle M^i, M^j \rangle = 0$, for all $i \neq j$, then we have the analogue of 2.c.3:

2.f.3. *Let M be an R^d-valued continuous local martingale satisfying $\langle M^i, M^j \rangle = 0$, for all $i \neq j$. Then*
(a) For $H \in \Lambda^2(M)$, $H \bullet M$ is a square integrable martingale satisfying

$$\left\| (H \bullet M)_t \right\|_{L^2(P)} = \left\| \int_0^t H_s \cdot dM_s \right\|_{L^2(P)} = \left\| 1_{[0,t]} H \right\|_{L^2(M)}.$$

(b) If $H \in L^2(M)$ then $H \bullet M \in \mathbf{H}^2$ is an L^2-bounded martingale and the map $H \in L^2(M) \mapsto H \bullet M \in \mathbf{H}^2$ is an isometry. If $\int_0^\infty H_s \cdot dM_s = (H \bullet M)_\infty$ denotes the last element of the martingale $H \bullet M$, then

$$\left\| \int_0^\infty H_s \cdot dM_s \right\|_{L^2(P)} = \left\| H \right\|_{L^2(M)}.$$

Proof. (a) For $t \geq 0$ set $U_j(t) = (H^j \bullet M^j)_t$, $j = 1, \ldots, d$. Then U_j is a square integrable martingale with $\left\| U_j(t) \right\|_{L^2(P)} = \left\| 1_{[0,t]} H^j \right\|_{L^2(M^j)}$ and $H \bullet M = \sum_{j=1}^d U_j$. See 2.c.3.(b). Thus $H \bullet M$ is a sum of square integrable martingales and hence itself such a martingale. Fix $t \geq 0$. Using 2.c.5, for $i \neq j$

$$E_P(U_i(t)U_j(t)) = E_P \left[(H^i \bullet M^i)_t (H^j \bullet M^j)_t \right] = E_P \left[\int_0^t H_s^i H_s^j d\langle M^i, M^j \rangle_s \right] = 0.$$

Consequently the random variables $U_j(t) \in L^2(P)$ are pairwise orthogonal and so

$$\left\|(H \bullet M)_t\right\|^2_{L^2(P)} = \left\|\sum_{j=1}^d U_j(t)\right\|^2_{L^2(P)} = \sum_{j=1}^d \left\|U_j(t)\right\|^2_{L^2(P)}$$
$$= \sum_{j=1}^d \left\|1_{[\![0,t]\!]} H^j\right\|^2_{L^2(M^j)} = \left\|1_{[\![0,t]\!]} H\right\|^2_{L^2(M)}.$$

(b) The last element Z_∞ of a martingale $Z \in \mathbf{H}^2$ satisfies $\|Z_\infty\|_{L^2} = \sup_t \|Z_t\|_{L^2}$. Thus (b) follows from (a) and the equality $\sup_{t\geq 0}\left\|1_{[\![0,t]\!]} H\right\|_{L^2(M)} = \|H\|_{L^2(M)}.$ ∎

2.f.4 Brownian motion.   Assume that W is a d-dimensional Brownian motion. Then W is a martingale and hence $L(W) = L^2_{loc}(W)$. Moreover each component W^j is a one dimensional Brownian motion and so $\langle W^j \rangle_s = s$. It follows that the space $L(W)$ of W-integrable processes consists exactly of all R^d-valued, progressively measurable processes H which satisfy

$$\int_0^t \|H_s\|^2 ds = \sum_{j=1}^d \int_0^t (H_s^j)^2 ds < \infty, \quad P\text{-as.}, \quad \forall\, t \geq 0.$$

Likewise $L^2(W)$ and $\Lambda^2(W)$ are the spaces of all R^d valued, progressively measurable processes H satisfying

$$E_P \int_0^\infty \|H_s\|^2 ds < \infty, \quad \text{respectively}, \quad E_P \int_0^t \|H_s\|^2 ds < \infty, \ \forall t > 0.$$

2.f.5. *Let W be an R^d-valued Brownian motion. For an R^d-valued, progressively measurable process H the following are equivalent:*
(a) $H \in L(W) = L^2_{loc}(W)$.
(b) There exist optional times $T_n \uparrow \infty$ such that $H^{T_n} \in L^2(W^{T_n})$, for all $n \geq 1$.
(c) There exist optional times $T_n \uparrow \infty$ with $E_P\left[\int_0^{T_n} \|H_s\|^2 ds\right] < \infty$, for all $n \geq 1$.
(d) There exist optional times $T_n \uparrow \infty$ such that $1_{[\![0,T_n]\!]} H \in L^2(W)$, for all $n \geq 1$.
(e) $\int_0^t \|H_s\|^2 ds < \infty$, P-as., for each $t > 0$.

Proof. This follows easily from 2.b.0, 2.b.1 if it is observed that $\langle W^j \rangle_s = s$, for all $1 \leq j \leq d$. ∎

3. ITO'S FORMULA

3.a Ito's formula. Let $X = (X^1, \ldots, X^d)$ be an R^d-valued process with continuously differentiable paths and consider the process $Y_t = f(X_t)$, where $f \in C^2(R^d)$. Let us write

$$D_j f = \frac{\partial f}{\partial x_j} \quad \text{and} \quad D_{ij} f = \frac{\partial^2 f}{\partial x_i \partial x_j}.$$

The process Y has continuously differentiable paths with

$$\frac{d}{dt} f(X_t(\omega)) = \sum_{j=1}^{d} D_j f(X_t(\omega)) \frac{d}{dt} X_t^j(\omega).$$

Fixing $\omega \in \Omega$ and integrating yields

$$f(X_t(\omega)) - f(X_0(\omega)) = \sum_{j=1}^{d} \int_0^t D_j f(X_s(\omega)) \frac{d}{ds} X_s^j(\omega) \, ds,$$

where this integral is to be interpreted pathwise. Written as

$$f(X_t) - f(X_0) = \sum_{j=1}^{d} \int_0^t D_j f(X_s) \, dX_s^j \tag{0}$$

this equation remains true if X is a continuous, bounded variation process. The situation becomes more complicated if the process X is a continuous semimartingale and hence no longer has paths which are of bounded variation on finite intervals in general. Then a new term appears on the right hand side of (0) (Ito's formula). We will give a very explicit derivation which shows clearly where the new term comes from.

3.a.0 Ito's formula. *Let $G \subseteq R^d$ be an open set, $X = (X^1, \ldots, X^d)$ a continuous semimartingale with values in G and $f \in C^2(G)$. Then*

$$f(X_t) - f(X_0) = \sum_{j=1}^{d} \int_0^t D_j f(X_s) dX_s^j + \frac{1}{2} \sum_{i,j=1}^{d} \int_0^t D_{ij} f(X_s) d\langle X^i, X^j \rangle_s, \tag{1}$$

P-as., for each $t \geq 0$.

Remark. Writing $f(X)$ to denote the process $f(X_t)$ we can rewrite (1) as

$$f(X) - f(X_0) = \sum_{j=1}^{d} D_j f(X) \bullet X^j + \frac{1}{2} \sum_{i,j=1}^{d} D_{ij} f(X) \bullet \langle X^i, X^j \rangle. \tag{2}$$

Proof. We may assume that the path $t \mapsto X_t(\omega)$ is continuous, for *every* $\omega \in \Omega$. If necessary the process X can be replaced with an indistinguishable version which has this property and this will leave all stochastic integrals unchanged (2.d.5). Note that the integrals exist by continuity of the integrands (2.d.4).

(a)   Assume first that F, K are compact sets such that $F \subseteq K^o \subseteq K \subseteq G$ and the range of X is contained in F. Fix $t \geq 0$ and let (Δ_n) be a sequence of partitions of the interval $[0, t]$ such that $\|\Delta_n\| \to 0$, as $n \uparrow \infty$. For $n \geq 1$ write $\Delta_n = \{0 = t_0^n < t_1^n < \ldots < t_{k-1}^n < t_k^n < \ldots < t_{k_n}^n = t\}$. Set $\epsilon = dist(F, K^c) > 0$ and

$$\Omega_m = \{\, \omega \in \Omega \mid \|X_{t_k^n}(\omega) - X_{t_{k-1}^n}(\omega)\| < \epsilon, \; \forall n \geq m, 1 \leq k \leq k_n \,\}.$$

If $\omega \in \Omega$, then the path $s \in [0, t] \to X_s(\omega)$ is uniformly continuous and so $\omega \in \Omega_m$, for some $m \geq 1$. Thus $\Omega_m \uparrow \Omega$, as $m \uparrow \infty$. It will thus suffice to show that (1) holds P-as. on the set Ω_m, for each $m \geq 1$.

Fix $m \geq 1$. If $\omega \in \Omega_m$, then $X_{t_k^n}(\omega) \in B_\epsilon(X_{t_{k-1}^n}(\omega))$ and hence the line segment from $X_{t_{k-1}^n}(\omega)$ to $X_{t_k^n}(\omega)$ is contained in the ball $B_\epsilon(X_{t_{k-1}^n}(\omega)) \subseteq K$, for all $n \geq m$ and all $1 \leq k \leq k_n$. Let $n \geq m$ and write

$$f(X_t) - f(X_0) = \sum_{k=1}^{k_n} \left[f(X_{t_k^n}) - f(X_{t_{k-1}^n}) \right]. \tag{3}$$

Consider $k \in \{1, \ldots, k_n\}$ and $\omega \in \Omega_m$. A second degree Taylor expansion for $f(x)$ centered at $x = X_{t_{k-1}^n}(\omega)$ yields

$$f(X_{t_k^n}) - f(X_{t_{k-1}^n}) = \sum_{j=1}^d D_j f(X_{t_{k-1}^n})(X_{t_k^n}^j - X_{t_{k-1}^n}^j)$$
$$+ \frac{1}{2} \sum_{i,j=1}^d D_{ij} f(\xi_{nk})(X_{t_k^n}^i - X_{t_{k-1}^n}^i)(X_{t_k^n}^j - X_{t_{k-1}^n}^j),$$

where the point $\xi_{nk} = \xi_{nk}(\omega)$ is on the line segment from $X_{t_k^n}(\omega)$ to $X_{t_{k-1}^n}(\omega)$. Note that this line segment is contained in K and that $D_{ij} f$ is uniformly continuous on K. Entering the above expansion into (3) and commuting the order of summation we can write

$$f(X_t) - f(X_0) = \sum_{j=1}^d A_j^n + \frac{1}{2} \sum_{i,j=1}^d B_{ij}^n,$$

where
$$A_j^n = \sum_{k=1}^{k_n} D_j f(X_{t_{k-1}^n})(X_{t_k^n}^j - X_{t_{k-1}^n}^j)$$

and
$$B_{ij}^n = \sum_{k=1}^{k_n} D_{ij} f(\xi_{nk})(X_{t_k^n}^i - X_{t_{k-1}^n}^i)(X_{t_k^n}^j - X_{t_{k-1}^n}^j),$$

at all points $\omega \in \Omega_m$. According to 2.e.1 we have $A_j^n \to \int_0^t D_j f(X_s) dX_s^j$ in probability, as $n \uparrow \infty$. Since limits in probability are uniquely determined P-as., it will now suffice to show that $B_{ij}^n \to \int_0^t D_{ij} f(X_s) d\langle X^i, X^j \rangle_s$ in probability on the set Ω_m, as $n \uparrow \infty$. To see this we will compare B_{ij}^n to the similar term

$$\tilde{B}_{ij}^n = \sum_{k=1}^{k_n} D_{ij} f(X_{t_{k-1}^n})(X_{t_k^n}^i - X_{t_{k-1}^n}^i)(X_{t_k^n}^j - X_{t_{k-1}^n}^j),$$

which is known to converge to $\int_0^t D_{ij} f(X_s) d\langle X^i, X^j \rangle_s$ in probability (2.e.5).

It will thus suffice to show that $\left|B_{ij}^n - \tilde{B}_{ij}^n\right| \to 0$ in probability on the set Ω_m, as $n \uparrow \infty$. Indeed, using the Cauchy Schwartz inequality,

$$\left|B_{ij}^n - \tilde{B}_{ij}^n\right| = \left|\sum_{k=1}^{k_n} \left(D_{ij}f(\xi_{nk}) - D_{ij}f(X_{t_{k-1}^n})\right)(X_{t_k^n}^i - X_{t_{k-1}^n}^i)(X_{t_k^n}^j - X_{t_{k-1}^n}^j)\right|$$

$$\leq C_{ij}^n \sum_{k=1}^{k_n} \left|X_{t_k^n}^i - X_{t_{k-1}^n}^i\right| \left|X_{t_k^n}^j - X_{t_{k-1}^n}^j\right| \leq C_{ij}^n B_i^n B_j^n,$$

where $\quad (B_i^n)^2 = \sum_{k=1}^{k_n} (X_{t_k^n}^i - X_{t_{k-1}^n}^i)^2, \; (B_j^n)^2 = \sum_{k=1}^{k_n} (X_{t_k^n}^j - X_{t_{k-1}^n}^j)^2$

and $\qquad\qquad C_{ij}^n = \sup_{1 \leq k \leq k_n} \left|D_{ij}f(\xi_{nk}) - D_{ij}f(X_{t_{k-1}^n})\right|.$

From the uniform continuity of $D_{ij}f$ on K it follows that $C_{ij}^n \to 0$, P-as. and hence in probability on the set Ω_m, as $n \uparrow \infty$. Moreover $B_i^n \to \langle X^i \rangle_t^{1/2} < \infty$ and $B_j^n \to \langle X^j \rangle_t^{1/2} < \infty$ in probability, according to I.11.b.0.(b). It follows that $\left|B_{ij}^n - \tilde{B}_{ij}^n\right| \to 0$ in probability on Ω_m, as $n \uparrow \infty$, as desired.

(b) Let us now deal with the general case. Choose a sequence (K_m) of compact sets such that $K_m \subseteq K_{m+1}^o$ and $G = \bigcup_m K_m$ and set $T_m = \inf\{ t > 0 : X_t \notin K_m \}$. By path continuity of X, (T_m) is a sequence of optional times such that $T_m \uparrow \infty$ on all of Π, as $m \uparrow \infty$. Since X_0 is constant we can choose m_0 such that $X_0 \in K_{m_0}^o$ and hence $X_t^{T_m} \in K_m$, for all $m \geq m_0$ and $t \geq 0$. Consider such m. Applying (a) in the form of equation (2) to the process X^{T_m} and observing that $g(X^T) = g(X)^T$, $\langle Y^T, Z^T \rangle = \langle Y, Z \rangle^T$ (I.11.b.1.(c)) and using 2.d.1.(d), we have

$$f(X)^{T_m} - f(X_0) = \sum_{j=1}^d \left(D_j f(X) \bullet X^j\right)^{T_m} + \frac{1}{2} \sum_{i,j=1}^d \left(D_{ij}f(X) \bullet \langle X^i, X^j \rangle\right)^{T_m}.$$

Let $m \uparrow \infty$ to obtain

$$f(X) - f(X_0) = \sum_{j=1}^d D_j f(X) \bullet X^j + \frac{1}{2} \sum_{i,j=1}^d D_{ij}f(X) \bullet \langle X^i, X^j \rangle. \; \blacksquare$$

3.a.1 Ito's formula. *Let $G \subseteq R^d$ be an open set, $T > 0$, $X = (X^1, \ldots, X^d)$ a continuous semimartingale with values in G and $f \in C^{1,2}([0,T] \times G)$. Then*

$$f(t, X_t) - f(0, X_0) = \int_0^t \frac{\partial f}{\partial s}(s, X_s)ds + \sum_{j=1}^d \int_0^t D_j f(s, X_s)dX_s^j$$

$$+ \frac{1}{2} \sum_{i,j=1}^d \int_0^t D_{ij}f(s, X_s)d\langle X^i, X^j \rangle_s,$$

P-as., for each $t \in [0,T]$.

Remark. The notation $f \in C^{1,2}([0,T] \times G)$ is to be interpreted as follows: the partial derivative $\partial f/\partial t$ exists on $(0,T) \times G$ and has a continuous extension to $[0,T] \times G$. Continuous partial derivatives $D_j f$, $D_{ij}f$ with respect to the remaining variables are assumed to exist on $[0,T] \times G$. This ensures that all partial derivatives are uniformly continuous on $[0,T] \times K$, for each compact subset $K \subseteq G$.

Proof. Consider a partition $\Delta_n = \{\, 0 = t_0^n < t_1^n < \ldots < t_{k-1}^n < t_k^n < \ldots < t_{k_n}^n = t \,\}$ of $[0, t]$ and write

$$f(t, X_t) - f(0, X_0) = \sum_{k=1}^{k_n} \left(f(t_k^n, X_{t_k^n}) - f(t_{k-1}^n, X_{t_{k-1}^n}) \right) =$$

$$\sum_{k=1}^{k_n} \left[\left(f(t_k^n, X_{t_k^n}) - f(t_{k-1}^n, X_{t_k^n}) \right) + \left(f(t_{k-1}^n, X_{t_k^n}) - f(t_{k-1}^n, X_{t_{k-1}^n}) \right) \right]$$

and
$$f(t_k^n, X_{t_k^n}) - f(t_{k-1}^n, X_{t_k^n}) = \frac{\partial f}{\partial t}(\eta_{nk}, X_{t_k^n})(t_k^n - t_{k-1}^n),$$

for some $\eta_{nk} = \eta_{nk}(\omega) \in (t_{k-1}^n, t_k^n)$. The summands $f(t_{k-1}^n, X_{t_k^n}) - f(t_{k-1}^n, X_{t_{k-1}^n})$ are dealt with exactly as in the proof of 3.a.0 (second degree Taylor expansion of $g(x) = f(t_{k-1}^n, x)$ around the point $x = X_{t_{k-1}^n}$). ∎

3.b Differential notation. Let us introduce some purely symbolic but nonetheless useful notation. If $X \in \mathcal{S}$ we write $dZ_t = H_t dX_t$ or more briefly $dZ = HdX$ if and only if $H \in L(X)$ and $Z_t = Z_0 + \int_0^t H_s dX_s$, for all $t \geq 0$, equivalently iff $H \in L(X)$ and $Z = Z_0 + H \bullet X$.

The equality $dZ = 0$ is to be interpreted as $dZ = 0dX$, for some $X \in \mathcal{S}$. Clearly then $dZ = 0$ if and only if $Z_t = Z_0$, $t \geq 0$, that is, if Z is a stochastic constant. By the associative law 2.d.2

$$dZ = HdX \text{ and } dX = KdY \quad \Rightarrow \quad dZ = HKdY. \tag{0}$$

According to 2.d.1.(f), $H \in L(X)$, $K \in L(Y)$, $Z = H \bullet X$ and $W = K \bullet Y$ imply that $HK \in L_{loc}^1(\langle X, Y \rangle)$ and $\langle H \bullet X, K \bullet Y \rangle_t = \int_0^t H_s K_s d\langle X, Y \rangle_s$, $t \geq 0$. In differential notation this can be written as

$$dZ = HdX, \text{ and } dW = KdY \quad \Rightarrow \quad d\langle Z, W \rangle = HKd\langle X, Y \rangle. \tag{1}$$

If we define the product $dZdW$ of the stochastic differentials dZ and dW as

$$dZdW = d\langle Z, W \rangle, \tag{2}$$

then (1) assumes the form $dZ = HdX$, $dW = KdY \Rightarrow dZdW = HKdXdY$. In particular $dZ = HdX \Rightarrow d\langle Z \rangle = (dZ)^2 = H^2(dX)^2 = H^2 d\langle X \rangle$. There is no analogue for the differential products $dXdY$ in classical integration theory on the line: If X and Y are locally of bounded variation then $\langle X, Y \rangle = 0$.

The above can be generalized to vector valued integrators X. If $X \in \mathcal{S}^d$, then we write $dZ = H \cdot dX$, iff $H \in L(X)$ and $Z = Z_0 + H \bullet X$, that is, $Z_t = Z_0 + \sum_{j=1}^d \int_0^t H_s^j dX_s^j$, for all $t \geq 0$. Note that then Z is a *scalar* semimartingale. The associative law (0) now assumes the form

$$dY = KdZ \text{ and } dZ = H \cdot dX \Rightarrow dY = (KH) \cdot dX,$$

whenever $X \in \mathcal{S}^d$, $H \in L(X)$, $K \in L(Z) = L(H \bullet X)$ (2.d.2). Here X and H are R^d-valued processes while Z and K are scalar processes. Thus KH is an R^d-valued process also. Likewise 2.d.1 in differential notation yields:

3.b.0. *Let* $Z \in \mathcal{S}$, $X, Y \in \mathcal{S}^d$, $H \in L(X)$, $K \in L(Y)$ *and* T *an optional time. Then*
(a) $d(H \bullet X) = H \cdot dX$.
(b) $dX^T = 1_{[0,T]} \cdot dX$.
(c) $d\langle Z, H \bullet X \rangle = H \cdot d\langle Z, X \rangle$.
(d) $d\langle H \bullet X, K \bullet Y \rangle = \sum_{i,j=1}^{d} H^i K^j d\langle X^i, Y^j \rangle$. ∎

Similarly Ito's formula 3.a.0, 3.a.1 can be written in differential form as follows:

3.b.1. *(a)* $d f(X_t) = \sum_{j=1}^{d} D_j f(X_t) dX_t^j + \frac{1}{2} \sum_{i,j=1}^{d} D_{ij} f(X_t) d\langle X^i, X^j \rangle_t$.
(b) $d f(t, X_t) = \frac{\partial f}{\partial t}(t, X_t) dt + \sum_{j=1}^{d} D_j f(t, X_t) dX_t^j$
$\qquad\qquad + \frac{1}{2} \sum_{i,j=1}^{d} D_{ij} f(t, X_t) d\langle X^i, X^j \rangle_t$. ∎

The assumptions are those of 3.a.0 in (a) and those of 3.a.1 in (b). Let us write down the special case where $X \in \mathcal{S}$ is a scalar semimartingale (d=1):

3.b.2. *(a)* $d f(X_t) = f'(X_t) dX_t + \frac{1}{2} f''(X_t) d\langle X \rangle_t$.
(b) $d f(t, X_t) = (\partial f/\partial t)(t, X_t) dt + (\partial f/\partial x)(t, X_t) dX_t + \frac{1}{2}(\partial^2 f/\partial x^2)(t, X_t) d\langle X \rangle_t$.

Remark. We do not assign any meaning to stochastic differentials HdX as individual objects, only to certain equations between them. These equations correspond in a precise manner to equations between stochastic integrals where the constituent objects are well defined. There is therefore nothing nonrigorous in the use of such equations between stochastic differentials in proofs and computations. The usual algebraic manipulations of these equations are supported by the linearity of the stochastic integral and the associativity property 2.d.2.

3.c Consequences of Ito's formula. As a first consequence of Ito's formula we show that the family $\mathcal{S}$ of continuous semimartingales is not only a real algebra but is in fact closed under the application of twice continuously differentiable functions:

3.c.0. *Let* G *be an open subset of* R^d, $X \in \mathcal{S}^d$ *with values in* G, $f \in C^2(G)$. *For each* $i = 1, \ldots, d$ *let* $X^i = M^i + A^i$ *be the semimartingale decomposition of* X^i, *especially* $A^i = u_{X^i}$. *Then* $Z = f(X)$ *is again a continuous semimartingale and its local martingale part* M_t *and compensator* $u_Z(t)$ *are given by*

$$M = Z_0 + \sum_{i=1}^{d} D_i f(X) \bullet M^i \quad and$$

$$u_Z = \sum_{i=1}^{d} D_i f(X) \bullet u_{X^i} + \frac{1}{2} \sum_{i,j=1}^{d} D_{ij} f(X) \bullet \langle X^i, X^j \rangle.$$

Proof. Writing $f(X)$ to denote the process $f(X_t)$ and using Ito's formula

$$\begin{aligned}
Z = f(X) &= Z_0 + \sum_{i=1}^{d} D_i f(X) \bullet X^i + \frac{1}{2} \sum_{i,j=1}^{d} D_{ij} f(X) \bullet \langle X^i, X^j \rangle \\
&= Z_0 + \sum_{i=1}^{d} D_i f(X) \bullet M^i \\
&\quad + \left\{ \sum_{i=1}^{d} D_i f(X) \bullet A^i + \frac{1}{2} \sum_{i,j=1}^{d} D_{ij} f(X) \bullet \langle X^i, X^j \rangle \right\} \\
&= M + A, \quad \text{where}
\end{aligned}$$

$$M = Z_0 + \sum_{i=1}^{d} D_i f(X) \bullet M^i \quad \text{and}$$

$$A = \sum_{i=1}^{d} D_i f(X) \bullet A^i + \frac{1}{2} \sum_{i,j=1}^{d} D_{ij} f(X) \bullet \langle X^i, X^j \rangle.$$

Here M is a continuous local martingale, since so are the M^i, and A is a continuous bounded variation process vanishing at zero. This shows that Z is a continuous semimartingale with semimartingale decomposition $Z = M + A$, as desired. ∎

Remark. In differential notation the formula for the compensator u_Z can be written as

$$du_Z(t) = \sum_{i=1}^{d} D_i f(X_t) du_{X^i}(t) + \frac{1}{2} \sum_{i,j=1}^{d} D_{ij} f(X_t) d\langle X^i, X^j \rangle_t.$$

Let $\mathcal{S}_+ = \{ X \in \mathcal{S} \mid X_t > 0, \ P\text{-as.}, \ \forall t \geq 0 \}$ denote the family of strictly positive continuous semimartingales on $(\Omega, \mathcal{F}, (\mathcal{F}_t), P)$.

3.c.1. *Let $X, Y \in \mathcal{S}$, $G_1, G_2 \subseteq R$ be open sets such that X and Y take values in G_1 and G_2 respectively, and $f \in C^2(G_1)$, $g \in C^2(G_2)$. Then*

(a) $\langle f(X), g(Y) \rangle_t = \int_0^t f'(X_s) g'(Y_s) d\langle X, Y \rangle_s$.

(b) $\langle X, g(Y) \rangle_t = \int_0^t g'(Y_s) d\langle X, Y \rangle_s$.

(c) If $M \in \mathcal{S}_+$, then $\langle X, \log(M) \rangle_t = \int_0^t M_s^{-1} d\langle X, M \rangle_s$.

(d) If $X \in \mathcal{S}_+$, then $\int_0^t X_s^{-1} dX_s = \log(X_t) - \log(X_0) + \frac{1}{2} \langle \log(X) \rangle_t$.

Proof. (a)   By Ito's formula we can write

$$f(X_t) = f(X_0) + \int_0^t f'(X_s) dX_s + \frac{1}{2} \int_0^t f''(X_s) d\langle X \rangle_s = (f'(X) \bullet X)_t + A_t,$$

where A is a continuous bounded variation process. A similar representation of $g(Y_t)$, recalling that bounded variation summands can be dropped from a covariation (I.11.b.1) and 2.d.1.(f), yields

$$\langle f(X), g(Y) \rangle_t = \langle f'(X) \bullet X, g'(Y) \bullet Y \rangle_t = \int_0^t f'(X_s) g'(Y_s) d\langle X, Y \rangle_s.$$

(b) now follows with $f(x) = x$. (c) follows from (b) with $Y = M$ and $g(y) = \log(y)$.
(d)   Since both sides of the equality in (d) are continuous semimartingales vanishing at zero, it will suffice to show that

$$X_t^{-1} dX_t = d\log(X_t) + \tfrac{1}{2} d\langle \log(X) \rangle_t. \tag{0}$$

Indeed, by the Ito formula

$$d\log(X_t) = X_t^{-1} dX_t - \tfrac{1}{2} X_t^{-2} d\langle X \rangle_t. \tag{1}$$

Using (a) with $X = Y$ and $f(x) = g(x) = \log(x)$ yields $d\langle \log(X) \rangle_t = X_t^{-2} d\langle X \rangle_t$. Thus (1) can be rewritten as (0). ∎

Let us rewrite the formulas 3.c.1 in differential form:

3.c.2. *With X, Y, f, g as in 3.c.1 we have*
(a) $d\langle f(X), g(Y)\rangle_t = f'(X_t)g'(Y_t)d\langle X, Y\rangle_t.$
(b) $d\langle X, g(Y)\rangle_t = g'(Y_t)d\langle X, Y\rangle_t.$
(c) *If $M \in \mathcal{S}_+$, then $d\langle X, log(M)\rangle_t = M_t^{-1}d\langle X, M\rangle_t.$* ∎

The next result shows that $\mathcal{S}$ is closed under multiplication and division and computes the compensator of a product of semimartingales. This is of course a special case of 3.c.0, but we include a separate proof.

3.c.3. *Let $X, Y \in \mathcal{S}$, $G \subseteq R$ open, $f \in C^2(G)$ and assume that X assumes values in G. Then*
(a) *$XY \in \mathcal{S}$ and $u_{XY}(t) = \int_0^t \left(X_s du_Y(s) + Y_s du_X(s)\right) + \langle X, Y\rangle_t.$*
(b) *$f(X) \in \mathcal{S}$ and $u_{f(X)}(t) = \int_0^t f'(X_s)du_X(s) + \frac{1}{2}\int_0^t f''(X_s)d\langle X\rangle_s.$*
(c) *If $X \in \mathcal{S}_+$, then $1/X \in \mathcal{S}$ and $u_{1/X}(t) = -\int_0^t X_s^{-2}du_X(s) + \frac{1}{2}\int_0^t X_s^{-3}d\langle X\rangle_s.$*

Remark. Equivalently $du_{XY}(t) = X_t du_Y(t) + Y_t du_X(t) + d\langle X, Y\rangle_t$, $du_{f(X)}(t) = f'(X_t)du_X(t) + f''(X_t)d\langle X\rangle_t$ and $du_{1/X}(t) = -X_t^{-2}du_X(t) + \frac{1}{2}X_t^{-3}d\langle X\rangle_t.$

Proof. Let $X = M + A$, $Y = N + B$ be the semimartingale decompositions of X and Y ($A = u_X$, $B = u_Y$). (a) The stochastic product rule yields

$$X_t Y_t = X_0 Y_0 + \int_0^t X_s dY_s + \int_0^t Y_s dX_s + \langle X, Y\rangle_t$$
$$= X_0 Y_0 + \int_0^t X_s dN_s + \int_0^t Y_s dM_s + \left\{\int_0^t X_s dB_s + \int_0^t Y_s dA_s + \langle X, Y\rangle_t\right\}$$
$$= K + C,$$

where $K_s = X_0 Y_0 + \int_0^t X_s dN_s + \int_0^t Y_s dM_s$ is a continuous local martingale and $C_t = \int_0^t X_s dB_s + \int_0^t Y_s dA_s + \langle X, Y\rangle_t$ is a continuous bounded variation process vanishing at zero. This shows that XY is a semimartingale with semimartingale decomposition $XY = K + C$, especially

$$u_{XY}(t) = C_t = \int_0^t X_s dB_s + \int_0^t Y_s dA_s + \langle X, Y\rangle_t, \quad \text{as desired.}$$

(b) The Ito formula yields

$$f(X_t) = f(X_0) + \int_0^t f'(X_s)dX_s + \frac{1}{2}\int_0^t f''(X_s)d\langle X\rangle_s$$
$$= f(X_0) + \int_0^t f'(X_s)dM_s + \left\{\int_0^t f'(X_s)dA_s + \frac{1}{2}\int_0^t f''(X_s)d\langle X\rangle_s\right\}$$
$$= L + D,$$

where $L_t = f(X_0) + \int_0^t f'(X_s)dM_s$ is a local martingale and the continuous bounded variation process $D_t = \int_0^t f'(X_s)dA_s + \frac{1}{2}\int_0^t f''(X_s)d\langle X\rangle_s$ vanishes at zero. This shows that $f(X)$ is a continuous semimartingale with semimartingale decomposition $f(X) = L + D$ and so $u_{f(X)}(t) = D_t$. (c) Use (b) with $f(x) = 1/x$. ∎

3.c.4. *Let $X, Y \in \mathcal{S}$ and assume that $H \in L(X) \cap L(Y)$. Then*
(a) $H \in L(XY)$ and
(b) *If $Y \in \mathcal{S}_+$, then $H \in L(X/Y)$.*

Proof. (a)   Since H is progressively measurable, it will suffice to show that

$$\int_0^T H_s^2 d\langle XY \rangle_s < \infty \quad \text{and} \quad \int_0^T |H_s|\, |du_{XY}(s)| < \infty, \quad P\text{-as.,} \qquad (2)$$

for each $T \geq 0$. The stochastic product rule $d(XY) = XdY + YdX + d\langle X, Y \rangle$ implies that the quadratic variation $\langle XY \rangle$ of the product XY satisfies

$$d\langle XY \rangle = \left[d(XY) \right]^2 = X^2 d\langle Y \rangle + Y^2 d\langle X \rangle + 2XY d\langle X, Y \rangle.$$

The first integral in (2) will thus be finite, if the integrals

$$\int_0^T H_s^2 X_s^2 d\langle Y \rangle_s, \quad \int_0^T H_s^2 Y_s^2 d\langle X \rangle_s, \quad \text{and} \quad \int_0^T H_s^2 X_s Y_s d\langle X, Y \rangle_s \qquad (3)$$

are all finite, P-as. on Ω. Since $H \in L(Y)$ we have $\int_0^T H_s^2 d\langle Y \rangle_s < \infty$, P-as., and the finiteness of the first integral in (3) now follows from the fact that the path $t \mapsto X_t^2(\omega)$ is continuous and hence bounded on the interval $[0, T]$, P-as. The finiteness of the second integral in (3) follows similarly. Using the Kunita-Watanabe inequality on the third integral yields

$$\left| \int_0^T (H_s X_s)(H_s Y_s) d\langle X, Y \rangle_s \right|^2 \leq \int_0^T H_s^2 X_s^2 d\langle Y \rangle_s \int_0^T H_s^2 Y_s^2 d\langle X \rangle_s < \infty,$$

P-almost surely, by the finiteness of the first two integrals in (3). Let us now turn to the second integral in (2). Recall from 3.c.3.(a) that $du_{XY}(t) = X du_Y(t) + Y du_X(t) + d\langle X, Y \rangle_t$. Consequently the associated total variation measures satisfy

$$|du_{XY}| \leq |X|\, |du_Y| + |Y|\, |du_X| + |d\langle X, Y \rangle|.$$

It will thus suffice to show that the integrals

$$\int_0^T |H_s X_s|\, |du_Y(s)|, \quad \int_0^T |H_s Y_s|\, |du_X(s)| \quad \text{and} \quad \int_0^T |H_s|\, |d\langle X, Y \rangle_s|$$

are all finite, P-as. The finiteness of the first integral follows from $H \in L^1_{loc}(u_Y)$ and the path continuity of X. The finiteness of the second integral is established similarly and, using the Kunita-Watanabe inequality on the third integral yields

$$\left(\int_0^T |H_s| \cdot 1\, |d\langle X, Y \rangle_s| \right)^2 \leq \int_0^T H_s^2 d\langle X \rangle_s \int_0^T 1\, d\langle Y \rangle_s$$

$$= \langle Y \rangle_T \int_0^T H_s^2 d\langle X \rangle_s < \infty, \quad P\text{-as.,}$$

since $H \in L(X)$.

(b)   In view of (a) it will suffice to show that $Y \in \mathcal{S}_+$ and $H \in L(Y)$ imply that $H \in L(1/Y)$. Assume that $Y \in \mathcal{S}_+$ and $H \in L(Y)$. We must show that the integrals

$$\int_0^T H_s^2 d\langle 1/Y\rangle_s \quad \text{and} \quad \int_0^T |H_s|\,|du_{1/Y}(s)| \tag{4}$$

are both finite P-as. We have $d\langle f(Y)\rangle_t = f'(Y_t)^2 d\langle Y\rangle_t$, for each function $f \in C^2(R_+)$ (3.c.1.(a)). Especially for $f(y) = 1/y$ it follows that $d\langle 1/Y\rangle_t = Y_t^{-4} d\langle Y\rangle_t$. Consequently

$$\int_0^T H_s^2 d\langle 1/Y\rangle_s = \int_0^T H_s^2 Y_s^{-4} d\langle Y\rangle_s.$$

The finiteness of this integral now follows from $H \in L(Y)$ and the fact that the continuous, positive path $t \mapsto Y_t(\omega)$ is bounded away from zero on the interval $[0, T]$. To deal with the second integral we must first find the compensator $u_{1/Y}$. 3.c.3.(b) with $f(y) = 1/y$ yields $du_{1/Y}(t) = -Y_t^{-2} du_Y(t) + Y_t^{-3} d\langle Y\rangle_t$. Thus the associated total variation measures satisfy

$$|du_{1/Y}(t)| \leq Y_t^{-2}|du_Y(t)| + Y_t^{-3} d\langle Y\rangle_t.$$

The finiteness of the second integral in (4) will thus follow if we can show that the integrals

$$\int_0^T |H_s|Y_t^{-2}|du_Y(t)| \quad \text{and} \quad \int_0^T |H_s|Y_t^{-3} d\langle Y\rangle_t$$

are both finite, P-as. which is an immediate consequence of $H \in L(Y)$ and the fact that the continuous, positive path $t \mapsto Y_t(\omega)$ is bounded away from zero on the interval $[0, T]$. This shows (b). ∎

3.d Stock prices. Let S_t denote the price of a stock at time $t \geq 0$. In simple models one views S as a continuous semimartingale satisfying the dynamics

$$dS_t = \mu S_t dt + \sigma S_t dB_t, \tag{0}$$

where B is a (one dimensional) Brownian motion and μ and σ are constants. According to our conventions regarding stochastic differentials, equation (0) is to be interpreted as $S_t = S_0 + \mu \int_0^t S_s ds + \sigma \int_0^t S_s dB_s$. Rewriting (0) purely formally as

$$\frac{dS_t}{S_t} = \mu dt + \sigma dB_t$$

suggests the following interpretation: μ is the instantaneous mean of the rate of return and σ^2 the instantaneous variance of the rate of return of the stock S. Being optimistic we seek a solution S_t of (0) which has the form $S_t = f(t, B_t)$, for some function $f = f(t, x) \in C^2(R^2)$. Here we want $f(0, B_0) = S_0$, that is $f(0, 0) = S_0$. With this, (0) can be rewritten as

$$d\,f(t, B_t) = \mu f(t, B_t)dt + \sigma f(t, B_t)dB_t. \tag{1}$$

By contrast, Ito's formula 3.b.2.(b) yields

$$d\,f(t, B_t) = \frac{\partial f}{\partial t}(t, B_t)dt + \frac{\partial f}{\partial x}(t, B_t)dB_t + \frac{1}{2}\frac{\partial^2 f}{\partial x^2}(t, B_t)d\langle B\rangle_t.$$

Since $\langle B\rangle_t = t$, this amounts to

$$d\,f(t, B_t) = \left[\frac{\partial f}{\partial t}(t, B_t) + \frac{1}{2}\frac{\partial^2 f}{\partial x^2}(t, B_t)\right]dt + \frac{\partial f}{\partial x}(t, B_t)dB_t.$$

A comparison with (2) shows that we want our function f to satisfy

$$(A) \quad \frac{\partial f}{\partial x} = \sigma f \quad \text{and} \quad (B) \quad \frac{\partial f}{\partial t} + \frac{1}{2}\frac{\partial^2 f}{\partial x^2} = \mu f.$$

From (A) it follows that $f(t, x) = C(t)e^{\sigma x}$ and this entered into (B) yields

$$C'(t)e^{\sigma x} + \frac{1}{2}\sigma^2 C(t)e^{\sigma x} = \mu C(t)e^{\sigma x}, \quad \text{that is,} \quad C'(t) = (\mu - \sigma^2/2)C(t)$$

with solution $C(t) = Ce^{(\mu-\sigma^2/2)t}$. Thus $f(t, x) = C(t)e^{\sigma x} = Ce^{(\mu-\sigma^2/2)t+\sigma x}$. From $f(0, 0) = S_0$ we obtain $C = S_0$. Altogether

$$\begin{aligned} f(t, x) &= S_0\, exp\{(\mu - \tfrac{\sigma^2}{2})t + \sigma x\} \quad \text{and so} \\ S_t &= f(t, B_t) = S_0\, exp\{(\mu - \tfrac{\sigma^2}{2})t + \sigma B_t\}. \end{aligned} \tag{2}$$

This approach does produce a solution of (0) but does not investigate the uniqueness of this solution. Better and more general results will be derived below (4.b.1, 4.b.2).

3.e Levi's characterization of Brownian motion.

3.e.0. *Let $B_t = (B_t^1, B_t^2 \ldots, B_t^d)$ be a Brownian motion on $(\Omega, \mathcal{F}, (\mathcal{F}_t), P)$. Then (a) $B_t^i B_t^j$ is a martingale, for all $i \neq j$. (b) $\langle B^i, B^j\rangle = 0$, for all $i \neq j$.*

Proof. Each coordinate process B_t^j is a one dimensional Brownian motion and hence a continuous, square integrable martingale (II.2.g.0). Especially $B_t^j \in L^2(P)$ and hence $B_t^i B_t^j \in L^1(P)$ for all i, j and $t \geq 0$. The covariation $\langle B^i, B^j\rangle$ is the unique continuous, bounded variation process A such that $A_0 = 0$ and $B^i B^j - A$ is a local martingale. Thus (b) follows from (a).

Let us now show (a). Assume that $i \neq j$. In order to see that $B_t^i B_t^j$ is a martingale we must show that $E_P\left[B_t^i B_t^j - B_s^i B_s^j | \mathcal{F}_s\right] = 0$. Write

$$B_t^i B_t^j - B_s^i B_s^j = (B_t^i - B_s^i)(B_t^j - B_s^j) + B_s^i(B_t^j - B_s^j) + B_s^j(B_t^i - B_s^i). \tag{0}$$

The first summand is a function of the increment $B_t - B_s$ and hence independent of the σ-field $\mathcal{F}_s$. Since the two factors are themselves independent we obtain

$$\begin{aligned} E_P\left[(B_t^i - B_s^i)(B_t^j - B_s^j)|\mathcal{F}_s\right] &= E_P\left[(B_t^i - B_s^i)(B_t^j - B_s^j)\right] \\ &= E_P\left[B_t^i - B_s^i\right]E_P\left[B_t^j - B_s^j\right] = 0. \end{aligned}$$

Moreover the $\mathcal{F}_s$-measurability of B_s^i, B_s^j implies that

$$E_P\left[B_s^i(B_t^j - B_s^j)|\mathcal{F}_s\right] = B_s^i E_P\left[B_t^j - B_s^j|\mathcal{F}_s\right] = 0 \quad \text{and}$$
$$E_P\left[B_s^j(B_t^i - B_s^i)|\mathcal{F}_s\right] = B_s^j E_P\left[B_t^i - B_s^i|\mathcal{F}_s\right] = 0.$$

Conditioning on the σ-field $\mathcal{F}_s$ in (0) now yields $E_P\left[B_t^i B_t^j - B_s^i B_s^j|\mathcal{F}_s\right] = 0.$ ∎

3.e.1 Levi's Theorem. *Let $B = (B^1, B^2, \ldots, B^d)$ be a continuous, R^d-valued local martingale. Then B is a Brownian motion on $(\Omega, \mathcal{F}, (\mathcal{F}_t), P)$ if and only if it satisfies*

$$\langle B^i \rangle_t = t \quad and \quad \langle B^i, B^j \rangle_t = 0, \qquad (1)$$

for all $t \geq 0$ and $i, j \in \{1, \ldots, d\}$ with $i \neq j$.

Proof. We have seen in 3.e.0 and II.2.g.0 that every Brownian motion B satisfies (1). Assume now conversely that the continuous local martingale B satisfies (1). We have to show that B is a Brownian motion. Since B is continuous by assumption, we have to show only that the increment $B_t - B_s$ is multivariate normal with mean zero and covariance matrix $C = (t - s)I$ and that $B_t - B_s$ is independent of the σ-field $\mathcal{F}_s$, for all s, t with $0 \leq s < t$. Fix $\alpha \in R^d$ and define the function $\phi_\alpha \in C^2(R^{d+1})$ as follows:

$$\phi_\alpha(t, x) = exp(i\alpha \cdot x + \tfrac{1}{2}\|\alpha\|^2 t), \quad x \in R^d, t \in R, \ (i^2 = -1).$$

Note that $\partial\phi_\alpha/\partial x_j = i\alpha_j\phi_\alpha$ and so $\partial^2\phi_\alpha/\partial x_j^2 = -\alpha_j^2\phi_\alpha$, for all $1 \leq j \leq d$. Since $\partial\phi_\alpha/\partial t = \tfrac{1}{2}\|\alpha\|^2\phi_\alpha$ it follows that

$$\frac{\partial\phi_\alpha}{\partial t} + \frac{1}{2}\sum_{j=1}^{d}\frac{\partial^2\phi_\alpha}{\partial x_j^2} = 0. \qquad (2)$$

Set $X_t = \phi_\alpha(t, B_t)$. Using Ito's formula and (1) and observing the cancellation induced by (2) yields

$$dX_t = \sum_{j=1}^{d}\frac{\partial\phi_\alpha}{\partial x_j}(t, B_t)dB_t^j \quad and \ so \quad X = X_0 + \sum_{j=1}^{d}\frac{\partial\phi_\alpha}{\partial x_j}(t, B_t)\bullet B^j$$

is a local martingale. Let $a > 0$. Then $|\phi_\alpha(t, x)| \leq exp(\tfrac{1}{2}\|\alpha\|^2 a)$ which implies $|X_t| \leq exp(\tfrac{1}{2}\|\alpha\|^2 a)$, for all $t \in [0, a]$. Thus $(X_t)_{t \in [0,a]}$ is uniformly bounded (and hence a square integrable) martingale. Since here $a > 0$ was arbitrary, it follows that X is a square integrable martingale.

This will now be used to verify the claims about the process B. Let $0 \leq s < t$. The covariance matrix and independence of $B_t - B_s$ from $\mathcal{F}_s$ will be investigated by means of the characteristic function $F_{(B_t - B_s)}(\alpha) = E_P[exp(i\alpha \cdot (B_t - B_s))]$. Indeed, the martingale property of X yields

$$E_P\left[exp\left(i\alpha \cdot B_t + \tfrac{1}{2}\|\alpha\|^2 t\right) \mid \mathcal{F}_s\right] = exp\left(i\alpha \cdot B_s + \tfrac{1}{2}\|\alpha\|^2 s\right).$$

Multiply with $exp\left(-i\alpha \cdot B_s - \tfrac{1}{2}\|\alpha\|^2 t\right)$. Since this random variable is bounded and $\mathcal{F}_s$-measurable it multiplies into the conditional expectation and we obtain

$$E_P\left[exp\left(i\alpha \cdot (B_t - B_s)\right) \mid \mathcal{F}_s\right] = exp\left(-\tfrac{1}{2}\|\alpha\|^2(t - s)\right). \qquad (3)$$

Here the right hand side is a constant independent of $\omega \in \Omega$. Integrating over Ω yields

$$E_P\big[exp\,(i\alpha \cdot (B_t - B_s))\big] = exp\,\big(-\tfrac{1}{2}\|\alpha\|^2(t - s)\big),$$

that is, the characteristic function of the increment $B_t - B_s$ satisfies

$$F_{(B_t - B_s)}(\alpha) = exp\,\big(-\tfrac{1}{2}\|\alpha\|^2(t - s)\big). \tag{4}$$

This shows that the increment $B_t - B_s$ is multivariate normal with mean zero and covariance matrix $C = (t - s)I$. It remains to be shown only that the increment $B_t - B_s$ is independent of the σ-field $\mathcal{F}_s$, or equivalently, that $B_t - B_s$ is independent of every $\mathcal{F}_s$-measurable random variable Z. Consider such Z. It will suffice to show that the characteristic function $F_{(B_t - B_s, Z)}$ of the R^{d+1}-valued random vector $(B_t - B_s, Z)$ factors as $F_{(B_t - B_s, Z)}(\alpha, \beta) = F_{B_t - B_s}(\alpha)F_Z(\beta)$, for all $\alpha \in R^d$, $\beta \in R$ (II.1.a). Indeed, for such α, β,

$$
\begin{aligned}
F_{(B_t - B_s, Z)}(\alpha, \beta) &= E_P\big[exp\,(i(B_t - B_s, Z) \cdot (\alpha, \beta))\big] \\
&= E_P\big[exp\,(i\beta Z + i\alpha \cdot (B_t - B_s))\big] \\
&= E_P\big[E_P\big[e^{i\beta Z}exp\,(i\alpha \cdot (B_t - B_s)) \mid \mathcal{F}_s\big]\big] \\
&= E_P\big[e^{i\beta Z}E_P\big[exp\,(i\alpha \cdot (B_t - B_s)) \mid \mathcal{F}_s\big]\big] = \text{ using (3) } = \\
&= E_P\big[e^{i\beta Z}exp\,\big(-\tfrac{1}{2}\|\alpha\|^2(t - s)\big)\big] \\
&= exp\,\big(-\tfrac{1}{2}\|\alpha\|^2(t - s)\big)E_P\big[e^{i\beta Z}\big] = \text{ using (4) } = \\
&= F_{(B_t - B_s)}(\alpha)F_Z(\beta), \quad \text{as desired.} \quad \blacksquare
\end{aligned}
$$

3.f The multiplicative compensator U_X.

3.f.0. *Let $X \in \mathcal{S}_+$. Then there is a unique continuous bounded variation process A such that $A_0 = 1$, $A > 0$ and X_t/A_t is a local martingale. The process A is called the multiplicative compensator of the semimartingale X and denoted $A = U_X$. The relationship to the (additive) compensator u_X of X is as follows:*

$$U_X(t) = exp\left(\int_0^t \frac{1}{X_s}du_X(s)\right) \quad \text{and} \quad u_X(t) = \int_0^t X_s d\,log(U_X(s)). \tag{0}$$

Proof. Uniqueness. Here we will also see how to find such a process A. Assume that A is a process with the above properties and set $Z = 1/A$. Since the continuous, positive bounded variation process A is P-as. pathwise bounded away from zero on finite intervals, it follows that $Z = 1/A$ is itself a continuous bounded variation process with $Z_0 = A_0 = 1$. Thus $\langle Z, X \rangle = 0$ and $u_Z = Z$. As ZX is a local martingale, $u_{ZX} = 0$ and formula 3.c.3.(a) for the compensator u_{ZX} yields

$$0 = du_{ZX}(t) = X_t dZ_t + Z_t du_X(t), \quad \text{that is,} \quad Z_s^{-1}dZ_s = -X_s^{-1}du_X(s).$$

Since Z is of bounded variation this can be rewritten as $d\,log(Z_s) = -X_s^{-1}du_X(s)$. Observing that $log(Z_0) = 0$ integration yields

$$log(Z_t) = -\int_0^t \frac{1}{X_s}du_X(s) \quad \text{and so} \quad log(A_t) = -log(Z_t) = \int_0^t \frac{1}{X_s}du_X(s).$$

This shows that a process A with the above properties must be given by the first formula in (0). In particular A is uniquely determined.

Existence. Set $A_t = exp\left(\int_0^t X_s^{-1}du_X(s)\right)$. We verify that A has the desired properties. We merely have to reverse the considerations of (a) above. Clearly A is a strictly positive, continuous bounded variation process with $A_0 = 1$. Set $Z = 1/A$. To show that ZX is a local martingale note that it is a continuous semimartingale and $Z_t = exp\left(-\int_0^t X_s^{-1}du_X(s)\right)$ and thus $d\,log(Z_s) = -X_s^{-1}du_X(s)$. Since Z is a bounded variation process, this can be rewritten as

$$Z_s^{-1}dZ_s = -X_s^{-1}du_X(s) \quad \text{and so} \quad X_sdZ_s + Z_sdu_X(s) = 0,$$

that is, $du_{ZX}(s) = 0$ and so $u_{ZX} = 0$. Thus ZX is a local martingale. It remains to verify the second equation in (0), that is, $du_X(t) = X_t\, d\,log(U_X(t))$. This follows at once from the first equation in (0) upon taking the logarithm, differentiating and multiplying with X_t. ∎

3.g Harmonic functions of Brownian motion. Let f be a C^∞-function on R^d and write $\nabla f = (\partial f/\partial x_1, \dots, \partial f/\partial x_d)'$ and $\triangle f = \sum_{j=1}^d \partial^2 f/\partial x_j^2$ as usual. If $B_t = (B_t^1, \dots, B_t^d)$ is a d-dimensional Brownian motion, the relations $\langle B^i, B^j \rangle_t = \delta_{ij}t$ combined with Ito's formula yield

$$d\,f(B_t) = \nabla f(B_t) \cdot dB_t + \triangle f(B_t)\,dt.$$

If now f is *harmonic*, that is, $\triangle f = 0$, then the second summand vanishes and it follows that $f(B_t)$ is a local martingale. In case $d = 2$ the function $f(x) = log(\|x\|)$ is harmonic albeit only on $R^2 \setminus \{0\}$. Let B be a 2-dimensional Brownian motion starting at some point x with $\|x\| > 1$. We have used in example I.8.a.6 that $X_t = log\|B_t\|$ is a local martingale.

To overcome the difficulty at the origin set $D_n = \{y \in R^2 \mid \|y\| \leq 1/n\}$ and $T_n = \inf\{t > 0 \mid B_t \in D_n\}$, for $n \geq 1$. Then T_n is a hitting time and hence optional (I.7.a.6, example 2). Since the range of the stopped process B^{T_n} is contained in $R^2 \setminus D_n$, Ito's formula can be applied and yields $d\,f(B_t^{T_n}) = \nabla f(B_t^{T_n}) \cdot dB_t^{T_n}$ and so the process $f(B)^{T_n}$ satisfies

$$f(B)^{T_n} = f(B^{T_n}) = f(x) + \nabla f(B^{T_n}) \bullet B^{T_n}$$

and is thus a local martingale. One can now show that the optional times T_n satisfy $T_n \uparrow \infty$, P-as. It follows that the process $f(B)$ is a local martingale.

4. CHANGE OF MEASURE

4.a Locally equivalent change of probability. Recall that $(\Omega, \mathcal{F}, (\mathcal{F}_t), P)$ is a filtered probability space with right continuous filtration $(\mathcal{F}_t)$ and that $\mathcal{F}_0$ consists of the null sets and their complements. A probability measure Q on $\mathcal{F}_\infty = \sigma(\bigcup_{t \geq 0} \mathcal{F}_t)$ is called *locally equivalent to P*, iff the restriction $Q|\mathcal{F}_t$ is equivalent to the restriction $P|\mathcal{F}_t$, for each $t \geq 0$; equivalently, iff the measures Q and P are equivalent on each σ-field $\mathcal{F}_t$, $t \geq 0$. This does not imply that P and Q are equivalent on $\mathcal{F}_\infty$. In fact they can be mutually singular on this larger σ-field. Easy examples will be encountered below (example 4.c.4). For $f \in L^1(P)$, $g \in L^1(Q)$ set

$$M_t = \frac{d(Q|\mathcal{F}_t)}{d(P|\mathcal{F}_t)}, \quad E_t^P(f) = E_P(f|\mathcal{F}_t) \quad \text{and} \quad E_t^Q(g) = E_Q(g|\mathcal{F}_t), \quad t \geq 0.$$

Let us recall from Bayes Theorem (I.8.b.0):
(a) M_t is a strictly positive P-martingale with $M_0 = 1$.
(b) For $f \in L^1(Q, \mathcal{F}_T)$ we have $E_t^Q(f) = E_t^P(M_T f)/M_t = E_t^P(M_T f)/E_t^P(M_T)$, $0 \leq t \leq T$.
(c) The adapted process (Z_t) is a Q-martingale (Q-local martingale) if and only if the process $(M_t Z_t)$ is a P-martingale (P-local martingale).
The process M is called the *density process* associated with the measures P and Q. For the remainder of this section we proceed under the following:

4.a.0 Assumption. *The density process M is continuous.*

Remark. More precisely we are assuming that M has a continuous version. According to I.7.b.3 M always has a right continuous version. If $(\mathcal{F}_t)$ is the augmented filtration generated by some Brownian motion, we will see in 5.c.4 below that every $(\mathcal{F}_t)$-adapted local martingale has a continuous version. Consequently assumption 4.a.0 is automatically satisfied for such filtrations.

4.a.1 Girsanov's Formula. *Assume that Q is locally equivalent to P and let X be a continuous P-semimartingale. Then X is also a continuous Q-semimartingale and its compensator u_X^Q with respect to Q is given by $u_X^Q = u_X^P + \langle X, log(M) \rangle$.*

Proof. Let B be any process and $\Psi \subseteq \Omega$ the set of all $\omega \in \Omega$ such that the path $t \mapsto B_t(\omega)$ is continuous and of bounded variation on all finite intervals. Clearly then $\Psi = \bigcap_n \Psi_n$, where Ψ_n is the set of all $\omega \in \Omega$ such that the path $t \mapsto B_t(\omega)$ is continuous and of bounded variation on the interval $[0, n]$. For $n \geq 1$, the set Ψ_n is in $\mathcal{F}_n$ and since P and Q are equivalent on $\mathcal{F}_n$, we have $P(\Psi_n) = 1$ if and only if $Q(\Psi_n) = 1$. It follows that $P(\Psi) = 1$ if and only if $Q(\Psi) = 1$, that is, B is a continuous bounded variation process with respect to P if and only if B is a continuous bounded variation process with respect to Q.

   Recall now that X is a Q-semimartingale if and only if there exists a continuous bounded variation process B vanishing at zero such that $X - B$ is a Q-local martingale in which case $B = u_X^Q$.

Now let B be any continuous bounded variation process vanishing at zero. Then $X - B$ is a Q-local martingale if and only if $(X - B)M$ is a P-local martingale, that is, $u^P_{(X-B)M} = 0$, equivalently $du^P_{(X-B)M} = 0$. Observing that $u^P_M = 0$ and $u^P_{X-B} = u^P_X - B$ and using formula 3.c.3.(a) for the compensator of a product, the equality

$$0 = du^P_{(X-B)M} = M_t du^P_{X-B}(t) + d\langle X - B, M \rangle_t$$
$$= M_t du^P_X(t) - M_t dB_t + d\langle X, M \rangle_t$$

is equivalent with $dB_t = du^P_X(t) + M_t^{-1}d\langle X, M \rangle_t = du^P_X(t) + d\langle X, log(M) \rangle_t$, that is, $B_t = u^P_X(t) + \langle X, log(M) \rangle_t$ which is indeed a bounded variation process vanishing at zero. Thus X is a Q-semimartingale with $u^Q_X = B = u^P_X + \langle X, log(M) \rangle$. ∎

Let us now show that stochastic integrals are invariant under change to a locally equivalent probability measure. With P, Q and $M_t = d(Q|\mathcal{F}_t)/d(P|\mathcal{F}_t)$, $t \geq 0$, as above, let X be a continuous P-semimartingale, $H \in L(X)$ and $I = (H \bullet X)^P$, that is, $I = \int_0^{\cdot} H_s dX_s$, where this integral process is computed with respect to the measure P. To show that $I = (H \bullet X)^Q$ also, that is, the integral process $H \bullet X$ is unaffected if we switch from the probability P to the locally equivalent probability Q, we first note the following universal property of the process I:

4.a.2. *The stochastic integral $I = (H \bullet X)^P$ is the unique continuous P-semimartingale satisfying*
(a) $I_0 = 0$, $u^P_I = H \bullet u^P_X$ and
(b) $\langle I, Y \rangle = H \bullet \langle X, Y \rangle$, for each continuous P-semimartingale Y.

Proof. Let $X = M + A$ be the P-semimartingale decomposition of X. Then $I = H \bullet X = H \bullet M + H \bullet A$, where here $H \bullet M$ is a continuous P-local martingale and $H \bullet A$ a continuous bounded variation process vanishing at zero. Thus I is a continuous P-semimartingale with $u^P_I = H \bullet A = H \bullet u^P_X$. This shows (a). Property (b) has already been verified in 2.d.1.(e).

Conversely it remains to be shown that (a) and (b) uniquely determine the continuous P-semimartingale I. Assume that I_1, I_2 are continuous P-semimartingales satisfying (a) and (b). Then $\langle I_1 - I_2, N \rangle = 0$, for each continuous P-semimartingale N and especially for $N = I_1 - I_2$, we obtain $\langle I_1 - I_2 \rangle = 0$. Thus $I_1 - I_2$ is a continuous bounded variation process and since this process vanishes at zero we have $I_1 - I_2 = u^P_{I_1 - I_2} = u^P_{I_1} - u^P_{I_2} = H \bullet u^P_X - H \bullet u^P_X = 0$, that is, $I_1 = I_2$. ∎

4.a.3. *Let P, Q, X be as above. Then*
(a) The space $L(X)$ is the same when computed with respect to P or Q.
(b) For $H \in L(X)$ we have $(H \bullet X)^P = (H \bullet X)^Q$.

Proof. Let us note first that the covariation $\langle X, Y \rangle$ is invariant under locally equivalent change of probability measure. This follows at once from the limit representation I.11.b.0.(b) and the fact that convergence in P-probability is equivalent with convergence in Q-probability for sequences of random variables all measurable with respect to the same σ-field $\mathcal{F}_t$, for some $t \geq 0$.

(a)   Let $X = L + A$ be the P-semimartingale decomposition of X $(A = u_X^P)$. The Q-semimartingale decomposition of X is given by $X = (X - u_X^Q) + u_X^Q$ and since $u_X^Q = A + \langle X, log(M) \rangle = A + \langle L, log(M) \rangle$ (4.a.1), this assumes the form $X = K + B$, where $K = L - \langle L, log(M) \rangle$ and $B = A + \langle L, log(M) \rangle$.

Thus $L(X) = L_{loc}^2(L) \cap L_{loc}^1(A)$, if computed with respect to P, whilst $L(X) = L_{loc}^2(K) \cap L_{loc}^1(B)$, if computed with respect to Q.

Since L and K differ by a continuous bounded variation process, we have $\langle K \rangle = \langle L \rangle$ and this implies $L_{loc}^2(K) = L_{loc}^2(L)$ by 2.b.2.(c). By symmetry it will now suffice to show that $L_{loc}^1(A) \subseteq L_{loc}^1(B)$.

Let $H \in L_{loc}^1(A)$, that is, H progressively measurable and $\int_0^t |H_s| \, |dA_s| < \infty$, P-as., for each $t \geq 0$. Fix $t \geq 0$. As $B = A + \langle X, log(M) \rangle$, we have

$$\int_0^t |H_s| \, |dB_s| \leq \int_0^t |H_s| \, |dA_s| + \int_0^t |H_s| \, |d\langle X, log(M) \rangle_s|.$$

Since the first summand on the right is P-as. and hence Q-as. finite, we need concern ourselves only with the second summand. By the Kunita-Watanabe inequality

$$\left(\int_0^t |H_s| \, |d\langle L, log(M) \rangle_s| \right)^2 \leq \langle log(M) \rangle_t \int_0^t |H_s|^2 d\langle L \rangle_s < \infty,$$

P-as. and hence Q-as., since $H \in L_{loc}^2(L)$. Thus $H \in L_{loc}^1(B)$. This shows (a).

(b)   Set $I = (H \bullet X)^P$. We claim that $I = (H \bullet X)^Q$ also. According to 4.a.2, we have to show that

(α) I is a continuous Q-semimartingale vanishing at zero such that

$\langle I, Y \rangle = H \bullet \langle X, Y \rangle$, for all continuous Q-semimartingales Y, and

(β) $u_I^Q = H \bullet u_X^Q$.

Here (α) follows from the fact that this is true if Q is replaced with P, the spaces of continuous semimartingales with respect to P respectively Q coincide and the covariation is the same whether computed relative to P or relative to Q. It thus remains to verify (β). Indeed, using (α), 4.a.1 and 4.a.2.(a),

$$u_I^Q = u_I^P + \langle I, log(M) \rangle = H \bullet u_X^P + H \bullet \langle X, log(M) \rangle$$
$$= H \bullet \left(u_X^P + \langle X, log(M) \rangle \right) = H \bullet u_X^Q. \quad \blacksquare$$

Let P, Q and $M_t = d(Q|\mathcal{F}_t)/d(P|\mathcal{F}_t)$, $t \geq 0$, be as above. The following is the analogue of Girsanov's formula 4.a.1 for the multiplicative compensator U_X of a positive continuous semimartingale X:

4.a.4. *Let $X \in \mathcal{S}_+$. Then $U_X^Q = U_X^P \, exp(\langle log(X), log(M) \rangle)$.*

Proof. Taking logarithms and passing to differentials using 3.f.0 and 3.c.2.(c), the equality 4.a.4 is seen to be equivalent with

$$X_t^{-1} du_X^Q(t) = X_t^{-1} du_X^P(t) + d\langle log(X), log(M) \rangle$$
$$= X_t^{-1} du_X^P(t) + X_t^{-1} d\langle X, log(M) \rangle. \tag{0}$$

Multiply with X_t and (0) becomes Girsanov's formula 4.a.1 in differential form. $\blacksquare$

4.b The exponential local martingale. Let L be a continuous local martingale with $L_0 = 0$. The *Doleans exponential* $Z = \mathcal{E}(L)$ of L is defined as

$$Z_t = \mathcal{E}_t(L) = exp\big(L_t - \tfrac{1}{2}\langle L\rangle_t\big).$$

We have a stochastic integral equation for Z:

4.b.0. *The process* $Z = \mathcal{E}(L)$ *satisfies* $Z_t = 1 + \int_0^t Z_s dL_s$ *and* $Z_0 = 1$. *Thus* Z *is a nonnegative local martingale and hence a supermartingale. Consequently* Z *is a martingale if and only if* $E(Z_t) = 1$, *for all* $t \geq 1$.

Proof. Set $\zeta_t = L_t - \tfrac{1}{2}\langle L\rangle_t$. Then $\zeta_0 = 0$ and ζ is a continuous semimartingale with local martingale part L. Thus $\langle\zeta\rangle = \langle L\rangle$. Ito's formula applied to $Z = exp(\zeta)$ now implies that

$$dZ_t = exp(\zeta_s)d\zeta_s + \tfrac{1}{2}exp(\zeta_s)d\langle\zeta\rangle_s = Z_s d\big(L_s - \tfrac{1}{2}\langle L\rangle_s\big) + \tfrac{1}{2}Z_s d\langle L\rangle_s = Z_s dL_s.$$

Since $Z_0 = 1$, it follows that $Z_t = 1 + \int_0^t Z_s dL_s$ and so Z is a local martingale. By definition $Z \geq 0$. The rest follows from I.8.a.7. ∎

Remark. In differential form the equation for Z reads $dZ_t = Z_t dL_t$. This is of course analogous to the nonstochastic exponential differential equation $dx(t) = x(t)dt$ with unique solution $x(t) = x(0)e^t$. This justifies our terminology. In analogy to the nonstochastic case we have:

4.b.1. *Let* L *be a continuous local martingale with* $L_0 = 0$ *and* $E_t = \mathcal{E}_t(L) = exp\big(L_t - \tfrac{1}{2}\langle L\rangle_t\big)$. *Then each solution* $X \in \mathcal{S}$ *of the exponential stochastic differential equation* $dX_s = X_s dL_s$ *has the form* $X_t = X_0 E_t$, *for all* $t \geq 0$.

Remark. Conversely, since $E_t = \mathcal{E}_t(L)$ is a solution of $dX_s = X_s dL_s$, the same is true of every process X_t of the form $X_t = X_0 E_t$.

Proof. Assume that $X \in \mathcal{S}$ satisfies $dX_s = X_s dL_s$. Then $U_t = X_t E_t^{-1}$ is a continuous semimartingale. Since $E_0 = 1$, we have $U_0 = X_0$ and must show that $U_t = U_0$, $t \geq 0$. Since U is a continuous semimartingale, this is equivalent with $dU_t = 0$. By the stochastic product rule

$$dU_t = X_t dE_t^{-1} + E_t^{-1}dX_t + d\langle X, E^{-1}\rangle_t. \tag{0}$$

From $dE_t = E_t dL_t$ and $dX_t = X_t dL_t$, that is, $E = 1 + E\bullet L$, $X = X_0 + X\bullet L$, we infer (using 3.c.2.(b) and 3.b.0.(d)) that

$$d\langle E\rangle_t = E_t^2 d\langle L\rangle_t \quad \text{and}$$
$$d\langle X, E^{-1}\rangle_t = -E_t^{-2}d\langle X, E\rangle_t = -E_t^{-2}X_t E_t \, d\langle L, L\rangle_t = -X_t E_t^{-1}d\langle L\rangle_t. \tag{1}$$

Furthermore, using Ito's formula and $dE_t = E_t dL_t$,

$$dE_t^{-1} = -E_t^{-2}dE_t + E_t^{-3}d\langle E\rangle_t = -E_t^{-1}dL_t + E_t^{-1}d\langle L\rangle_t.$$

Consequently the term $X_t dE_t^{-1}$ in (0) becomes $-X_t E_t^{-1}dL_t + X_t E_t^{-1}d\langle L\rangle_t$. Because of $dX_t = X_t dL_t$, the term $E_t^{-1}dX_t$ in (0) becomes $X_t E_t^{-1}dL_t$. Thus (1) shows that all terms in (0) cancel to yield $dU_t = 0$, as desired. ∎

4.b.2. *Let V be a continuous, R^d-valued local martingale and $\gamma \in L(V)$. Then the general solution $X \in S$ of the exponential stochastic differential equation*

$$dX_t = X_t \gamma(t) \cdot dV_t \qquad (2)$$

has the form $X_t = X_0 \mathcal{E}_t(\gamma \bullet V)$.

Proof. Rewrite (2) as $dX_t = X_t d(\gamma \bullet V)_t$ and use 4.b.0, 4.b.1 with $L = \gamma \bullet V$. ∎

We are now interested in conditions under which the Doleans exponential $Z = \mathcal{E}(L)$ is not only a local martingale but in fact a martingale. We start with the following easy condition:

4.b.3. *Let L be a continuous local martingale with $L_0 = 0$. If $\langle L \rangle_t \le C(t) < \infty$ on Ω, for some nondecreasing (deterministic) function $C : [0, \infty) \to [0, \infty)$, then the Doleans exponential $Z = \mathcal{E}(L)$ is a martingale with $E_P(Z_t^2) \le 4e^{C(t)}$. If more strongly $\langle L \rangle_t \le C$, for all $t \ge 0$, where the constant C does not depend on t, then the martingale Z is L^2-bounded.*

Proof. For $t \ge 0$ set $Y_t = \mathcal{E}_t(2L) = exp\big(2L_t - \frac{1}{2}\langle 2L \rangle_t\big) = exp\big(2L_t - 2\langle L \rangle_t\big)$. Then we have

$$Z_t^2 = exp\big(2L_t - \langle L \rangle_t\big) = Y_t \, exp\,(\langle L \rangle_t) \le Y_t e^{C(t)}.$$

Moreover Z and Y are continuous local martingales (4.b.1). Let (T_n) be a sequence of optional times which simultaneously reduces Z and Y to a martingale. Fix $t \ge 0$ and $n \ge 1$. The nondecreasing nature of the function $C(t)$ implies that

$$Z_{t \wedge T_n}^2 \le Y_{t \wedge T_n} e^{C(t \wedge T_n)} \le e^{C(t)} Y_{t \wedge T_n},$$

where the factor $exp(C(t))$ no longer depends on $\omega \in \Omega$. Applying the L^2-maximal inequality (I.7.e.1.(b) with $p = 2$) to the martingale $(Z_{s \wedge T_n})_s$ we obtain

$$E_P \left(\sup_{s \in [0,t]} Z_{s \wedge T_n}^2 \right) \le 4 E_P \left(Z_{t \wedge T_n}^2 \right) \le 4 e^{C(t)} E_P \big(Y_{t \wedge T_n} \big) = 4 e^{C(t)} E_P(Y_0) = 4 e^{C(t)}.$$

Let $n \uparrow \infty$. Then $T_n \uparrow \infty$ and this implies that $\sup_{s \in [0,t]} Z_{s \wedge T_n}^2 \uparrow \sup_{s \in [0,t]} Z_s^2$ and so

$$E_P \big(\sup_{s \in [0,t]} Z_{s \wedge T_n}^2 \big) \uparrow E_P \big(\sup_{s \in [0,t]} Z_s^2 \big), \qquad P\text{-as.}$$

It follows that

$$E_P \left(\sup_{s \in [0,t]} Z_s^2 \right) \le 4 e^{C(t)}. \qquad (3)$$

Thus $E_P(Z_t^2) \le 4e^{C(t)}$, for all $t \ge 0$. Moreover (3) implies that $\sup_{s \in [0,t]} |Z_s| \in L^1(P)$, for all $t \ge 0$, from which it follows that the local martingale Z is in fact a martingale (I.8.a.4). ∎

4.b.4 Example. Let W be a one dimensional Brownian motion, μ a constant and $L = \mu \bullet W$, that is, $L_t = \int_0^t \mu \, dW_s = \mu W_t$. Then $\langle L \rangle_t = \big(\mu^2 \bullet \langle W \rangle \big)_t = \int_0^t \mu^2 ds = \mu^2 t$ and this satisfies the assumption of 4.b.3. Consequently

$$Z_t = \mathcal{E}_t(L) = exp\big(L_t - \tfrac{1}{2}\langle L \rangle_t\big) = exp\left(\mu W_t - \tfrac{1}{2}\mu^2 t\right), \qquad t \ge 0,$$

is a martingale.

If L is a continuous local martingale adapted to the augmented filtration generated by some Brownian motion, we have the following stronger condition 4.b.4. The proof will be postponed till section 4.d.

4.b.5 Abstract Novikov Condition. *Let M be a continuous local martingale with $M_0 = 0$ and assume that $E_P\big[exp(\frac{1}{2}\langle M\rangle_t)\big] < \infty$, $0 \le t < \infty$. Then $Z = \mathcal{E}(M)$ is a martingale.* ∎

4.c Girsanov's theorem. Assume that the probability measure Q is locally equivalent to P and set $M_t = d(Q|\mathcal{F}_t)/d(P|\mathcal{F}_t)$, $t \ge 0$. Let W be a d-dimensional Brownian motion on $(\Omega, \mathcal{F}, (\mathcal{F}_t), P)$. Clearly W cannot be expected to be a Brownian motion with respect to Q also. We will see however that W differs from a Q-Brownian motion (a Brownian motion on $(\Omega, \mathcal{F}, (\mathcal{F}_t), Q)$) only by a bounded variation process. Indeed W is an (R^d-valued) P-semimartingale and consequently a Q-semimartingale. Thus

$$W^Q := W - u_W^Q$$

is a Q-local martingale and since the compensator u_W^Q is an (R^d-valued) bounded variation process, we have

$$\big\langle (W^i)^Q\big\rangle_t = \big\langle W^i\big\rangle_t = t \quad \text{and} \quad \big\langle (W^i)^Q, (W^j)^Q\big\rangle_t = \big\langle W^i, W^j\big\rangle_t = 0,$$

for all $i, j \in \{1, 2, \ldots, d\}$ with $i \ne j$. From Levi's characterization of d-dimensional Brownian motion (3.e.1) it follows that W^Q is a Brownian motion with respect to Q. Since W is a P-martingale we have $u_W^P = 0$ and Girsanov's formula 4.a.1 now yields the compensator u_W^Q as

$$u_W^Q = u_W^P + \langle W, log(M)\rangle = \langle W, log(M)\rangle,$$

under the assumption 4.a.0 that M is continuous. Here

$$\langle W, log(M)\rangle = (\langle W^1, log(M)\rangle, \langle W^2, log(M)\rangle, \ldots, \langle W^d, log(M)\rangle), \qquad (0)$$

in accordance with 2.f.eq.(1). Thus, the Q-Brownian motion W^Q assumes the form

$$W^Q = W - \langle W, log(M)\rangle. \qquad (1)$$

Assume now that the martingale M satisfies $M = \mathcal{E}(\gamma \bullet W)$, equivalently (4.b.2),

$$\frac{dM_t}{M_t} = \gamma(t) \cdot dW_t, \qquad (2)$$

for some process $\gamma \in L(W)$. Let γ_j and W^j denote the components of the R^d-valued processes γ and W. Then M is automatically continuous and by definition of the exponential local martingale we have $log(M) = \gamma \bullet W - A = \sum_{i=1}^{d} \gamma_i \bullet W^i - A$, where A is the continuous, bounded variation process $A = \frac{1}{2}\langle \gamma \bullet W\rangle$. From (0) and

$$\langle W^j, log(M)\rangle = \Big\langle W^j, \sum_{i=1}^{d} \gamma_i \bullet W^i\Big\rangle$$

$$= \sum_{i=1}^{d} \gamma_i \bullet \langle W^j, W^i\rangle = \int_0^{\cdot} \gamma_j(s)ds = \Big(\int_0^{\cdot} \gamma(s)ds\Big)_j$$

it follows that

$$\langle W, log(M)\rangle_t = \int_0^t \gamma(s)ds. \qquad (3)$$

Thus the Q-Brownian motion W^Q in (1) assumes the form $W_t^Q = W_t - \int_0^t \gamma(s)ds$. We can summarize these observations as follows:

4.c.0. *Let W be a d-dimensional Brownian motion on $(\Omega, \mathcal{F}, (\mathcal{F}_t), P)$, Q a probability locally equivalent to P and assume that the density process $M_t = d(Q|\mathcal{F}_t)/d(P|\mathcal{F}_t)$ satisfies $M = \mathcal{E}(\gamma \bullet W)$, that is,*
$$\frac{dM_t}{M_t} = \gamma(t) \cdot dW_t, \quad t \geq 0,$$

for some $\gamma \in L(W)$. Then the process $W_t^Q = W_t - \int_0^t \gamma(s)ds$ is a Brownian motion on $(\Omega, \mathcal{F}, (\mathcal{F}_t), Q)$. ∎

Remarks. (1) Note that $\gamma \bullet W = \sum_j \gamma_j \bullet W^j$. The bilinearity of the covariation 2.c.1.(f) and $\langle W^i, W^j \rangle_t = \delta_{ij}t$, now show that $\langle \gamma \bullet W \rangle$ is the process

$$\langle \gamma \bullet W \rangle = \langle \gamma \bullet W, \gamma \bullet W \rangle = \sum_{ij} \gamma_i \gamma_j \bullet \langle W^i, W^j \rangle = \sum_j \int_0^\cdot \gamma_j^2(s)ds = \int_0^\cdot \|\gamma(s)\|^2 ds.$$

Thus our assumption on the martingale M can be written more explicitly as

$$M_t = \mathcal{E}_t(\gamma \bullet W) = exp\big((\gamma \bullet W)_t - \tfrac{1}{2}\langle \gamma \bullet W \rangle_t\big)$$
$$= exp\left(\int_0^t \gamma(s) \cdot dW_s - \tfrac{1}{2}\int_0^t \|\gamma(s)\|^2 ds\right), \quad t \geq 0,$$

for some process $\gamma \in L(W)$, that is, γ is R^d-valued, progressively measurable and satisfies $\int_0^t \|\gamma(s)\|^2 ds < \infty$, for all $t \geq 0$. In this case we have seen that W differs from a Q-Brownian motion $\tilde{W}$ by some bounded variation process A, that is, there exist a Q-Brownian motion $\tilde{W}$ and a bounded variation process A such that $W - A = \tilde{W}$. Here W is a continuous Q-semimartingale and $\tilde{W}$ a Q-local martingale. Thus the process A is uniquely determined as $A = u_W^Q$. This also shows that the Q-Brownian motion $\tilde{W}$ is uniquely determined (as $\tilde{W} = W - u_W^Q = W^Q$).

In applications the process γ is frequently at hand already. Since M is a strictly positive P-martingale, theorem 5.e.1 below shows that $\gamma \in L(W)$ with $M = \mathcal{E}(\gamma \bullet W)$ always exists if the filtration $(\mathcal{F}_t)$ is the augmented filtration generated by the Brownian motion W.

(2) A frequent application of 4.c.0 is as follows. A process $r(t)$ is given satisfying the dynamics
$$d\,r(t) = \alpha(t)dt + \beta(t) \cdot dW_t \tag{4}$$

driven by some P-Brownian motion W. Additional considerations may now force us to replace the underlying probability measure P with some locally equivalent probability measure Q. The problem is to find the dynamics satisfied by the process $r(t)$ with respect to the new probability measure Q. Finding a process γ satisfying (2) we have the Q-Brownian motion W^Q given by (1) with stochastic differential dW_t^Q satisfying
$$dW_t = dW_t^Q + \gamma(t)dt.$$

This transforms (4) into $d\,r(t) = \big[\alpha(t) + \beta(t) \cdot \gamma(t)\big]dt + \beta(t) \cdot dW_t^Q$, which represent the dynamics of $r(t)$ under the new probability Q, since W^Q is a Brownian motion with respect to Q.

Conversely, starting with the dynamics (4) we may want to eliminate the so called *drift term* $\alpha(t)dt$. To do this we would look for a process $\gamma \in L(W)$ such that $\alpha(t) + \beta(t) \cdot \gamma(t) = 0$ and the question now becomes if there exists a probability measure Q, locally equivalent to P, such that $\tilde{W}_t = W_t - \int_0^t \gamma(s)ds$ is a Brownian motion with respect to Q. In this case we would have $dW_t = d\tilde{W}_t + \gamma(t)dt$ and substituting this into (4) yields the dynamics of $r(t)$ under the probability measure Q as $dr(t) = \beta(t) \cdot d\tilde{W}_t$.

In particular then the process $r(t)$ would be a Q-local martingale. Here we make use of the fact that stochastic integrals (and hence stochastic differentials) are not affected if we change from the probability P to a locally equivalent probability Q. This naturally leads us to consider the

Converse of 4.c.0. Suppose we have a P-Brownian motion W and some bounded variation process A. Is it possible to find a probability measure Q, locally equivalent to P, such that $W - A$ is a Q-Brownian motion? A positive answer for a sufficiently large class of processes A will be quite interesting, since a Brownian motion has many pathwise properties almost surely with respect to the underlying probability measure.

The measure Q, defined on $\mathcal{F}_\infty$, will frequently have to be *singular* with respect to P on $\mathcal{F}_\infty$ despite being equivalent to P on all σ-fields $\mathcal{F}_t$, $0 \leq t < \infty$. See example 4.c.4 below. This points to the fact that the construction of the measure Q on the σ-field $\mathcal{F}_\infty$ is nontrivial.

In the greatest generality we are given a P-Brownian motion W and a continuous, bounded variation process A and we seek a probability Q on $\mathcal{F}_\infty$, locally equivalent to P, such that $W - A$ is a Q-Brownian motion. Reversing the above steps, we need to find the martingale M which is to be the candidate for $M_t = d(Q|\mathcal{F}_t)/d(P|\mathcal{F}_t)$ and thus are led to solve the equation $A = \langle W, log(M) \rangle$ for M. In this generality it is not clear how M can be derived from A. However, in the special case

$$A_t = \int_0^t \gamma(s)ds, \quad \text{where } \gamma \in L(W),$$

the above considerations lead us to define

$$M_t = \mathcal{E}_t(\gamma \bullet W) = \mathcal{E}_t \left(\int_0^{\cdot} \gamma(s)dW_s \right) = exp \left(\int_0^t \gamma(s)dW_s - \tfrac{1}{2} \int_0^t \|\gamma(s)\|^2 ds \right).$$

Then M is a supermartingale and is a martingale if and only if $E_P(M_t) = 1$, for all $t \geq 0$ (4.b.0).

To simplify matters considerably let us assume that our time horizon T is finite, that is, we are interested in all processes only on the finite interval $[0, T]$. Define the measure $Q = Q_T$ on the σ-field $\mathcal{F}_T$ by means of

$$\frac{dQ}{d(P|\mathcal{F}_T)} = M_T, \quad \text{equivalently,} \quad Q(A) = E_P(M_T 1_A), \ A \in \mathcal{F}_T. \tag{5}$$

Since Q must be a probability measure, we must have $E_P(M_T) = 1$. Since M is a supermartingale with $M_0 = 1$ this is equivalent with $E_P(M_t) = 1$, for all $t \in [0, T]$, that is, $M_t = \mathcal{E}_t(\gamma \bullet W)$ must be a martingale on $[0, T]$.

4.c.1. *Let $T > 0$, W be a P-Brownian motion on $[0, T]$ and $\gamma \in L(W)$. Assume that $M_t = \mathcal{E}_t(\gamma \cdot W)$ is a P-martingale on $[0, T]$. Define the measure $Q = Q_T$ on $\mathcal{F}_T$ by means of (5). Then the process*

$$\tilde{W}_t = W_t - \int_0^t \gamma(s)ds, \ t \in [0, T]$$

is a Q-Brownian motion on $[0, T]$.

Proof. Since the processes M and $d(Q|\mathcal{F}_t)/d(P|\mathcal{F}_t)$ are both martingales on $[0, T]$ which agree at time $t = T$ (by definition of Q), we have $M_t = d(Q|\mathcal{F}_t)/d(P|\mathcal{F}_t)$, for all $t \in [0, T]$. Thus 4.c.0 applies and shows that $\tilde{W}$ is a Q-Brownian motion on $[0, T]$. ∎

The situation becomes more complicated, if we want our measure Q to be defined on the much larger σ-field $\mathcal{F}_\infty$. We then have to assume that $M = \mathcal{E}(\gamma \bullet W)$ is a P-martingale on $[0, \infty)$, equivalently (4.b.1) that $E_P(M_t) = 1$, for all $t \geq 0$. For $t \geq 0$ define the measure Q_t on $\mathcal{F}_t$ by

$$dQ_t/d(P|\mathcal{F}_t) = M_t, \quad \text{equivalently,} \quad Q_t(A) = E_P(M_t 1_A), \ A \in \mathcal{F}_t. \qquad (6)$$

Since M is a martingale, the measures Q_t, $t \geq 0$, defined above are consistent in the sense that $Q_t|\mathcal{F}_s = Q_s$, for $s \leq t$. Consequently they define a finitely additive measure Q on the subfield $\mathcal{G} = \bigcup_{t \geq 0} \mathcal{F}_t$ of the σ-field $\mathcal{F}_\infty$ by means of $Q(A) = \lim_{t \uparrow \infty} Q_t(A)$, $A \in \mathcal{G}$. Since $\mathcal{G}$ generates the σ-field $\mathcal{F}_\infty$, Q will extend uniquely to a probability measure on $\mathcal{F}_\infty$ if and only if Q is countably additive on $\mathcal{G}$ (Caratheodory's Extension Theorem). This extension Q then satisfies $Q_t = Q|\mathcal{F}_t$ and consequently

$$\frac{d(Q|\mathcal{F}_t)}{d(P|\mathcal{F}_t)} = \frac{dQ_t}{d(P|\mathcal{F}_t)} = M_t,$$

for all $t \geq 0$. The proof of 4.c.1 then goes through for an infinite time horizon. Unfortunately the countable additivity of Q on $\mathcal{G}$ is a nontrivial problem. It is automatically satisfied, if the probability space $(\Omega, \mathcal{F}, (\mathcal{F}_t), P)$ is d-dimensional path space $(C^d, \mathcal{C}^d)$ equipped with the Wiener measure P and the augmented filtration generated by the Brownian motion W. We will not use this result. For a proof the reader is referred to [PTH, theorem 4.2].

4.c.2 Girsanov's Theorem. *Let $(\Omega, \mathcal{F}, (\mathcal{F}_t), P)$ be path space with its canonical filtration and the Wiener measure P, W the associated canonical P-Brownian motion (identity map), $\gamma \in L(W)$ and assume that $M_t = \mathcal{E}_t(\gamma \bullet W)$ is a martingale. For $t \geq 0$ define the measure Q_t on $\mathcal{F}_t$ by means of (6). Then there is a unique probability measure Q on $\mathcal{F}_\infty$ such that $Q|\mathcal{F}_t = Q_t$ and hence $d(Q|\mathcal{F}_t)/d(P|\mathcal{F}_t) = M_t$, for all $t \geq 0$. With respect to this measure Q the process $\tilde{W}_t = W_t - \int_0^t \gamma(s)ds$, $t \geq 0$, is a Q-Brownian motion.* ∎

4.c.3 Remark. We can think of this as follows: with respect to the original measure P, our process W_t is a Brownian motion with zero drift. With respect to the new measure Q, $W_t = \tilde{W}_t + \int_0^t \gamma(s)ds$ is a Brownian motion plus a drift $\int_0^t \gamma(s)ds$, which can depend on the entire history of the path followed by W_t. In differential notation

$$dW_t = \gamma(s)ds + d\tilde{W}_t.$$

It is common to refer to $\gamma(s)$ as the drift coefficient. Note that the filtrations $\mathcal{F}_t^W$ and $\mathcal{F}_t^{\tilde{W}}$ generated by the Brownian motions W_t and $\tilde{W}_t$ will in general be different. This is a nuisance whenever we want to apply the martingale representation theorems to be developed below, since these assume adaptedness with respect to the filtration generated by the representing Brownian motion. The two filtrations do coincide, however, if the drift process $\int_0^t \gamma(s)ds$ is deterministic (independent of $\omega \in \Omega$).

4.c.4 Example. The following special case of 4.c.2 will be useful later: let W be a one dimensional Brownian motion and μ a real number and set $\gamma(t) = \mu$, that is, we consider the case of a nonstochastic, constant drift rate process. Then $(\gamma \bullet W)_t = \int_0^t \gamma(s)dW_s = \mu W_t$ and $\langle \gamma \bullet W \rangle_t = \langle \mu W \rangle_t = \mu^2 t$ and so

$$M_t = \mathcal{E}_t(\gamma \bullet W) = exp\left(\int_0^t \gamma(s)dW_s - \tfrac{1}{2} \int_0^t \gamma^2(s)ds \right) = exp(\mu W_t - \tfrac{1}{2}\mu^2 t)$$

is a martingale (4.b.4). Consequently Girsanov's theorem can be applied and yields that $\tilde{W}_t = W_t - \int_0^t \gamma(s)ds = W_t - \mu t$ is Brownian motion with respect to the probability measure Q^μ corresponding to M, that is, the unique probability measure on $\mathcal{F}_\infty$ satisfying $Q^\mu(A) = E_P(1_A M_t)$, for all $A \in \mathcal{F}_t$ and $t \geq 0$.

In other words, with respect to the probability measure Q^μ, the original process W_t is a Brownian motion plus a drift μt: $W_t = \tilde{W}_t + \mu t$. Even in this simple example the locally equivalent measure $Q = Q^\mu$ is singular with respect to the original measure P on $\mathcal{F}_\infty$. Indeed $W_t/t \to 0$, as $t \uparrow \infty$, P-as., since W is a Brownian motion with respect to P. On the other hand $W_t/t = \tilde{W}_t/t + \mu \to \mu$, as $t \uparrow \infty$, Q-as., since $\tilde{W}$ is a Brownian motion with respect to Q (II.2.g.2). The measures P and Q are thus mutually singular and concentrated on the disjoint sets $[W_t/t \to 0]$ and $[W_t/t \to \mu]$ in $\mathcal{F}_\infty$. It is no coincidence that these sets are in the σ-field $\mathcal{F}_\infty$, but not in any $\mathcal{F}_t$, $0 \leq t < \infty$. In fact P and Q are equivalent on each $\mathcal{F}_t$, $t \in [0,\infty)$. In our example

$$\frac{d(Q|\mathcal{F}_t)}{d(P|\mathcal{F}_t)} = M_t = exp(\mu W_t - \tfrac{1}{2}\mu^2 t), \quad t \geq 0.$$

4.c.5 Wald's Identity. *Let M_t and Q^μ be as in 4.c.5 and T an optional time satisfying $P(T < \infty) = 1$. Then $Q^\mu(T < \infty) = E_P(M_T) = E_P\left[exp(\mu W_T - \tfrac{1}{2}\mu^2 T) \right]$.*

Proof. Let $n \geq 1$. Then the Optional Sampling Theorem yields $E_P(M_n \mid \mathcal{F}_{n\wedge T}) = M_{n\wedge T}$. Since $[T \leq n] \in \mathcal{F}_{n\wedge T} \subseteq \mathcal{F}_n$, the definition of Q^μ yields

$$Q^\mu(T \leq n) = E_P\left(1_{[T \leq n]} M_n \right) = E_P\left(1_{[T \leq n]} M_{n\wedge T} \right) = E_P\left(1_{[T \leq n]} M_T \right).$$

Letting $n \uparrow \infty$ it follows that $Q^\mu(T < \infty) = E_P(M_T) = E_P\left[exp(\mu W_T - \tfrac{1}{2}\mu^2 T) \right]$. ∎

4.d The Novikov condition. We now turn to a more powerful condition which ensures that the Doleans exponential $Z_t = \mathcal{E}_t(L)$ of a local martingale L is in fact a martingale. Here it is assumed that L is adapted to the augmented filtration generated by some Brownian motion.

4.d.0 Abstract Novikov Condition. *Let L be a continuous local martingale with $L_0 = 0$ which is adapted to the augmented filtration generated by some Brownian motion and assume that*

$$E_P\left[exp(\tfrac{1}{2}\langle L\rangle_t)\right] < \infty, \quad \forall 0 \leq t < \infty. \tag{0}$$

Then $Z_t = \mathcal{E}_t(L) = exp\left(L_t - \tfrac{1}{2}\langle L\rangle_t\right)$ is a martingale.

Proof. It will suffice to show that $E(Z_t) = 1$, for all $t \geq 0$ (4.b.0). Note first that (0) implies $P(\langle L\rangle_t < \infty) = 1$.

According to 5.a.4 below we can choose a Brownian motion W on a suitable enlargement $(\Omega_1, \mathcal{G}, P_1, (\mathcal{G}_t))$ of the original filtered probability space $(\Omega, \mathcal{G}, P, (\mathcal{G}_t))$ such that $L_t = W_{\langle L\rangle_t}$ and such that each $\langle L\rangle_t$ is a $(\mathcal{G}_t)$-optional time. This will allow us to reduce the general case $Z_t = exp\left(L_t - \tfrac{1}{2}\langle L\rangle_t\right)$ to the special case of the well known basic exponential martingale $exp\left(\mu W_t - \tfrac{1}{2}\mu^2 t\right)$ (4.c.4) via an application of Wald's identity.

Let $b < 0$ and set $T_b = \inf\{\, s \geq 0 \mid W_s - s = b\,\}$. Then T_b is a $(\mathcal{G}_t)$-optional time. Since the process $W_s - s$ has continuous paths and satisfies $W_s - s \to -\infty$, as $s \uparrow \infty$, we have $P(T_b < \infty) = 1$ and $T_b \uparrow \infty$, as $b \downarrow -\infty$, P-as.

Set $\mu = 1$. The process $W_s - s = W_s - \mu s$ is a one dimensional Brownian motion with respect to the measure Q^μ of example 4.c.4 and since one dimensional Brownian motion hits all values we have $Q^\mu(T_b < \infty) = 1$. Wald's identity now implies that

$$E_P\left(e^{W_{T_b} - \frac{1}{2}T_b}\right) = Q^\mu(T_b < \infty) = 1. \tag{1}$$

Note that $W_{T_b} - T_b = b$, by definition of the optional time T_b, that is

$$W_{T_b} - \tfrac{1}{2}T_b = b + \tfrac{1}{2}T_b, \tag{2}$$

and so $E_P\left(exp(b + \tfrac{1}{2}T_b)\right) = 1$, that is,

$$E_P\left(exp(\tfrac{1}{2}T_b)\right) = e^{-b}. \tag{3}$$

Recall that $Y_s = exp(\mu W_s - \tfrac{1}{2}\mu^2 s) = e^{W_s - s/2}$ is a martingale and hence, by the Optional Sampling Theorem, so is the process $N_s = Y_{s \wedge T_b}$.

Let us note that $Y_0 = 1$ and hence $E(N_s) = E(N_0) = E(Y_0) = 1$, $s \geq 0$. Since $P(T_b < \infty) = 1$ we have

$$N_\infty = \lim_{s \uparrow \infty} N_s = Y_{T_b} = e^{W_{T_b} - \frac{1}{2}T_b},$$

with convergence P-as. According to (1) we have $E_P(N_\infty) = 1$. Let us now show that N_∞ is a last element for the martingale N. Fix $s \geq 0$. Then $N_s = E_P(N_k|\mathcal{F}_s)$, for all $k \geq s$. Fatou's Lemma (I.2.b.8 with $h = 0$) yields

$$N_s = \lim_k E_P(N_k|\mathcal{F}_s) = \liminf_k E_P(N_k|\mathcal{F}_s) \leq E_P\left(\liminf_k N_k \mid \mathcal{F}_s\right)$$
$$= E_P(N_\infty|\mathcal{F}_s), \quad P\text{-as.}$$

Since $E_P[E_P(N_\infty|\mathcal{F}_s)] = E_P(N_\infty) = 1 = E_P(N_s)$ it follows that $N_s = E_P(N_\infty|\mathcal{F}_s)$. Thus N_∞ is a last element for the martingale N which is thus uniformly integrable. Consequently the Optional Sampling Theorem can be applied with all optional times τ to yield $E_P(Y_{\tau \wedge T_b}) = E_P(N_\tau) = E_P(N_0) = 1$, that is,

$$E_P\left(exp(W_{\tau \wedge T_b} - \tfrac{1}{2}\tau \wedge T_b)\right) = 1. \tag{4}$$

Now fix $t \in [0, \infty)$ and apply (4) to the optional time $\tau = \langle L \rangle_t$ observing that

$$\tau \wedge T_b = \begin{cases} T_b & \text{on } [T_b \le \tau] = [T_b \le \langle L \rangle_t] \\ \langle L \rangle_t & \text{on } [T_b > \tau] = [T_b > \langle L \rangle_t]. \end{cases}$$

Using (2) it follows that

$$W_{\tau \wedge T_b} - \tfrac{1}{2}\tau \wedge T_b = \begin{cases} b + \tfrac{1}{2}T_b & \text{on } [T_b \le \tau] = [T_b \le \langle L \rangle_t] \\ L_t - \tfrac{1}{2}\langle L \rangle_t & \text{on } [T_b > \tau] = [T_b > \langle L \rangle_t]. \end{cases}$$

With the notation $E(X; A) = E(1_A X)$ we can rewrite (4) as

$$E_P\left(exp(b + \tfrac{1}{2}T_b); [T_b \le \langle L \rangle_t]\right) + E_P\left(exp(L_t - \tfrac{1}{2}\langle L \rangle_t); [T_b > \langle L \rangle_t]\right) = 1. \tag{5}$$

Now let $b \downarrow -\infty$. Then $T_b \uparrow \infty$ and so $1_{[T_b > \langle L \rangle_t]} \uparrow 1$, P-as. By Monotone Convergence the second expectation in (5) converges to $E_P\left(exp(L_t - \tfrac{1}{2}\langle L \rangle_t)\right) = E_P(Z_t)$. The first expectation satisfies

$$E_P\left(exp(b + \tfrac{1}{2}T_b); [T_b \le \langle L \rangle_t]\right) \le E_P\left(exp(b + \tfrac{1}{2}\langle L \rangle_t)\right)$$
$$= e^b E_P\left(exp(\tfrac{1}{2}\langle L \rangle_t)\right) \to 0,$$

as $b \downarrow -\infty$ (recall (1)). Thus (5) implies that $E_P(Z_t) = 1$, as desired. ∎

Application to Girsanov's Theorem. It remains to apply this condition to decide when the drift rate process $\gamma(s)$ satisfies the assumption of Girsanov's Theorem 4.c.2. Here we are dealing with the special case of the continuous local martingale $L = \gamma \bullet W$, where W is some d-dimensional Brownian motion. For this local martingale we have

$$\langle L \rangle_t = \int_0^t \|\gamma(s)\|^2 ds,$$

and consequently the Doleans exponential $Z = \mathcal{E}(L)$ assumes the form

$$Z_t := \mathcal{E}_t(L) = exp(L_t - \frac{1}{2}\langle L \rangle_t) = exp\left(\int_0^t \gamma(s) \cdot dB_s - \frac{1}{2}\int_0^t \|\gamma(s)\|^2 ds\right).$$

Thus 4.d.0 specialized to the above local martingale $L = \mathcal{E}(\gamma \cdot W)$ yields

4.d.1 Novikov Condition. *Let W be some d-dimensional Brownian motion and $\gamma \in L(W)$. Then the supermartingale $Z = \mathcal{E}(\gamma \bullet W)$ is a martingale if the following (sufficient) condition is satisfied:*

$$E_P\left[exp\left(\frac{1}{2}\int_0^t \|\gamma(s)\|^2 ds\right)\right] < \infty, \quad \forall t \geq 0. \blacksquare$$

Remark. In the context of a finite time horizon (4.c.1) $Z = \mathcal{E}(\gamma \bullet W)$ has to be a martingale only on the finite interval $[0, T]$. This is ensured by the condition

$$E_P\left[exp\left(\frac{1}{2}\int_0^T \|\gamma(s)\|^2 ds\right)\right] < \infty.$$

The proof in the case of a finite time horizon is similar to the proof of 4.d.0 with some simplifications.

5. REPRESENTATION OF CONTINUOUS LOCAL MARTINGALES

5.a Time change for continuous local martingales. Consider a uniformly integrable martingale $(M_t, \mathcal{F}_t)$ and let $\{\, T(s) \mid s \geq 0 \,\}$ be a nondecreasing family of $(\mathcal{F}_t)$-optional times. Then $\big(M_{T(s)}, \mathcal{F}_{T(s)}\big)$ is a martingale by the Optional Sampling Theorem. The family $\{T(s)\}$ of optional times can be viewed as a stochastic process $T : \Omega \times [0, +\infty) \rightarrow [0, +\infty)$ and as such can be considered to be a stochastic, that is, path dependent time change for the martingale $(M_t, \mathcal{F}_t)$. Conversely a stochastic process $T : \Omega \times [0, +\infty) \rightarrow [0, +\infty)$ can serve as such a time change, if it is nondecreasing and the random variable $T(s)$ is an $(\mathcal{F}_t)$-optional time, for each $s \geq 0$. The nondecreasing nature of T ensures that $\mathcal{F}_{T(s)} \subseteq \mathcal{F}_{T(t)}$, for $s \leq t$, that is, the family $\{\mathcal{F}_{T(s)}\}$ is a filtration on $(\Omega, \mathcal{F}, P)$.

5.a.0. *Let* $T : \Omega \times [0, +\infty) \rightarrow [0, +\infty)$ *be a nondecreasing stochastic process such that* $T(s)$ *is an* $(\mathcal{F}_t)$-*optional time, for each* $s \geq 0$. *If* T *is right continuous, then so is the filtration* $(\mathcal{F}_{T(s)})$.

Proof. We may assume that every path of T is right continuous. Indeed T is indistinguishable from a process $\tilde{T}$ which has this property and then $\tilde{T}(s)$ is again $(\mathcal{F}_t)$-optional and $\mathcal{F}_{T(s)} = \mathcal{F}_{\tilde{T}(s)}$, for each $s \geq 0$, since the filtration $(\mathcal{F}_t)$ is augmented. Now let $s_n \downarrow s \geq 0$. Then $T(s_n) \downarrow T(s)$ and it follows that $\mathcal{F}_{T(s_n)} \downarrow \mathcal{F}_{T(s)}$ (I.7.a.3.(f)). $\blacksquare$

We will now see that for each continuous local martingale M there exists a suitable time change T such that $\big(M_{T(s)}, \mathcal{F}_{T(s)}\big)$ is a Brownian motion W. Moreover the local martingale M can be recovered from W via an inverse time change $S = S(t)$.

Let us try to find such a time change T. Set $Y_s = M_{T(s)}$. Since Y is a Brownian motion, T must satisfy $\langle Y \rangle_s = s$. If M were an $\mathbf{H}^2$-martingale, then $M_t^2 - \langle M \rangle_t$ would be a uniformly integrable martingale and so $Y_s^2 - \langle M \rangle_{T(s)} = M_{T(s)}^2 - \langle M \rangle_{T(s)}$ a martingale, according to the Optional Sampling Theorem. Thus $\langle Y \rangle_s = \langle M \rangle_{T(s)}$ and so T would have to satisfy $\langle M \rangle_{T(s)} = s$. This suggests that we define

$$T(s) = \inf\{\, t \geq 0 \mid \langle M \rangle_t > s \,\}.$$

It will be seen in 5.a.3 below that this definition works in great generality. We need some preparation.

5.a.1. *Let* $f : [0, \infty) \rightarrow [0, \infty)$ *be continuous and nondecreasing with* $f(0) = 0$ *and* $\lim_{t \uparrow \infty} f(t) = \infty$. *Set* $T(s) = \inf\{\, t \geq 0 \mid f(t) > s \,\}$, $s \geq 0$. *Then*
(a) T *is nondecreasing, right continuous and satisfies* $f(T(s)) = s$ *and* $T(f(s)) \geq s$.
(b) *If* $\phi : [0, \infty) \rightarrow R$ *is a continuous function which satisfies*

$$0 \leq a < b, \ f(a) = f(b) \quad \Rightarrow \quad \phi(a) = \phi(b) \tag{0}$$

then $\phi(T(s))$ *is continuous and we have* $\phi(T(f(s))) = \phi(s)$.

Remark. If f is strictly increasing, T is simply the inverse function of f. In general T jumps through intervals of constancy of f, that is, if f is constant on the interval

$[a, b]$, then $T(f(a)) \geq b$. Thus the assumption (0) on the function ϕ is needed (consider the function $\phi(x) = x$).

Proof. (a) Let $0 \leq s < r$ and choose $t_n \downarrow T(r)$ such that $f(t_n) > r$. Then $f(T(r)) = \lim_n f(t_n) \geq r$, by continuity of f. On the other hand, if $f(t) > r$, then $T(r) \leq t$ and so $f(T(r)) \leq f(t)$. Thus $f(T(r)) \leq \inf\{ f(t) \mid f(t) > r \} = r$. It follows that $f(T(r)) = r$.

As $f(t_n) > r > s$ we have $T(s) \leq t_n$ and so $T(s) \leq \inf_n t_n = T(r)$. To show that $T(f(r)) \geq r$ choose $q_n \downarrow T(f(r))$ with $f(q_n) > f(r)$ and so $q_n > r$. It follows that $T(f(r)) = \inf_n q_n \geq r$.

It remains to be shown only that T is right continuous. Assume that $s_n \downarrow s$. Then $T(s_n) \downarrow x = \inf_n T(s_n) \geq T(s)$. We have to show only that $x \leq T(s)$. Choose $t_m \downarrow T(s)$ with $f(t_m) > s$. Fix $m \geq 1$ and choose $n \geq 1$ such that $f(t_m) > s_n$. Then $x \leq T(s_n) \leq t_m$. Letting $m \uparrow \infty$ we conclude that $x \leq T(s)$.

(b) Let $\phi : [0, \infty) \to R$ be a continuous function which satisfies (0). From (a) it follows that $\phi(T(s))$ is right continuous. To show that $\phi(T(s))$ is left continuous, let $0 \leq s_n \uparrow s$ and set $r = \sup_n T(s_n)$. Then $T(s_n) \uparrow r$ and consequently $\phi(T(s_n)) \to \phi(r)$ and we need to show only that $\phi(r) = \phi(T(s))$. According to (0) this will follow from $f(r) = f(T(s))$, i.e., $f(r) = s$.

Since $T(s_n) \uparrow r$, the continuity of f and (a) imply that $s_n = f(T(s_n)) \to f(r)$, that is, $f(r) = \lim_n s_n = s$. This shows the continuity of $\phi(T(s))$. It remains to be verified that $\phi(T(f(s))) = \phi(s)$. Using (0) it suffices to show $f(T(f(s))) = f(s)$ and this in turn follows from $f(T(s)) = s$ upon replacing s with $f(s)$. ∎

5.a.2. *(a) If M is a continuous square integrable martingale with $M_0 = 0$, then $E(M_\tau^2) = E(\langle M \rangle_\tau)$, for each bounded optional time $\tau : \Omega \to [0, \infty)$.*
(b) If M is a continuous local martingale with $M_0 = 0$, then $E(M_\tau^2) \leq E(\langle M \rangle_\tau)$, for each optional time $\tau : \Omega \to [0, \infty)$ satisfying $P(\tau < \infty)$.

Proof. (a) Let M be a continuous square integrable martingale with $M_0 = 0$. Then $N_t = M_t^2 - \langle M \rangle_t$ is a martingale (I.11.b.2.(b)). If τ is any bounded optional time, the Optional Sampling Theorem yields $E(N_\tau) = E(N_0) = 0$, i.e., $E(M_\tau^2) = E(\langle M \rangle_\tau)$, as desired.

(b) Assume now that M is a continuous local martingale with $M_0 = 0$ and let (T_n) be a sequence of optional times such that $T_n \uparrow \infty$, P-as., and $M_t^{T_n} = M_{t \wedge T_n}$ is a square integrable martingale, for each $n \geq 1$ (I.8.a.5, note $M_0 = 0$). If τ is a bounded optional time, then (a) yields

$$E\left[\left(M_\tau^{T_n} \right)^2 \right] = E\left[\langle M^{T_n} \rangle_\tau \right],$$

for all $n \geq 1$. Let $n \uparrow \infty$. Since the quadratic variation $\langle M \rangle$ is an increasing process, we have $0 \leq \langle M^{T_n} \rangle_\tau = \langle M \rangle_\tau^{T_n} = \langle M \rangle_{\tau \wedge T_n} \uparrow \langle M \rangle_\tau$ and so

$$E\left(\langle M^{T_n} \rangle_\tau \right) \uparrow E\left(\langle M \rangle_\tau \right),$$

by monotone convergence. Also $M_\tau^{T_n} \to M_\tau$, P-as., and so, using Fatou's Lemma,

$$E(M_\tau^2) = E\left(\liminf_n \left(M_\tau^{T_n}\right)^2\right) \leq \liminf_n E\left(\left(M_\tau^{T_n}\right)^2\right)$$
$$= \liminf_n E\left(\langle M^{T_n}\rangle_\tau\right) = E\left(\langle M\rangle_\tau\right).$$

This shows (b) for bounded optional times τ. If now $P(\tau < \infty) = 1$, then the above shows that
$$E\left(M_{\tau \wedge n}^2\right) \leq E\left(\langle M\rangle_{\tau \wedge n}\right) \leq E\left(\langle M\rangle_\tau\right), \quad \forall n \geq 1.$$

Letting $n \uparrow \infty$ it follows that $E(M_\tau^2) \leq E(\langle M\rangle_\tau)$ as above. ∎

5.a.3 Theorem. *Let $M = (M_t, \mathcal{F}_t)$ be a continuous local martingale with $M_0 = 0$ and $\langle M\rangle_\infty = \lim_{t\uparrow\infty}\langle M\rangle_t = \infty$, P-as. Set $T(s) = \inf\{t \geq 0 \mid \langle M\rangle_t > s\}$ and $\mathcal{G}_s = \mathcal{F}_{T(s)}$, $s \geq 0$. Then*

(a) Each $T(s)$ is an $(\mathcal{F}_t)$-optional time and the stochastic process $T = T(s,\omega)$ is nondecreasing and right continuous. $(\mathcal{G}_s)$ is a right continuous and augmented filtration. Moreover $\langle M\rangle_t$ is a $(\mathcal{G}_s)$-optional time, for each $t \geq 0$.

(b) The process $W_s = M_{T(s)}$ is a Brownian Motion on $(\Omega, \mathcal{F}, (\mathcal{G}_s), P)$ satisfying $M_t = W_{\langle M\rangle_t}$, for all $t \geq 0$.

Remark. Note that W is a Brownian motion relative to the filtration $(\mathcal{G}_s)$ and not the original filtration $(\mathcal{F}_s)$.

Proof. (a) The definition and nondecreasing property of $\langle M\rangle$ imply $[T(s) < r] = [\langle M\rangle_r > s] \in \mathcal{F}_r$, since the process $\langle M\rangle$ is $(\mathcal{F}_t)$-adapted. Thus $T(s)$ is $(\mathcal{F}_t)$-optional. From 5.a.1 applied to $f(s) = \langle M\rangle_s(\omega)$ it follows that the path $s \mapsto T(s,\omega)$ is nondecreasing and right continuous P-as. 5.a.0 now shows that $(\mathcal{G}_s)$ is a right continuous and augmented filtration.

Recall that $\mathcal{G}_s = \mathcal{F}_{T(s)} = \{A \subseteq \Omega \mid A \cap [T(s) < r] \in \mathcal{F}_r, \forall r \geq 0\}$ and fix $t \geq 0$. To see that the random variable $\langle M\rangle_t : \Omega \to [0,\infty)$ is $(\mathcal{G}_s)$-optional, we have to show that $[\langle M\rangle_t < s] \in \mathcal{G}_s$; equivalently, $A = [\langle M\rangle_t < s] \cap [T(s) < r] \in \mathcal{F}_r$, for each $r \geq 0$. From $[T(s) < r] = [\langle M\rangle_r > s]$ it follows that $A = [\langle M\rangle_t < s] \cap [\langle M\rangle_r > s]$. This set is empty if $t \geq r$ and is in $\mathcal{F}_r$, if $t < r$. This proves (a).

(b) The process $W_s = M_{T(s)}$ is $(\mathcal{G}_s)$-adapted and right continuous (by the continuity of M and the right continuity of T). To see that W is a Brownian motion on $(\Omega, \mathcal{F}, (\mathcal{G}_s), P)$ it will now suffice to show that W is a continuous local martingale which satisfies $\langle W\rangle_t = t$ (3.e.1).

To deal with the continuity of W, fix $\omega \in \Omega$, set $\phi(t) = M_t(\omega)$ and consider the path $s \mapsto W_s(\omega) = M_{T(s)(\omega)}(\omega) = \phi(T(s)(\omega))$. Using 5.a.1 with $f(t) = \langle M\rangle_t(\omega)$, the continuity of the path $s \mapsto W_s(\omega) = \phi(T(s)(\omega))$ will follow if we can show that ϕ satisfies (0) above, that is,

$$0 \leq a < b, \ \langle M\rangle_a(\omega) = \langle M\rangle_b(\omega) \quad \Rightarrow \quad M_a(\omega) = M_b(\omega)$$

with probability one. This has been verified in I.9.b.7. Thus W is a continuous process.

Next we show that W is a square integrable martingale. Fix $r > 0$ and set $N_t = M_{t \wedge T(r)}$, that is, $N = M^{T(r)}$. Then N is a continuous local martingale with respect to the filtration $(\mathcal{F}_t)$ (I.8.a.2.(c)) with $N_0 = M_0 = 0$. Note

$$\langle N \rangle_t = \langle M \rangle_t^{T(r)} = \langle M \rangle_{t \wedge T(r)} \leq r,$$

for all $t \geq 0$, by definition of the optional time $T(r)$. Thus $\langle N \rangle_\infty \leq r$ and in particular this random variable is integrable. According to I.9.c.0 it follows that N and $N_t^2 - \langle N \rangle_t$ are uniformly integrable martingales. Since $\{T(t)\}_{t \in [0,r]}$ is an increasing family of $(\mathcal{F}_t)$-optional times, the Optional Sampling Theorem applied to the uniformly integrable martingale $(N_t, \mathcal{F}_t)$ shows that

$$W_t = M_{T(t)} = M_{T(t) \wedge T(r)} = N_{T(t)}, \quad t \in [0, r],$$

is an $\mathcal{F}_{T(t)} = \mathcal{G}_t$-martingale.

Let $t \in [0, r]$. Then $E(W_t^2) = E\big(N_{T(t)}^2\big) \leq E\big(\langle N \rangle_{T(t)}\big) \leq r < \infty$ (5.a.2.(b)). Thus $(W_t, \mathcal{G}_t)_{t \in [0,r]}$ is a square integrable martingale. Moreover

$$\langle N \rangle_{T(t)} = \big\langle M^{T(r)} \big\rangle_{T(t)} = \langle M \rangle_{T(t)}^{T(r)} = \langle M \rangle_{T(t) \wedge T(r)} = \langle M \rangle_{T(t)} = t,$$

by definition of the optional time $T(t)$. Let $0 \leq s < r$. The Optional Sampling Theorem applied to the uniformly integrable martingale $(N_t^2 - \langle N \rangle_t, \mathcal{F}_t)$ now yields

$$E(W_r^2 - r \mid \mathcal{G}_s) = E\big(N_{T(r)}^2 - r \mid \mathcal{F}_{T(s)}\big) = E\big(N_{T(r)}^2 - \langle N \rangle_{T(r)} \mid \mathcal{F}_{T(s)}\big)$$
$$= N_{T(s)}^2 - \langle N \rangle_{T(s)} = W_s^2 - s.$$

Thus $W_t^2 - t$ is a $\mathcal{G}_t$-martingale and it follows that $\langle W \rangle_t = t$, as desired. ∎

If the condition $\langle M \rangle_\infty = \lim_{t \uparrow \infty} \langle M \rangle_t = \infty$ is not satisfied, the filtered probability space $(\Omega, \mathcal{F}, (\mathcal{F}_t), P)$ has to be enlarged and the representing Brownian motion W based on the enlarged space:

5.a.4 Theorem. *Let $M = (M_t, \mathcal{F}_t)_t$ be a continuous local martingale with $M_0 = 0$. Then there exists a Brownian motion $(W_s, \mathcal{G}_s)$ on an enlargement of the probability space $(\Omega, \mathcal{F}, (\mathcal{F}_t), P)$ such that $\mathcal{G}_{\langle M \rangle_t} \supseteq \mathcal{F}_t$, the quadratic variation $\langle M \rangle_t$ is a $(\mathcal{G}_s)$-optional time and $M_t = W_{\langle M \rangle_t}$, for all $t \geq 0$.*

Proof. see [KS problem 3.4.7, p175]. ∎

5.b Brownian functionals as stochastic integrals. Let $W_t = (W_t^1, \ldots, W_t^d)$ be a d-dimensional Brownian motion on the filtered probability space $(\Omega, \mathcal{F}, (\mathcal{F}_t), P)$. Let $\mathcal{N}$ denote the family of all P-null sets. We shall now assume that

$$\mathcal{F}_t = \mathcal{F}_t^W = \sigma(\mathcal{N} \cup \sigma(W_s; s \le t))$$

is the augmented (and thus right continuous) filtration generated by the Brownian motion W. In particular $\mathcal{F}_\infty = \mathcal{F}_\infty^W = \sigma(\mathcal{N} \cup \sigma(W_s; s \ge 0))$.

A *Brownian functional* is a measurable function $\xi : (\Omega, \mathcal{F}_\infty) \to R$, that is, an $\mathcal{F}_\infty$-measurable real valued function of the Brownian path $\omega \in \Omega$.

Recall from 2.f.5 that $L^2(W)$ denotes the space of all progressively measurable processes H satisfying
$$\|H\|_{L^2(M)}^2 = E_P\left[\int_0^\infty \|H_s\|^2 ds\right] < \infty.$$

If W is a one dimensional Brownian motion, then $L^2(W)$ is the Hilbert space $L^2(\Pi, \mathcal{P}_g, \mu_W)$ and so is complete. The subspace of all predictable processes $H \in L^2(W)$ is the Hilbert space $L^2(\Pi, \mathcal{P}, \mu_W)$ and is thus a closed subspace of $L^2(W)$. This fact remains true for general W since then $L^2(W) = L^2(W^1) \times \ldots \times L^2(W^d)$. Let $H \in L^2(W)$. Then the last element $(H \bullet W)_\infty$ of the martingale $H \bullet W \in \mathbf{H}^2$ satisfies (2.f.3.(b))

$$\left\|(H \bullet W)_\infty\right\|_{L^2(P)}^2 = \|H \bullet W\|_{\mathbf{H}^2}^2 = \|H\|_{L^2(W)}^2 = E_P\left[\int_0^\infty H_s^2 ds\right] < \infty. \quad (0)$$

Thus $\xi_0 = \int_0^\infty H_s \cdot dW_s$ is a Brownian functional which satisfies $\xi_0 \in L^2(\Omega, \mathcal{F}_\infty, P)$ and $E_P(\xi_0) = 0$. We will now see that conversely each square integrable Brownian functional $\xi \in L^2(\Omega, \mathcal{F}_\infty, P)$ can be represented as

$$\xi = E_P(\xi) + \int_0^\infty H_s \cdot dW_s = E_P(\xi) + (H \bullet W)_\infty \quad (1)$$

for some *predictable* process $H \in L^2(W)$. First we exhibit some Brownian functionals which can be so represented:

5.b.0. *Let K be a bounded, left continuous, R^d-valued process and $t \ge 0$. Then the random variable $Z_t = \mathcal{E}_t(K \bullet W)$ can be represented as $Z_t = E_P(Z_t) + (H \bullet W)_\infty$, for some predictable process $H \in L^2(W)$.*

Proof. Choose the constant C such that $\|K\| \le C$. Then

$$\langle K \bullet W \rangle_t = \int_0^t \|K_s\|^2 ds \le Ct$$

and so $Z = \mathcal{E}(K \bullet W)$ is a martingale (4.b.3) satisfying $Z_0 = 1 = E_P(Z_t)$ and $dZ_t = Z_t d(K \bullet W)_t = Z_t K_t \cdot dW_t$, that is, in integral form,

$$Z_t = 1 + \int_0^t Z_s K_s \cdot dW_s = E(Z_t) + \int_0^\infty H_s \cdot dW_s,$$

where $H_s = 1_{[0,t]}(s)Z_s K_s$. Thus we need to verify only that H is a predictable process in $L^2(W)$. The left continuity of K and the continuity of Z imply that H is left continuous and hence predictable (1.a.1.(b)). According to 4.b.3 we have $E_P(Z_t^2) \leq 4e^{Ct}$. Moreover $H_s^2 = 0$, for $s > t$, and $H_s^2 \leq C^2 Z_s^2$ and so $E_P(H_s^2) \leq C^2 E_P(Z_s^2) \leq 4C^2 e^{Cs}$, for all s. An application of Fubini's theorem now yields

$$\|H\|_{L^2(W)}^2 = E_P \int_0^t H_s^2 ds = \int_0^t E_P(H_s^2)ds \leq \int_0^t 4C^2 e^{Cs}ds < \infty.$$

Thus $H \in L^2(W)$. ∎

5.b.1. *Let* $x \in R$, $\lambda = (\lambda_1, \lambda_2, \ldots, \lambda_{nd}) \in R^{nd}$ *and* $0 = t_0 < t_1 < \ldots < t_n$. *Then*

$$exp\left(x \sum_{i=1}^d \sum_{j=1}^n \lambda_{(i-1)n+j}(W_{t_j}^i - W_{t_{j-1}}^i)\right) \in L^p(P), \quad \forall p > 0.$$

Proof. Set $f_x = exp\left(x \sum_{i=1}^d \sum_{j=1}^n \lambda_{(i-1)n+j}(W_{t_j}^i - W_{t_{j-1}}^i)\right)$. Then $f_x^p = f_{px}$, for all $p > 0$. Thus it suffices to show that $f_x \in L^1(P)$, for all $x \in R$. Recall that the coordinate processes W_t^i of W are independent, one dimensional Brownian motions. Thus the increments $W_{t_j}^i - W_{t_{j-1}}^i$, $i = 1, \ldots, d$; $j = 1, \ldots, n$, are independent and it follows that

$$E_P\left[\prod_{i,j} exp\left(x\lambda_{(i-1)n+j}(W_{t_j}^i - W_{t_{j-1}}^i)\right)\right] =$$
$$\prod_{i,j} E_P\left[exp\left(x\lambda_{(i-1)n+j}(W_{t_j}^i - W_{t_{j-1}}^i)\right)\right].$$

As the increments $W_{t_j}^i - W_{t_{j-1}}^i$ are one dimensional normal variables with mean zero, it remains to be shown only that $E_P\left[e^{rN}\right] = \int_R e^{rt} P_N(dt) < \infty$, for each such variable N and all $r \in R$. The verification using the normal density is left to the reader. ∎

To simplify the technical details we conduct the proof of the representation result indicated in (1) first for a one dimensional Brownian motion W:

5.b.2 Theorem. *Let* W *be a one dimensional Brownian motion. If* $\xi \in L^2(\Omega, \mathcal{F}_\infty, P)$ *is a square integrable Brownian functional, then there exists a unique predictable process* $H \in L^2(W)$ *such that*

$$\xi = E_P(\xi) + \int_0^\infty H_s dW_s = E_P(\xi) + (H \bullet W)_\infty.$$

Remark. Uniqueness here means uniqueness as an element of the space $L^2(W)$.

Proof. Uniqueness. If $H, K \in L^2(W)$ satisfy $(H \bullet W)_\infty = \xi - E_P(\xi) = (K \bullet W)_\infty$ then $((H-K) \bullet W)_\infty = 0$ and the isometric property (0) implies $\|H-K\|_{L^2(W)} = 0$

Existence. Let $\mathcal{X}$ denote the family of all random variables $\xi \in L^2(\Omega, \mathcal{F}_\infty, P)$ which can be represented as above. The linearity of the expectation and the stochastic integral imply that $\mathcal{X} \subseteq L^2(\Omega, \mathcal{F}_\infty, P)$ is a subspace. According to 5.b.0 we have $\xi = \mathcal{E}_t(K \bullet W) \in \mathcal{X}$, for each $t \geq 0$ and each bounded, left continuous process K.

Let us show now that the subspace $\mathcal{X} \subseteq L^2(\Omega, \mathcal{F}_\infty, P)$ is closed. Let $(\xi_n) \subseteq \mathcal{X}$, $\xi \in L^2(\Omega, \mathcal{F}_\infty, P)$ and assume $\xi_n \to \xi$. We must show that $\xi \in \mathcal{X}$. Since convergence in L^2 implies convergence of the means, we have $E_P(\xi_n) \to E_P(\xi)$. For each $n \geq 1$ let $H^{(n)} \in L^2(W)$ be a predictable process such that $\xi_n = E_P(\xi_n) + (H^{(n)} \bullet W)_\infty$ and hence $(H^{(n)} \bullet W)_\infty = \xi_n - E_P(\xi_n)$. The isometric property (0) implies that

$$
\begin{aligned}
\left\| H^{(n)} - H^{(m)} \right\|_{L^2(W)} &= \left\| \left((H^{(n)} - H^{(m)}) \bullet W \right)_\infty \right\|_{L^2(P)} \\
&= \left\| (\xi_n - E_P(\xi_n)) - (\xi_m - E_P(\xi_m)) \right\|_{L^2(P)} \\
&\leq \left\| \xi_n - \xi_m \right\|_{L^2(P)} + \left| E_P(\xi_n) - E_P(\xi_m) \right|.
\end{aligned}
$$

Thus $(H^{(n)})$ is a Cauchy sequence and hence convergent in $L^2(W)$. Since the subspace of predictable $H \in L^2(W)$ is closed in $L^2(W)$, there exists a predictable process $H \in L^2(W)$ such that $H^{(n)} \to H$ in $L^2(W)$.

Then $(H^{(n)} \bullet W)_\infty \to (H \bullet W)_\infty$, in $L^2(P)$, by the isometric property (0) on the one hand, and $(H^{(n)} \bullet W)_\infty = \xi_n - E_P(\xi_n) \to \xi - E_P(\xi)$, in $L^2(P)$, on the other hand. It follows that $\xi - E_P(\xi) = (H \bullet W)_\infty$ and consequently $\xi \in \mathcal{X}$, as desired. Thus $\mathcal{X}$ is a closed subspace of $L^2(\Omega, \mathcal{F}_\infty, P)$.

It will now suffice to show that the subspace $\mathcal{X} \subseteq L^2(\Omega, \mathcal{F}_\infty, P)$ is dense, equivalently $\mathcal{X}^\perp = \{ \eta \in L^2(\Omega, \mathcal{F}_\infty, P) \mid E_P(\eta \xi) = 0, \forall \xi \in \mathcal{X} \} = \{0\}$. Let $\eta \in \mathcal{X}^\perp$. Then

$$
E_P \left(\eta \, \mathcal{E}_t(K \bullet W) \right) = 0, \tag{2}
$$

for all bounded, left continuous processes K and $t \geq 0$, since $\xi = \mathcal{E}_t(K \bullet W) \in \mathcal{X}$, for such K and t.

To exploit (2), let $0 = t_0 < t_1 < \ldots < t_n$, $x \in R$ and $\lambda = (\lambda_1, \lambda_2, \ldots, \lambda_n) \in R^n$ be arbitrary and consider the deterministic process $K = \sum_{j=1}^n x \lambda_j 1_{(t_{j-1}, t_j]}$. Clearly K is bounded and left continuous. Fix any real number $t > t_n$. Then $(K \bullet W)_t = x \sum_{j=1}^n \lambda_j (W_{t_j} - W_{t_{j-1}})$ and

$$
\langle K \bullet W \rangle_t = \int_0^t K_s^2 ds = \int_0^{t_n} K_s^2 ds = D,
$$

where D is a constant, since the process K does not depend on $\omega \in \Omega$. It follows that

$$
\begin{aligned}
\mathcal{E}_t(K \bullet W) &= exp \left((K \bullet W)_t - \tfrac{1}{2} \langle K \bullet W \rangle_t \right) \\
&= C \, exp \left(x \sum_{j=1}^n \lambda_j (W_{t_j} - W_{t_{j-1}}) \right), \quad t > t_n,
\end{aligned} \tag{3}
$$

where $C = exp(-\tfrac{1}{2} D)$. Thus (2) implies that

$$
E_P \left[\eta \, exp \left(x \sum_{j=1}^n \lambda_j (W_{t_j} - W_{t_{j-1}}) \right) \right] = 0. \tag{4}
$$

Let Q denote the (signed) measure on $\mathcal{F}_\infty$ defined by $dQ = \eta dP$. Then (4) can be rewritten as

$$E_Q\left[exp\left(x \sum_{j=1}^n \lambda_j (W_{t_j} - W_{t_{j-1}}) \right) \right] = 0. \tag{5}$$

Let Θ be the map $\Theta : \omega \in \Omega \mapsto (W_{t_1}(\omega) - W_{t_0}(\omega), \dots, W_{t_n}(\omega) - W_{t_{n-1}}(\omega)) \in R^n$ and w denote the variable $w = (w_1, \dots, w_n) \in R^n$. Then (5) can be rewritten as

$$0 = \int_\Omega exp\big(x(\lambda \cdot \Theta(\omega))\big) \, Q(d\omega) = \int_{R^n} exp(x(\lambda \cdot w)) \, [\Theta(Q)](dw), \tag{6}$$

where $\Theta(Q)$ denotes the image of the measure Q under the map Θ on R^n. Now the function

$$\phi(z) = \int_{R^n} exp(z(\lambda \cdot w)) \, [\Theta(Q)](dw), \quad z \in C,$$

is easily seen to be an entire function. From the Dominated Convergence Theorem it follows that ϕ is continuous. To get a dominating function, note that 5.b.1 implies that the function $f(w) = exp(x(\lambda \cdot w))$ is in $L^1(\Theta(Q))$, for all $x \in R$. Thus the integrand is bounded by the function $1 \vee exp(r|\lambda \cdot w|) \in L^1(\Theta(Q))$, for all $|z| \leq r$. Using Fubini's Theorem, one then verifies that the line integral of ϕ over all smooth closed curves in the complex plane is zero. Thus ϕ is analytic in the plane.

According to (6), ϕ vanishes on the real line and thus must vanish everywhere. In particular for $z = i$ we obtain

$$\widehat{\Theta(Q)}(\lambda) = \int_\Omega exp(i(\lambda \cdot w)) \, [\Theta(Q)](dw) = 0,$$

where $\widehat{\Theta(Q)}$ denotes the Fourier transform of the measure $\Theta(Q)$ on R^n. Since $\lambda \in R^n$ was arbitrary, it follows that $\Theta(Q) = 0$. This in turn implies that Q vanishes on the σ-field

$$\sigma\big(W_{t_1} - W_{t_0}, \dots, W_{t_n} - W_{t_{n-1}}\big) = \sigma\big(W_{t_1}, W_{t_2} - W_{t_1}, \dots, W_{t_n} - W_{t_{n-1}}\big)$$
$$= \sigma\big(W_{t_1}, W_{t_2}, \dots, W_{t_n}\big).$$

Recall that $\mathcal{N}$ denotes the family all P-null sets. Then Q vanishes on $\mathcal{N}$. Thus Q vanishes on the union of $\mathcal{N}$ and the σ-fields $\sigma\big(W_{t_1}, W_{t_2}, \dots, W_{t_n}\big)$ which is a π-system generating the domain $\mathcal{F}_\infty$ of Q. The usual application of the π-λ-theorem (appendix B.3) now shows that $Q = 0$. From $dQ = \eta dP$ we now conclude that $\eta = 0$, P-as., as desired. ∎

Let us now turn to the multidimensional case and indicate the necessary changes in the proof:

5.b.3 Theorem. *If* $\xi \in L^2(\Omega, \mathcal{F}_\infty, P)$ *then there exists a unique predictable process* $H \in L^2(W)$ *such that*

$$\xi = E_P(\xi) + \int_0^\infty H_s \cdot dW_s = E_P(\xi) + (H \bullet W)_\infty. \tag{7}$$

Proof. Uniqueness. As in the proof of 5.b.2. *Existence.* Let $\mathcal{X}$ be the space of all $\xi \in L^2(\Omega, \mathcal{F}_\infty, P)$ which can be represented as in (8). As in the proof of 5.b.2 we see that $\mathcal{X}$ is a closed subspace of $L^2(\Omega, \mathcal{F}_\infty, P)$ which contains all the random variables $\xi = \mathcal{E}_t(K \bullet W)$, where $t \geq 0$ and K is a bounded, left continuous, R^d-valued process. It remains to be shown that $\mathcal{X}$ is dense in $L^2(\Omega, \mathcal{F}_\infty, P)$, that is, $\mathcal{X}^\perp = \{0\}$. Let $\eta \in \mathcal{X}^\perp$. Then

$$E_P\left[\eta \mathcal{E}_t(K \bullet W)\right] = 0, \tag{8}$$

for all bounded, left continuous, R^d-valued processes K and $t \geq 0$. We must show that $\eta = 0$, P-as., and introduce the measure Q on $\mathcal{F}_\infty$ by means of $dQ = \eta dP$. It will then suffice to show that Q vanishes on $\mathcal{F}_\infty$. Since the union of the P-null sets and the σ-fields

$$
\begin{aligned}
\mathcal{F}_{t_1 t_2 \ldots t_n} &= \sigma(W^1_{t_1}, \ldots, W^1_{t_n}, W^2_{t_1}, \ldots, W^2_{t_n}, \ldots, W^d_{t_1}, \ldots, W^d_{t_n}) \\
&= \sigma(W^1_{t_1} - W^1_{t_0}, \ldots, W^1_{t_n} - W^1_{t_{n-1}}, \ldots, W^d_{t_1} - W^d_{t_0}, \ldots, W^d_{t_n} - W^d_{t_{n-1}})
\end{aligned}
$$

(note $W_{t_0} = 0$), where $0 = t_0 < t_1 < \ldots < t_n$, is a π-system generating the σ-field $\mathcal{F}_\infty$, it will suffice to show that $Q|\mathcal{F}_{t_1 t_2 \ldots t_n} = 0$, for all sequences of real numbers $0 = t_0 < \ldots < t_n$. Fix such a sequence of real numbers and consider the random vector $\Theta : \Omega \to R^{nd}$ defined by

$$\Theta = \left(W^1_{t_1} - W^1_{t_0}, \ldots, W^1_{t_n} - W^1_{t_{n-1}}, \ldots, W^d_{t_1} - W^d_{t_0}, \ldots, W^d_{t_n} - W^d_{t_{n-1}}\right).$$

To see that Q vanishes on $\mathcal{F}_{t_1 t_2 \ldots t_n} = \sigma(\Theta)$, it will suffice to show that the image measure $\Theta(Q)$ vanishes on R^{nd}. To see this, we show that the Fourier transform

$$\widehat{\Theta(Q)}(\lambda) = \int_{R^{nd}} exp(i(\lambda \cdot w))\Theta(Q)(dw) = 0, \quad \text{for all } \lambda \in R^{nd}.$$

From (8) and the definition of Q we have

$$E_Q\left[\mathcal{E}_t(K \bullet W)\right] = 0, \tag{9}$$

for all bounded, left continuous, R^d-valued processes K and $t \geq 0$. Fix $x \in R$, $\lambda \in R^{nd}$ and consider the deterministic, bounded, left continuous process $K = (K^1, K^2, \ldots, K^d)$ defined by

$$K^i = \sum_{j=1}^n x\lambda_{(i-1)n+j} 1_{(t_{j-1}, t_j]}, \quad i = 1, \ldots, d.$$

A computation similar to the one in the proof of 5.b.2 now shows that

$$\mathcal{E}_t(K \bullet W) = C \, exp\left(x \sum_{i=1}^d \sum_{j=1}^n \lambda_{(i-1)n+j}\left(W^i_{t_j} - W^i_{t_{j-1}}\right)\right), \quad t > t_n, \tag{10}$$

for some constant C. From (9) and (10) we conclude

$$
\begin{aligned}
\int_{R^{nd}} exp(x(\lambda \cdot w))\left[\Theta(Q)\right](dw) &= \int_\Omega exp(x(\lambda \cdot \Theta(\omega)))q(d\omega) \\
&= E_Q\left[exp\left(x \sum_{i=1}^d \sum_{j=1}^n \lambda_{(i-1)n+j}\left(W^i_{t_j} - W^i_{t_{j-1}}\right)\right)\right] = 0. \quad \blacksquare
\end{aligned}
$$

5.c Integral representation of square integrable Brownian martingales. Let $W_t = (W_t^1, \ldots, W_t^d)$ be a d-dimensional Brownian motion on the filtered probability space $(\Omega, \mathcal{F}, (\mathcal{F}_t), P)$ and assume that $\mathcal{F}_t = \mathcal{F}_t^W$ is the augmented (and thus right continuous) filtration generated by the Brownian motion W. In consequence an adapted process is now adapted to the Brownian filtration $(\mathcal{F}_t^W)$. To stress this point a (local) martingale adapted to the Brownian filtration $(\mathcal{F}_t^W)$ will be called a *Brownian (local) martingale*.

Let us recall that $L^2(W)$ is the space of all progressively measurable processes H which satisfy

$$\|H\|_{L^2(W)}^2 = E_P \int_0^\infty \|H_s\|^2 ds < \infty.$$

If $H \in L^2(W)$, then $H \bullet W \in \mathbf{H}_0^2$ and the map $H \in L^2(W) \mapsto H \bullet W \in \mathbf{H}^2$ is an isometry and so $\|(H \bullet W)_\infty\|_{L^2(P)} = \|H \bullet W\|_{\mathbf{H}^2} = \|H\|_{L^2(W)}$.

The space $\Lambda^2(W)$ consists of all progressively measurable processes H satisfying $1_{[0,t]}H \in L^2(W)$, for all $t \geq 0$. If $H \in \Lambda^2(W)$, then $H \bullet W$ is a square integrable Brownian martingale satisfying $(H \bullet W)_t = \left((1_{[0,t]}H) \bullet W\right)_\infty$ (see 2.f.0.(d)) and so

$$\|(H \bullet W)_t\|_{L^2(P)} = \|1_{[0,t]}H\|_{L^2(W)}, \quad \forall t \geq 0. \tag{0}$$

Finally $L(W) = L_{loc}^2(W)$ consists of all progressively measurable processes H such that $1_{[0,\tau_n]}H \in L^2(W)$, for some sequence of optional times (τ_n) satisfying $\tau_n \uparrow \infty$, P-as., as $n \uparrow \infty$ (2.f.5). We have $L^2(W) \subseteq \Lambda^2(W) \subseteq L(W)$. In each of these spaces two processes H, K are identified if they satisfy $E_P \int_0^\infty \|H_s - K_s\|^2 ds = 0$; equivalently, if $H(s, \omega) = K(s, \omega)$, for $\lambda \times P$-ae. $(s, \omega) \in R_+ \times \Omega$, where λ denotes Lebesgue measure on R_+.

If $H \in \Lambda^2(W)$, then $H \bullet W$ is a square integrable Brownian martingale. We shall now prove that conversely each square integrable Brownian martingale M can be represented as $M = H \bullet W$, for some *predictable* process $H \in \Lambda^2(W)$. According to I.7.b.3 the martingale M has a right continuous version and we will therefore assume that M itself is right continuous. Let us now gather some auxiliary facts.

5.c.0. *Let $H \in L^2(W)$, $n \geq 1$ and $\xi = (H \bullet W)_\infty$. Then $E(\xi|\mathcal{F}_t) = (H \bullet W)_t$, for all $t \geq 0$.*

Proof. Simply because $\xi = (H \cdot W)_\infty$ is by definition the last element of the $\mathbf{H}^2$-martingale $H \bullet W$ (2.f.3). ∎

5.c.1. *Let τ_n be a sequence of optional times such that $\tau_n \uparrow \infty$, P-as., as $n \uparrow \infty$, and $H^{(n)} \in L^2(W)$, $n \geq 1$, a sequence of predictable processes such that*

$$1_{[0,\tau_n]}H^{(n)} = 1_{[0,\tau_n]}H^{(n+1)} \text{ in } L^2(W), \quad n \geq 1. \tag{1}$$

Then there exists a unique predictable process $H \in L(W)$ such that $1_{[0,\tau_n]}H = 1_{[0,\tau_n]}H^{(n)}$ in $L^2(W)$, for all $n \geq 1$. If the τ_n are nonstochastic (constant) times, then $H \in \Lambda^2(W)$.

Remark. Uniqueness here means uniqueness as an element of $L(W)$, that is, uniqueness pointwise, $\lambda \times P$-as. on the set $\Pi = R_+ \times \Omega$.

Proof. Choose a P-null set $A \subseteq \Omega$ such that $\tau_n(\omega) \uparrow \infty$, as $n \uparrow \infty$, for all $\omega \in A^c$. Then $A \in \mathcal{F}_0$ and consequently the set $N_0 = [0, \infty) \times A \subseteq \Pi = R_+ \times \Omega$ is predictable. It is obviously a $\lambda \times P$-null set.

From (1) it follows that $H^{(n+1)} = H^{(n)}$, $\lambda \times P$-as. on the set $[\![0, \tau_n]\!] \subseteq \Pi$. Consequently there exists a predictable $\lambda \times P$-null set $N_1 \subseteq \Pi$ such that $H_s^{(n)}(\omega) = H_s^{(n+1)}(\omega)$, for all $(s, \omega) \in N_1^c$ with $s \leq \tau_n(\omega)$ and all $n \geq 1$. Let $N = N_0 \cup N_1$. Then N is a predictable $\lambda \times P$-null set. Cutting everything off to zero outside N, we can define the process H as follows:

$$H = 1_{N^c} H^{(n)} \text{ on } [\![0, \tau_n]\!].$$

If $(t, \omega) \in N^c$, we have $\tau_n(\omega) \uparrow \infty$, as $n \uparrow \infty$, and $H_t^{(n)}(\omega) = H_t(\omega)$, whenever $\tau_n(\omega) \geq t$, especially $H_t^{(n)}(\omega) \to H_t(\omega)$, as $n \uparrow \infty$. Thus $1_{N^c} H^{(n)} \to H$, pointwise on all of Π, and it follows that the process H is predictable.

Note that $H = H^{(n)}$, $\lambda \times P$-as. on the stochastic interval $[\![0, \tau_n]\!]$ and so $1_{[\![0, \tau_n]\!]} H = 1_{[\![0, \tau_n]\!]} H^{(n)} \in L^2(W)$, for all $n \geq 1$. Thus $H \in L(W)$ (2.f.5). $\blacksquare$

5.c.2. *(a) Let $H, K \in L(W)$. If $H \bullet W = K \bullet W$, then $H = K$ in $L(W)$.*
(b) If $H, K \in L^2(W)$ and $(H \bullet W)_\infty = (K \bullet W)_\infty$, then $H = K$ in $L^2(W)$.

Proof. (a) By linearity it will suffice to show that $H \bullet W = 0$ implies that $H = 0$ in $L(W)$. Assume $H \bullet W = 0$. Then $0 = \langle H \bullet W \rangle_t = \int_0^t \|H_s\|^2 ds$, P-as., for all $t \geq 0$. Thus $E_P \int_0^\infty \|H_s\|^2 ds = 0$, that is, $H = 0$ in $L(W)$.

(b) This follows from $\|((H - K) \bullet W)_\infty\|_{L^2(P)} = \|H - K\|_{L^2(W)}$. $\blacksquare$

5.c.3 Theorem. *Let M be a square integrable Brownian martingale with $M_0 = 0$. Then there exists a unique predictable process $H \in \Lambda^2(W)$ such that $M = H \bullet W$, that is, $M_t = \int_0^t H_s \cdot dW_s$, P-as., for all $t \geq 0$. The process H is in $L^2(W)$ if and only if M is L^2-bounded, that is, $M \in \mathbf{H}^2$.*

Proof. The uniqueness of H follows immediately from 5.c.2 if we observe that identification of processes in $L(W)$ and $\Lambda^2(W) \subseteq L(W)$ is the same.

Existence. Let $n \geq 1$ and note that $E(M_n) = E(M_0) = 0$. Then $M_n \in L^2(\Omega, \mathcal{F}_n, P)$ and according to 5.b.3 there exists a predictable process $H^{(n)} \in L^2(W)$ such that $M_n = (H^{(n)} \bullet W)_\infty$. The martingale property of M and 5.c.0 imply that

$$M_t = E(M_n | \mathcal{F}_t) = (H^{(n)} \bullet W)_t = \left(1_{[0,t]} H^{(n)} \bullet W\right)_\infty, \quad \forall 0 \leq t \leq n,$$

and so $\quad \left(1_{[0,n]} H^{(n)} \bullet W\right)_\infty = M_n = \left(1_{[0,n]} H^{(n+1)} \bullet W\right)_\infty, \quad \forall n \geq 1.$
The isometric property (0) now shows that $1_{[0,n]} H^{(n)} = 1_{[0,n]} H^{(n+1)}$ in $L^2(W)$. Thus there exists $H \in \Lambda^2(W)$ such that $1_{[0,n]} H = 1_{[0,n]} H^{(n)}$, for all $n \geq 1$ (5.c.1), and so
$$M_t = (H \bullet W)_t, \quad \forall t \geq 0.$$

If $H \in L^2(W)$ then $M = H \bullet W \in \mathbf{H}^2$. Conversely, $M = H \bullet W \in \mathbf{H}^2$ and (0) imply $\|H\|_{L^2(W)} = \sup_{t \geq 0} \|1_{[0,t]} H\|_{L^2(W)} = \sup_{t \geq 0} \|(H \bullet W)_t\|_{L^2(P)} = \|H \bullet W\|_{\mathbf{H}^2} = \|M\|_{\mathbf{H}^2} < \infty$ (see (0)). Thus $H \in L^2(W)$. $\blacksquare$

Remark. Thus the map $H \mapsto H \bullet W$ identifies the space $\Lambda^2(W)$ with the space of all $(\mathcal{F}_t^W)$-adapted, square integrable martingales vanishing at zero. The restriction of this map to $L^2(W)$ is an isometric isomorphism of $L^2(W)$ with $\mathbf{H}_0^2$.

5.c.4 Corollary. *Each Brownian local martingale M has a continuous version.*

Proof. (a) Assume first that M is a square integrable martingale. Then there exists a process $H \in \Lambda^2(W)$ such that $M_t = (H \bullet W)_t$, P-as., for all $t \geq 0$. Thus the process $H \bullet W$ is a continuous version of M.

(b) Assume now that M is a martingale and fix $T > 0$. According to I.7.b.3 M has a right continuous version and we may therefore assume that M itself is right continuous. It will now suffice to show that the restriction of M to the interval $[0, T]$ is in fact continuous. Choose a sequence of square integrable random variables $M_T^{(n)}$ such that $E_P|M_T^{(n)} - M_T| < 2^{-n}$, for all $n \geq 1$. Then $L_t^{(n)} = E_P(M_T^{(n)}|\mathcal{F}_t)$, $t \in [0, T]$, is a square integrable Brownian martingale (Jensen's inequality) and hence has a continuous version $M_t^{(n)}$. Applying the maximal inequality I.7.e.1.(a) to the right continuous martingale $X_t = M_t^{(n)} - M_t$ we obtain

$$P\left(\sup_{t \in [0,T]}|M_t^{(n)} - M_t| \geq 1/n\right) \leq nE_P\left(|M_T^{(n)} - M_T|\right) \leq n2^{-n},$$

for all $n \geq 1$. Since the sum of these probabilities converges, the Borel Cantelli lemma yields $P\left(\sup_{t \in [0,T]}|M_t^{(n)} - M_t| \geq 1/n \text{ io.}\right) = 0$, and so

$$\sup_{t \in [0,T]}|M_t^{(n)} - M_t| \to 0, \quad P\text{-as., as } n \uparrow \infty.$$

Thus the sequence $(M^{(n)})$ of continuous martingales converges P-as. pathwise uniformly on $[0, T]$ to the martingale M. It follows that M is continuous on $[0, T]$.

(c) Finally, let M be a Brownian local martingale and (T_n) a reducing sequence of optional times. Then $T_n \uparrow \infty$, P-as., as $n \uparrow \infty$ and M^{T_n} is a Brownian martingale and hence has a continuous version $K^{(n)}$, for each $n \geq 1$. It follows that

$$K_t^{(n)} = M_{t \wedge T_n} = M_{t \wedge T_{n+1}} = K_t^{(n+1)}, \quad P\text{-as. on the set } [t \leq T_n]. \qquad (2)$$

By continuity of the $K^{(n)}$ the exceptional null set here can be made independent of t and n and we can thus choose a null set $N \subseteq \Omega$ such that $T_n(\omega) \uparrow \infty$, as $n \uparrow \infty$ and $K_t^{(n)}(\omega) = K_t^{(n+1)}(\omega)$, for all $n \geq 1$, $t \geq 0$ and all $\omega \in [t \leq T_n] \cap N^c$. In other words $K_t^{(n)} = K_t^{(n+1)}$ on the set $[\![0, T_n]\!] \cap (R_+ \times N^c)$. We can thus define the process L as

$$L = 1_{N^c} K^{(n)} \text{ on } [\![0, T_n]\!], \; n \geq 1.$$

Then L has continuous paths. Let $t \geq 0$. Then $L_t = K_t^{(n)} = M_{t \wedge T_n} = M_t$, P-as. on the set $[t \leq T_n]$, for all $n \geq 1$. Since the union of these sets is the complement of a null set it follows that $L_t = M_t$, P-as., and hence L is a version of M. $\blacksquare$

Remark. The proof of (b) shows that a right continuous Brownian martingale is itself continuous.

5.d Integral representation of Brownian local martingales. We now turn to an analogue of 5.c.3 for Brownian local martingales, that is, local martingales adapted to the Brownian filtration. Let $W_t = (W_t^1, \ldots, W_t^d)$ be a d-dimensional Brownian motion on the filtered probability space $(\Omega, \mathcal{F}, (\mathcal{F}_t), P)$ and assume that $\mathcal{F}_t = F_t^W$ is the augmented (and thus right continuous) filtration generated by the Brownian motion W as above.

5.d.0 Theorem. *Let M_t be a Brownian local martingale with $M_0 = 0$. Then there exists a unique predictable process $H \in L(W)$ such that $M = H \bullet W$, that is,*

$$M_t = \int_0^t H_s \cdot dB_s, \quad P\text{-}as., \quad t \geq 0. \tag{0}$$

Proof. The uniqueness of H as an element of $L(W)$ follows immediately from 5.c.2. *Existence.* According to 5.c.4, M has a continuous version and we may therefore assume that M is itself continuous. We can thus find a sequence (τ_n) of optional times such that $\tau_n \uparrow \infty$ and $M(n) = M^{\tau_n}$ is a uniformly bounded martingale and hence a martingale in $\mathbf{H}^2$, for each $n \geq 1$ (I.8.a.5, note $M_0 = 0$).

Fix $n \geq 1$ and note that $M(n)_t = M_{t \wedge \tau_n}$. Applying the representation theorem 5.c.3 we can find a predictable process $H^{(n)} \in L^2(W)$ such that

$$M(n) = H^{(n)} \bullet W.$$

Using 2.c.0.(d) as well as $M(n) = M(n)^{\tau_n} = M(n+1)^{\tau_n}$ we can now write

$$\begin{aligned} \left(1_{[\![0,\tau_n]\!]} H^{(n)}\right) \bullet W = \left(H^{(n)} \bullet W\right)^{\tau_n} &= M(n)^{\tau_n} = M(n) \\ &= M(n+1)^{\tau_n} = \left(1_{[\![0,\tau_n]\!]} H^{(n+1)}\right) \bullet W. \end{aligned} \tag{1}$$

The isometric property of the map $H \in L^2(W) \mapsto H \bullet W \in \mathbf{H}^2$ now shows that we have $1_{[\![0,\tau_n]\!]} H^{(n)} = 1_{[\![0,\tau_n]\!]} H^{(n+1)}$ in $L^2(W)$, for all $n \geq 1$. According to 5.c.1 there exists a predictable process $H \in L(W)$ such that

$$1_{[\![0,\tau_n]\!]} H = 1_{[\![0,\tau_n]\!]} H^{(n)} \quad \text{in } L^2(W),$$

for all $n \geq 1$. From (1) and 2.c.0.(d) we now have

$$M^{\tau_n} = M(n) = \left(1_{[\![0,\tau_n]\!]} H^{(n)}\right) \bullet W = \left(1_{[\![0,\tau_n]\!]} H\right) \bullet W = (H \bullet W)^{\tau_n}.$$

Letting $n \uparrow \infty$ it follows that $M = H \bullet W$. ∎

Let us note the following interesting consequence:

5.d.1. *Let $K \in L(W)$ be any progressively measurable process. Then there exists a predictable process $H \in L(W)$ such that $K = H$ in $L(W)$, that is,*

$$K = H, \quad \lambda \times P\text{-}as. \text{ on the set } \Pi = R_+ \times \Omega.$$

Proof. Simply represent the Brownian local martingale $M = K \bullet W$ as in 5.d.0 and then use the uniqueness result 5.c.2. ∎

5.e Representation of positive Brownian martingales. We continue with the assumptions of sections 5.c, 5.d. Let us call a martingale M *positive* if it satisfies $M_t > 0$, P-as., for every $t \geq 0$.

5.e.0. *Let* $\gamma \in L(W)$ *and* $M \in \mathcal{S}$. *Then the equality* $M = \mathcal{E}(\gamma \bullet W)$ *is equivalent with* $M_0 = 1$ *and* $dM_t = M_t \gamma_t \cdot dW_t$.

Proof. See 4.b.2. ∎

5.e.1. *A positive Brownian martingale* M *can be represented in the form*

$$M_t = \mathcal{E}_t(\gamma \bullet W) = exp\left(\int_0^t \gamma_s \cdot dW_s - \frac{1}{2} \int_0^t \|\gamma_s\|^2 ds \right), \quad t \geq 0,$$

for some predictable, R^d-*valued process* $\gamma \in L(W)$.

Proof. According to 5.c.4, M has a continuous version and we may therefore assume that M is itself continuous. According to 5.e.0 it will suffice to find a process $\gamma \in L(W)$ satisfying $dM_t = M_t \gamma_t \cdot dW_t$. Using 5.d.0 we can write $M_t = \int_0^t H_s \cdot dW_s$, $t \geq 0$, for some predictable process $H \in L(W)$. Then

$$\int_0^t \|H_s\|^2 ds < \infty, \quad P\text{-as.}, \quad \forall t \geq 0, \tag{0}$$

and $dM_t = H_t \cdot dW_t = M_t \gamma_t \cdot dW_t$, where $\gamma_t = M_t^{-1} H_t$. It remains to be shown only that γ is a predictable process in $L(W)$. Since M is continuous it is predictable. Since H is also predictable, it follows that γ is predictable. Thus it remains to be shown only that

$$\int_0^t \|\gamma_s\|^2 ds < \infty, \quad P\text{-as.}, \quad \forall t \geq 0.$$

This follows immediately from (1) and the fact that the positive and continuous paths $s \in [0, t] \mapsto M_s(\omega)$ are bounded away from zero, P-as. on Ω. ∎

5.f Kunita-Watanabe decomposition. The representation results above assume that the local martingale to be represented is adapted to the augmented filtration generated by the representing Brownian motion. If this is not the case, we still have a decomposition result. We shall thus no longer assume that our filtration $(\mathcal{F}_t)$ is the augmented filtration generated by some Brownian motion W.

Let us call two continuous local martingales M, N *orthogonal* $(M \perp N)$ iff the covariation process $\langle M, N \rangle$ is identically zero, that is, iff the product MN is a local martingale.

If M and N are square integrable martingales, then $M_t N_t - \langle M, N \rangle_t$ is a martingale (I.11.b.2). Thus $M \perp N$ if and only if the product MN is a martingale.

Assume now that $M_0 = 0$ or $N_0 = 0$, that is, $M_0 N_0 = 0$. If τ is a bounded optional time and $T > 0$ a number such that $\tau \leq T$, then $M_\tau = E_P[M_T | \mathcal{F}_\tau]$. Since all conditional expectation operators are contractions on $L^2(P)$ (I.2.b.15) it follows that $M_\tau \in L^2(P)$. Likewise $N_\tau \in L^2(P)$ and consequently $M_\tau N_\tau \in L^1(P)$. According to I.9.c.4, $M_t N_t$ is a martingale if and only if $E_P[M_\tau N_\tau] = E_P[M_0 N_0] = 0$, that is, $M_\tau \perp N_\tau$ in $L^2(P)$, for all bounded optional times τ:

5.f.0. *Let M, N be continuous, square integrable martingales with $M_0 N_0 = 0$. Then $M \perp N$ if and only if $M_\tau \perp N_\tau$ in $L^2(P)$, for all bounded optional times τ.* ∎

In particular $M \perp N$ implies that $M_t \perp N_t$ in $L^2(P)$, for all $t \geq 0$. If $M, N \in \mathbf{H}^2$ are L^2-bounded martingales, this implies $M_\infty \perp N_\infty$ in $L^2(P)$, that is, $M \perp N$ in $\mathbf{H}^2$, since $M_t \to M_\infty$ and $N_t \to N_\infty$ in $L^2(P)$, as $t \uparrow \infty$ (square integrability of the maximal function of an $\mathbf{H}^2$-martingale and Dominated Convergence Theorem). Thus our notion of orthogonality of continuous local martingales M, N is stronger than orthogonality in $\mathbf{H}_0^2$, when specialized to martingales $M, N \in \mathbf{H}_0^2$.

Let W be an R^d-valued Brownian motion. Recall that $L^2(W)$ is a Hilbert space of progressively measurable, R^d-valued processes H, the subspace of all predictable processes $H \in L^2(W)$ is closed, the map

$$H \in L^2(W) \mapsto (H \bullet W)_\infty \in L^2(P) \tag{0}$$

is an isometry and $\Lambda^2(W)$ is the space of all progressively measurable, R^d-valued processes H such that $1_{[0,t]} H \in L^2(W)$, for all $t > 0$. If $H \in \Lambda^2(W)$ and $t > 0$, then $(H \bullet W)_t = \left(1_{[0,t]} H \bullet W \right)_\infty$, and so, using the isometry (0),

$$\left\| (H \bullet W)_t \right\|^2_{L^2(P)} = \left\| 1_{[0,t]} H \right\|^2_{L^2(W)} = E_P \int_0^t \left\| H_s \right\|^2 ds.$$

Fix $T > 0$ and set

$$\mathcal{I}_T(W) = \left\{ (H \bullet W)_T \mid H \in \Lambda^2(W) \text{ is predictable} \right\} \subseteq L^2(P).$$

If $H \in \Lambda^2(W)$ then $(H \bullet W)_T = (\tilde{H} \bullet W)_\infty$, where $\tilde{H} = 1_{[0,T]} H \in L^2(W)$ (2.f.0.(d)) satisfies $1_{[0,T]} \tilde{H} = \tilde{H}$. It follows that $\mathcal{I}_T(W)$ is the image under the isometry (0) of the subspace $L_T^2(W) = \left\{ H \in L^2(W) \mid H = 1_{[0,T]} H \right\} \subseteq L^2(W)$. As $L_T^2(W) \subseteq L^2(W)$ is a closed subspace ($H = 1_{[0,T]} H$ is equivalent with $1_{(T,\infty)} H = 0$) it follows that the subspace $\mathcal{I}_T(W) \subseteq L^2(P)$ is closed also. Letting

$$\mathcal{I}(W) = \left\{ H \bullet W \mid H \in \Lambda^2(W) \text{ is predictable} \right\}$$

we have $\mathcal{I}_T(W) = \left\{ I_T \mid I \in \mathcal{I}(W) \right\}$. Each integral process $I \in \mathcal{I}(W)$ is a continuous square integrable martingale vanishing at zero. If the underlying filtration $(\mathcal{F}_t)$ is the augmented filtration generated by the Brownian motion W, then it follows from 5.c.3 that conversely every continuous, square integrable martingale vanishing at zero is in $\mathcal{I}(W)$. In general we have the following decomposition result:

5.f.1. *Every continuous, square integrable martingale M has a unique decomposition $M = H \bullet W + Z$, where $H \in \Lambda^2(W)$ is predictable and Z is a square integrable martingale which is orthogonal to every martingale in $\mathcal{I}(W)$. If $M \in \mathbf{H}^2$, then $H \in L^2(W)$, $Z \in \mathbf{H}^2$ and $\|M\|_{\mathbf{H}^2}^2 = \|H\|_{L^2(W)}^2 + \|Z\|_{\mathbf{H}^2}^2$.*

Remark. Uniqueness of the decomposition here means that the process H is uniquely determined as an element of $\Lambda^2(W)$ and Z is unique up to indistinguishability.

Proof. Let M be a continuous, square integrable martingale.
Uniqueness. Assume that $H \bullet W + Z = M = K \bullet W + X$, where $H, K \in \Lambda^2(W)$ are predictable and Z, X continuous, square integrable martingales orthogonal to each martingale in $\mathcal{I}(W)$. Then $Z_0 = X_0 = M_0$ and hence $Z_0 - X_0 = 0$. Moreover the martingale $(H - K) \bullet W = Z - X$ is orthogonal to itself, i.e., $\langle Z - X \rangle = 0$. From this it follows that $Z - X$ is constant in time and so $Z - X = 0$. Thus $H \bullet W = K \bullet W$ and consequently $H = K$ in $\Lambda^2(W)$ (5.c.2).
Existence. It will suffice to establish the decomposition $M_t = (H \bullet W)_t + Z_t$, $t \in [0, T]$, for each finite time horizon $T > 0$. The independence of H and Z of T then follows from 5.c.1 and the uniqueness above.

Fix $T > 0$. Then $M_T \in L^2(P)$ and since $\mathcal{I}_T(W) \subseteq L^2(P)$ is a closed subspace, we have a decomposition
$$M_T = (H \bullet W)_T + Z_T, \tag{1}$$

where $H \in \Lambda^2(W)$ and $Z_T \perp \mathcal{I}_T(W)$. Now set $Z_t = E(Z_T | \mathcal{F}_t)$, $t \in [0, T]$. Since M, $H \bullet W$ and Z are all martingales on $[0, T]$, (1) implies that

$$M_t = (H \bullet W)_t + Z_t, \quad t \in [0, T].$$

The continuity of the martingale Z now follows from the continuity of M and $H \bullet W$. The square integrability of Z_T implies the square integrability of the martingale Z on $[0, T]$ (I.2.b.15). Thus it remains to be shown only that $Z \perp \mathcal{I}(W)$ on $[0, T]$. Let $K \in \Lambda^2(W)$. We must show that $Z \perp K \bullet W$ on $[0, T]$, equivalently (5.f.0)

$$E_P[Z_\tau (K \bullet W)_\tau] = 0,$$

for all optional times $\tau \leq T$. Consider such an optional time τ. Since conditional expectation operators are contractions on $L^2(P)$ we have $Z_\tau = E(Z_T | \mathcal{F}_\tau) \in L^2(P)$ and likewise $(K \bullet W)_\tau \in L^2(P)$ and so $Z_\tau (K \bullet W)_\tau \in L^1(P)$. Set $\tilde{K} = 1_{[0,\tau]} K \in L^2(W)$. Then

$$(K \bullet W)_\tau = (\tilde{K} \bullet W)_T \in \mathcal{I}_T(W)$$

(2.c.0.(d)). Note that $Z_\tau = E_P(Z_T | \mathcal{F}_\tau)$ and the $\mathcal{F}_\tau$-measurable, square integrable factor $(K \bullet W)_\tau$ satisfies $E_P[Z_T | \mathcal{F}_\tau](K \bullet W)_\tau = E_P[Z_T (K \bullet W)_\tau | \mathcal{F}_\tau]$ (I.2.b.10). It follows that

$$E_P[Z_\tau (K \bullet W)_\tau] = E_P[E_P[Z_T | \mathcal{F}_\tau](K \bullet W)_\tau] = E_P[E_P[Z_T (K \bullet W)_\tau | \mathcal{F}_\tau]]$$
$$= E_P[Z_T (K \bullet W)_\tau] = E_P[Z_T (\tilde{K} \bullet W)_T] = 0,$$

as desired. The last equality holds since $(\tilde{K} \bullet W)_T \in \mathcal{I}_T(W)$ and $Z_T \perp \mathcal{I}_T(W)$.

Assume now that $M \in \mathbf{H}^2$. The orthogonality of $H \bullet W$ and Z implies that $(H \bullet W)_t \perp Z_t$ in $L^2(P)$ and so, using 2.f.3.(a),

$$\|M\|_{\mathbf{H}^2}^2 \geq \|M_t\|_{L^2(P)}^2 = \|(H \bullet W)_t\|_{L^2(P)}^2 + \|Z_t\|_{L^2(P)}^2$$

$$= \int_0^t \|H_s\|^2 ds + \|Z_t\|_{L^2(P)}^2,$$

for all $t \geq 0$. Taking the supremum over all $t \geq 0$, we see that $H \in L^2(W)$, $Z \in \mathbf{H}^2$ and we have $\|M\|_{\mathbf{H}^2}^2 = \|H\|_{L^2(W)}^2 + \|Z\|_{\mathbf{H}^2}^2$. ∎

6. MISCELLANEOUS

6.a Ito processes. A continuous semimartingale X is called an *Ito process* if it satisfies $X(t) = X(0) + \int_0^t \mu(s)ds + \int_0^t \nu(s) \cdot dW_s$, equivalently

$$dX(t) = \mu(t)dt + \nu(t) \cdot dW_t, \quad t \geq 0, \tag{0}$$

for some d-dimensional Brownian motion W and processes $\mu \in L(\mathbf{t})$ and $\nu \in L(W)$. Here $\mathbf{t}$ denotes the process $\mathbf{t}(t) = t$. The relation (0) is commonly referred to as the *dynamics* of X. It follows from (0) that the compensator of X is given by

$$u_X(t) = \int_0^t \mu(s)ds.$$

The processes $\mu(t)$ and $\nu(t)$ are called the *drift* and *instantaneous volatility* of X respectively. This terminology will be justified in section 6.b. The Ito process X is a local martingale if and only if its drift is zero. The following special case of (0)

$$dL(t) = L(t)\mu(t)dt + L(t)\lambda(t) \cdot dW_t, \tag{1}$$

with drift and volatility proportional to the size of the random quantity, is the basic dynamics dealt with in finance. Since drift and volatility depend on the process L it is not immediately clear that a solution L exists, but 6.a.0 below shows that it does under suitable assumptions on the processes μ and λ.

The process $\lambda(t)$ is called the *instantaneous proportional* (or *percentage*) *volatility* of L. We will see below that the dynamics (1) implies that the process $L(t)$ is strictly positive and that $X(t) = log(L(t))$ is an Ito process.

6.a.0. *Let* $\mu \in L(\mathbf{t})$, $\lambda \in L(W)$ *and* L *be a continuous semimartingale. Then the following are equivalent:*
(a) $dL(t) = L(t)\mu(t)dt + L(t)\lambda(t) \cdot dW_t$.
(b) $L(t) = L(0)exp\left(\int_0^t \mu(s)ds\right)\mathcal{E}_t(\lambda \bullet W)$.
(c) *The process* L *is strictly positive and satisfies*
  $d\,log(L(t)) = \left(\mu(t) - \frac{1}{2}\|\lambda(t)\|^2\right)dt + \lambda(t) \cdot dW_t$.
In this case the multiplicative compensator U_L *of* L *is given by*

$$U_L(t) = exp\left(\int_0^t \mu(s)ds\right).$$

Proof. (a)$\Rightarrow$(b) Set $B(t) = exp\left(-\int_0^t \mu(s)ds\right)$. Then $dB(t) = -\mu(t)B(t)dt$. Thus multiplying the equality $dL(t) - L(t)\mu(t)dt = L(t)\lambda(t) \cdot dW_t$ with $B(t)$ it follows that $B(t)dL(t) + L(t)dB(t) = B(t)L(t)\lambda(t) \cdot dW_t$. Setting $X(t) = B(t)L(t)$, observing that $B(t)$ is a bounded variation process and using the stochastic product rule, this becomes $dX(t) = X(t)\lambda(t) \cdot dW_t$ with unique solution (4.b.2)

$$X(t) = X(0)\mathcal{E}_t(\lambda \bullet W) = X(0)exp\left(-\frac{1}{2}\int_0^t \|\lambda(s)\|^2 ds + \int_0^t \lambda(s) \cdot dW_s\right).$$

Note now that $X(0) = L(0)$ and divide by $B(t)$ to obtain (b).

(b)$\Rightarrow$(c): Obvious. (c)$\Rightarrow$(a): Assuming (c) set $Z(t) = log(L(t))$. Then $L(t) = e^{Z(t)}$ and Ito's formula yields

$$dL(t) = e^{Z(t)}dZ(t) + \tfrac{1}{2}e^{Z(t)}d\langle Z \rangle_t = L(t)dZ(t) + \tfrac{1}{2}L(t)d\langle Z \rangle_t. \qquad (2)$$

Here $dZ(t) = \big(\mu(t) - \tfrac{1}{2}\|\lambda(t)\|^2\big)dt + \lambda(t) \cdot dW_t$, by assumption, and consequently $d\langle Z \rangle_t = \|\lambda(t)\|^2 dt$. Entering this into (2) we obtain

$$\begin{aligned}
dL(t) &= L(t)\big[\big(\mu(t) - \tfrac{1}{2}\|\lambda(t)\|^2\big)dt + \lambda(t) \cdot dW_t\big] + \tfrac{1}{2}L(t)\|\lambda(t)\|^2 dt \\
&= L(t)\mu(t)dt + L(t)\lambda(t) \cdot dW_t,
\end{aligned}$$

as in (a). Assume now that (a)-(c) are satisfied and set $U(t) = exp\big(\int_0^t \mu(s)ds\big)$. Then U is a continuous bounded variation process with $U(0) = 1$. Moreover (b) implies that $L(t)/U(t) = L(0)\mathcal{E}_t(\lambda \bullet W)$ is a local martingale. It follows that $U(t) = U_L(t)$ is the multiplicative compensator of L. ∎

Remark. We are mainly interested in the equivalence of (a) and (c). However the intermediate step (b) was necessary to see that the dynamics (a) implies the positivity of the process L. If this were known beforehand, the equivalence of (a) and (c) could be established by direct application of Ito's formula. Rewriting (0) as

$$\frac{dL(t)}{L(t)} = \mu(t)dt + \lambda(t) \cdot dW_t$$

suggests that $\mu(t)$ should be interpreted as the instantaneous rate of return of $L(t)$ at time t. This interpretation is also supported by formula 6.a.0.(b), if we recall that the local martingale $K_t = \mathcal{E}_t(\lambda \bullet W)$ is driftless.

6.a.1. *Let Y be a continuous semimartingale satisfying $dY(t) = Y(t)\sigma(t) \cdot dW_t$, where W is a d-dimensional Brownian motion and σ is a bounded, progressively measurable R^d-valued process. Then Y is a square integrable martingale. Moreover, setting $Y_t^* = \sup_{s \in [0,t]} Y(s)$ we have $E\big[(Y_t^*)^2\big] < \infty$ and consequently*

$$E\left(\int_0^t \sigma(s)^2 Y(s)^2 ds\right) < \infty, \quad t \geq 0.$$

Proof. Choose a constant C with $|\sigma| \leq C$. Using 6.a.0 with $\mu = 0$ we see that $Y(t) = Y(0)\mathcal{E}_t(L)$, where $L = \sigma \bullet W$. Since $\langle L \rangle_t = \int_0^t \|\sigma(s)\|^2 ds \leq C^2 t$, Y is a square integrable martingale (4.b.3). Now the L^2-maximal inequality implies that $E\big[(Y_t^*)^2\big] \leq 4E\big[Y(t)^2\big] < \infty$ (I.7.e.1.(b)) and this in turn implies that

$$E\left(\int_0^t \sigma(s)^2 Y(s)^2 ds\right) \leq E\left((Y_t^*)^2 \int_0^t \sigma(s)^2 ds\right) \leq C^2 t\, E\big[(Y_t^*)^2\big] < \infty. \quad ∎$$

Next we consider the dynamics (0) with drift $\mu(t) = 0$ and nonstochastic volatility $\sigma(t)$. In this case the distribution of the random vector $X(T)$ can be identified:

6.a.2. *Let W be a d-dimensional Brownian motion, $T > 0$ and $\sigma_j : [0, T] \to R^d$, $1 \le j \le n$, continuous functions. Then $\sigma_j \in L(W)$. Set $Y_j = \int_0^T \sigma_j(s) \cdot dW_s$ and $Y = (Y_1, \dots, Y_n)$. Then the random vector Y has a multinormal distribution $N(0, C)$ with covariance matrix $C_{ij} = \int_0^T \sigma_i(t) \cdot \sigma_j(t) dt$.*

Proof. (A) Let $n = 1$, write $\sigma_1(t) = \sigma(t)$ and set $\Sigma^2 = C_{11} = \int_0^T \|\sigma(s)\|^2 ds$. We must show that Y has distribution $N(0, \Sigma^2)$. To do this we compute the characteristic function $\hat{Y}(\lambda) = E\left[e^{i\lambda Y}\right]$. Set $Z_t = \int_0^t \sigma(s) \cdot dW_s$ (thus $Y = Z_T$) and note that Z_t is a mean zero continuous martingale with $\langle Z \rangle_t = \int_0^t \|\sigma(s)\|^2 ds$ and hence

$$d\langle Z \rangle_t = \|\sigma(t)\|^2 dt.$$

Now fix $\lambda \in R$ and set $f(w) = e^{i\lambda w}$ and $u(t) = \hat{Z}_t(\lambda) = E\left[e^{i\lambda Z_t}\right] = E(f(Z_t))$. Since $f'(w) = i\lambda f(w)$ and $f''(w) = -\lambda^2 f(w)$, Ito's formula yields

$$f(Z_t) = f(Z_0) + \int_0^t f'(Z_s)dZ_s + \frac{1}{2}\int_0^t f''(Z_s)d\langle Z \rangle_s$$

$$= 1 + \int_0^t f'(Z_s)dZ_s - \frac{\lambda^2}{2}\int_0^t f(Z_s)\|\sigma(s)\|^2 ds.$$

Here $\int_0^t f'(Z_s)dZ_s$ is a continuous mean zero martingale. Thus, taking expectations using Fubini's theorem and the nonstochastic nature of the process $\|\sigma(s)\|^2$ yields

$$u(t) = E(f(Z_t)) = 1 - \frac{\lambda^2}{2}E\left(\int_0^t f(Z_s)\|\sigma(s)\|^2 ds\right)$$

$$= 1 - \frac{\lambda^2}{2}\int_0^t \|\sigma(s)\|^2 E(f(Z_s))ds = 1 - \frac{\lambda^2}{2}\int_0^t \|\sigma(s)\|^2 u(s)ds.$$

The function $u(t)$ is continuous and hence so is the integrand $\|\sigma(s)\|^2 u(s)$. Thus, upon differentiating we obtain the following differential equation for u:

$$u'(t) = -\frac{\lambda^2}{2}\|\sigma(t)\|^2 u(t) \quad \text{with solution} \quad u(t) = u(0)exp\left(-\frac{\lambda^2}{2}\int_0^t \|\sigma(s)\|^2 ds\right).$$

Since $f(Z_0) = 1$ we have $u(0) = E(f(Z_0)) = 1$. Now let $t = T$. Then

$$\hat{Y}(\lambda) = \hat{Z}_T(\lambda) = u(T) = exp\left(-\frac{\lambda^2}{2}\int_0^T \|\sigma(s)\|^2 ds\right) = exp\left(-\frac{\lambda^2\Sigma^2}{2}\right),$$

which is the characteristic function of a one dimensional $N(0, \Sigma^2)$-variable.

(B) Now let $n \ge 1$. To see that Y is a Gaussian random vector, it will suffice to show that $h(Y)$ is a normal variable, for each linear functional $h : R^n \to R$. Such h has the form $h(y) = \alpha_1 y_1 + \dots + \alpha_n y_n$, $y \in R^n$, for some scalars $\alpha_1, \dots, \alpha_n$. Then

$$h(Y) = \sum_{i=1}^n \alpha_i Y_i = \sum_{i=1}^n \alpha_i \int_0^T \sigma_i(s) \cdot dW_s = \int_0^T \rho(s) \cdot dW_s,$$

where $\rho = \sum_{i=1}^{n} \alpha_i \sigma_i$ is a process as in step (A). It follows that $h(Y)$ is a normal random variable. Thus Y is Gaussian. It remains to compute the covariance matrix C of Y. Since the coordinates Y_i are mean zero variables we have $C_{ij} = E(Y_i Y_j)$. Using 2.c.5 it follows that

$$C_{ij} = E\left[\left(\int_0^T \sigma_i(s) \cdot dW_s\right)\left(\int_0^T \sigma_j(s) \cdot dW_s\right)\right] = \int_0^T \sigma_i(s) \cdot \sigma_j(s)ds. \; \blacksquare$$

Remark. Using 5.a.3 it is possible to shorten the proof of the one dimensional case: Fix $T > 0$, define $\sigma(t) = \sigma(T) + t - T$, for $t > T$, and set $Y(t) = \int_0^t \sigma(s) \cdot dW_s$, for all $t \geq 0$. Then Y is a continuous local martingale with deterministic quadratic variation $\langle Y \rangle_t = \int_0^t \sigma(s)^2 ds \uparrow \infty$, as $t \uparrow \infty$. According to 5.a.3 we can write $Y(t) = B_{\langle Y \rangle_t}$, for some Brownian motion $B = (B_t, \mathcal{G}_t)$, where the filtration $(\mathcal{G}_t)$ is defined as in 5.a.3. The nonstochastic nature of the quadratic variation $\langle Y \rangle_t$ now implies that $Y(T)$ is normal with mean zero and variance $\Sigma^2 = \langle Y \rangle_T = \int_0^T \sigma(t)^2 dt$, as desired. $\blacksquare$

6.b Volatilities. Let $T > 0$ and S be a strictly positive continuous semimartingale on $[0, T]$. Set $Z_t = log(S_t)$ and

$$V(t, T) = \sqrt{\langle S \rangle_T - \langle S \rangle_t} = \sqrt{\langle S \rangle_t^T}, \quad \text{as well as}$$

$$\Sigma(t, T) = \sqrt{\langle Z \rangle_T - \langle Z \rangle_t} = \sqrt{\langle Z \rangle_t^T}, \quad t \in [0, T].$$

From the representation as the limit in probability

$$\langle S \rangle_t^T = \lim_{\|\Delta\| \to 0} \sum \left(S_{t_k} - S_{t_{k-1}}\right)^2, \quad \text{and}$$

$$\langle Z \rangle_t^T = \lim_{\|\Delta\| \to 0} \sum \left(Z_{t_k} - Z_{t_{k-1}}\right)^2 = \lim_{\|\Delta\| \to 0} \sum \left(log\left(S_{t_k}/S_{t_{k-1}}\right)\right)^2,$$

where the limits are taken over all partitions $\Delta = \{t_k\}$ of $[t, T]$, it is clear that $\langle S \rangle_t^T$ and $\langle Z \rangle_t^T = \langle log(Y) \rangle_t^T$ are measures of the aggregate absolute respectively percentage volatility of the process S_t over the interval $[t, T]$.

Note that this quadratic variation does not change when computed with respect to some equivalent probability measure. This fact will be important when applied to models of financial markets. Here S_t will be a security price. Realizations of the paths of S are governed by the market probability P but the significant probability measures in the theory are measures which are different from but equivalent to P.

It is thus useful to know that the volatility of S with respect to these measures coincides with the volatility of S with respect to the market probability P and can thus be estimated from market data. If S is an Ito process satisfying

$$dS_t = \mu(t)dt + \nu(t) \cdot dW_t, \quad t \in [0, T],$$

where $W_t = (W_t^1, \ldots, W_t^d)$ is a d-dimensional Brownian motion on $(\Omega, \mathcal{F}, (\mathcal{F}_t), P)$ and $\nu \in L(W)$, then $d\langle S \rangle_t = \|\nu(t)\|^2 dt$ and so

$$V^2(t, T) = \int_t^T \|\nu(s)\|^2 ds \quad \text{and so} \quad dV^2(0, t) = \|\nu(t)\|^2 dt.$$

Thus $\|\nu(t)\|^2$ is a density for $V^2(0,t)$. We will refer to the process $\nu(t)$ as the volatility process of S. If S is a security price the Brownian motions W_t^k should be thought of as *risk factors* and the components $\nu_k(t)$ as intensities with which these risk factors affect the price S.

Assume that $\nu(t)$ never vanishes and set $u(s) = \nu(s)/\|\nu(s)\|$ and $V = u \bullet W$. Then $\|\nu(t)\|dV_t = \nu(t) \cdot dW_t$ and V is a continuous local martingale with $V_0 = 0$. Moreover $\langle V \rangle_t = \int_0^t \|u(s)\|^2 ds = t$ and hence V is a one dimensional Brownian motion (3.e.1). In short

6.b.0. *If $\nu(t)$ never vanishes, we can write $\nu(t) \cdot dW_t = \|\nu(t)\|dV_t$, where the process V_t is a one dimensional Brownian motion on $(\Omega, \mathcal{F}, (\mathcal{F}_t), P)$.* ∎

In terms of the one dimensional Brownian motion V, the dynamics of S now assumes the form
$$dS_t = \mu(t)dt + \|\nu(t)\|dV_t.$$

Similar observations apply to the *proportional* volatility. Here we start from a dynamics
$$\frac{dS_t}{S_t} = \mu(t)dt + \sigma(t) \cdot dW_t, \quad t \in [0,T],$$

where $\sigma \in L(W)$. Recall that $Z_t = log(S_t)$ and so, according to 6.a.0,

$$dZ_t = \left(\mu(t) - \tfrac{1}{2}\|\sigma(t)\|^2\right)dt + \sigma(t) \cdot dW_t.$$

Thus $d\langle Z \rangle_t = \|\sigma(t)\|^2 dt$. From this it follows that $\langle Z \rangle_T - \langle Z \rangle_t = \int_t^T \|\sigma(s)\|^2 ds$ and hence
$$\Sigma^2(t,T) = \int_t^T \|\sigma(s)\|^2 ds \quad \text{and so} \quad d\Sigma^2(0,t) = \|\sigma(t)\|^2 dt.$$

Thus $\|\sigma(t)\|^2$ is a density for $\Sigma^2(0,t)$. We will refer to the process $\sigma(t)$ as the (proportional) volatility process of S. The dynamics of S now can be rewritten as

$$\frac{dS_t}{S_t} = \mu(t)dt + \|\sigma(t)\|dV_t,$$

where V_t is a one dimensional Brownian motion. In the literature the term (proportional) volatility is often reserved for the numerical process $\|\sigma(t)\|$. The components W^j of the underlying Brownian motion are then referred to as *factors* and the vectorial process $\sigma(t)$ as the *factor loading*. We will on occasion refer to the process $\|\sigma(t)\|$ as the *numerical (proportional) volatility* of S.

6.c Call option lemmas.

6.c.0. *Let x, Σ, R be positive real numbers and Y a standard normal variable. Then*

$$E\left[\left(x\,e^{\Sigma Y-\frac{1}{2}\Sigma^2}-Ke^{-R}\right)^+\right]=x\,N(d_1)-Ke^{-R}N(d_2)=e^{-R}\left[f\,N(d_1)-K\,N(d_2)\right],$$

where $f=xe^R,\quad d_1=\dfrac{log(f/K)+\frac{1}{2}\Sigma^2}{\Sigma},\quad d_2=d_1-\Sigma=\dfrac{log(f/K)-\frac{1}{2}\Sigma^2}{\Sigma}$

and $N(d)=P(Y\le d)$ is the standard normal distribution function.

Proof. Set $U=x\,exp(\Sigma Y-\frac{1}{2}\Sigma^2)-Ke^{-R}$. Then

$$U>0\quad\text{if and only if}\quad Y>d=\left(ln(K/f)+\tfrac{1}{2}\Sigma^2\right)/\Sigma.$$

Thus $\quad E\left[U^+\right]=E\left[U;[U>0]\right]=E\left[\left(x\,e^{\Sigma Y-\frac{1}{2}\Sigma^2}-Ke^{-R}\right);[Y>d]\right]$

$$=I_1-I_2,\quad\text{where}$$

$$I_1=xE\left(e^{\Sigma Y-\frac{1}{2}\Sigma^2};[Y>d]\right)\quad\text{and}\quad I_2=E\left(Ke^{-R};[Y>d]\right).$$

Recall that $1-N(d)=N(-d)$, because of the symmetry of the standard normal density. It follows that

$$I_2=Ke^{-R}P(Y>d)=Ke^{-R}\left(1-N(d)\right)=Ke^{-R}N(-d)=Ke^{-R}N(d_2).$$

Moreover, using $P_Y(dy)=(2\pi)^{-1/2}exp(-y^2/2)dy$, we have

$$x^{-1}I_1=\int_d^\infty(2\pi)^{-\frac{1}{2}}exp\left(-\tfrac{y^2}{2}+\Sigma y-\tfrac{1}{2}\Sigma^2\right)dy=\int_d^\infty(2\pi)^{-\frac{1}{2}}exp\left(-\tfrac{1}{2}(y-\Sigma)^2\right)dy$$

$$=\int_{d-\Sigma}^\infty(2\pi)^{-\frac{1}{2}}e^{-y^2/2}dy=(1-N(d-\Sigma))=N(\Sigma-d)=N(d_1).\ \blacksquare$$

6.c.1. *Let X_n, X be random variables on $(\Omega,\mathcal{F},P)$ and $\mathcal{G}\subseteq\mathcal{F}$ a sub-σ-field. Assume that X_n is independent of $\mathcal{G}$, for all $n\ge1$, and $X_n\to X$, P-as. Then X is independent of $\mathcal{G}$.*

Proof. It will suffice to show that X is independent of Z, equivalently that the characteristic function $F_{(X,Z)}(s,t)$ factors as $F_{(X,Z)}(s,t)=F_X(s)F_Z(t)$, for each $\mathcal{G}$-measurable random variable Z. Consider such Z. By assumption we have $F_{(X_n,Z)}(s,t)=F_{X_n}(s)F_Z(t)$, for all $n\ge1$.

Let now $n\uparrow\infty$. Then $F_{(X_n,Z)}(s,t)=E_P\left(e^{i(sX_n+tZ)}\right)\to F_{(X,Z)}(s,t)$ and likewise $F_{X_n}(s)\to F_X(s)$ by the Dominated Convergence Theorem. It follows that $F_{(X,Z)}(s,t)=F_X(s)F_Z(t)$. $\blacksquare$

Let now $(W_t)_{t\in[0,T]}$ be a d-dimensional Brownian motion on the filtered probability space $(\Omega,\mathcal{F},(\mathcal{F}_t),P)$. Then the increment W_t-W_s is independent of $\mathcal{F}_s$, for all $0\le s<t$.

6.c.2. *Let $0 \le t < T$ and $\sigma : [t, T] \to R^d$ be a continuous function. Then the random variable $X = \int_t^T \sigma(s) \cdot dW_s$ is independent of the σ-field $\mathcal{F}_t$.*

Proof. Let Δ_n be a sequence of partitions of the interval $[t, T]$ such that $\|\Delta_n\| \to 0$ as $n \uparrow \infty$. According to 2.e.0 we have

$$S_{\Delta_n}(\sigma, W) = \sum_{t_j \in \Delta_n} \sigma(t_{j-1}) \cdot (W_{t_j} - W_{t_{j-1}}) \to X$$

in probability, as $n \uparrow \infty$. Indeed this convergence will be almost sure if (Δ_n) is replaced with a suitable subsequence. The independence of $W_{t_j} - W_{t_{j-1}}$ from $\mathcal{F}_t$ now shows that $S_{\Delta_n}(\sigma, W)$ is independent of $\mathcal{F}_t$, for all $n \ge 1$, and 6.c.2 follows from 6.c.1. ∎

Consider now a strictly positive, continuous semimartingale S. Assume that the process $Z(t) = log(S(t))$ satisfies the dynamics

$$dZ(t) = \mu(t)dt + \sigma(t) \cdot dW_t, \tag{0}$$

for some *deterministic* processes $\mu \in L(\mathbf{t})$ and $\sigma \in L(W)$ and set

$$m(t, T) = \int_t^T \mu(s)ds \quad \text{and}$$
$$\Sigma(t, T) = \sqrt{\langle Z \rangle_t^T} = \left(\int_t^T \|\sigma(s)\|^2 ds \right)^{1/2}, \quad t \in [0, T]. \tag{1}$$

6.c.3. *Let $K > 0$ and assume that $\Sigma(t, T) > 0$, for all $t \in [0, T)$ and $K > 0$. Let $A = [S(T) > K] = [Z(T) > log(K)]$. Then*

(i) $\qquad\qquad E_P[1_A|\mathcal{F}_t] = N(d), \qquad and$

(ii) $\quad E[(S(T) - K)^+|\mathcal{F}_t] = S(t)e^{m(t,T) + \frac{1}{2}\Sigma^2(t,T)} N(d_1) - KN(d_2), \quad where$

$$d = d_2 = \frac{log(S(t)/K) + m(t,T)}{\Sigma(t,T)} \quad and \quad d_1 = d + \Sigma(t,T), \quad for \ all \ t \in [0, T).$$

Proof. Fix $t \in [0, T)$. Let us split $Z(T)$ into a summand which is $\mathcal{F}_t$-measurable and another summand which is independent of the σ-field $\mathcal{F}_t$. Write $m(0, T) = m(0, t) + m(t, T)$ and $\Sigma^2(0, T) = \Sigma^2(0, t) + \Sigma^2(t, T)$. From (0) it follows that

$$Z(T) = Z(0) + \int_0^T \mu(s)ds + \int_0^T \sigma(s) \cdot dW_s$$
$$= Z(t) + m(t, T) + \int_t^T \sigma(s)dW_s = X(t) + Y(t), \quad where \tag{2}$$
$$X(t) = Z(t) + m(t, T) \quad and \quad Y(t) = \int_t^T \sigma(s) \cdot dW_s.$$

Since σ is nonstochastic, $Y(t)$ is independent of $\mathcal{F}_t$ (6.c.2) and is a mean zero normal variable with variance $\Sigma^2(t, T)$, that is, $Y(t)/\Sigma^2(t, T)$ is a standard normal variable (6.a.2). To simplify notation let us write $m = m(t, T)$ and $\Sigma = \Sigma(t, T)$.

(i) We have $A = [X(t) + Y(t) > log(K)]$ and consequently $1_A = f(X(t), Y(t))$, where $f(x, y) = 1_{\tilde{A}}$ with $\tilde{A} = [x + y > log(K)] \subseteq R^2$.

Since $X(t)$ is $\mathcal{F}_t$-measurable while $Y(t)$ is independent of $\mathcal{F}_t$, the conditional expectation $E_P[1_A|\mathcal{F}_t] = E_P[f(X(t), Y(t)) \mid \mathcal{F}_t]$ can be computed by leaving $X(t)$ unchanged while integrating $Y(t)$ out according to its distribution under P (I.2.b.11), that is,

$$E_P[1_A|\mathcal{F}_t] = E_P[f(X(t), Y(t)) \mid \mathcal{F}_t] = \int_R f(X(t), y) P_{Y(t)}(dy)$$

$$= F(t, X(t)), \quad \text{where}$$

$$F(t, x) = \int_R f(x, y) P_{Y(t)}(dy) = P_{Y(t)}(\tilde{A}) = P_{Y(t)}([y > log(K) - x])$$

$$= P(Y(t) > log(K) - x) = P\left(\frac{Y(t)}{\Sigma} < \frac{log(K) - x}{\Sigma}\right)$$

$$= 1 - N\left(\frac{log(K) - x}{\Sigma}\right) = N\left(\frac{x - log(K)}{\Sigma}\right).$$

As $X(t) = Z(t) + m = log(S(t)) + m$ it follows that $E_P[1_A|\mathcal{F}_t] = F(t, X(t)) = N(d)$, with $d = (X(t) - log(K))/\Sigma = (log(S(t)/K) + m)/\Sigma$.

(ii) Set $Y = Y(t)/\Sigma$ and note that $S(T) = e^{Z(T)} = e^{X(t)}e^{Y(t)}$. Thus

$$E\left[(S(T) - K)^+|\mathcal{F}_t\right] = E\left[\left(e^{X(t)}e^{Y(t)} - K\right)^+ \Big| \mathcal{F}_t\right] = G(t, X(t)), \quad \text{where}$$

$$G(t, x) = \int_R \left(e^x e^y - K\right)^+ P_{Y(t)}(dy) = E_P\left[\left(e^x e^{Y(t)} - K\right)^+\right]$$

$$= E_P\left[\left(e^{x + \frac{1}{2}\Sigma^2}e^{\Sigma Y - \frac{1}{2}\Sigma^2} - K\right)^+\right].$$

Using 6.c.0 with $R = 0$ and x replaced with $e^{x + \frac{1}{2}\Sigma^2}$ it follows that $G(t, x) = e^{x + \frac{1}{2}\Sigma^2}N(d_1) - KN(d_2)$ with $d_1 = (x - log(K) + \Sigma^2)/\Sigma$ and $d_2 = d_1 - \Sigma$. Replace x with $X(t) = log(S(t)) + m$ to obtain

$$E\left[(S(T) - K)^+|\mathcal{F}_t\right] = G(t, X(t)) = S(t)e^{m + \frac{1}{2}\Sigma^2}N(d_1) - KN(d_2),$$

where $d_1 = (log(S(t)/K) + m + \Sigma^2)/\Sigma$ and $d_2 = d - \Sigma$ as desired. ∎

6.d Log-Gaussian processes. Let W be a d-dimensional Brownian motion on the filtered probability space $(\Omega, \mathcal{F}, (\mathcal{F}_t), P)$.

6.d.0. *Let M be a continuous local martingale such that the quadratic variation $\langle M \rangle$ is nonstochastic. Then M is a square integrable Gaussian martingale.*

Proof. According to 5.a.4 we can write $M_t = B_{\langle M \rangle_t}$ for some Brownian motion B on a suitable enlargement of the filtered probability space $(\Omega, \mathcal{F}, (\mathcal{F}_t), P)$. The result follows, since B is a square integrable Gaussian martingale. ∎

Remark. The converse is also true: if M is a square integrable Gaussian martingale, then the quadratic variation process $\langle M \rangle$ is nonstochastic.

6.d.1. *If the process $\sigma \in L(W)$ is nonstochastic, then the integral process $\sigma \bullet W$ is a square integrable Gaussian martingale.*

Proof. In this case $\sigma \bullet W$ is a continuous local martingale with nonstochastic quadratic variation $\langle \sigma \bullet W \rangle_t = \int_0^t \|\sigma(s)\|^2 ds$. ∎

6.d.2. *If the continuous semimartingale X has nonstochastic compensator u_X and quadratic variation $\langle X \rangle$, then X is a Gaussian process.*

Proof. Let $X = M + A$ be the semimartingale decomposition of X ($u_X = A$). Then $\langle M \rangle = \langle X \rangle$ is nonstochastic and so M is a square integrable Gaussian martingale (6.d.0). Since the process A is nonstochastic, it follows that X is a square integrable Gaussian process. ∎

Let us call a positive process X *log-Gaussian* if the process $log(X)$ is Gaussian.

6.d.3. *Let X be a positive, continuous local martingale such that the quadratic variation process $\langle log(X) \rangle$ is nonstochastic. Then X is a log-Gaussian process.*

Remark. Note that $log(X)$ is not a local martingale in general.

Proof. Set $Z_t = log(X_t)$ and note that $d\langle Z \rangle_t = X_t^{-2} d\langle X \rangle_t$ (3.c.2.(c)). Assume that the quadratic variation $\langle Z \rangle$ is nonstochastic. Since Z is a continuous semimartingale it will now suffice to show that the compensator u_Z is nonstochastic also. Using the compensator formula 3.c.3.(b) and observing that $u_X = 0$, we have

$$du_Z(t) = X_t^{-1} du_X(t) - \tfrac{1}{2} X_t^{-2} d\langle X \rangle_t = -\tfrac{1}{2} d\langle Z \rangle_t.$$

Consequently $u_Z = -\tfrac{1}{2}\langle Z \rangle_t$ is nonstochastic. ∎

6.d.4. *Let $\sigma \in L(W)$ be nonstochastic and assume that the process $L \in \mathcal{S}$ satisfies $dL(t) = L(t)\sigma(t) \cdot dW_t$. Then $L \in \mathcal{S}_+$ is a log-Gaussian process.*

Proof. L is positive and $d\,log(L(t)) = -\tfrac{1}{2}\|\sigma(t)\|^2 dt + \sigma(t) \cdot dW_t$ (6.a.0); equivalently, $log(L(t)) = A_t + (\sigma \bullet W)_t$, where the process $A_t = log(L(0)) - \tfrac{1}{2}\int_0^t \|\sigma(s)\|^2 ds$ is nonstochastic. According to 6.d.1 the process $\sigma \bullet W$ is Gaussian and hence so is the process $log(L(t))$. ∎

6.e Processes with finite time horizon. In the study of financial markets we will fix a finite time horizon $T > 0$ and consider a filtered probability space $(\Omega, \mathcal{F}, (\mathcal{F}_t)_{t \in [0,T]}, P)$ with $\mathcal{F} = \mathcal{F}_T$ and processes $X = X(t, \omega) : [0, T] \times \Omega \to \overline{R} \ (R^d)$ defined on the finite time interval $[0, T]$.

Such a process X will be called a continuous local martingale, semimartingale, etc. on $[0, T]$ if the process $\tilde{X}(t) = X(t \wedge T)$, $t \geq 0$, is a continuous local martingale, semimartingale, etc. on the filtered probability space $(\Omega, \mathcal{F}, (\mathcal{F}_{t \wedge T})_{t \geq 0}, P)$. In other words we extend the filtration $(\mathcal{F}_t)$ and the process X to the interval $[0, \infty)$ by setting $\mathcal{F}_t = \mathcal{F}_T$ and $X(t) = X(T)$, for all $t > T$.

Note that $\tilde{X}^T = \tilde{X}$. If X is a continuous semimartingale, then the semimartingale decomposition $\tilde{X} = M + A$ of the extension $\tilde{X}$ satisfies $M = M^T$ and $A = A^T$, thus $d\langle M \rangle_t = du_{\tilde{X}}(t) = 0$, for $t > T$.

We now set $L(X) = L(\tilde{X})$ and $H \bullet X = H \bullet \tilde{X}$, for all $H \in L(X)$. The integrands $H \in L(X)$ are processes defined on $[0, \infty)$ but their behaviour for $t > T$ is irrelevant, since $\tilde{X} = \tilde{X}^T$. In other words the stochastic differential $dX = d\tilde{X}$ satisfies $dX(t) = 0$, for $t > T$ in the sense that

$$\int_0^t H(s) dX(s) = (H \bullet \tilde{X})_t = (H \bullet \tilde{X}^T)_t = (H \bullet \tilde{X})_t^T = \int_0^{t \wedge T} H(s) dX(s).$$

For example, if $X = M$ is a scalar local martingale, then $L(X) = L^2_{loc}(M)$ is the space of all progressively measurable processes H satisfying

$$\int_0^T H_s^2 d\langle M \rangle_s < \infty, \quad P\text{-as.}$$

Chapter IV: Application to Finance **211**

CHAPTER IV

Application to Finance

1. THE SIMPLE BLACK SCHOLES MARKET

1.a The model. Consider a market trading only two securities, a bond with principal one and a stock. Let us identify these securities with their price processes and let B_t and S_t denote the prices of the bond and stock at time $t \in [0, T]$ respectively. Here T denotes the finite time horizon. All trading is assumed to stop at time T. We now make several assumptions about our market:

(a) Securities can be bought and sold short in unlimited quantities and are infinitely divisible (that is, any fraction of a security can be bought or sold short).

(b) There are no transaction costs.

(c) The bond and stock satisfy
$$dB_t = r(t)B_t dt, \ B_0 = 1 \quad \text{and}$$
$$dS_t/S_t = \mu(t)dt + \sigma(t)dW_t, \ S_0 = x, \tag{0}$$

respectively, where $r, \sigma : [0, T] \to R_+$ and $\mu : [0, T] \to R$ are continuous functions (deterministic processes), W is a Brownian motion on the filtered probability space $(\Omega, \mathcal{F}, (\mathcal{F}_t), P)$ and $(\mathcal{F}_t)$ the augmented filtration generated by W. Recall that this filtration is right continuous (II.2.f.0).

Clearly then $B_t = exp\left(\int_0^t r(s)ds\right)$. In our simple model the bond is nonstochastic, that is, B_t is a constant for all $t \in [0, T]$. Because of the nondecreasing nature of B_t bondholders are subject to no risk. An investment in the bond can be liquidated at any time without incurring a loss. Consequently r is called the *risk-free rate of return*.

The equation for the stock price can also easily be solved. Recalling that $\sigma(t)dW_t = d(\sigma \bullet W)_t$ we can rewrite it as $dS_t - \mu(t)S_t dt = S_t d(\sigma \bullet W)_t$. Multiply with $m(t) = exp(-\int_0^t \mu(s)ds)$, set $X_t = m(t)S_t$ and use the stochastic product rule to obtain $dX_t = X_t d(\sigma \bullet W)_t$ with unique solution $X_t = X_0 \mathcal{E}_t(\sigma \bullet W)$ (III.4.b.1). Observing that $X_0 = S_0$ and multiplying with $m(t)^{-1} = exp(\int_0^t \mu(s)ds)$ this becomes

$$S_t = S_0 \, exp\left(\int_0^t \mu(s)ds\right) \mathcal{E}_t(\sigma \bullet W)$$
$$= S_0 \, exp(\int_0^t (\mu(s) - \tfrac{1}{2}\sigma^2(s))ds + \int_0^t \sigma(s)dW_s). \tag{1}$$

Since here $\mathcal{E}_t(\sigma \bullet W)$ is a martingale with constant mean one and $S_0 = x$ a constant, taking expectations yields $E(S_t) = S_0 exp(\int_0^t \mu(s)ds)$ and we can thus regard $\mu(t)$

as the instantaneous expected rate of return on the stock S at time t. On the other hand the equality $d\langle log(S)\rangle_t = \sigma^2(t)dt$ allows us to view $\sigma(t)$ as the instantaneous percentage volatility of S at time t (see III.6.b).

An investment of $1/B_t$ dollars into the bond at time zero grows to one dollar at time t in riskless fashion and so represents the value at time zero of one dollar to be received at time t. Thus $1/B_t$ is the discount factor allowing us to express prices in constant, time zero dollars. For example $S_t^B = S_t/B_t$ is the stock price process expressed in such constant dollars. This discounting eliminates an inflationary drift in prices, which is a consequence of the fact that money is lent for interest, and is a necessary first step toward transforming the price processes B_t, S_t into *martingales* with respect to some suitable equivalent probability measure P_B on $\mathcal{F}_T$. Note that the discounted bond $B_t^B = B_t/B_t = 1$ is already a martingale in any probability measure. A short computation involving the stochastic product rule yields

$$dS_t^B = \sigma(t)S_t^B\left[\sigma(t)^{-1}(\mu(t) - r(t))dt + dW_t\right]. \tag{2}$$

1.b Equivalent martingale measure. To eliminate the drift $(\mu - r)S_t^B$ from 1.a.eq.(2) set $W_t^B = \int_0^t \gamma(s)ds + W_t$, where $\gamma = (\mu - r)/\sigma$ (recall that σ is assumed to be strictly positive). Then $dW_t^B = \sigma(t)^{-1}(\mu(t) - r(t))dt + dW_t$ and so 1.a.eq.(2) can be rewritten as

$$dS_t^B = \sigma(t)S_t^B dW_t^B. \tag{0}$$

The expected rate of return μ on the stock has disappeared. Equation (0) solves as $S_t^B = S_0\mathcal{E}_t(\sigma \bullet W^B)$ (III.4.b.1). It is now desirable to find a probability measure P_B in which W_t^B is a Brownian motion, for then (0) can be regarded as the dynamics of the process S_t^B under the probability P_B and S_t^B is a P_B-martingale.

Using III.4.c.0 such a probability P_B is easily found. As $W_t^B = W_t + \int_0^t \gamma(s)ds$ it will suffice to determine P_B such that the density process $M_t = d(P_B|\mathcal{F}_t)/d(P|\mathcal{F}_t)$ satisfies $dM_t = -\gamma(t)M_t dW_t$, equivalently $M_t = \mathcal{E}_t(-\gamma \bullet W)$, for all $t \in [0, T]$. Since M and $\mathcal{E}(-\gamma \bullet W)$ are both martingales on $[0, T]$ it suffices to have

$$\frac{dP_B}{dP} = \mathcal{E}_T(-\gamma \bullet W) = exp\left(-\int_0^T \gamma(s)dW_s - \frac{1}{2}\int_0^T \gamma(s)^2 ds\right)$$

and this defines a suitable probability measure P_B on $\mathcal{F}_T$. The condition $\gamma \in L(W)$ of III.4.c.0 is satisfied since γ is continuous.

The precise nature of this Radon-Nykodym derivative is not important. The crucial property is the fact that $dP_B/dP > 0$ and hence the probability measure P_B is actually *equivalent* to the original probability measure P. We note

1.b.0. *The discounted price processes $B_t^B = 1$, S_t^B are martingales with respect to the probability P_B.* ∎

For this reason P_B is called the *equivalent martingale measure*. As $S_t = B_t S_t^B$ equation (0) implies

$$dS_t/S_t = r(t)dt + \sigma(t)dW_t^B. \tag{1}$$

Since W_t^B is a Brownian motion with respect to P_B, this equation is the dynamics of S_t under P_B. Note that the switch to the equivalent martingale measure P_B has replaced the expected rate of return μ of S under P with the risk-free rate of return r on the bond. With respect to P_B the expected yield of every asset is the risk-free yield r. This corresponds to a world where every investor is risk neutral: the possibility of greater gain exactly compensates a risk neutral investor for greater risk so that no expected return greater than the risk-free return is demanded of any asset. In consequence P_B is also called the *risk neutral probability*. By contrast the original probability P will now be called the *market probability*.

Remark. The nonstochastic nature of γ implies that the Brownian motion $W_t^B = W_t + \int_0^t \gamma(s)ds$ generates the same augmented filtration $(\mathcal{F}_t)$ as the original Brownian motion W. This is not generally the case for more complicated Girsanov transformations and is important in the application of martingale representation theorems.

1.c Trading strategies and absence of arbitrage. A *trading strategy* (dynamic portfolio) is a predictable R^2-valued process $\phi_t = (K_t, H_t)$, $t \in [0, T]$, satisfying $K \in L(B)$ and $H \in L(S)$. This requirement ensures that the stochastic differentials KdB and HdS are defined. Because of the special nature of our processes B and S it is easily seen to be equivalent with the condition

$$\int_0^T |K_t|dt + \int_0^T H_t^2 dt < \infty, \quad P\text{-as.}$$

The process ϕ is to be interpreted as a continuously changing portfolio holding K_t units of the bond and H_t units of the stock at time t. The coefficients K and H are called the *portfolio weights*. Thus

$$V_t(\phi) = K_t B_t + H_t S_t \tag{0}$$

is the price of this portfolio at time t. Such a portfolio is called *tame*, if the price process $V_t(\phi)$ is bounded below, that is, $V_t(\phi) \geq C > -\infty$, for all $0 \leq t \leq T$ and some constant C. Consider now a portfolio $\phi = (K, H)$ which holds a constant number of shares of the bond and the stock except for a single rebalancing of the portfolio at time t_0; in other words assume that

$$K_t = \begin{cases} a_-, & t \leq t_0, \\ a_+, & t > t_0, \end{cases} \quad \text{and} \quad H_t = \begin{cases} b_-, & t \leq t_0, \\ b_+, & t > t_0, \end{cases}$$

where a_-, a_+, b_-, b_+ are constants. The rebalancing at time t_0 will be called *self-financing*, if money is neither injected nor withdrawn from the portfolio. In other words the position at time t_0 is sold and the proceeds immediately invested into the new position. This is of course equivalent with the requirement $V_{t_0}(\phi) = a_+ B_{t_0} + b_+ S_{t_0}$ which in turn is equivalent with the equality

$$\Delta V_t(\phi) = V_t(\phi) - V_{t_0}(\phi) = a_+(B_t - B_{t_0}) + b_+(S_t - S_{t_0}) = K_t \Delta B_t + H_t \Delta S_t, \quad t > t_0.$$

This leads to the following fundamental definition:

1.c.0 Definition. *The trading strategy $\phi = (K, H)$ is called self-financing if it satisfies*

$$dV_t(\phi) = K_t dB_t + H_t dS_t.$$

Such a strategy ϕ is to be interpreted as a portfolio which is continuously rebalanced without injection or withdrawal of funds. A transfer of funds takes place only at the time of its inception. The self-financing condition can also be written as

$$V_t(\phi) = V_0(\phi) + \int_0^t (K_u dB_u + H_u dS_u), \quad t \in [0, T].$$

Note that the discounted price process $V_t^B(\phi) = V_t(\phi)/B_t$ of a trading strategy $\phi = (K, H)$ has the form $V_t^B(\phi) = K_t + H_t S_t^B$.

1.c.1. *let $\phi_t = (K_t, H_t)$ be a tame trading strategy. Then ϕ is self-financing if and only if the discounted portfolio price process satisfies $dV_t^B(\phi) = H_t dS_t^B$.*

Proof. Write $V_t = V_t(\phi)$. From $V_t^B = K_t + H_t S_t^B$ and the stochastic product rule it follows that

$$dV_t^B = dK_t + H_t dS_t^B + S_t^B dH_t + d\langle H, S^B\rangle_t. \tag{1}$$

Observing that $dS_t^B = -rS_t B_t^{-1} dt + B_t^{-1} dS_t$ we can write $S_t^B = S_0 + \int_0^t dS_r^B = A_t + (B^{-1} \bullet S)_t$, where A is a continuous bounded variation process. Consequently $\langle H, S^B\rangle = \langle H, B^{-1} \bullet S\rangle = B^{-1} \bullet \langle H, S\rangle$, in other words $d\langle H, S^B\rangle_t = B_t^{-1} d\langle H, S\rangle_t$. Thus (1) can be rewritten as

$$dV_t^B = H_t dS_t^B + \left[dK_t + S_t^B dH_t + B_t^{-1} d\langle H, S\rangle_t\right]. \tag{2}$$

Similarly from $V_t = K_t B_t + H_t S_t$, the stochastic product rule and the bounded variation property of B,

$$\begin{aligned} dV_t &= K_t dB_t + B_t dK_t + H_t dS_t + S_t dH_t + d\langle H, S\rangle_t \\ &= K_t dB_t + H_t dS_t + \left[B_t dK_t + S_t dH_t + d\langle H, S\rangle_t\right] \\ &= K_t dB_t + H_t dS_t + B_t\left[dK_t + S_t^B dH_t + B_t^{-1} d\langle H, S\rangle_t\right]. \end{aligned}$$

Using (2) the last bracket can be rewritten as $dV_t^B - H_t dS_t^B$. Consequently

$$dV_t = K_t dB_t + H_t dS_t + B_t\left(dV_t^B - H_t dS_t^B\right)$$

and 1.c.1 follows. ∎

Remark. Let us call a trading strategy ϕ *static* if it is (pathwise) constant, that is, the coefficients $K_t = K_0$ and $H_t = H_0$ do not depend on t. Then, obviously,

$$dV_t(\phi) = d\left(K_0 B_t + H_0 S_t\right) = K_0 dB_t + H_0 dS_t,$$

that is, ϕ is self-financing. Let us now gather the crucial facts about self-financing trading strategies:

1.c.2. *Let ϕ be a self-financing trading strategy. Then*
(a) $V_t^B(\phi)$ is a P_B-local martingale.
(b) If ϕ is tame, then $V_t^B(\phi)$ is a P_B-supermartingale.
(c) If $V_t(\phi)$ is a bounded variation process, then $dV_t(\phi) = r(t)V_t(\phi)dt$.

Proof. (a) From $dV_t^B(\phi) = H_t dS_t^B$ we conclude that $V^B(\phi) = V_0(\phi) + H \bullet S^B$ and (a) follows. (b) A local martingale which is bounded below is a supermartingale (I.8.a.7). (c) If $V_t(\phi)$ is a bounded variation process the same is true of the process $V_t^B(\phi)$ which is a P_B-local martingale and must therefore be constant in time (I.9.b.1) and so $dV_t^B = 0$. It follows that

$$dV_t = d(B_t V_t^B) = V_t^B dB_t + B_t dV_t^B = r(t)B_t V_t^B dt = r(t)V_t dt. \ \blacksquare$$

Remarks. Properties (b), (c) have interesting interpretations. A tame trading strategy ϕ is a strategy which does not tolerate unbounded losses. In other words, a maximum loss is known in advance. In this case, according to (b), $V_t(\phi) = B_t Z_t$, where Z_t is a P_B-supermartingale. Thus, under the equivalent martingale measure P_B, such a strategy is expected to do no better than the bond B.

   If the price process $V_t(\phi)$ has paths of bounded variation, then the strategy ϕ is called *riskless*. Thus property (c) states that a riskless self-financing portfolio must earn the risk-free rate of return. In our model $dV_t = K_t dB_t + H_t dS_t = K_t dB_t + \mu(t)H_t S_t dt + \sigma(t)H_t S_t dW_t$ and hence the risk-free property can only happen in the trivial case $\sigma H = 0$ but the same principle applies in more general models.

Arbitrage strategies. A trading strategy ϕ is called an arbitrage strategy if it is self-financing and satisfies

$$V_0(\phi) = 0, V_T(\phi) \geq 0 \text{ and } P(V_T(\phi) > 0) > 0.$$

Such a strategy can be originated and maintained until time T without funds, carries no risk ($V_T(\phi) \geq 0$) and leads to a positive payoff with positive probability.

   It is generally believed that arbitrage strategies do not exist in real financial markets. This belief is based on the conviction that the appearance of an arbitrage strategy will lead market players to try to exploit it on a very large scale. This trading will then move prices in such a way as to make the arbitrage opportunity disappear.

   Example 1.c.3 below shows that arbitrage strategies exist in our market. However we will be able to show that no *tame* arbitrage strategy exists (1.c.4). This fact will be an immediate consequence of the existence of the equivalent martingale measure P_B. The tameness condition means that a bound on the credit necessary to maintain the strategy throughout its lifetime is known in advance.

1.c.3 Example. [KS, 1.2.3] Even when betting against subfair odds, winning strategies can be found by sufficiently increasing the stakes on each bet. Let us first bet repeatedly on the outcome $X_n = +1$ of a loaded coin labelled $+1/-1$

with probabilities $P(X_n = +1) = p$, $P(X_n = -1) = q$, $n \geq 1$. Recalling that $2^n = 1 + \sum_{k=0}^{n-1} 2^k$ we bet 2^{n-1} dollars on the nth throw of the coin. This nets winnings of 1 dollar at time $\tau = \inf\{\, n \geq 1 \mid X_n = 1 \,\}$, where

$$E(\tau) = \sum_{n=0}^{\infty} nP(\tau = n) = \sum_{n=0}^{\infty} nq^{n-1}p = p\,\frac{1}{(1-q)^2} = \frac{1}{1-q} < \infty.$$

Even though the expected time to our winnings of 1 is finite, the stopping time τ is not bounded and we must therefore be prepared to bet arbitrarily long. Likewise intermediate losses are unbounded also.

In a continuous setting such strategies can be implemented on finite time intervals $[0, T]$. Consider the simple Black Scholes market with $r = \mu = 0$ and $\sigma = 1$. In this case $B_t = 1$, $dS_t = S_t dW_t$ and $S_t = exp(W_t - t/2)$, $t \in [0, T]$. Note that the assets B, S are already martingales with respect to the market probability P. The stochastic integral

$$I(t) = \int_0^t \frac{1}{\sqrt{T-s}} dW_s$$

is a local martingale on $[0, T)$ with quadratic variation

$$\langle I \rangle_t = \int_0^t \frac{1}{T-s} ds = log\left(\frac{T}{T-t}\right).$$

Observe that $s = log\left(T/(T-t)\right)$ if and only if $t = t(s) = T(1-e^{-s})$ with increasing $t(s) : [0, \infty) \mapsto [0, T)$. It follows that $J(s) = I\big(t(s)\big)$ is a continuous local martingale on $[0, \infty)$ with quadratic variation $\langle J \rangle_s = \langle I \rangle_{t(s)} = s$ and hence is a Brownian motion on $[0, \infty)$. In particular $\rho_\alpha = \inf\{\, s > 0 \mid J(s) = \alpha \,\} < \infty$ almost surely, for each real number α. This in turn shows that

$$\tau_\alpha = \inf\{\, t > 0 \mid I(t) = \alpha \,\} < T$$

and so $I(T \wedge \tau_\alpha) = \alpha$ almost surely. Now let $\phi = (K, H)$ be a trading strategy satisfying $K_t = I(t \wedge \tau_\alpha) - H_t S_t$. Then

$$V_t(\phi) = K_t + H_t S_t = I(t \wedge \tau_\alpha) = \int_0^t (T-s)^{-1/2} 1_{[s \leq \tau_\alpha]} dW_s,$$

especially $V_0(\phi) = 0$, $V_T(\phi) = \alpha$ and $dV_t(\phi) = (T-t)^{-1/2} 1_{[t \leq \tau_\alpha]} dW_t$. From $dB_t = 0$ and $dS_t = S_t dW_t$ it now follows that the self-financing condition assumes the form

$$H_t S_t dW_t = K_t dB_t + H_t dS_t = dV_t(\phi) = \frac{1}{\sqrt{T-t}} 1_{[t \leq \tau_\alpha]} dW_t$$

and this can be satisfied by setting $H_t = \left(S_t \sqrt{T-t}\right)^{-1} 1_{[t \leq \tau_\alpha]}$. With K_t defined as above, ϕ is a self-financing strategy allowing us to reach an arbitrary amount of α dollars at time T almost surely with no initial investment at time zero. This strategy is not tame. In fact

1.c.4. *In the simple Black Scholes market tame arbitrage strategies do not exist.*

Proof. Let ϕ be a tame, self-financing trading strategy with $V_T^B(\phi) \geq 0$ and $V_0^B(\phi) = 0$. Then $V_t^B(\phi)$ is a P_B-supermartingale, in particular $E_{P_B}\left(V_T^B(\phi)\right) \leq E_{P_B}\left(V_0^B(\phi)\right) = 0$. Therefore $V_T^B(\phi) = 0$, P_B-as. and hence also P-as. Consequently ϕ cannot be an arbitrage strategy. ∎

1.c.5. *Let ϕ be a self-financing trading strategy. If $V_T(\phi) = 0$ and $|V_t(\phi)| \leq C$, $t \in [0, T]$, for some constant C, then $V_t(\phi) = 0$, for all $t \in [0, T]$.*

Proof. Write $V_t^B = V_t^B(\phi) = V_t(\phi)/B_t$. Then V_t^B is a P_B-local martingale which is uniformly bounded and hence a martingale (I.8.a.4). From $V_T^B = 0$ and the martingale property it now follows that $V_t^B = 0$, P_B-as. and hence P-as., for all $t \in [0, T]$. ∎

1.c.6 Law of One Price. *Let ψ, χ be self-financing trading strategies and assume that $V_T(\psi) = V_T(\chi)$. If $|V_T(\psi) - V_T(\chi)| \leq C$, $t \in [0, T]$, for some constant C, then $V_t(\psi) = V_t(\chi)$ for all $t \in [0, T]$.*

Proof. Apply 1.c.5 to the strategy $\phi = \psi - \chi$. ∎

2. PRICING OF CONTINGENT CLAIMS

2.a Replication of contingent claims. A *contingent claim* h maturing at time T is an $\mathcal{F}_T$-measurable random variable. The value $h(\omega)$ is the payoff at time T of the claim h in the state $\omega \in \Omega$. It is assumed that our claim h has a payoff only at the time T of maturity. The claim h is called a (European) option if it is nonnegative

Note that h can be any measurable function of the entire path $t \in [0,T] \mapsto S_t(\omega)$. Thus we call the risky asset the *asset underlying the claim* h. The payoff h is contingent on or in some way derived from the price process of the underlying asset. In consequence contingent claims are also called *derivatives*.

Many contingent claims occurring in practice do not depend on the entire path $t \in [0,T] \mapsto S_t(\omega)$ but are in fact deterministic functions $h = f(S_T)$ of the stock price S_T at the time T of maturity only.

Examples of such contingent claims are the *forward contract* for purchase of the asset at time T for a strike price K ($h = f(S_T) = S_T - K$), the European *call option* on the asset S with maturity T and strike price K ($h = f(S_T) = (S_T - K)^+$) and the European *put option* on the asset S with maturity T and strike price K ($h = f(S_T) = (S_T - K)^-$).

Replication and pricing. A self-financing trading strategy ϕ is said to *replicate* the contingent claim h if it satisfies $V_T(\phi) = h$ and the discounted process $V_t^B(\phi)$ is a P_B-martingale (rather than only a P_B-local martingale), equivalently if

$$V_t^B(\phi) = E_{P_B}\left[h/B_T \mid \mathcal{F}_t\right], \quad \text{for all } t \in [0,T]. \tag{0}$$

The claim h is called *replicable*, if there exists a replicating strategy for h. Multiplying (0) with B_t we obtain

$$V_t(\phi) = B_t E_{P_B}\left[h/B_T \mid \mathcal{F}_t\right], \quad \text{for all } t \in [0,T],$$

for each replicating strategy ϕ of h. This leads us to define the *arbitrage price* $\pi = \pi(h)$ of a *replicable* contingent claim h to be the process

$$\pi_t(h) = B_t E_{P_B}\left[h/B_T \mid \mathcal{F}_t\right], \quad \text{for all } t \in [0,T]. \tag{1}$$

In other words we set $\pi_t(h) = V_t(\phi)$, where ϕ is any replicating strategy for h. Consider such a strategy ϕ and let us see why this equality should hold at time $t = 0$, that is, why we should have $\pi_0(h) = V_0(\phi)$ (the general case is argued in section 4.a below).

Assume we wish to enlarge our market by trading the claim h according to some price process π_t. If $\pi_0(h) > V_0(\phi)$ we sell short the claim h, go long the strategy ϕ at time $t = 0$ and invest the surplus into the riskless bond. This is a self-financing strategy yielding the certain profit $(\pi_0(h) - V_0(\phi))B_T$ at time T. If $\pi_0(h) < V_0(\phi)$ we follow the opposite strategy. In any case we have an arbitrage strategy in the enlarged market which we wish to avoid.

Note that this argument is not conclusive in the abstract generality of our model, since in general only *tame* arbitrage strategies can be ruled out. However, the price processes of all strategies that can be implemented in real financial markets are bounded and hence tame.

Equation (1) is called the *risk neutral valuation formula* since expectations are taken with respect to the risk neutral probability P_B rather than the market probability P. Let us note that the arbitrage price $\pi_t(h)$ is linear in h.

If the claim h is not replicable, then the arbitrage price of h is not defined. If h is replicable, then $h/B_T = V_T^B(\phi)$ for some P_B-martingale $V_t^B(\phi)$ and so in particular h/B_T is P_B-integrable. In our simple Black Scholes market the converse is true also:

2.a.0. *If the contingent claim h is P_B-integrable, then it is replicable.*

Proof. Set $M_t = E_{P_B}[h/B_T|\mathcal{F}_t]$. Let $\phi = (K, H)$ be a trading strategy and write $V_t = V_t(\phi)$. Then ϕ replicates h if and only if $K_t + H_t S_t^B = V_t^B = M_t$, for all $0 \le t \le T$. It will thus suffice to determine the process H_t, since we can then set $K_t = M_t - H_t S_t^B$.

To find H_t recall that the self-financing condition for ϕ is equivalent with $dV_t^B = H_t dS_t^B$, that is in integral form, $V_t^B = V_0 + \int_0^t H_s dS_s^B$, for all $t \in [0, T]$. Combining this with the above we see that we must have

$$M_t = V_t^B = V_0 + \int_0^t H_s dS_s^B, \quad \forall t \in [0, T].$$

This now indicates how to obtain the process H_t. Recall that $(\mathcal{F}_t)$ is also the augmented filtration generated by the Brownian motion W_t^B. By the martingale representation theorem III.5.d.0 the $(\mathcal{F}_t)$-martingale M_t can be represented as

$$M_t = M_0 + \int_0^t J_s dW_s^B, \quad t \in [0, T], \tag{2}$$

for some predictable process $J \in L(W^B)$. Recalling that $dS_s^B = \sigma S_s^B dW_s^B$ we can rewrite (2) as $M_t = M_0 + \int_0^t J_s/(\sigma S_s^B) dS_s^B$ and so we want

$$M_0 + \int_0^t J_s/(\sigma S_s^B) dS_s^B = M_t = V_0 + \int_0^t H_s dS_s^B,$$

for all $t \in [0, T]$. This implies that $M_0 = V_0$ and indicates that we should define

$$H_s = J_s/(\sigma S_s^B), \quad K_s = M_s - H_s S_s^B \quad \text{and} \quad \phi = (K, H).$$

Then $M_t = M_0 + \int_0^t H_s dS_s^B$. Let us show that ϕ is a trading strategy, that is $K \in L(B)$ and $H \in L(S)$. From the dynamics $dS_t = S_t(\mu dt + \sigma dW_t)$ we conclude that $du_S(s) = \mu S_s ds$ and $d\langle S \rangle_s = \sigma^2 S_s^2 ds$. The process $J \in L(W^B)$ satisfies

$$\int_0^T J_s^2 ds < \infty, \quad P_B\text{-as.} \tag{3}$$

Thus $\int_0^T H_s^2 d\langle S\rangle_s = \int_0^T J_s^2 B_s^2 ds < \infty$ and $\int_0^T |H_s| |du_S(s)| = \int_0^T |\sigma^{-1}\mu J_s| B_s ds < \infty$, P-as., and so $H \in L(S)$. Likewise $K_s = M_s - H_s S_s^B = M_s - J_s/\sigma$. From (3) it follows that $J \in L(B)$ and the continuity of M (III.5.c.4) now implies that $K \in L(B)$.

Directly from its definition the trading strategy ϕ satisfies $V_t^B(\phi) = M_t$, $t \in [0,T]$. In particular $V_t^B(\phi)$ is a martingale. Moreover, for $t = T$, it follows that $V_T(\phi) = B_T M_T = h$. It remains to be checked only that the strategy ϕ is self-financing. Indeed from $M_t = M_0 + \int_0^t H_s dS_s^B$ it follows that

$$dV_t^B(\phi) = dM_t = H_t dS_t^B, \quad \text{as desired.} \quad \blacksquare$$

Remark. Many actually traded derivatives are deterministic functions $h = f(S_T)$ of the price of the underlying asset at the time T of maturity of the derivative. As we shall see later it is possible to derive explicit formulas for the hedging strategy $\phi_t = (K_t, H_t)$ without relying on the martingale representation theorem.

A naive approach to derivatives pricing would try to compute the price c_t of the derivative at time t as the expected payoff $\pi_t = B_t B_T^{-1} E[h|\mathcal{F}_t]$ of the derivative at maturity T discounted back to time t.

However the arbitrage pricing argument shows that this conditional expectation *has to be computed with respect to the equivalent martingale measure* P_B and not with respect to the market probability P. In the simple Black Scholes model P_B as constructed above is the *unique* eqivalent probability measure with respect to which the price processes of the market assets are martingales.

Thus arbitrage pricing forces us to change the original probability to the equivalent martingale measure P_B. We have already seen that this corresponds to passage into a world where all investors are risk neutral and the expected yield on every security is the risk-free yield.

Forward contracts and forward prices. The pricing of the forward contract for the purchase of the stock S at time T for the strike price K is particularly simple. Here $h = f(S_T) = S_T - K$. Recalling that S_t^B is a P_B-martingale, the arbitrage price π_t of this contract is given by

$$\begin{aligned}
\pi_t &= B_t E_{P_B}[h/B_T \mid \mathcal{F}_t] = B_t E_{P_B}[S_T/B_T \mid \mathcal{F}_t] - K B_t B_T^{-1} \\
&= B_t E_{P_B}[S_T^B \mid \mathcal{F}_t] - K B_t B_T^{-1} = B_t S_t^B - K B_t B_T^{-1} \\
&= S_t - K B_t B_T^{-1}.
\end{aligned}$$

It is easy to give a self-financing, even static, portfolio replicating this forward contract:

long: one share of S,   short: K/B_T riskless bonds.

The long position grows to S_T at time T while the short position grows to K at time T. The price of this portfolio at time t is equal to $V_t = S_t - K B_t B_T^{-1}$ and so $V_t^B = S_t^B - K/B_T$ is a P_B-martingale.

The *forward price* F_t of the stock S for delivery at time T is that strike price $F_t = K$ which makes the value π_t of the above forward contract at time t equal to zero. Solving for K we obtain $F_t = S_t B_t^{-1} B_T = B_T S_t^B$. This is nothing but the price S_t transported forward from time t to time T using the accrual factor $B_t^{-1} B_T$. Since the discounted price process S_t^B is a P_B-martingale, we can write this as

$$F_t = B_T S_t^B = B_T E_{P_B}\left[S_T^B \mid \mathcal{F}_t\right] = E_{P_B}\left[S_T \mid \mathcal{F}_t\right].$$

Forward price. *The forward price F_t at time t of the stock S for delivery at time T is given by $F_t = S_t B_t^{-1} B_T = E_{P_B}\left[S_T \mid \mathcal{F}_t\right]$.*

European puts and calls. Let $h = S_T - K$ be the forward contract for the purchase of one share of S at strike price K at time T. Then the claim $h^+ = (S_T - K)^+$ is called the European call on S with strike price K exercisable at time T. Obviously this is the value at time T of the right (without obligation) to purchase one share of S for the strike price K. Likewise the claim $h^- = (S_T - K)^-$ is called the European put on S with strike price K exercisable at time T and is the value at time T of the right (without obligation) to sell one share of S for the strike price K.

Recalling that the arbitrage price $\pi_t(h)$ is linear and observing that $h = h^+ - h^-$ yields the following relation for the call and put price processes $C_t = \pi_t(h^+)$ and $P_t = \pi_t(h^-)$: $S_t - KB_t B_T^{-1} = \pi_t(h) = \pi_t(h^+) - \pi_t(h^-) = C_t - P_t$. In short we have the so called

Put-Call Parity. $S_t + P_t - C_t = KB_t B_T^{-1}$, *for all $t \in [0, T]$.*

2.b Derivatives of the form $h = f(S_T)$. Consider a contingent claim h of the form $h = f(S_T)$, where $f : R \to R$ is some function and assume that $h \in L^1(P_B)$. Then h is replicable and we will now try to compute the arbitrage price process

$$\pi_t(h) = B_t E_{P_B}[h/B_T \mid \mathcal{F}_t] = B_t B_T^{-1} E_{P_B}[h|\mathcal{F}_t]. \tag{0}$$

Since here expectations are taken with respect to the equivalent martingale measure P_B it will be useful to start from the dynamics

$$dS_t/S_t = r(t)dt + \sigma(t)dW_t^B$$

(1.b.eq.(1)) driven by the P_B-Brownian motion W_t^B with solution

$$S_t = S_0 \, exp\left(\int_0^t r(s)ds - \frac{1}{2}\int_0^t \sigma^2(s)ds + \int_0^t \sigma(s)dW_s^B\right). \tag{1}$$

Let $t < T$ and write

$$S_T = S_t\left(\frac{S_T}{S_t}\right) = S_t \, exp\left(\int_t^T r(s)ds - \frac{1}{2}\int_t^T \sigma^2(s)ds + \int_t^T \sigma(s)dW_s^B\right).$$

Setting

$$R(t,T) = \int_t^T r(s)ds \quad \text{and} \quad \Sigma(t,T) = \left(\int_t^T \sigma^2(s)ds\right)^{1/2},$$

we can rewrite this as

$$S_T = S_t\left(\frac{S_T}{S_t}\right) = S_t\, exp\left(R(t,T) - \frac{1}{2}\Sigma^2(t,T) + \Sigma(t,T)Y\right), \tag{2}$$

where $Y = \Sigma(t,T)^{-1}\int_t^T \sigma(s)dW_s^B$. According to III.6.a.2 the stochastic integral $\int_t^T \sigma(s)dW_s^B$ is a normal random variable with mean zero and variance $\int_t^T \sigma^2(s)ds = \Sigma^2(t,T)$. Consequently Y is a standard normal variable under the probability P_B which is independent of the conditioning σ-field $\mathcal{F}_t$ in (0) (III.6.c.2). Writing $h = f(S_T) = f\left(S_t\, exp\left(R(t,T) - \frac{1}{2}\Sigma^2(t,T) + \Sigma(t,T)Y\right)\right)$, (0) becomes

$$\pi_t(h) = B_tB_T^{-1}E_{P_B}\left[f\left(S_t\, exp\left(R(t,T) - \frac{1}{2}\Sigma^2(t,T) + \Sigma(t,T)Y\right)\right)\bigg|\mathcal{F}_t\right].$$

Since here S_t is $\mathcal{F}_t$-measurable while Y is independent of the σ-field $\mathcal{F}_t$ this conditional expectation can be computed by integrating out the variable Y according to its distribution $P_Y^B(dy)$ under the probability P_B (I.2.b.11); in other words

$$\pi_t(h) = B_tB_T^{-1}\int_R f\left(S_t\, exp\left(R(t,T) - \frac{1}{2}\Sigma^2(t,T) + \Sigma(t,T)y\right)\right)P_Y^B(dy)$$

$$= F(t,S_t), \quad \text{where}$$

$$F(t,x) = B_tB_T^{-1}\int_R f\left(x\cdot exp\left(R(t,T) - \frac{1}{2}\Sigma^2(t,T) + \Sigma(t,T)y\right)\right)P_Y^B(dy).$$

Recalling that $B_tB_T^{-1} = exp(-R(t,T))$ we can write

$$F(t,x) = exp(-R(t,T))E_{P_B}\left[f\left(x\cdot exp\left(R(t,T) - \frac{1}{2}\Sigma^2(t,T) + \Sigma(t,T)Y\right)\right)\right].$$

In this form the precise nature of the probability P_B is no longer relevant. It is relevant only that Y is a standard normal variable under P_B. Thus we can summarize these findings as follows:

2.b.0. *Assume that the derivative $h = f(S_T)$ satisfies $h \in L^1(\mathcal{F}_T, P_B)$. Then the arbitrage price $\pi_t(h)$ can be written as $\pi_t(h) = F(t,S_t)$, where*

$$F(t,x) = exp(-R(t,T))E\left[f\left(x\cdot exp\left(R(t,T) - \frac{1}{2}\Sigma^2(t,T) + \Sigma(t,T)Y\right)\right)\right], \tag{3}$$

for some standard normal variable Y. ∎

The function $F(t,x)$ will later be seen to satisfy certain partial differential equations. We should think of $F(t,x)$ as the price of h at time t given that $S_t = x$.

European call. We are now in a position to the derive the Black-Scholes formula for the arbitrage price $\pi_t(h)$ of a European call h with strike price K and maturity T. Here $f(u) = (u - K)^+$ and multiplying through with the leftmost exponential in (3) yields $\pi_t(h) = F(t, S_t)$, where

$$F(t, x) = E\left[\left(x \cdot exp\left[\Sigma(t, T)Y - \tfrac{1}{2}\Sigma(t, T)^2\right] - Ke^{-R(t,T)}\right)^+\right], \qquad (4)$$

for some standard normal variable Y. Evaluating $F(t, x)$ using III.6.c.0 with $\Sigma = \Sigma(t, T)$ and $R = R(t, T)$ we obtain

$$F(t, x) = x\,N(d_1) - Ke^{-R(t,T)}\,N(d_2) = e^{-R(t,T)}\left[g\,N(d_1) - K\,N(d_2)\right],$$

where $g = xe^{R(t,T)}$,

$$d_1 = \frac{log(g/K) + \tfrac{1}{2}\Sigma(t, T)^2}{\Sigma(t, T)}, \quad d_2 = d_1 - \Sigma(t, T) = \frac{log(g/K) - \tfrac{1}{2}\Sigma(t, T)^2}{\Sigma(t, T)}$$

and $N(d) = P(Y \le d)$ is the standard normal distribution function. To find the Black-Scholes call price replace x with S_t and note that then $g = S_t e^{R(t,T)} = S_t B_t^{-1} B_T$ becomes the forward price $F_t = S_t B_t^{-1} B_T$ of the asset S at time t. Thus

2.b.1 Black-Scholes call price. *The European call* $h = (S_T - K)^+$ *has arbitrage price* $C_t = S_t N(d_1) - Ke^{-R(t,T)} N(d_2) = e^{-R(t,T)}\left[F_t\,N(d_1) - K\,N(d_2)\right]$*, where*

$$d_1 = \frac{log(F_t/K) + \tfrac{1}{2}\Sigma(t, T)^2}{\Sigma(t, T)}, \quad d_2 = \frac{log(F_t/K) - \tfrac{1}{2}\Sigma(t, T)^2}{\Sigma(t, T)}$$

and $F_t = S_t e^{R(t,T)} = S_t B_t^{-1} B_T$ *is the forward price at time t of the underlying asset S for delivery at time T.*

Remark. Alternatively this can be written as $C_t = F(t, S_t)$, where

$$F(t, x) = xN(d_1) - Ke^{-R(t,T)}N(d_2),$$

$$d_1 = \frac{log(x/K) + R(t, T) + \tfrac{1}{2}\Sigma(t, T)^2}{\Sigma(t, T)} \quad \text{and} \quad d_2 = \frac{log(x/K) + R(t, T) - \tfrac{1}{2}\Sigma(t, T)^2}{\Sigma(t, T)}.$$

Here $F(t, x)$ is the price of our call option at time t given that $S_t = x$.

European put. Solving in the put call parity $S_t + P_t - C_t = Ke^{-R(t,T)}$ for the put price P_t and using $1 - N(d) = N(-d)$ yields

$$P_t = e^{-R(t,T)}\left[K\,N(-d_2) - F_t\,N(-d_1)\right],$$

where d_1 and d_2 and F_t are as in 2.b.1. More examples will be treated below in the context of stochastic interest rates (examples 4.d.2, 4.d.3, 4.d.4).

Historic volatility. A crucial input in the evaluation of the call price 2.b.1 is the quantity $\Sigma(t,T)$. Assume that S follows the dynamics $dS_t = \mu(t)S_t dt + \sigma(t)S_t dW_t$ under the market probability P (the volatilities of S under P and P_B are the same). Then $d\log(S_t) = \left(\mu(t) - \frac{1}{2}\sigma(t)^2\right)dt + \sigma(t)dW_t$ (III.6.a.0) and so $d\langle\log(S)\rangle_t = \sigma(t)^2 dt$. Consequently

$$\Sigma^2(t,T) = \int_t^T \sigma^2(s)ds = \langle\log(S)\rangle_t^T = \langle\log(S)\rangle_T - \langle\log(S)\rangle_t$$

is the aggregate volatility of $\log(S)$, that is, the aggregate percentage volatility of the stock price S over the remaining life of the call option (the interval $[t,T]$). Thus an application of 2.b.1 at time t necessitates the prediction of the future aggregate volatility $\langle\log(S)\rangle_t^T$.

Let us assume now that $\mu(t) = \mu$ and $\sigma(t) = \sigma$ are constant. Then $\Sigma(t,T) = \sigma\sqrt{T-t}$ and the problem of predicting $\langle\log(S)\rangle_t^T$ becomes the problem of estimating the parameter σ. Under the restrictive assumptions of our model this can be done by using historic observations of the stock price S_t. If $\mu(t) = \mu$ and $\sigma(t) = \sigma$, then $\log(S_t) = \log(S_0) + (\mu - \frac{1}{2}\sigma^2)t + \sigma W_t$ and so, for $t_k < t_{k+1}$,

$$\log(S_{t_{k+1}}) - \log(S_{t_k}) = (\mu - \tfrac{1}{2}\sigma^2)(t_{k+1} - t_k) + \sigma(W_{t_{k+1}} - W_{t_k}).$$

From this it follows that the return $\log(S_{t_{k+1}}) - \log(S_{t_k})$ over the interval $[t_k, t_{k+1}]$ is normal with mean $m = (\mu - \frac{1}{2}\sigma^2)(t_{k+1} - t_k)$ and variance $s^2 = \sigma^2(t_{k+1} - t_k)$.

Now split any past time interval $[a,b]$ of length $b-a = T-t$ into N subintervals $[t_k, t_{k+1}]$ of equal length $t_{k+1} - t_k = \delta$. Set $X_k = \log(S_{t_{k+1}}) - \log(S_{t_k})$. Then the X_k are independent normal variables with identical distribution $N((\mu - \frac{1}{2}\sigma^2)\delta, \sigma^2\delta)$. Thus the observed values of the X_k can be viewed as independent random draws from a normal distribution with variance $\sigma^2\delta$. The standard statistical estimator for this variance is the quantity

$$\sigma^2\delta = \frac{1}{N}\sum_{k=0}^{N-1}(X_k - \overline{X})^2 = \frac{1}{N}\sum_{k=1}^{N-1}X_k^2 - \overline{X}^2,$$

where $\overline{X} = \frac{1}{N}\sum_{k=1}^{N-1}X_k$. It is convenient to use the denominator N rather than $N-1$ as is usual. Here $\overline{X} \cong (\mu - \frac{1}{2}\sigma^2)\delta$ and so $\overline{X}^2$ is very small if δ is small. This term can therefore be neglected and we estimate

$$\sigma^2\delta = \frac{1}{N}\sum_{k=1}^{N-1}X_k^2.$$

Multiplying with N and observing that $N\delta = T - t$ we obtain the predictor

$$\langle\log(S)\rangle_t^T = \sigma^2(T-t) = \sum_{k=1}^n X_k^2 = \sum_{k=1}^{N-1}\left(\log(S_{t_{k+1}}) - \log(S_{t_k})\right)^2$$

in pleasant agreement with the definition of this quadratic variation.

2.c Derivatives of securities paying dividends. So far we have assumed that the stock S does not pay a dividend. This was important in the definition of a self-financing trading strategy, which in turn is the basis for arbitrage arguments. When considering opportunities for riskless profit the dividend stream accruing to the holder of an asset paying dividends must be taken into account.

Let us assume now that the asset S pays a dividend continuously at the yield $q(t)$ assumed to be a deterministic function of time. In other words we assume that the dividend process D_t satisfies

$$dD_t = q(t)S_t dt.$$

Here D_t is to be interpreted as the total amount of dividend received up to time t. An example of such an asset is a foreign currency. In this case $q(t)$ is the foreign risk-free rate.

A trading strategy $\phi_t = (K_t, H_t)$ holding K_t units of the riskless bond and H_t units of the dividend paying stock S at time t will now be called *self-financing*, if the corresponding portfolio price process $V_t(\phi) = K_t B_t + H_t S_t$ satisfies

$$dV_t(\phi) = K_t dB_t + H_t dS_t + q(t)H_t S_t dt.$$

Set $Q(t,T) = \int_t^T q(s)ds$, $A_t = e^{-Q(t,T)}$ and $S_t^1 = A_t S_t = S_t e^{-Q(t,T)}$. Then A_t is a nonstochastic, bounded variation process satisfying $dA_t = q(t)A_t dt$ and $A_T = 1$. Using the stochastic product rule and 1.a.eq.(1) we have

$$\begin{aligned} dS_t^1 &= A_t dS_t + S_t dA_t = A_t dS_t + q(t)A_t S_t dt \\ &= A_t S_t[\mu(t)dt + \sigma(t)dW_t] + q(t)A_t S_t dt \qquad (0)\\ &= S_t^1[(\mu(t) + q(t))dt + \sigma(t)dW_t]. \end{aligned}$$

Thus S_t^1 follows a geometric Brownian motion with time dependent nonstochastic parameters. We can thus view S_t^1 as the price process of a new stock. Let $\psi_t = (K_t, H_t/A_t)$ be a trading strategy taking positions in the bond and the new stock S_t^1. The corresponding price process $V_t(\psi)$ satisfies

$$V_t(\psi) = K_t B_t + (H_t/A_t)S_t^1 = K_t B_t + H_t S_t = V_t(\phi),$$

that is, ϕ and ψ have the same price process. From (0) it follows that $dS_t^1 = A_t(dS_t + q(t)S_t dt)$. If ϕ is self-financing, then

$$\begin{aligned} dV_t(\psi) = dV_t(\phi) &= K_t dB_t + H_t(dS_t + q(t)S_t dt) \\ &= K_t dB_t + (H_t/A_t)dS_t^1. \end{aligned}$$

This is the self-financing condition for the trading strategy ψ if the new stock S_t^1 is assumed to pay no dividend. Let us call the asset S^1 the *dividend-free reduction* of S. Then we have seen:

For each self-financing trading strategy $\phi_t = (K_t, H_t)$ taking positions in the dividend paying asset S the corresponding trading strategy $\psi_t = (K_t, H_t/A_t)$ taking positions in the dividend-free reduction S^1 of S is also self-financing and satisfies $V_t(\psi) = V_t(\phi)$, $t \in [0, T]$.

Let now $h = f(S_T)$ be any derivative of the dividend paying asset S_t which depends only on the terminal value of S. Because of $A_T = 1$ we have $S_T = S_T^1$. Thus $h = f(S_T) = f(S_T^1)$ is the very same derivative of the dividend-free reduction S^1 of S.

If the trading strategy ϕ replicates the derivative $h = f(S_T)$ then the trading strategy ψ replicates $h = f(S_T^1)$ viewed as a derivative of S^1. Thus, letting c_t respectively c_t^1 denote the arbitrage price processes of $h = f(S_T) = f(S_T^1)$ considered as a derivative of the dividend paying asset S respectively of the dividend-free reduction S^1 of S, we have

$$c_t = V_t(\phi) = V_t(\psi) = c_t^1, \quad t \in [0, T].$$

If explicit formulas are already known for the case of a dividend-free asset, the price process c_t of h as a derivative of a dividend paying asset S can be obtained by simply replacing S_t with its dividend-free reduction S_t^1 and using the corresponding formulas for S_t^1. Consider the following examples:

Forward price. The forward price F_t (at time t) for delivery of S at time T is the strike price K which makes the value of the forward contract on S maturing at time T equal to zero. This forward contract is a derivative $h = f(S_T) = S_T - K$ of S_t of the above form. Thus the forward price F for delivery of S at time T equals the forward price F^1 for delivery of the dividend-free reduction S^1 of S, that is,

$$F_t = F_t^1 = S_t^1 e^{R(t,T)} = S_t e^{R(t,T) - Q(t,T)}.$$

European calls and puts. Replacing S_t with S_t^1 in 2.b.1 amounts to replacing the forward price $F_t = S_t e^{R(t,T)}$ with $F_t^1 = S_t^1 e^{R(t,T)} = S_t e^{R(t,T) - Q(t,T)}$, which is the forward price of S_t as a dividend paying asset. Thus we see that the formulas 2.b.1 of the European call and put prices remain unchanged in the case of a dividend paying asset (when expressed in terms of the forward price F_t of this asset):

$$C_t = e^{-R(t,T)} \big[F_t\, N(d_1) - K\, N(d_2) \big], \quad P_t = e^{-R(t,T)} \big[K\, N(-d_2) - F_t\, N(-d_1) \big],$$

$$\text{where} \quad d_1 = \frac{log(F_t/K) + \tfrac{1}{2}\Sigma(t,T)^2}{\Sigma(t,T)} \quad \text{and} \quad d_2 = \frac{log(F_t/K) - \tfrac{1}{2}\Sigma(t,T)^2}{\Sigma(t,T)},$$

the only difference being in the computation of the forward price F of S for delivery at time T: $F_t = S_t e^{R(t,T) - Q(t,T)}$.

In the computation of the forward price the change from a dividend-free asset to a dividend paying asset can simply be made by replacing the risk-free yield $r(t)$ with the difference $r(t) - q(t)$. Note carefully however that the European call and put prices for a dividend paying asset cannot be obtained from those of a dividend-free asset by simply replacing $r(t)$ with $r(t) - q(t)$.

Equivalent martingale measure: In the case of a dividend-free asset the equivalent martingale measure P_B made the discounted price process of the asset into a martingale with the crucial consequence being that the discounted price process of a self-financing trading strategy ϕ is a P_B- local martingale (and a martingale under suitable, not very restrictive conditions on the coefficients K_t, H_t of ϕ). Thus an appropriate notion for an equivalent martingale measure in the case of a dividend paying asset is as an equivalent probability with respect to which the discounted price processes of self-financing trading strategies taking positions in this asset are local martingales.

Because of the equality $V_t^B(\phi) = V_t^B(\psi)$, where ϕ and ψ are as above, this will be true of an equivalent martingale measure for the dividend-free reduction S^1 of S. Since the price process S_t^1 satisfies

$$dS_t^1 = S_t^1\big((\mu(t) + q(t))dt + \sigma(t)dW_t\big)$$

this equivalent martingale measure P_B replaces the yield $\mu(t) + q(t)$ of the dividend-free reduction S_t^1 of S_t with the risk-free yield $r(t)$. Equivalently, P_B replaces the yield $\mu(t)$ of S_t with the difference $r(t) - q(t)$.

With this notion of equivalent martingale measure P_B the forward price F of S for delivery at time T can again be written as

$$F_t = F_t^1 = E_{P_B}\big[S_T^1|\mathcal{F}_t\big] = E_{P_B}\big[S_T|\mathcal{F}_t\big],$$

exactly as in the dividend-free case (recall $S_T^1 = S_T$).

Put call parity. Since European puts and calls on S have the same price processes as the corresponding puts and calls on S^1, the put call parity assumes the form $S_t^1 + P_t - C_t = Ke^{-R(t,T)}$, that is,

$$C_t - P_t = S_t e^{-Q(t,T)} - Ke^{-R(t,T)}.$$

3. THE GENERAL MARKET MODEL

Let $T^* > 0$ be finite, $(\Omega, \mathcal{F}, (\mathcal{F}_t)_{t \in [0,T^*]}, P)$ a filtered probability space, $\mathcal{F} = \mathcal{F}_{T^*}$. The filtration $(\mathcal{F}_t)$ is assumed to be augmented and right continuous and the σ-field $\mathcal{F}_0$ is trivial and hence all $\mathcal{F}_0$-measurable random variables constant. This is in accordance with our intuition that at time $t = 0$ (the present) the values of all processes can be observed and are thus not subject to uncertainty.

Recall that our theory of stochastic integration can handle only continuous integrators. Some naturally occurring local martingales M however are not necessarily continuous. This is the case for instance if $M_t = d(Q|\mathcal{F}_t)/d(P|\mathcal{F}_t)$ is the density process of an absolutely continuous measure $Q << P$ on $\mathcal{F}$. This process is merely known to have a right continuous version with left limits. In order to force such processes into the scope of our integration theory, we make the following assumption, which is not uncommon in the theory of mathematical finance:

3.0 Assumption. *$(\mathcal{F}_t)$ is the augmented filtration generated by some (not necessarily one dimensional) Brownian motion.*

In consequence every $(\mathcal{F}_t)$-adapted local martingale is automatically continuous (III.5.c.4).

3.a Preliminaries. Recall the conventions of III.6.e regarding processes with finite time horizons and let $\mathcal{S}$ denote the family of all continuous semimartingales on $(\Omega, \mathcal{F}, (\mathcal{F}_t)_{t \in [0,T^*]}, P)$ and $\mathcal{S}_+$ denote the family of all semimartingales $S \in \mathcal{S}$ satisfying $S(t) > 0$, P-as., for all $t \in [0, T^*]$.

To deal with markets trading infinitely many securities we need a slight extension of the vectorial stochastic integral of section III.2.f. Let I be an index set, not necessarily finite, and let $\mathcal{S}^I$ denote the family of all vectors $B = (B_i)_{i \in I}$, with $B_i \in \mathcal{S}$, for all $i \in I$.

For $B \in \mathcal{S}^I$ let $L(B)$ denote the family of all vectors $\theta = (\theta_i)_{i \in I}$ such that $\theta_i \in L(B_i)$, for all $i \in I$, and $\theta_i \neq 0$, for only finitely many $i \in I$. Note that $L(B)$ is a vector space. If $\theta \in L(B)$, the integral process $Y = \int \theta \cdot dB = \theta \bullet B$ is defined as $Y = \theta \bullet B = \sum_{i \in I} \theta_i \bullet B_i$, that is,

$$Y(t) = \int_0^t \theta(s) \cdot dB(s) = \sum_{i \in I} \int_0^t \theta_i(s) dB_i(s) \tag{0}$$

(the sum is finite). Here the stochastic differential dB is interpreted to be the vector $dB = (dB_i)_{i \in I}$ and the stochastic differential $\theta \cdot dB = \sum_i \theta_i dB_i$ is computed as expected. As in the one dimensional case the equality $dY = \theta \cdot dB$ is equivalent with $Y(t) = Y(0) + (\theta \bullet B)(t)$.

The vector valued process $\theta = (\theta_i)_{i \in I}$ is called *continuous*, *progressively measurable* and *locally bounded* if each component θ_i has the corresponding property. If θ is progressively measurable and locally bounded and satisfies $\theta_i = 0$, for all but finitely many $i \in I$, then $\theta \in L(B)$ and this condition is satisfied in particular if θ is continuous.

Call B a *local martingale* if each component B_i is a local martingale. In this case set $L^2_{loc}(B) = L(B)$ and let $\Lambda^2(B)$ and $L^2(B)$ denote the space of all vectors $\theta \in L(B)$ such that $\theta_i \in \Lambda^2(B_i)$ respectively $\theta_i \in L^2(B_i)$, for all $i \in I$. Then $L^2(B) \subseteq \Lambda^2(B) \subseteq L^2_{loc}(B) = L(B)$.

Assume that B is a local martingale. If $\theta \in L(B)$, then $Y = \theta \bullet B$ is a local martingale. If $\theta \in L^2(B)$ ($\theta \in \Lambda^2(B)$), then $Y = \theta \bullet B$ is a martingale in $\mathbf{H}^2$ (a square integrable martingale). All this follows from the corresponding facts in the one dimensional case.

We now have two versions of the stochastic product rule for vectorial stochastic differentials. Assume that $\theta, B \in \mathcal{S}^I$ and $\theta_i = 0$, for all but finitely many $i \in I$. Then $\theta \cdot B = \sum_i \theta_i B_i$ is defined and we have

$$d(\theta \cdot B) = \theta \cdot dB + B \cdot d\theta + d\langle \theta, B \rangle,$$

where $\langle \theta, B \rangle = \sum_i \langle \theta_i, B_i \rangle$. If $\xi \in \mathcal{S}$ and $B \in \mathcal{S}^I$, then $\xi B \in \mathcal{S}^I$ and we have the vectorial equation

$$d(\xi B) = \xi dB + B d\xi + d\langle \xi, B \rangle, \tag{1}$$

where $\langle \xi, B \rangle$ is the vector $\left(\langle \xi, B_i \rangle \right)_{i \in I}$ and $B d\xi$ is the vector $\left(B_i d\xi \right)_{i \in I}$. This follows simply from the one dimensional stochastic product rule applied to each coordinate. If $Y = \theta \bullet B$, then $\langle \xi, Y \rangle = \theta \bullet \langle \xi, B \rangle$, equivalently

$$d\langle \xi, Y \rangle_t = \theta(t) \cdot d\langle \xi, B \rangle_t, \tag{2}$$

with $d\langle \xi, B \rangle = \left(d\langle \xi, B_i \rangle \right)_{i \in I}$ as above.

3.b Markets and trading strategies. A *market* is a vector $B = (B_i)_{i \in I}$ of continuous, strictly positive semimartingales $B_i \in \mathcal{S}_+$ on the filtered probability space $(\Omega, \mathcal{F}, (\mathcal{F}_t)_{t \in [0,T^*]}, P)$. Here I is an index set, not necessarily finite. The number T^* is the finite time horizon at which all trading stops. The semimartingales B_i are to be interpreted as the price processes of securities, which are traded in B, with $B_i(t)$ being the cash price of security B_i at time t. We will call X a *security in B*, if $X = B_i$, for some $i \in I$. The probability P will be called the *market probability* to be interpreted as the probability controlling the realization of events and paths observed in the market. We make the following assumptions:

(a) The securities in B do not pay dividends or any other cashflows to their holder.
(b) Our market is frictionless and perfectly liquid, that is, there are no transaction costs or trading restrictions, securities are infinitely divisible and can be bought and sold in unlimited quantities.

Trading strategies. A *trading strategy* θ in B is an element $\theta \in L(B)$ to be interpreted as follows: the strategy invests in (finitely many of) the securities B_i, $i \in I$, with $\theta_i(t)$ being the number of shares of the security B_i held at time t. The value (cash price) $V_t(\theta)$ of this portfolio at time t is given by the inner product

$$V_t(\theta) = (\theta \cdot B)(t) = \sum_i \theta_i(t) B_i(t).$$

Note that the integrability condition $\theta_i \in L(B_i)$ is automatically satisfied if θ_i is locally bounded, especially if θ_i is continuous. If the market B is allowed to vary, we will write (θ, B) to denote a trading strategy investing in B and $V_t(\theta, B)$ to denote its value at time t. Thus $L(B)$ is the family of all trading strategies in B and this family is a vector space.

A trading strategy θ is called *nonnegative* respectively *tame*, if it satisfies

$$V_t(\theta) \geq 0, \quad \text{respectively}, \quad V_t(\theta) \geq m > -\infty, \quad P\text{-as.,}$$

for all $t \in [0, T^*]$ and some constant m. The existence of a lower bound for the value of a tame strategy means that an upper bound for the credit necessary to maintain the strategy during its entire life is known at the time of its inception. A linear combination with nonnegative, constant coefficients of tame (nonnegative) trading strategies is itself a tame (nonnegative) trading strategy.

As a simple example consider optional times $0 \leq \tau_1 \leq \tau_2 \leq T^*$ and recall that $]\!]\tau_1, \tau_2]\!]$ denotes the stochastic interval $\{ (\omega, t) \in \Omega \times R_+ \mid \tau_1(\omega) < t \leq \tau_2(\omega) \}$. Consider the following trading strategy investing only in the asset B_j with weight $\theta_j = 1_{]\!]\tau_1, \tau_2]\!]}$ ($\theta_i = 0$, for $i \neq j$). This strategy buys one share of B_j at time $\tau_1(\omega)$ and sells at time $\tau_2(\omega)$. Because of assumptions (a) and (b) the cumulative gains in this position up to time t are given by

$$G(t) = B_j(t \wedge \tau_2) - B_j(t \wedge \tau_1) = \int_0^t \theta_j(s) dB_j(s) = \int_0^t \theta(s) \cdot dB(s).$$

By linearity the cumulative gains up to time t from trading according to a trading strategy θ, which is a linear combination of strategies as above, is similarly given by the stochastic integral $G(t) = \int_0^t \theta(s) \cdot dB(s)$. By approximation a case can be made that this integral should be so interpreted for every trading strategy $\theta \in L(B)$ (III.2.c.7 and localization). This motivates the following definition: The strategy θ is called *self-financing* (in B) if it satisfies

$$V_t(\theta) = V_0(\theta) + \int_0^t \theta(s) \cdot dB(s), \quad t \in [0, T^*]. \tag{0}$$

Note that this can also be written as $V_t(\theta) = V_0(\theta) + (\theta \bullet B)(t)$. Thus the self financing condition means that the strategy can be implemented at time zero for a cost of $\theta(0) \cdot B(0)$ and thereafter the value of the portfolio evolves according to the gains and losses from trading only, that is, money is neither injected into nor withdrawn from the position. From (0) it follows that $V_t(\theta)$ is a continuous semimartingale. In differential form the self-financing condition can be written as

$$dV_t(\theta) = \theta(t) \cdot dB(t), \quad \text{equivalently}, \quad d(\theta \cdot B)(t) = \theta(t) \cdot dB(t).$$

A linear combination with constant coefficients of self-financing trading strategies is itself a self-financing trading strategy.

The simplest example of a self-financing trading strategy θ is a buy and hold strategy: At time zero buy $\theta_i(0)$ shares of security B_i and hold to the time horizon. Here the coefficients θ_i are constants and the self-financing condition $d(\theta \cdot B) = \theta \cdot dB$ follows from the linearity of the stochastic differential.

Arbitrage. A trading strategy θ is called an *arbitrage*, if it is self-financing and satisfies $V_0(\theta) = 0$, $V_{T^*}(\theta) \geq 0$, P-as., and $P\big(V_{T^*}(\theta) > 0\big) > 0$. Thus such a strategy can be implemented at no cost and allows us to cash out at time T^* with no loss and with a positive probability of a positive gain (free lunch). Such strategies can be shown to exist in very simple, reasonable markets (see example 1.c.3). Thus, in general, arbitrage can be ruled out only in restricted families of self-financing trading strategies.

Let $\underline{S}(B)$ denote the family of all tame, self-financing trading strategies in B. Note that $\underline{S}(B)$ is a convex cone in the space $L(B)$ of all trading strategies in B. If the market B is a local martingale, let $S^2(B)$ denote the family of all self-financing trading strategies $\theta \in L^2(B)$ and note that $S^2(B)$ is a subspace of $L^2(B)$.

Let us now develop the simplest properties of self-financing trading strategies. Since a trading strategy θ invests in only finitely many securities in B we assume (for the remainder of section 3.b) that the market $B = (B_1, B_2, \ldots, B_n)$ is finite. For a process $\xi \in \mathcal{S}$ we set $\xi B = (\xi B_1, \ldots, \xi B_n)$.

3.b.0 Numeraire invariance of the self-financing condition. *Let $\xi \in \mathcal{S}_+$ and $\theta \in L(B) \cap L(\xi B)$. Then θ is self-financing in B if and only if it is self-financing in the market ξB.*

Proof. By assumption θ is a trading strategy in both B and ξB. Assume now that θ is self-financing in B. Then $(\theta \cdot B)(t) = (\theta \cdot B)(0) + (\theta \bullet B)(t)$, thus $\langle \xi, \theta \cdot B \rangle = \langle \xi, \theta \bullet B \rangle = \theta \bullet \langle \xi, B \rangle$ and so $d\langle \xi, \theta \cdot B \rangle = \theta \cdot d\langle \xi, B \rangle$. To see that θ is self-financing in the market ξB we have to show that $d\big(\theta \cdot (\xi B)\big) = \theta \cdot d(\xi B)$. Indeed

$$d\big(\theta \cdot (\xi B)\big) = d\big(\xi(\theta \cdot B)\big) = \xi d(\theta \cdot B) + (\theta \cdot B)d\xi + d\langle \xi, \theta \cdot B \rangle$$
$$= \xi \theta \cdot dB + \theta \cdot (Bd\xi) + \theta \cdot d\langle \xi, B \rangle$$
$$= \theta \cdot \big[\xi dB + Bd\xi + d\langle \xi, B \rangle\big] = \theta \cdot d(\xi B).$$

Thus θ is self-financing in the market ξB. The converse follows by symmetry (replace ξ with $1/\xi$ and B with ξB). $\blacksquare$

Remarks. (a) The market ξB can be viewed as a version of the market B, where security prices are no longer cash prices, but are expressed as a multiple of the *numeraire process* $1/\xi$: $B(t) = \big(\xi(t)B(t)\big)\big(1/\xi(t)\big)$. In this sense 3.b.0 shows that the self-financing condition is unaffected by a change of numeraire.
(b) If $\theta_i \in L(\xi)$, $i = 1,\ldots,n$, then $\theta \in L(B)$ if and only if $\theta \in L(\xi B)$. See III.3.c.4.

3.b.1 Corollary. *Let $j \in \{1, \ldots, n\}$ and assume that $\theta \in L(B) \cap L(B/B_j)$. Then θ is self-financing in B if and only if*

$$\theta_j(t) = \theta_j(0) + \sum_{i \neq j} \left(\theta_j(0) \frac{B_i(0)}{B_j(0)} - \theta_i(t) \frac{B_i(t)}{B_j(t)} + \int_0^t \theta_i(s) d\left(\frac{B_i}{B_j}\right)(s) \right). \quad (1)$$

Proof. θ is self-financing in B if and only if θ is self-financing in B/B_j which is equivalent with

$$\theta(t) \cdot \frac{B(t)}{B_j(t)} = \theta(0) \frac{B(0)}{B_j(0)} + \int_0^t \theta_i(s) \cdot d\left(\frac{B}{B_j}\right)(s), \quad \text{equivalently,}$$

$$\sum_{i=1}^n \theta_i(t) \frac{B_i(t)}{B_j(t)} = \sum_{i=1}^n \theta_i(0) \frac{B_i(0)}{B_j(0)} + \sum_{i=1}^n \int_0^t \theta_i(s) d\left(\frac{B_i}{B_j}\right)(s).$$

Noting that $d\left(B_i/B_j\right)(s) = 0$, for $i = j$, this is equivalent with

$$\theta_j(t) + \sum_{i \neq j} \theta_i(t) \frac{B_i(t)}{B_j(t)} = \theta_j(0) + \sum_{i \neq j} \theta_i(0) \frac{B_i(0)}{B_j(0)} + \sum_{i \neq j} \int_0^t \theta_i(s) d\left(\frac{B_i}{B_j}\right)(s),$$

which, after rearrangement of terms, is (1). ∎

Remark. This means that the coefficients θ_i, $i \neq j$, of a self-financing trading strategy can be chosen arbitrarily if the coefficient θ_j is adjusted accordingly. In more practical terms, the security B_j is used to finance the positions in the remaining securities.

3.c Deflators. A process $\xi \in \mathcal{S}_+$ is called a *deflator* for the market $B = (B_i)$, if ξB_i is a P-martingale, for each $i \in I$. The market B is called *deflatable* (DF) if there exists a deflator ξ for B.

Similarly a *local deflator* for B is a process $\xi \in \mathcal{S}_+$ such that ξB_i is a P-local martingale, for each $i \in I$. The market B is called *locally deflatable* (LDF) if it admits a local deflator ξ.

3.c.0. *Let ξ be a local deflator for B and θ be a self-financing trading strategy in the market B. If $\theta \in L(\xi B)$, then $\xi(t) V_t(\theta)$ is a local martingale.*

Proof. Assume that $\theta \in L(\xi B)$. By the numeraire invariance of the self-financing condition θ is also a self-financing trading strategy in the market ξB. Thus

$$\xi(t) V_t(\theta, B) = \xi(t) \theta(t) \cdot B(t) = V_t(\theta, \xi B) = V_0(\theta, \xi B) + \int_0^t \theta(s) \cdot d(\xi B)(s)$$

and the result now follows from the fact that ξB is a vector of local martingales and hence the integral process $\theta \bullet (\xi B)$ a local martingale. ∎

Remark. If θ_j is the buy and hold strategy investing in B_j, then $V_t(\theta_j) = B_j(t)$ and $\xi V_t(\theta_j)$ is a local martingale by definition of a local deflator for B. Thus 3.c.0 can be viewed as an extension of this property to certain other self-financing trading strategies. The buy and hold strategy θ_j is in $L(\xi B)$ since it is continuous and hence locally bounded. However, in general $L(B) \neq L(\xi B)$, that is, the markets B and ξB do not have the same trading strategies.

Note that each deflator ξ for B is also a local deflator for B. If B admits a local deflator ξ, then certain arbitrage strategies in B are ruled out:

3.c.1. *If ξ is a local deflator for B, then there are no arbitrage strategies in the spaces $S^2(\xi B)$ and $\underline{S}(\xi B)$.*

Proof. If $\theta \in \underline{S}(\xi B)$, then $V_t(\theta, \xi B) = V_0(\theta, \xi B) + \big(\theta \bullet (\xi B)\big)(t)$ is a P-local martingale which is bounded below and hence is a supermartingale (I.8.a.7). If $\theta \in S^2(\xi B)$, then $V_t(\theta, \xi B)$ is a square integrable P-martingale. In every case $V_t(\theta, \xi B)$ has a nonincreasing mean. Thus $V_0(\theta, \xi B) = 0$ and $V_{T^*}(\theta, \xi B) \geq 0$ combined with $E(V_{T^*}(\theta, \xi B)) \leq E(V_0(\theta, \xi B)) = 0$ implies that $V_{T^*}(\theta, \xi B) = 0$, P-as. Thus θ cannot be an arbitrage strategy in the market ξB. ∎

3.c.1 rules out arbitrage strategies in $S^2(\xi B)$ and $\underline{S}(\xi B)$. Now assume that θ is an arbitrage strategy in B. Then θ will be an arbitrage strategy in $S^2(\xi B)$ respectively $\underline{S}(\xi B)$ if it is an element of $S^2(\xi B)$ respectively $\underline{S}(\xi B)$. This follows from $V_t(\theta, \xi B) = \xi(t) V_t(\theta, B)$. By the numeraire invariance of the self-financing condition θ will be in $S^2(\xi B)$ whenever it is in $L^2(\xi B)$. If θ is in $\underline{S}(B)$ it need not be in $\underline{S}(\xi B)$ even if it is a trading strategy in the market ξB. If $V_t(\theta, B)$ is bounded below, the same need not be true of $V_t(\theta, \xi B) = \xi(t) V_t(\theta, B)$. However if $V_t(\theta, B) \geq 0$, then $V_t(\theta, \xi B) \geq 0$. Thus, if θ is a nonnegative trading strategy in $\underline{S}(B) \cap L(\xi B)$, then $\theta \in \underline{S}(\xi B)$. Note that the integrability condition $\theta \in L(B)$ is automatically satisfied (for every market B) if the process θ is locally bounded.

Consequently 3.c.1 rules out the existence of arbitrage strategies θ in B which either satisfy $\theta \in L^2(\xi B)$ or which are nonnegative strategies satisfying $\theta \in L(\xi B)$. Example 1.c.3 shows that arbitrage can occur even in a very simple market B with deflator $\xi = 1$, i.e., in which the securities are already martingales under the market probability P.

For the remainder of section 3.c, let $B = (B_0, B_1, \ldots, B_n)$ be a finite market and let us develop conditions for the existence of a local deflator ξ for B. Recall that the compensator u_X of a process $X \in \mathcal{S}$ is the unique continuous bounded variation process such that $u_X(0) = 0$ and $X - u_X$ is a P-local martingale. Similarly the multiplicative compensator U_X of a process $X \in \mathcal{S}_+$ is the unique positive continuous bounded variation process such that $U_X(0) = 1$ and X/U_X is a P-local martingale. The compensator u_X and multiplicative compensator U_X are related by

$$\frac{du_X}{X} = \frac{dU_X}{U_X} \qquad \text{(III.3.f.0)}. \tag{0}$$

3.c.2. *Let $X \in \mathcal{S}_+$ and $Y \in \mathcal{S}$. Then the equality $u_X = -\langle X, Y \rangle$ is equivalent with $U_X = exp\left(-\langle log(X), Y \rangle\right)$.*

Proof. The second equality is equivalent with $log(U_X) = -\langle log(X), Y \rangle$. As both processes vanish at zero this is equivalent with $d\,log(U_X) = -d\langle log(X), Y \rangle$. Using that U_X is a bounded variation process and III.3.c.2.(b) this can be written as $dU_X(t)/U_X(t) = -X_t^{-1}d\langle X, Y \rangle_t$, equivalently (using (0)), $du_X(t) = -d\langle X, Y \rangle_t$. As both u_X and $\langle X, Y \rangle$ vanish at zero this is equivalent with $u_X = -\langle X, Y \rangle$. ∎

3.c.3. *Let $j \in \{0, 1, \ldots, n\}$, $\xi, C \in \mathcal{S}_+$ and assume that ξB_j is a P-local martingale. Then the following are equivalent:*
(a) ξC is a P-local martingale.
(b) $u_{C/B_j} = -\langle \frac{C}{B_j}, log(\xi B_j) \rangle$.
(c) $U_{C/B_j} = exp\left(-\langle log(\frac{C}{B_j}), log(\xi B_j) \rangle\right)$.

Proof. The equivalence of (b) and (c) follows from 3.c.2. Let us now show the equivalence of (a) and (b). Write $\xi C = (C/B_j)(\xi B_j)$ and note that $u_{\xi B_j} = 0$. Thus, using III.3.c.3.(a) and III.3.c.2.(c),

$$
\begin{aligned}
du_{\xi C} = du_{(C/B_j)(\xi B_j)} &= (C/B_j)du_{\xi B_j} + \xi B_j du_{C/B_j} + d\langle C/B_j, \xi B_j \rangle \\
&= \xi B_j \left[du_{C/B_j} + (\xi B_j)^{-1}d\langle C/B_j, \xi B_j \rangle \right] \\
&= \xi B_j \left[du_{C/B_j} + d\langle C/B_j, log(\xi B_j) \rangle \right] \\
&= \xi B_j d\left[u_{C/B_j} + \langle (C/B_j), log(\xi B_j) \rangle \right].
\end{aligned}
$$

The equivalence of (a) and (b) follows since ξC is a P-local martingale if and only if $du_{\xi C} = 0$. ∎

3.c.4 Theorem. *Fix $j \in \{0, 1, \ldots, n\}$. Then the market B is LDF if and only if there exists a process $\xi \in \mathcal{S}_+$ such that*

$$
\begin{aligned}
u_{C/B_j} &= -\langle \tfrac{C}{B_j}, log(\xi B_j) \rangle, \quad equivalently \\
U_{C/B_j} &= exp\left(-\langle log(\tfrac{C}{B_j}), log(\xi B_j) \rangle\right),
\end{aligned}
\tag{1}
$$

for all $C = B_0, B_1, \ldots, B_n$. Moreover if ξ is such a process then $\xi/U_{\xi B_j}$ is a local deflator for B.

Proof. The equivalence of the equalities in (1) follows from 3.c.4. If B is LDF and ξ a local deflator for B (consequently ξB_j a local martingale), then 3.c.5 yields (1) for all $C = B_1, B_2, \ldots, B_n$.
Conversely assume that $\xi \in \mathcal{S}_+$ is a process satisfying

$$
u_{C/B_j} = -\langle \tfrac{C}{B_j}, log(\xi B_j) \rangle,
\tag{2}
$$

for all $C = B_0, B_1, \ldots, B_n$ and set $\zeta = \xi/U_{\xi B_j}$. We must show that ζ is a local deflator for B. Note first that ζB_j is a local martingale. Moreover $log(\zeta B_j) = log(\xi B_j) - log(U_{\xi B_j})$, where the process $log(U_{\xi B_j})$ is a continuous bounded variation process. Consequently (2) still holds when ξ is replaced with ζ since this does not change the quadratic variation on the right. Thus 3.c.3 implies that ζC is a local martingale, for all $C = B_0, B_1, \ldots, B_n$. ∎

3.d Numeraires and associated equivalent probabilities. Assume that ξ is a local deflator for the market B, that is, ξB is a P-local martingale. Let $A \in \mathcal{S}_+$ and set $X^A(t) = X(t)/A(t)$, for each process $X \in \mathcal{S}$. Then the market $B^A = (B_i^A(t))_i$ can be viewed as a version of the market B where the prices of securities are now expressed as multiples of the numeraire process A rather than as cash prices. The numeraire A need not be a security in B.

Assume that ξA is a P-martingale. Define the measure P_A on $\mathcal{F} = \mathcal{F}_{T^*}$ as

$$P_A(E) = E_P\left[((\xi A)(T^*)/(\xi A)(0))1_E\right], \quad \text{for all sets } E \in \mathcal{F}.$$

Then P_A is absolutely continuous with respect to P with strictly positive Radon-Nikodym derivative

$$dP_A/dP = (\xi A)(T^*)/(\xi A)(0). \tag{0}$$

Consequently the measure P_A is equivalent to P. Set

$$Z_A(t) = (\xi A)(t)/(\xi A)(0), \quad t \in [0, T^*].$$

Then Z_A is a P-martingale with $Z_A(0) = 1$ and so $E_P[Z_A(T^*)] = E_P[Z_A(0)] = 1$. It follows that P_A is a probability measure. Let

$$M_t = \frac{d(P_A|\mathcal{F}_t)}{d(P|\mathcal{F}_t)}, \quad t \in [0, T^*], \tag{1}$$

where $P_A|\mathcal{F}_t$ and $P|\mathcal{F}_t$ denote the restrictions of P_A respectively P to the σ-field $\mathcal{F}_t$ as usual. Then M_t is a martingale with $M_{T^*} = Z_A(T^*)$. Thus

$$M_t = Z_A(t) = (\xi A)(t)/(\xi A)(0), \quad \text{for all } t \in [0, T^*]. \tag{2}$$

P_A is called the *A-numeraire probability* (associated with the deflator ξ). The change from cash to other numeraires in the computation of prices is an extremely useful technique (see the ubiquitous use of forward prices and the forward martingale measure (3.f) below).

3.d.0. *Let $0 \le t \le T^*$, h an $\mathcal{F}_t$-measurable random variable and X be any $(\mathcal{F}_t)$-adapted process. Then*
(a) $h/A(t) \in L^1(P_A)$ if and only if $\xi(t)h \in L^1(P)$.
(b) $X^A(t)$ is a P_A-martingale if and only if $\xi(t)X(t)$ is a P-martingale.
(c) $X^A(t)$ is a P_A-local martingale if and only if $\xi(t)X(t)$ is a P-local martingale.
(d) If $0 \le s \le t$ and $h/A(t) \in L^1(P_A)$, then

$$A(s)E_{P_A}\left[h/A(t)|\mathcal{F}_s\right] = (1/\xi(s))E_P\left[\xi(t)h|\mathcal{F}_s\right].$$

Proof. This follows from Bayes' Theorem I.8.b.0 and (2) above. For example:
(b) $X^A(t)$ is a P_A-martingale if and only if $M_t X^A(t) = \xi(t)X(t)/\xi(0)A(0)$ is a P-martingale. Here $\xi(0)$ and $A(0)$ are constants (convention about $\mathcal{F}_0$).
(d) If $h/A(t) \in L^1(P_A)$, then

$$E_{P_A}\left[h/A(t)|\mathcal{F}_s\right] = \frac{E_P\left[M_t h/A(t)|\mathcal{F}_s\right]}{M_s}.$$

Using that $M_t = [\xi(t)A(t)]/[\xi(0)A(0)]$, $M_s = [\xi(s)A(s)]/[\xi(0)A(0)]$, cancelling the constant $\xi(0)A(0)$ and multiplying with $A(s)$ yields (d). ∎

3.d.1. *Let $A, C \in \mathcal{S}_+$ be any two numeraires such that ξA, ξC are P-martingales, $0 \le t \le T^*$, h an $\mathcal{F}_t$-measurable random variable and X any $(\mathcal{F}_t)$-adapted process. Then*
(a) $h/A(t) \in L^1(P_A)$ if and only if $h/C(t) \in L^1(P_C)$.
(b) $X^A(t)$ is a P_A-martingale if and only if $X^C(t)$ is a P_C-martingale.
(c) $X^A(t)$ is a P_A-local martingale if and only if $X^C(t)$ is a P_C-local martingale.
(d) If $0 \le s \le t$ and $h/A(t) \in L^1(P_A)$, then

$$A(s)E_{P_A}\left[h/A(t)|\mathcal{F}_s\right] = C(s)E_{P_C}\left[h/C(t)|\mathcal{F}_s\right].$$

Proof. This follows from 3.d.0. For example: (b) Both are equivalent with $\xi(t)X(t)$ being a P-martingale.
(d) Both sides of the equation are equal to $(1/\xi(s))E_P\left[\xi(t)h|\mathcal{F}_s\right]$. ∎

Formula (d) will be referred to as the *symmetric numeraire change formula*.

Local martingale measures. Let $A \in \mathcal{S}_+$. An *A-martingale measure (A-local martingale measure)* for B is a probability measure Q on $\mathcal{F} = \mathcal{F}_{T^*}$ which is equivalent to the market probability P and such that the process $B_i^A(t)$ is a Q-martingale (Q-local martingale), for each security B_i in B.

3.d.2. *Let $A \in \mathcal{S}_+$, Q a probability on $\mathcal{F}_{T^*}$ equivalent to P and*

$$M_t = d(Q|\mathcal{F}_t)/d(P|\mathcal{F}_t), \quad t \in [0, T^*].$$

Then Q is an A-(local) martingale measure for B if and only if $\xi(t) = M_t^A$ is a (local) deflator for B. In this case $Q = P_A$ is the A-numeraire measure associated with the deflator ξ.

Proof. By Bayes' Theorem, $B_i^A(t)$ is a Q-martingale (Q-local martingale) if and only if $M_t B_i^A(t) = \xi(t)B_i(t)$ is a P-martingale (P-local martingale), for each security $B_i \in B$. Thus, if ξ is a deflator (local deflator) for B, then Q is an A-martingale measure (A-local martingale measure).

Conversely, if Q is an A-martingale measure (A-local martingale measure) then ξ will be a deflator (local deflator) for B if it is a continuous process. However since M_t is a martingale adapted to the Brownian filtration $(\mathcal{F}_t)$, it is continuous (III.5.c.4), and the continuity of ξ follows.

Assume now that $\xi(t) = M_t^A$ is a local deflator for B. Note $M_t = \xi(t)A(t)$. Since M_t is a martingale with mean 1 and M_0 is a constant, we have $\xi(0)A(0) = M_0 = 1$. Hence $dQ/dP = M_{T^*} = \xi(T^*)A(T^*) = \xi(T^*)A(T^*)/\xi(0)A(0)$ and so $Q = P_A$. ∎

3.d.3 Remark. If ξ is a local deflator for B then the market probability P itself is the local martingale measure $P = P_A$ for the process $A = 1/\xi \in \mathcal{S}_+$.

Thus there exists a deflator ξ for the market B if and only if there exists an A-martingale measure for B, for some process $A \in \mathcal{S}_+$. In this case there exists an A-martingale measure for B, for every process $A \in \mathcal{S}_+$ such that ξA is a P-martingale.

Moreover, if a process $A \in \mathcal{S}_+$ is fixed, then $\xi = M^A$ defines a one to one correspondence between A-martingale measures (A-local martingale measure) for B and deflators (local deflators) ξ for B such that $\xi(0)A(0) = 1$ and ξA is a P-martingale. In this sense deflators for B and (equivalent) martingale measures associated with numeraires are the same concept.

Riskless bond and spot martingale measure. A *riskless bond* in B is a security $B_0 \in B$ which is of bounded variation and satisfies $B_0(0) = 1$. It is the bounded variation property of the price process which makes investment in this security less risky. If B is locally deflatable, then B can contain at most one riskless bond. Indeed, if ξ is any local deflator for B, then the local martingale property of ξB_0 combined with $B_0(0) = 1$ implies that $B_0 = 1/U_\xi$.

Conversely, if B is locally deflatable and ξ a local deflator for B, then $B_0 = 1/U_\xi$ is a continuous bounded variation process such that $B_0(0) = 1$ and ξB_0 is a P-local martingale. Thus B_0 can be added to B as a riskless bond and ξ will remain a deflator for the enlarged market.

Assume now that B is locally deflatable. As we have just seen we may assume that B contains a riskless bond B_0. B_0 is then a distinguished numeraire asset. A B_0-*(local)* martingale measure for B is called a *(local) spot martingale measure* for B. If a (local) deflator ξ for B is fixed, then the B_0-numeraire measure $P_0 = P_{B_0}$ (associated with the deflator ξ) is a (local) spot martingale measure for B and is referred to as *the* (local) spot martingale measure for B. From $B_0 = 1/U_\xi$ it follows that P_0 has density $dP_0/dP = (\xi B_0)(T^*)/(\xi B_0)(0) = \xi(T^*)/\xi(0)U_\xi(T^*)$.

3.d.4. Let $A \in \mathcal{S}_+$, Q an A-local martingale measure for B, $M_t = d(Q|\mathcal{F}_t)/d(P|\mathcal{F}_t)$, $\xi = M^A$ and $\theta \in L(B) \cap L(\xi B)$ a self-financing trading strategy. Then

(a) $V_t^A(\theta)$ is a Q-local martingale.

(b) There is no arbitrage $\theta \in L(B) \cap L(\xi B)$ such that the process $V_t^A(\theta)$ is bounded below.

Remark. The integrability condition $\theta \in L(B) \cap L(\xi B)$ is automatically satisfied if θ is locally bounded.

Proof. (a) According to 3.c.0 the process $M_t V_t^A(\theta) = \xi(t)V_t(\theta)$ is a P-local martingale and hence $V_t^A(\theta)$ a Q-local martingale (3.d.0.(c)).

(b) Let $\theta \in L(B) \cap L(\xi B)$ be self-financing such that the process $V_t^A = V_t^A(\theta)$ is bounded below. Then V_t^A is a Q-local martingale and hence a Q-supermartingale (I.8.a.7). In particular the mean $E_Q[V_t^A]$ is nonincreasing.

Assume now that $V_{T^*}^A \geq 0$ and $Q[V_{T^*}^A > 0] > 0$. Then $E_Q[V_0^A] \geq E_Q[V_{T^*}^A] > 0$. Thus $V_0(\theta) \neq 0$ and θ cannot be an arbitrage strategy. ∎

3.d.5. *Let $A \in \mathcal{S}_+$ and assume that B admits an A-local martingale measure Q. Then the market B^A does not admit arbitrage in the cone $\underline{S}(B^A)$.*

Proof. Let Q be an A-local martingale measure and $\theta \in \underline{S}(B^A)$ with $V_0(\theta) = 0$. In particular θ is a trading strategy investing in the market B^A. From the self-financing property of θ we have $V_t(\theta) = V_0(\theta) + (\theta \bullet B^A)_t = (\theta \bullet B^A)_t$, where the integral process $\theta \bullet B^A$ is computed with respect to the probability P. Recall from III.4.a.3 that B^A-integrability of θ and the stochastic integral $\theta \bullet B^A$ do not change when we switch to the equivalent probability Q. Under Q however the integrator B^A is a local martingale and so $V(\theta) = \theta \bullet B^A$ is a local martingale and hence a supermartingale since it is bounded below (I.8.a.7). Thus the mean $E_Q[V_t(\theta)]$ is nonincreasing. Consequently $E_Q[V_{T^*}(\theta)] \leq E_Q[V_0(\theta)] = 0$. Thus we cannot have $V_{T^*}(\theta) \geq 0$ and $Q[V_{T^*}(\theta) > 0] > 0$ and so θ cannot be an arbitrage strategy. ∎

3.e Absence of arbitrage and existence of a local spot martingale measure. Let $B = (B_0, B_1, \ldots, B_n)$ be a finite market. From 3.d.5 we know that the existence of an A-local martingale measure Q for B rules out arbitrage strategies in the space $\underline{S}(B^A)$. Let us now investigate the converse: Does the absence of arbitrage in $\underline{S}(B^A)$ imply the existence of an A-local martingale measure?

We will assume that the numeraire A is a security in the market B. Then the market B^A contains the riskless bond $A^A(t) = 1$. Equivalently, replacing the market B with B^A, we may assume that

$$B_0(t) = A(t) = 1$$

and seek an equivalent probability Q on $\mathcal{F} = \mathcal{F}_{T^*}$ such that all assets B_i in B are Q-local martingales. Let us call such Q a *local martingale measure* for B (a local 1-martingale measure in previous terminology).

It turns out that it suffices to have no arbitrage in a much smaller space of trading strategies than $\underline{S}(B)$. Indeed, let $\mathcal{V}$ be the space of all trading strategies $\theta \in S(B)$ such that the process $V_t(\theta)$ is *uniformly bounded*, that is, $|V_t(\theta)| \leq C$ for some constant C and all $t \in [0, T^*]$ and let

$$V = \{ V_{T^*}(\theta) \mid \theta \in \mathcal{V} \} \subseteq L^\infty(\Omega, \mathcal{F}, P)$$

be the space of all terminal payoffs $h = V_{T^*}(\theta)$ of the trading strategies $\theta \in \mathcal{V}$. Write $L^\infty = L^\infty(\Omega, \mathcal{F}, P)$, $L^p = L^p(\Omega, \mathcal{F}, P)$ and $L^0 = L^0(\Omega, \mathcal{F}, P)$. Recall that L^0 is simply the space of all $\mathcal{F}$-measurable random variables.

The space $\mathcal{V}$ contains sufficiently many trading strategies to imply properties for the asset processes B_i themselves. Consider an asset B_i in B. Since the process B_i is not necessarily bounded, $\mathcal{V}$ will not in general contain the buy and hold strategy investing in B_i. However, fixing $k > |B_i(0)|$ and setting

$$\tau_k = \inf\{ t > 0 : |B_i(t)| > k \}, \tag{0}$$

we have $|B_i(t \wedge \tau_k)| \leq k$, $t \in [0, T^*]$, by continuity of B_i. If τ is any optional time with values in $[0, T^*]$, let $\rho_k = \tau \wedge \tau_k$ and consider the strategy $\theta = (\theta_0, \ldots, \theta_n)$ investing only in $B_0 = 1$ and B_i, buying one share of B_i at time zero, selling this at time ρ_k, with the proceeds buying shares of B_0 and holding these until time T^*. More formally

$$\theta_j = 0, \ j \neq 0, i, \quad \theta_i = 1_{[0, \rho_k]}, \quad \theta_0 = 1_{]\rho_k, T^*]} B_i(\rho_k). \tag{1}$$

We claim that $\theta \in \mathcal{V}$. Clearly $V_t(\theta) = B_i(t \wedge \rho_k)$ is uniformly bounded. Let us now verify that θ is self-financing. Indeed, since $dB_0(s) = 0$, we have

$$V_t(\theta) = B_i(t \wedge \rho_k) = B_i(0) + \int_0^{t \wedge \rho_k} 1 \, dB_i(s)$$

$$= V_0(\theta) + \int_0^t \left\{ 1_{[0, \rho_k]} dB_i(s) + 1_{]\rho_k, T^*]} B_i(\rho_k) dB_0(s) \right\}$$

$$= V_0(\theta) + \int_0^t \theta(s) \cdot dB(s), \quad \text{as desired.}$$

Price functional. Assume that there is no arbitrage in $\mathcal{V}$. If $\theta \in \mathcal{V}$, the element $h = V_{T^*}(\theta) \in V$ can be thought of as a random payoff (claim) at time T^* which can be implemented at time zero at cost $V_0(\theta)$ by trading according to the strategy θ. It is now tempting to define the *price* $\pi_0(h)$ at time zero of h as $\pi_0(h) = V_0(\theta)$. To see that this price is well defined, we must show that $\theta, \phi \in \mathcal{V}$ and $V_{T^*}(\theta) = h = V_{T^*}(\phi)$ implies that $V_0(\theta) = V_0(\phi)$. To this end it will suffice to show that $\theta \in \mathcal{V}$ and $V_{T^*}(\theta) \geq 0$ implies that $V_0(\theta) \geq 0$. The proof of this is very similar to the proof of the following

$$\theta \in \mathcal{V}, \ V_{T^*}(\theta) \geq 0, \ V_{T^*}(\theta) \neq 0 \quad \Rightarrow \quad V_0(\theta) > 0, \tag{2}$$

which is needed below and which follows easily from the absence of arbitrage in $\mathcal{V}$. Note first that $\mathcal{V}$ contains the strategy ρ which buys one share of the asset $B_0 = 1$ at time zero and holds until time T^*. Assume now that (contrary to (2)) $\theta \in \mathcal{V}$, $V_{T^*}(\theta) \geq 0$, $V_{T^*}(\theta) \neq 0$ (hence $P[V_{T^*}(\theta) > 0] > 0$) but $V_0(\theta) \leq 0$. Set $a = -V_0(\theta) \geq 0$ and consider the strategy $\chi = \theta + a\rho \in \mathcal{V}$ going long θ at time zero and using the surplus a to buy and hold shares of B_0. Then χ has zero cost at time zero and payoff $V_{T^*}(\chi) = V_{T^*}(\theta) + a \geq V_{T^*}(\theta)$. Thus χ is an arbitrage in $\mathcal{V}$.

For a subspace $W \subseteq L^p(P)$, $1 \leq p \leq \infty$, let $W_+ = \{h \in W \mid h \geq 0\}$ and call a linear functional π on W *strictly positive*, if $h \in W_+$, $h \neq 0$ implies $\pi(h) > 0$. Here $h = 0$ means $h = 0$, P-as. Let q be the exponent conjugate to p, defined by $(1/p) + (1/q) = 1$.

If Q is any measure on $\mathcal{F}$ which is absolutely continuous with respect to P and satisfies $m = dQ/dP \in L^q$, then $\pi(h) = E_Q(h) = E_P(mh)$ defines a positive linear functional on L^p. This functional is strictly positive if and only if $m > 0$, P-as., that is, iff Q is equivalent to P.

Recall that $V_0(\theta)$ is a constant (assumption 1.0). Consequently the pricing functional $\pi_0 : h = V_{T^*}(\theta) \in V \mapsto \pi_0(h) = V_0(\theta) \in R$ is well defined and is a *strictly positive* linear functional on V. We need

3.e.0. *Each positive linear functional π on L^p is continuous.*

Proof.   Assume that the positive linear functional π on L^p is discontinuous and choose a sequence $(f_n) \subseteq L^p$ such that $\left\| f_n \right\|_{L^p} = 1$ and $\pi(f_n) \geq n2^n$, for all $n \geq 1$. Set $g_n = |f_n|$ and $g = \sum_n 2^{-n} g_n \in L^p$ (the series converges absolutely). Then $g \geq 2^{-n} g_n \geq 2^{-n} f_n$ and the positivity of π implies that $\pi(g) \geq 2^{-n} \pi(f_n) \geq n$, for all $n \geq 1$. This contradicts the finiteness of $\pi(g)$. ∎

Assume now that Q is a local martingale measure for B. If $\theta \in \mathcal{V}$, then $V_t(\theta) = V_0(\theta) + (\theta \bullet B)_t$, $t \in [0, T^*]$, where $\theta \bullet B$ can be interpreted to be a stochastic integral with respect to Q. Thus $V_t(\theta)$ is a uniformly bounded Q-local martingale and hence a Q-martingale. Consequently, for $h = V_{T^*}(\theta) \in V$,

$$\pi_0(h) = V_0(\theta) = E_Q\big[V_0(\theta)\big] = E_Q\big[V_{T^*}(\theta)\big] = E_Q(h).$$

If in addition the Radon-Nikodym derivative $m = dQ/dP$ is in L^q, then $\pi(h) = E_Q(h) = E_P(mh)$, $h \in L^p$, defines an extension of π_0 from $V \subseteq L^\infty \subseteq L^p$, to a *strictly positive* linear functional π on L^q. The measure Q can be recovered from this extension via $Q(A) = \pi(1_A)$, $A \in \mathcal{F}$.

Conversely assume we have a strictly positive extension π of π_0 from V to L^p. Then π is continuous and so there is a function $m \in L^q$ such that $\pi(h) = E_P(mh)$, for all $h \in L^p$. Then $Q(A) = \pi(1_A) = E_P(m1_A)$, $A \in \mathcal{F}$, defines a measure Q which is absolutely continuous with respect to P and has Radon-Nikodym derivative $m \in L^q$ and satisfies $\pi(h) = E_P(mh) = E_Q(h)$, for all $h \in L^p$. Because of the strict positivity of π, Q is equivalent with P. Note that V contains the buy and hold strategy investing in $B_0 = 1$. Thus $1 \in V$ and $\pi_0(1) = 1$. Consequently $Q(\Omega) = \pi(1) = \pi_0(1) = 1$ and so Q is a probability measure.

Finally let us verify that Q is a local martingale measure for B. Since $B_0 = 1$ we have to show only that B_i is a Q-local martingale, for all $i = 1, \ldots, n$. Consider the asset B_i and let $\theta \in V$ be the trading strategy defined in (0), (1). It satisfies $V_0(\theta) = B_i(0)$ and $h = V_{T^*}(\theta) = B_i(\rho_k) = B_i(\tau \wedge \tau_k)$. Thus

$$E_Q\big[B_i(\tau \wedge \tau_k)\big] = E_Q(h) = \pi(h) = \pi_0(h) = B_i(0) = E_Q\big[B_i(0)\big].$$

This is true for each optional time τ with values in $[0, T^*]$. According to I.9.c.4 this shows that $B_i(t \wedge \tau_k)$ is a Q-martingale (indexed by $t \in [0, T^*]$). Since the optional times τ_k satisfy $\tau_k \uparrow \infty$, as $k \uparrow \infty$, it follows that B_i is a Q-local martingale (recall the conventions in III.6.e). We have now seen:

If there is no arbitrage in $\mathcal{V}$, then there exists a local martingale measure Q for B with $dQ/dP \in L^q(P)$ if and only if the pricing functional $\pi_0 : V \to R$ has an extension to a strictly positive linear functional on $L^p(P)$.

It is known that the absence of arbitrage in $\mathcal{V}$ alone does not imply the existence of a local martingale measure for B [DS, example 7.7, p509]. The above suggests that we should strengthen the no arbitrage condition in such a manner as to ensure

that the price functional π_0 extends to a strictly positive linear functional on L^p. To this end we introduce the notion of p-approximate arbitrage in $\mathcal{V}$. Recall that $L^p(P)_+ = \{ f \in L^p(P) \mid f \geq 0 \}$ and let $C_p = L^p(P)_+ \setminus \{0\}$.
A *p-approximate arbitrage* is a sequence $(\theta_n) \subseteq \mathcal{V}$ such that
(a) $V_0(\theta_n) = 0$, for all $n \geq 1$, and
(b) there exists a sequence $(f_n) \subseteq L^p(P)$ and $f \in C_p$ such that $f_n \leq V_{T^*}(\theta_n)$, for all $n \geq 1$, and $f_n \to f$ in L^p-norm.
In particular then $\pi_0\big(V_{T^*}(\theta)\big) = V_0(\theta) = 0$, that is, $V_{T^*}(\theta) \in ker(\pi_0)$, for each $n \geq 1$. The above terminology arises from the fact that the $h_n = V_{T^*}(\theta_n)$ are payoffs at time T^* which can be implemented at no cost at time zero via self-financing trading strategies $\theta_n \in \mathcal{V}$ and yet these payoffs are no less than functions f_n converging to a nonnegative function f which is nonzero and hence positive with positive probability. In particular if θ is an arbitrage strategy in $\mathcal{V}$, then the sequence $\theta_n = \theta$ is a p-approximate arbitrage in $\mathcal{V}$, for all $p \geq 1$. Simply let $f_n = V_{T^*}(\theta_n)$, $n \geq 1$.

The market B is called *strongly arbitrage free of order p $(SAF(p))$* if it does not admit a p-approximate arbitrage in $\mathcal{V}$. If B is $SAF(p)$, then there is no arbitrage in $\mathcal{V}$.

Let $p_1 < p_2$. Then $L^{p_2} \subseteq L^{p_1}$ and the inclusion map $L^{p_2} \hookrightarrow L^{p_1}$ is continuous. From this it follows that each p_2-approximate arbitrage is also a p_1-approximate arbitrage. Consequently the condition $SAF(p_1)$ implies $SAF(p_2)$, that is, the condition $SAF(p)$ becomes weaker as $p \uparrow \infty$ and is weakest for $p = \infty$.

Assume that there is no arbitrage in $\mathcal{V}$ and hence the pricing functional π_0 is defined. Observing that a function $f_n \in L^p$ satisfies $f_n \leq V_{T^*}(\theta_n)$ for some strategy $\theta_n \in \mathcal{V}$ with $V_0(\theta_n) = 0$ if and only if $f_n \in ker(\pi_0) - L_+^p$, it is easily seen that the condition $SAF(p)$ is equivalent with

$$\overline{ker(\pi_0) - L_+^p} \cap L_+^p = \{0\} \quad \text{equivalently} \quad \overline{ker(\pi_0) - C_p} \cap C_p = \emptyset.$$

Assume now that B is $SAF(p)$ and $1 \leq p < \infty$. Then the space $L^p(P)$ is separable and so Clark's separation theorem (appendix A.3) implies the existence of a continuous linear functional π_1 on $L^p(P)$ such that $\pi_1 = 0$ on $ker(\pi_0)$ and $\pi_1 > 0$ on C_p, that is, π_1 is a strictly positive linear functional on $L^p(P)$. Recall that $1 \in \mathcal{V}$ and $\pi_0(1) = 1$ and let $h \in \mathcal{V}$ be arbitrary. Then $h - \pi_0(h)1 \in ker(\pi_0)$ and consequently $\pi_1\big(h - \pi_0(h)1\big) = 0$, that is,

$$\pi_1(h) = \pi_1(1)\pi_0(h).$$

Here $\lambda = \pi_1(1) > 0$. It follows that the functional $\pi = \lambda^{-1}\pi_1$ satisfies $\pi = \pi_0$ on $\mathcal{V}$. Consequently π is an extension of π_0 to a strictly positive linear functional on $L^p(P)$. As seen above this implies that $Q(A) = \pi(1_A)$, $A \in \mathcal{F}$, defines a local martingale measure for B with $dQ/dP \in L^q(P)$.

Conversely, if Q is a local martingale measure for B with $dQ/dP \in L^q(P)$, then B is $SAF(p)$. In fact, for such Q, $\pi(h) = E_Q(h)$, $h \in L^p(P)$, defines an extension of π_0 to a strictly positive linear functional on $L^p(P)$. Assume now that (θ_n) is an approximate arbitrage in $\mathcal{V}$, $h_n = V_{T^*}(\theta_n)$ and $f_n, f \in L^p(P)$ are such that $f_n \leq h_n$ and $f_n \to f \in C_p$ in L^p-norm. Since π is strictly positive and extends π_0, it follows that

$$\pi(f_n) \leq \pi(h_n) = \pi_0(h_n) = 0 \quad \text{and} \quad \pi(f_n) \to \pi(f) > 0,$$

a contradiction. Thus the existence of a local martingale measure Q for B with $dQ/dP \in L^q(P)$ implies that B is $SAF(p)$. We can summarize these findings as follows:

3.e.1 Theorem. *Assume that $B = (B_0, \ldots, B_n)$ is a finite market containing the riskless bond $B_0 = 1$, $1 \leq p < \infty$ and q is the exponent conjugate to p. Then the following are equivalent:*
(i) B is $SAF(p)$.
(ii) There exists a local martingale measure Q for B with $dQ/dP \in L^q(P)$.
(iii) There exists a local deflator ξ for B with $\xi(T^*) \in L^q(P)$.

Proof. The equivalence of (i) and (ii) has been seen above. For the equivalence of (ii) and (iii) see section 3.d.3 ($\xi(t) = E_P[dQ/dP \mid \mathcal{F}_t]$, $\xi(T^*) = dQ/dP$). ∎

Remark. We really do not care whether the Radon-Nikodym derivative of a local martingale measure Q for B is in $L^q(P)$ but this is a consequence of the condition $SAF(p)$. This suggests that $SAF(p)$ is too strong if all we want is a local martingale measure for B. Indeed, this condition was formulated so as to be able to apply Clark's Extension Theorem and thus to stay within the bounds of reasonably simple functional analysis.

The conditions $SAF(p)$ become increasingly weaker as $p \uparrow \infty$ and one wonders what happens for $p = \infty$. This case is inaccessible to our means, as $L^\infty(P)$ is not a separable space. If B is a finite market with locally bounded asset prices and time horizon $T^* = 1$ the existence of an equivalent local martingale measure is equivalent to the condition NFLVR (no free lunch with vanishing risk) defined as follows:

> *There does not exist a sequence (θ_n) of self-financing trading strategies in B satisfying $V_0(\theta_n) = 0$, $V_1(\theta_n)^- \to 0$ uniformly and $V_1(\theta_n) \to f$, P-as., as $n \uparrow \infty$, for some function $f \geq 0$ with $P(f > 0) > 0$.*

The reader is referred to [DS, Corollary 1.2, p479].

3.f Zero coupon bonds and interest rates. To introduce certain notions frequently encountered in the financial literature consider a market B (not necessarily finite) equipped with a riskless bond B_0 of the form

$$B_0(t) = exp\left(\int_0^t r(s)ds\right), \tag{0}$$

where r is a process in $L(\mathbf{t})$. The value $r(t)$ should then be thought of as the (annualized) rate at time t for riskless borrowing over the infinitesimal time interval $[t, t + dt]$. $B_0(t)$ should be thought of as the price process of a strategy continuously rolling over risk-free loans over infinitesimal time intervals at the rate $r(t)$. Among existing financial instruments the money market account comes closest to this abstraction.

The process $r(t)$ is then called the *short rate process*. We assume that the market B is locally deflatable and admits a local deflator ξ for B such that ξB_0 is a martingale. Fix such a deflator ξ and let $P_0 = P_{B_0}$ denote the corresponding local spot martingale measure.

3.f.0. *Let θ be a self-financing trading strategy in B such that $\theta \in L(\xi B)$. If the price process $V_t(\theta)$ is of bounded variation, then $V_t(\theta) = V_0(\theta)B_0(t)$.*

Proof. Write $V(t) = V_t(\theta)$. According to 3.c.0, ξV is a P-local martingale and so V/B_0 a P_0-local martingale (3.d.0.(c)). The bounded variation property now implies that $V(t)/B_0(t)$ is constant in time (I.9.b.1) and the result follows. ∎

Remark. So far we only used that B_0 has bounded variation paths. From $dB_0(t) = r(t)B_0(t)dt$, it follows that $dV_t(\theta) = r(t)V_t(\theta)dt$. This result is frequently stated as follows: a riskless and self-financing strategy must earn the risk-free rate of return.

Zero coupon bonds. A *zero coupon bond expiring at time T* is a process $B_T \in \mathcal{S}_+$ satisfying $B_T(T) = 1$. We are not interested in a zero coupon bond after its time of expiration; however it lives on until the time horizon. In a real market this feature can be duplicated by simply rolling over expiring zero coupon bonds into the money market account.

A zero coupon bond B_T is useful as a numeraire asset only if $\xi(t)B_T(t)$ is a martingale. This assumption is satisfied automatically if B_T is a security in B and ξ is in fact a deflator for B. If $\xi(t)B_T(t)$ is a martingale, then $\xi(t)B_T(t) = E_P[\xi(T)B_T(T) \mid \mathcal{F}_t] = E_P[\xi(T) \mid \mathcal{F}_t]$, that is,

$$B_T(t) = \xi(t)^{-1}E_P[\xi(T) \mid \mathcal{F}_t], \quad \forall t \in [0, T],$$

and so B_T is uniquely determined on the interval $[0, T]$. This leads us to define the canonical zero coupon bond $B(t, T)$ as

$$B(t, T) = \xi(t)^{-1}E_P[\xi(T) \mid \mathcal{F}_t], \quad \forall t \in [0, T^*]. \tag{1}$$

Then $\xi(t)B(t,T)$ is a martingale adapted to the Brownian filtration $(\mathcal{F}_t)$ and hence continuous. Since ξ is strictly positive, so is the process $B(t,T)$. Clearly $B(T,T) = 1$. Thus $B(t,T)$ is in fact a zero coupon bond.

From 3.d.0.(b) it follows that $B_0(t)^{-1}B(t,T)$ is a P_0-martingale (indexed by t). Combined with $B(T,T) = 1$ this implies that $B_0(t)^{-1}B(t,T) = E_{P_0}[B_0(T)^{-1} \mid \mathcal{F}_t]$, that is,

$$B(t,T) = B_0(t)E_{P_0}[B_0(T)^{-1} \mid \mathcal{F}_t], \quad t \in [0,T]. \tag{2}$$

Commuting the $\mathcal{F}_t$-measurable factor $B_0(t)$ into the conditional expectation and using (0) to infer that $B_0(t)B_0(T)^{-1} = exp(-\int_t^T r(s)ds)$, this can be written as

$$B(t,T) = E_{P_0}\left[exp(-\int_t^T r(s)ds) \mid \mathcal{F}_t\right]. \tag{3}$$

Remark. If the short rate process $r(t)$ is nonstochastic, equation (2) becomes $B(t,T) = B_0(t)/B_0(T)$ or $B(t,T) = B_t B_T^{-1}$ in the notation of section 2, which proceeds under this assumption.

Forward rates. In keeping with prevailing customs we choose one year as the unit of time and express all rates of interest as annualized rates, that is, as rates of return over one year.

Now let $t \leq T < U \leq T^*$. By trading in zero coupon bonds we can implement at time t a loan of one dollar (to a hypothetical issuer of zero coupon bonds) over the future time interval $[T,U]$: at time t sell one zero coupon bond maturing at time T and with the proceeds $B(t,T)$ buy $B(t,T)/B(t,U)$ zero coupon bonds maturing at time U. With the understanding that the zero coupon bonds are redeemed at the time of maturity, this strategy induces the following cash flows:

$$\begin{array}{ccc} 0 & -1 & B(t,T)/B(t,U) \\ \bullet & \bullet & \\ t & T & U \end{array} \tag{4}$$

The annualized, continuously compounded rate $R = f(t,T,U)$ of interest on this loan is given by the equation $1 \cdot e^{R(U-T)} = B(t,T)/B(t,U)$, that is

$$f(t,T,U) = \frac{log\, B(t,T) - log\, B(t,U)}{U - T}.$$

The quantity $f(t,T,U)$ is called the *forward rate* at time t for risk-free borrowing over the interval $[T,U]$. Assuming that the zero coupon bond $B(t,T)$ is pathwise differentiable in the tenor T, we can let $U \downarrow T$ to obtain the *instantaneous forward rate* $f(t,T)$ at time t for risk-free borrowing over the infinitesimal time interval $[T, T+dt]$ as

$$f(t,T) = -\frac{\partial}{\partial T} log\, B(t,T) = -\frac{(\partial/\partial T)B(t,T)}{B(t,T)}. \tag{5}$$

If $f(t,T)$ is a (pathwise) continuous function of T it follows that

$$log\, B(t,T) = log\, B(t,t) + \int_t^T \frac{\partial}{\partial s} log\, B(t,s)ds = -\int_t^T f(t,s)ds,$$

whence
$$B(t,T) = exp\big(-\int_t^T f(t,s)ds\big)$$

which agrees with the interpretation of $(f(t,s))_{s\in[t,T]}$ as the development over the interval $[t,T]$ of the instantaneous risk-free rate anticipated at time t.

If the short rate process $r(t)$ is bounded and continuous, then the differentiability of $B(t,T)$ with respect to T follows from the representation (3). Indeed, under this assumption the derivative $(\partial/\partial T)B(t,T)$ can be computed by commuting $\partial/\partial T$ with the conditional expectation in (3) yielding

$$\tfrac{\partial}{\partial T}B(t,T) = E_{P_0}\left[-r(T)exp\big(-\int_t^T r(s)ds\big) \mid \mathcal{F}_t\right]. \tag{6}$$

Especially for $T = t$ we obtain $\tfrac{\partial}{\partial T}B(t,T)\big|_{T=t} = -r(t)$. Thus (5) and $B(t,t) = 1$ yield
$$f(t,t) = r(t),$$

also in accordance with intuition. Since these results will not be used in the sequel we omit a formal justification of the interchange of differentiation and conditional expectation in (6). Such a justification can be based on the dominated convergence theorem for conditional expectations (I.2.b.9). The reader who objects to the fluid introduction of assumptions (continuity and boundedness of the short rate process) may take solace in the fact that the subject of short rates and continuously compounded forward rates will not be pursued any further. Instead we will focus on Libor rates.

Forward Libor. The simple annualized rate of interest $L(t,T,U)$ implied by the zero coupon bond prices $B(t,T)$, $B(t,U)$ via the cash flow diagram (4) is given by the equation
$$\frac{B(t,T)}{B(t,U)} = 1 + \delta L(t,T,U), \tag{7}$$

where $\delta = U - T$, and is called *forward Libor at time t for the interval* $[T,U]$. If $t = T$ we call this rate *Libor set at time T* and denote it more simply by $L(T)$ with the understanding that the period $\delta = U - T$, over which Libor is set, is clear from the context. The definition then simplifies to $B(T,U)^{-1} = 1 + \delta L(T)$. Libor rates are the most fundamental interest rates and will be studied in section 5.

Forward Martingale Measures. Let $T \in (0,T^*]$. Then $A(t) = B(t,T)$ is a numeraire asset such that ξA is a martingale. Thus the A-local martingale measure P_A is defined and its restriction P_T to the σ-field $\mathcal{F}_T$ given by

$$\frac{dP_T}{dP} = \frac{(\xi A)(T)}{(\xi A)(0)} = \frac{\xi(T)B(T,T)}{\xi(0)B(0,T)}.$$

The measure P_T is called the *forward local martingale measure at date T*. If ξ is in fact a deflator (rather than a local deflator) for B, then we will call P_T the forward martingale measure at date T.

If $S(t)$ is any asset in B, then $S^A(t) = S(t)/B(t,T)$ should be interpreted as the price of S at time t expressed in constant time T dollars (dollars deliverable at time T). This price is called the *forward price* at time t *of* S deliverable at time T and denoted $F_S(t,T) = S(t)/B(t,T)$. We will see below that this price is related to forward contracts in the same way as the corresponding notion in section 2.a.

Likewise, if B_0 is a riskless bond for B, $S^0(t) = S(t)/B_0(t)$ is called the discounted price of S at time t and should be interpreted as the price of S at time t expressed in constant time zero dollars.

In the theory of pricing European options the short rate process and even the riskless bond (and with it the spot martingale measure P_0) can be dispensed with. However the family of zero coupon bonds and associated forward martingale measures are indispensable.

3.g General Black-Scholes model and market price of risk. Let us consider a finite market $B = (B_1, \ldots, B_n)$ and assume that the processes B_j are Ito processes satisfying
$$\frac{dB_j(t)}{B_j(t)} = \mu_j(t)dt + \sigma_j(t) \cdot dW_t, \quad 1 \le j \le n,$$

where $W_t = (W_t^1, \ldots, W_t^d)$ is a Brownian motion on $[0, T^*]$ with $d \le n$, $\mu_j \in L(\mathbf{t})$ and $\sigma_j \in L(W)$, $1 \le j \le n$. Using III.6.a.0 this can be rewritten as

$$
\begin{aligned}
d\log(B_j(t)) &= \left(\mu_j(t) - \tfrac{1}{2}\|\sigma_j(t)\|^2\right)dt + \sigma_j(t) \cdot dW_t \\
&= \left(\mu_j(t) - \tfrac{1}{2}\|\sigma_j(t)\|^2\right)dt + \sum_{k=1}^{d} \sigma_{jk}(t)dW_t^k.
\end{aligned}
\tag{0}
$$

Let us investigate when the market B admits a local deflator ξ which is itself an Ito process satisfying
$$\frac{d\xi(t)}{\xi(t)} = -r(t)dt - \phi(t) \cdot dW_t, \tag{1}$$

for some processes $r \in L(\mathbf{t})$ and $\phi \in L(W)$. If S is any Ito process satisfying

$$\frac{dS(t)}{S(t)} = \mu_S(t)dt + \sigma_S(t) \cdot dW_t, \tag{2}$$

for some processes $\mu_S \in L(\mathbf{t})$ and $\sigma_S \in L(W)$, then

$$
\begin{aligned}
d(\xi S)(t) &= \xi(t)dS(t) + S(t)d\xi(t) + d\langle \xi, S\rangle_t \\
&= \xi(t)S(t)\mu_S(t)dt + \xi(t)S(t)\sigma_S(t) \cdot dW_t \\
&\quad - S(t)\xi(t)r(t)dt - S(t)\xi(t)\phi(t) \cdot dW_t - \xi(t)S(t)\sigma_S(t) \cdot \phi(t)dt \\
&= \xi(t)S(t)\left[\mu_S(t) - r(t) - \sigma_S(t) \cdot \phi(t)\right]dt + \xi(t)S(t)\left(\sigma_S(t) - \phi(t)\right) \cdot dW_t.
\end{aligned}
$$

Thus ξS is a local martingale if and only if

$$\mu_S(t) - r(t) - \sigma_S(t) \cdot \phi(t) = 0, \tag{3}$$

and in this case we see that S and the local martingale ξS satisfy

$$dS(t)/S(t) = \big(r(t) + \phi(t) \cdot \sigma_S(t)\big)dt + \sigma_S(t) \cdot dW_t \quad \text{and}$$
$$d(\xi S)(t)/(\xi S)(t) = \big(\sigma_S - \phi\big)(t) \cdot dW_t, \quad \text{that is,} \tag{4}$$
$$(\xi S)(t) = (\xi S)(0)\mathcal{E}_t\left[(\sigma_S - \phi)\bullet W\right].$$

Set $\mu(t) = (\mu_1(t), \ldots, \mu_n(t))'$, $1_n = (1, 1, \ldots, 1)' \in R^n$ and let $\sigma(t)$ denote the $n \times d$-matrix with rows $\sigma_j(t)'$. It follows from (3) that ξ is a local deflator for B if and only if $\mu_j(t) - r(t) - \sigma_j(t) \cdot \phi(t) = 0$, for all $1 \le j \le n$, that is

$$\sigma(t)\phi(t) = \mu(t) - r(t)1_n. \tag{5}$$

Thus B is LDF with a local deflator ξ of the form (1) if and only if there exist processes $r \in L(\mathbf{t})$, $\phi \in L(W)$ satisfying (5). From (1) it follows that $U_\xi(t) = exp\big(-\int_0^t r(s)ds\big)$ and so the unique riskless bond $B_0 = 1/U_\xi$ associated with the deflator ξ has the form

$$B_0(t) = exp\big(\int_0^t r(s)ds\big). \tag{6}$$

The process $r(t)$ is then interpreted to be the short rate process, that is, $r(t)$ is the continuously compounded rate for lending over the infinitesimal time interval $[t, t+dt]$. It is customary to specify the short rate process $r \in L(\mathbf{t})$ as an additional structural element of the market B and B_0 is then defined to be the riskless bond given by (6) but not assumed to be a security of B. Indeed, if B were to contain a riskless bond, the volatility matrix σ would contain a zero row, an undesirable flaw.

If the short rate process $r(t)$ is specified, the existence of a local deflator ξ of the form (1) is equivalent with the existence of a process $\phi \in L(W)$ satisfying (5), equivalently $\mu_j(t) - r(t) - \sigma_j(t) \cdot \phi(t) = 0$, for all $j = 1, \ldots, n$. Such a process ϕ is called a *market price of risk process*. This terminology arises as follows: Rewrite (0) as

$$B_j(t) = B_j(0)exp\left(\int_0^t \mu_j(s)ds\right)\mathcal{E}_t(\sigma_j \bullet W).$$

Under mild conditions on the process σ_j the exponential local martingale $\mathcal{E}_t(\sigma_j \bullet W)$ is a martingale, that is, a process which is neither expected to increase or decrease. In this case the process $\mu_j(t)$ can be viewed as the continuously compounded expected return process on the security $B_j(t)$.

The Brownian motion $W_t = (W_t^1, \ldots, W_t^d)$ represents the source of random shocks to the instantaneous returns $d\log(B_j(t))$ and the components $\sigma_{jk}(t)$ of $\sigma_j(t)$ measure the intensity of the shocks $\sigma_{jk}(t)dW_t^k$ and consequently the risk inherent in the security B_j. Rewriting (2) (for $S = B_j$) as

$$\mu_j(t) - r(t) = \sigma_j(t) \cdot \phi(t) = \sum_{k=1}^d \sigma_{jk}(t)\phi_k(t)$$

we see that the process $\phi(t)$ relates this risk to the excess of the expected return on the security B_j over the risk-free rate $r(t)$.

The market B together with a short rate process $r \in L(\mathbf{t})$ and a market price of risk process $\phi \in L(W)$ satisfying (5) is called the *general Black Scholes market*. This market is locally deflatable, and ξ defined by (1) and normalized by $\xi(0) = 1$ is a local deflator for B. Explicitly

$$\xi(t) = exp\big(-\textstyle\int_0^t r(s)ds\big)\mathcal{E}_t\big(-\phi\bullet W\big) = B_0(t)^{-1}\mathcal{E}_t\big(-\phi\bullet W\big). \tag{7}$$

If the matrix $\sigma(t)$ has full rank (and hence $\sigma(t)'\sigma(t)$ is invertible) at all points (t,ω) then multiplication of (5) with $(\sigma(t)'\sigma(t))^{-1}\sigma(t)'$ on the left implies that we must have $\phi(t) = (\sigma(t)'\sigma(t))^{-1}\sigma(t)'\big(\mu(t) - r(t)1_n\big)$. In this case the market price of risk process is uniquely determined (by the short rate, security returns and volatilities in B). Conditions have to be placed on $\sigma(t)$, $\mu(t)$ and $r(t)$ to ensure that $\phi \in L(W)$. According to (4) the deflated securities ξB_j satisfy

$$(\xi B_j)(t) = (\xi B_j)(0)\mathcal{E}_t\big[(\sigma_j - \phi)\bullet W\big].$$

Under mild conditions on the processes σ_j, ϕ, the exponential local martingale $\mathcal{E}_t\big[(\sigma_j - \phi)\bullet W\big]$ is in fact a martingale, for all $j = 1,\ldots, n$. In this case ξ given by (7) is in fact a deflator for the General Black-Scholes market B. We shall assume that ξB_0 is a martingale and hence the spot martingale measure P_0 is defined.

Consider now the zero coupon bond $B(t,T) = \xi(t)^{-1}E_P\big(\xi(T) \mid \mathcal{F}_t\big)$ expiring at time T. According to III.5.e.1 the strictly positive $(\mathcal{F}_t)$-adapted martingale $\xi(t)B(t,T)$ can be represented as

$$\xi(t)B(t,T) = \xi(0)B(0,T)\mathcal{E}_t(\alpha\bullet W), \quad t \in [0,T], \tag{8}$$

for some process $\alpha \in L(W)$. Setting $b(t,T) = \alpha(t) + \phi(t)$ we obtain

$$\xi(t)B(t,T) = \xi(0)B(0,T)\mathcal{E}_t\big((b(\cdot,T) - \phi)\bullet W\big), \quad t \in [0,T]. \tag{9}$$

From (1) and (8) combined with III.6.a.0 it follows that

$$d\,log\xi(t) = -\big(r(t) + \tfrac{1}{2}\|\phi(t)\|^2\big)dt - \phi(t)\cdot dW_t,$$
$$d\,log\big(\xi(t)B(t,T)\big) = -\tfrac{1}{2}\|\alpha(t)\|^2 dt + \alpha(t)\cdot dW_t.$$

Upon subtraction, $d\,logB(t,T) = \big[r(t) + \tfrac{1}{2}\big(\|\phi(t)\|^2 - \|\alpha(t)\|^2\big)\big]dt + b(t,T)\cdot dW_t$ and so

$$\frac{d\,B(t,T)}{B(t,T)} = \big[r(t) + \tfrac{1}{2}\big(\|\phi(t)\|^2 - \|\alpha(t)\|^2 + \|b(t,T)\|^2\big)\big]dt + b(t,T)\cdot dW_t$$

Since here $\|\phi(t)\|^2 - \|\alpha(t)\|^2 + \|b(t,T)\|^2 = \|\phi(t)\|^2 - \|b(t,T) - \phi(t)\|^2 + \|b(t,T)\|^2 = 2\phi(t)\cdot b(t,T)$ this simplifies to

$$\frac{d\,B(t,T)}{B(t,T)} = \big[r(t) + \phi(t)\cdot b(t,T)\big]dt + b(t,T)\cdot dW_t. \tag{10}$$

From (7) and (8) we have

$$\xi(t)B_0(t) = \mathcal{E}_t\left(-\phi \bullet W\right) \quad \text{and}$$
$$\xi(t)B(t,T) = \xi(0)B(0,T)\mathcal{E}_t\left[(b(\cdot,T) - \phi) \bullet W\right]. \tag{11}$$

Dynamics under the spot and forward martingale measure. Assume now that ξS is a local martingale and so (4) and (5) hold. Since ξ is a local deflator for B this is true in particular for every asset S in B, but also for example for $S(t) = B(t,T)$. For later use we shall now determine the dynamics of S under the spot martingale measure P_0 and the forward martingale measure P_T. To do this we must switch from the P-Brownian motion W to Brownian motions W_t^0, W_t^T with respect to P_0 respectively P_T by means of III.4.c.0. Recall that $\xi(0)B_0(0) = 1$. Thus the spot martingale measure P_0 is defined by $dP_0/dP = \xi(T^*)B_0(T^*) = \mathcal{E}_{T^*}\left(-\phi \bullet W\right)$. Using (11) it follows that

$$M_t^0 = \frac{d(P_0|\mathcal{F}_t)}{d(P|\mathcal{F}_t)} = \xi(t)B_0(t) = \mathcal{E}_t(-\phi \bullet W), \quad t \in [0, T^*].$$

According to III.4.c.0 it follows that $W_t^0 = W_t + \int_0^t \phi(s)ds$ is a Brownian motion on $(\Omega, \mathcal{F}, (\mathcal{F}_t), P_0)$. Obviously $dW_t = dW_t^0 - \phi(t)dt$. Substitute this into (2) and recall from (3) that $\mu_S(t) - \sigma_S(t) \cdot \phi(t) = r(t)$. This yields the dynamics of S under P_0 as

$$\frac{dS(t)}{S(t)} = \left(\mu_S(t) - \sigma_S(t) \cdot \phi(t)\right)dt + \sigma_S(t) \cdot dW_t^0 = r(t)dt + \sigma_S(t) \cdot dW_t^0. \tag{12}$$

Thus S has drift $r(t)$ under the spot martingale measure P_0. The volatility remains unchanged as always when we switch to some locally equivalent probability. Using (11) the forward martingale measure P_T on the σ-field $\mathcal{F}_T$ is defined by

$$\frac{dP_T}{dP} = \frac{\xi(T)B(T,T)}{\xi(0)B(0,T)} = \mathcal{E}_T\left[(b(\cdot,T) - \phi) \bullet W\right].$$

Thus $\quad M_t^T = \dfrac{d(P_T|\mathcal{F}_t)}{d(P|\mathcal{F}_t)} = \dfrac{\xi(t)B(t,T)}{\xi(0)B(0,T)} = \mathcal{E}_t\left[(b(\cdot,T) - \phi) \bullet W\right], \quad t \in [0, T].$

According to III.4.c.0 it follows that $W_t^T = W_t - \int_0^t \left(b(s,T) - \phi(s)\right)ds$ is a Brownian motion on $(\Omega, \mathcal{F}, (\mathcal{F}_t), P_T)$. We have $dW_t = dW_t^T + \left(b(t,T) - \phi(t)\right)dt$. Substituting this into (2) yields the dynamics of S under P_T as

$$\frac{dS(t)}{S(t)} = \left(r(t) + \sigma_S(t) \cdot b(t,T)\right)dt + \sigma_S(t) \cdot dW_t^T. \tag{13}$$

Especially for $S(t) = B(t,T)$ (then $\sigma_S(t) = b(t,T)$) we obtain

$$\frac{dB(t,T)}{B(t,T)} = \left(r(t) + \|b(t,T)\|^2\right)dt + b(t,T) \cdot dW_t^T. \tag{14}$$

Finally let us determine the dynamics of the forward price $F_S(t,T) = S(t)/B(t,T)$ under the forward martingale measure P_T. From (13) and (14) we obtain

$$d\,logS(t) = \left(r(t) + \sigma_S(t) \cdot b(t,T) - \tfrac{1}{2}\|\sigma_S(t)\|^2\right)dt + \sigma_S(t) \cdot dW_t^T \quad \text{and}$$
$$d\,logB(t,T) = \left(r(t) + \tfrac{1}{2}\|b(t,T)\|^2\right)dt + b(t,T) \cdot dW_t^T.$$

Subtraction yields $d\,logF_S(t,T) = -\tfrac{1}{2}\|\sigma_S(t) - b(t,T)\|^2 dt + \left(\sigma_S(t) - b(t,T)\right) \cdot dW_t^T$, from which it follows (III.6.a.0) that

$$\frac{d\,F_S(t,T)}{F_S(t,T)} = \left(\sigma_S(t) - b(t,T)\right) \cdot dW_t^T. \tag{15}$$

By assumption ξS is a P-local martingale and so $F_S(t,T) = S(t)/B(t,T)$ a P_T-local martingale (3.d.0.(c)). This explains the absence of the drift term.

4. PRICING OF RANDOM PAYOFFS AT FIXED FUTURE DATES

Let B be a market containing zero coupon bonds of all maturities $T \in (0, T^*]$ and ξ a local deflator for B such that ξB_j is a martingale, for each zero coupon bond B_j in B.

4.a European options. Fix a time $T \in (0, T^*]$ and let $B|T$ denote the market based on the filtered probability space $(\Omega, (\mathcal{F}_t)_{t \in [0,T]}, P)$ resulting from B by restricting the security processes in B to the interval $[0, T]$. Thus all trading stops at time T in the market $B|T$.

Lemma. *Let* $\tau : \Omega \to [0, T]$ *be an optional time and* ϕ *a trading strategy satisfying* $V_t(\phi) = \int_\tau^t \phi(s) \cdot dB(s)$, *P-as. on the set* $[\tau < t]$, *for all* $t \in [0, T]$. *Then the trading strategy* $\chi = 1_{]\tau, T]} \phi$ *is self-financing.*

Proof. Note that $V_t(\chi) = 1_{[\tau < t]} V_t(\phi)$ especially $V_0(\chi) = 0$. Thus we must show that $V_t(\chi) = \int_0^t \chi(s) \cdot dB(s)$, *P*-as., for all $t \in [0, T]$. Consider such t and note that $\chi = 0$ and so $\int_0^t \chi(s) \cdot dB(s) = 0 = V_t(\chi)$, *P*-as. on the set $[t \leq \tau]$ (III.2.d.4). Likewise on the set $[\tau < t]$ we have

$$V_t(\chi) = V_t(\phi) = \int_\tau^t \phi(s) \cdot dB(s) = \int_0^t 1_{]\tau, T]}(s)\phi(s) \cdot dB(s) = \int_0^t \chi(s) \cdot dB(s). \blacksquare$$

4.a.0. *Let* ψ_1, ψ_2 *be self-financing trading strategies with* $V_T(\psi_1) = V_T(\psi_2)$. *Then*
(a) $V_t(\psi_1) = V_t(\psi_2)$, *for all* $t \in [0, T]$, *or*
(b) there is arbitrage in the market $B|T$.

Proof. Assume that (b) is not true, set $\psi = \psi_1 - \psi_2$ and let $\epsilon > 0$. To establish (a) it will suffice to show that the optional time $\tau = \inf\{ t \in [0, T] \mid V_t(\psi) > \epsilon \} \wedge T$ satisfies $P(\tau < T) = 0$. Let ρ be the trading strategy which buys one share of the zero coupon bond $B(t, T)$ maturing at time T and holds this to time T. Set $Z = V_\tau(\phi)/B(\tau, T)$ and consider the trading strategy

$$\chi = 1_{]\tau, T]} Z\rho - 1_{]\tau, T]}\psi = 1_{]\tau, T]}\phi,$$

where $\phi = 1_{]\tau, T]} Z\rho - \psi$. Following the strategy χ we wait until time τ. If $\tau = T$ we do nothing. If $\tau < T$ we short the portfolio ψ (long ψ_2, short ψ_1) and invest the proceeds into the zero coupon bond $B(t, T)$. The self-financing property of ψ implies that

$$V_t(\psi) = V_0(\psi) + \int_0^t \psi(s) \cdot dB(s), \quad \forall t \in [0, T], \quad \text{and so}$$

$$V_\tau(\psi) = V_0(\psi) + \int_0^\tau \psi(s) \cdot dB(s).$$

Subtraction yields $\int_\tau^t \psi(s) \cdot dB(s) = V_t(\psi) - V_\tau(\psi)$, *P*-as. on the set $[\tau < t]$. Likewise the $\mathcal{F}_\tau$-measurability of Z and III.2.d.0.(i) imply that $\int_\tau^t 1_{]\tau, T]}(s) Z\rho(s) \cdot dB(s) =$

$\int_0^t Z1_{]\tau,T]}(s)dB(s,T) = Z(B(t,T) - B(t \wedge \tau, T))$. It follows that

$$\int_\tau^t \phi(s) \cdot dB(s) = Z(B(t,T) - B(\tau,T)) - \left(V_t(\psi) - V_\tau(\psi)\right)$$
$$= ZB(t,T) - V_t(\psi) = V_t(\phi),$$

P-as. on the set $[\tau < t]$. The preceding Lemma now shows that the strategy χ is self-financing. Since $V_0(\chi) = 0$ and $V_T(\chi) = Z > 0$, on the set $[\tau < T]$, we must have $P(\tau < T) = 0$. ∎

Remark. From example 1.c.3 we know that such arbitrage χ can coexist with the local deflator ξ for B. Thus we cannot conclude alternative (a) in 4.a.0. Additional assumptions on ϕ, θ are necessary.

4.a.1 Law of One Price. *Let ϕ, θ be trading strategies. If $\xi(t)\left(V_t(\phi) - V_t(\theta)\right)$ is a P-martingale, then $V_T(\phi) = V_T(\theta)$ implies that $V_t(\phi) = V_t(\theta)$, for all $t \in [0,T]$.*

Proof. Set $D_t = V_t(\phi) - V_t(\theta)$ and assume that $D_T = 0$. The martingale property of $\xi(t)D_t$ then implies that $D_t = 0$, that is, $V_t(\phi) = V_t(\theta)$, for all $t \in [0,T]$. ∎

Remark. If ϕ, θ are self-financing, then the processes $\xi(t)V_t(\phi)$ and $\xi(t)V_t(\theta)$ and hence the difference $\xi(t)\left(V_t(\phi) - V_t(\theta)\right)$ are P-local martingales (3.c.0). If in addition the maximal function $\sup_{t\in[0,T]} \xi(t)\left|V_t(\phi) - V_t(\theta)\right|$ is integrable, then $\xi(t)\left(V_t(\phi) - V_t(\theta)\right)$ is a P-martingale (I.8.a.4).

Options and replication. A *European option* exercisable at time T is a nonnegative, $\mathcal{F}_T$-measurable random variable h. The quantity $h(\omega)$ is the payoff received by the option holder at time T if the market is in state ω. The nonnegativity of h is the mathematical expression of the fact that holders of options traded in existing financial markets do not exercise an option unless it is in the money, that is, unless this results in a positive payoff. The $\mathcal{F}_T$-measurability corresponds to the fact that the uncertainty regarding the payoff $h(\omega)$, if exercised, is resolved by time T.

A trading strategy θ in $B|T$ is said to *replicate* the option h, if it is self-financing, $\xi(t)V_t(\theta)$ is a martingale and $V_T(\theta) = h$. Necessarily then $\xi(t)V_t(\theta) = E_P\left[\xi(T)V_T(\theta)|\mathcal{F}_t\right]$, that is

$$V_t(\theta) = \xi(t)^{-1}E_P\left[\xi(T)h|\mathcal{F}_t\right], \quad t \in [0,T]. \tag{0}$$

The option h is said to be *replicable* if and only if there exists a trading strategy θ in $B|T$ replicating h. Recall that for a self-financing trading strategy θ, the process $\xi(t)V_t(\theta)$ is automatically a P-local martingale; however to obtain formula (0) we need the stronger martingale condition.

Assume now that h is replicated by the trading strategy θ. To determine what the price $\pi_t(h)$ of the claim h at time $t \leq T$ should be, let us assume that we decide to trade h in our market according to some price process $\pi(t)$. To avoid arbitrage we must have $\pi(T) = h = V_T(\theta)$ and so $\pi(t) = V_t(\theta) = \xi(t)^{-1}E_P\left[\xi(T)h|\mathcal{F}_t\right]$, for all

$t \in [0, T]$ (4.a.0 with $\psi_1 = \theta$ and ψ_2 being the buy and hold strategy investing in h). This leads us to define the *arbitrage price* of h as

$$\pi_t(h) = \xi(t)^{-1} E_P\big[\xi(T)h \mid \mathcal{F}_t\big], \quad t \in [0, T]. \tag{1}$$

For later use we define $\pi_t(h)$ as in (1), even if h is not replicable. However then $\pi_t(h)$ can no longer be interpreted as the arbitrage price process of the claim h. Using 3.d.0.(d) with $A(t) = B(t, T)$ (then $A(T) = 1$), we see that

$$\pi_t(h) = B(t, T) E_{P_T}\big[h | \mathcal{F}_t\big], \quad t \in [0, T], \tag{2}$$

where P_T denotes the forward martingale measure at date T. If B contains a riskless bond B_0 such that ξB_0 is a martingale (and hence the spot martingale measure P_0 is defined), a similar application of 3.d.0.(d) with $A(t) = B_0(t)$ yields

$$\pi_t(h) = B_0(t) E_{P_0}\big[h/B_0(T) \mid \mathcal{F}_t\big], \quad t \in [0, T]. \tag{3}$$

Formula (2) points to the importance of the forward martingale measure P_T. The switch between forward martingale measures at different dates $S < T$ is made as follows:

4.a.2. *Let $0 \le t \le S < T$ and assume that h is $\mathcal{F}_S$-measurable. Then*
(a) $B(t, S) E_{P_S}[B(S, T) h \mid \mathcal{F}_t] = B(t, T) E_{P_T}[h \mid \mathcal{F}_t]$, if $h \ge 0$ or $h \in L^1(P_T)$.
(b) $B(t, S) E_{P_S}[h | \mathcal{F}_t] = B(t, T) E_{P_T}[h/B(S, T) \mid \mathcal{F}_t]$, if $h \ge 0$ or $h \in L^1(P_S)$.

Remark. Looking at formula (a) consider h as a random payoff occurring at time T. The right hand side evaluates this payoff at time t according to (2). The left hand side first discounts this payoff back to time S and then evaluates the discounted payoff at time t according to (2). A similar interpretation is possible for formula (b). Consider h as a payoff occurring at time S.

Proof. (b) Apply the symmetric numeraire change formula 3.d.1.(d) to the market $B|S$ and the numeraires $A(t) = B(t, S)$ and $C(t) = B(t, T)$. Noting that $A(S) = 1$ the symmetric numeraire change formula 3.d.1.(d)

$$A(t) E_{P_A}[h/A(S)|\mathcal{F}_t] = C(t) E_{P_C}[h/C(S)|\mathcal{F}_t]$$

yields $B(t, S) E_{P_S}[h|\mathcal{F}_t] = B(t, T) E_{P_T}[h/B(S, T)|\mathcal{F}_t]$.
(a) Simply replace h with $B(S, T)h$ in (b). ∎

4.a.3. *Let θ be a self-financing trading strategy such that $V_T(\theta) = h$ and $A \in \mathcal{S}_+$ a numeraire such that ξA is a martingale. Then θ replicates h if and only if $V_t^A(\theta) = V_t(\theta)/A(t)$ is a P_A-martingale.*

Proof. According to 3.d.0.(b), $V_t^A(\theta)$ is a P_A-martingale if and only if $\xi(t)V_t(\theta)$ is a P-martingale. ∎

4.b Forward contracts and forward prices. A *forward contract* for delivery of an asset Z in B at date T with strike price K obliges the holder of the contract to buy this asset at time T for K dollars thereby inducing a single cash flow $h = Z_T - K$ at time T. The *forward price* at time t for delivery of the asset Z at time T is defined to be that strike price K, which makes the value of the forward contract equal to zero at time t. The payoff $h = Z_T - K$ at time T can be implemented at time zero via the following self-financing trading strategy θ:

At time t buy one unit of the asset Z, sell K units of the zero coupon bond maturing at time T and hold until time T.

The Law of One Price suggests that the arbitrage price $\pi_t(h)$ of this forward contract at time $t \leq T$ be defined as $\pi_t(h) = V_t(\theta) = Z_t - KB(t,T)$. Setting this equal to zero and solving for K, we obtain the forward price $F_Z(t,T)$ at time t for delivery of the asset Z at time T as

$$F_Z(t,T) = \frac{Z_t}{B(t,T)}. \tag{0}$$

If $Z_t/B(t,T)$ is in fact a P_T-martingale (rather than only a local martingale), then (0) can be rewritten as

$$F_Z(t,T) = E_{P_T}\left[Z_T | \mathcal{F}_t\right]. \tag{1}$$

4.c Option to exchange assets. Fix $K > 0$ and let h be the European option to receive one unit of the asset S_1 in exchange for K units of the asset S_2 at time T. The payoff h of this option is given by $h = (S_1(T) - KS_2(T))^+$. If $S_2(t) = B(t,T)$ is the zero coupon bond maturing at time T, then $h = (S_1(T) - K)^+$ is the European call on S_1 with strike price K exercisable at time T, that is, the payoff at time T of the right to buy one share of S_1 for K dollars at time T.

Let us introduce the *exercise set* $A = \{\omega \in \Omega \mid S_1(T)(\omega) > KS_2(T)(\omega)\}$ that is the set of all states in which our option is exercised at time T. Then $h = (S_1(T) - KS_2(T))1_A$ and, assuming that this claim is replicable, its arbitrage price process $\pi_t(h)$ can be written as

$$\pi_t(h) = \xi(t)^{-1}E_P\left[\xi(T)S_1(T)1_A \mid \mathcal{F}_t\right] - K\xi(t)^{-1}E_P\left[\xi(T)S_2(T)1_A \mid \mathcal{F}_t\right]. \tag{0}$$

Let us now use the assets S_1, S_2 themselves as numeraires. Assume that the processes ξS_1, ξS_2 are martingales and hence the probabilities P_{S_1}, P_{S_2} defined Using 3.d.0.(d) with $h = S_j(T)1_A$, we can write $\xi(t)^{-1}E_P\left[\xi(T)S_j(T)1_A \mid \mathcal{F}_t\right] = S_j(t)E_{P_{S_j}}[1_A|\mathcal{F}_t]$, $j = 1,2$, and thus (0) becomes

$$\pi_t(h) = S_1(t)E_{P_{S_1}}[1_A|\mathcal{F}_t] - KS_2(t)E_{P_{S_2}}[1_A|\mathcal{F}_t]. \tag{1}$$

To get a more specific formula we need to make further assumptions on our market model. Assume that we are in the setting of the general Black-Scholes model of 3.g with a deflator ξ satisfying

$$\frac{d\xi(t)}{\xi(t)} = -r(t)dt - \phi(t) \cdot dW(t),$$

where W_t is a Brownian motion with respect to the market probability P generating the (augmented) filtration $(\mathcal{F}_t)$. The assets S_j are assumed to follow the dynamics

$$\frac{dS_j(t)}{S_j(t)} = \mu_j(t)dt + \sigma_j(t) \cdot dW(t), \quad j = 1, 2. \tag{2}$$

Then
$$\frac{d(\xi S_j)(t)}{(\xi S_j)(t)} = \big(\sigma_j(t) - \phi(t)\big) \cdot dW(t), \quad j = 1, 2 \tag{3}$$

(see 3.g.eq.(4)). Set $Z_t = log\big(S_1(t)/S_2(t)\big)$ and write the exercise set A as

$$A = \big[\, Z_T > log(K)\,\big]. \tag{4}$$

To evaluate the conditional expectations in (1) we must find the distribution of Z_T under the probabilities P_{S_j}, $j = 1, 2$. From (3) it follows that

$$d\,log(\xi S_j)(t) = -\frac{1}{2}\|\alpha_j(t)\|^2 dt + \alpha_j(t) \cdot dW(t), \tag{5}$$

where $\alpha_j(t) = \sigma_j(t) - \phi(t)$. Thus

$$\begin{aligned} dZ(t) &= d\,log(\xi S_1)(t) - d\,log(\xi S_2)(t) \\ &= \frac{1}{2}\big(\|\alpha_2(t)\|^2 - \|\alpha_1(t)\|^2\big)\,dt + (\alpha_1(t) - \alpha_2(t)) \cdot dW_t. \end{aligned} \tag{6}$$

To determine the conditional expectation $E_{P_{S_1}}[1_A|\mathcal{F}_t]$ we use III.4.c.0 to determine the dynamics of Z under the measure P_{S_1}. By definition of the measure P_{S_1} we have
$$M_t := \frac{d\,(P_{S_1}|\mathcal{F}_t)}{d\,(P|\mathcal{F}_t)} = \frac{(\xi S_1)(t)}{(\xi S_1)(0)}, \quad t \in [0, T],$$

and consequently, from (3), $\qquad \dfrac{dM_t}{M_t} = \alpha_1(t) \cdot dW_t.$

According to III.4.c.0 it follows that $W_t^{S_1} = W_t - \int_0^t \alpha_1(s)ds$ is a P_{S_1}-Brownian motion on $\big(\Omega, \mathcal{F}, (\mathcal{F}_t), P_{S_1}\big)$. Obviously $dW_t = \alpha_1(t)dt + dW_t^{S_1}$. Substituting this into (6) we find that

$$\begin{aligned} d\,Z(t) &= \left[\frac{1}{2}\big(\|\alpha_2\|^2 - \|\alpha_1\|^2\big) + (\alpha_1 - \alpha_2) \cdot \alpha_1\right]dt + (\alpha_1 - \alpha_2) \cdot dW_t^{S_1} \\ &= \frac{1}{2}\|\alpha_1 - \alpha_2\|^2 dt + (\alpha_1 - \alpha_2) \cdot dW_t^{S_1}, \end{aligned} \tag{7}$$

with respect to the measure P_{S_1} (i.e., for a P_{S_1}-Brownian motion $W_t^{S_1}$). We now make the following *assumption*: The process $\alpha_1(t) - \alpha_2(t) = \sigma_1(t) - \sigma_2(t)$ is *nonstochastic*. Then III.6.c.3 can be applied to the dynamics (7) to compute the conditional expectation $E_{P_{S_1}}\left[1_A|\mathcal{F}_t\right]$. Because of the special nature of the drift term in (7) the quantities $m(t,T)$, $\Sigma(t,T)$ from III.6.c.3 become

$$\Sigma^2(t,T) = \int_t^T \|(\alpha_1 - \alpha_2)(s)\|^2 ds \quad \text{and} \quad m(t,T) = \tfrac{1}{2}\Sigma^2(t,T)$$

and it follows that

$$E_{P_{S_1}}\left[1_A|\mathcal{F}_t\right] = N(d_1) \quad \text{where} \quad d_1 = \frac{\log\big(S_1(t)/KS_2(t)\big) + \tfrac{1}{2}\Sigma^2(t,T)}{\Sigma(t,T)}.$$

A similar computation starting from the equation

$$d\,Z(t) = -\frac{1}{2}\|(\alpha_1 - \alpha_2)\|^2 dt + (\alpha_1 - \alpha_2)\cdot dW_t^{S_2}$$

under the measure P_{S_2} yields $E_{P_{S_2}}\left[1_A|\mathcal{F}_t\right] = N(d_2)$, where

$$d_2 = \frac{\log\big(S_1(t)/KS_2(t)\big) - \tfrac{1}{2}\Sigma^2(t,T)}{\Sigma(t,T)} = d_1 - \Sigma(t,T).$$

Thus we have the option price

$$\pi_t(h) = S_1(t)N(d_1) - K\,S_2(t)N(d_2),$$

where d_1, d_2 are given as above. We can summarize these findings as follows:

4.c.0 Margrabe's Formula. *Assume that the asset prices $S_j(t)$, $j = 1,2$, follow the dynamics (2) above and that the process $\sigma_1 - \sigma_2$ is deterministic and satisfies $\Sigma^2(t,T) = \int_t^T \|(\sigma_1 - \sigma_2)(s)\|^2 ds > 0$, for all $t \in [0,T)$. Then the option $h = \big(S_1(T) - KS_2(T)\big)^+$ to exchange assets has arbitrage price process*

$$\pi_t(h) = S_1(t)N(d_1) - KS_2(t)N(d_2), \quad t \in [0,T),$$

where N is the standard normal cumulative distribution function and d_1, d_2 are as above.

Remark. From (6) it follows that the quantity $\Sigma^2(t,T)$ can also be written as

$$\Sigma^2(t,T) = \langle Z\rangle_t^T = \big\langle log\big(S_1/S_2\big)\big\rangle_t^T$$

and is thus a measure of the aggregate (percentage) volatility of S_1/S_2 on the interval $[t,T]$ under the market probability P, that is, realized in the market. If $S_2(t)$ is the zero coupon bond $B(t,T)$, then $h = \big(S_1(T) - K\big)^+$ is the European call on S_1 with strike price K. In this case the quotient $S_1(t)/S_2(t)$ is the *forward price* $F_{S_1}(t,T)$ of S_1 deliverable at time T and consequently the crucial quantity $\|(\sigma_1 - \sigma_2)(t)\|$ the volatility of the forward price of S_1 and not of S_1 itself.

The reader will note that the term structure of interest rates does not enter our formula unless one of the assets S_1, S_2 is a zero coupon bond. The reason is that the claim h can be replicated by a trading strategy θ investing in the assets S_1, S_2 only. Indeed our formula for the price $\pi_t(h)$ indicates as possible weights

$$\theta_1 = N(d_1) \quad \text{and} \quad \theta_2 = -KN(d_2)$$

for S_1 and S_2 respectively. Let us verify that this strategy is self-financing. By the numeraire invariance of the self-financing condition it will suffice to show that θ is self-financing in the market ξB, that is, that $d\big(\theta \cdot (\xi B)\big) = \theta \cdot d(\xi B)$. Now in general

$$d\big(\theta \cdot (\xi B)\big) = \theta \cdot d(\xi B) + \xi B \cdot d\theta + d\langle \theta, \xi B \rangle \tag{8}$$

and so we must show that $\qquad \xi B \cdot d\theta + d\langle \theta, \xi B \rangle = 0.$ (9)

Since $\big(\theta \cdot (\xi B)\big)(t) = \xi(t)\pi_t(h) = E_P\big[\xi(T)h \mid \mathcal{F}_t\big]$ is a martingale, $d\big(\theta \cdot (\xi B)\big)$ and $\theta \cdot d(\xi B)$ are known to be the stochastic differentials of local martingales. Thus (8) shows that the bounded variation terms on the left of (9) automatically cancel. It will thus suffice to show that the local martingale part of the stochastic differential $B \cdot d\theta = S_1 d\theta_1 + S_2 d\theta_2$ vanishes. We may assume that $K = 1$. Then

$$\theta_1 = N(d_1) = \frac{1}{\sqrt{2\pi}} \int_{-\infty}^{d_1(t,S_1,S_2)} e^{-u^2/2} du,$$

$$\theta_2 = -N(d_2) = -\frac{1}{\sqrt{2\pi}} \int_{-\infty}^{d_2(t,S_1,S_2)} e^{-u^2/2} du, \quad \text{where}$$

$$d_1(t, s_1, s_2) = \frac{\log(s_1) - \log(s_2) + \frac{1}{2}\Sigma^2(t,T)}{\Sigma(t,T)}, \quad \text{and}$$

$$d_2(t, s_1, s_2) = \frac{\log(s_1) - \log(s_2) - \frac{1}{2}\Sigma^2(t,T)}{\Sigma(t,T)}, \quad \text{for } s_1, s_2 \in R.$$

Writing $X \sim Y$ if $X - Y$ is a bounded variation process and using similar notation for stochastic differentials, Ito's formula yields

$$d\theta_1 \sim \frac{\partial N(d_1)}{\partial s_1}(t, S_1, S_2)dS_1 + \frac{\partial N(d_1)}{\partial s_2}(t, S_1, S_2)dS_2, \quad \text{and}$$

$$d\theta_2 \sim -\frac{\partial N(d_2)}{\partial s_1}(t, S_1, S_2)dS_1 - \frac{\partial N(d_2)}{\partial s_2}(t, S_1, S_2)dS_2. \tag{10}$$

Here $\qquad \dfrac{\partial N(d_1)}{\partial s_1} = (2\pi)^{-\frac{1}{2}}e^{-d_1^2/2}\dfrac{\partial d_1}{\partial s_1} = (2\pi)^{-\frac{1}{2}}e^{-d_1^2/2}\dfrac{1}{s_1\Sigma(t,T)}.$

Likewise $\qquad \dfrac{\partial N(d_1)}{\partial s_2} = -(2\pi)^{-\frac{1}{2}}e^{-d_1^2/2}\dfrac{1}{s_2\Sigma(t,T)}.$

Similarly

$$\frac{\partial N(d_2)}{\partial s_1} = (2\pi)^{-\frac{1}{2}} e^{-d_2^2/2} \frac{1}{s_1 \Sigma(t,T)}, \qquad \frac{\partial N(d_2)}{\partial s_2} = -(2\pi)^{-\frac{1}{2}} e^{-d_2^2/2} \frac{1}{s_2 \Sigma(t,T)}.$$

Thus, from (10),

$$(2\pi)^{\frac{1}{2}} \Sigma(t,T) S_1 d\theta_1 \sim e^{-d_1^2/2} dS_1 - e^{-d_1^2/2} \frac{S_1}{S_2} dS_2, \quad \text{and}$$

$$(2\pi)^{\frac{1}{2}} \Sigma(t,T) S_2 d\theta_2 \sim -e^{-d_2^2/2} \frac{S_2}{S_1} dS_1 + e^{-d_2^2/2} dS_2,$$

which, upon addition, yields

$$(2\pi)^{\frac{1}{2}} \Sigma(t,T) \big[S_1 d\theta_1 + S_2 d\theta_2 \big] \sim$$

$$\left(e^{-d_1^2/2} - e^{-d_1^2/2} \frac{S_2}{S_1} \right) dS_1 + \left(e^{-d_2^2/2} - e^{-d_2^2/2} \frac{S_1}{S_2} \right) dS_2 \sim \qquad (11)$$

$$e^{-d_1^2/2} \left(1 - e^{\frac{1}{2}(d_1^2 - d_2^2)} \frac{S_2}{S_1} \right) dS_1 + e^{-d_2^2/2} \left(1 - e^{\frac{1}{2}(d_2^2 - d_1^2)} \frac{S_1}{S_2} \right) dS_2.$$

Noting now that

$$\frac{1}{2}(d_1^2 - d_2^2) = (d_1 - d_2)\frac{d_1 + d_2}{2} = \Sigma(t,T)\frac{d_1 + d_2}{2} = log(S_1/S_2),$$

we see that the coefficients of dS_1, dS_2 on the right of (11) vanish and consequently $B \cdot d\theta = S_1 d\theta_1 + S_2 d\theta_2 \sim 0$, as desired. Thus θ is self-financing. The self-financing property of θ is no accident. See 4.e.0 below. By its very definition this strategy replicates the arbitrage price of h on the entire interval $[0,T)$. The reader will have noticed that the weights θ_1, θ_2 are not defined at time $t = T$. Thus $V_t(\theta)$ is not defined for $t = T$. However $\xi(t)V_t(\theta) = E_P\big[\xi(T)h \mid \mathcal{F}_t\big]$ is a continuous martingale and the martingale convergence theorem I.7.c.0 shows that $\xi(t)V_t(\theta) \to \xi(T)h$ and hence $V_t(\theta) \to h$ almost surely, as $t \uparrow T$. Thus defining the weights $\theta_1(T)$, $\theta_2(T)$ in any fashion such that $V_T(\theta) = h$ will extend the self-financing property of θ from the interval $[0,T)$ to all of $[0,T]$.

In the case of a European call on S_1 ($S_2(t) = B(t,T)$) the replicating strategy invests in S_1 and the zero coupon bond $B(t,T)$ expiring at time T. Indeed, if interest rates are stochastic the call *cannot* be replicated investing in S_1 and the risk-free bond except under rather restrictive assumptions and even then the corresponding portfolio weights have to be chosen differently (see 4.f.3 below).

4.d Valuation of non-path-dependent European options in Gaussian models.
Consider a European option h of the form $h = f(S_1(T), S_2(T), \ldots, S_k(T))$ exercisable at time T, where $S_1(t), S_2(t), \ldots, S_k(t)$ are any assets (possibly zero coupon bonds). We *assume* that the claim h is *attainable* and that we are in the setting of the general Black Scholes market of section 3.g. Let $F_j(t) = S_j(t)/B(t,T)$ denote the forward price of the asset S_j deliverable at time T and recall that P_T denotes the forward martingale measure at time T. The price process $\pi_t(h)$ of h can then be computed as

$$\pi_t(h) = B(t,T)E_{P_T}[h|\mathcal{F}_t], \quad t \in [0,T]. \tag{0}$$

Since $S_j(T) = F_j(T)$ the option h can also be written as

$$h = f\big(F_1(T), F_2(T), \ldots, F_k(T)\big). \tag{1}$$

The forward prices $F_j(t)$ are P_T-local martingales and hence (in the context of 3.g) follow a driftless dynamics

$$\frac{dF_j(t)}{F_j(t)} = \gamma_j(t) \cdot dW_t^T, \quad \text{equivalently}$$

$$d(logF_j(t)) = -\frac{1}{2}\|\gamma_j(t)\|^2 dt + \gamma_j(t) \cdot dW_t^T \tag{2}$$

under the forward martingale measure P_T, that is, for some Brownian motion W_t^T on $(\Omega, \mathcal{F}, (\mathcal{F}_t)_{t \in [0,T]}, P_T)$. Integration yields

$$F_j(t) = F_j(0)exp\left(\int_0^t \gamma_j(s) \cdot dW_s^T - \frac{1}{2}\int_0^t \|\gamma_j(s)\|^2 ds\right), \quad t \in [0,T]. \tag{3}$$

The use of forward prices and the forward martingale measure eliminates interest rates from explicit consideration. All the necessary information about interest rates is contained in the numeraire asset $A(t) = B(t,T)$. To make (3) useful for the computation of the conditional expectation (0) we make the following

(G) *Gaussian assumption*: The volatility processes γ_j are nonstochastic.

The forward price $F_j(t)$ is then a log-Gaussian process with respect to the forward martingale measure P_T (III.6.d.4). Likewise assumption (G) implies that the deflated processes ξS_j are log Gaussian processes with respect to the market probability P (3.g.eq.(4) and III.6.d.4).

To compute the conditional expectation (0) with h as in (1) it will be convenient to write the vector $\big(F_1(T), F_2(T), \ldots, F_k(T)\big)$ as a function of some vector measurable with respect to $\mathcal{F}_t$ and another vector independent of $\mathcal{F}_t$. Using (3) for $t = t, T$ we see that

$$F_j(T) = F_j(t)exp\left(\int_t^T \gamma_j(s) \cdot dW_s^T - \frac{1}{2}\int_t^T \|\gamma_j(s)\|^2 ds\right)$$

$$= F_j(t)exp\left(\zeta_j(t,T) - \frac{1}{2}C_{jj}\right), \quad \text{where} \tag{4}$$

$$\zeta_j(t,T) = \int_t^T \gamma_j(s) \cdot dW_s^T \quad \text{and} \quad C_{ij} = \int_t^T \gamma_i(s) \cdot \gamma_j(s)ds = \langle log(F_i), log(F_j) \rangle_t^T.$$

Fix $t \in [0,T]$. Combining (0), (1) and (4) we obtain

$$\pi_t(h) = B(t,T)E_{P_T}\left[f\big(F_1(t)e^{\zeta_1(t,T)-\frac{1}{2}C_{11}}, \ldots, F_k(t)e^{\zeta_k(t,T)-\frac{1}{2}C_{kk}}\big) \mid \mathcal{F}_t \right]. \qquad (5)$$

Note now that the vector $(F_1(t), \ldots, F_k(t))$ is $\mathcal{F}_t$-measurable, while the vector $(\zeta_1(t,T), \ldots, \zeta_k(t,T))$ is independent of $\mathcal{F}_t$ with distribution $N(0,C)$ (III.6.a.2 III.6.c.2). Thus the conditional expectation (5) is computed by integrating out the vector $(\zeta_1(t,T), \ldots, \zeta_k(t,T))$ according to its distribution while leaving the vector $(F_1(t), \ldots, F_k(t))$ unaffected (I.2.b.11); in short

$$\pi_t(h) = B(t,T) \int_{R^k} f\big(F_1(t)e^{x_1-\frac{1}{2}C_{11}}, \ldots, F_k(t)e^{x_k-\frac{1}{2}C_{kk}}\big) N(0,C)(dx). \qquad (6)$$

Let us now reduce this integral to an integral with respect to the standard multi-normal distribution $N(0,I)(dx) = n_k(x)dx = (2\pi)^{-\frac{k}{2}}e^{-\frac{1}{2}\|x\|^2}dx$.

To do this we represent the covariance matrix C in the form $C = A'A$, for some $k \times k$ matrix A, that is we write

$$C_{ij} = \int_t^T \gamma_i(s) \cdot \gamma_j(s)ds = \theta_i \cdot \theta_j,$$

where $\theta_j = c_j(A)$ is the jth column of the matrix A. Especially then $C_{ii} = \|\theta_i\|^2$. Using II.1.a.7 we can now rewrite (6) as

$$\pi_t(h) = B(t,T) \int_{R^k} f\big(F_1(t)e^{\theta_1 \cdot x - \frac{1}{2}\|\theta_1\|^2}, \ldots, F_k(t)e^{\theta_k \cdot x - \frac{1}{2}\|\theta_k\|^2}\big) n_k(x)dx. \qquad (7)$$

Replacing x with $-x$ and noting that $e^{-\theta_j \cdot x - \frac{1}{2}\|\theta_j\|^2} = n_k(x+\theta_j)/n_k(x)$, (7) can be rewritten as

$$\pi_t(h) = B(t,T) \int_{R^k} f\left(F_1(t)\frac{n_k(x+\theta_1)}{n_k(x)}, \ldots, F_k(t)\frac{n_k(x+\theta_k)}{n_k(x)} \right) n_k(x)dx. \qquad (8)$$

4.d.0 Theorem. *Assume that the assets $S_1(t), \ldots, S_k(t)$ follow the dynamics (2) and that the Gaussian assumption (G) holds. Then the price process $\pi_t(h)$ of an attainable European claim $h = f(S_1(T), \ldots, S_k(T))$ maturing at time T is given by equation (8), where $F_j(t) = S_j(t)/B(t,T)$ is the forward price of the asset S_j, the vectors $\theta_j = \theta_j(t,T) \in R^k$ are chosen so that*

$$C_{ij} = \langle log(F_i), log(F_j) \rangle_t^T = \int_t^T \gamma_i(s) \cdot \gamma_j(s)ds = \theta_i \cdot \theta_j$$

and $n_k(x) = (2\pi)^{-\frac{k}{2}}e^{-\frac{1}{2}\|x\|^2}$ is the standard normal density in R^k. ∎

Homogeneous case. In case the function $f = f(s_1, s_2, \ldots, s_k)$ is homogeneous of degree one, formula (8) simplifies as follows:

$$\pi_t(h) = \int_{R^k} f\big(S_1(t)n_k(x+\theta_1), \ldots, S_k(t)n_k(x+\theta_k)\big) dx. \qquad (9)$$

The zero coupon bond $B(t, T)$ drops out and any explicit dependence on the rate of interest disappears. We have seen this before in the formula for the price of an option to exchange assets. In the Black Scholes call price formula the rate of interest enters only since one of the assets is in fact the zero coupon bond with the same maturity as the call option.

We will apply 4.d.0 to several options depending on two assets S_1, S_2 (k=2). Recall that $N(d) = \int_{-\infty}^{d} n_1(t)dt$ denotes the (one dimensional) cumulative normal distribution function and that the two dimensional standard normal density n_2 satisfies $n_2(x) = n_2(x_1, x_2) = n_1(x_1)n_1(x_2)$. The following Lemma will be useful:

4.d.1 Lemma. *Let r be a real number, $\theta, w \in R^2$ and $G = \{x \in R^2 \mid x \cdot w \le r\} \subseteq R^2$. Then*

$$\int_G n_2(x + \theta)dx = N\left(\frac{r + \theta \cdot w}{\|w\|}\right).$$

Proof: Let $e_1 = (1, 0)' \in R^2$ and A be the (linear) rotation of R^2 which satisfies $Aw = \|w\|e_1$. Then A is a unitary map, that is, $A' = A^{-1}$. Consider the substitution $x = A^{-1}u$. Using the rotational invariance of Lebesgue measure, the fact that A is an isometry and that the standard normal density $n_2(x)$ depends on x only through the norm $\|x\|$, it follows that

$$\int_G n_2(x + \theta)dx = \int_{AG} n_2(A^{-1}u + \theta)du = \int_{AG} n_2(A^{-1}(u + A\theta))du$$

$$= \int_{AG} n_2(u + A\theta)du.$$

Here $u \in AG \iff A'u \in G \iff (A'u) \cdot w \le r \iff u \cdot (Aw) \le r \iff u_1\|w\| \le r$. Thus $AG = \{u \in R^2 \mid u_1 \le r/\|w\|\}$. Set $u = (u_1, u_2)$, $A\theta = (\alpha_1, \alpha_2) \in R^2$. Then $n_2(u + A\theta) = n_1(u_1 + \alpha_1)n_1(u_2 + \alpha_2)$ and the special nature of the domain AG now implies that

$$\int_G n_2(x + \theta)dx = \int_{AG} n_2(u + A\theta)du$$

$$= \left(\int_{[u_1 \le r/\|w\|]} n_1(u_1 + \alpha_1)du_1\right)\left(\int_R n_1(u_2 + \alpha_2)du_2\right).$$

Since the second integral in this product is equal to one it follows that

$$\int_G n_2(x + \theta)dx = \int_{[t \le r/\|w\| + \alpha_1]} n_1(t)dt = N\left(\frac{r}{\|w\|} + \alpha_1\right). \qquad (10)$$

Finally $\qquad \alpha_1 = (A\theta) \cdot e_1 = \theta \cdot (A'e_1) = \theta \cdot (A^{-1}e_1) = \theta \cdot \dfrac{w}{\|w\|}$

and so 4.d.1 follows from (10). ∎

Consider now an option $h = f(S_1, S_2)$ which depends on two assets. Here the dimension $k = 2$ and the vectors $\theta_1, \theta_2 \in R^2$ satisfy

$$\|\theta_1\|^2 = \int_t^T \|\gamma_1(s)\|^2 ds = \langle log(F_1)\rangle_t^T, \quad \|\theta_2\|^2 = \int_t^T \|\gamma_2(s)\|^2 ds = \langle log(F_2)\rangle_t^T,$$

and
$$\theta_1 \cdot \theta_2 = \int_t^T \gamma_1(s) \cdot \gamma_2(s) ds = \langle log(F_1), log(F_2)\rangle_t^T,$$

from which it follows that $\Sigma^2(t, T) := \|\theta_1 - \theta_2\|^2 = \int_t^T \|\gamma_1(s) - \gamma_2(s)\|^2 ds$. Set $Y(t) = S_1(t)/S_2(t) = F_1(t)/F_2(t)$ and $Z(t) = log(Y(t))$. From (2)

$$dZ(t) = -\frac{1}{2}\left(\|\gamma_1(t)\|^2 - \|\gamma_2(t)\|^2\right) + (\gamma_1(t) - \gamma_2(t)) \cdot dW_t^T,$$

and so $d\langle Z\rangle_t = \|\gamma_1(t) - \gamma_2(t)\|^2 dt$. Thus $\Sigma^2(t, T) = \int_t^T \|\gamma_1(s) - \gamma_2(s)\|^2 ds = \langle Z\rangle_t^T$ as in Margrabe's formula 4.c.0.

4.d.2 Example. *Option to exchange assets.* The option to receive, at time T, one unit of asset S_1 in exchange for K units of asset S_2 has payoff

$$h = f(S_1(T), S_2(T)) = (S_1(T) - KS_2(T))^+ = (S_1(T) - KS_2(T))1_{[S_1(T) \geq KS_2(T)]}$$

which is homogeneous of degree one in S_1, S_2. Let us see if we can derive Margrabe's formula 4.c.0 from (9) above. Entering $f(s_1, s_2) = (s_1 - Ks_2)1_{[s_1 \geq Ks_2]}$ into (9) yields

$$\pi_t(h) = \int_G (S_1(t)n_2(x + \theta_1) - KS_2(t)n_2(x + \theta_2))dx$$

$$= S_1(t)\int_G n_2(x + \theta_1)dx - KS_2(t)\int_G n_2(x + \theta_2)dx,$$

where $G = \{ x \in R^2 \mid S_1(t)n_2(x + \theta_1) \geq KS_2(t)n_2(x + \theta_2) \}$. Thus $x \in G$ if and only if

$$\frac{n_2(x + \theta_1)}{n_2(x + \theta_2)} = exp\left(-\frac{1}{2}\left[\|x + \theta_1\|^2 - \|x + \theta_2\|^2\right]\right) \geq \frac{KS_2(t)}{S_1(t)},$$

equivalently
$$\frac{1}{2}\left[\|x + \theta_1\|^2 - \|x + \theta_2\|^2\right] \leq log\left(\frac{S_1(t)}{KS_2(t)}\right),$$

that is
$$x \cdot (\theta_1 - \theta_2) \leq log\left(\frac{S_1(t)}{KS_2(t)}\right) - \frac{1}{2}(\|\theta_1\|^2 - \|\theta_2\|^2).$$

Thus $G = \{ x \in R^2 \mid x \cdot w \leq r \}$, where $w = \theta_1 - \theta_2$ and

$$r = log\left(\frac{S_1(t)}{KS_2(t)}\right) - \frac{1}{2}(\|\theta_1\|^2 - \|\theta_2\|^2).$$

From 4.d.1 $\int_G n_2(x + \theta_1)dx = N(d_1)$ and $\int_G n_2(x + \theta_2)dx = N(d_2)$ and so

$$\pi_t(h) = S_1(t)N(d_1) - KS_2(t)N(d_2),$$

where $d_1 = (r + \theta_1 \cdot w)/\|w\|$ and $d_2 = (r + \theta_2 \cdot w)/\|w\|$. Recalling from (10) that $\|w\| = \|\theta_1 - \theta_2\| = \Sigma(t, T)$ and observing that

$$r + \theta_1 \cdot w = log\left(\frac{S_1(t)}{KS_2(t)}\right) + \frac{1}{2}\|w\|^2 \quad \text{and} \quad r + \theta_2 \cdot w = log\left(\frac{S_1(t)}{KS_2(t)}\right) - \frac{1}{2}\|w\|^2,$$

it follows that

$$d_1 = \frac{log\left(S_1(t)/KS_2(t)\right) + \frac{1}{2}\Sigma^2(t, T)}{\Sigma(t, T)} \quad \text{and} \quad d_2 = d_1 - \Sigma(t, T),$$

as in formula 4.c.0 above. Note that we can also write these quantities as

$$d_{1,2} = \frac{log(F_1(t)/F_2(t)) - log(K) \pm \frac{1}{2}\langle log(F_1/F_2)\rangle_t^T}{\sqrt{\langle log(F_1/F_2)\rangle_t^T}}. \quad \blacksquare$$

4.d.3 Example. *Digital option.* Consider the option $h = 1_{[S_1(T) \geq KS_2(T)]}$. Since the function $f(s_1, s_2) = 1_{[s_1 \geq Ks_2]}$ satisfies $f(\alpha s_1, \alpha s_2) = f(s_1, s_2)$, 4.d.0 simplifies to

$$\pi_t(h) = B(t, T)\int_{R^2} f\left(S_1(t)n_2(x + \theta_1), S_2(t)n_2(x + \theta_2)\right)n_2(x)dx$$

$$= B(t, T)\int_G n_2(x)dx = B(t, T)\, N\left(\frac{r}{\|w\|}\right),$$

where G, r and w are as in 4.d.2. Set $\rho = r/\|w\|$. As $\|w\| = \sqrt{\langle log(F_1/F_2)\rangle_t^T}$ and

$$r = log\left(\frac{S_1(t)}{KS_2(t)}\right) - \frac{1}{2}(\|\theta_1\|^2 - \|\theta_2\|^2)$$

$$= log\left(F_1(t)/F_2(t)\right) - log(K) + \frac{1}{2}(\langle log(F_2)\rangle_t^T - \langle log(F_1)\rangle_t^T),$$

we obtain $\pi_t(h) = B(t, T)N(\rho)$, where

$$\rho = \frac{log\left(F_1(t)/F_2(t)\right) - log(K) + \frac{1}{2}(\langle log(F_2)\rangle_t^T - \langle log(F_1)\rangle_t^T)}{\sqrt{\langle log(F_1/F_2)\rangle_t^T}}. \tag{11}$$

Comparing this with the formula $\pi_t(h) = B(t, T)E_{P_T}(h|\mathcal{F}_t)$ shows that $N(\rho)$ is the (conditional) exercise probability $N(\rho) = E_{P_T}(h|\mathcal{F}_t) = P_T\left(S_1(T) \geq KS_2(T) \mid \mathcal{F}_t\right)$ under the forward martingale measure P_T. In case $S_2(t) = B(t, T)$ the option payoff becomes $h = 1_{[S_1(T) \geq K]}$, $F_2(t) = 1$ and consequently (11) simplifies to

$$\rho = \frac{log\left(F_1(t)\right) - log(K) - \frac{1}{2}\langle log(F_1)\rangle_t^T}{\sqrt{\langle log(F_1)\rangle_t^T}}. \quad \blacksquare$$

4.d.4 Example. *Power option.* Let now $h = S_1(T)^\lambda S_2(T)^\mu 1_{[S_1(T) \geq KS_2(T)]}$, where $\lambda, \mu \in R$. Let G, r and w be as in 4.d.2. As the function $f(s_1, s_2) = s_1^\lambda s_2^\mu 1_{[s_1 \geq Ks_2]}$ satisfies $f(\alpha s_1, \alpha s_2) = \alpha^{\lambda+\mu} f(s_1, s_2)$, 4.d.0 simplifies to

$$\pi_t(h) = B(t,T)^{1-(\lambda+\mu)} \int_{R^2} f\big(S_1(t)n_2(x+\theta_1), S_2(t)n_2(x+\theta_2)\big) n_2(x)^{1-(\lambda+\mu)} dx$$

$$= B(t,T)^{1-(\lambda+\mu)} S_1(t)^\lambda S_2(t)^\mu \int_G n_2(x+\theta_1)^\lambda n_2(x+\theta_2)^\mu n_2(x)^{1-(\lambda+\mu)} dx$$

$$= B(t,T) F_1(t)^\lambda F_2(t)^\mu \int_G n_2(x+\theta_1)^\lambda n_2(x+\theta_2)^\mu n_2(x)^{1-(\lambda+\mu)} dx.$$

Set $U = exp\big[-\tfrac{1}{2}\big(\lambda(1-\lambda)\|\theta\|_1^2 + \mu(1-\mu)\|\theta\|_2^2 - 2\lambda\mu\,\theta_1 \cdot \theta_2\big)\big]$. By straightforward computation $n_k(x+\theta_1)^\lambda n_k(x+\theta_2)^\mu n_k(x)^{1-(\lambda+\mu)} = Un_k(x + \lambda\theta_1 + \mu\theta_2)$ and so, using 4.d.1,

$$\pi_t(h) = UB(t,T)F_1(t)^\lambda F_2(t)^\mu \int_G n_k(x + \lambda\theta_1 + \mu\theta_2) dx$$

$$= UB(t,T)F_1(t)^\lambda F_2(t)^\mu N\Big[\|w\|^{-1}\big(r + (\lambda\theta_1 + \mu\theta_2) \cdot w\big)\Big].$$

Since $w = \theta_1 - \theta_2$ and $r = log(F_1(t)/F_2(t)) - log(K) - \tfrac{1}{2}(\|\theta_1\|^2 - \|\theta_2\|^2$ we have

$$r + (\lambda\theta_1 + \mu\theta_2) \cdot w = r + \lambda\|\theta_1\|^2 + (\mu - \lambda)\theta_1 \cdot \theta_2 - \mu\|\theta_2\|^2$$

$$= log(F_1(t)/F_2(t)) - log(K) + (\lambda - \tfrac{1}{2})\|\theta_1\|^2 + (\mu - \lambda)\theta_1 \cdot \theta_2 + (\tfrac{1}{2} - \mu)\|\theta_2\|^2.$$

Recalling $\|\theta_1\|^2 = \langle log(F_1)\rangle_t^T$, $\|\theta_2\|^2 = \langle log(F_2)\rangle_t^T$, $\theta_1 \cdot \theta_2 = \langle log(F_1), log(F_2)\rangle_t^T$ and $\|w\| = \langle log(F_1/F_2)\rangle_t^T$, the option price assumes the form

$$\pi_t(h) = UB(t,T)F_1(t)^\lambda F_2(t)^\mu N(q), \quad \text{where}$$

$$U = exp\Big[-\tfrac{1}{2}\big(\lambda(1-\lambda)\langle log(F_1)\rangle_t^T + \mu(1-\mu)\langle log(F_2)\rangle_t^T - 2\lambda\mu\langle log(F_1), log(F_2)\rangle_t^T\big)\Big]$$

and $\quad q = \Big[log\big(F_1(t)/F_2(t)\big) - log(K) + (\lambda - \tfrac{1}{2})\langle log(F_1)\rangle_t^T + (\tfrac{1}{2} - \mu)\langle log(F_2)\rangle_t^T$

$$+ (\mu - \lambda)\langle log(F_1), log(F_2)\rangle_t^T\Big] \Big/ \sqrt{\langle log(F_1/F_2)\rangle_t^T}. \quad\blacksquare$$

Remark. Here $\langle log(F_j)\rangle_t^T$ is the aggregate percentage volatility of the forward price F_j that is left from current time t to the time T of expiry of the option. It is incorrect to use the volatilities of the cash prices S_j instead. The two are the same only if the zero coupon bond $A(t) = B(t,T)$ is a bounded variation process.

Note that $\langle log(F_j)\rangle_t^T = \int_t^T \|\gamma_j(s)\|^2 ds$, $\langle log(F_1), log(F_2)\rangle_t^T = \int_t^T \gamma_1(s) \cdot \gamma_2(s) ds$ and

$$\langle log(F_1/F_2)\rangle_t^T = \langle log(F_1)\rangle_t^T + \langle log(F_2)\rangle_t^T - 2\langle log(F_1), log(F_2)\rangle_t^T$$
$$= \int_t^T \|\gamma_1(s) - \gamma_2(s)\|^2 ds.$$

The following notation is frequently employed in the literature: set $\sigma_j = \|\gamma_j\|$ (the numerical volatility of the forward price $F_j(t)$) and $\rho_{ij} = (\gamma_i/\|\gamma_i\|) \cdot (\gamma_j/\|\gamma_j\|)$. The dynamics of the forward prices $F_j(t)$ then becomes

$$dF_j(t) = F_j(t)\sigma_j(t) dV_j^T(t)$$

for P_T-Brownian motions $V_j^T(t)$ defined by $dV_j^T(t) = \|\gamma_j(t)\|^{-1}\gamma_j(t) \cdot dW_t^T$ which are one dimensional and correlated by $d\langle V_i^T, V_j^T\rangle_t = \rho_{ij}(t) dt$ (III.6.b.0). Then

$$\langle log(F_j)\rangle_t^T = \int_t^T \sigma_j^2(s) ds, \quad \langle log(F_1), log(F_2)\rangle_t^T = \int_t^T (\sigma_1\sigma_2\rho_{12})(s) ds$$

and
$$\langle log(F_1/F_2)\rangle_t^T = \int_t^T (\sigma_1^2 + \sigma_2^2 - 2\sigma_1\sigma_2\rho_{12})(s) ds.$$

4.e Delta hedging. A replicating strategy θ for a European option h is also called a *hedge* for h with the interpretation that a seller of h will trade in the market according to θ to hedge the random payoff h at time T.

Assume now that A is a numeraire asset such that ξA is a martingale. Then the local martingale measure P_A is defined. Assume that the market B contains only finitely many securities and that A is a security of B and write $B = (A, B_1, \ldots, B_n)$. For a process $X(t)$ we write $X^A(t) = X(t)/A(t)$ as usual.

Now let h be a European option exercisable at time T and write $\pi_t(h) = \xi(t)^{-1} E_P[\xi(T)h|\mathcal{F}_t]$, $t \in [0, T]$. Then $\xi(t)\pi_t(h)$ is a P-martingale and hence $\pi_t^A(h)$ a P_A-martingale (3.d.0.(b)).

4.e.0 Delta Hedging. *Assume that the process $\pi_t^A(h)$ can be written in the form*

$$\pi_t^A(h) = F(t, B^A(t)) = F(t, B_1^A(t), \ldots, B_n^A(t)), \quad t \in [0, T], \tag{0}$$

for some function $F = F(t, b) = F(t, b_1, \ldots, b_n) \in C^{1,2}([0, T] \times R_+^n)$. Let $\theta(t) = (K(t), H_1(t), \ldots, H_n(t))$ be the trading strategy investing in $B = (A, B_1, \ldots, B_n)$ defined by

$$H_j(t) = \frac{\partial F}{\partial b_j}(t, B_j^A(t)) \quad and \quad K(t) = F(t, B^A(t)) - \sum_{j=1}^n H_j(t) B_j^A(t).$$

Then θ is a replicating strategy for h.

Remark. Here $F = F(t, b) \in C^{1,2}([0, T] \times R_+^n)$ is to be interpreted as in III.3.a.1, that is, F is continuous on $[0, T] \times R_+^n$, the partial derivative $\partial f/\partial t$ exists on $(0, T) \times R_+^n$

and has a continuous extension to $[0, T] \times R_+^n$. Continuous second order partial derivatives are assumed to exist with respect to the remaining variables.

Proof. By definition
$$V_t^A(\theta) = K(t) + \sum\nolimits_{j=1}^n H_j(t) B_j^A(t) = F(t, B^A(t)) = \pi_t^A(h).$$

Thus $V_t^A(\theta)$ is a P_A-martingale with $V_T^A(\theta) = \pi_T^A(h)$ and so $V_T(\theta) = \pi_T(h) = h$. From 3.d.0.(b) it follows that $\xi(t) V_t(\theta)$ is a P-martingale and thus we have to show only that θ is self-financing. By the numeraire invariance of the self-financing condition it will suffice to show that θ is self-financing in the market $B^A = (1, B_1^A, \ldots, B_n^A)$. Since $dB^A = (0, dB_1^A, \ldots, dB_n^A)'$ the self-financing condition for θ assumes the form
$$dV_t(\theta, B^A) = d(\theta \cdot B^A) = \theta \cdot dB^A = \sum\nolimits_{j=1}^n H_j dB_j^A. \tag{1}$$

Indeed, since $V_t(\theta, B^A) = V_t^A(\theta) = F(t, B^A(t))$, Ito's formula III.3.a.1 yields
$$\begin{aligned} dV_t(\theta, B^A) &= dC(t) + \sum\nolimits_{j=1}^n \frac{\partial F}{\partial b_j}(t, B_j^A(t)) dB_j^A(t) \\ &= dC(t) + \sum\nolimits_{j=1}^n H_j(t) dB_j^A(t), \end{aligned} \tag{2}$$

for some continuous bounded variation process C with $C(0) = 0$. In integral form
$$V_t(\theta, B^A) = V_0(\theta, B^A) + C(t) + \sum\nolimits_{j=1}^n (H_j \bullet B_j^A)(t).$$

Here $V_t(\theta, B^A) = V_t^A(\theta)$ is a P_A-martingale and the processes $H_j \bullet B_j^A$ are P_A-local martingales (as the B_j^A are P_A-local martingales). It follows that $C(t) = C(0) = 0$, $t \in [0, T]$, and (2) simplifies to yield (1). $\blacksquare$

The weights H_j given to the underlying assets B_j in this strategy are derivatives $\partial F / \partial b_j (t, B^A(t))$ of the relative price $\pi_t^A(h)$ of h with respect to the relative price B_j^A at time t. In other words $H_j(t)$ is the first order sensitivity of the relative price of h to the relative price of the underlying asset B_j at time t. These sensitivities are the so called *deltas* of the option h at time t. Therefore our replicating strategy θ is also called *delta hedging*. The numeraire asset A is used to keep the portfolio value equal to the option price $\pi_t(h)$ at all times.

   In practice the zero coupon bond $A(t) = B(t, T)$ is the most useful numeraire. In this case the relevant prices to be used in the computation of option deltas and hedging coefficients are the forward prices for delivery at time T. Common market practice however uses the cash prices instead, that is, one writes $\pi_t(h) = C(t, B(t))$ and uses the sensitivities $(\partial C / \partial b_j)(t, B(t))$ as portfolio weights. This is justifiable only if the numeraire A is nonstochastic, in which case
$$\pi_t(h) = A(t) \pi_t^A(h) = A(t) F(t, B^A(t)) = C(t, B(t)),$$

where $C(t, b) = A(t) F(t, A(t)^{-1} b)$, for $(t, b) \in [0, T] \times R_+^n$, and so $(\partial C / \partial b_j)(t, b) = (\partial F / \partial b_j)(t, A(t)^{-1} b)$ from which it follows that
$$\frac{\partial C}{\partial b_j}(t, B(t)) = \frac{\partial F}{\partial b_j}(t, B^A(t)).$$

Note that the numeraire asset $A(t) = 1$ is in B only if interest rates are zero.

4.f Connection with partial differential equations. We continue in the setting of the general Black Scholes market of 3.g. Let S be an asset in B and consider a European option h of the form $h = f(S_T)$ exercisable at time T. Let $A(t) = B(t,T)$ be the zero coupon bond maturing at time T and write $X^A(t) = X(t)/A(t)$ as usual.

Switching to the numeraire A, that is, replacing the cash price S_t with the forward price $S_t^A = F_S(t,T)$ of the asset S allows us to incorporate stochastic rates of interest without extra effort. As we will see below this relies on the fact that $A(T) = 1$ is nonstochastic. The zero coupon bond $A(t) = B(t,T)$ is essentially the only numeraire in B with this property.

From 3.g.eq.(15) combined with III.6.b.0 we know that the forward price S_t^A follows a dynamics

$$dS_t^A = S_t^A \sigma(t) dV_t^T, \quad t \in [0,T] \tag{0}$$

under the forward martingale measure P_T, where $\sigma \in L(V^T)$ is the volatility of the forward price of S under the forward martingale measure P_T (and hence also under the market probability P) and V_t^T is a one dimensional Brownian motion on $(\Omega, \mathcal{F}, (\mathcal{F}_t), P_T)$. Since the numeraire A satisfies $A_T = 1$ and hence $S_T = S_T^A$, the option h can also be written as $h = f(S_T^A)$. We now make the following assumption: *The process $\sigma(t)$ is nonstochastic and continuous.*

If h is replicable, then the arbitrage price $\pi_t(h)$ of h satisfies $\pi_t^A(h) = E_{P_T}\left[h|\mathcal{F}_t\right]$ and hence is a P_T-martingale satisfying $\pi_T^A(h) = h$. We shall however not assume that h is replicable. Nonetheless the process $\pi_t^A(h) = E_{P_T}\left[h|\mathcal{F}_t\right]$ can be considered and we shall attempt to write $\pi_t^A(h)$ in the form

$$\pi_t^A(h) = F\left(t, S_t^A\right), \quad t \in [0,T],$$

for some function $F = F(t,s) \in C^{1,2}([0,T] \times R_+)$ (to be interpreted as in III.3.a.1) and see what this implies for the function F. By Ito's formula III.3.a.1,

$$d\pi_t^A(h) = \frac{\partial F}{\partial t}\left(t, S_t^A\right)dt + \frac{\partial F}{\partial s}\left(t, S_t^A\right)dS_t^A + \frac{1}{2}\frac{\partial^2 F}{\partial s^2}\left(t, S_t^A\right)d\left\langle S^A\right\rangle_t.$$

From (0) we have $d\left\langle S^A\right\rangle_t = \left(S_t^A\right)^2 \sigma^2(t)dt$ and entering this and (0) into (1) yields

$$
\begin{aligned}
d\pi_t^A(h) = &\left[\frac{\partial F}{\partial t}\left(t, S_t^A\right) + \frac{1}{2}(S_t^A)^2 \sigma^2(t)\frac{\partial^2 F}{\partial s^2}\left(t, S_t^A\right)\right]dt \\
&+ S_t^A \sigma(t)\frac{\partial F}{\partial s}\left(t, S_t^A\right)dV_t^T.
\end{aligned}
\tag{1}
$$

Since $\pi_t^A(h)$ is a P_T-martingale, the drift term must vanish and we obtain

$$\frac{\partial F}{\partial t}\left(t, S_t^A\right) + \frac{1}{2}\left(S_t^A\right)^2 \sigma^2(t)\frac{\partial^2 F}{\partial s^2}\left(t, S_t^A\right) = 0.$$

This suggests that we consider solutions $F = F(t, s) \in C^{1,2}([0,T] \times R_+)$ of the PDE

$$\frac{\partial F}{\partial t} + \frac{1}{2}s^2\sigma^2(t)\frac{\partial^2 F}{\partial s^2} = 0. \tag{2}$$

Recalling that $h = f(S_T^A)$, the requirement $F(T, S_T^A) = \pi_T^A(h) = h = f(S_T^A)$ leads to the boundary condition

$$F(T, s) = f(s). \tag{3}$$

Note that it is the driftless nature of equation (0) which makes the partial differential equation (2) so simple.

Conversely, let us assume we have a solution $F = F(t, s) \in C^{1,2}([0,T] \times R_+)$ of (2) satisfying the boundary condition (3) and set

$$U_t = F\left(t, S_t^A\right), \quad t \in [0,T].$$

Then $U_T = F(T, S_T^A) = f(S_T^A) = h$. Recall now that $\pi_t^A(h)$ is a P_T-martingale satisfying $\pi_T^A(h) = h = U_T$. If we can show that U_t is a P_T-martingale also, it will follow that

$$\pi_t^A(h) = E_{P_T}[h \mid \mathcal{F}_t] = U_t = F\left(t, S_t^A\right), \quad t \in [0,T],$$

establishing the desired representation for the process $\pi_t^A(h)$. Note that this implies

$$\pi_t(h) = A(t)F\left(t, S_t^A\right) = B(t,T)F\left(t, S(t)/B(t,T)\right), \quad t \in [0,T].$$

To ensure that U_t is in fact a P_T-martingale we must put one more constraint on the solution F of (2). We assume that *the partial derivative $\partial F/\partial s$ is bounded on* $[0,T] \times R_+$. Ito's formula now yields the expansion (1) for $dU_t = dF\left(t, S_t^A\right)$ with collapsing drift term, that is, $dU_t = \sigma(t)S_t^A(\partial F/\partial s)\left(t, S_t^A\right)dV_t^T$, equivalently

$$U_t = U_0 + \int_0^t \sigma(v)S_v^A\frac{\partial F}{\partial s}\left(v, S_v^A\right)dV_v^T. \tag{4}$$

The nonstochastic and continuous volatility σ in (0) is bounded on $[0,T]$. Thus, according to III.6.a.1, the dynamics (0) implies that

$$E_{P_T}\left[\int_0^T \sigma^2(t)\left(S_t^A\right)^2 dt\right] < \infty.$$

Since the partial derivative $\partial F/\partial s$ is bounded, it follows from this that

$$E_{P_T}\left[\int_0^T \left(\sigma(t)S_t^A\frac{\partial F}{\partial s}\left(t, S_t^A\right)\right)^2 dt\right] < \infty$$

also. But this ensures that U_t given by (4) is a (square integrable) P_T-martingale on $[0,T]$, as desired. This shows that $\pi_t^A(h) = E_{P_T}[h \mid \mathcal{F}_t] = F\left(t, S_t^A\right)$, $t \in [0,T]$.

Thus 4.e.0 applies to show that a replicating strategy $\theta_t = (K_t, H_t)$ for h which invests in the asset vector (A_t, S_t), that is, in the numeraire asset and the underlying asset, is given by

$$H_t = \frac{\partial F}{\partial s}\left(t, S_t^A\right) \quad \text{and} \quad K_t = F\left(t, S_t^A\right) - H_t S_t^A. \tag{5}$$

We can summarize these findings as follows:

4.f.0. *Let* $h = f(S_T)$ *be a European option on some asset* S_t *satisfying* (0) *with continuous, nonstochastic volatility* $\sigma(t)$. *If* $F = F(t,s) \in C^{1,2}([0,T] \times R_+)$ *is any solution of the PDE*

$$\frac{\partial F}{\partial t} + \frac{1}{2}s^2\sigma^2(t)\frac{\partial^2 F}{\partial s^2} = 0$$

satisfying the boundary condition $F(T,s) = f(s)$ *and with bounded partial derivative* $\partial F/\partial s$, *then* h *is replicable and the price process* $\pi_t(h)$ *can be written as*

$$\pi_t(h) = B(t,T)F\left(t, S(t)/B(t,T)\right), \quad t \in [0,T].$$

A replicating strategy $\theta(t) = (K_t, H_t)$ *for* h *investing in the vector* $(A_t, S_t) = (B(t,T), S_t)$ *is given by* (5). ∎

The weight H_t given to the underlying asset S_t in this strategy is the derivative $(\partial F/\partial s)\left(t, S_t^A\right)$ of the forward price of h with respect to the forward price of S at time t. This weight would not be correct if the cash prices were used instead.

4.f.1 Remarks. (a) The use of the forward price S_t^A and the evaluation of h via the forward martingale measure P_T has the advantage of eliminating interest rates from explicit consideration. The necessary information about interest rates is packed into the numeraire asset $A(t) = B(t,T)$. The forward price S_t^A is the price of S at time t expressed in constant time T dollars. Note that the critical input, namely the volatility process $\sigma(t)$, does not change when we pass from the market probability P to any equivalent probability. Thus σ is the volatility of the forward price S_t^A realized in the market.

An evaluation of h as $\pi_t(h) = B_0(t)E_{P_0}\left[B_0(T)^{-1}h \mid \mathcal{F}_t\right]$ based on the dynamics of the discounted cash price $S(t)/B_0(t)$ under the spot martingale measure P_0 does not offer this advantage and necessitates assumptions on the spot rate process $r(t)$. For the valuation of a cashflow occurring at a single future date T, the time T-forward martingale measure P_T is superior to the spot martingale measure P_0.

(b) Equation (3) does not have constant coefficients even if $\sigma(t)$ is constant. In this case however we can derive a constant coefficient PDE if we use a slightly different setup: The logarithmic transform $Z_t = log\left(S_t^A\right)$ simplifies (0) to

$$dZ_t = -\tfrac{1}{2}\sigma^2(t)dt + \sigma(t)dV_t^T \tag{6}$$

and we write now $\pi_t^A(h) = H(t, Z_t)$, $t \in [0,T]$, for some function $H = H(t,z) \in C^{1,2}([0,T] \times R_+)$ and see what PDE the function H has to satisfy. From (6) we have

$$d\langle Z \rangle_t = \sigma(t)^2 dt, \tag{7}$$

and entering this into the expansion

$$d\pi_t^A(h) = dH(t, Z_t) = \frac{\partial H}{\partial t}(t, Z_t)dt + \frac{\partial H}{\partial z}(t, Z_t)dZ_t + \frac{1}{2}\frac{\partial^2 H}{\partial z^2}(t, Z_t)d\langle Z \rangle_t$$

yields
$$d\,\pi_t^A(h) = \left[\frac{\partial H}{\partial t}(t, Z_t) - \frac{1}{2}\sigma^2(t)\frac{\partial H}{\partial z}(t, Z_t) + \frac{1}{2}\sigma^2(t)\frac{\partial^2 H}{\partial z^2}(t, Z_t)\right] dt$$
$$+ \sigma(t)\frac{\partial H}{\partial z}(t, Z_t)dV_t^T.$$

Since $\pi_t^A(h) = E_{P_T}[h \mid \mathcal{F}_t]$ is a P_T-martingale, the drift term must vanish and we obtain
$$\frac{\partial H}{\partial t}(t, Z_t) - \frac{1}{2}\sigma^2(t)\frac{\partial H}{\partial z}(t, Z_t) + \frac{1}{2}\sigma^2(t)\frac{\partial^2 H}{\partial z^2}(t, Z_t) = 0.$$

This suggests that we consider solutions $H = H(t, z) \in C^{1,2}([0, T] \times R_+)$ of the PDE
$$\frac{\partial H}{\partial t} - \frac{\sigma^2}{2}\frac{\partial H}{\partial z} + \frac{\sigma^2}{2}\frac{\partial^2 H}{\partial z^2} = 0. \tag{8}$$

The requirement $H(T, Z_T) = \pi_T^A(h) = h = f(S_T^A) = f\left(e^{Z_T}\right)$ translates into the boundary condition
$$H(T, z) = f(e^z). \tag{9}$$

Conversely, if $H = H(t, z) \in C^{1,2}([0, T] \times R_+)$ is a solution of (8) satisfying (9), we can show that
$$\pi_t^A(h) = H(t, Z_t), \quad \forall\, t \in [0, T],$$

under a suitable additional assumption on the partial derivative $\partial H/\partial z$. To determine this condition let us investigate the relation between the function $F = F(t, s)$ from (2) and $H = H(t, z)$ above. In fact the relation $Z_t = log(S_t^A)$ suggests that the PDEs (2) and (8) are related via the transformation $z = log(s)$. In fact it is straightforward to show that the substitution $z = log(s)$ transforms (8) into (2). Thus the boundedness of $\partial F/\partial s$ corresponds to the boundedness of $e^{-z}\partial H/\partial z$.

Higher dimensional PDEs. The above approach can also be extended to options $h = f(S_1(T), \ldots, S_n(T))$ depending on a vector $S(t) = (S_1(t), \ldots, S_n(t))'$ of assets. Starting from
$$dS_j^A(t) = S_j^A(t)\sigma_j(t) \cdot dW_t^T, \quad 1 \leq j \leq n, \tag{10}$$

where W_t^T is an n-dimensional P_T-Brownian motion and the $\sigma_j : [0, T] \to R^n$ are continuous functions, note $d\langle S_i^A, S_j^A\rangle_t = S_i^A(t)S_j^A(t)\,\sigma_i(t) \cdot \sigma_j(t)dt$ and try a representation
$$\pi_t^A(h) = F\left(t, S^A(t)\right) = F\left(t, S_1^A(t), \ldots, S_n^A(t)\right), \tag{11}$$

for some function $F = F(t, s) = F(t, s_1, \ldots, s_n) \in C^{1,2}([0, T] \times R_+^n)$. This yields the PDE
$$\frac{\partial F}{\partial t} + \frac{1}{2}\sum\nolimits_{ij} s_i s_j \sigma_i(t) \cdot \sigma_j(t)\frac{\partial^2 F}{\partial s_i \partial s_j} = 0 \tag{12}$$

with boundary condition
$$F(T, s) = f(s), \tag{13}$$

where $s = (s_1, \ldots, s_n)$. An argument similar to the above shows that conversely (12), (13) combined with the boundedness of all the partial derivatives $\partial F/\partial s_j$ suffices to establish the representation (11). Note that we have already solved the

PDE (12), (13) in 4.d.eq.(7) above. We have $d\langle log(S_i^A), log(S_j^A)\rangle_t = \sigma_i(t)\cdot\sigma_j(t)dt$ which follows from (10). Thus the process $\sigma_i(t)\cdot\sigma_j(t)$ is the instantaneous covariation of $log(S_i^A)$ and $log(S_j^A)$. A replicating strategy θ for h invests in the vector $(A(t), S_1(t),\ldots, S_n(t))$ with weights $\theta(t) = (K(t), H_1(t),\ldots, H_n(t))$ given by

$$H_j(t) = \frac{\partial F}{\partial s_j}(t, S^A(t)) \quad \text{and} \quad K(t) = F(t, S^A(t)) - \sum_j H_j(t)S_j^A(t).$$

Continuous dividends. Assume now that the asset S_j pays a continuous dividend $D_j(t)$ satisfying $dD_j(t) = q_j(t)S_j(t)dt$ and let $h = f(S_1(T),\ldots, S_n(T))$ be as above. From the discussion in 2.c we know that the option price remains unaffected if the assets $S_j(t)$ are replaced with their dividend-free reductions $\tilde{S}_j(t) = S_j(t)C_j(t)$ with $C_j(t) = exp(-\int_t^T q_j(s)ds)$. In other words

$$\pi_t(h) = A(t)F(t, \tilde{S}_1^A(t),\ldots, \tilde{S}_n^A(t)) = A(t)F(t, S_1^A(t)C_1(t),\ldots, S_n^A(t)C_n(t)),$$

where the function $F = F(t, \tilde{s}_1,\ldots, \tilde{s}_n) \in C^{1,2}([0,T]\times R_+^n)$ satisfies

$$\frac{\partial F}{\partial t} + \frac{1}{2}\sum_{ij}\tilde{s}_i\tilde{s}_j\sigma_i(t)\cdot\sigma_j(t)\frac{\partial^2 F}{\partial \tilde{s}_i\partial \tilde{s}_j} = 0$$

with boundary condition $F(T, \tilde{s}) = f(\tilde{s})$. This appears to be the most efficient approach to dealing with continuous dividends as it shows that the same valuation PDE can be used as in the dividend-free case if the formula for the option price is adjusted accordingly. However if it is desired to write the option price in terms of the dividend paying assets $S_j(t)$ as $\pi_t(h) = A(t)G(t, S_1^A(t),\ldots, S_n^A(t))$, the corresponding PDE for the function $G = G(t, s_1,\ldots, s_n)$ can also be derived.

The equality $F(t, \tilde{S}_1^A(t),\ldots, \tilde{S}_n^A(t)) = \pi_t^A(h) = G(t, S_1^A(t),\ldots, S_n^A(t))$ suggests that we should have $F(t, \tilde{s}_1,\ldots, \tilde{s}_n) = G(t, s_1,\ldots, s_n)$, where the variables $\tilde{s}$ and s are related by

$$s_j = C_j(t)^{-1}\tilde{s}_j = exp(\int_t^T q_j(s)ds)\tilde{s}_j.$$

From this it follows that $\partial s_j/\partial t = -s_jq_j(t)$ and $\partial s_j/\partial \tilde{s}_j = C_j(t)^{-1}$ and so

$$\frac{\partial F}{\partial t} = \frac{\partial G}{\partial t} + \sum_j \frac{\partial G}{\partial s_j}\frac{\partial s_j}{\partial t} = \frac{\partial G}{\partial t} - \sum_j s_jq_j(t)\frac{\partial G}{\partial s_j},$$

$$\frac{\partial F}{\partial \tilde{s}_j} = \frac{\partial G}{\partial s_j}\frac{\partial s_j}{\partial \tilde{s}_j} = \frac{\partial G}{\partial s_j}C_j(t)^{-1}.$$

It follows that $\partial^2 F/\partial \tilde{s}_i\partial \tilde{s}_j = (\partial^2 G/\partial s_i\partial s_j)C_i(t)^{-1}C_j(t)^{-1}$ and consequently $\tilde{s}_i\tilde{s}_j\partial^2 F/\partial \tilde{s}_i\partial \tilde{s}_j = s_is_j\partial^2 G/\partial s_i\partial s_j$. Entering this into the PDE for F yields

$$\frac{\partial G}{\partial t} - \sum_j s_jq_j(t)\frac{\partial G}{\partial s_j} + \frac{1}{2}\sum_{ij}s_is_j\sigma_i(t)\cdot\sigma_j(t)\frac{\partial^2 G}{\partial s_i\partial s_j} = 0$$

with boundary condition $G(T, s) = f(s)$.

Remark. Our PDEs are related to the heat equation $\partial H / \partial \tau = \frac{1}{2} \sum_j \partial^2 H / \partial u_j^2$. Consider (12), (13) with constant volatilities $\sigma_i \in R^n$. Introduce the new variables $(\tau, u) = (\tau, u_1, \ldots, u_n)$ defined by $t = T - \tau$ and $s_i = exp(\sigma_i \cdot u + \frac{1}{2} \tau \|\sigma_i\|^2)$, $1 \leq i \leq n$. Then the function $H(\tau, u) = F(t, s_1, \ldots, s_n)$ satisfies the heat equation.

4.f.2 Valuation PDE for barrier options. We consider the case of a single asset S. Let $Z_t = (t, S_t)$, $G \subseteq [0, T] \times R_+$ be a relatively open set with $Z_0 \in G$ and $\tau = \inf\{ t > 0 \mid Z_t \in bdry(G) \}$ the time at which Z_t hits the boundary of G. Note that Z_t hits the boundary of G before time T and so $\tau \leq T$. Let $f = f(t, s)$ be a continuous function on the boundary of G and consider the option h with payoff $f(\tau, S_\tau)$ at time T. The payoff of h receivable at time T is determined when the process Z hits the boundary of G (the barrier).

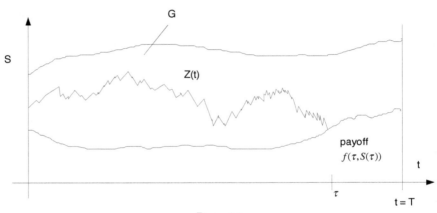

Figure 4.1

To establish the proper valuation PDE for this option we work from the dynamics

$$dS_t = r(t)S_t dt + \sigma(t)S_t dW_t^0 \tag{14}$$

of S under the spot martingale measure P_0 with deterministic short rate process $r(t)$ and volatility $\sigma(t)$. The riskless bond $B_t = exp\left(\int_0^t r(s)ds\right)$ is then nonstochastic also and so the option price $\pi_t(h)$ satisfies

$$\pi_t(h) = B_t E_{P_0}\left[h/B_T \mid \mathcal{F}_t\right] = B_t B_T^{-1} E_{P_0}[h|\mathcal{F}_t]. \tag{15}$$

Set $V_t = F(t \wedge \tau, S_{t \wedge \tau})$ where $F = F(t, s) \in C^{1,2}(\overline{G})$ (continuous on the closure of G, $C^{1,2}$ on $G \cap (0, T) \times R_+$). If V is a P_0-martingale satisfying $V_T = h = E_{P_0}[h|\mathcal{F}_T]$ then it follows that $V_t = E_{P_0}[h|\mathcal{F}_t]$ and so

$$\pi_t(h) = B_t B_T^{-1} E_{P_0}[h|\mathcal{F}_t] = B_t B_T^{-1} V_t = B_t B_T^{-1} F(t \wedge \tau, S_{t \wedge \tau}), \quad \forall t \in [0, T]. \tag{16}$$

The requirement $V_T = h$ can be rewritten as $F(\tau, S_\tau) = f(\tau, S_\tau)$ and is satisfied if F satisfies the boundary condition

$$F = f \quad \text{on} \quad bdry(G). \tag{17}$$

According to III.2.d.0.(c) we have $d(t \wedge \tau) = 1_{[\![0,\tau]\!]}(t)dt$,

$$d S_t^\tau = 1_{[\![0,\tau]\!]}(t)dS_t = 1_{[\![0,\tau]\!]}(t)r(t)S_t dt + 1_{[\![0,\tau]\!]}(t)\sigma(t)S_t dW_t^0 \quad \text{and}$$

$$d\langle S^\tau \rangle_t = d\langle S \rangle_t^\tau = 1_{[\![0,\tau]\!]}(t)d\langle S \rangle_t = 1_{[\![0,\tau]\!]}(t)\sigma(t)^2 S_t^2 dt,$$

and so Ito's formula yields

$$dV_t = \frac{\partial F}{\partial t}(t \wedge \tau, S_t^\tau)\, d(t \wedge \tau) + \frac{\partial F}{\partial s}(t \wedge \tau, S_t^\tau)\, d(S^\tau)_t + \frac{1}{2}\frac{\partial^2 F}{\partial s^2}(t \wedge \tau, S_t^\tau)\, d\langle S^\tau \rangle_t$$

$$= 1_{[\![0,\tau]\!]}(t)\left\{ \frac{\partial F}{\partial s}(t \wedge \tau, S_t^\tau)\,\sigma(t)S_t dW_t^0 + \right.$$

$$\left. \left[\frac{\partial F}{\partial t}(t \wedge \tau, S_t^\tau) + r(t)S_t\frac{\partial F}{\partial s}(t \wedge \tau, S_t^\tau) + \frac{1}{2}\sigma(t)^2 S_t^2\frac{\partial^2 F}{\partial s^2}(t \wedge \tau, S_t^\tau) \right] dt \right\}.$$

If now $F = F(t,s)$ satisfies the PDE

$$\frac{\partial F}{\partial t} + r(t)s\frac{\partial F}{\partial s} + \frac{1}{2}\sigma(t)^2 s^2\frac{\partial^2 F}{\partial s^2} = 0, \tag{18}$$

this collapses to $dV_t = (\partial F/\partial s)(t \wedge \tau, S_{t\wedge\tau})\,\sigma(t)S_t dW_t^0$ implying that V is a P_0-local martingale. If in addition the partial derivative $\partial F/\partial s$ is bounded, it follows that V is a square integrable P_0-martingale. In this case we have the representation

$$\pi_t(h) = B_t B_T^{-1} F(t \wedge \tau, S_{t\wedge\tau}), \quad t \in [0,T],$$

for the option price $\pi_t(h)$.

4.f.3 Hedging the call. Let $h = (S_T - K)^+$ be the call on S_T with strike price K. In the proof of Margrabe's formula 4.c.0 we have seen that the process $\pi_t(h) = B(t,T)E_{P_T}[h|\mathcal{F}_t]$ is given by $\pi_t(h) = S_t N(d_1) - KB(t,T)N(d_2)$ and so

$$\pi_t^A(h) = S_t^A N(d_1) - KN(d_2), \quad t \in [0,T], \quad \text{where}$$

$$d_1 = \frac{\log\left(S_t^A/K\right) + \frac{1}{2}\Sigma^2(t,T)}{\Sigma(t,T)}, \quad d_2 = d_1 - \Sigma(t,T), \quad \Sigma^2(t,T) = \int_t^T \|\sigma(s)\|^2 ds$$

and $A_t = B(t,T)$. Here $\|\sigma(s)\|$ is the volatility process of the forward price S_t^A. This did not use the replicability of h (only the interpretation of $\pi_t(h)$ as the arbitrage price of h does). Thus $\pi_t^A(h) = F(t, S_t^A)$ where $F(t,s) = sN(d_1(s)) - KN(d_2(s))$,

$$d_1 = \frac{\log(s/K) + \frac{1}{2}\Sigma^2(t,T)}{\Sigma(t,T)}, \quad d_2 = d_1 - \Sigma(t,T),$$

and $\Sigma(t, T)$ does not depend on s. A straightforward computation shows that $\partial F/\partial s = N(d_1(s))$. Thus the pricing formula

$$\pi_t(h) = S_t N(d_1) - K A_t N(d_2) \tag{19}$$

already yields the correct weights for hedging the call in the underlying asset S_t and the zero coupon bond $A_t = B(t, T)$ (delta hedging). A long call will be hedged by being short S_t and long the bond $B(t, T)$.

These weights are not correct if the long side of the hedge invests in the riskless bond (investing the difference $\pi_t(h) - S_t N(d_1)$ in the riskless bond), unless the short rate $r(t)$ is nonstochastic. To see this, let us derive the correct weights for hedging the call with the underlying asset and the riskless bond $B_0(t)$. Write $X_t^0 = X(t)/B_0(t)$, for each process X. Starting from the dynamics

$$dS_t^0 = S_t^0 \sigma(t) \cdot dW_t^0, \quad \text{and} \quad dA_t^0 = A_t^0 \beta(t) \cdot dW_t^0, \tag{20}$$

under the spot martingale measure P_0 (W_t^0 a two dimensional Brownian motion on $(\Omega, \mathcal{F}, (\mathcal{F}_t), P_0)$ and $\sigma = \sigma_S$, $\beta(t) = b(t, T)$ in the terminology of 3.g), straightforward computations yield

$$dS_t^A = S_t^A \left\{ (\beta - \sigma) \cdot \beta dt + (\sigma - \beta) \cdot dW_t^0 \right\}. \tag{21}$$

Assume now that $\phi_t = (\tilde{K}_t, \tilde{H}_t)$ is a replicating strategy for our call investing in the assets $(B_0(t), S(t))$. Then, writing $\pi_t = \pi_t(h)$, we have $d\pi_t^0 = dV_t^0(\phi) = \tilde{H}_t dS_t^0$ since ϕ is self-financing. Likewise, if $\theta_t = (K_t, H_t)$ is any trading strategy investing in the assets (A_t, S_t) which replicates h, then $d\pi_t^A = dV_t^A(\theta) = H_t dS_t^A$.

Suitable weights $H_t = N(d_1)$ and $K_t = -KN(d_2)$ for such a strategy are already known from (19) and we would like to derive suitable weights $\tilde{H}_t$, $\tilde{K}_t$ for ϕ from these. To do this, note that $\pi_t^0 = A_t^0 \pi_t^A$ and thus, by the stochastic product rule,

$$d\pi_t^0 = A_t^0 d\pi_t^A + \pi_t^A dA_t^0 + d\langle A^0, \pi^A \rangle_t. \tag{22}$$

We will now reduce the left and right hand sides to stochastic differentials with respect to W_t^0 and compare coefficients. On the left we have

$$d\pi_t^0 = \tilde{H}_t dS_t^0 = \tilde{H}_t S_t^0 \sigma \cdot dW_t^0. \tag{23}$$

To simplify the right hand side, we compute the summands one by one. First

$$d\pi_t^A = H_t dS_t^A = H_t S_t^A \left\{ (\beta - \sigma) \cdot \beta dt + (\sigma - \beta) \cdot dW_t^0 \right\} \tag{24}$$

from (21). Multiplying this with A_t^0 and observing that $A_t^0 S_t^A = S_t^0$, we obtain

$$A_t^0 d\pi_t^A = H_t S_t^0 \left\{ (\beta - \sigma) \cdot \beta dt + (\sigma - \beta) \cdot dW_t^0 \right\}. \tag{25}$$

From (20)

$$\pi_t^A dA_t^0 = \pi_t^A A_t^0 \beta \cdot dW_t^0 = \pi_t^0 \beta \cdot dW_t^0 \tag{26}$$

and finally, from (20) and (24), observing again that $A_t^0 S_t^A = S_t^0$,

$$d\langle A^0, \pi^A \rangle_t = H_t S_t^0 (\sigma - \beta) \cdot \beta dt. \tag{27}$$

Entering $(25), (26), (27)$ into (22) we obtain $d\pi_t^0 = \{ H_t S_t^0 (\sigma - \beta) + \pi_t^0 \beta \} \cdot dW_t^0$. Comparing this to (23) yields $\tilde{H}_t S_t^0 \sigma = H_t S_t^0 (\sigma - \beta) + \pi_t^0 \beta$, equivalently

$$\tilde{H}_t \sigma = H_t (\sigma - \beta) + \pi_t^S \beta. \tag{28}$$

Assume now that the vectors $\sigma(t)$ and $\beta(t)$ are linearly independent, for all $t \in [0, T]$. Then (28) implies in particular that $\pi_t^S = H_t$, that is, $V_t(\theta) = \pi_t = H_t S_t$ and so $K_t = 0$ in contradiction to $K_t = -KN(d_1)$. Thus, in this case, there is no process $\tilde{H}_t$ satisfying (28) and consequently a replicating strategy ϕ hedging the call by investing in $(B_0(t), S(t))$ does not exist.

However such a replicating strategy does exist, if we assume that *the same one dimensional* Brownian motion V_t drives both the asset S_t and the zero coupon bond $A_t = B(t, T)$, that is, if we assume the dynamics

$$dS_t^0 = S_t^0 \sigma_1(t) dV_t \quad \text{and} \quad dA_t^0 = A_t^0 \sigma_2(t) dV_t,$$

instead of (20). Computations which are identical to the ones above (σ, β and W_t^0 replaced with σ_1, σ_2 and V_t) lead to the equation $\tilde{H}_t \sigma_1 = H_t (\sigma_1 - \sigma_2) + \pi_t^S \sigma_2$ with scalar processes σ_1, σ_2, which can be solved for $\tilde{H}_t$ as

$$\tilde{H}_t = H_t + \sigma_2 \sigma_1^{-1} (\pi_t^S - H_t). \tag{29}$$

From (19) it is known that $H_t = N(d_1)$ and $\pi_t = S_t N(d_1) - K A_t N(d_2)$ and so $\pi_t^S - H_t = -K A_t S_t^{-1} N(d_2)$ with the notation of section 4.c.0. With this (29) yields

$$\tilde{H}_t = N(d_1) - K \sigma_2 \sigma_1^{-1} A_t S_t^{-1} N(d_2) = N(d_1) - K \sigma_2 \sigma_1^{-1} B(t, T) S_t^{-1} N(d_2)$$

as the correct number of shares of the asset S_t to hold short when hedging a long call $h = (S_T - K)^+$ by investing in $S(t)$ and the riskless bond $B_0(t)$.

5. INTEREST RATE DERIVATIVES

Fix a sequence of dates (*tenor structure*) $0 < T = T_0 < T_1 < \ldots < T_n < T^*$ and consider a market B containing each zero coupon bond $B(t, T_j)$ and admitting a local deflator ξ such that $\xi(t)B(t, T_j)$ is a martingale and so the forward martingale measure P_{T_j} is defined at each date T_j, $0 \leq j \leq n$.

Set $\delta_j = T_{j+1} - T_j$, $0 \leq j < n$, and assume that $0 \leq t \leq T = T_0$. Recall that Libor $L(T_j)$ set at time T_j (for the accrual period $[T_j, T_{j+1}]$) is defined as

$$B(T_j, T_{j+1})^{-1} = 1 + \delta_j L(T_j). \tag{0}$$

One dollar at time T_j buys $B(T_j, T_{j+1})^{-1}$ zero coupon bonds maturing at time T_{j+1} with payoff $B(T_j, T_{j+1})^{-1}$ at time T_{j+1}. Thus $L(T_j)$ is a simple rate of interest expressed in annualized form. The dates $T_0, \ldots, T_{n-1}$ are called the *reset dates* (i.e., dates at which Libor is reset) and the dates $T_1, \ldots, T_n$ are called the *settlement dates* (i.e., dates where interest payments are made (for Libor settled in arrears)).

5.a Floating and fixed rate bonds. The *floating rate bond* FLB (with principal 1) is a security which pays the coupon $c_j = \delta_j L(T_j)$ at time T_{j+1}, $0 \leq j < n$ and returns the principal 1 at time T_n. Let FLB_t denote the value of this random cash flow at time $t \leq T = T_0$ and $c_j(t)$ the value at time t of the jth coupon payment c_j. Clearly then

$$FLB_t = B(t, T_n) + \sum_{j=0}^{n-1} c_j(t). \tag{1}$$

Moreover, evaluating the coupon $c_j = \delta_j L(T_j) = B(T_j, T_{j+1})^{-1} - 1$ (payable at time T_{j+1}) at time t using the time T_{j+1}-forward martingale measure $P_{T_{j+1}}$ in accordance with 4.a.eq.(2) yields

$$c_j(t) = B(t, T_{j+1}) E_{P_{T_{j+1}}} \left[B(T_j, T_{j+1})^{-1} - 1 \big| \mathcal{F}_t \right]$$
$$= B(t, T_{j+1}) E_{P_{T_{j+1}}} \left[B(T_j, T_{j+1})^{-1} \big| \mathcal{F}_t \right] - B(t, T_{j+1}).$$

Using 4.a.2.(b) to switch to the forward martingale measure P_{T_j} yields

$$c_j(t) = B(t, T_j) E_{P_{T_j}} \left[1 \big| \mathcal{F}_t \right] - B(t, T_{j+1}) = B(t, T_j) - B(t, T_{j+1}).$$

Entering this into (1) and telescoping the sum yields

$$FLB_t = B(t, T_0).$$

Here it was assumed that $t \leq T = T_0$. If $t \in (T_j, T_{j+1}]$, then $FLB_t = B(t, T_{j+1})$. In particular the floating rate bond FLB has value 1 at each reset date T_j.

The fixed rate bond $FRB(\kappa)$ (with coupon rate κ and principal 1) pays the fixed coupon $c_j = \delta_j \kappa$ at time T_{j+1}, $j = 0, \ldots, n - 1$ and returns the principal 1 at time T_n. Consequently its value $FRB_t(\kappa)$ at time $t \leq T$ satisfies

$$FRB_t(\kappa) = B(t, T_n) + \sum_{j=0}^{n-1} \delta_j \kappa B(t, T_{j+1}). \tag{2}$$

5.b Interest rate swaps. Interest rate swaps exchange fixed rate coupons for floating rate coupons on a nominal principal which we shall always assume to be equal to one. Such a swap is called a *payer* respectively *receiver swap* according as the fixed rate coupons are payed or received.

Recall from section 3.f that *forward Libor* $L(t, T_j)$ at time $t \leq T_j$ for the accrual period $[T_j, T_{j+1}]$ is the simple annualized rate defined by

$$\frac{B(t, T_j)}{B(t, T_{j+1})} = 1 + \delta_j L(t, T_j). \tag{0}$$

The holder of a *forward payer swap* $FS(\kappa)$ *with fixed rate* κ is obliged to pay the fixed rate coupon $\delta_j \kappa$ and receives the floating rate coupon $\delta_j L(T_j)$ at time T_{j+1} for the accrual period $[T_j, T_{j+1}]$, $j = 0, \ldots, n-1$. Here the fixed rate κ is a simple annualized rate.

In other words, such a swap pays coupons at the fixed rate κ on a nominal principal of 1 and receives floating rate coupons over the accrual periods $[T_j, T_{j+1}]$. The floating (Libor) rate is reset at the beginning of each accrual period and payments are exchanged at the end of each accrual period (settlement in arrears). The forward payer swap $FS(\kappa)$ is called simply a *payer swap* if accrual periods are to commence immediately, that is, if current time t satisfies $t = T = T_0$. Let $FS_t(\kappa)$ denote the value at time $t \leq T$ of such a forward payer swap. A forward receiver swap is defined similarly with fixed coupons received and floating coupons paid.

It is clear that the cashflows of a payer swap are identical to the cashflows induced by the following portfolio: long the floating rate bond FLB and short the fixed rate bond $FRB(\kappa)$ with face value 1 and coupon rate κ. Thus the value $FS_t(\kappa)$ at time t of the payer swap is given by

$$FS_t(\kappa) = FLB_t - FRB_t(\kappa) = B(t, T) - \sum_{j=0}^{n-1} \delta_j \kappa B(t, T_{j+1}) - B(t, T_n). \tag{1}$$

The $(n\text{-}period)$ *forward swap rate* $\kappa(t, T, n)$ is now defined to be that fixed rate κ making the value of the foward payer swap $FS_t(\kappa)$ at time t equal to zero and so, from (1),

$$\kappa(t, T, n) = \frac{B(t, T) - B(t, T_n)}{\sum_{j=0}^{n-1} \delta_j B(t, T_{j+1})}. \tag{2}$$

Consequently a payer swap with accrual periods to commence at time $T = T_0$ can be entered into at any time $t \leq T$ at no cost, if the fixed rate κ is chosen to be the forward swap rate $\kappa(t, T, n)$. Thus we have

$$FS_t(\kappa) = B(t, T) - \sum_{j=0}^{n-1} \delta_j \kappa B(t, T_{j+1}) - B(t, T_n)$$

and

$$0 = B(t, T) - \sum_{j=0}^{n-1} \delta_j \kappa(t, T, n) B(t, T_{j+1}) - B(t, T_n),$$

by definition of the forward swap rate $\kappa(t,T,n)$. Subtraction now yields

$$FS_t(\kappa) = \sum_{j=0}^{n-1} \delta_j\big(\kappa(t,T,n) - \kappa\big)B(t,T_{j+1}). \tag{3}$$

The *swap rate* is the forward swap rate $\kappa(t,T,n)$ for $t=T$, that is, the fixed rate κ at which a payer swap can be initiated immediately at no cost. From (2) we see that the swap rate $\kappa(T,T,n)$ satisfies

$$\kappa(T,T,n) = \frac{1 - B(t,T_n)}{\sum_{j=0}^{n-1} \delta_j B(t,T_{j+1})}. \tag{4}$$

5.c Swaptions. Recall that the forward payer swap $FS(\kappa)$ satisfies

$$FS_t(\kappa) = B(t,T) - \sum_{j=0}^{n-1} \delta_j\kappa B(t,T_{j+1}) - B(t,T_n) = B(t,T) - \sum_{j=0}^{n-1} c_j B(t,T_{j+1}),$$

where
$$c_j = \begin{cases} \delta_j\kappa, & \text{if } j < n-1 \\ 1 + \delta_j\kappa, & \text{if } j = n-1. \end{cases}$$

The *payer swaption* $PS(\kappa)$ is the European option exercisable at time T to enter at no cost into the payer swap $FS(\kappa)$ commencing at time T, that is, $PS(\kappa)$ is a European call exercisable at time T with strike price zero on the payer swap $FS(\kappa)$ starting at the time of exercise. Thus $PS(\kappa)$ is a European option with payoff

$$FS_T(\kappa)^+ = \left(1 - \sum_{j=0}^{n-1} c_j B(T,T_{j+1})\right)^+ \tag{0}$$

at time T. This is the payoff of the European put exercisable at time T with strike price 1 on the coupon bearing bond with coupons c_j at the settlement dates T_{j+1}, $0 \le j < n$ (the last coupon contains the principal). Alternatively, using

$$FS_t(\kappa) = \sum_{j=0}^{n-1} \delta_j\big(\kappa(t,T,n) - \kappa\big)B(t,T_{j+1})$$

and observing that the term $\kappa(t,T,n) - \kappa$ does not depend on the summation index this payoff can be written as

$$FS_T(\kappa)^+ = \sum_{j=0}^{n-1} \delta_j B(T,T_{j+1})\big(\kappa(T,T,n) - \kappa\big)^+ \tag{1}$$

and can be viewed as the payoff of a portfolio of $\delta_0, \delta_1, \ldots, \delta_{n-1}$ European calls on the forward swap rate $\kappa(t,T,n)$ with strike price κ all of which must be exercised at the same time T and have payoffs deferred to times $T_1, T_2, \ldots, T_n$ respectively.

Similarly the *receiver swaption* $RS(\kappa)$ is the European option exercisable at time T to enter at no cost into the receiver swap $-FS(\kappa)$ commencing at time T, that is, $RS(\kappa)$ is a European call exercisable at time T with strike price zero on the receiver swap $-FS(\kappa)$ starting immediately. Thus $RS(\kappa)$ is a European option with payoff $\left(-FS_T(\kappa)\right)^+$ and so the value of the portfolio $PS(\kappa) - RS(\kappa)$ at time T is given by

$$FS_T(\kappa)^+ - \left(-FS_T(\kappa)\right)^+ = FS_T(\kappa).$$

Let $PS_t(\kappa)$ and $RS_t(\kappa)$ denote the arbitrage price processes of $PS(\kappa)$ and $RS(\kappa)$ respectively. Then $\xi(t)PS_t(\kappa)$, $\xi(t)RS_t(\kappa)$ and $\xi(t)FS_t(\kappa)$ are all P-martingales and hence the Law of One Price 4.a.1 applies and shows that

$$PS_t(\kappa) - RS_t(\kappa) = FS_t(\kappa), \quad t \in [0, T], \tag{2}$$

in analogy to the put-call parity. Note that the payoff of the receiver swaption $RS(\kappa)$ at time T can be written as

$$\left(-FS_T(\kappa)\right)^+ = \left(\sum_{j=0}^{n-1} c_j B(T, T_{j+1}) - 1\right)^+$$

and is thus seen to be identical with the payoff of the European call with strike price 1 exercisable at time T on the coupon bearing bond with coupons c_j at times T_{j+1}, $j = 0, \ldots, n-1$ (the principal is in the last coupon). Consequently the receiver swaption $RS(\kappa)$ can be viewed as a European call with strike 1 exercisable at time T on this coupon bearing bond.

The *forward swaptions* $PS(\hat{T}, \kappa)$, $RS(\hat{T}, \kappa)$ are European options exercisable at time $\hat{T} \le T$ to enter at no cost into the payer respectively receiver swaps $FS(\kappa)$, $-FS(\kappa)$ commencing at the later date T. They can thus be viewed as European calls with strike price zero exercisable at time $\hat{T}$ on the forward payer respectively receiver swaps $FS(\kappa)$, $-FS(\kappa)$. Consequently $PS(\hat{T}, \kappa)$ has payoff

$$FS_{\hat{T}}(\kappa)^+ = \sum_{j=0}^{n-1} \delta_j B(\hat{T}, T_{j+1})\left(\kappa(\hat{T}, T, n) - \kappa\right)^+ \tag{3}$$

at time $\hat{T}$. This can be interpreted as the payoff of a portfolio of $\delta_0, \delta_1, \ldots, \delta_{n-1}$ European calls on the forward swap rate $\kappa(t, T, n)$ with strike price κ, all of which must be exercised at the same time $\hat{T}$ and have payoffs deferred to times $T_1, T_2, \ldots, T_n$ respectively. A similar interpretation as a portfolio of European puts on the forward swap rate $k(t, T, n)$, all of which must be exercised at the same time and have payments deferred to the settlement dates, is possible for the forward receiver swaption $RS(\hat{T}, \kappa)$. Again we have the put call parity

$$PS_t(\hat{T}, \kappa) - RS_t(\hat{T}, \kappa) = FS_t(\kappa), \quad t \in [0, \hat{T}]. \tag{4}$$

Evaluating the payoff (3) at any time $t \le \hat{T}$ using the forward martingale measure $P_{\hat{T}}$, we obtain the price $PS_t(\hat{T}, \kappa)$ of the forward payer swaption $PS(\hat{T}, \kappa)$ as

$$PS_t(\hat{T}, \kappa) = \sum_{j=0}^{n-1} \delta_j B(t, \hat{T}) E_{P_{\hat{T}}}\left[B(\hat{T}, T_{j+1})\left(\kappa(\hat{T}, T, n) - \kappa\right)^+ | \mathcal{F}_t\right]. \tag{5}$$

Using 4.a.2.(a) this can be rewritten as

$$PS_t(\hat{T}, \kappa) = \sum_{j=0}^{n-1} \delta_j B(t, T_{j+1}) E_{P_{T_{j+1}}}\left[\left(\kappa(\hat{T}, T, n) - \kappa\right)^+ | \mathcal{F}_t\right]. \tag{6}$$

5.d Interest rate caps and floors. Interest rate caps (floors) are instruments designed to provide upper (lower) bounds for the coupon payments on a floating rate bond. An interest rate cap protects a floating rate borrower against an increase in Libor while an interest rate floor protects a floating rate lender from a decrease in Libor past a certain strike level κ. More precisely the *forward cap FC(\kappa)* with strike level κ is the random cash flow paying the caplets

$$Cpl(T_j, \kappa) = \delta_j(L(T_j) - \kappa)^+ = \left(\frac{1}{B(T_j, T_{j+1})} - (1 + \delta_j \kappa) \right)^+$$

at the settlement times T_{j+1}, $0 \le j < n$. In other words this security pays that portion of the floating rate coupons which corresponds to the excess of Libor above the strike level κ and thus protects a floating rate borrower of one dollar against an increase of Libor above κ.

The *forward cap* is simply called a *cap* if accrual periods are to commence immediately, that is, if current time t satisifies $t = T = T_0$. Evaluating the caplet $Cpl(T_j, \kappa)$ (payable at time T_{j+1}) at time $t \le T = T_0$ using the forward martingale measure at the settlement time T_{j+1} yields

$$Cpl_t(T_j, \kappa) = B(t, T_{j+1}) E_{P_{T_{j+1}}} \left[\left(B(T_j, T_{j+1})^{-1} - (1 + \delta_j \kappa) \right)^+ | \mathcal{F}_t \right]$$

$$= B(t, T_{j+1}) E_{P_{T_{j+1}}} \left[B(T_j, T_{j+1})^{-1} (1 - \kappa_j B(T_j, T_{j+1}))^+ | \mathcal{F}_t \right],$$

where $\kappa_j = 1 + \delta_j \kappa$. Using formula 4.a.2.(b) to switch to the forward martingale measure P_{T_j} at time T_j, we can write this as

$$Cpl_t(T_j, \kappa) = B(t, T_j) E_{P_{T_j}} \left[(1 - \kappa_j B(T_j, T_{j+1}))^+ | \mathcal{F}_t \right]$$

$$= \kappa_j B(t, T_j) E_{P_{T_j}} \left[(\kappa_j^{-1} - B(T_j, T_{j+1}))^+ | \mathcal{F}_t \right].$$

Note that this is the value at time t of κ_j European puts exercisable at time T_j on zero coupon bonds maturing at time T_{j+1} with strike price $1/\kappa_j$. The price $FC_t(\kappa)$ at time t of the forward cap $FC(\kappa)$ is given by

$$FC_t(\kappa) = \sum_{j=0}^{n-1} Cpl_t(T_j, \kappa).$$

Thus the forward cap $FC(\kappa)$ can be viewed as a portfolio of European puts exercisable at the reset times on zero coupon bonds maturing at the following settlement times. The *forward floor FF(\kappa)* with strike rate κ is the random cashflow paying the floorlets

$$Fll(T_j, \kappa) = \delta_j(\kappa - L(T_j))^+$$

at the settlement times T_{j+1}, $0 \le j < n$. In other words the floor $FF(\kappa)$ pays that portion of the floating rate coupons which corresponds to the excess of the strike rate κ above Libor and consequently protects the holder of a floating rate bond against a decline in Libor below the strike level κ. The equality $x^+ - (-x)^+ = x^+ - x^- = x$ yields

$$Cpl(T_j, \kappa) - Fll(T_j, \kappa) = \delta_j\left[(L(T_j) - \kappa)^+ - (\kappa - L(T_j))^+\right] = \delta_j\left[L(T_j) - \kappa\right]. \quad (0)$$

The quantity on the right is the payment received at settlement date T_{j+1} by the holder of a forward payer swap $FS(\kappa)$. Evaluating the payments in (0) at time t and summing them up yields

$$FC_t(\kappa) - FF_t(\kappa) = FS_t(\kappa), \quad t \in [0, T]. \quad (1)$$

5.e Dynamics of the Libor process. Consider a market $B = (B_0, B_1, \ldots, B_n)$ admitting a deflator ξ such that ξB_n is a P-martingale. Then the numeraire measure $P_n := P_{B_n}$ is defined and satisfies

$$M_t := \frac{d(P_n|\mathcal{F}_t)}{d(P|\mathcal{F}_t)} = \frac{\xi(t)B_n(t)}{\xi(0)B_n(0)}, \quad t \in [0, T^*]. \quad (0)$$

If we interpret B_j as the zero coupon bond $B(t, T_j)$, then P_n plays the role of the forward martingale measure P_{T_n} at the terminal date T_n. Fix a sequence $(\delta_i)_{i=0}^{n-1}$ of positive numbers δ_i and set

$$B_i/B_{i+1} = 1 + \delta_i L_i, \quad i = 0, \ldots, n - 1.$$

The process $L(t) = \big(L_0(t), \ldots, L_{n-1}(t)\big)$ is an abstract version of the process of forward Libor rates in section 5.b.eq.(0). Let $0 \le i < n$. Then $\xi B_{i+1} L_i = \delta_i^{-1}\big(\xi B_i - \xi B_{i+1}\big)$ is a local martingale. Using 3.c.3 with $j = i + 1$ and $C = B_{i+1} L_i = B_j L_i$ (thus $C/B_j = L_i$) we obtain

$$u_{L_i} = -\langle L_i, log(\xi B_{i+1})\rangle. \quad (1)$$

By definition of the L_j we have $B_{i+1} = B_n(1 + \delta_{i+1} L_{i+1}) \ldots (1 + \delta_{n-1} L_{n-1})$ and consequently

$$0 = u_{L_i} + \langle L_i, log(\xi B_{i+1})\rangle$$
$$= u_{L_i} + \langle L_i, log(\xi B_n)\rangle + \sum_{j=i+1}^{n-1} \langle L_i, log(1 + \delta_j L_j)\rangle. \quad (2)$$

Since $\langle L_i, log(1 + \delta_j L_j)\rangle_t = \int_0^t \frac{\delta_j}{1 + \delta_j L_j(s)} d\langle L_i, L_j\rangle_s$ (III.3.c.1.(c)), we can rewrite (2) as

$$u_{L_i}(t) + \langle L_i, log(\xi B_n)\rangle_t = -\sum_{j=i+1}^{n-1} \int_0^t \frac{\delta_j}{1 + \delta_j L_j(s)} d\langle L_i, L_j\rangle_s. \quad (3)$$

Assume now that the forward Libor processes $L_i(t)$ are Ito processes satisfying

$$dL_i(t) = L_i(t)\mu_i(t)dt + L_i(t)\nu_i(t) \cdot dW_t^n, \quad 0 \le i < n, \quad (4)$$

where W^n is a d-dimensional Brownian motion on $(\Omega, \mathcal{F}, (\mathcal{F}_t), P_n)$, $\mu_i \in L(\mathbf{t})$ and $\nu_i \in L(W^n)$. Then (4) represents the dynamics of $L_i(t)$ under the forward martingale measure P_n and the process ν_i is the proportional volatility of L_i. We will now see that the existence of the local deflator ξ for B implies that the drift processes $\mu_i(t)$ are uniquely determined by the volatility processes $\nu_i(t)$. Let $u_{L_i}^n = u_{L_i}^{P_n}$ denote the compensator of L_i with respect to the probability P_n. Since W^n is a P_n-Brownian motion (4) implies that $d\,u_{L_i}^n(t) = L_i(t)\mu_i(t)dt$ and so we can rewrite (4) as

$$dL_i(t) = d\,u_{L_i}^n(t) + L_i(t)\nu_i(t) \cdot dW_t^n, \quad 0 \le i < n. \tag{5}$$

By Girsanov's formula III.4.a.1 the compensators $u_{L_i} = u_{L_i}^P$ and $u_{L_i}^n = u_{L_i}^{P_n}$ with respect to P and P_n are related by $u_{L_i}^n = u_{L_i} + \langle L_i, log(M) \rangle = u_{L_i} + \langle L_i, log(\xi B_n) \rangle$. With this (3) becomes

$$u_{L_i}^n(t) = -\sum_{j=i+1}^{n-1} \int_0^t \frac{\delta_j d \langle L_i, L_j \rangle_s}{1 + \delta_j L_j(s)}, \quad \text{that is,} \quad d\,u_{L_i}^n(t) = -\sum_{j=i+1}^{n-1} \frac{\delta_j d \langle L_i, L_j \rangle_t}{1 + \delta_j L_j(t)}.$$

Putting this into (5) and observing that $d \langle L_i, L_j \rangle_t = L_i(t)L_j(t)\nu_i(t) \cdot \nu_j(t)dt$ (from (4)) we can rewrite (5) as

$$d\,L_i(t) = -\sum_{j=i+1}^{n-1} \frac{\delta_j L_i(t)L_j(t)\,\nu_i(t) \cdot \nu_j(t)}{1 + \delta_j L_j(t)}\,dt + L_i(t)\nu_i(t) \cdot dW_t^n, \tag{6}$$

$$i = 0, 1, \ldots, n-1.$$

This relation was derived under the assumption of the existence of a local deflator ξ for B and will thus be called the *arbitrage free dynamics* of the forward Libor process $L(t) = \big(L_0(t), \ldots, L_{n-1}(t)\big)$ under the forward martingale measure P_n.

5.f Libor models with prescribed volatilities. Fix a tenor structure $0 = T_0 < T_1 < \ldots < T_n$, set $\delta_i = T_{i+1} - T_i$ and let $\nu_i(t)$, $0 \le i < n$, be any bounded, progressively measurable processes.

We now turn to the construction of a deflatable market $B = (B_0, B_1, \ldots, B_n)$ such that the associated Libor processes L_i are Ito processes with proportional volatilities $\nu_i(t)$ and fit a given initial term structure $\big(L_0(0), L_1(0), \ldots, L_{n-1}(0)\big)$. Since the process B_i should be thought of as the zero coupon bond $B(t, T_i)$, we also want to satisfy the zero coupon bond constraint $B_i(T_i) = 1$.

Rather than constructing the zero coupon bonds B_i directly, we construct first a solution $L(t)$ of 5.e.eq.(6). Noting that the equation for L_i only involves the processes $L_i, \ldots, L_{n-1}$, while the equation for L_{n-1},

$$dL_{n-1}(t) = L_{n-1}(t)\nu_{n-1}(t) \cdot dW_t^n, \tag{0}$$

does not involve any other process, we can define the solution processes L_i using backward induction starting with L_{n-1}.

The initial values $L_i(0)$ are chosen as needed (for example letting $L_i(0)$ be the forward Libor rate for the ith accrual interval observed in the market at time $t = 0$). This flexibility of choosing the initial value $L_i(0)$ makes the problem of fitting the model to an observed Libor term structure trivial. Moreover the dynamics 5.e.eq.(6) ensures the strict positivity of the processes L_i, thus avoiding the common problem of negative interest rates.

Having constructed $L_0, \ldots, L_{n-1}$, set $Y_i = (1 + \delta_i L_i) \ldots (1 + \delta_{n-1} L_{n-1})$ and choose the process $B_n \in \mathcal{S}_+$ so that $B_n(T_n) = 1$. Define $B_i = B_n Y_i$, $0 \le i < n$. This ensures that the L_i are the Libor processes associated with the B_i. Recall that we also want to ensure that $B_i(T_i) = B_n(T_i) Y_i(T_i) = 1$ and this can be effected by choosing B_n so that $B_n(T_i) = 1/Y_i(T_i)$, that is, the process B_n should interpolate the random variables $1/Y_i(T_i)$ at times $T_0, T_1, \ldots, T_{n-1}$. This is possible, since the processes $L_0, \ldots, L_{n-1}$ are already at hand before the choice of B_n has to be made.

Finally, to verify the existence of a deflator, we show that the quotients B_i/B_n are all martingales with respect to the underlying probability measure Q (interpreted as being the forward martingale measure P_n of 5.e.).

To carry this out, let W_t^n be a d-dimensional Brownian motion on some filtered probability space $(\Omega, \mathcal{F}, (\mathcal{F}_t)_{t \in [0, T^*]}, Q)$ (the measure Q plays the role of P_n above). Define the process L_{n-1} as the solution of (0), explicitly (III.6.a.0):

$$L_{n-1}(t) = L_{n-1}(0)\mathcal{E}_t\big(\nu_{n-1} \bullet W^n\big)$$
$$= L_{n-1}(0)exp\left(-\frac{1}{2}\int_0^t \|\nu_{n-1}(s)\|^2 ds + \int_0^t \nu_{n-1}(s) \cdot dW_s^n\right).$$

Note that L_{n-1} is a strictly positive process. Assume strictly positive processes $L_{n-1}, L_{n-2}, \ldots, L_{i+1}$ have been defined already. Define the process L_i as the solution of 5.e.eq.(6), that is,

$$dL_i(t) = L_i(t)\mu_i(t)dt + L_i(t)\nu_i(t) \cdot dW_t^n, \quad \text{where}$$

$$\mu_i(t) = -\sum_{j=i+1}^{n-1} \frac{\delta_j L_j(t)}{1 + \delta_j L_j(t)} \nu_i(t) \cdot \nu_j(t).$$

Setting
$$\gamma_i(t) = \sum_{j=i+1}^{n-1} \frac{\delta_j L_j(t)}{1 + \delta_j L_j(t)} \nu_j(t), \quad 0 \le i < n$$

$(\gamma_{n-1}(t) = 0)$, we have $\mu_i(t) = -\gamma_i(t) \cdot \nu_i(t)$ and so

$$dL_i(t) = -L_i(t)\gamma_i(t) \cdot \nu_i(t)dt + L_i(t)\nu_i(t) \cdot dW_t^n. \tag{1}$$

Note that the drift term $\mu_i(t)$ depends only on $L_{i+1}, \ldots, L_{n-1}$ and is bounded. Explicitly (III.6.a.0):
$$L_i(t) = L_i(0)exp\left(\int_0^t \mu_i(s)ds\right) \mathcal{E}_t\big(\nu_i \bullet W^n\big)$$

and so L_i is a strictly positive process. This completes the construction of the processes $L_0, \ldots, L_{n-1}$ and we can now proceed as outlined above. To see that our market B is deflatable it remains to be shown only that the quotients

$$\frac{B_k}{B_n} = Y_k = (1 + \delta_k L_k) \ldots (1 + \delta_{n-1} L_{n-1}) \tag{2}$$

are all Q-martingales. To do this we examine the dynamics of Y_k under Q. Taking logarithms we have $log(Y_k) = \sum_{i=k}^{n-1} log(1 + \delta_i L_i)$, where

$$d\,log(1 + \delta_i L_i) = \frac{\delta_i}{1 + \delta_i L_i} dL_i - \frac{1}{2}\left(\frac{\delta_i}{1 + \delta_i L_i}\right)^2 d\langle L_i \rangle.$$

Here $d\langle L_i \rangle_t = L_i(t)^2 \|\nu_i(t)\|^2 dt$ (from 5.e.eq.(6)). Thus

$$d\,log(1 + \delta_i L_i) = \frac{\delta_i}{1 + \delta_i L_i} dL_i - \frac{1}{2}\left\|\frac{\delta_i L_i}{1 + \delta_i L_i}\nu_i\right\|^2 dt.$$

Substituting the right hand side of (1) for dL_i and observing that

$$\frac{\delta_i L_i(t)}{1 + \delta_i L_i(t)}\nu_i(t) = \gamma_{i-1}(t) - \gamma_i(t) \quad \text{we obtain}$$

$$
\begin{aligned}
d\,log(1 + \delta_i L_i) &= -\gamma_i \cdot \frac{\delta_i L_i}{1 + \delta_i L_i}\nu_i\,dt - \frac{1}{2}\|\gamma_{i-1} - \gamma_i\|^2 dt + \frac{\delta_i L_i}{1 + \delta_i L_i}\nu_i(t)\cdot dW_t^n \\
&= \left[-\gamma_i \cdot (\gamma_{i-1} - \gamma_i) - \frac{1}{2}\|\gamma_{i-1} - \gamma_i\|^2\right] dt + \frac{\delta_i L_i}{1 + \delta_i L_i}\nu_i(t)\cdot dW_t^n \\
&= \frac{1}{2}\left[\|\gamma_i\|^2 - \|\gamma_{i-1}\|^2\right] dt + \frac{\delta_i L_i}{1 + \delta_i L_i}\nu_i(t)\cdot dW_t^n.
\end{aligned}
$$

Summing this over all $i = k, \ldots, n-1$ and observing that $\gamma_{n-1} = 0$ we obtain

$$d\,log(Y_k(t)) = -\frac{1}{2}\|\gamma_{k-1}(t)\|^2 dt + \gamma_{k-1}(t)\cdot dW_t^n, \tag{3}$$

which is equivalent with $dY_k(t) = Y_k(t)\gamma_{k-1}(t)\cdot dW_t^n$ (III.6.a.0). Since $\gamma_{k-1}(t)$ is bounded, this implies that Y_k is a square integrable martingale (III.6.a.1).

Here Q is interpreted to be the forward martingale measure P_n. Any probability P equivalent to Q on $\mathcal{F}_{T*}$ can now serve as the market probability. Setting $N(t) = d(Q|\mathcal{F}_t)/d(P|\mathcal{F}_t)$, a deflator ξ is then given by $\xi(t) = N_t^{B_n} = N(t)/B_n(t)$ and Q becomes the forward martingale measure P_n (see 3.d.2). It will be useful to determine the dynamics of $L_{k-1}(t)$ under the measure $P_k = P_{B_k}$ (to be interpreted as the forward martingale measure at the end of the accrual period for L_{k-1}). As usual we use III.4.c.0 to switch from the $Q = P_n$-Brownian motion W_t^n to P_k-Brownian motion W_t^k. To do this, we set

$$M_k(t) = \frac{d(P_k|\mathcal{F}_t)}{d(Q|\mathcal{F}_t)} = c\frac{B_k(t)}{B_n(t)} = cY_k(t), \quad \text{where } c = 1/Y_k(0) \text{ is a constant.}$$

Then $d\log(M_k(t)) = d\log(Y_k(t)) = -\frac{1}{2}\|\gamma_{k-1}(t)\|^2 dt + \gamma_{k-1}(t) \cdot dW_t^n$, and thus $dM_k(t) = M_k(t)\gamma_{k-1}(t) \cdot dW_t^n$. By III.4.c.0 it follows that $W_t^k = W_t^n - \int_0^t \gamma_{k-1}(s)ds$ is a P_k-Brownian motion. Obviously

$$dW_t^k = dW_t^n - \gamma_{k-1}(t)dt. \tag{4}$$

The dynamics (1) of $L_{k-1}(t)$ can now be written as

$$\frac{dL_{k-1}(t)}{L_{k-1}(t)} = -\gamma_{k-1}(t) \cdot \nu_{k-1}(t)dt + \nu_{k-1}(t) \cdot dW_t^n = \nu_{k-1}(t) \cdot dW_t^k, \tag{5}$$

as expected in analogy to (0). If the volatility processes $\nu_i(t)$ are nonstochastic, then the market B is called the *log-Gaussian Libor model*. It then follows from (5) that the forward Libor process $L_{k-1}(t)$ is a log-Gaussian square integrable martingale under the forward martingale measure P_k (III.6.a.1, III.6.d.4).

5.g Cap valuation in the log-Gaussian Libor model. The log-Gaussian Libor model B of 5.f is perfectly suited for the valuation of the forward cap $FC(\kappa)$ with strike rate κ by means of an explicit formula. Recalling that Libor $L(T_j)$ set at time T_j corresponds to $L_j(T_j)$ in our model, the jth caplet $Cpl(T_j, \kappa)$, payable at time T_{j+1}, assumes the form $Cpl(T_j, \kappa) = \delta_j(L_j(T_j) - \kappa)^+$. Consequently its arbitrage price at time $t \leq T_0$ is given by

$$Cpl_t(T_j, \kappa) = \delta_j B_{j+1}(t) E_{P_{j+1}}\left[(L_j(T_j) - \kappa)^+ | \mathcal{F}_t\right]. \tag{0}$$

Using the dynamics $d\log(L_j(t)) = -\frac{1}{2}\|\nu_j(t)\|^2 dt + \nu_j(t) \cdot dW_t^{j+1}$ of $L_j(t)$ under the forward martingale measure P_{j+1} and III.6.c.3 to compute the conditional expectation in (0) we obtain

$$Cpl_t(T_j, \kappa) = \delta_j B_{j+1}(t)\left[L_j(t)N(d_1(j)) - \kappa N(d_2(j))\right], \quad \text{where} \tag{1}$$

$$d_{1,2}(j) = \frac{\log(L_j(t)/\kappa) \pm \frac{1}{2}\Sigma^2(t, T_j)}{\Sigma(t, T_j)} \quad \text{and} \quad \Sigma(t, T_j) = \left(\int_t^{T_j} \|\nu_j(s)\|^2 ds\right)^{\frac{1}{2}}. \tag{2}$$

It follows that the price at time $t \leq T_0$ of the forward cap $FC(\kappa)$ is given by

$$FC_t(\kappa) = \sum_{j=0}^{n-1} Cpl_t(T_j, \kappa) = \sum_{j=0}^{n-1} \delta_j B_{j+1}(t)\left[L_j(t)N(d_1(j)) - \kappa N(d_2(j))\right] \tag{3}$$

with $d_{1,2}(j)$ as in (2). Note that here the processes $B_{j+1}(t)$ and $L_j(t)$ are models of the zero coupon bonds $B(t, T_{j+1})$ and forward Libor rates $L(t, T_j)$ observable in the markets. The forward floor $FF(\kappa)$ can now be valued using equation (1) of 5.d. In order to be able to obtain similarly simple formulas for the valuation of swaptions we now turn to models of the market B of zero coupon bonds in which forward swap rates have suitably simple dynamics.

5.h Dynamics of forward swap rates. Consider a market $B = (B_0, B_1, \ldots, B_n)$ with deflator ξ such that each ξB_i is a P-martingale and hence the numeraire measures $P_i := P_{B_i}$ are all defined. Fix a sequence $(\delta_i)_{i=0}^{n-1}$ of positive numbers δ_i and introduce the following processes

$$B_{i,n} = \sum_{j=i+1}^{n} \delta_{j-1} B_j, \quad S_i = \frac{B_i - B_n}{B_{i,n}}, \quad \text{and}$$

$$s_{ij} = \sum_{k=j}^{n-1} \delta_k \prod_{u=i+1}^{k} (1 + \delta_{u-1} S_u), \quad s_i = s_{ii}, \quad 0 \le i \le j \le n - 1,$$

with the understanding that empty sums are zero and empty products equal to one. The interpretation is again as follows: the numbers δ_j are the lengths of the accrual periods $\delta_j = T_{j+1} - T_j$ associated with some tenor structure $0 \le T_0 < T_1 < \ldots < T_n$, $B_j(t)$ is the zero coupon bond $B(t, T_j)$, P_j the forward martingale measure at the date T_j and $S_i(t)$ the $(n-i)$-period forward swap rate $\kappa(t, T_i, n-i)$ associated with a swap along the tenor structure $T_i < T_{i+1} < \ldots < T_n$ (5.b.eq.(2)). However this interpretation is not necessary for the results of this section. Let us note that

$$s_i = \sum_{k=i}^{n-1} \delta_k \prod_{u=i+1}^{k} (1 + \delta_{u-1} S_u)$$

and consequently we have the following backward recursion:

$$\begin{aligned} s_{n-1} &= \delta_{n-1} \quad \text{and} \\ s_{i-1} &= \delta_{i-1} + (1 + \delta_{i-1} S_i) s_i, \quad 1 \le i \le n - 1. \end{aligned} \tag{0}$$

Using backward induction on i it now follows that

$$B_{i,n} = B_n s_i, \quad 0 \le i \le n - 1. \tag{1}$$

Indeed, for $i = n - 1$, $B_{i,n}/B_n = B_{n-1,n}/B_n = \delta_{n-1} = s_{n-1}$ and, assuming that $B_{i,n} = B_n s_i$, we have

$$\begin{aligned} B_n s_{i-1} &= B_n(\delta_{i-1} + (1 + \delta_{i-1} S_i) s_i) = B_n \delta_{i-1} + (1 + \delta_{i-1} S_i) B_{i,n} \\ &= B_n \delta_{i-1} + B_{i,n} + \delta_{i-1}(B_i - B_n) = B_{i,n} + \delta_{i-1} B_i = B_{i-1,n}. \end{aligned}$$

From this it follows easily that

$$B_i = B_n(1 + S_i s_i). \tag{2}$$

Note that the process $\xi B_{i,n}$ is a P-martingale and hence the numeraire measure $P_{i,n} = P_{B_{i,n}}$ is defined. This measure will be called the $(n-i)$-*period forward swap measure.* According to 5.d.0.(b), $B_k/B_{i,n}$ is a $P_{i,n}$-martingale, for all $k = 0, 1, \ldots, n$. It follows that S_i is a $P_{i,n}$-martingale and consequently the compensator of S_i with respect to $P_{i,n}$ vanishes:

$$u_{S_i}^{P_{i,n}} = 0. \tag{3}$$

Let us now compute the compensator $u^n_{S_i} = u^{P_n}_{S_i}$ of S_i under the forward martingale measure P_n. Set

$$M_t = \frac{d(P_n|\mathcal{F}_t)}{d(P_{i,n}|\mathcal{F}_t)} = c\frac{B_n(t)}{B_{i,n}(t)}, \quad t \in [0, T^*],$$

where c is a normalizing constant. Then, by Girsanov's formula III.4.a.1 and III.3.c.1.(c)

$$u^n_{S_i}(t) = u^{P_{i,n}}_{S_i}(t) + \langle S_i, log(M)\rangle_t = \langle S_i, log(B_n/B_{i,n})\rangle_t$$

$$= -\langle S_i, log(s_i)\rangle_t = -\int_0^t \frac{1}{s_i(r)} d\langle S_i, s_i\rangle_r. \tag{4}$$

To compute $d\langle S_i, s_i\rangle$ set $Z_k = log \prod_{u=i+1}^k (1 + \delta_{u-1}S_u) = \sum_{u=i+1}^k log(1 + \delta_{u-1}S_u)$ and note that then $s_{ij} = \sum_{k=j}^{n-1} \delta_k e^{Z_k}$. In particular $s_i = \sum_{k=i}^{n-1} \delta_k e^{Z_k}$ and so, using III.3.c.2.(b),

$$d\langle S_i, s_i\rangle = \sum_{k=i}^{n-1} \delta_k d\langle S_i, e^{Z_k}\rangle = \sum_{k=i}^{n-1} \delta_k e^{Z_k} d\langle S_i, Z_k\rangle$$

$$= \sum_{k=i}^{n-1} \delta_k e^{Z_k} \sum_{u=i+1}^k d\langle S_i, log(1 + \delta_{u-1}S_u)\rangle$$

$$= \sum_{k=i}^{n-1} \delta_k e^{Z_k} \sum_{u=i+1}^k \frac{\delta_{u-1}}{1 + \delta_{u-1}S_u} d\langle S_i, S_u\rangle.$$

Commuting the order of summation and writing j instead of u we obtain

$$d\langle S_i, s_i\rangle = \sum_{j=i+1}^{n-1} \frac{\delta_{j-1}}{1 + \delta_{j-1}S_j} \sum_{k=j}^{n-1} \delta_k e^{Z_k} d\langle S_i, S_j\rangle = \sum_{j=i+1}^{n-1} \frac{\delta_{j-1}s_{ij}}{1 + \delta_{j-1}S_j} d\langle S_i, S_j\rangle. \tag{5}$$

Entering this into (4) we see that

$$u^n_{S_i}(t) = -\int_0^t \sum_{j=i+1}^{n-1} \frac{\delta_{j-1}s_{ij}(r)}{(1 + \delta_{j-1}S_j(r))s_i(r)} d\langle S_i, S_j\rangle_r. \tag{6}$$

Assume now that the forward swap rates S_i satisfy a dynamics of the form

$$dS_i(t) = S_i(t)\mu_i(t)dt + S_i(t)\nu_i(t) \cdot dW^n_t, \quad 0 \le i \le n - 1, \tag{7}$$

where W^n_t is a P_n-Brownian motion. Then

$$d\langle S_i, S_j\rangle_t = S_i(t)S_j(t)\nu_i(t) \cdot \nu_j(t)dt \quad \text{and} \quad S_i(t)\mu_i(t)dt = du^n_{S_i}(t).$$

Using (6) we can now rewrite (7) as

$$dS_i(t) = -\sum_{j=i+1}^{n-1} \frac{\delta_{j-1}s_{ij}(t)S_i(t)S_j(t)}{(1 + \delta_{j-1}S_j(t))s_i(t)} \nu_i(t) \cdot \nu_j(t)dt + S_i(t)\nu_i(t) \cdot dW^n_t. \tag{8}$$

This dynamics has been derived under the assumption of the existence of a deflator ξ for B (giving rise to the numeraire measures P_n, $P_{i,n}$) and will therefore be called the *arbitrage free dynamics* of the forward swap rate S_i under the forward martingale measure P_n. As in the case of the Libor dynamics we have seen that in the absence of arbitrage the drift is determined by the volatility.

As in the Libor case the system of equations (8) is triangular: the equation for $i = n - 1$ is

$$dS_{n-1} = S_{n-1}\nu_{n-1} \cdot dW_t^n$$

while in general the equation for S_i only contains the processes $S_i, S_{i+1}, \ldots, S_{n-1}$. This feature makes these equations amenable to a solution by backwards induction, a construction to which we now turn.

5.i Swap rate models with prescribed volatilities. Fix a tenor structure $0 = T_0 < T_1 < \ldots < T_n$ and set $\delta_i = T_{i+1} - T_i$, $i = 0, 1, \ldots, n - 1$. Let $\nu_i(t)$, $i = 0, 1, \ldots, n - 1$, be any bounded, progressively measurable processes and let us turn to the construction of a deflatable market $B = (B_0, B_1, \ldots, B_n)$ such that the associated swap rate processes S_i are Ito processes with proportional, R^d-valued, volatilities $\nu_i(t)$ and fit a given initial term structure $\big(S_0(0), S_1(0), \ldots, S_{n-1}(0)\big)$. Since the process B_i should be thought of as the zero coupon bond $B(t, T_i)$, we also want to satisfy the zero coupon bond constraint $B_i(T_i) = 1$.

As in the Libor case the idea is to solve the swap rate dynamics 5.h.eq.(8) recursively starting with $i = n - 1$ and then to derive the zero coupon bonds B_i from the forward swap rates S_i. In detail, let W_t^n be an R^d-valued Brownian motion on $(\Omega, \mathcal{F}, (\mathcal{F}_t)_{t \in [0, T^*]}, Q)$ (the measure Q plays the role of the forward martingale measure P_n of 5.h) and define S_{n-1} as the solution of $dS_{n-1} = S_{n-1}\nu_{n-1} \cdot dW_t^n$, that is,

$$S_{n-1}(t) = S_{n-1}(0)\mathcal{E}_t\big(\nu_{n-1} \bullet W^n\big), \qquad (0)$$

and let, for $0 \le i \le n - 2$, S_i be the solution of

$$d S_i = -\sum_{j=i+1}^{n-1} \frac{\delta_{j-1} s_{ij} S_i S_j}{(1 + \delta_{j-1} S_j) s_i} \nu_i \cdot \nu_j dt + S_i(t)\nu_i(t) \cdot W_t^n \qquad (1)$$

$$= S_i \mu_i dt + S_i \nu_i \cdot dW_t^n,$$

where $\qquad \mu_i = -\sum_{j=i+1}^{n-1} \frac{\delta_{j-1} s_{ij} S_j}{(1 + \delta_{j-1} S_j) s_i} \nu_i \cdot \nu_j \qquad$ and

$$s_{ij} = \sum_{k=j}^{n-1} \delta_k \prod_{u=i+1}^{k} (1 + \delta_{u-1} S_u), \quad s_i = s_{ii}, \quad 1 \le i \le j \le n - 1.$$

As in 5.h this implies the backward recursion

$$s_{n-1} = \delta_{n-1} \quad \text{and} \qquad (2)$$
$$s_{i-1} = \delta_{i-1} + \big(1 + \delta_{i-1} S_i\big) s_i, \quad 1 \le i \le n - 1.$$

Explicitly S_i is given by
$$S_i(t) = S_i(0) exp \left(\int_0^t \mu_i(r) dr \right) \mathcal{E}_t(\nu_i \bullet W^n).$$

This defines the processes S_i, s_{ij}, s_i, for all $0 \le i \le j \le n-1$ and we now turn to the definition of the zero coupon bonds B_i. Let B_n be any continuous Q-semimartingale satisfying
$$B_n(T_i) = \frac{1}{1 + S_i(T_i)s_i(T_i)} \tag{3}$$

and set $B_i = (1 + S_i s_i)B_n$ in accordance with equation (2) of 5.h. Then (3) ensures that B_i satisfies the zero coupon bond constraint $B_i(T_i) = 1$. An easy backward induction using (2) shows that $S_i = (B_i - B_n)/B_{i,n}$ ensuring that S_i is the intended forward swap rate associated with the zero coupon bonds B_i. To see that the market $B = (B_0, B_1, \ldots, B_n)$ is arbitrage free, it will suffice to show that the ratios

$$B_i/B_n = 1 + S_i s_i$$

are all Q-martingales. Indeed, from the dynamics (1),

$$s_i dS_i = -\sum_{j=i+1}^{n-1} \frac{\delta_{j-1} s_{ij} S_i S_j}{1 + \delta_{j-1} S_j} \nu_i \cdot \nu_j dt + s_i S_i \nu_i \cdot dW_t^n.$$

As in 5.h (equation (5)) the definition of s_i implies

$$d\langle S_i, s_i \rangle = \sum_{j=i+1}^{n-1} \frac{\delta_{j-1} s_{ij}}{1 + \delta_{j-1} S_j} d\langle S_i, S_j \rangle = \sum_{j=i+1}^{n-1} \frac{\delta_{j-1} s_{ij} S_i S_j}{1 + \delta_{j-1} S_j} \nu_i \cdot \nu_j dt$$

and so, by addition,
$$s_i dS_i + d\langle S_i, s_i \rangle = S_i s_i \nu_i \cdot dW_t^n. \tag{4}$$

Now we claim that
$$ds_i = \gamma_i \cdot dW_t^n \tag{5}$$

with processes $\gamma_i \in L(W)$ satisfying the recursion

$$\gamma_{n-1} = 0 \quad \text{and} \quad \gamma_{i-1} = (1 + \delta_{i-1} S_i)\gamma_i + \delta_{i-1} S_i s_i \nu_i. \tag{6}$$

Indeed, proceeding by backward induction, (5), (6) are true for $i = n - 1$ since $s_{n-1} = \delta_{n-1}$. Assume now that $ds_i = \gamma_i \cdot dW_t^n$ where $\gamma_i \in L(W^n)$. Then, using the recursion (2) and the stochastic product rule,

$$\begin{aligned} ds_{i-1} &= (1 + \delta_{i-1} S_i)ds_i + \delta_{i-1} s_i dS_i + \delta_{i-1} d\langle S_i, s_i \rangle \\ &= (1 + \delta_{i-1} S_i)\gamma_i \cdot dW_t^n + \delta_{i-1} \left[s_i dS_i + d\langle S_i, s_i \rangle \right] \\ &= (1 + \delta_{i-1} S_i)\gamma_i \cdot dW_t^n + \delta_{i-1} S_i s_i \nu_i \cdot dW_t^n \\ &= \gamma_{i-1} \cdot dW_t^n, \end{aligned}$$

where $\gamma_{i-1} = (1 + \delta_{i-1} S_i)\gamma_i + \delta_{i-1} S_i s_i \nu_i \in L(W^n)$, as desired. Let us now write this relation as

$$ds_i = s_i \sigma_i \cdot dW_t^n, \quad \text{where} \quad \sigma_i = \gamma_i/s_i. \tag{7}$$

We claim that the processes σ_i are bounded. Indeed $\sigma_{n-1} = 0$ and if $\sigma_i = \gamma_i/s_i$ is bounded, then

$$\sigma_{i-1} = \frac{\gamma_{i-1}}{s_{i-1}} = \left(\frac{s_i}{s_{i-1}} + \delta_{i-1}\frac{S_i s_i}{s_{i-1}}\right)\left(\frac{\gamma_i}{s_i}\right) + \delta_{i-1}\left(\frac{S_i s_i}{s_{i-1}}\right)\nu_i$$

is bounded also, since $s_i \leq s_{i-1}$ and ν_i, $S_i s_i/s_{i-1}$ are both bounded; indeed

$$\frac{S_i s_i}{s_{i-1}} = \frac{S_i s_i}{\delta_{i-1} + (1 + \delta_{i-1}S_i)s_i} \leq \frac{1}{\delta_{i-1}} < \infty.$$

The boundedness of the σ_i follows by backward induction. Thus the dynamics (7) implies that s_i is a square integrable Q-martingale, for all $1 \leq i \leq n-1$ (III.6.a.1). The relation $s_{i-1} = \delta_{i-1} + (1 + \delta_{i-1}S_i)s_i$ now shows that $S_i s_i$ is a square integrable Q-martingale as well. Consequently $B_i/B_n = 1 + S_i s_i$ is a square integrable Q martingale, as desired.

Here Q is to be interpreted as the forward martingale measure P_n. Any probability P equivalent to Q on $\mathcal{F}_{T^*}$ can now serve as the market probability. Setting $N(t) = d(Q|\mathcal{F}_t)/d(P|\mathcal{F}_t)$ a deflator ξ is given by $\xi(t) = N_t^{B_n} = N(t)/B_n(t)$ and Q then becomes the forward martingale measure P_n (see 3.d.2).

For the valuation of swaptions we will need the dynamics of the forward swap rate S_i under the forward swap measure $P_{i,n}$. Since the B_j/B_n are Q-martingales the forward swap rate $S_i = (B_i - B_n)/B_{i,n}$ is a $P_{i,n}$-martingale (see 5.d.1.(b)). Set

$$M_t = \frac{d(P_{i,n}|\mathcal{F}_t)}{d(Q|\mathcal{F}_t)} = \frac{d(P_{i,n}|\mathcal{F}_t)}{d(P_n|\mathcal{F}_t)} = c\frac{B_{i,n}(t)}{B_n(t)} = cs_i(t), \quad t \in [0, T^*],$$

where c is a normalizing constant. Then, using (7),

$$dM_t = c\,ds_i(t) = cs_i(t)\sigma_i(t) \cdot dW_t^n = M_t\sigma_i(t) \cdot dW_t^n.$$

According to III.4.c.0 it follows that $W_t^{i,n} = W_t^n - \int_0^t \sigma_i(r)dr$ is a $P_{i,n}$-Brownian motion. Obviously $dW_t^n = dW_t^{i,n} + \sigma_i(t)dt$. Entering this into (1) we see that

$$dS_i = S_i\tilde{\mu}_i dt + S_i\nu_i \cdot dW_t^{i,n},$$

for some process $\tilde{\mu}_i(t)$. However, since S_i is a $P_{i,n}$-martingale, the drift term must vanish and we obtain

$$dS_i = S_i\nu_i \cdot dW_t^{i,n} \tag{8}$$

as the dynamics of S_i under the forward swap measure $P_{i,n}$. If the volatility processes $\nu_i(t)$ are nonstochastic, then the above market $B = (B_0, B_1, \ldots, B_n)$ is called the *log-Gaussian swap rate model*. The forward swap rate S_i is then a square integrable log-Gaussian martingale under $P_{i,n}$ (III.6.a.1, III.6.d.4).

5.j Valuation of swaptions in the log-Gaussian swap rate model. Continuing with the terminology of 5.h and assuming that the volatilities $\nu_i(t)$ are nonstochastic, let $t \leq \hat{T} \leq T = T_0$. The payoff $FS_{\hat{T}}(\kappa)^+$ of the forward payer swaption $PS(\hat{T}, \kappa)$ at time $\hat{T}$ can be written as

$$FS_{\hat{T}}(\kappa)^+ = \sum_{j=0}^{n-1} \delta_j B(\hat{T}, T_{j+1})(\kappa(\hat{T}, T, n) - \kappa)^+ = B_{0,n}(\hat{T})(S_0(\hat{T}) - \kappa)^+.$$

Using the symmetric numeraire change formula 5.d.1.(d) and $B(\hat{T}, \hat{T}) = 1$ the arbitrage price $PS_t(\hat{T}, \kappa)$ of this swaption at time $t \leq \hat{T}$ is given by

$$
\begin{aligned}
PS_t(\hat{T}, \kappa) &= B(t, \hat{T})E_{P_{\hat{T}}}\left[B_{0,n}(\hat{T})(S_0(\hat{T}) - \kappa)^+ \mid \mathcal{F}_t\right] \\
&= B_{0,n}(t)E_{P_{0,n}}\left[(S_0(\hat{T}) - \kappa)^+ \mid \mathcal{F}_t\right].
\end{aligned}
\tag{0}
$$

Set $Z(t) = log(S_0(t))$. From the dynamics $dS_0(t) = S_0(t)\nu_0(t) \cdot dW_t^{0,n}$ it follows that

$$dZ(t) = -\frac{1}{2}\|\nu_0(t)\|^2 dt + \nu_0(t) \cdot dW_t^{0,n}.$$

Thus, using III.6.c.3,

$$E_{P_{0,n}}\left[(S_0(\hat{T}) - \kappa)^+ | \mathcal{F}_t\right] = S_0(t)N(d_1) - \kappa N(d_2),$$

where $\quad d_{1,2} = \dfrac{log(S_0(t)/\kappa) \pm \frac{1}{2}\Sigma^2(t, \hat{T})}{\Sigma(t, \hat{T})} \quad$ and $\quad \Sigma(t, \hat{T}) = \left(\displaystyle\int_t^{\hat{T}} \|\nu_0(t)\|^2 dt\right)^{1/2}.$

Consequently $PS_t(\hat{T}, \kappa) = B_{0,n}(t)(S_0(t)N(d_1) - \kappa N(d_2))$ with $d_{1,2}$ as above. Recalling that

$$B_{0,n}(t) = \sum_{i=1}^{n} \delta_{j-1}B_j(t) = \sum_{i=1}^{n} \delta_{j-1}B(t, T_j) \quad \text{and} \quad S_0(t) = \kappa(t, T, n)$$

we can summarize these findings as follows:

Black Swaption formula. *Let $\nu(t)$ denote the (proportional) volatility of the forward swap rate $\kappa(t, T, n)$. Under the assumptions of the log-Gaussian swap rate model the price $PS_t(\hat{T}, \kappa)$ of the forward payer swaption $PS(\hat{T}, \kappa)$ at time $t \leq \hat{T} \leq T = T_0$ is given by*

$$PS_t(\hat{T}, \kappa) = \sum_{j=1}^{n} \delta_{j-1}B(t, T_j)(\kappa(t, T, n)N(d_1) - \kappa N(d_2)),$$

where $d_{1,2} = \dfrac{log(\kappa(t, T, n)/\kappa) \pm \frac{1}{2}\Sigma^2(t, \hat{T})}{\Sigma(t, \hat{T})} \quad$ and $\quad \Sigma(t, \hat{T}) = \left(\displaystyle\int_t^{\hat{T}} \|\nu(s)\|^2 ds\right)^{\frac{1}{2}}.$ ∎

Remark. This formula is in accordance with our interpretation of the payer swap $PS(\hat{T}, \kappa)$ as a portfolio of $\delta_0, \delta_1, \ldots, \delta_{n-1}$ European calls on the forward swap rate

$\kappa(t, T, n)$ with strike price κ all of which must be exercised at the same time $\hat{T}$ and have payoffs deferred to times $T_1, T_2, \ldots, T_n$ respectively (see section 5.c).

It is not hard to derive the relation between the forward Libor rates $L_i(t)$ and forward swap rates $S_i(t)$: As $B_i/B_n = (1 + \delta_i L_i)(1 + \delta_{i+1} L_{i+1}) \ldots (1 + \delta_{n-1} L_{n-1})$ and consequently

$$B_{i,n}/B_n = \sum_{j=i+1}^{n} \delta_{j-1} \frac{B_j}{B_n} = \sum_{j=i+1}^{n} \delta_{j-1} \prod_{u=j}^{n-1}(1 + \delta_u L_u),$$

and $B_i = B_n(1 + S_i s_i)$, we obtain

$$S_i = \frac{B_i - B_n}{B_{i,n}} = \frac{B_i/B_n - 1}{B_{i,n}/B_n} = \frac{\prod_{u=i}^{n-1}(1 + \delta_u L_u) - 1}{\sum_{j=i+1}^{n} \delta_{j-1} \prod_{u=j}^{n-1}(1 + \delta_u L_u)}$$

and
$$L_i = \delta_i^{-1}\left(\frac{B_i}{B_{i+1}} - 1\right) = \delta_i^{-1}\left(\frac{1 + S_i s_i}{1 + S_{i+1} s_{i+1}} - 1\right).$$

It follows that the volatilities of the forward swap rates S_i cannot be nonstochastic, if the volatilities of the forward Libor rates L_i are nonstochastic and conversely. In other words the assumptions of the log-Gaussian Libor and swap rate models are mutually contradictory.

5.k Replication of claims. So far we have computed the arbitrage price $\pi_t(h)$ of a European claim h without investigation whether the claim h is replicable. However, under suitable assumptions on the Libor respectively swap rate volatilities ν_i, all relevant claims are in fact replicable. To simplify notation we assume that the time horizon T^* satisfies $T^* = 1$.

Consider a finite market $B = (B_0, B_1, \ldots, B_n)$ on $(\Omega, \mathcal{F}, (\mathcal{F}_t)_{t \in [0,1]}, P)$ with local deflator ξ such that ξB_n is a martingale and so the equivalent martingale measure $P_n = P_{B_n}$ is defined. Let $u_n^n(t)$ denote the P_n-compensator of the semimartingale B_n and set $B/B_n = (B_0/B_n, \ldots, B_n/B_n)'$ and $\tilde{B}/B_n = (B_0/B_n, \ldots, B_{n-1}/B_n)'$. Assume that

(i) W_t^n is a d-dimensional P_n-Brownian motion with $d \le n$ and that $(\mathcal{F}_t)$ is the (augmented) filtration generated by W_t^n,

(ii) $|du_n^n|(t) + d\langle B_n \rangle_t = \alpha(t)dt$, for some pathwise bounded, measurable process α,

(iii) $d(\tilde{B}/B_n) = \rho dW^n$, for some pathwise continuous, $Mat_{n \times d}(R)$-valued process ρ which is of full rank d along P_n-almost every path.

Remark. Note that $\tilde{B}/B_n$ is a vector of P_n-martingales. This justifies the driftless nature of the dynamics in assumption (iii).

5.k.0. *For every European claim h such that $h/B_n(1) \in L^1(\mathcal{F}_1, P_n)$ there exists a self-financing strategy $\theta \in L(B) \cap L(B/B_n)$ such that $h = V_1(\theta)$ and $V_t^{B_n}(\theta)$ is a P_n-martingale. In particular the claim h is replicable in B.*

Proof. Set $c(t) = E_{P_n}[h/B_n(1) \mid \mathcal{F}_t]$, $t \in [0,1]$. Then $c(t)$ is an $(\mathcal{F}_t)$-adapted P_n-martingale and by assumption (i) and the martingale representation theorem

III.5.d.0 there exists a process $\gamma \in L(W^n)$ such that

$$c(t) = c_0 + \int_0^t \gamma(s) \cdot dW_s^n. \tag{0}$$

Now let ψ be the pathwise continuous $Mat_{n \times d}(R)$-valued process $\psi = \rho(\rho'\rho)^{-1}$. Note that the inverse $(\rho'\rho)^{-1}$ exists along P_n-ae. path by assumption (iii). We have $\rho'\psi = Id_{d \times d}$. The pathwise continuity implies that ψ is pathwise bounded, that is,

$$K = \sup_{t \in [0,1]} \|\psi(t)\| < \infty, \quad P_n\text{-as. on } \Omega.$$

Set $\beta = \psi\gamma$ and write $\beta = (\beta_0, \beta_1, \ldots, \beta_{n-1})$. Then $\rho'\beta = \gamma \in L(W^n)$. Recalling that the stochastic differential $\beta \cdot d(B/B_n)$ is computed as a dot product of column vectors (rather than as a matrix product), it follows that $\beta \cdot d(\tilde{B}/B_n) = \beta \cdot (\rho dW^n) = \rho'\beta \cdot dW^n = \gamma \cdot dW^n$ (especially $\beta \in L(\tilde{B}/B_n)$) and so

$$c(t) = c_0 + \int_0^t \gamma(s) \cdot dW_s^n = c_0 + \int_0^t \beta(s) \cdot d(\tilde{B}/B_n)(s);$$

in other words $\qquad\qquad dc(t) = \beta(t) \cdot d(\tilde{B}/B_n)(t). \tag{1}$

Now let $\theta = (\beta_0, \beta_1, \ldots, \beta_{n-1}, \theta_n)$, where

$$\theta_n(t) = c(t) - B_n(t)^{-1} [\beta_0(t)B_0(t) + \ldots + \beta_{n-1}(t)B_{n-1}(t)].$$

Then $\qquad\qquad\qquad \theta(t) \cdot B(t) = B_n(t)c(t). \tag{2}$

From $\beta \in L(\tilde{B}/B_n)$ and $d(B_n/B_n) = 0$ it follows that $\theta \in L(B/B_n)$. Let us now show that $\theta_i \in L(B_n)$, for all $i = 0, \ldots, n$. Since $\|\beta(s)\|^2 \le \|\psi(s)\|^2 \|\gamma(s)\|^2 \le K^2 \|\gamma(s)\|^2$ and $\gamma \in L(W^n)$ we have

$$\int_0^1 \|\beta(s)\|^2 ds \le K^2 \int_0^1 \|\gamma(s)\|^2 ds < \infty, \quad P_n\text{-as.} \tag{3}$$

and so $\qquad\qquad\qquad \int_0^1 \theta_i^2(s) ds < \infty, \quad P_n\text{-as.,} \tag{4}$

for all $i = 0, \ldots, n-1$. To verify (4) for $i = n$ we use the inequality $(a_0 + a_1 + \ldots + a_n)^2 \le (n+1)(a_0^2 + a_1^2 + \ldots + a_n^2)$ (convexity of $f(t) = t^2$) and the pathwise boundedness of $c(t)$ and $B_i(t)/B_n(t)$ to obtain

$$\theta_n^2(t) \le (n+1) \left[c_t^2 + \beta_0^2(t) \left(\frac{B_0(t)}{B_n(t)} \right)^2 + \ldots + \beta_{n-1}^2(t) \left(\frac{B_{n-1}(t)}{B_n(t)} \right)^2 \right]$$

$$\le D\|\beta(t)\|^2 + (n+1)c_t^2,$$

where the random variable D is finitely valued, P_n-as. From this it follows that $\int_0^1 \theta_n^2(s)ds < \infty$, P_n-as. Next we claim that

$$\theta_i \in L(B_n), \quad \text{for all } i = 0, 1, \dots, n. \tag{5}$$

Set $M = \sup_{t \in [0,1]} \alpha(t) < \infty$, P_n-as. Then

$$\int_0^1 |\theta_i(s)||du_n^n(s)| + \int_0^1 \theta_i^2(s)d\langle B_n \rangle_s \leq \int_0^1 |\theta_i(s)|\alpha(s)ds + \int_0^1 \theta_i^2(s)\alpha(s)ds$$

$$\leq \left(\int_0^1 \theta_i^2(s)ds \right)^{1/2} \left(\int_0^1 \alpha^2(s)ds \right)^{1/2} + M \int_0^1 \theta_i^2(s)ds$$

$$\leq M \left(\int_0^1 \theta_i^2(s)ds \right)^{1/2} + M \int_0^1 \theta_i^2(s)ds < \infty, \quad P_n\text{-as.}$$

This shows (5). Since $\theta \in L(B/B_n)$ it now follows that $\theta \in L(B)$ (III.3.c.4), that is, θ is a trading strategy in B. From (2) we have $V_t^{B_n}(\theta) = c(t)$ and consequently $V_t^{B_n}(\theta)$ is a P_n-martingale with $V_1(\theta) = h$. It thus remains to be shown only that θ is self-financing. Since $\theta \in L(B/B_n)$ and the self-financing condition is numeraire invariant, it will suffice to show that θ is self-financing in B/B_n. Indeed, using (2) and (1),

$$d\big(\theta \cdot (B/B_n)\big)(t) = dc(t) = \beta(t) \cdot d\big(\tilde{B}/B_n\big)(t) = \theta(t) \cdot d\big(B/B_n\big)(t),$$

as desired. Here the second equality holds since $d(B_n/B_n) = 0$ and θ and β agree in all but the last coordinate. $\blacksquare$

Let us now apply 5.k.1 to the Libor and swap rate models of 5.f, 5.i. Recall that the probability Q in these models plays the role of the forward martingale measure P_n. Let ν_i be the volatility processes of 5.f, 5.i and let ν be the $Mat_{d \times n}(R)$-valued process with columns ν_i, $0 \leq i < n$ (the volatility matrix).

Application to the Libor model. Let $Y_i = B_i/B_n$ as in 5.f. Equations (2), (3) of 5.f show that

$$d(B_i/B_n) = \rho_i \cdot dW^n, \quad \text{where} \quad \rho_i = \sum_{k=i}^{n-1} Y_i \frac{\delta_k L_k}{1 + \delta_k L_k} \nu_k, \tag{6}$$

$0 \leq i < n$. In short

$$d(\tilde{B}/B_n) = \rho' dW^n,$$

where ρ is the $Mat_{d \times n}(R)$-valued process with columns ρ_i. From (6) we see that $\rho = \nu A$, where A is the triangular $Mat_{n \times n}(R)$-valued process with entries

$$A_{ki} = \begin{cases} Y_i \dfrac{\delta_k L_k}{1 + \delta_k L_k}, & \text{if } i \leq k \leq n-1 \\ 0, & \text{if } 0 \leq k < i. \end{cases}$$

The diagonal elements of A are nonzero and consequently the matrix A is invertible. It follows that ρ' is of full rank whenever the volatility matrix ν is of full rank. Likewise, by continuity of the L_k, the process ρ' has continuous paths whenever this is true of the process ν. Recall also that there is considerable freedom in the choice of the process B_n in the construction of the Libor model of 5.f.

Assume that the process B_n in the Libor market B of 5.f is chosen such that assumption (ii) is satisfied and the volatility matrix ν has continuous, full rank paths, P_n-as. Then B satisfies the assumptions of 5.k.1. Thus each European claim h exercisable at time $T = 1$ such that $h/B_n(1) \in L^1(\mathcal{F}_1, P_n)$ is replicable in B.

Application to the swap rate model. In the swap market B of 5.i we have $B_i/B_n = 1 + S_i s_i$ and consequently equations (4), (5) of 5.i and the stochastic product rule yield

$$d\big(B_i/B_n\big) = d\big(S_i s_i\big) = \big(S_i \gamma_i + S_i s_i \nu_i\big) \cdot dW^n = \rho_i \cdot dW^n,$$

where $\rho_i = S_i \gamma_i + S_i s_i \nu_i$. In other words

$$d\big(\tilde{B}/B_n\big) = \rho' dW^n,$$

where ρ is the $Mat_{d \times n}(R)$-valued process with columns ρ_i. The recursion

$$\gamma_{n-1} = 0, \quad \gamma_{i-1} = (1 + \delta_{i-1} S_i) \gamma_i + \delta_{i-1} S_i s_i \nu_i$$

shows that each column vector γ_i is a linear combination (with stochastic coefficients) of the column vectors ν_k, $k = i+1, \ldots, n-1$. It follows that

$$\rho_i = S_i \gamma_i + S_i s_i \nu_i = \sum_{k=i}^{n-1} A_{ki} \nu_i$$

with continuous stochastic processes A_{ki} satisfying $A_{ii} = S_i s_i$. Thus $\rho = \nu A$, where the $n \times n$ matrix $A = (A_{ki})$ satisfies $A_{ki} = 0$, $k < i$ and $A_{ii} = S_i s_i$. In particular A is triangular with nonzero diagonal elements and hence invertible. As for the Libor model this implies the following:

Assume that the process B_n in the swap market B of 5.i is chosen such that assumption (ii) is satisfied and the volatility matrix ν has continuous, full rank paths, P_n-as. Then the market B satisfies the assumptions of 5.k.1 and consequently each European claim h exercisable at time $T = 1$ such that $h/B_n(1) \in L^1(\mathcal{F}_1, P_n)$ is replicable in B.

APPENDIX

A. Separation of convex sets. Separation theorems deal with the extent to which disjoint convex sets in a locally convex space can be separated by hyperplanes, equivalently by continuous linear functionals. We will limit ourselves to normed spaces and the separation of a cone from a disjoint subspace. Let X be a normed real vector space. A subset $C \subseteq X$ is called a *cone* if it satisfies the following two conditions:

(a) $x \in C$ and $\lambda > 0$ implies $\lambda x \in C$.

(b) $x, y \in C$ implies $x + y \in C$.

If C and K are cones in X, then so is the set $C + K$. Each cone is a convex set. If B is any convex set in X, then $\cup_{t>0} tB$ is a cone in X, in fact the smallest cone containing B, that is, the cone generated by B.

A.1. *Let $H \subseteq X$ be a closed subspace. If $dim(X/H) > 1$, then the set $X \setminus H$ is pathwise connected.*

Proof. The quotient space X/H is a normed space of dimension at least two. Let $Q : X \to X/H$ be the quotient map and let $a, b \in X \setminus H$ be arbitrary. Then the elements $Q(a), Q(b) \in X/H$ are nonzero and can therefore be connected by a continuous path γ in X/H which does not pass through the origin (this is where we use $dim(X/H) > 1$). Then the composition $\gamma \circ Q$ is a continuous path in $X \setminus H$ connecting a and b. ∎

Let us recall some elementary facts concerning continuous linear functionals on X. If $H \subseteq X$ is a subspace with $dim(X/H) = 1$ then H is a maximal proper subspace of X and since the closure of H is a subspace containing H, H is either closed or dense in X. Moreover there exists a linear functional π on X such that $ker(\pi) = H$ (consider the quotient map $Q : X \to X/H \cong R$) and π is continuous if and only if $H = ker(\pi)$ is closed in X. If A is any subset, C an open subset of X then the set $A + C = \cup_{a \in A}(a + C)$ is open in X.

A.2. *Let $C \subseteq X$ be an open cone and $M \subseteq X$ a subspace such that $M \cap C = \emptyset$. Then there exists a continuous linear functional π on X such that $\pi = 0$ on M and $\pi > 0$ on C.*

Proof. We may assume that C is nonempty. From Zorn's lemma it follows that there exists a subspace $H \subseteq X$, which is maximal with respect to inclusion subject to the conditions $M \subseteq H$ and $H \cap C = \emptyset$. Since C is open, it follows that $\overline{H} \cap C = \emptyset$. By maximality we must have $H = \overline{H}$, that is, H is closed.

The sets $C - H$ and $H - C$ are open, disjoint and contained in the set $X \setminus H$. Let $x \in X \setminus H$. By maximality of H the subspace $span(H \cup \{x\})$ must intersect C. Thus there exist $h \in H$ and $t \in R$ such that $h + tx \in C$. We cannot have $t = 0$, since $H \cap C = \emptyset$. If $t > 0$, then $x \in C - H$. If $t < 0$, then $x \in H - C$. We have thus shown that $X \setminus H$ is the union of the two disjoint open sets $C - H$ and $H - C$. Thus the set $X \setminus H$ is not connected. From A.1 it follows that we must have $dim(X/H) = 1$.

Since H is closed, H is the kernel of a continuous linear functional π on X. Especially then $\pi = 0$ on M. The set C does not intersect $H = ker(\pi)$ and is convex. From this it follows that π cannot assume both positive and negative values on C. Thus either $\pi > 0$ on C or $\pi < 0$ on C. In the latter case replace π with $-\pi$ to obtain the desired functional. ∎

If the cone C is not open, then it is much harder to obtain the strict positivity of π on C ($\pi(x) > 0$, for all $x \in C$). If X is a separable Banach space, then the following argument of Clark yields the desired functional:

A.3 Clark's Separation Theorem. *Let X be a separable Banach space, $M \subseteq X$ a subspace and $C \subseteq X$ a cone. Then the following are equivalent:*

(i) *There exists a continuous linear functional π on X such that $\pi = 0$ on M and $\pi > 0$ on C.*

(ii) $\overline{M - C} \cap C = \emptyset$.

Remark. Here $\pi > 0$ on C means that $\pi(x) > 0$, for all $x \in C$, that is, π is strictly positive on C.

Proof. We may assume that C is nonempty, since otherwise (i) and (ii) are simply both true. (i)$\Rightarrow$(ii): Since $\pi \leq 0$ on $\overline{M - C}$ and $\pi > 0$ on the set C, we must have $\overline{M - C} \cap C = \emptyset$.

(i)$\Rightarrow$(ii): Assume now that $\overline{M - C} \cap C = \emptyset$ and let $x \in C$ be arbitrary. Then there exists an open ball B centered at x such that $B \cap (M - C) = \emptyset$. Then the cone $\cup_{t>0} tB$ generated by B is open and thus so is the cone

$$C(x) = C + \cup_{t>0} tB.$$

We claim that $C(x) \cap M = \emptyset$. Indeed, if $y \in C(x) \cap M$, then $y = c + tb$, for some $c \in C$, $b \in B$ and $t > 0$. Then $b = t^{-1}(y-c) \in M-C$ contradicting $B \cap (M-C) = \emptyset$.

Applying A.2 to the subspace M and the open cone $C(x)$ yields a continuous linear functional π_x on X satisfying $\pi_x = 0$ on M and $\pi_x > 0$ on $C(x)$. If the cone $C(x)$ were known to contain C we would now be finished, but in fact there is no reason to believe that this is true.

As it is, we note that $x = \frac{1}{2}x + \frac{1}{2}x \in C(x)$ and so $\pi_x(x) > 0$. Renormalizing if necessary, we may assume that $\|\pi_x\| = 1$. Thus we have the subset

$$P = \{ \pi_x \mid x \in C \} \subseteq X_1^*$$

of the unit ball X_1^* of the normed dual X^*. When equipped with the weak*-topology this unit ball is compact (Alaoglu's theorem) and metrizable (since X is separable, see [Rb, 3.15,3.16]). A subspace of a compact metric space is separable. Thus there exists a sequence $(\pi_{x_i}) \subseteq P$ which is weak* dense in P. Consequently, for each $x \in C$, there exists an index i such that

$$\left| \pi_x(x) - \pi_{x_i}(x) \right| < \pi_x(x),$$

and so in particular $\pi_{x_i}(x) > 0$. Now let π be the continuous linear functional $\pi = \sum_i 2^{-i} \pi_{x_i}$ (the series converges absolutely in the norm of X^*). Then $\pi = 0$ on M and $\pi(x) > 0$, for all $x \in C$. ∎

B. The basic extension procedure. Let $(\Omega, \mathcal{F}, P)$ be a probability space. A subset $\mathcal{I} \subseteq \mathcal{F}$ will be called a *family of generators for* $\mathcal{F}$ if $\mathcal{F}$ is the σ-field generated by $\mathcal{I}$ ($\mathcal{F} = \sigma(\mathcal{I})$). The following problem arises frequently in the development of probability theory:

We wish to establish some property $Q(f)$ for all nonnegative, $\mathcal{F}$-measurable functions f on Ω and it is easy to establish this property for all indicator functions $f = 1_A$ of suitably simple sets A forming a family $\mathcal{I}$ of generators for the σ-field $\mathcal{F}$. The extension of the property Q from such f to all nonnegative, measurable f naturally falls into two steps:

(I) Extend Q from generators $A \in \mathcal{I}$ to all sets $A \in \mathcal{F}$.

(II) Extend Q from indicator functions $f = 1_A$ to all nonnegative measurable functions f on Ω.

Usually one also wants to extend Q to suitable measurable functions which are not necessarily nonnegative, but this last extension is often accomplished by merely writing such f as a difference $f = f^+ - f^-$ of the nonnegative functions $f^+ = f1_{[f>0]}$, $f^- = -f1_{[f<0]}$. The purpose of this section is to provide a theorem which makes this extension procedure automatic in all cases to which it can be applied.

Consider step (I) and let us write $Q(A)$ instead of $Q(1_A)$. Since $Q(A)$ is known to be true for all sets A in a family $\mathcal{I}$ such that $\mathcal{F} = \sigma(\mathcal{I})$, it would suffice to show that the family of sets

$$\mathcal{L}_0 = \{ A \in \mathcal{F} \mid Q(A) \text{ is true} \} \tag{0}$$

is a σ-field, that is, contains the empty set and is closed under complements and arbitrary countable unions. However one can usually only show that $\mathcal{L}$ is closed under *disjoint* countable unions. This leads to the following definition:

A family $\mathcal{L}$ of subsets of Ω is called a λ-*system on* Ω, if it contains the empty set and is closed under complements and countable *disjoint* unions, that is, if

(i) $\emptyset \in \mathcal{L}$,

(ii) $A \in \mathcal{L} \Rightarrow A^c = \Omega \setminus A \in \mathcal{L}$,

(iii) If $(A_n) \subseteq \mathcal{L}$ is any disjoint sequence, then $A = \bigcup_n A_n \in \mathcal{L}$.

It is clear from our definition that every σ-field on Ω is a λ-system on Ω. Let us now return to extension step (I). We wish to show that $\mathcal{L}_0 \supseteq \mathcal{F}$ and it is usually easy to prove that $\mathcal{L}_0$ is a λ-system containing some family $\mathcal{I}$ of generators for $\mathcal{F}$. Consequently $\mathcal{L}_0$ contains the λ-system $\lambda(\mathcal{I})$ generated by $\mathcal{I}$, that is, the smallest λ-system containing $\mathcal{I}$. Thus the question becomes if $\lambda(\mathcal{I}) = \mathcal{F}$, that is, $\lambda(\mathcal{I}) = \sigma(\mathcal{I})$. It turns out (B.2 below) that this is automatically the case, if the family $\mathcal{I}$ is closed under finite intersections. Let us call π-*system on* Ω any family of subsets of Ω which is closed under finite intersections.

B.1. *Let $\mathcal{L}$ be a λ-system on Ω. Then*
(a) $E, F \in \mathcal{L}$ *and* $E \subseteq F$ *implies* $F \setminus E \in \mathcal{L}$.
(b) $(E_n) \subseteq \mathcal{L}$ *and* $E_n \uparrow E$ *implies* $E \in \mathcal{L}$.
(c)   *If $\mathcal{L}$ is also a π-system, then $\mathcal{L}$ is in fact a σ-field.*

Proof. (a)   If $E \subseteq F$, then F^c and E are disjoint and $F \setminus E = (F^c \cup E)^c$.
(b)   Assume that $E_n \in \mathcal{L}$, for each $n \geq 1$, and $E_n \uparrow E$, as $n \uparrow \infty$, that is, $E_1 \subseteq E_2 \subseteq E_3 \subseteq \ldots$ and $E = \bigcup_n E_n$. Then E is the countable *disjoint* union $E = \bigcup_{n \geq 1} B_n$, where $B_1 = E_1$ and $B_n = E_n \setminus E_{n-1}$, for all $n > 1$. According to (a) we have $B_n \in \mathcal{L}$, for all $n \geq 1$. Thus $E \in \mathcal{L}$.
(c)   Assume now that $\mathcal{L}$ is also a π-system. Then $\mathcal{L}$ is closed under finite unions and also under monotone limits (according to (b)) and consequently under arbitrary countable unions. ∎

B.2. *Let $\mathcal{I}$ be a π-system on Ω. Then $\lambda(\mathcal{I}) = \sigma(\mathcal{I})$.*

Proof. Let $\mathcal{L}$ be the λ-system $\lambda(\mathcal{I})$ generated by $\mathcal{I}$. Then $\mathcal{L}$ contains $\mathcal{I}$. Since the σ-field $\sigma(\mathcal{I})$ generated by $\mathcal{I}$ is a λ-system containing $\mathcal{I}$, we have $\mathcal{L} \subseteq \sigma(\mathcal{I})$. To see the reverse inclusion it will suffice to show that $\mathcal{L}$ is a σ-field. According to B.1.(c), it will suffice to show that $\mathcal{L}$ is a π-system. We do this in three steps:

(i) $E \in \mathcal{I}$ and $F \in \mathcal{I}$ implies $E \cap F \in \mathcal{L}$,
(ii) $E \in \mathcal{L}$ and $F \in \mathcal{I}$ implies $E \cap F \in \mathcal{L}$,   and
(iii) $E \in \mathcal{L}$ and $F \in \mathcal{L}$ implies $E \cap F \in \mathcal{L}$.

(i)   If $E, F \in \mathcal{I}$, then $E \cap F \in \mathcal{I} \subseteq \mathcal{L}$, since $\mathcal{I}$ is a π-system by assumption.
(ii)   Let $\mathcal{L}_1 = \{ E \subseteq \Omega : E \cap F \in \mathcal{L}, \forall F \in \mathcal{I} \}$. We must show that $\mathcal{L}_1 \supseteq \mathcal{L} = \lambda(\mathcal{I})$. According to (1) we have $\mathcal{I} \subseteq \mathcal{L}_1$. Thus it will suffice to show that $\mathcal{L}_1$ is a λ-system.
     Clearly $\emptyset \in \mathcal{L}_1$, since $\emptyset \in \mathcal{L}$. Assume now that $E \in \mathcal{L}_1$, that is, $E \cap F \in \mathcal{L}$, for all $F \in \mathcal{I}$. We wish to show that $E^c \in \mathcal{L}_1$. Let $F \in \mathcal{I}$ be arbitrary. Then $E^c \cap F = F \setminus E = F \setminus (E \cap F)$. Here $F, E \cap F \in \mathcal{L}$ and $E \cap F \subseteq F$. According to B.1.(a) this implies that $E^c \cap F = F \setminus (E \cap F) \in \mathcal{L}$. Since this is true for every set $F \in \mathcal{I}$, we have $E^c \in \mathcal{L}_1$.
     Finally, let $(E_n) \subseteq \mathcal{L}_1$ be any disjoint sequence and $E = \bigcup_n E_n$. We must show that $E \in \mathcal{L}_1$, that is, $E \cap F \in \mathcal{L}$, for each $F \in \mathcal{I}$. Let $F \in \mathcal{I}$. Then $E_n \cap F \in \mathcal{L}$, since $E_n \in \mathcal{L}_1$, for all $n \geq 1$. Consequently $(E_n \cap F)_n$ is a disjoint sequence contained in the λ-system $\mathcal{L}$. Thus $E \cap F = \bigcup_n (E_n \cap F) \in \mathcal{L}$.
(iii)   Let $\mathcal{L}_2 = \{ F \subseteq \Omega : E \cap F \in \mathcal{L}, \forall E \in \mathcal{L} \}$. We must show that $\mathcal{L}_2 \supseteq \mathcal{L} = \lambda(\mathcal{I})$. According to *(ii)* we have $\mathcal{I} \subseteq \mathcal{L}_2$. Thus it will suffice to show that $\mathcal{L}_2$ is a λ-system. This proof is similar to the proof of *(ii)* and is omitted. ∎

The following is a convenient reformulation of B.2:

B.3 π-λ Theorem. *Let $\mathcal{I}$ be a π-system on Ω and $\mathcal{L}$ a λ-system on Ω. If $\mathcal{L}$ contains $\mathcal{I}$, then $\mathcal{L}$ contains the σ-field generated by $\mathcal{I}$.* ∎

The π-λ-Theorem handles extension step (I) above. All that is necessary is to find a π-system $\mathcal{I}$ of generators for $\mathcal{F}$ such that the truth of $Q(A)$ can be verified for each set $A \in \mathcal{I}$ and subsequently to show that the family $\mathcal{L}_0 = \{ A \in \mathcal{F} \mid Q(A) \text{ is true} \}$ is a λ-system on Ω. Extension step (II) from indicator functions $f = 1_A$ to all nonnegative measurable functions f is then usually straightforward. However it is convenient to have a theorem which handles both extension steps (I) and (II) simultaneously. To this end we introduce the following notion:

A family $\mathcal{C}$ of nonnegative $\mathcal{F}$-measurable functions on Ω is called a λ-*cone* on Ω, if it satisfies the following conditions:

(α) $\mathcal{C}$ contains the constant function 1.

(β) If $f, g \in \mathcal{C}$ are bounded and $f \leq g$ then $g - f \in \mathcal{C}$.

(γ) If $f_n \in \mathcal{C}$ and $\alpha_n \geq 0$, for all $n \geq 1$, then $f = \sum_n \alpha_n f_n \in \mathcal{C}$.

B.4 Extension Theorem. *Let $\mathcal{C}$ be a λ-cone on Ω. Assume that $1_A \in \mathcal{C}$, for each set A in some π-system $\mathcal{I}$ generating the σ-field $\mathcal{F}$. Then $\mathcal{C}$ contains every nonnegative measurable function f on Ω.*

Proof. Let $\mathcal{L} = \{ A \in \mathcal{F} \mid 1_A \in \mathcal{C} \}$. We claim that $\mathcal{L}$ is a λ-system on Ω. From (α) and (β) above it follows that $0 \in \mathcal{C}$ and hence $\emptyset \in \mathcal{L}$. If $A \in \mathcal{L}$, then $1_A \in \mathcal{C}$ and so $1_{A^c} = 1 - 1_A \in \mathcal{C}$ (according to (β)), that is, $A^c \in \mathcal{L}$. Finally, if $(A_n) \subseteq \mathcal{L}$ is any disjoint sequence and $A = \bigcup_n A_n$, then $1_{A_n} \in \mathcal{C}$, for each $n \geq 1$ and so $1_A = \sum_n 1_{A_n} \in \mathcal{C}$, that is $A \in \mathcal{L}$.

Thus $\mathcal{L}$ is a λ-system containing $\mathcal{I}$. Since $\mathcal{I}$ is a π-system by assumption, the π-λ Theorem yields that $\mathcal{L} \supseteq \sigma(\mathcal{I}) = \mathcal{F}$. Thus $1_A \in \mathcal{C}$, for every set $A \in \mathcal{F}$. From (γ) it now follows that $\mathcal{C}$ contains all nonnegative simple functions on Ω.

Let now f be a nonnegative measurable function on Ω and choose a sequence (f_n) of simple functions on Ω such that $f_n \uparrow f$ pointwise, as $n \uparrow \infty$. Using (γ), $f_{k+1} - f_k \in \mathcal{C}$, for all $k \geq 1$, and

$$f = \lim_n f_n = \lim_n \left(f_1 + \sum_{k=1}^{n-1}(f_{k+1} - f_k) \right) = f_1 + \sum_{k=1}^{\infty}(f_{k+1} - f_k) \in \mathcal{C}. \quad ∎$$

Let us illustrate this extension procedure in several examples:

B.5 Image measure theorem. Let $(\Omega', \mathcal{F}')$ be a measurable space, that is, Ω' a set and $\mathcal{F}'$ a σ-field on Ω', and $X : (\Omega, \mathcal{F}, P) \to (\Omega', \mathcal{F}')$ a measurable map. Then the image P_X of the measure P under X is the measure on $\mathcal{F}'$ defined by $P_X(A) = P(X^{-1}(A))$, $A \in \mathcal{F}'$. This measure is also called the distribution of X under P.

B.5.0. (a) $E_{P_X}(f) = E_P(f \circ X)$, for each measurable function $f \geq 0$ on Ω'.
(b) If f is an arbitrary measurable function on Ω', then $f \in L^1(P_X)$ if and only if $f \circ X \in L^1(P)$ and in this case again $E_{P_X}(f) = E_P(f \circ X)$.

Proof. (a) Let $\mathcal{C}$ be the family of all nonnegative measurable functions f on Ω' which satisfy $E_{P_X}(f) = E_P(f \circ X)$. For an indicator function $f = 1_A$, $A \in \mathcal{F}'$, this equality is satisfied by the definition of the image measure P_X. Thus $1_A \in \mathcal{C}$ for all sets $A \in \mathcal{F}'$. Moreover it is easily seen that $\mathcal{C}$ is a λ-cone on Ω'. Property (α) of a λ-cone is trivial and properties (β) and (γ) follow from the linearity and the σ-additivity of the integral (over nonnegative series). Thus $\mathcal{C}$ contains every nonnegative measurable function on Ω'.
(b) This follows from (a) by writing $f = f^+ - f^-$. ∎

B.6 Measurability with respect to $\sigma(X)$. Let $(\Omega', \mathcal{F}')$ and $X : (\Omega, \mathcal{F}, P) \to (\Omega', \mathcal{F}')$ be as above and let $\sigma(X)$ be the σ-field generated by X on Ω, that is, $\sigma(X)$ is the smallest σ-field on Ω with respect to which X is measurable. It is easily seen that $\sigma(X) = \{ X^{-1}(A) \mid A \in \mathcal{F}' \}$.

B.6.0. *A function $f : \Omega \to \overline{R}$ is measurable with respect to $\sigma(X)$ if and only if f has the form $f = g \circ X$, for some measurable function $g : \Omega' \to \overline{R}$.*

Proof. If $f = g \circ X$ with g as above, then f is $\sigma(X)$-measurable since a composition of measurable maps is measurable. Conversely let $\mathcal{C}$ be the family of all functions f on Ω which can be written in the form $f = g \circ X$, with $g : \Omega' \to [0, +\infty]$ measurable. Thus each function $f \in \mathcal{C}$ is nonnegative.

We want to show that $\mathcal{C}$ contains every nonnegative, $\sigma(X)$-measurable function f on Ω. Indeed, if B is any set in $\sigma(X)$, then $B = X^{-1}(A)$ and so $1_B = 1_A \circ X$, for some set $A \in \mathcal{F}'$. Thus $1_B \in \mathcal{C}$. Moreover $\mathcal{C}$ is again easily seen to be a λ-cone on Ω.

Only property (β) of a λ-cone is not completely straightforward: Let $f, h \in \mathcal{C}$ be bounded and assume that $f \leq h$. Choose a constant M such that $0 \leq f \leq h \leq M$ and write $f = g \circ X$ and $h = k \circ X$, where $h, k : \Omega' \to [0, +\infty]$ are measurable. Then $f = f \wedge M = (g \wedge M) \circ X$ and likewise $h = (k \wedge M) \circ X$. Thus we may assume that g and k are bounded as well, especially finitely valued. In particular then the difference $k - g$ is defined and we have $h - f = (k - g) \circ X$, where the function $k - g$ is measurable on Ω' but is not known to be nonnegative. However $h - f \geq 0$ implies that $h - f = (k - g)^+ \circ X$. Thus $h - f \in \mathcal{C}$. Applying B. to the probability space $(\Omega, \sigma(X), P)$ with $\mathcal{I} = \sigma(X)$ shows that $\mathcal{C}$ contains every nonnegative $\sigma(X)$-measurable function on Ω.

If f is any $\sigma(X)$-measurable function on Ω write $f = f^+ - f^-$ and $f^+ = h_1 \circ X$, $f^- = h_2 \circ X$, for some measurable functions $h_1, h_2 : \Omega' \to [0, +\infty]$. Note that it does not follow that $f = h \circ X$ with $h = h_1 - h_2$, since this difference may not be defined on all of Ω'.

The sets $[f > 0]$, $[f < 0]$ are in $\sigma(X)$ and so there exist sets $A_1, A_2 \in \mathcal{F}'$ such that $[f > 0] = X^{-1}(A_1)$ and $[f < 0] = X^{-1}(A_2)$. Then $[f > 0] = X^{-1}(A_1 \setminus A_2)$ and $[f < 0] = X^{-1}(A_2 \setminus A_1)$ and we may therefore assume that the sets A_1 and A_2 are disjoint.

Note that $1_{[f>0]} = 1_{A_1} \circ X$ and so $f^+ = f^+ 1_{[f>0]} = g_1 \circ X$ with $g_1 = h_1 1_{A_1}$. Likewise $f^- = g_2 \circ X$ with $g_2 = h_2 1_{A_2}$. The measurable functions $g_1, g_2 : \Omega' \to [0, +\infty]$ satisfy $g_1 g_2 = 0$ and so the difference $g = g_1 - g_2 : \Omega' \to \overline{R}$ is defined. Clearly $f = g \circ X$. ∎

Remark. Let $X = (X_1, X_2, \ldots, X_n)' : (\Omega, \mathcal{F}, P) \to R^n$ be a random vector and $\sigma(X_1, \ldots, X_n)$ denote the smallest σ-field on Ω making each X_j measurable. Then X is measurable with respect to any σ-field $\mathcal{G}$ on Ω if and only if each component X_j is $\mathcal{G}$-measurable. From this it follows that $\sigma(X) = \sigma(X_1, \ldots, X_n)$. Applying B.6.0 we obtain

B.6.1. *A function* $f : \Omega \to \overline{R}$ *is* $\sigma(X_1, X_2, \ldots, X_n)$*-measurable if and only if* $f = g(X_1, X_2, \ldots, X_n)$ *for some measurable function* $g : R^n \to \overline{R}$. ∎

B.7 Uniqueness of finite measures. Let $\mathcal{I}$ be a π-system on Ω which generates the σ-field $\mathcal{F}$ and contains the set Ω. Then

B.7.0. *If the finite measures* P, P' *on* $\mathcal{F}$ *satisfy* $P(A) = P'(A)$, *for all sets* $A \in \mathcal{I}$, *then* $P = P'$.

Proof. The family $\mathcal{L} = \{\, A \in \mathcal{F} \mid P(A) = P'(A) \,\}$ is a λ-system containing $\mathcal{I}$. To see that $\mathcal{L}$ is closed under complements we use $\Omega \in \mathcal{I} \subseteq \mathcal{L}$ and the finiteness of P and P'. By the π-λ Theorem $\mathcal{L} \supseteq \mathcal{F}$. Thus $P(A) = P'(A)$, for all sets $A \in \mathcal{F}$, that is, $P = P'$. ∎

B.8 Fubini's theorem. Let $(\Omega_j, \mathcal{F}_j, P_j)$, $j = 1, 2$, be probability spaces and $(\Omega, \mathcal{F}, P)$ the product space $(\Omega_1, \mathcal{F}_1, P_1) \times (\Omega_2, \mathcal{F}_2, P_2)$. In other words $\Omega = \Omega_1 \times \Omega_2$, $\mathcal{F} = \mathcal{F}_1 \times \mathcal{F}_2$ the product σ-field, that is, the σ-field generated by the measurable rectangles $A_1 \times A_2$ with $A_j \in \mathcal{F}_j$, $j = 1, 2$, and $P = P_1 \times P_2$ the product measure, that is, the unique probability measure on $\mathcal{F}$ satisfying $P(A) = P_1(A_1) P_2(A_2)$, for each measurable rectangle $A = A_1 \times A_2 \in \mathcal{F}$.

For a function $f : \Omega \to \overline{R}$ and $x \in \Omega_1$, $y \in \Omega_2$ we define the sections $f_x : \Omega_2 \to \overline{R}$ and $f_y : \Omega_1 \to \overline{R}$ by $f_x(y) = f_y(x) = f(x, y)$.

B.8.0 Fubini's theorem. *Let* $f : \Omega \to [0, +\infty]$ *be measurable with respect to the product σ-field $\mathcal{F}$. Then the sections f_x and f_y are $\mathcal{F}_2$-measurable respectively $\mathcal{F}_1$-measurable, for each $x \in \Omega_1$ respectively $y \in \Omega_2$ and we have*

$$\int_{\Omega_1} E_{P_2}(f_x) \, P_1(dx) = E_P(f) = \int_{\Omega_2} E_{P_1}(f_y) \, P_2(dy). \tag{1}$$

Proof. Let $\mathcal{C}$ be the family of all nonnegative measurable functions f on the product Ω such that the sections f_x and f_y are $\mathcal{F}_2$-measurable respectively $\mathcal{F}_1$-measurable, for each $x \in \Omega_1$ respectively $y \in \Omega_2$ and such that equation (1) holds. From the linearity and σ-additivity of the integral, it follows that $\mathcal{C}$ is a λ-cone on Ω. We wish to show that $\mathcal{C}$ contains every nonnegative measurable function f on Ω. Since the measurable rectangles $A = A_1 \times A_2$, $A_j \in \mathcal{F}_j$, $j = 1, 2$, form a π-system of generators for the product σ-field $\mathcal{F}$, it will now suffice to show that $\mathcal{C}$ contains every such measurable rectangle A (or rather its indicator function 1_A).

Since $1_A(x, y) = 1_{A_1}(x)1_{A_2}(y)$, the sections $(1_A)_x$ and $(1_A)_y$ are given by $(1_A)_x = 1_{A_1}(x)1_{A_2}$ and $(1_A)_y = 1_{A_2}(y)1_{A_1}$, for each $x \in \Omega_1$, $y \in \Omega_2$. The measurability claim follows immediately and equation (1) reduces to the definition of the product measure P. $\blacksquare$

B.9 Approximation of sets by generators.   Let us now show that the sets in the σ-field $\mathcal{F} = \sigma(\mathcal{A})$ generated by some field of sets $\mathcal{A}$ can be approximated by sets in $\mathcal{A}$ in the following sense:

B.9.0. *Let $(\Omega, \mathcal{F}, P)$ be a probability space and $\mathcal{A} \subseteq \mathcal{F}$ a field of sets generating the σ-field $\mathcal{F}$. Then, for each set $E \in \mathcal{F}$ and $\epsilon > 0$, there exists a set $A \in \mathcal{A}$ such that $P(A \triangle E) < \epsilon$.*

Proof. Let $\mathcal{L}$ be the family of all sets $E \subseteq \Omega$ which can be approximated by sets in $\mathcal{A}$ as in B.9.0. We wish to show that $\mathcal{L} \supseteq \mathcal{F}$. Since $\mathcal{L}$ contains the π-system $\mathcal{A}$ generating $\mathcal{F}$, it will suffice to show that $\mathcal{L}$ is a λ-system of subsets of Ω. Indeed, we have $\emptyset \in \mathcal{A} \subseteq \mathcal{L}$ and the equality $A^c \triangle E^c = A \triangle E$ shows that $\mathcal{L}$ is closed under complements. It remains to be shown only that $\mathcal{L}$ is closed under countable disjoint unions.

Let $(E_n)_{n \geq 1} \subseteq \mathcal{L}$ be a disjoint sequence, $E = \bigcup_n E_n$ and $\epsilon > 0$ be arbitrary. As $\sum_n P(E_n) = P(E) \leq 1$ we can choose N such that $\sum_{n > N} P(E_n) < \epsilon/2$. For $1 \leq n \leq N$ choose $A_n \in \mathcal{A}$ such that $P(A_n \triangle E_n) < \epsilon/2^{n+1}$ and set $A = \bigcup_{n \leq N} A_n \in \mathcal{A}$. Then, from the inclusion

$$A \triangle E \subseteq \bigcup_{n \leq N}(A_n \triangle E_n) \cup \bigcup_{n > N} E_n$$

we obtain $P(A \triangle E) \leq \sum_{n \leq N} P(A_n \triangle E_n) + \sum_{n > N} P(E_n) < \epsilon$. Thus $E \in \mathcal{L}$. $\blacksquare$

B.10 Independence.   Let $\mathcal{G}$ be a sub-σ-field of $\mathcal{F}$. Recall that an event $B \in \mathcal{F}$ is called *independent* of $\mathcal{G}$, if $P(A \cap B) = P(A)P(B)$, for all events $A \in \mathcal{G}$. Likewise a sub-σ-field $\mathcal{S}$ of $\mathcal{F}$ is called independent of $\mathcal{G}$ if each event $B \in \mathcal{S}$ is independent of $\mathcal{G}$. Finally a random vector X is called independent of $\mathcal{G}$ if the σ-field $\sigma(X)$ is independent of $\mathcal{G}$.

B.10.0. *If the event B satisfies $P(A \cap B) = P(A)P(B)$, for all events A in some π-system generating the σ-field $\mathcal{G}$, then B is independent of $\mathcal{G}$.*

Proof. Fix B and let $\mathcal{I} \subseteq \mathcal{G}$ be a π-system with $\mathcal{G} = \sigma(\mathcal{I})$ such that $P(A \cap B) = P(A)P(B)$, for all $A \in \mathcal{I}$. We have to show that this equality holds for all sets $A \in \mathcal{G}$. Let $\mathcal{L}$ be the family of all sets $A \in \mathcal{F}$ such that $P(A \cap B) = P(A)P(B)$. We have $\mathcal{L} \supseteq \mathcal{I}$ and want to show that $\mathcal{L} \supseteq \mathcal{G}$. By the π-λ Theorem it will suffice to show that $\mathcal{L}$ is a λ-system of subsets of Ω.

Clearly $\emptyset \in \mathcal{L}$. If $A \in \mathcal{L}$, then $P(A^c \cap B) = P(B \setminus (A \cap B)) = P(B) - P(A \cap B) = P(B) - P(A)P(B) = P(A^c)P(B)$. Thus $A^c \in \mathcal{L}$. Finally, let $(A_n) \subseteq \mathcal{L}$ be a disjoint sequence and $A = \bigcup_n A_n$. Then $P(A \cap B) = P(\bigcup_n (A_n \cap B)) = \sum_n P(A_n \cap B) = \sum_n P(A_n)P(B) = P(A)P(B)$. Thus $A \in \mathcal{L}$. ∎

B.10.1. *Let $\mathcal{A}, \mathcal{B}, \mathcal{S}$ be sub-σ-fields of $\mathcal{F}$ and assume that $\mathcal{S}$ is independent of $\mathcal{A}$.*
(a) If $\mathcal{B}$ is independent of $\sigma(\mathcal{A} \cup \mathcal{S})$ then $\mathcal{S}$ is independent of $\sigma(\mathcal{A} \cup \mathcal{B})$.
(b) $\mathcal{S}$ is independent of $\sigma(\mathcal{A} \cup \mathcal{N})$, where $\mathcal{N}$ is the family of P-null sets.

Proof. (a) Assume that $\mathcal{B}$ is independent of $\sigma(\mathcal{A} \cup \mathcal{S})$. The family $\mathcal{I} = \{A \cap B \mid A \in \mathcal{A}, B \in \mathcal{B}\}$ is a π-system generating the σ-field $\sigma(\mathcal{A} \cup \mathcal{B})$. According to B.10.0 it will now suffice to show that $P(S \cap A \cap B) = P(S)P(A \cap B)$, for all sets $A \in \mathcal{A}$ and $B \in \mathcal{B}$. Indeed, for such A and B we have

$$P(S \cap A \cap B) = P(S \cap A)P(B) = P(S)P(A)P(B) = P(S)P(A \cap B),$$

where the first equality uses the independence of $\mathcal{B}$ from $\sigma(\mathcal{A} \cup \mathcal{S})$, the second the independence of $\mathcal{S}$ from $\mathcal{A}$ and the third the independence of $\mathcal{B}$ from $\mathcal{A}$.

(b) Let $\mathcal{B} = \sigma(\mathcal{N})$. Then the σ-field $\mathcal{B}$ consists of the P-null sets and their complements and is therefore independent of every other σ-field. According to (a), $\mathcal{S}$ is independent of $\sigma(\mathcal{A} \cup \mathcal{B}) = \sigma(\mathcal{A} \cup \mathcal{N})$. ∎

C. Positive semidefinite matrices. Let $\{e_1, e_2, \ldots, e_n\}$ denote the standard basis of R^n. Elements of R^n are viewed as column vectors and t', C' denote the transpose of a vector t respectively matrix C. Recall that a real $n \times n$ matrix C is called *symmetric* if it satisfies $C = C'$ in which case it admits an orthonormal basis $\{f_1, f_2, \ldots, f_n\} \subseteq R^n$ consisting of eigenvectors of C. Let $\lambda_1, \ldots, \lambda_n$ be the associated eigenvalues and let the eigenvectors f_j be numbered such that $\lambda_1, \ldots \lambda_k \neq 0$ and $\lambda_{k+1} = \lambda_{k+2} = \ldots = \lambda_n = 0$.

Given that this is the case, let U be the $n \times n$ matrix whose columns are the eigenvectors f_j: $c_j(U) = Ue_j = f_j$, $j = 1, 2, \ldots, n$. Then U is an orthogonal matrix, that is, U is invertible and $U^{-1} = U'$. We claim that U diagonalizes the matrix C in the sense that $U^{-1}CU = diag(\lambda_j)$, where $diag(\lambda_j)$ denotes the diagonal matrix with entries $\lambda_1, \ldots, \lambda_n$ down the main diagonal. Indeed, $U^{-1}CUe_i = U^{-1}Cf_i = \lambda_i U^{-1} f_i = \lambda_i e_i = diag(\lambda_j)e_i$, for all $i = 1, 2, \ldots, n$. Recall that an $n \times n$ matrix C is called *positive semidefinite* if it satisfies

$$(Ct, t) = t'Ct = \sum_{i,j=1}^{n} C_{ij}t_i t_j \geq 0, \quad \forall t = (t_1, t_2, \ldots, t_n)' \in R^n.$$

By contrast to the case of complex scalars this does not imply that the matrix C is symmetric, as the example of the matrix $C = \begin{pmatrix} 1 & 2 \\ 0 & 1 \end{pmatrix}$ shows.

If C is symmetric and positive semidefinite, then $\lambda_j = \lambda_j \|f_j\|^2 = (\lambda_j f_j, f_j) = (C f_j, f_j) \geq 0$ and it follows that $\lambda_1, \lambda_2, \ldots \lambda_k > 0$ and $\lambda_{k+1} = \lambda_{k+2} = \ldots = \lambda_n = 0$. It is now easily seen that C can be written as $C = QQ'$, for some $n \times n$ matrix Q. Indeed $Q = U\, diag(\sqrt{\lambda_j})$ yields such a matrix Q: From $U^{-1}CU = diag(\lambda_j)$ it follows that

$$C = U\, diag(\lambda_j)U^{-1} = U\, diag(\lambda_j)U' = \big(U\, diag(\sqrt{\lambda_j})\big)\big(U\, diag(\sqrt{\lambda_j})\big)' = QQ'.$$

Indeed it is even true that C has a positive squareroot (i.e., Q above can be chosen to be symmetric and positive semidefinite). We do not need this. The relation $C = QQ'$ will be the key in the proof of the existence of Gaussian random variables with arbitrary parameters $m \in R^n$ and C a symmetric, positive semidefinite $n \times n$ matrix.

Let us note that the matrix $Q = U\, diag(\sqrt{\lambda_j})$ satisfies $range(Q) = range(C)$. Indeed, using the equality $CU = U\, diag(\lambda_j)$, we have $range(C) = range(CU) = range(U\, diag(\lambda_k)) = span\{Ue_1, Ue_2, \ldots, Ue_k\} = range(Q)$.

D. Kolmogoroff Existence Theorem.

Compact classes and countable additivity. Let E be a set. A family $\mathcal{K}_0$ of subsets of E has the *finite intersection property*, if $K_0 \cap K_1 \cap \ldots \cap K_n \neq \emptyset$, for each finite subfamily $\{K_0, K_1, \ldots, K_n\} \subseteq \mathcal{K}_0$.

A *compact class* on E is now a family $\mathcal{K}$ of subsets of E such that $\bigcap_{K \in \mathcal{K}_0} K \neq \emptyset$, for each subfamily $\mathcal{K}_0 \subseteq \mathcal{K}$, which has the finite intersection property, that is,

$$\mathcal{K}_0 \subseteq \mathcal{K} \text{ and } K_0 \cap \ldots \cap K_n \neq \emptyset,$$

for each finite subfamily $\{K_0, \ldots, K_n\} \subseteq \mathcal{K}_0, \quad \Rightarrow \quad \bigcap_{K \in \mathcal{K}_0} K \neq \emptyset.$

In more familiar terms: If we set $\mathcal{S} = \{K^c = E \setminus K : K \in \mathcal{K}\}$, then $\mathcal{K}$ is a compact class on E if and only if every cover of E by sets in $\mathcal{S}$ has a finite subcover. Thus the family of closed subsets of a compact topological space E is always a compact class on E. Similarly the family of all compact subsets of a Hausdorff space E is also a compact class on E. Here the Hausdorff property is needed to make all compact sets closed. These compact classes are closed under finite unions.

D.1. *Let $\mathcal{K}$ be a compact class on the set E. Then*
(a) *Every subfamily of $\mathcal{K}$ is again a compact class on E.*
(b) *There is a topology on E in which E is compact and such that $\mathcal{K}$ is contained in the family of all closed subsets of E.*
(c) *There is a compact class $\mathcal{K}_1$ on E such that $\mathcal{K} \subseteq \mathcal{K}_1$ and $\mathcal{K}_1$ is closed under finite unions.*
(d) *The family of all finite unions of sets in $\mathcal{K}$ is again a compact class on E.*

Proof. (a) is clear. (b) Set $\mathcal{S} = \{K^c \mid K \in \mathcal{K}\}$, then every cover of E by sets in $\mathcal{K}$ has a finite subcover. By the Alexander Subbasis Theorem E is compact in the topology generated by $\mathcal{S}$ as a subbasis on E. Clearly every set $K \in \mathcal{K}$ is closed in this topology. (c) Let $\mathcal{K}_1$ be the family of all closed subsets of E in the topology of (c). (d) follows from (c) and (a). ∎

D.2. *Let $\mathcal{A}$ be a field of subsets of E, $\mu : \mathcal{A} \to [0, +\infty)$ a finite, finitely additive set function on $\mathcal{A}$ and $\mathcal{K} \subseteq \mathcal{A}$ a compact class on E. If μ is inner regular with respect to $\mathcal{K}$ in the sense that*

$$\mu(A) = \sup\{ \mu(K) \mid K \in \mathcal{K}, K \subseteq A \}, \quad \text{for all sets } A \in \mathcal{A},$$

then μ is countably additive on $\mathcal{A}$.

Proof. Since μ is already finitely additive and $\mu(E) < +\infty$, the countable additivity of μ is implied by the following condition:

$$(D_n)_{n=1}^{\infty} \subseteq \mathcal{A}, \ D_n \downarrow \emptyset \quad \Rightarrow \quad \mu(D_n) \downarrow 0. \tag{0}$$

To verify (0) consider such a sequence $(D_n)_{n=1}^{\infty} \subseteq \mathcal{A}$ and let $\epsilon > 0$ be arbitrary. For each $n \geq 1$ choose a set $K_n \in \mathcal{K}$ such that

$$K_n \subseteq D_n \quad \text{and} \quad \mu(D_n \setminus K_n) < \epsilon/2^n.$$

As $\bigcap_{n \geq 1} D_n = \emptyset$ it follows that $\bigcap_{n \geq 1} K_n = \emptyset$. Since $\mathcal{K}$ is a compact class, it follows that $\bigcap_{n \leq N} K_n = \emptyset$, for some finite number N. Then $n \geq N$ implies

$$D_n \subseteq D_N = D_N \setminus \bigcap_{j=1}^{N} K_j = \bigcup_{j=1}^{N}(D_N \setminus K_j) \subseteq \bigcup_{j=1}^{N}(D_j \setminus K_j)$$

and so $\mu(D_n) \leq \sum_{j=1}^{N} \mu(D_j \setminus K_j) < \sum_{j=1}^{N} \epsilon/2^j < \epsilon$. Thus $\mu(D_n) \to 0$, as $n \uparrow \infty$. ∎

Products. Let E be a compact Hausdorff space, $\mathcal{E}$ the Borel σ-field on E and I any index set. The product $\Omega = E^I$ is then the family of all functions $\omega : I \to E$. We write $\omega(t) = \omega_t$, $t \in I$, and $\omega = (\omega_t)_{t \in I}$. Equipped with the product topology Ω is again a compact Hausdorff space by Tychonoff's Theorem.

For $t \in I$ we have the projection (coordinate map) $\pi_t : \omega \in \Omega \to \omega(t) \in E$. The product σ-field $\mathcal{E}^I$ on $\Omega = E^I$ is then defined to be the σ-field $\sigma(\pi_t, t \in I)$ generated by the coordinate maps π_t. It is characterized by the following universal property: a map X from any measurable space into $(E^I, \mathcal{E}^I)$ is measurable if and only if $\pi_t \circ X$ is measurable for each $t \in I$.

More generally, for all subsets $H \subseteq J \subseteq I$, we have the natural projections

$$\pi_H : \Omega = E^I \to \Omega_H = E^H \quad \text{and} \quad \pi_{JH} : \Omega_J = E^J \to \Omega_H = E^H$$

which are measurable with respect to the product σ-fields and satisfy

$$\pi_H = \pi_{JH} \circ \pi_J, \quad H \subseteq J \subseteq I.$$

In this notation $\pi_t = \pi_H$, where $H = \{t\}$. Let $\mathcal{H}(I)$ denote the family of all *finite* subsets of I. For each set $H = \{t_1, t_2, \ldots, t_n\} \in \mathcal{H}(I)$ we have

$$\pi_H(\omega) = (\omega_{t_1}, \omega_{t_2}, \ldots, \omega_{t_n}) \in \Omega_H = E^H.$$

If $H \in \mathcal{H}(I)$ and $B_H \in \mathcal{E}_H$, then the subset $Z = \pi_H^{-1}(B_H) \subseteq \Omega$ is called the *finite dimensional cylinder with base B_H*. This cylinder is said to be represented on the set $H \in \mathcal{H}(I)$. The cylinder $Z = \pi_H^{-1}(B_H)$ also satisfies

$$Z = \pi_H^{-1}(B_H) = \pi_J^{-1}\big(\pi_{JH}^{-1}(B_H)\big) = \pi_J^{-1}(B_J),$$

where $B_J = \pi_{JH}^{-1}(B_H) \in \mathcal{E}_J$. In other words, the cylinder $Z = \pi_H^{-1}(B_H)$ can be represented on every set $J \in \mathcal{H}(I)$ with $J \supseteq H$. Thus any two cylinders Z_1, Z_2 can be represented on the same set $H \in \mathcal{H}(I)$. Since

$$\big(\pi_H^{-1}(B_H)\big)^c = \pi_H^{-1}(B_H^c) \quad \text{and} \quad \pi_H^{-1}(B_H) \cap \pi_H^{-1}(C_H) = \pi_H^{-1}(B_H \cap C_H)$$

it follows that the family $\mathcal{Z} = \{\, \pi_H^{-1}(B_H) \subseteq \Omega \mid H \in \mathcal{H}(I) \text{ and } B_H \in \mathcal{E}_H \,\}$ of finite dimensional cylinders is a field of subsets of Ω. Clearly the finite dimensional cylinders generate the product σ-field $\mathcal{E}^I$.

If we merely need a π-system of generators for the product σ-field $\mathcal{E}^I$ we can manage with a far smaller family of sets. A *finite dimensional rectangle* is a set Z of the form

$$Z = \bigcap_{t \in H} \pi_t^{-1}(E_t) = \bigcap_{t \in H} [\pi_t \in E_t],$$

where $H \in \mathcal{H}(I)$ and $E_t \in \mathcal{E}$, for all $t \in H$. Thus Z is the cylinder based on the rectangle $B_H = \prod_{t \in H} E_t \in \mathcal{E}^H$. The finite dimensional rectangles in $\mathcal{E}^I$ no longer form a field but they are still a π-system generating the product σ-field $\mathcal{E}^I$.

Indeed, the set H in the definition of Z can be enlarged, by setting $E_t = E$ for the new elements t, without altering Z. Thus any two finite dimensional rectangles can be represented on the same set $H \in \mathcal{H}(I)$ and from this it follows easily that the intersection of any two finite dimensional rectangles is another such rectangle.

Each finite dimensional rectangle is in $\mathcal{E}^I$ and thus the σ-field $\mathcal{G}$ generated by the finite dimensional rectangles satisfies $\mathcal{G} \subseteq \mathcal{E}^I$. On the other hand each coordinate map π_t is $\mathcal{G}$ measurable and this implies $\mathcal{E}^I \subseteq \mathcal{G}$. Thus $\mathcal{E}^I = \mathcal{G}$.

Finite dimensional rectangles are extremely basic events and a σ-field on the product space E^I will not be useful unless it contains them all. In this sense the product σ-field $\mathcal{E}^I$ is the smallest useful σ-field on E^I. It has the following desirable property: a probability measure Q on $\mathcal{E}^I$ is uniquely determined by its values on finite dimensional rectangles in $\mathcal{E}^I$. Usually, when such a measure Q is to be constructed to reflect some probabilistic intuition, it is clear what Q has to be on finite dimensional rectangles and this then determines Q on all of $\mathcal{E}^I$. If such uniqueness does not hold, the problem arises which among all possible candidates best reflects the underlying probabilistic intuition.

The product topology on $\Omega = E^I$ provides us with two more σ-fields on Ω, the Baire σ-field (the σ-field generated by the continuous (real valued) functions on Ω) and the Borel σ-field $\mathcal{B}(\Omega)$ (the σ-field generated by the open subsets of Ω).

Let us say that a function $f = f(\omega)$ on Ω depends only on countably many coordinates of the point $\omega = (\omega_t)_{t \in I} \in \Omega$ if there exists a countable subset $I_0 \subseteq I$ such that $f(\omega) = f(\tilde{\omega})$, for all $\omega, \tilde{\omega} \in \Omega$ with $\omega|_{I_0} = \tilde{\omega}|_{I_0}$.

Likewise a subset $A \subseteq \Omega$ is said to depend only on countably many coordinates if this is true of its indicator function 1_A, equivalently, if there exists a countable subset $I_0 \subseteq I$ such that $\omega \in A \Longleftrightarrow \tilde{\omega} \in A$, for all $\omega, \tilde{\omega} \in \Omega$ with $\omega|_{I_0} = \tilde{\omega}|_{I_0}$.

D.3. *(a) The product σ-field $\mathcal{E}^I$ is the Baire σ-field on Ω and thus is contained in the Borel σ-field $\mathcal{B}(\Omega)$. If I is countable, then $\mathcal{B}(\Omega) = \mathcal{E}^I$.*
(b) Every set A in the product σ-field $\mathcal{E}^I$ depends only on countably many coordinates. Thus, if I is uncountable, then $\mathcal{B}(\Omega) \neq \mathcal{E}^I$.
(c) Every function $f = f(\omega) : \Omega \to R$ which is measurable with respect to the product σ-field $\mathcal{E}^I$ on Ω depends only on countably many coordinates of the point $\omega = (\omega_t)_{t \in I} \in \Omega$. In particular this is true for all continuous functions on Ω.

Proof. (a)   Since each coordinate map π_t is continuous, the product σ-field $\mathcal{E}^I$ is contained in the Baire σ-field on Ω.

To see the reverse inclusion let $C^r(\Omega)$ denote the real algebra of all continuous functions $f : \Omega \to R$. It will suffice to show that every function $f \in C^r(\Omega)$ is in fact measurable with respect to the product σ-field $\mathcal{E}^I$. This is certainly true of the projections π_t, $t \in I$, and of the constant function 1 and hence of every function in the subalgebra $\mathcal{A} \subseteq C^r(\Omega)$ generated by these functions. By the measurability of pointwise limits, every pointwise limit of functions in $\mathcal{A}$ is measurable for the product σ-field $\mathcal{E}^I$ on Ω.

Thus it remains to be shown only that every function $f \in C^r(\Omega)$ can be represented as a pointwise limit of functions in $\mathcal{A}$. In fact the subalgebra $\mathcal{A} \subseteq C^r(\Omega)$ separates points on Ω and contains the constants and is thus even uniformly dense in $C^r(\Omega)$, by the Stone Weierstrass Theorem.

Assume now that I is countable. Then so is the family $\mathcal{H}(I)$. The family

$$\mathcal{G} = \{ \pi_H^{-1}(G_H) \mid H \in \mathcal{H}(I), G_H \subseteq \Omega_H \text{ open} \} \tag{1}$$

is a basis for the product topology on Ω. An arbitrary union of such basic sets with fixed index set H is a set of the same form. Thus any open set $G \subseteq \Omega$ can be written as a union of basic open sets with *distinct* index sets H and any such union is necessarily countable, by the countability of $\mathcal{H}(I)$. Thus, if G is any open subset of Ω, then G is a countable union of basic open sets as in (1). Each such basic open set is a finite dimensional cylinder and hence in the product σ-field $\mathcal{E}^I$. Thus $G \in \mathcal{E}^I$ and it follows that $\mathcal{B}(\Omega) \subseteq \mathcal{E}^I$.

(b)   The family $\mathcal{F}_0$ of all subsets $A \subseteq \Omega$, which depend only on countably many coordinates, is easily seen to be a σ-field containing all finite dimensional cylinders $Z = \pi_H^{-1}(B_H)$, $H \in \mathcal{H}(I)$, $B_H \in \mathcal{E}_H$ (such a cylinder depends only on the coordinates in the set H) and hence the entire product σ-field $\mathcal{E}^I$.

Note now that a singleton set $A = \{\omega\} \subseteq \Omega$ depends on all coordinates. Thus, if I is uncountable, then the product σ-field $\mathcal{E}^I$ contains no singleton sets. The Borel σ-field $\mathcal{B}(\Omega)$ on the other hand contains all singleton sets since these are closed (the product $\Omega = E^I$ is again Hausdorff).

(c)   The family $\mathcal{C}$ of all nonnegative functions $f : \Omega \to R$ which depend on only finitely many coordinates is easily seen to be a λ-cone on Ω containing the indicator function of every finite dimensional rectangle (see (b)). Since these rectangles form a π-system generating the product σ-field $\mathcal{E}^I$, $\mathcal{C}$ contains every nonnegative, $\mathcal{E}^I$-measurable function $f : \Omega \to R$ (B.4). The extension to arbitrary $\mathcal{E}^I$-measurable $f : \Omega \to R$ is trivial. ∎

Projective families of probability measures. Let P be a probability measure on the product space $(\Omega, \mathcal{E}) = (E^I, \mathcal{E}^I)$. For each subset $H \in \mathcal{H}(I)$ the image measure $P_H = \pi_H(P)$ is defined on the finite product $(\Omega_H, \mathcal{E}_H) = (E^H, \mathcal{E}^H)$ as $P_H(B_H) = P(\pi_H^{-1}(B_H))$, for all sets $B_H \in \mathcal{E}_H$.

The measures P_H, $H \in \mathcal{H}(I)$, are called the *finite dimensional marginal distributions* of P. The relation $\pi_H = \pi_{JH} \circ \pi_J$ implies the following consistency relation for these marginal distributions:

$$\pi_{JH}(P_J) = \pi_{JH}(\pi_J(P)) = \pi_H(P) = P_H,$$
$$\text{for all } H, J \in \mathcal{H}(I) \text{ with } H \subset J. \tag{2}$$

Conversely assume that for each set $H \in \mathcal{H}(I)$, P_H is a probability measure on the the finite product $(E^H, \mathcal{E}^H)$. We wonder whether there exists a probability measure P on the product space $(E^I, \mathcal{E}^I)$ such that $\pi_H(P) = P_H$, for all $H \in \mathcal{H}(I)$, that is such that the finite dimensional marginal distributions of P are the measures P_H, $H \in \mathcal{H}(I)$. Clearly such a measure P can exist only if the measures P_H satisfy the consistency relation (2). If this relation is satisfied we call the family $(P_H)_{H \in \mathcal{H}(I)}$ *projective*. The projective property of the measures $(P_H)_{H \in \mathcal{H}(I)}$ is also sufficient for the existence of the measure P on $\mathcal{E}^I$ under very general assumptions. We do not need this result in full generality. The proof can be simplified greatly if suitable conditions are imposed on the measurable space $(E, \mathcal{E})$.

D.4 Definition. *The measurable space $(E, \mathcal{E})$ is called standard if there exists a metric on E which makes E compact and $\mathcal{E}$ the Borel σ-field on E.*

Remark. If there exists a bimeasurable isomorphism $\phi : (T, \mathcal{B}(T)) \to (E, \mathcal{E})$, where T is any compact metric space and $\mathcal{B}(T)$ the Borel σ-field on T, then obviously $(E, \mathcal{E})$ is a standard measurable space.

We will now exhibit such an isomorphism $\phi : (T, \mathcal{B}(T)) \to (R, \mathcal{B}(R))$, where $T = [-1, 1]$. Such ϕ induces an isomorphism $\phi_d : (T^d, \mathcal{B}(T^d)) \to (R^d, \mathcal{B}(R^d))$. We will then have shown that $(R^d, \mathcal{B}(R^d))$ is a standard measurable space, for all $d \geq 1$.

Set $A_n = [-1/n, -1/(n+1)[\cup]1/(n+1), 1/n]$, $B_n = [-n, -(n-1)[\cup]n-1, n]$ and $\phi_n(t) = n(n+1)t - sgn(t)$, $t \in A_n$, $n \geq 1$, where $sgn(t) = +1$, if $t > 0$, and $sgn(t) = -1$, if $t < 0$, as usual. Note that $\phi_n : A_n \to B_n$ is a bimeasurable isomorphism, for all $n \geq 1$. Moreover $T = [-1, 1]$ is the disjoint union $\{0\} \cup \bigcup A_n$ and R is the disjoint union $\{0\} \cup \bigcup B_n$. Set $\phi = \sum 1_{A_n} \phi_n$, that is, $\phi : T \to R$ satisfies $\phi(0) = 0$ and $\phi = \phi_n$ on A_n. It follows that $\phi : (T, \mathcal{B}(T)) \to (R, \mathcal{B}(R))$ is a bimeasurable isomorphism.

D.5. *Let T be a compact metric space and P a probability measure on the Borel σ-field $\mathcal{B}(T)$ of T. Then every Borel set $A \subseteq T$ satisfies*

$$P(A) = \sup\{\, P(K) \mid K\,compact,\ K \subseteq A \,\}. \tag{3}$$

Proof. It is not hard to show that the family $\mathcal{G}$ of all Borel sets $B \subseteq T$ such that both sets $A = B, B^c$ satisfy (3) is a σ-field [DD, 7.1.2]. Any open set $G \subseteq T$ is the increasing union of the compact sets $K_n = \{\, x \in T \mid dist(x, G^c) \geq 1/n \,\}$ and consequently $P(K_n) \uparrow P(G)$, $n \uparrow \infty$. Thus $G \in \mathcal{G}$. It follows that $\mathcal{G}$ contains every Borel subset of T. ∎

D.6 Kolmogoroff Existence Theorem. *Let $(E, \mathcal{E})$ be a standard measurable space. If $(P_H)_{H \in \mathcal{H}(I)}$ is a projective family of probability measures on $\big((\Omega_H, \mathcal{E}_H)\big)_{H \in \mathcal{H}(I)}$ then there exists a unique probability measure P on the product space $(E^I, \mathcal{E}^I)$ such that $P_H = \pi_H(P)$, for all sets $H \in \mathcal{H}(I)$.*

Proof. The condition $P_H = \pi_H(P)$, for all sets $H \in \mathcal{H}(I)$, uniquely determines P on cylinders and hence on the entire product σ-field $\mathcal{E}^I$ (the cylinders form a π-system of generators for $\mathcal{E}^I$). To see the existence of P define the set function P_0 on the field $\mathcal{Z}$ of finite dimensional cylinders as

$$P_0(Z) = P_H(B_H), \quad Z = \pi_H^{-1}(B_H) \in \mathcal{Z}, H \in \mathcal{H}(I), B_H \in \mathcal{E}_H.$$

It must be shown that P_0 is well defined. Indeed if $Z = \pi_H^{-1}(B_H) = \pi_K^{-1}(B_K)$ with sets $H, K \in \mathcal{H}(I)$ and $B_H \in \mathcal{E}_H$, $B_K \in \mathcal{E}_K$, set $J = H \cup K \in \mathcal{H}(I)$ and note that $Z = \pi_H^{-1}(B_H) = \pi_J^{-1}\big(\pi_{JH}^{-1}(B_H)\big)$ and likewise $Z = \pi_K^{-1}(B_K) = \pi_J^{-1}\big(\pi_{JK}^{-1}(B_K)\big)$ and thus

$$\pi_J^{-1}\big(\pi_{JH}^{-1}(B_H)\big) = \pi_J^{-1}\big(\pi_{JK}^{-1}(B_K)\big).$$

Since the projection π_J is surjective, it follows that $\pi_{JH}^{-1}(B_H) = \pi_{JK}^{-1}(B_K)$ and consequently, by the projective property of the measures P_H, $H \in \mathcal{H}(I)$,

$$P_H(B_H) = P_J\big(\pi_{JH}^{-1}(B_H)\big) = P_J\big(\pi_{JK}^{-1}(B_K)\big) = P_K(B_K),$$

as desired. Clearly $P_0(\Omega) = 1$. It will now suffice to show that the set function $P_0 : \mathcal{Z} \to [0,1]$ is countably additive, for then it extends to a probability measure P on the σ-field $\mathcal{E}^I$ generated by the field $\mathcal{Z}$ of cylinders and this extension obviously satisfies $P_H = \pi_H(P)$, for all sets $H \in \mathcal{H}(I)$.

Clearly P_0 is finitely additive on $\mathcal{Z}$. To see countable additivity, equip E with a metric with which it becomes a compact space such that $\mathcal{E}$ is the Borel σ-field on E. Then each finite product $\Omega_H = E^H$ is compact and $\mathcal{E}_H = \mathcal{E}^H = \mathcal{B}(\Omega_H)$ is the Borel σ-field on Ω_H. Moreover the Borel probability measure P_H on Ω_H is automatically inner regular with respect to the family of compact subsets of Ω_H (D.5). Thus for each cylinder $Z = \pi_H^{-1}(B_H) \in \mathcal{Z}$, $H \in \mathcal{H}(I)$, $B_H \in \mathcal{E}_H$, we have

$$P_0(Z) = P_H(B_H) = \sup\{\, P_H(K_H) \mid K_H \subseteq B_H, K_H \text{ compact} \,\}$$
$$= \sup\{\, P_0(\pi_H^{-1}(K_H)) \mid K_H \subseteq B_H, K_H \text{ compact} \,\}.$$

This shows that P_0 is inner regular with respect to the family

$$\mathcal{K} = \{\, \pi_H^{-1}(K_H) \mid H \in \mathcal{H}(I), K_H \subseteq B_H, K_H \text{ compact}\,\} \subseteq \mathcal{Z}.$$

If $H \in \mathcal{H}(I)$ and K_H is a compact subset of B_H then the set $\pi_H^{-1}(K_H)$ is closed in the compact product space $\Omega = E^I$ and hence itself compact. Thus $\mathcal{K}$ is contained in the family of compact subsets of Ω and hence is a compact class. The countable additivity of P_0 now follows according to D.1. ∎

BIBLIOGRAPHY

[Ca]   K. L. CHUNG (1974), *A Course in Probability Theory*, Academic Press.

[Cb]   K. L. CHUNG (1974), *Lectures from Markov Processes to Brownian Motion*, Heidelberg, Springer-Verlag.

[CRS]   Y. CHOW, H. ROBBINS, D SIEGMUND (1991), *The Theory of Optimal Stopping*, New York, Dover.

[CW]   K.L. CHUNG, R. J. WILLIAMS (1990), *Introduction to Stochastic Integration*, New York, Springer-Verlag.

[DB]   F. DELBAEN, Representing Martingale Measures when Asset Prices are Continuous and Bounded,*Mathematical Finance* Vol. 2, No. 2 (1992), 107-130.

[DD]   R. M. DUDLEY (1989), *Real Analysis and Probability*, Belmont, WadsworthBrooks/Cole.

[DF]   D. DUFFIE (1996), *Dynamic Asset Pricing Theory*, New Haven, Princeton University Press.

[DS]   F. DELBAEN, W. SCHACHERMAYER, A General Version of the Fundamental Theorem of Asset Pricing, *Math. Ann.* 300, 463-520.

[DT]   R. DURRETT (1996), *Stochastic Calculus, a Practical Introduction*, Boca Raton, CRC Press.

[J]   F. JAMSHIDIAN, Libor and Swap Market Models and Measures, *Finance and Stochastics* 1 (1997), 293-330.

[K]   N.V. KRYLOV (1995), *Introduction to the Theory of Diffusion Processes*, Providence, American Mathematical Society.

[KS]   I. KARATZAS, S. SHREVE (1988), *Brownian Motion and Stochastic Calculus*, Heidelberg, Springer-Verlag.

[MR]   M. MUSIELA, M. RUTKOVSKI (1998), *Martingale Methods in Financial Modelling*, Heidelberg, Springer-Verlag.

[P]   P. PROTTER (1990), *Stochastic Integration and Differential Equations*, Heidelberg, Springer-Verlag.

[PTH]   K. R. PARTHASARATHY (1967), *Probability Measures on Metric Spaces*, New York, Academic Press.

[Ra]   W. RUDIN (1966), *Real and Complex Analysis*, New York, McGraw-Hill.

[Rb]   W. RUDIN (1973), *Functional Analysis*, New York, McGraw-Hill.

[RY]   D. REVUZ, M. YOR. (1999), *Continuous Martingales and Brownian Motion*, Heidelberg, Springer-Verlag.

INDEX

For Product Safety Concerns and Information please contact our EU
representative GPSR@taylorandfrancis.com
Taylor & Francis Verlag GmbH, Kaufingerstraße 24, 80331 München, Germany

www.ingramcontent.com/pod-product-compliance
Ingram Content Group UK Ltd.
Pitfield, Milton Keynes, MK11 3LW, UK
UKHW021621240425

457818UK00018B/677

* 9 7 8 0 3 6 7 4 5 5 4 3 9 *